Lecture Notes in Computer Science   11281

Commenced Publication in 1973
Founding and Former Series Editors:
Gerhard Goos, Juris Hartmanis, and Jan van Leeuwen

More information about this series at http://www.springer.com/series/7410

Vinod Ganapathy · Trent Jaeger
R. K. Shyamasundar (Eds.)

Information Systems Security

14th International Conference, ICISS 2018
Bangalore, India, December 17–19, 2018
Proceedings

 Springer

Editors
Vinod Ganapathy
Indian Institute of Science
Bangalore, India

R. K. Shyamasundar
Indian Institute of Technology Bombay
Mumbai, India

Trent Jaeger
Pennsylvania State University
University Park, PA, USA

ISSN 0302-9743   ISSN 1611-3349   (electronic)
Lecture Notes in Computer Science
ISBN 978-3-030-05170-9   ISBN 978-3-030-05171-6   (eBook)
https://doi.org/10.1007/978-3-030-05171-6

Library of Congress Control Number: 2018962541

LNCS Sublibrary: SL4 – Security and Cryptology

This Springer imprint is published by the registered company Springer Nature Switzerland AG
The registered company address is: Gewerbestrasse 11, 6330 Cham, Switzerland

Preface

This volume contains the papers presented at the 14th International Conference on Information Systems Security (ICISS 2018), held at the Indian Institute of Science, Bengaluru, Karnataka, India, during December 17–19, 2018. In response to the call for papers, 53 submissions were received. One submission was withdrawn by the authors while a second one was desk-rejected, leaving a total of 51 papers to be evaluated by the Program Committee. All submissions were evaluated on the basis of the novelty and significance of their scientific content. The Program Committee, comprising 47 members, reviewed all submissions via a single-blind review process. Each paper was reviewed by three or more reviewers and discussed. After discussions, the committee selected a total of 23 papers for presentation at the conference. The papers covered a wide range of topics as is reflected in the list of papers in this volume.

In addition to the peer-reviewer papers, we were also fortunate to have four eminent speakers delivering keynote presentations at the conference: Venkatramanan Siva Subrahmanian (Dartmouth University), Atul Prakash (University of Michigan–Ann Arbor), Prateek Saxena (National University of Singapore), and Sriram Rajamani (Microsoft Research India). The program also consisted of two tutorials: one by Nishanth Chandran and Divya Gupta (Microsoft Research India), and a second one by Somesh Jha (University of Wisconsin–Madison). We are really thankful to these speakers for taking time off from their busy schedules and contributing to ICISS 2018.

Many individuals contributed to making ICISS 2018 a success, and it is a pleasure to thank them. We are thankful to all members of the Program Committee and all external reviewers for their efforts in reviewing the papers and participating in the discussion and selection process. We thank the Steering Committee, our publicity chair (Anu Mary Chacko of NIT Calicut), and the Web team (Rounak Agarwal, Aditya Shukla and Kripa Shanker, of IISc Bangalore). We thank Kushael and Shankar from the Department of Computer Science and Automation, IISc Bangalore, for providing administrative support and taking care of many logistical details. Needless to say, we are thankful to all the authors who submitted their work to ICISS 2018, and our keynote speech and tutorial speakers who accepted our invitation to present at the conference.

We were fortunate to receive financial support for the conference from Sonata Software, IISc Bangalore, and Microsoft Research India. We are thankful to Omprakash Subbarao (Sonata Software), Y. Narahari (IISc Bangalore), and the team of Chiranjib Bhattacharyya (IISc Bangalore), Sriram Rajamani, Satish Sangameswaran, and Christina Gould-Sandhu (Microsoft Research India) for providing financial sponsorship. We also appreciate the support of Springer, in particular Alfred Hofmann and Anna Kramer, in publishing the proceedings as well as the monetary support for the conference. We would also like to acknowledge EasyChair for their conference management system, which was freely used to manage the process of paper submissions and reviews.

We hope that you find these proceedings interesting and useful in your own research.

October 2018

Vinod Ganapathy
Trent Jaeger
R. K. Shyamasundar

Organization

Program Committee

Vijay Atluri	Rutgers University, USA
Gogul Balakrishnan	Google, USA
Arati Baliga	Persistent Systems, India
Mridul Sankar Barik	Jadavpur University, India
Lorenzo Cavallaro	Royal Holloway, London, UK
Sambuddho Chakravarty	IIIT-Delhi, India
Frederic Cuppens	IMT Atlantique, France
Ashok Kumar Das	IIIT-Hyderabad, India
Lorenzo DeCarli	Worcester Polytechnic Institute, USA
Rinku Dewri	University of Denver, USA
Mohan Dhawan	IBM Research India
Adam Doupe	Arizona State University, USA
Earlence Fernandes	University of Washington, USA
Vinod Ganapathy	IISc Bangalore, India
Vijay Ganesh	University of Waterloo, Canada
Siddharth Garg	New York University, USA
Kanchi Gopinath	IISc Bangalore, India
Trent Jaeger	Pennsylvania State University, USA
Sushil Jajodia	George Mason University, USA
Suman Jana	Columbia University, USA
Aniket Kate	Purdue University, USA
Ram Krishnan	University of Texas-San Antonio, USA
Subhomoy Maitra	ISI-Kolkata, India
Pratyusa Manadhata	HP Labs, USA
Debdeep Mukhopadhyay	IIT-Kharagpur, India
Divya Muthukumaran	Imperial College London, UK
Adwait Nadkarni	College of William and Mary, USA
Eiji Okamoto	University of Tsukuba, Japan
Biswabandan Panda	IIT-Kanpur, India
Arpita Patra	IISc Bangalore, India
Goutam Paul	ISI-Kolkata, India
Phu Phung	University of Dayton, USA
Atul Prakash	University of Michigan–Ann Arbor, USA
Indrakshi Ray	Colorado State University, USA
Bimal Roy	ISI-Kolkata, India
Diptikalyan Saha	IBM-Research India
R. Sekar	StonyBrook University, USA
Sandeep Shukla	IIT-Kanpur, India

Anoop Singhal	National Institute of Standards and Technology, USA
Arunesh Sinha	University of Michigan–Ann Arbor, USA
Pramod Subramanyan	IIT-Kanpur, India
Laszlo Szekeres	Google, USA
Mohit Tiwari	University of Texas at Austin, USA
Mahesh Tripunitara	University of Waterloo, Canada
Venkatakrishnan V. N.	University of Illinois, Chicago, USA
Hayawardh Vijayakumar	Samsung Research, USA
Stijn Volckaert	University of California, Irvine, USA
Vinod Yegneswaran	SRI International, USA

Additional Reviewers

Bruhadeshwar Bezawada
Ayantika Chatterjee
Warren Connell
Sabrina De Capitani di Vimercati
Akshar Kaul
Manish Kesarwani
Haining Wang

Keynote Abstracts

Bots, Socks, and Vandals: An Overview of Malicious Actors on the Web

V. S. Subrahmanian

Department of Computer Science and Institute for Security, Technology,
and Society, Dartmouth College, Hanover NH 03755, USA
vs@dartmouth.edu

Abstract. In this paper, we discuss four types of malicious actors on social platforms and online markets: bots, sockpuppets, individuals committing review fraud, and vandals.

Keywords: Social media · Bots · Sockpuppets · Wikipedia · Vandals

Online social networks and e-commerce platforms are increasingly targeted by malicious actors with a wide variety of goals. Bots on Twitter may seek to illicitly influence opinion. Sock-puppet accounts on online discussion forums (e.g. discussion threads on online news articles) may help push certain points of view. Vandals on Wikipedia may seek to inject false material into otherwise legitimate pages. Review fraud in online forums may illicitly promote a product or destroy a competing product's reputation.

The bulk of this talk will focus on identifying review fraud in online e-commerce platforms such as Amazon, eBay and Flipkart. Because an increase of 1 star in a product rating can, on average, lead to a 5–9% increase in revenues, vendors have strong incentives to generate fake reviews. We will present both an unsupervised model as well as a supervised model to identify users who generate fake reviews. We show that our framework, called REV2 [3], produces high performance in real world experiments. In addition, a report of 150 review fraud accounts on Flipkart was independently evaluated by Flipkart's anti-fraud team who reported that 127 of the predictions were correct.

Sockpuppet accounts – multiple accounts operated by a single individual or corporate "puppetmaster" – are also a popular mechanism used to inappropriately sway opinion in online platforms. For instance, social "botnets" [4] commonly use multiple "sock" accounts to implement coordinated bots. Sockpuppet accounts are also commonly used by trolls. I will report on recent work [2] on the characteristics and properties of sockpuppet accounts through a study that involves data from the Disqus platform. Disqus powers discussion threads and forums on a host of news and other websites. Sockpuppets are often used in such contexts to artificially boost an opinion or artificially generate controversy. I will also briefly discuss the use of bots in real world influence campaigns along with methods to detect them [1, 4].

Third, I will discuss the problem of vandals on Wikipedia. Though research has been done previously on automated methods to detect acts of vandalism on Wikipedia, we describe VEWS, a Wikipedia Vandal Early Warning System that seeks to detect vandals as early as possible and preferably before they commit any acts of vandalism.

We show that VEWS outperforms prior work – but that when combined with prior work, it predicts vandals with very high accuracy.

The talk will conclude with a discussion of different types of malicious actors on the web.

References

1. Dickerson, J.P., Kagan, V., Subrahmanian, V.: Using sentiment to detect bots on twitter: are humans more opinionated than bots? In: Proceedings of the 2014 IEEE/ACM International Conference on Advances in Social Networks Analysis and Mining, pp. 620–627. IEEE Press (2014)
2. Kumar, S., Cheng, J., Leskovec, J., Subrahmanian, V.: An army of me: sockpuppets in online discussion communities. In: Proceedings of the 26th International Conference on World Wide Web, pp. 857–866. International World Wide Web Conferences Steering Committee (2017)
3. Kumar, S., Hooi, B., Makhija, D., Kumar, M., Faloutsos, C., Subrahmanian, V.: Rev2: fraudulent user prediction in rating platforms. In: Proceedings of the Eleventh ACM International Conference on Web Search and Data Mining, pp. 333–341. ACM (2018)
4. Subrahmanian, V.S., et al.: The darpa twitter bot challenge. Computer 49(6), 38–46 (2016). https://doi.org/10.1109/MC.2016.183

Robust Physical-World Attacks on Deep Learning Visual Classifiers and Detectors (Invited Talk)

Atul Prakash

Computer Science Division, University of Michigan,
Ann Arbor, MI 48109, USA
aprakash@umich.edu

Abstract. Recent studies show that the state-of-the-art deep neural networks (DNNs) are vulnerable to adversarial examples, resulting from small-magnitude perturbations added to the input [1, 5, 6, 8, 10, 12]. Given that that emerging physical systems are using DNNs in safety-critical situations such as autonomous driving, adversarial examples could mislead these systems and cause dangerous situations. It was however unclear if these attacks could be effective in practice with real-world objects [7], with some researchers finding that the attacks fail to translate to physical world in practice [9]. We report on some of our findings [2, 3] for generating such adversarial examples that can be physically realized using techniques such as stickers placed on real-world traffic signs. With a perturbation in the form of only black and white stickers, we modified real stop signs, causing targeted misclassification in over 80% of video frames obtained on a moving vehicle (field test) for state-of-the-art image classifiers, LISA-CNN and GTSRB-CNN. Our recent results [4] suggest that object detectors, such as YOLO [11], are also susceptible to physical perturbation attacks. I discuss some of the implications of the work on the design of robust classifiers and detectors for safety-critical applications.

Keywords: Adversarial machine learning · Input perturbation
Physical attacks · Deep learning · Security · Robust classifiers · Robust detectors

References

1. Carlini, N., Wagner, D.: Towards evaluating the robustness of neural networks. In: 2017 IEEE Symposium on Security and Privacy (SP), pp. 39–57. IEEE (2017)
2. Eykholt, K., et al.: Robust physical-world attacks on deep learning visual classification. In: Proceedings of Computer Vision and Pattern Recognition Conference (CVPR 2018). IEEE, June 2018. (Supersedes arXiv preprint arXiv:1707.08945, August 2017)
3. Eykholt, K., et al.: GitHub Repo on Robust Physical Perturbations Code. https://github.com/evtimovi/robust_physical_perturbations
4. Eykholt, K., et al.: Attacking object detectors with adversarial stickers. In: Proceedings of 12th Usenix Workshop on Offensive Technologies (WOOT), Baltimore, MD, (arXiv:1807.07769) (supersedes arXiv:1712.08062), August 2018

5. Goodfellow, I.J., Shlens, J., Szegedy, C.: Explaining and harnessing adversarial examples. arXiv preprint arXiv:1412.6572 (2014)
6. Kos, J., Fischer, I., Song, D.: Adversarial examples for generative models. arXiv preprint arXiv:1702.06832 (2017)
7. Kurakin, A., Goodfellow, I., Bengio, S.: Adversarial examples in the physical world. arXiv preprint arXiv:1607.02533 (2016)
8. Liu, Y., Chen, X., Liu, C., Song, D.: Delving into transferable adversarial examples and black-box attacks. arXiv preprint arXiv:1611.02770 (2016)
9. Lu, J., Sibai, H., Fabry, E., Forsyth, D.: No need to worry about adversarial examples in object detection in autonomous vehicles. arXiv preprint arXiv:1707.03501 (2017)
10. Papernot, N., McDaniel, P., Jha, S., Fredrikson, M., Celik, Z.B., Swami, A.: The limitations of deep learning in adversarial settings. In: 2016 IEEE European Symposium on Security and Privacy (EuroS&P), pp. 372–387. IEEE (2016)
11. Redmon, J., Farhadi, A.: YOLO9000: better, faster, stronger. CoRR, abs/1612.08242 (2016)
12. Sabour, S., Cao, Y., Faghri, F., Fleet, D.J.: Adversarial manipulation of deep representations. arXiv preprint arXiv:1511.05122 (2015)

Specifying and Checking Data Use Policies

Sriram K. Rajamani

Microsoft Research, Bengaluru, India
sriram@microsoft.com

Cloud computing has changed the goals of security and privacy research. The primary concerns have shifted to protecting data in terms of not only who gets to access data, but also how they use it. While the former can be specified using access control logics, the latter is relatively a new topic and relatively unexplored.

We describe a language called Legalese, which we designed to specify data use policies in cloud services. Legalese [1] uses propositional logic together with type-state to specify constraints on data use, retention and combination of data. Next, we describe a notion called Information Release Confinement (IRC) [2], which can be used to specify that data does not leave a region except through specific channels such as API calls. IRC has been used to specify and verify confidentiality of cloud services that use Intel SGX enclaves. Finally, we speculate on combining these two approaches to specify and check stateful policies on data use in cloud services.

References

1. Sen, S., Guha, S., Datta, A., Rajamani, S.K., Tsai, J.Y., Wing, J.M.: Bootstrapping Privacy Compliance in Big Data Systems. In: IEEE Symposium on Security and Privacy, pp. 327–34 (2014)
2. Sinha, R., et al.: A design and verification methodology for secure isolated regions. In: PLDI, pp. 665–681 (2016)

Contents

Privacy

Client Security and Authentication

Invited Keynote

Ubiquitous Computing

A Characterization of the Mass Surveillance Potential of Road Traffic Monitors

Kirk Boyer, Hao Chen, Jingwei Chen, Jian Qiu, and Rinku Dewri[✉]

Department of Computer Science, University of Denver, Denver, CO, USA
rdewri@cs.du.edu

Abstract. Modern technology allows for the detection and identification of a vehicle passing through specific locations on a road network. The most prominent technology in use leverages cameras capable of high speed image capture, back-end extraction of plate numbers, and real time membership queries in multiple databases. Various parties have a vested interest in making use of the kind of data produced by such systems, in particular to deter risky driving, analyze traffic patterns, enable unmanned toll collection, and aid law enforcement agencies. In this paper, we proceed to assess the mass surveillance potential arising from the type and frequency of data collected in these systems. We show that even when restricted to information only about the structure of a road network, one can begin to set up an effective network of traffic monitoring devices to infer the travel destinations of individuals up to a concerning level of precision. We develop a tracker placement algorithm to corroborate this claim, and provide a quantitative evaluation of the privacy risks generated by the network of trackers determined by this algorithm.

Keywords: Location privacy · Mass surveillance · ALPR

1 Introduction

A recurring theme in privacy is that the development of technologies that provide new useful forms of data often inadvertently provide access, even if indirectly, to information that is much more personal than originally intended or hoped. One such technology is automatic vehicle detection and identification, which can be used for traffic control and enforcement, monitoring accidents, toll collection, criminal pursuits, and gathering intelligence, among others. The technology is undoubtedly powerful and is beneficial for local administration and public safety services. It has seen different levels of adoption, ranging from local municipalities to large scale nationwide deployments.

As real-time image recognition technology evolves and becomes cost-effective, the installation of monitoring devices in road networks is only expected to increase. There is already a circulating argument from privacy groups that the

© Springer Nature Switzerland AG 2018
V. Ganapathy et al. (Eds.): ICISS 2018, LNCS 11281, pp. 3–23, 2018.
https://doi.org/10.1007/978-3-030-05171-6_1

deployment of more and more vehicle tracking devices in disparate localities could finally amalgamate into a large scale mass surveillance network. While some networks are large enough that real time tracking is surmised to be possible (e.g. the UK's National ANPR Data Center [15]), other road networks across much of the developed world are slowly being converted to smart infrastructures aided with traffic cameras and back-end vehicle identification systems [19]. In the midst of continuous deployments, it is often difficult to comprehend when the state of traffic monitoring technology crosses the thin line between public good and personal privacy.

In this paper, we present the first known study to quantitatively assess the mass tracking potential of traffic monitoring devices. We explore how the number and geographic locations of vehicle identification cameras (or trackers in general) impact the real time tracking of a moving vehicle on a road network. Since roadways are hierarchically designed, placing trackers in specific high usage junctions can add more value from a surveillance standpoint than others. In addition, we seek to obtain a quantitative characterization of the privacy implications of such tracking, primarily as related to the locations visited by an individual.

We first develop a tracker placement algorithm that favors nodes that are central to the fastest paths joining locations on a road network graph. In this context, there are the competing interests of placing trackers at frequently passed locations, and preventing the clustering of trackers in a small region. Second, we propose four metrics to evaluate the surveillance coverage of a specific set of trackers, their effectiveness in being able to continuously track a vehicle, and consequently how much location uncertainty remains about the destinations of a travel path. An empirical evaluation of the placement algorithm with respect to these metrics in a 100 square mile area of the Denver metropolitan area of Colorado, USA suggests that, with as few as 100 trackers, one can achieve an 80% coverage, and location uncertainties close to a mile. The location privacy risks are worrisome if the number of trackers crosses into the thousands—using 1000 trackers, 97.6% of tested paths could be tracked, with most destination nodes being traceable to within 2000 ft.

The remainder of the paper is organized as follows. We present background on the tracking methodology, and insights into the design of our tracker placement algorithm in Sects. 2 and 3. Section 4 presents the four evaluation metrics. We present the experimental setup in Sect. 5, followed by empirical results in Sect. 6. Section 7 discusses some related work in the domain. Finally, we conclude the paper in Sect. 8 with a discussion on potential refinements.

2   Road Traffic Monitoring

A road network is modeled as a directed graph $G = \langle V, E \rangle$ consisting of a vertex (node) set V and an edge set E. A node is present for each road intersection. However, nodes are typically present between two intersections as well when the path connecting them is not a straight line. This helps maintain the shape of roadways when visualized as a planar graph, and also enables accurate computation of the distance between two intersection nodes. An edge represents a road segment between two adjacent nodes. Nodes can be annotated with positioning data, and edges can be annotated with length and speed limit. Figure 1 depicts a road network graph plotted based on the latitude and longitude positions of corresponding nodes.

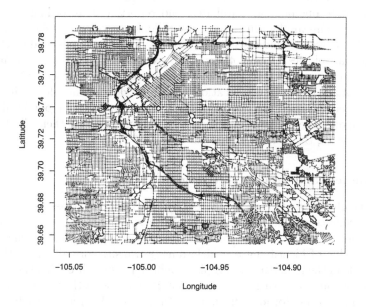

Fig. 1. An example road network graph.

Travel on a road network is often dictated by shortest time and fewer turns, instead of shortest length [8]. As such, a typical path between two nodes shows a hierarchy of road types, starting at local streets, joining on to higher capacity, but fewer, collector and arterial roadways, and finally to a limited number of expressways for long distance travel [1]. This pattern results in certain road segments being utilized with much higher frequency than others.

2.1 Traffic Monitoring

Several types of traffic cameras supplement a modern road transportation infrastructure. The most common of these is a traffic detection camera, deployed at intersections to detect the presence of traffic and accordingly activate traffic lights. Such cameras are monitored in real time by the local administration, who also decides whether the footage is recorded. The availability of cost-effective high-resolution cameras opens the possibility of performing other recognition tasks on the captured images, such as passenger face detection and vehicle identification (number plate). Another category of cameras that is deployed enforces different traffic regulations such as red lights, speed limits, restricted vehicle lanes, occupancy limits, and tollways. These cameras could be supplemented with additional hardware, such as a flash light or a radio transceiver, depending on the task for which they are set up. Since a penalty is often levied on violators, the ability to perform vehicle identification is rudimentary in such deployments. An Automated License Plate Recognition (ALPR) system can perform such a task by automatically extracting a vehicle's plate number from a captured image, comparing it to one or more databases, and reporting or recording the results [7]. ALPR systems are known to be in use to look for stolen vehicles, or vehicles registered to persons of interest, gather intelligence on criminals, and track fleets of commercial vehicles, among others. They exist as locally managed small-scale systems, and also as nationwide deployments (e.g. UK's National ANPR Data Center). Not all ALPR camera locations are public domain knowledge due to the nature of their intended use cases. ALPR systems also have the potential to act as mass surveillance systems, although it is difficult to assess their effectiveness without knowing the camera locations.

2.2 Trackers and Tracker Activations

A primary objective of this work is to gather a preliminary assessment on the mass surveillance potential of traffic monitoring cameras. We abstract out the type of camera in use, and use the term *tracker* to mean any monitoring device that is capable of identifying a vehicle during transit. Formally, a tracker is a special node in the road network graph. A vehicle passing through a tracker node is then analogous to making an entry into a database with the vehicle's identity, the tracker's location (or identifier), and a timestamp. We refer to such an event as a *tracker activation*. Multiple activations can originate from a tracker at the same time instance, meaning that a tracker is fast enough to identify multiple high-speed vehicles passing through the node at the same time. We assume that trackers are omni-directional (works irrespective of the direction of approach towards the node). A vehicle traveling through a road network generates tracker activations as it passes through tracker nodes, effectively generating a timestamped trace of its locations on the road network.

2.3 Path Reconstruction

Given a road network $G = \langle V, E \rangle$, let the ordered set $P = \{v_1, v_2, ..., v_l\}$ represent a path of length l, where $v_i \in V$, for $i = 1...l$, and $v_i \rightarrow v_{i+1} \in E$, for $i = 1...(l-1)$. Here, v_1 is the source (start) and v_l is the destination (end) node of the path, also referred to as the boundary nodes of the path. Let $T \subseteq V$ designate a set of tracker nodes. Then, $P \cap T$ represents the trackers that are activated by path P. The ordering of elements in this intersection is done as per their ordering in P. Let $\tilde{P} = P \cap T = \{v_{t_1}, v_{t_2}, ..., v_{t_s}\}$ be the ordered set of activated trackers. v_{t_1} and v_{t_s} are the corresponding boundary nodes of this set.

An entity monitoring tracker activations will observe a time series of tracker activations for each vehicle. This series can be split into multiple subsequences by observing the time difference between two successive activations – if the time difference is much larger than the time required to travel between the two trackers, then it is reasonable to split the series at this point.

Given a set of activated trackers $\tilde{P}$ obtained after splitting as above, a monitoring entity can attempt to reconstruct P based on standard notions of optimal travel time. Let $\mathsf{op}(v, v')$ denote the optimal path from source v to destination v'. The optimal path between two nodes is often the fastest path, unless it is exceedingly longer than the shortest path. For the purpose of this study, we will mean the fastest path in all our uses of the op function. One way to reconstruct P from $\tilde{P}$ is to concatenate the optimal paths between successive trackers in $\tilde{P}$. The reconstructed path, denoted as P', is given as

$$P' = \mathsf{op}(v_{t_1}, v_{t_2}) \cup \ ... \ \cup \mathsf{op}(v_{t_{s-1}}, v_{t_s}),$$

where the union operations are order-preserving. Observe that if tracker activations are generated by vehicles following the fastest path from a source to a destination, then the reconstruction is simply $P' = \mathsf{op}(v_{t_1}, v_{t_s})$. The quality of a reconstruction is then dependent on the proximity of a vehicle's tracker activations to the source and destination nodes, which in turn is dependent on the placement of trackers in the road network.

3   Tracker Placement

A trivial method to ensure that a reconstructed path exactly matches the underlying true path is to convert every node in the network to a tracker. Thereafter, the tracker activations will indicate the exact path ($P' = \tilde{P} = P$), and no reconstruction is necessary. Another alternative would be to only convert the intersection nodes to trackers, and then calculate the optimal path between two trackers as the path containing no intermediate intersections. Clearly, both solutions are cost-prohibitive.

We explore the problem of placing trackers under the situation when the number of trackers, n_T, is pre-decided. Thereafter, given a road network graph G and a positive integer n_T, determine n_T nodes to be converted to trackers such that the accuracy of path reconstructions is maximized. Specific algorithms can be tailored to maximize specific accuracy metrics; however, our approach in this initial study is to develop a generic method free from any specific metric, and then evaluate its performance with respect to different metrics. The design of specific algorithms targeting specific objective functions is left for a future study.

3.1   Frequency Based Placement

One generic approach to place the trackers is to choose nodes in the decreasing order of their frequency of use in paths. The approach is promising due to the hierarchical nature of roadways, and the conformance of driving patterns to this hierarchy in terms of path selection [18]. The node frequencies can be obtained from structural properties of the road network, or through a sampling of traffic flow using temporary devices such as pneumatic road tubes. We consider the betweenness centrality measure of connected graphs for the former [3]. The betweenness value of a node v captures the inclusion of v in the optimal paths between any pair of nodes. If $\mathcal{P}(v_a, v_b)$ represents all optimal paths from node v_a to v_b, then the betweenness value of a node v is given as

$$\beta(v) = \sum_{v \neq v_a \neq v_b} \frac{|\{P | P \in \mathcal{P}(v_a, v_b) \text{ and } v \in P\}|}{|\mathcal{P}(v_a, v_b)|}. \tag{1}$$

It can be reasonably assumed that a road network will be a connected graph. Hence, $|\mathcal{P}(v_a, v_b)| > 0$, for all v_a, v_b in the above formulation; otherwise, we ignore such pairs of nodes in the computation. Recall that we use the fastest path(s) as the optimal ones.

Node frequencies can also be obtained from available traffic count data. While betweenness accounts for paths between all pairs of nodes, and treats all such paths equally, frequency information derived from traffic counts can capture travel patterns specific to localities (e.g. a local store), central commercial locations (e.g. a business district in the city), and temporal variations throughout the day. In the following discussion, we will use the term *node frequency* to mean either betweenness or traffic count depending on the context.

3.2   Minimal Separation Between Trackers

Given the set of nodes ordered by their frequencies, the first n_T nodes can be converted to trackers so that tracker activations are triggered for a large number of paths. However, neighboring road network nodes tend to cluster together when sorted based on their frequencies. A high frequency node often has adjoining frequently used road segments. Figure 2 illustrates the issue with a toy example. Consider the four paths originating in S and terminating in A, B, C and D. Assume that each hop (moving along an edge) takes constant time. Based on the four paths, if the two highest frequency nodes are converted to trackers (leftmost figure), then node A would be 1 hop away from a tracker activation, node B would be 2 hops away, and nodes C and D will be 3 hops away. However, the average hop count can be reduced by forcing the trackers to have some minimal separation, instead of being adjacent to each other. The center and right figures show the hop counts when using a separation of 2 hops between trackers. Motivated by this observation, we choose nodes in decreasing order of their frequencies, but skip a node if a tracker already exists within some predefined distance of the node.

3.3   Waves

Minimal separating distances help disperse trackers throughout a road network. However, if the specified distance is too large, there is a possibility that the entire set of nodes is exhausted before n_T nodes are chosen as trackers. To alleviate this issue, we can restart the selection process on the remaining nodes using a smaller separating distance than in the previous iteration. Hence, our approach

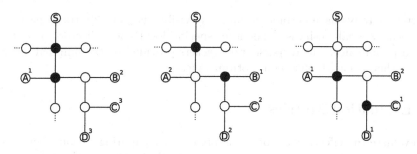

Fig. 2. Introducing separation between trackers (solid circles) can help improve reconstruction effectiveness.

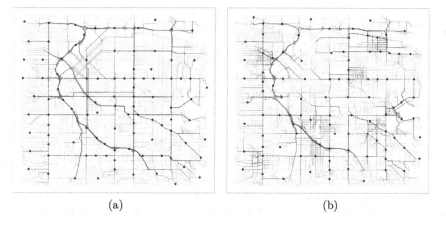

Fig. 3. Tracker placement using minimal separating distances and waves. Frequencies are from (a) betweenness values, and (b) traffic counts highlighting local visits.

runs the selection process in waves (iterations) until n_T nodes have been chosen. The steps for the entire approach can be summarized as follows.

1. Let V_{sorted} be an ordered set of vertices sorted in decreasing order of their frequencies, $T = \phi$, $\boldsymbol{d} = (d_1, d_2, ..., d_w = 0)$ be a sequence of decreasing values to be used as separating distances, and dist be a distance function between nodes. Let $wave = 1$ and $V_{rejected} = \phi$.
2. Remove the first node $v \in V_{sorted}$. Add v to T if for all $v' \in T$, dist$(v, v') > d_{wave}$; otherwise add v to $V_{rejected}$ (tail end).
3. If $V_{sorted} = \phi$, increment $wave$ by 1, set $V_{sorted} = V_{rejected}$ and then $V_{rejected} = \phi$.
4. If $|T| < n_T$, repeat from step 2.

Figure 3 illustrates the result of placing 100 trackers on a road network graph of the Denver metropolitan area in Colorado, USA. In both plots, frequently used roadways are depicted using a darker shade. For Fig. 3a, the fastest paths between all pairs of nodes have been considered. As a result, all highways and arterial roadways have become prominently visible. For Fig. 3b, travel paths are to a nearby local business. Therefore, specific local and collector roads have gained prominence. The dispersion of trackers provided by the minimal separation method is clearly visible in both instances.

4   Evaluation Metrics

We evaluate the effectiveness of our approach by computing various metrics on the reconstructed paths corresponding to a set $\mathcal{P}_{test}$ of test paths. Given a set of tracker nodes T, we compute the reconstructed path P_i' for each test path $P_i \in \mathcal{P}_{test}$ as detailed in Sect. 2.3.

4.1   Reconstruction Coverage

An ill-placed set of trackers will fail to overlap with most paths. As a result, no activations will be triggered, thereby leading to no reconstruction. For mass surveillance, the more reconstructions that a set of trackers can effectuate, the better is the underlying placement. Reconstruction coverage captures this aspect as the fraction of test paths for which a reconstruction is possible.

$$Coverage = \frac{|\{P|P \in \mathcal{P}_{test} \text{ and } P \cap T \neq \phi\}|}{|\mathcal{P}_{test}|}. \tag{2}$$

Coverage does not consider the quality of a reconstruction. Even a single tracker activation is considered a successful tracking event under this metric, although no path reconstruction is possible with a single tracker activation.

4.2   Path Coverage

The path coverage metric measures the fraction of the total distance in a path $P_i \in \mathcal{P}_{test}$ that has been accurately covered by the corresponding reconstructed path P_i'. If $P_i = \{v_{i1}, v_{i2}, ..., v_{il}\}$ and $P_i' = \{v_{i1}', v_{i2}', ..., v_{il'}'\}$, then

$$Path\,Coverage(P_i) = \frac{\sum_{k=1}^{l'-1} \text{dist}(v_{ik}', v_{i(k+1)}')}{\sum_{k=1}^{l-1} \text{dist}(v_{ik}, v_{i(k+1)})}. \tag{3}$$

This metric is appropriate when the test path P_i is also an optimal path as per the op function used during the path reconstruction. When using fastest paths, we clearly have $P_i' \subseteq P_i$ and the metric signifies the fraction of travel distance for which the vehicle's location can be accurately tracked in real time.

4.3   Boundary Activation Distance

We often associate a higher privacy value to the locations and neighborhoods that we visit, instead of the path we take to arrive at such destinations. While high frequency nodes operating as trackers can provide good reconstruction and path coverage, the associated privacy risks can be minimal if a path's source and destination are difficult to infer from a reconstruction. As such the boundary activation distance metric quantifies the average distance between the two corresponding boundary nodes in the real and the reconstructed paths. If $P_i = \{v_{i1}, v_{i2}, ..., v_{il}\}$ and $P_i' = \{v_{i1}', v_{i2}', ..., v_{il'}'\}$, then

$$Boundary\ Activation(P_i) = \frac{1}{2}\left(\mathsf{dist}(v_{i1}, v_{i1}') + \mathsf{dist}(v_{il}, v_{il'}')\right). \qquad (4)$$

Tracker activations happening closer to the source and destination nodes of a path will result in a smaller boundary activation distance, thereby providing smaller areas of uncertainties on the source and destination of a path.

4.4   Tracker Period

The real time tracking potential of a set of trackers can be characterized in a manner similar to that in the boundary activation distance metric. Instead of considering the location uncertainty only at the boundary nodes, the tracker period metric considers the uncertainty along the entire path as the average distance traveled between two successive tracker activations. If $P_i \cap T = \{v_{it_1}, v_{it_2}, ..., v_{it_s}\}$ are the activated tracker nodes, then

$$Tracker\ Period(P_i) = \frac{1}{s-1}\sum_{k=1}^{s-1} \mathsf{op_{len}}(v_{it_k}, v_{it_{k+1}}), \qquad (5)$$

where $\mathsf{op_{len}}(v_a, v_b)$ is the length (travel distance) of the optimal path from node v_a to v_b. A well dispersed set of trackers will generate a consistent tracker period for a majority of the test paths.

Average values for path coverage, boundary activation distance and tracker period can be computed over the test paths in $\mathcal{P}_{test}$. In addition, summary statistics such as median and quartiles are useful in observing the variation in the metrics' values over different paths.

5   Experimental Setup

We perform the empirical evaluation of our approach on a road network graph spanning an approximately 100 square mile area of Denver, Colorado, USA (Fig. 1). The graph spans between latitudes 39.654518°N and 39.790931°N, and longitudes 105.053195°W and 104.867402°W. It consists of 40,253 vertices and 83,599 directed edges. Each node is labeled with its latitude and longitude coordinates. Each edge is labeled with the geodesic distance between the two nodes,

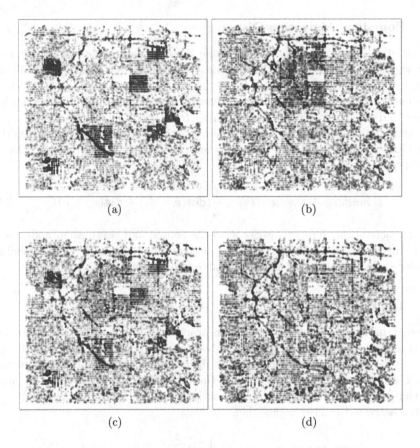

Fig. 4. Source and destination nodes of 10,000 test paths in four different generation models—(a) local (b) central (c) mix (d) free. See text for model descriptions.

a road segment type value, and the speed limit on the road segment. We compute the time required to travel a road segment (edge) by dividing the distance by the speed limit. Distances between nodes (the dist function) are computed using the Vincenty inverse formula for ellipsoid, which is available as the gdist function in the Imap R package. The implementation is done as a single threaded R application, running on a laptop with a 3.1 GHz Intel Core i7 processor, 16 GB memory, and OSX 10.10.5. Graph operations, such as finding fastest paths and betweenness centrality values, are performed using the igraph 1.2.1 R package.

We consider four probabilistic node selection models, and generate 10,000 test paths from each. For test path generation, we divide the graph area into a 10×10 grid of cells, and assign a probability of selection to each cell. Nodes are chosen by first choosing a cell as per the assigned probabilities, and then randomly picking a node within the chosen cell. In the *free* model, equal probabilities are assigned to each cell, and source/destination pairs are chosen accordingly. For the *central* model, specific cells in the Denver business district are assigned

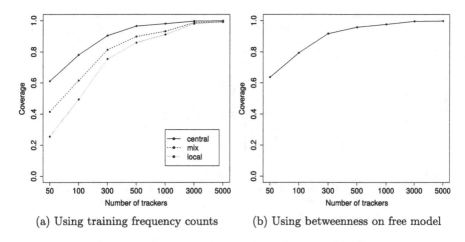

(a) Using training frequency counts   (b) Using betweenness on free model

Fig. 5. Coverage evaluation.

a significantly higher probability of selection. Once a source (or destination) node is chosen based on these probabilities, the other node is chosen similar to as in the free model. This results in most paths being directed towards, or away from, a central area in the city. In the *local* model, few cells containing locally prominent shopping stores are first identified. A source node is chosen as in the free model. The destination node is then chosen from the closest locally prominent cell. Finally, the *mix* model contains paths of types generated in both the central and the local models. The sampled source and destination nodes of the paths in the four models are depicted in Fig. 4. The fastest path between a chosen source and destination pair is taken as the respective test path. The generated paths are usually the same as obtained from road navigation services.

We implemented our approach to place trackers based on both the betweenness centrality measure, as well as traffic counts. In the absence of real traffic count data, we obtained the counts for the latter from a set of training paths generated in a manner similar to that of test paths. We generated separate sets of 10,000 training paths from each of the local, central and mix models, and computed the node frequencies in each case from the corresponding training paths set. Unless stated otherwise, the free model test paths are used to evaluate the trackers placed based on betweenness values, while the local, central and mix model test paths are used to evaluate trackers placed based on frequency counts computed from the respective training paths.

We present results for tracker counts (n_T) of 50, 100, 300, 500, 1000, 3000, and 5000, using a separation distance vector of $d = (1, 0.5, 0.25, 0.1, 0)$ mile for all but the case of $n_T = 50$. For $n_T = 50$, we start with a separation distance of 2 miles, followed by the listed values. Where appropriate, metrics are computed only on the test paths for which a reconstruction is possible.

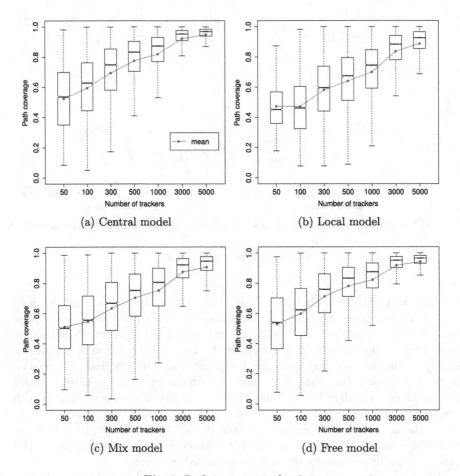

Fig. 6. Path coverage evaluation.

6   Results

In the following, we first report results on the mass surveillance potential of the tracker placement approach, and later discuss some parameter influence.

6.1   Mass Tracking

Reconstruction Coverage. Figure 5 shows the reconstruction coverage of the placement algorithm in the four models. Except in the local model, some form of reconstruction becomes possible for 80% or more of the test paths with 300 or more trackers. The coverage is also reasonably good in the mix and free models for as few as 100 trackers. The local model requires more trackers to achieve coverage similar to the central or mix models. This is expected since traffic is more likely to be restricted to localities, and hence trackers have mostly local

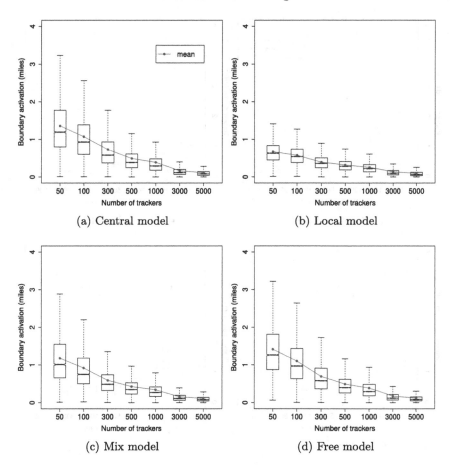

Fig. 7. Boundary activation distance evaluation.

utility. A tracker has better overall utility when it can be on the path of local as well as centrally directed traffic, as in the central and mix models.

Path Coverage. The path coverage statistics on the fraction of covered test paths (reconstruction possible) for each model are depicted in Fig. 6. We report summary statistics using a boxplot, which shows the minimum, first quartile, median, third quartile, and maximum values. In general, the results for the local model lie somewhere between that of the central and mix models, with the free model statistics being similar or better than those in the mix model. An average path coverage of 60–70% is achieved with 300 trackers, with 75% of the test paths being reconstructed with at least a 50% path coverage (the local model is slightly lower). While the minimum and maximum values fluctuate, the quartile boundaries show a general increasing trend with increasing number of trackers.

Boundary Activation Distance. From the standpoint of source and destination privacy, the boundary activation distance is a critical measure. Path source

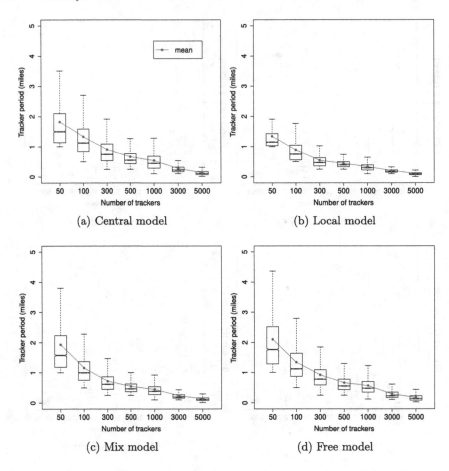

(a) Central model

(b) Local model

(c) Mix model

(d) Free model

Fig. 8. Tracker period evaluation.

and destination is within an average of less than a mile from the closest tracker activations when using 300 trackers. The uncertainty reduces to half a mile or less with 500 trackers. The interquartile range in most cases is itself half a mile or less, indicating that the metric's value even with the observed variations is concernedly low. It can be seen that the metric has much lower values in the local model compared to the other models. This is because trackers in this model locally serve a smaller targeted region, and the source nodes are often in the close vicinity.

Tracker Period. The uncertainty in continuous tracking is depicted in terms of the tracker period metric in Fig. 8. Although the values are slightly larger than the boundary activation distances, the trends are similar in nature. Effectively, tracker activations happen every mile or less (on an average) with 300 or more trackers. The quartile values are indicative of a good dispersion of trackers across the entire area.

In summary, the evaluation indicates that trackers placed based on node frequencies have a significant mass tracking potential with as few as 100 or 300 trackers. A vehicle can also be localized to a small region at all times, which can have adverse implications in terms of location privacy. The potential is amplified almost to the extent of targeted tracking when deploying more than 1000 trackers is no longer cost-prohibitive. Comparatively, using the betweenness centrality measure (as in the free model evaluation) provides similar effectiveness as when using traffic counts. The advantage is that betweenness is a structural property of the graph, and does not require sample data of traffic counts. Hence, this approach is more generic and attractive. Of course, to be robust, the betweenness approach should perform reasonably well even when test paths follow specific distributions, as in the central, mix, or local models (Sect. 6.3).

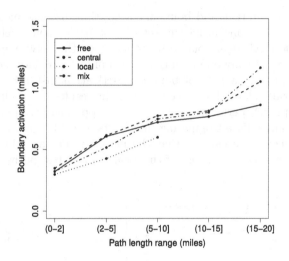

Fig. 9. Path length versus boundary activation distance when using 300 trackers.

6.2 Impact of Path Length

The test paths used in the evaluations range from 0–10 miles in the local model, and 0–20 miles in the other three models. It is imperative to ask if the boundary activation distance statistics have been skewed due to significantly differing performance in long and short paths. Figure 9 depicts the mean boundary activation distance in subsets of test paths grouped by path length. While we observe a tendency for the boundary activation distance to slowly grow with longer paths, the absolute values themselves are within half a mile of the collective mean. We do not consider this variation to be significant enough that it can alleviate any pertinent privacy concerns when traveling longer distances.

Table 1. Performance of the betweenness approach with 300 trackers on different model specific test paths.

	Boundary activation distance		Coverage
	Mean (miles)	Variance	
Free	0.69	0.21	0.92
Central	0.72	0.22	0.91
Local	0.50	0.08	0.55
Mix	0.64	0.18	0.72

6.3   Impact of Path Distributions

Table 1 shows the coverage and boundary activation distance means/variances resulting from evaluations using the set of test paths from each of the four models when 300 trackers are placed based solely on the betweenness centrality measures. We have already observed that the approach provides more than 90% coverage and less than a mile of boundary activation distance on test paths generated uniformly at random (free model). The results here indicate that the betweenness approach performs at par with an approach executed with model specific traffic counts data. Comparing the results in Table 1 and those in Figs. 5 and 7 (300 trackers), we can see that the metric values are almost identical, except for a lower coverage in case of the local model's test paths.

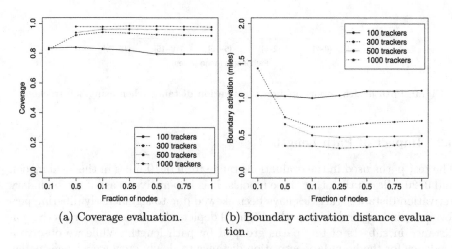

(a) Coverage evaluation.   (b) Boundary activation distance evaluation.

Fig. 10. Impact of considering a reduced set of nodes for tracker placement.

6.4   Candidate Nodes for Tracker Placement

The betweenness centrality values (and frequency of node usage in general) of a road network follow a heavy tailed distribution. For example, in the Denver area graph we use here, 75% of the sum of the betweenness values comes from that of only 12.5% of the most frequently used nodes in the network. Since our approach enforces minimal separation between trackers, it is possible that, within a wave, nodes that are insignificant in terms of their centrality in fastest paths gets chosen as trackers. It therefore begs the question of whether tracking performance can be improved by restricting the choice of trackers to few most frequently used nodes only. Figure 10 depicts the coverage and mean boundary activation distance on the free model test paths when trackers are chosen from the top 1%, 5%, 10%, 25%, 50%, 75% and 100% nodes sorted by their betweenness values. Since the total number of nodes is 40,253, results are unavailable when restricting to the top 1% of nodes while requiring 500 or 1000 trackers. We observe minor, but insignificant, improvements when restricting to the top 10–25% of the nodes. Clearly, restricting to too few nodes will nullify the advantages of the minimal separation approach owing to the iterative reduction of the separation distance.

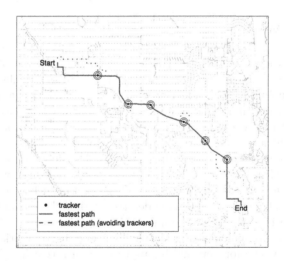

Fig. 11. A tracking avoidance example.

6.5   Tracking Avoidance

As the final experiment, we explored how the travel time will be affected if tracker locations are known, and an attempt is made to travel along the fastest path that avoids the tracker nodes. As shown in Fig. 11, an avoidance path could simply include rerouting in the vicinity of the tracker nodes, or separate (potentially slower) subpaths altogether. Depending on the source and destination of a path,

Table 2. Impact of avoiding trackers on travel time and connectivity.

(a) Mean percentage increase in travel time

	Number of trackers						
	50	100	300	500	1000	3000	5000
free	12.9	20.5	32.8	47.7	60.3	100.1	108.9
central	11.6	19.4	30.7	45.6	53.8	103.9	50.2
local	17.2	26.3	39.0	62.2	99.7	200.4	61.9
mix	12.1	19.3	32.9	50.3	62.4	97.2	45.9

(b) Percentage of test paths with no avoidance path

	Number of trackers						
	50	100	300	500	1000	3000	5000
free	2.4	4.5	9.1	18.8	28.0	94.4	99.7
central	2.0	3.8	7.5	15.9	26.9	96.1	99.8
local	3.3	4.1	12.7	16.4	30.0	85.9	99.1
mix	1.4	3.4	10.0	17.9	27.1	91.1	98.9

it is also possible that an avoidance path is impossible since a node critical to the connectivity between the boundary nodes has been marked as a tracker. Table 2 shows the average percentage increase in travel time of the various test paths in the four models (trackers placed by the default approaches). We observe an average of ≈30% increase in travel time with 300 trackers in place. In addition, ≈10% of the test paths have no avoidance paths. The travel time may not be too bad, but the path itself can be inconvenient on a regular basis! The values become significantly worse for 1000 or more trackers.

7 Related Work

The issue of privacy in automated traffic enforcements has received significant attention from academicians and civil liberty groups alike. Blumberg et al. highlighted that automated vehicle identification systems should be designed to cater no more information than what is necessary to enforce traffic laws [2]. To such an end, they proposed a camera-free protocol for traffic monitoring where the identity of a vehicle can be learned only if it violated a traffic law. The Australian Privacy Foundation argued that automated vehicle identification can be inaccurate, and thereby result in unreasonable, embarrassing, or even dangerous, conclusions for law-abiding citizens [4]. The effect of such social implications can be much greater than the possible deterrence that the technology can have on criminals. Besides, the ability to link vehicle sightings to travel patterns can expose individuals to malicious uses such as theft and discrimination, in addition to creating the avenue for personal habits to be scrutinized in a legal proceeding [5]. The absence of national standards and policies for transportation data storage and access can make it a challenging task to assure privacy and accountability to the traveling public. A key challenge that has been identified in this context is to succinctly define terms such as "casual observation" and "targeted surveillance" [9]. Irrespective of the numerous privacy preservation proposals offered, adoption has been minimal, and the threat continues to grow [6,17].

The usage of centrality measures to capture traffic flows has been explored earlier in the context of urban transportation planning. Kazerani and Winter argued that human agents demonstrate travel behavior that cannot be captured with topological characteristics of a road network alone. As such, centrality measures based on traditional notions of shortest path are insufficient [12,13]. Further, sources and destinations of travel are not uniformly distributed, and change over time, which contradicts the premise behind measures such as betweenness. We partially observed the impact of these dynamics in our study; albeit, the advantages of pursuing non-generic measures was minimal in mass tracking, at least when working with fixed trackers only. In fact, in a large scale study involving 360,000 San Francisco Bay area users and 680,000 Boston area users spanning a three week period, nodes with the top 25% of betweenness and degree values were reported to be of topological importance from a driving standpoint [18]. Park and Yilmaz observed that node centrality in downtown versus residential locations can be quite different owing to the presence of alternative pathways in the grid-like design of the former [16]. Gao et al. also reported a similar conclusion when attempting to understand urban traffic-flow characteristics [10]. As a consequence in this work, attempts to monitor traffic inside a core urban area will require the placement of more trackers. Combining multiple centrality measures to understand traffic flow can also be useful [11].

The closest work with respect to determining ideal tracker locations on a road network is in a recent study by Ma et al. [14]. Their approach operates on a grid of blocks overlaid on the road network, and identifies prominent blocks based on factors such as number of unique vehicles crossing a block, amount of vehicle traffic, time when a vehicle is out of surveillance, and average camera-hit intervals. The placement strategy is tied to a set of already available GPS traces—a dependency that we sought to avoid in this study.

8   Conclusion and Future Work

Through this work, we have demonstrated that existing traffic monitoring capabilities hold the potential to support a high-precision mass surveillance network without the need for an excessive level of investment. Our node tracker placement algorithm can determine critical locations on a road network that are often parts of high traffic routes, and also disperse trackers over a region to enable a large coverage. Results suggest that more disclosure is needed in how and where traffic monitoring locations are chosen in an evolving infrastructure so as to ensure that evaluations of the nature performed here can be carried out to quantitatively assess potential privacy risks.

In this work, we approached tracker placement as a static problem. However, traffic patterns change at different times of the day, creating a varying distribution of node usage frequencies. Although we have demonstrated that the betweenness approach adapts well to specific distributions, it remains to be evaluated if tracking capabilities are enhanced when mobile trackers can be deployed. Mobile trackers can change locations depending on changing traffic patterns and have the potential to address low coverage areas dynamically. What mix of fixed and mobile trackers can provide an attractive solution is an interesting direction to explore.

Traffic cameras are currently deployed mostly in accident prone and high crime areas. Our placement algorithm targets good surveillance possibility. With access to a database of cameras with their deployed locations, we can assess where the current mass tracking capabilities stand in a region of interest. Such a study can hopefully provide a much needed quantitative dimension to the debate on service versus privacy in the transportation infrastructure.

References

1. American Association of State Highway and Transportation Officials: A Guide for Achieving Flexibility in Highway Design, chap. 1.4.1 Functional Classification (2004)
2. Blumberg, A.J., Keeler, L.S., Shelat, A.: Automated traffic enforcement which respects "driver privacy". In: Proceedings of 2005 IEEE Intelligent Transportation Systems, pp. 941–946 (2005)
3. Brandes, U.: A faster algorithm for betweenness centrality. J. Math. Sociol. **25**(2), 163–177 (2001)
4. Clarke, R.: The covert implementation of mass vehicle surveillance in Australia. In: Proceedings of the Fourth Workshop on the Social Implications of National Security, pp. 45–59 (2009)
5. Cottrill, C.D.: Examining privacy and surveillance in urban areas: a transportation context. In: Proceedings of 3rd Hot Topics in Privacy Enhancing Technologies, pp. 1–13 (2010)
6. Crump, C.: You are being tracked: how license plate readers are being used to record Americans' movements. Technical report. American Civil Liberties Union (2013)
7. Du, S., Ibrahim, M., Shehata, M., Badawy, W.: Automatic license plate recognition (ALPR): a state-of-the-art review. IEEE Trans. Circuits Syst. Video Technol. **23**(2), 311–325 (2013)
8. Duckham, M., Kulik, L.: "Simplest" paths: automated route selection for navigation. In: Proceedings of the International Conference on Spatial Information Theory, pp. 169–185 (2003)
9. Fries, R.N., Gahrooei, M.R., Chowdhury, M., Conway, A.J.: Meeting privacy challenges while advancing intelligent transportation systems. Transp. Res. Part C: Emerg. Technol. **25**, 34–45 (2012)
10. Gao, S., Wang, Y., Gao, Y., Liu, Y.: Understanding urban traffic-flow characteristics: a rethinking of betweenness centrality. Environ. Plan. B: Urban Anal. City Sci. **40**(1), 135–153 (2013)
11. Jayasinghe, A., Sano, K., Nishiuchi, H.: Explaining traffic flow patterns using centrality measures. Int. J. Traffic Transp. Eng. **5**(2), 134–149 (2015)
12. Kazerani, A., Winter, S.: Can betweenness centrality explain traffic flow? In: Proceedings of the 12th AGILE International Conference on Geographic Information Science, pp. 1–9 (2009)
13. Kazerani, A., Winter, S.: Modified betweenness centrality for predicting traffic flow. In: Proceedings of the 10th International Conference on GeoComputation, pp. 1–5 (2009)
14. Ma, X., et al.: Vehicle traffic driven camera placement for better metropolis security surveillance. IEEE Intell. Syst. (2018, preprint)

15. Mandeville, B.: Automatic number plate recognition (ANPR) strategy 2016–2020. Technical report. National Police Chef's Council, UK (2016)
16. Park, K., Yilmaz, A.: A social network analysis approach to analyze road networks. In: Proceedings of the ASPRS Annual Conference (2010)
17. Schwartz, A.: Chicago's video surveillance cameras: a pervasive and poorly regulated threat to our privacy. Nortwestern J. Technol. Intellect. Prop. **11**(2), 47 (2012)
18. Wang, P., Hunter, T., Bayen, A.M., Schechtner, K., González, M.C.: Understanding road usage patterns in urban areas. Nat. Sci. Rep. **2**, 1001 (2012)
19. Wikipedia: Automatic number-plate recognition, 13 August 2018. https://en.wikipedia.org/wiki/Automatic_number-plate_recognition#Usage

SecSmartLock: An Architecture and Protocol for Designing Secure Smart Locks

Bhagyesh Patil[✉], Parjanya Vyas, and R. K. Shyamasundar

Department of Computer Science and Engineering,
Indian Institute of Technology Bombay, Mumbai, India
{bhagyeshpatil,parjanya}@iitb.ac.in, shyamasundar@gmail.com

Abstract. The Internet of Things (IoT) has become widespread in home to industrial environments. Smart locks are one of the most popular IoT devices that have been in use. Smart locks rely on smartphones to ease the burden of physical key management. Concerns that include privacy risks as well as access through unreliable devices have been raised regarding smart locks. A number of attacks have been identified based on the weaknesses in the system design of the smart locks. For example, several security vulnerabilities have been found in one of the popular architectures for smart locks called DGC (Device-Gateway-Cloud) architecture. Efforts have also been made to mitigate these attacks as much as possible. In this paper, we propose a new smart lock framework called SecSmart-Lock, that overcomes the above attacks and thus, prevents the possibility of unauthorized access to the user's premises. The proposed framework includes an architecture along with a secure communication protocol that can be used to implement marketable smart locks and server as fundamental guidelines to enhance the future research on secure smart locks. We establish proof of security of the proposed smart lock architecture and protocol. To demonstrate the practicality of our approach, we have implemented a prototype smart lock simulated using an Android smartphone along with a companion Android application. Advantages of our approach over other approaches follow from our comparison with other prominent solutions in the literature. We also highlight our implementation along with its' performance.

Keywords: Internet of Things · Smart locks · Security

1 Introduction

Internet of Things (IoT) has arrived in the houses of users converting their homes to smart homes. Smart homes support various desirable features, such as voice-controlled devices [22] and remote-controlled door locks [18]. Recently, Amazon has launched amazon key [1], which enables a person from Amazon to deliver goods to customer's home just by scanning QR code on the package and

© Springer Nature Switzerland AG 2018
V. Ganapathy et al. (Eds.): ICISS 2018, LNCS 11281, pp. 24–43, 2018.
https://doi.org/10.1007/978-3-030-05171-6_2

pressing *unlock* in a mobile app. Amazon then checks its' servers to make sure the right associate and the package are present at the right place. A camera is connected with the lock that records the package delivery that can be viewed later (for varieties of forensics). While such functionalities provide significant convenience to their users, they also raise new security and privacy risks. Further explorations are being done for increasing user convenience, but additional efforts in the direction of ensuring users' privacy or safeguarding unauthorized access of premises are also needed when using such gadgets.

As end users with relatively limited experience and awareness about the involved risks have more and more control over the smart devices and their security policies, threats also increase. Thus, security of these devices needs to be realized through proper configuration of smart home functions including setting access passwords or granting access to devices (i.e., electronic door locks). This should be done with a clear assessment of issues involving personal safety and data privacy [16].

Several smart locks are available in the market based on Device-Gateway-Cloud (DGC) architecture such as August [2], Danalock [3], Okidokeys [7], and Kevo [6]. These locks do not have direct connectivity with the Internet. They rather communicate with a user's smartphone and uses it as a gateway to access cloud. Examining the network architectures and access control policies used by these smart lock systems, an attacker can evade revocation mechanisms and access logging procedures. The automatic unlocking protocols used by August and Danalock can often undesirably unlock the door by accident or in the presence of an adversary [18].

In this paper, we propose a new architecture and protocol for smart locks called SecSmartLock that provides provable security guarantees and mitigates attacks such as Revocation Evasion and Access Log Evasion that are possible on popular smart locks based on DGC architecture. The proposed mechanism is generic enough to be implemented using any operating system that allow developing applications for IoT devices and smartphones. We have designed and implemented a prototype in which the lock has an Android OS that can be easily integrated to locks with minimal hardware requirements. The lock is operated by an Android application given to end users. End users are divided in four different categories of users which are owner, authorized user, recurring guest or temporary guest. The Android application provides functionalities such as giving unconditional or conditional accesses, revoking accesses, unlocking remotely via Bluetooth or accessing logs based on the category of user. An authority for the lock, who is henceforth referred to as the owner, could provide or revoke conditional or unconditional access to users and view logs in addition to unlocking the lock via Bluetooth. Other categories of users can unlock the lock, provided an optional condition specified by the owner is met. For instance, conditions could include allowing access on a specific date and time only, or allowing a temporary one time access. Advantages of our approach over other approaches [18] follow from our comparative study.

Rest of the paper is organized as follows: Sect. 2 describes the components and functionalities of Smart locks as well as the DGC architecture followed by Sect. 3 describing the possible security attacks on smart locks. Section 4 then describes the proposed smart lock architecture along with its operational details and the functionalities provided. Section 5 describes the security claims and their argumentative proofs followed by Sect. 6 that shows the performance evaluation of the developed prototype. Section 7 shows a comparison of our work with the relevant aspects of the research works available in the literature. Finally, Sect. 8 provides the concluding remarks and describes the future work.

2 Background

In this section, we describe the Device-Gateway-Cloud(DGC) architecture, which is an underlying architecture used by various smart locks presently available in the market. We are concerned only with the smart locks based on DGC architecture. Thus, we do not discuss other locks such as digital locks that require a fixed PIN to be entered.

2.1 Device-Gateway-Cloud (DGC) Architecture

Smart locks based on DGC architecture [18] consist of three components:

- An electronic deadbolt which is installed on the door.
- A mobile device which is used to control the lock.
- A remote web server which has information such as authorized users.

In DGC architecture, the electronic deadbolt does not have a direct connection to the Internet. Instead, smart locks rely on the user's device for Internet connectivity. The user's device acts as a *gateway* for smart locks that relays information between the remote web servers and the deadbolt. The information is only exchanged when the user's device is in Bluetooth range of the deadbolt.

Figure 1 illustrates the DGC architecture used in smartlocks such as August, Danalock, Kevo, and Okidokeys. Note that smart locks themselves do not connect to the Internet. Rather, they connect to a user's phone via Bluetooth and expect the smart phone to be connected to the Internet, where it will be able to push and pull relevant information and updates (such as updates to the lock's software or a new digital key).

2.2 Functionalities

Digital Keys: The owner(O) of a smart lock can issue a *digital key* to another user(U). This key decides the level of access O has given to U. There are four access levels:

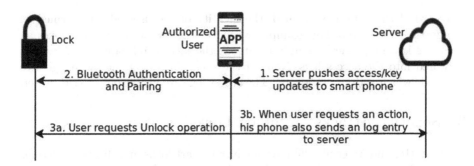

Fig. 1. Device-gateway-cloud architecture.

Owner: The owner of the smart lock is at this access level. The person with *owner* key can lock and unlock the smart lock at any time and his/her permissions can only be revoked by the manufacturer of the lock. The Owner has the capability to grant and revoke the access of the smart lock from other users at any time. The owner can access all the administrative functionalities provided by lock manufacturers such as viewing access logs or issuing digital keys.

Resident: The residents of the home are issued *Resident* level access keys. They can lock and unlock the door at any time but they do not have access to administrative functionalities provided by smart lock manufacturers (for instance, they cannot issue digital keys to other users).

Recurring Guest: *Recurring guest* keys are issued to the users who are allowed to enter the home during a fixed time window. This time is set by the owner while issuing the access. It is useful when a person (such as house cleaner) enters the home during a fixed time interval (for instance, 9–11am everyday).

Temporary Guest: The *Temporary guest* keys are given to users to whom you want to give access for a short period of time (say for a day or two).

2.3   Operations

1. **Unlocking Mechanism**
   Whenever an authorized user gets into the range of the lock, the door can be unlocked.
   - In August and Danalock, there is automatic unlocking process in which the user does not have to use the mobile application of smart lock. If user is in range of the lock then the lock gets automatically unlocked.
   - In Kevo, the touch-to-unlock mechanism is being used. In this, the user has to touch the deadbolt to activate the unlocking process. If an authorized device is inside the Bluetooth range, then the lock gets unlocked.
2. **Logging Mechanism**
   All the actions performed by any of the authorized users without any exception are stored on the server in terms of access log. Log entries include a

record of the action performed, the identity of the user who performed it, and the time-stamp. For example, whenever the owner grants or revokes an access key, or a user attempts to unlock the lock, a relevant log entry gets stored into the access logs. None of the users, including the owner, gets to decide which actions get logged. The access logs are visible only to the owner.

3   Security Attacks on Smart Locks

Ho et al. [18] and Ye et al. [26] have analyzed smart locks and discussed various security threats and attacks possible on them. Some of the attacks possible on smart locks are described below:

Revocation Evasion: A **revoked attacker** is an attacker who had legitimate access to the smart lock in past but his/her access is now revoked. For example, a home cleaner worker who has been relieved of duty. In this attack, the revocation mechanism can be evaded by the attacker and the attacker can still open the smart lock. This attack is possible on all locks based on DGC architecture when availability is favored over consistency.

Danalock allows users to interact with the lock even when it is not Internet connected. This is necessary as an authorized user should be able to unlock the lock even when the Danalock's servers are unreachable (e.g. Internet outage).

In Danalock and other locks that are based on DGC architecture, the key revocation mechanism works by having the remote server push a revocation message to the revoked user's phone. But if the phone is in airplane mode, then this information cannot be pushed by the server and the lock remains unaware of the revocation. This means that a revoked user can evade revocation by simply switching his/her device to airplane mode.

Access Log Evasion: The integrity of recorded logs is very important for forensics purposes. An adversary should not be able to tamper or alter the access logs or be able to prevent his/her interaction with the lock from being recorded. This attack can be performed by blocking all packets going to the remote server.

In Danalock and other locks based on DGC architecture, the lock relies on the user's device to communicate the details of interaction to the remote server. If the user's device is in airplane mode, then all the packets can be blocked, meaning, they could not reach the remote server. Additionally, the lock is assumed to be stateless and hence, does not store any information about the access. This means, even after a later point when a legitimate user interacts with lock the information cannot be pushed to the server.

Relay Attacks: In a **relay attacker** threat model, an attacker 'A1' has a companion 'A2'. One of them is near an authorized user and the other is near the smart lock. Both 'A1' and 'A2' have Bluetooth devices that can also communicate over long distances and transmit data.

In Kevo, when a relay attacker 'A1' is near the lock, he taps Kevo's deadbolt face to begin touch-to-unlock procedure. Using his Bluetooth relay device, he captures the Bluetooth authentication challenge message and relays(e.g. over

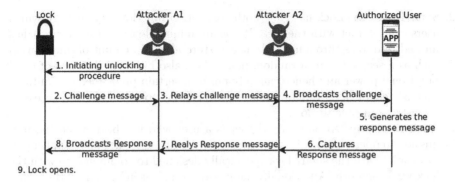

Fig. 2. Relay attack.

Internet) it to his companion 'A2' who is near the authorized user. Upon receiving the relay message, 'A2' broadcasts it, captures the response message from authorized user's device and relays this response back to 'A1', who then broadcasts it to the smart lock and the lock gets unlocked. The attack is illustrated in Fig. 2.

Danalock and August use geo-fencing [5] design which makes relay attacks more difficult, but the attack is still possible. In this attack, the attacker's 'A' and 'B' both should conduct a Bluetooth relay attack against the authorized user and smart lock, and spoof a false geo-location onto authorized user's phone. The smart lock applications query passive geo-location (such as WLAN-based positioning [17], based on nearby Wi-Fi network ids) once every few minutes and occasionally use GPS to confirm this location. Thus, a relay attacker can still gain unauthorized access by first conducting a location spoofing attack on authorized user's phone and then proceeding with a regular relay attack.

Unintentional Unlocking: All the locks provide some kind of automatic unlocking procedure, but this brings in the possibility of a physical attack. The range of communication of lock can be boosted by an attacker by using available methods [23], and if the authorized user is at few meters distance then his device can come in the range of communication that could lead to unlocking the lock.

4 Architecture and Protocol Description

In this section, we describe a new architecture and protocol for secure smart locks called SecSmartLock. The proposed architecture is illustrated in Fig. 3, which includes the following components:

1. Owner: The owner is an authoritative figure that owns the smart lock. Owner can provide conditional or unconditional access to users. Users can open the smart lock provided that the preset condition as specified by the owner, is satisfied. Additionally, owner can also access the recorded log entries of actions performed on the smart lock.

2. SmartLock: The Lock has Bluetooth connection functionality through which users can interact with the lock. It has an unique identity of it's own. It has limited resources through which, it can store a small amount of information such as a secret key or a random nonce. It is also bounded in terms of computational power and hence can only perform certain predefined trivial tasks such as generating a random nonce or decrypting tokens. Lock has access to a trusted and precise clock.
3. Authorized user: An authorized user is a user who has been given the permission to open the lock by the lock owner. He also have a mobile application associated with the smart lock specifically designed to communicate with the lock via Bluetooth. Additionally, he possesses a "Token" given by the owner on their smartphones, which identifies him as an authorized user.
4. Camera: An independent camera connected directly to the central server is installed to watch over the lock. The lock notifies the camera whenever an action is being performed via Bluetooth connection. The camera records all the attempts made to open the lock and constantly uploads them to the server.

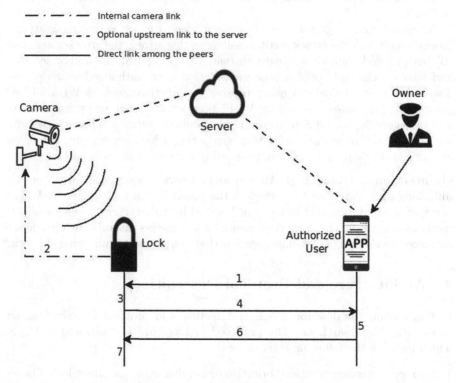

Fig. 3. The SecSmartLock architecture and protocol. The steps are enumerated as described in operational phase from Sect. 4.1.

5. Server: The central server that stores the information of access logs recorded by the camera.

4.1   Protocol Description

The protocol of SecSmartLock is divided in two phases - (i) Initialization phase and (ii) Operation phase. These phases can described in detail as follows:

Initialization Phase

1. A secret key (SK_L) is created using a CCA-secure symmetric key encryption scheme [21] and shared between the lock and the owner before installing the smart lock on the door. The lock stores SK_L in its local memory.
2. A Public-Secret key pair (PK_U, SK_U) is created by all the authorized users using a CPA-secure public key encryption scheme [14]. Every user sends their public key to the owner along with a digital certificate issued by a trusted certifying authority. Owner stores the identity of every user (a phone number or an IMEI number can serve as a unique identity) along with PK_U after validating the digital certificate.
3. Owner creates a 'token' for each user that includes all the information about the user's identity and conditions for granting access to the user.
4. Owner sends the token to all authorized users. Users keep the tokens stored in their smartphones for using them later to open the smart lock.

Operation Phase

1. The application residing in the user's smartphone sends the locally stored token to the lock.
2. Lock notifies the camera via Bluetooth connection that an attempt is being made to open the lock. Camera starts recording for a pre determined amount of time and updates the log entry to the server.
3. Lock validates the token by decrypting it using SK_L and generates a random number referred to as an authentication nonce(N_A). Lock gets PK_U from the decrypted token and encrypts N_A appended with a unique identity of the lock ID_L using PK_U.
4. Lock sends encrypted $N_A + ID_L$ to the user.
5. User decrypts the message using SK_U and validates that the message is indeed from lock by checking the ID_L.
6. User sends the decrypted N_A back to the lock.
7. If the decrypted N_A matches with the one sent earlier, the lock opens otherwise the access is denied.

4.2 Token Creation

The token is the most important component of the designed architecture and determines the authority to open the lock, given by the owner. The token essentially is an encrypted XML (Extensible markup language) [13] file. The file includes the tags: Name, Mobile/IMEI number, Designation, Allowed Days, Allowed Time, Allowed Dates, Creation Date and Public Key (PK_U) of the user.

- **Name**: Name of the person for whom token is created.
- **Mobile/IMEI number**: Mobile number or IMEI number of the person's smartphone for whom token is created. This serves as an identity of the user.
- **Designation**: It can be Owner, Resident, Recurring (Allowed on a certain days of week at a certain time) and Temporary (Allowed On particular dates).
- **Allowed Days**: For Recurring guests. On which days the person is allowed to enter.
- **Allowed Time**: For Recurring guests. During what time duration the person is allowed to enter.
- **Allowed Dates**: For Temporary guests. On what Dates the person is allowed to enter.
- **Creation Date**: Creation Date of Token.
- **Public Key** (PK_U): Public Key of the authorized user.

An XML file containing all the above specified entries is created and encrypted with the symmetric key SK_L using a CCA-secure encryption scheme [21]. We call this encrypted XML file a *token*.

4.3 User Validation

The CCA-security of the symmetric key encryption scheme ensures that successful decryption of the token means that the token is not forged. Hence, the first step of validation is done by trying to decrypt the message. After decrypting the token the lock checks all the tags in XML. Following scenarios are possible:

- **Scenario 1.** If the user is not authorized user (decryption fails) then lock remains unopened.
- **Scenario 2.** If the user is *Owner*, then he/she has unconditional access and can open the lock whenever he/she desires.
- **Scenario 3.** If the user is *Resident*, then also he/she has unconditional access.
- **Scenario 4.** If the user is *Recurring Guest*, then *Allowed Days* and *Allowed Time* fields are checked and compared with the clock. If the current day and time falls inside the days and time interval mentioned in the token, then the user will be allowed.
- **Scenario 5.** If the user is a Temporary guest, then Allowed Dates and time interval (if specified) fields are checked. If they match with the current date and time, then the user has the access.

After checking whether the user has access for the current time a random number called authentication nonce N_A will be generated. N_A along with the lock's unique identity ID_L will be encrypted by user's public key PK_U mentioned in the token and sent to the user. User decrypts the message using the secret key SK_U and validates that the message is indeed from the lock by checking the lock id. Then, User sends the decrypted random authentication nonce back to the lock. The locks compares it with the nonce sent earlier and opens if it matches, otherwise the access is denied. This authentication mechanism is designed to prevent man-in-the-middle and token stealing attacks that are described in Sect. 5.

4.4 Communication Through Bluetooth

The developed smartphone application facilitates the communication with the lock via Bluetooth. For sending the token, the user uses the application interface. A server-client model is used for establishing the connection. The Lock act as a server which is always up for accepting the tokens users acting as clients. This connection is set up using a UUID [8] (Universal unique identifier) which is used to identify the communication channel. The same UUID is used at the server and the client side.

The connection between the camera and the lock is also established via Bluetooth. A different UUID is used for this communication channel. Here camera acts as a server which is always up for accepting a notification from the lock, which acts as a client.

4.5 Mitigating Attacks

The attacks discussed in Sect. 3, are possible because of the server being not able to communicate with the lock. Even if it communicates, it has to use the device as a gateway which increases the latency as the authorized users information has to be sent to lock through device. If the lock is directly connected to the Internet, then exposure to the Internet can create a passage for the intruders. This increases lock's vulnerability to large-scale remote compromises and could allow remote adversaries to directly access and exploit vulnerabilities in the lock.

SecSmartLock does not require a remote server to communicate the details of authorized users and access logs to and from the lock. It validates the authorized users through the random authentication nonce. Access logs are stored to the server by an independent camera connected to the lock through Bluetooth. The lock does not have any direct exposure to the Internet for server connectivity. The Camera collects the information (such as access logs, and recordings) and updates this information on the remote server. In our mechanism, only owner has credentials to login. Other users do not have a need of id and password for login, thus giving them minimal exposure to the application.

5 Security Guarantees

In this section, we describe various security claims and their corresponding proofs that depict the security guarantees provided by the proposed architecture and protocol.

5.1 Unforgebility of Tokens

Claim: No-one but the owner can create authentic tokens.
Assumptions:

1. The shared secret key (SK_L) between the owner and lock is indeed a secret.
2. The symmetric key encryption scheme used does not allow CCA attacks [24] (i.e., it is CCA-secure).

Proof:

- Owner 'O' creates a token and encrypts it using the shared secret key by the CCA-secure symmetric key encryption scheme.
- 'O' passes the encrypted token to an authorized user 'U'.
- Above steps are repeated polynomial number of times.
- Assume, that 'U' can now create a new valid authentic token for an unauthorized user 'U$_1$' that successfully decrypts for a valid token for 'U$_1$' by the lock.
- This contradicts the definition of CCA-security of the encryption mechanism.
- Hence, no one but the owner 'O' can create authentic tokens.

5.2 Security Against Leaking Tokens

Claim: Lock mechanism remains secure, even if tokens are stolen.
Assumptions:

1. All secret keys are kept secret.
2. Public key encryption scheme used does not allow CPA attacks [12] (i.e., it is CPA-secure).

Proof:

- Let 'A' be an attacker who has stolen a token from an authorized user 'U'.
- In order to successfully open the lock 'A' provides the token to the lock.
- Lock generates a random authentication nonce, and sends it to 'A' after encrypting it with U's public key PK_U.
- Now, 'A' must reply back with decrypted nonce, which can only be achieved if 'A' has U's secret key SK_U which contradicts with our assumption or the definition of CPA security.
- Hence, lock mechanism remains secure even if tokens are captured or stolen.

5.3   Prevention of the Man-in-the-Middle (MITM) Attack

Claim: The MITM attack in its true sense is not relevant to the proposed protocol and a translation of MITM attack to suit the scenario fails to succeed.
Assumptions:

1. All secret keys are kept secret.
2. The authorized user is trusted.

Proof:

- Man-in-the-middle attack is an attack to fool one of the communicating parties by impersonating a forged identity of the other party, and break the confidentiality of every future communication.
- Here the only part of the protocol that involves active two way communication is authenticating the user interacting with lock via random nonce.
- Note that this involves **only** validation and no further communication.
- Hence, MITM attack in its true sense, is not relevant to our case.
- An attempt to translate the MITM attack for our scenario yields an attack as shown in Fig. 4. Here, an attacker 'A' attempts to fool the lock by assuming identity of an authorized user 'U'. A sends a stolen token to the lock and also maintains a parallel connection with U, who knows the identity of A but is unaware of his malicious intentions. When the lock sends the encrypted $N_A + ID_L$ to A, he forwards it to an unaware U as a normal encrypted message. U decrypts it and finds the ID_L along with the nonce. U now recognizes A as an attacker as the message came from lock, and aborts the connection preventing the attack.
- For the above attack to be successful, either A should know the secret key of U, or U proceeds to provide decrypted nonce to A, even after realizing A's malicious intention. Both of these contradict with the described assumptions.
- The only way this attack succeeds is that A assumes the identity of lock while communicating with U and of U while communicating with lock. In this case, the attack becomes a relay attack.
- Relay attacks are only relevant in the case when the system provides an auto-unlocking mechanism. Unlike other smart lock systems, SecSmartLock does not provide any form of auto-unlocking, making the relay attacks irrelevant.

From the above discussion, we can conclude:

Corollary: Relay attack does not have any relevance in our architecture.

5.4   Impossibility of Log Evasion

Claim: Evading logs is not possible.
Assumptions:

1. Camera device is continuously connected with the lock through Bluetooth and is getting a clear view of the lock at required orientation without any obstructions.

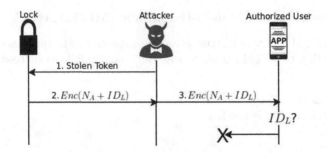

Fig. 4. Translated man-in-the-middle attack.

2. Camera consistently records and uploads the recordings to the server.
3. Camera system and the uplink to server are secure.

Proof:

- Logs are maintained by a separate camera device which has a totally independent storage system and connectivity to the server.
- The lock always notifies the camera as soon as it receives a token.
- Hence, only ways logs can be evaded (apart from physically damaging any devices) are either to disrupt the Bluetooth connection between lock and camera, or the connection between the camera and the server, both of which contradicts with our assumptions.

5.5   Revocation

Claim: Remote revocation of authorized users is possible.
Assumptions:
We need an addendum as follows to the described mechanism for remote revocation to be possible. Figure 5 illustrates the required additions.

1. In addition to the secret key, lock and central server also share a secret random nonce called central nonce (N_C). The lock and the central server both stores N_C locally.
2. In the last step of operation phase of the protocol, the authenticated user requests an encrypted N_C from server.
3. The server encrypts the N_C by the shared secret key SK_L using the CCA-secure secret key encryption and sends it to the authorized user via a secure communication channel after checking the user's validity.
4. The user in turn passes the encrypted N_C along with decrypted N_A to the lock. Lock decrypts $Enc(N_C)$ using the SK_L and compares both N_A and N_C with their respective locally stored copies. If both of them matches, the lock opens, else the access is denied.
5. To ensure availability in case of Internet outage, or unavailability of central server, a master PIN is available with the owner through which lock can be opened anytime. Only the owner knows the master PIN and uses it only in emergency situations. Owner always resets it after using it.

Additionally, we also assume the following:

1. All the secret keys remain secret.
2. Central server is trusted.
3. The communication between user and central server is through a secure and authenticated channel.

Proof:

- In the final step of authentication, the user needs $Enc(N_C)$ from the central server. If the user's access is revoked, the central server will never provide the encrypted nonce and the final authentication step would never succeed provided the keys and the nonce remain secret. Note that, here we do not trust the application that resides in a potentially hostile environment of the revoked user's smartphone.
- We prefer consistency over availability in normal scenarios. If the central server is not reachable by the user's application then the lock will not open. For emergency conditions, we have a master PIN for the lock that can be entered (by getting it from the owner manually) into the lock anytime without going through the regular authenticating mechanism.

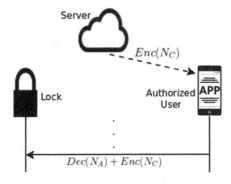

Fig. 5. Additions to the mechanism for allowing Revocation.

6 Performance Analysis

The performance evaluation of our lock mechanism focuses on the resources consumed by the smart lock on an Android platform, which includes Power and CPU usage. We used GameBench profiler (ver 5.0.2) [4] available on Google Play store for the measurements of these parameters. We also measure the time taken by the lock application to perform cryptographic operations, and end-to-end time starting from initiation of unlock operation till lock actually opens.

The time taken for performing cryptographic operations is calculated by finding the difference between the time when lock receives the token and the time just before the lock sends the encrypted nonce to the user. This time includes three operations performed by the lock - decrypting and validating the token, generating random authentication nonce N_A and encrypting N_A using PK_U extracted from the token. Here, the decryption of token is done using the symmetric key encryption, whereas encryption is performed by the public key encryption. Note that these are the most expensive operations in terms of resource utilization performed by the lock. The end-to-end time shows the total response time a user experiences. This includes time taken for initialization of Bluetooth connection, all validation and authentication operations and packet transfers over established Bluetooth communication channel.

To measure the resource consumption by the lock, we tested the lock in three different scenarios.

Test 1: When the lock was idle and no requests for unlocking the lock were issued by any user.

Test 2: When the lock received a request from users every 2 min.

Test 3: When the lock received two simultaneous requests from different users every 1 min.

Table 1. Performance measurements of the lock using the test cases defined in above.

Metrics	Test 1	Test 2	Test 3
Power usage	2689.02 mW	2856.08 mW	3128.85 mW
CPU usage	2.26%	5.61%	8.96%
Cryptographic operations time	-	342 ms	464 ms
End-to-end time	-	773 ms	1027 ms

Table 1 shows the measurements of resources used by the lock. We performed each of the aforementioned test cases 5 times, each for 20 min and took an average to get the final results. Before doing each of these experiments, we perform a fresh boot and a clean install to preserve the test-bed across all the experiments. For the experiments, the lock was tested on Motorola Nexus 6 device containing Qualcomm APQ8084 Snapdragon 805 quad-core processor, 3 GB RAM, and Android version 7.1.1 (Nougat).

In the test case 1, the power consumption and CPU usage are less because the lock is idle and no requests are issued by any user. Only the Bluetooth server waiting for requests is consuming power and CPU.

In contrast, test cases 2 and 3 shows, increased power and CPU consumption as the lock starts receiving requests from users. It works for performing cryptographic operations of decryption, random number generation and encryption and starts sending as well as receiving Bluetooth packets. In test case 3, we did the load testing and found the lock works well even if simultaneous requests are issued giving each user desired result.

Another parameter on which we test our implementation is how fast it performs the cryptographic primitives and what is the total response time experienced by the user. We found that to decrypt the token, generate random nonce and encrypt it using the PKE scheme the lock takes 342 ms in test case 2 and 464 ms in test case 3 whereas the end-to-end time for test case 2 is 773 ms and for test case 3 is 1027 ms. The time is increased in test case 3 as two sets of operations are simultaneously performed by the lock.

The memory required by the lock remains constant as the lock only stores a shared secret key locally. It does not increase with the number of requests. We also tested whether the practical security matches the theoretical claims that we made by tampering the token and sending it to the lock for an unauthorized access, but the lock was able to detect the tampered token and did not open.

We have evaluated our approach and found that it mitigates the attacks and does not give access to unauthorized users. We also evaluated the functioning of our lock and did the load testing on it, which gave successful results indicating many users (which also included attackers) can successfully interact with the lock at the same time without affecting the security guarantees. The results show that the CPU and power consumption by the lock is relatively small and the time taken to perform the cryptographic operations by lock is also less making the lock a suitable candidate for a secure, yet resource and power limited IoT device.

7   Related Wok

In this section, we explore similar work available in the literature and compare relevant aspects of our work with them. As we propose an abstract architecture and a protocol for secure smart locks which can be used to design and implement smart locks as an end product, we do not focus on the vulnerabilities due to bugs in the implementation.

The Grey project at CMU deployed a digital lock system for their office doors in their department [10,11]. The project considered a setting where the access credentials were scattered across different administrative entities in a non-trivial distributed system. They designed device enabled authorization techniques can prove to a lock that it is authorized. This system took a long time to identify the authorized user. The project uses features of phones available during that time. Smartphones have now evolved a lot since then with various resources and features. Along with smartphones, user requirements have also changed. The findings from the Grey project guided us for developing a secure and user friendly interface with fast authorization.

Kim et al. in their research [20] have proposed access control policies for future smart homes (smart lights, smart door locks). They proposed four access control groups: full control, restricted control, partial control, and minimal control. The levels given by them can be seen in today's smart locks with different names but with similar access controls policies. Ur et al. in their study [25] found that the audit logs with visuals (photographs, recordings) are beneficial to customers. They discussed directions for auditing interfaces that could improve home security without impacting privacy.

Denning et al. [15] talk about the broader aspects of security and privacy in smart homes and the importance of it. They discuss the attack surface possible because of unprofessional administration to maintain and control smart home devices. In contrast, our work studies the security and privacy risks posed by external adversaries. Ye et al. in their work [26] discussed various attacks possible on smart locks. Their case study was based on August lock and does not cover the general smart lock architecture.

The work done by Ho et al. [18] tries to solve the problems with the existing framework of the locks by proposing an approach based on eventual consistency which improves DGC architecture. This model decides when to allow access to user in case of server unavailability. Their design stores the access logs not pushed to the server and a list of authorized users which gets updated whenever an honest user with Internet connectivity interacts with the lock.

1. Their design only allows a revoked attacker to maintain unauthorized access as long as no legitimate user uses the lock. As soon as an honest user interacts with the lock, the server will be able to update the lock with the latest list of authorized user. In contrast, our approach requires the user to compulsorily connect with the server, which in turn sends an encrypted central nonce which has to be sent to the lock for validation. If the owner wants to revoke access of a user, it blacklists that user from server, which in turn denies to provide encrypted nonce to the blacklisted user. Due to unavailability of freshly encrypted nonce, the final step of authentication will never get completed and the lock will not open, thus, preventing revoked attacker from accessing the lock. In their approach the revoked attacker has a time window in which he can go and access the lock but in our approach, we prefer consistency over availability and we do not open the lock if the server is not reachable and is not able to send the central nonce to the user. Instead, for emergency situations, we provide a mechanism of master PIN, to override the normal authentication to ensure availability.

2. In their design all access log events will reach the server and will be available for the lock owners to view once an owner interact with the lock. Thus, an attacker can only hide her lock interactions for a limited amount of time. In contrast, in our approach, the logs are updated to servers by an independent camera, so the server will always have the updated access logs at any point in time.

3. The NFC based and distance bounding approach proposed in their design avoids relay attacks. But both these approaches require additional hardware integrated to the lock and are also shown to be prone to geo-location spoofing attacks. Our approach does not provide any auto-unlocking facilities, thus making the relay attacks irrelevant as discussed in Sect. 5.3.

4. Their approach relies on the application being trusted to perform all the operations correctly. The application resides in a potentially adversarial environment and might be tampered with to deviate from the protocol. Bugs in the application would pose a serious threat and to completely get rid of such security vulnerabilities, one needs to formally verify the application to

be completely secure and error free. In contrast our approach does not trust the application at all and only relies on the central server being trusted and the keys being secret which are reasonable assumptions.

Additionally, to ensure the tamperproofness of the lock, it is possible to include an alarm system on the lines of proposal in [9]. The alarm system would set off if someone tries to tamper with the lock physically, or enter the master pin incorrectly for a constant (e.g., 3) number of times consecutively. This mechanism is much simpler and practically implementable than the other mechanisms described in [18]. Moreover, it requires minimal additional hardware (the alarm system) that is easily available and can be integrated with the smart lock with very little added cost.

8 Conclusion and Future Work

In this paper, we first discuss the need for security measures in the smart homes. We focus on the attacks that are possible on the smart locks based on Device-Gateway-Cloud architecture due to flaws in the system and protocol design.

We have proposed a novel architecture and protocol for smartlocks accompanied by smartphone applications. The proposed mechanism prevents the described attacks while providing a fast and user friendly interface. The designed system requires very limited resources and hardware requirements from the smart locks making it suitable for resource bound IoT devices. Additionally, we also provide claims and their argumentative proofs that demonstrate the provable security guarantees given by the proposed architecture.

From the security evaluation results of our implementation, we conclude that it prevents the attacks possible in earlier architectures, and thus provides a robust architectures as compared to existing approaches. We also measured the performance of the implementation by performing load testing on it, which has provided good results establishing that several users can interact with the lock at the same time. The lock responded with appropriate response to each of the users and the attackers could not breach the security even while parallel sessions were active. We did the performance testing based on varying test cases and found the resource utilization in terms of CPU and power consumption as well as the time taken for doing the cryptographic operations to be quite minimal.

To sum up, we conclude that the proposed smart lock architecture provide better security than the available designs. Moreover, the proposed design can also help to ensure the security of other similar IoT devices.

We are working on refining the revocation mechanism to make it more robust and concrete. We are extending our architecture and protocol such that it encompasses IoT devices other than smart locks and helps provide provable security guarantees. In fact, information flow considerations as done in [19], will enable us to consider generalized IoT applications for realizing security properties. We intend to extend our implementation of the architecture to operating systems other than Android.

Acknowledgement. The work was done as part of Information Security Research and Development Centre (ISRDC) at IIT Bombay, funded by MEITY, Government of India. We also thank the anonymous reviewers for providing their insights and valuable feedback.

References

1. Amazon key. https://www.amazon.com/key. Accessed 25 July 2018
2. August. https://www.august.com/. Accessed 24 July 2018
3. Danalock. https://www.danalock.com/. Accessed 24 July 2018
4. Gamebench. https://www.gamebench.net/. Accessed 29 July 2018
5. Geo-fencing. https://en.wikipedia.org/wiki/Geo-fence. Accessed 26 July 2018
6. Kwikset kevo smart lock. http://www.kwikset.com/kevo/default. Accessed 24 July 2018
7. Okidokeys. https://www.okidokeys.com/. Accessed 24 July 2018
8. Uuid. https://en.wikipedia.org/wiki/Universally_unique_identifier. Accessed 26 July 2018
9. Arora, N., Shyamasundar, R.: PGSP: a protocol for secure communication in peer-to-peer system. In: 2005 IEEE Wireless Communications and Networking Conference, vol. 4, pp. 2094–2099. IEEE (2005)
10. Bauer, L., Cranor, L.F., Reiter, M.K., Vaniea, K.: Lessons learned from the deployment of a smart phone-based access-control system. In: Proceedings of the 3rd Symposium on Usable Privacy and Security, pp. 64–75. ACM (2007)
11. Bauer, L., Garriss, S., McCune, J.M., Reiter, M.K., Rouse, J., Rutenbar, P.: Device-enabled authorization in the grey system. In: Zhou, J., Lopez, J., Deng, R.H., Bao, F. (eds.) ISC 2005. LNCS, vol. 3650, pp. 431–445. Springer, Heidelberg (2005). https://doi.org/10.1007/11556992_31
12. Biryukov, A.: Chosen plaintext attack. In: van Tilborg, H.C.A., Jajodia, S. (eds.) Encyclopedia of Cryptography and Security, pp. 205–206. Springer, Boston (2011). https://doi.org/10.1007/978-1-4419-5906-5
13. CBray, T., Paoli, J., Sperberg-McQueen, C.M., Maler, E., Yergeau, F.: Extensible Markup Language (XML) 1.0 (2008)
14. Canetti, R., Halevi, S., Katz, J.: A forward-secure public-key encryption scheme. In: Biham, E. (ed.) EUROCRYPT 2003. LNCS, vol. 2656, pp. 255–271. Springer, Heidelberg (2003). https://doi.org/10.1007/3-540-39200-9_16
15. Denning, T., Kohno, T.: Empowering consumer electronic security and privacy choices: navigating the modern home. In: Symposium on Usable Privacy and Security (SOUPS) (2013)
16. Fernandes, E., Jung, J., Prakash, A.: Security analysis of emerging smart home applications. In: 2016 IEEE Symposium on Security and Privacy (SP), pp. 636–654. IEEE (2016)
17. Gonikberg, M.: Wlan-based positioning system. US Patent 9,125,165, 1 September 2015
18. Ho, G., Leung, D., Mishra, P., Hosseini, A., Song, D., Wagner, D.: Smart locks: lessons for securing commodity internet of things devices. In: Proceedings of the 11th ACM on Asia Conference on Computer and Communications Security, pp. 461–472. ACM (2016)

19. Khobragade, S., Narendra Kumar, N.V., Shyamasundar, R.K.: Secure synthesis of IoT via readers-writers flow model. In: Negi, A., Bhatnagar, R., Parida, L. (eds.) ICDCIT 2018. LNCS, vol. 10722, pp. 86–104. Springer, Cham (2018). https://doi.org/10.1007/978-3-319-72344-0_5

20. Kim, T.H.J., Bauer, L., Newsome, J., Perrig, A., Walker, J.: Challenges in access right assignment for secure home networks. In: HotSec (2010)

21. Kurosawa, K., Desmedt, Y.: A new paradigm of hybrid encryption scheme. In: Franklin, M. (ed.) CRYPTO 2004. LNCS, vol. 3152, pp. 426–442. Springer, Heidelberg (2004). https://doi.org/10.1007/978-3-540-28628-8_26

22. Mittal, Y., Toshniwal, P., Sharma, S., Singhal, D., Gupta, R., Mittal, V.K.: A voice-controlled multi-functional smart home automation system. In: 2015 Annual IEEE India Conference (INDICON), pp. 1–6. IEEE (2015)

23. Mohebbi, B.B.: Short range booster with multiple antennas. US Patent 8,478,191, 2 July 2013

24. Rackoff, C., Simon, D.R.: Non-interactive zero-knowledge proof of knowledge and chosen ciphertext attack. In: Feigenbaum, J. (ed.) CRYPTO 1991. LNCS, vol. 576, pp. 433–444. Springer, Heidelberg (1992). https://doi.org/10.1007/3-540-46766-1_35

25. Ur, B., Jung, J., Schechter, S.: The current state of access control for smart devices in homes. In: Workshop on Home Usable Privacy and Security (HUPS), HUPS 2014 (2013)

26. Ye, M., Jiang, N., Yang, H., Yan, Q.: Security analysis of internet-of-things: a case study of august smart lock. In: 2017 IEEE Conference on Computer Communications Workshops (INFOCOM WKSHPS), pp. 499–504. IEEE (2017)

A Novel Multi-factor Authentication Protocol for Smart Home Environments

K. Nimmy[(⊠)], Sriram Sankaran, and Krishnashree Achuthan

Center for Cybersecurity Systems and Networks,
Amrita Vishwa Vidyapeetham, Amritapuri, Kollam, India
{nimmy,srirams}@am.amrita.edu, krishna@amrita.edu

Abstract. User authentication plays an important role in smart home environments in which devices are interconnected through the Internet and security risks are high. Most of the existing research works for remote user authentication in smart homes fail in one way or the other in combating common attacks specifically smartphone capture attack. Robust authentication method which can uniquely identify the smartphones of users can thwart unauthorized access through the physical capture of smartphones. Existing studies demonstrate that Photo Response Non-Uniformity (PRNU) of a smartphone can be used to uniquely identify the device with an error rate less than 0.5%. Based on these results, we propose a multi-factor user authentication protocol based on Elliptic Curve Cryptography (ECC) and secret sharing for smart home environments. We leverage face biometric and PRNU to make it resilient to common attacks. Moreover, the proposed protocol achieves mutual authentication among all participating entities and thereby ensures the legitimacy of all the participating entities. Subsequently, a session key is established for secure communication between the users and the devices. Our analysis of the proposed protocol shows that it provides significantly better security than the existing schemes with a reasonable overhead. In addition, it provides better usability by alleviating the burden of users from memorizing passwords and carrying additional mechanisms such as smart cards.

Keywords: Mutual authentication · PRNU · Secret sharing
Smart home · IoT · ECC

1 Introduction

Strong user authentication is the best way to secure smart home as smart devices are subject to numerous security threats from inside or outside of the home network. As the smart devices become pervasive and interconnected, the attack surface on a device increases. Recently, security vulnerabilities have been identified in connected devices of smart homes. Vulnerabilities present in these devices may lead to unauthorized access to the entire home network. For instance, any unauthorized access to a smart oven or smart lock can create a fire hazard or

© Springer Nature Switzerland AG 2018
V. Ganapathy et al. (Eds.): ICISS 2018, LNCS 11281, pp. 44–63, 2018.
https://doi.org/10.1007/978-3-030-05171-6_3

a burglary risk respectively [12,23]. Moreover, vulnerabilities have been discovered in the protocols that are used in the smarthome devices such as ZWave and ZigBee [13,19]. In particular, there have been numerous flaws identified in the OAuth protocol which is the de-facto protocol for authentication and authorization [6].

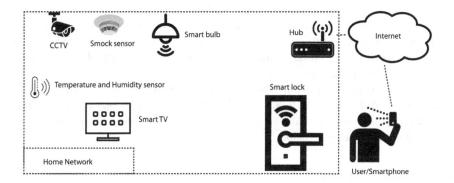

Fig. 1. Smart home environment

Unauthorized access can happen when adversaries gain physical access to the smartphone to impersonate as legitimate users. Robust mutual authentication protocols are the countermeasures against unauthorized access to smart home networks [1]. Most of the existing protocols for the remote user authentication are not secure against attacks such as smartphone capture attack, smart device capture attack, insider attack, and impersonation attacks [16,25,29,30]. A multi-factor authentication scheme which combines more than one method of authentication can provide an additional layer of security to combat these attacks. This necessitates the design of a protocol which can uniquely identify the user as well as the smartphone.

The Photo Response Non-Uniformity (PRNU) of the digital camera image is a hardware fingerprint that can be used to uniquely identify smartphones [7]. The advantage of using PRNU is that it may be difficult to launch an attack using any other smartphone other than the legitimate one. An extensive analysis has been performed to prove that PRNU of a smartphone camera is highly intrinsic that single image is sufficient to uniquely identify the device with an error rate less than 0.5% [3]. Thus, PRNU can be used in conjunction with cryptographic primitives for providing security in smart homes.

Motivated by these observations, we propose a novel multi-factor authentication protocol for smart home environments. The authentication process requires only a face image of the user which is captured at the time of authentication. The freshness of the image is verified at every authentication attempt by performing image analysis which is a method to access the metadata of the image. Apart from establishing a session key, the proposed protocol achieves forward secrecy and mutual authentication among all participating entities.

1.1 Our Contributions

Our contributions are summarized as follows:

1. We propose a novel multi-factor authentication protocol for smart home environments. Unauthorized physical access to the device is prevented by verifying the PRNU of the face image and performing face recognition. The freshness of the image is ensured using image analysis. The proposed protocol avoids the need for a password or smart card based authentication, hence removes the security risk of stolen credentials. Users can conveniently authenticate by capturing their own face images. This preserves usability of the proposed scheme by reducing the registration overhead.
2. Formal security verification using SPAN+AVISPA (Security Protocol ANimator for Automated Validation of Internet Security Protocols and Applications) [2,14] shows that the proposed protocol is resilient to replay and Man-In-The-Middle attacks.

1.2 Network Model

The network model as depicted in Fig. 1 consists of users U_i $(i = 1..n)$ who want to access and control the smart devices D_j $(j = 1..m)$ through the hub G. We assume that the public and private key pairs are generated at the deployment of the devices and applications. We also assume that the devices are registered at the hub in off-line mode. Also, we assume that the hub G is completely trusted and the sensitive information stored in the G are protected from adversaries. Moreover, the keys are stored in a secure key storage area in the internal storage of the smartphone which will make it difficult for the attacker to extract the keys [9].

1.3 Threat Model

We use Dolev-Yao threat model in our proposed protocol [11]. According to this model, an adversary is capable of performing the following actions:

– Adversary can obtain any message passing through the network.
– Adversary is an active eavesdropper who can tap the channel to obtain messages and then modify or delete messages to prevent the protocol from achieving its goals.

1.4 Related Work

A real-time smartphone authentication protocol utilizing the PRNU was proposed by Ba et al. [3]. Their approach significantly reduces the registration overhead of the authentication scheme. However, their scheme is not resilient to smartphone capture attack.

Recently, several authentication protocols for IoT have been proposed based on traditional encryption schemes. Sankaran et al. [24] proposed a lightweight security framework for IoTs using Identity based Cryptography focusing on identity and data tampering attacks. Tewari *et al.* [27] proposed a mutual authentication protocol based on ECC for IoT devices. Their scheme considers only the authentication of IoT devices to the server.

Santoso *et al.* [25] proposed a protocol based on ECC for smarthome systems. This protocol is vulnerable to replay attacks as the messages lack the presence of timestamps, nonces or counters. Kumar *et al.* [18] proposed a lightweight session-key establishment scheme in smart home environments. Their scheme lacks forward secrecy as the compromise of long term key can lead to the compromise of session keys. Moreover, it does not provide mutual authentication between the user and smart device as well as user and hub. Wazid *et al.* [30] proposed a remote user authenticated key establishment protocol for smart home environments. According to them, the session key will be compromised if the device is captured by an adversary. This shows that their protocol lacks forward secrecy and thereby vulnerable to smart device capture attack. Moreover, the absence of identity of the entity in the message sent from smart devices can lead to a denial of service attack.

Challa *et al.* [5] proposed an ECC-based three-factor user authentication and key agreement protocol for wireless health care sensor networks. This scheme lacks forward secrecy and does not provide mutual authentication among all participating entities. Chifor *et al.* [8] proposed a lightweight authorization stack for smart home IoT applications, where a cloud-connected device relays input commands to a user's smartphone for authorization. This scheme addresses security issues in the context of an untrusted cloud platform. Zhang *et al.* [31] proposed matrix-based cross-layer key establishment protocol for smart homes. The protocol establishes a session key only between the smart devices for further communication.

In contrast, we propose multi-factor user authentication protocol which provides mutual authentication among all participating entities. In addition, it ensures forward secrecy and is resilient to smartphone capture attack. The proposed protocol avoids the need for passwords and smart cards and thereby enhances the usability.

2 Background

2.1 PRNU Fingerprint

The Photo-Response Non-Uniformity (PRNU) of an image is used to forensically link an image to a digital camera in digital forensics. The non-uniform sensitivity of a digital camera to light causes PRNU [20]. The image I captured using a digital camera is represented using the following equation:

$$I = I^0 + I^0 K + \theta$$

where K is the camera PRNU fingerprint, I^0 is the actual optical view and θ represents other noise components such as shot noise and read-out noise [3]. In

order to extract the fingerprint, a denoising filter such as BM3D [10], is applied
to the image and subtracted from I as follows

$$W_I = I - F(I)$$

where W_I is the extracted noise residue. The PRNU fingerprint, $\hat{K}$, is obtained
by averaging the noise residues of multiple images captured using the following
equation:

$$\hat{K} = \frac{\sum_{i=1}^{N} W_i I_i}{\sum_{i=1}^{N} (I_i)^2}$$

where $\hat{K}$ is the estimated fingerprint which contains a small noise factor δ,
$\hat{K} = K + \delta$, where K is the real finger print. A correlation, $corr(K, \hat{K})$ of the
estimated PRNU fingerprint and the real fingerprint is computed to identify the
device.

2.2 Secret Sharing

A secret sharing scheme is a method by which a secret is distributed as shares
to participants such that only authorized subsets of participants can reconstruct
the secret. In a (t, n) threshold secret sharing scheme, the secret S, is distributed
among n participants such that any t ($t <= n$) of the participants can recover
the secret from their shares. Geometric problems can also be used as a basis
for secret sharing schemes [28]. Let the secret S be the coordinates of a fixed
point on a given line l which intersects the y axis at the secret point $(0, S)$. The
coordinates of l are denoted by $(1, S + R)$ and $(2, S + 2R)$, where R is a random
slope. Line l can be determined using any of the two points and its intersection
with y axis will result in the secret. When two parties mutually authenticate
with each other using secret sharing, the number of participants is $n = 2$ and
number of shares required to reconstruct the secret is $t = 2$. The two shares can
be constructed using the following equations:

$$s_1 = (S + R) \bmod p$$
$$s_2 = (S + 2R) \bmod p$$

where p is a prime number. The shares s_1 and s_2 are combined to reconstruct
the secret using the following equation:

$$S = (2 \times s_1 - s_2) \bmod p$$

The shares are kept by participating entities and this avoids the risk of stolen
credentials. The shares are combined and compared against the stored value at
the time of registration and individual shares give little or no knowledge about
the secret [22].

2.3   Elliptic Curve Cryptography

Elliptic curve cryptography (ECC) is a set of public key encryption methods based on the algebraic structure of elliptic curves over finite fields. An elliptic curve $E(F_p)$ over the finite field F_p is defined by equation $y^2 = x^3 + ax + b \bmod p$, where $a, b \in F_p$ and $4a^3 + 27b^2 \neq 0$, together with a special point O, called the point at infinity (or zero point) [17, 21].

Consider A and B are the two communicating parties who agree upon the Elliptic curve and a generator P whose order be n such that $nP = P + P + ... + P(n times) = O$. Let n_A and n_B be the private keys chosen by A and B respectively. The public keys for A and B are given by

$$K_A = n_A P, K_B = n_B P$$

To encrypt a message M, A uses B's public key, K_B and sends the message. The ciphertext C is computed as given in the following equation:

$$C = (kP,\ M + kK_B)$$

where k is a random number. B decrypts the message using the following equation:

$$M = M + kK_B - n_B kP$$

3   The Proposed Scheme

We propose a novel multi-factor authentication protocol for smart home environments based on Elliptic Curve Cryptography (ECC). ECC provides high level of security with lesser key size and less storage space. The main entities of this protocol include the user U_i who uses the smartphone for the entire communication, the hub G and smart device D_j. The protocol consists of three phases: user registration phase, the mutual authentication phase, and PRNU update phase. The mutual authentication among the participating entities is established using secret sharing. The two shares are kept by the pair of entities and both shares are required to reconstruct the secret. The advantage of using this method is that the adversary who captures a share gains little knowledge about the secret. Also, this avoids the need for pre-shared keys which are used to exchange the secret. The notations used in the protocol are given in Table 1.

3.1   User Registration Phase

The registration phase is depicted in Fig. 2. The users are required to register at the hub before proceeding to the mutual authentication phase. In addition, face recognition is performed to uniquely identify users. The freshness of the image is verified using image analysis (*iminfo* in MATLAB). This function returns a structure containing information about the image I_m. The *DateTimeOriginal* field gives the date and time of the face image. This timestamp is then compared with the timestamp of the message. If it lies within a threshold it is assured that the image is not replayed. We describe the steps for the user registration phase below.

Table 1. Notations used in the protocol

Notation	Description
U_i, D_j, G	i^{th} user, j^{th} device, Hub
I	Face image of the user
I_m	Metadata of the image I
K_x, K_{x-}	Public and private key pair of x
$E_{K_x}\{y\}$	Public key encryption of y using the key K_x
ID_{U_i}, ID_{D_j}, ID_G	Identities of the ith user, j^{th} device and the hub
p	A large prime
P	A point in the elliptic curve
P_{D_j}, P_{U_i}	Ephemeral public keys of jth device and i^{th} user
n_{U_i}, n_{D_i}	Ephemeral private keys of ith user and j^{th} device
S_{U_iG}	Secret in $[0, p]$ created by the ith user and the hub
S_{D_iG}	Secret created by the jth smart device and the hub.
s_i	Share stored by the ith user
s_{G_i}	Share stored by the hub corresponding to the ith user
s_j	Share stored by the jth smart device
s_{G_j}	Share stored by the the hub corresponding to the jth device
N_{xi}	i^{th} Nonce chosen by x
T_{xi}	i^{th} Timestamp chosen by x
C_j	The challenge given by the hub to the jth device
R	Random number in $[0, p]$
Res_j	The response, $Res_j = C_j \oplus R_j \oplus s_j$, loaded in the device
K_S	Session key established between the user and the device
$h(.)$	A one way hash function
$Sig_x(.)$	Signature of x
Z	Token issued to the device for the user

Step 1: User captures photo of her face using the smartphone and chooses an identity ID_{U_i}. Smartphone sends this information to the hub in the following way. The signature $SI_{U_i} = Sig_{U_i}(ID_{U_i}, ID_G, I)$ is computed using the private key K_{U_i-}.

Step 2: The chosen identity ID_{U_i}, identity of the hub ID_G, image I, timestamp T_U, nonce N_U and signature SI_{U_i} are encrypted using the public key K_G and sent to the hub.

Step 3: Upon successful verification, the hub ensures that the image is not tampered in transit. It then verifies the timestamp T_U by checking whether $T_U - T \le \Delta T$ where T is the current timestamp and ΔT is the maximum transmission delay. If the timestamp lies within the threshold, hub performs image analysis. Otherwise, the hub aborts the execution of the protocol. If the

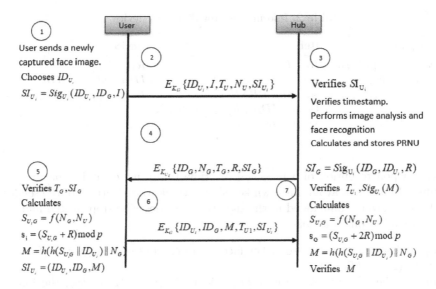

Fig. 2. Registration phase

timestamp of the image is within a threshold, it performs face recognition. On successful verification, the hub computes the PRNU of the image and stores the information.

Step 4: The hub generates a random nonce N_G, random number R and signs N_G, R along with the identities $SI_G = Sig_G(ID_G, ID_{U_i}, N_G, R)$ and sends along with current timestamp T_G encrypted using the public key of the user K_{U_i} to the user U_i.

Step 5: Upon successful verification, user computes the secret $S_{U_iG} = f(N_U, N_G)$, share $s_i = (S_{U_iG} + R) \bmod p$ and estimates $M = h(h(S_{U_iG}||ID_{U_i})||N_G)$.

Step 6: User sends M along with identity ID_{U_i}, the identity of the hub ID_G, current timestamp T_{U1}, and signature $SI_{U_i} = Sig_{U_i}(ID_{U_i}, ID_G, M)$, encrypted using the public key K_G to the hub. User stores the following information corresponding to the hub G $\{ID_G, K_G, h(S_{U_iG}||ID_G), s_i\}$.

Step 7: Upon successful verification, the registration phase is completed. It then stores $\{ID_{U_i}||h(S_{U_iG}||ID_{U_i})||s_G\}$.

After the registration phase, the information which gets stored at the user's smartphone, hub and smart device is given in Table 2.

3.2 Mutual Authentication Phase

The mutual authentication phase is depicted in Fig. 3. This phase is invoked when users access a device in the smart home. Users need to authenticate to the hub to access any device in the home network. At the end of a successful run of this protocol mutual authentication is achieved among the user, hub, and the

Table 2. Information stored at each device

Smartphone	Hub	Device
ID_G, $h(S_{U_iG}\|\|ID_G)$, s_i	K_G, K_{G-}	K_{D_j}, K_{D_j-}
K_{U_i}, K_{U_i-}, K_G	User: ID_{U_i}, $h(S_{U_iG}\|\|ID_{U_i})$,	ID_{D_j}, $h(S_{D_jG}\|\|ID_G)$
	s_{G_i}, K_{U_i}, $PRNU$, I_m	$Res_j = C_j \oplus R_j \oplus s_{D_i}$, K_{D_i}
	Device: ID_{D_j}, $h(S_{D_jG}\|\|ID_{D_j})$,	
	s_{G_j}, C_j, R_j, K_{D_j}	

device. Upon reception of a message, the timestamp, nonce and signature are verified. In order to avoid unknown key share attack, the identities of the sender and the receiver are included in the signature. We describe steps in the mutual authentication phase as follows:

Step 1: User captures photo of her face I and computes the signature $SI_{U_i} = Sig_{U_i}(ID_{U_i}, ID_G, I)$

Step 2: The identity of the user ID_{U_i}, identity of the Hub ID_G, the image I, nonce N_{U1}, timestamp T_{U1}, and signature SI_{U_i} are encrypted using the public key K_G and sent to the hub.

Step 3: Upon successful verification, the Hub performs image analysis to ensure the freshness and origin of the image. hub computes PRNU of the received image I and compares it with the stored value. It also performs the face recognition. If any of these processes fail, the hub prompts the user to resend the message. On successful completion, the user is successfully authenticated to the hub.

Step 4: Hub sends its share s_{G_i} along with its identity ID_G, identity of the user ID_{U_i}, timestamp T_{G1}, nonce N_{G1} and signature $SI_G = Sig_G(ID_G, ID_{U_i}, s_G, N_{G1})$ encrypted using the public key K_{U_i} to the user.

Step 5: The user reconstructs the secret by computing $S_{U_iG} = (2 \times s_{G_i} - s_i) mod\ p$. A hash value $h(S_{U_iG}\|\|ID_G)$ is computed and compared with the stored value. On successful verification, the user computes $M = h(h(S_{U_iG}\|\|ID_{U_i})\|\|N_{G1})$ and signature $SI_{U_i} = Sig_{U_i}(ID_{U_i}, ID_G, M)$ and selects a device to connect to. At this step, the hub is authenticated to the user and mutual authentication between the hub and the user is successfully achieved.

Step 6: Upon successful verification in the above step, user encrypts a message which contains the identity of the user ID_{U_i}, identity of the hub ID_G, identity of the device ID_{D_j}, M, nonce N_{U2}, timestamp T_{U2} and signature SI_{U_i}, and sends to the hub using the public key K_G.

Step 7: The hub retrieves $h(S_{U_iG}\|\|ID_{U_i})$ corresponding to the identity ID_{U_i} and computes $M = h(h(S_{U_iG}\|\|ID_{U_i})\|\|N_{G1})$ and $SI_G = Sig_G(ID_G, ID_{D_j}, C_j, N_{G2})$. It then verifies M and on successful verification, proceeds to the next step. Otherwise, hub aborts the execution of the protocol.

Step 8: The hub retrieves the challenge C_j and sends a message to the device encrypted using the public key K_{D_j}. The message contains the identity of the

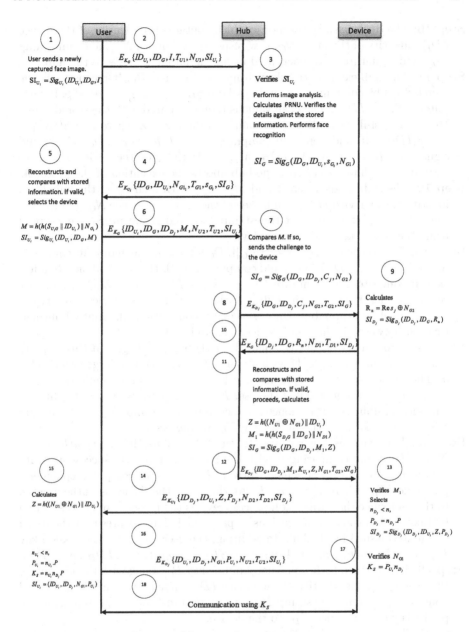

Fig. 3. Mutual authentication phase

hub ID_G, identity of the device ID_{D_j}, challenge C_j, nonce N_{G2}, timestamp T_{G2} and signature SI_G.

Step 9: Upon receiving the challenge, device retrieves Res_j and computes $R_n = Res_j \oplus N_{G2}$ and signature $SI_{D_j} = Sig_{D_j}(ID_{D_j}, ID_G, R_n)$.

Step 10: The device sends a response which contains the identity of the device ID_{D_j}, identity of the hub ID_G, new response R_n, nonce N_{D_1}, and timestamp T_{D_1}, and signature SI_{D_j} encrypted using the public key K_G to the hub.

Step 11: The hub extracts the share from the response R_n. It reconstructs the secret S_{D_jG} by combining s_{G_j} and s_j where $S_{D_jG} = (2s_{G_j} - s_j) mod\ p$. It computes $h(S_{D_jG}||ID_D)$. The hash value is then compared with the stored value. Upon successful verification, hub computes the token Z where $Z = h((N_{U_1} \oplus N_{G_1})||ID_{U_i})$. In addition, hub computes $M_1 = h(h(S_{D_jG}||ID_G)||N_{D_2})$ and signature $SI_G = Sig_G(ID_G, ID_{D_j}, M_1, Z)$. At this step the device is authenticated to the hub. Otherwise, the hub aborts the execution of the protocol.

Step 12: The hub sends token Z and M_1 along with identity of the hub ID_G, identity of the device ID_{D_j}, public key of the user K_{U_i}, nonce N_{G_1} (which was sent in the 4th step), current timestamp T_{G3}, and signature SI_G, encrypted using the public key K_{D_j}, to the device.

Step 13: The device retrieves $h(S_{D_jG}||ID_G)$ from its memory. It computes $M_1 = h(h(S_{D_jG}||ID_G)||N_{D_1})$ and compares it with the received one. In addition, it computes the signature $SI_{D_j} = Sig_{D_j}(ID_{D_j}, ID_{U_i}, Z, P_{D_j})$. On successful verification of M, the hub is authenticated to the device. Otherwise, the protocol is terminated. Upon successful completion, the mutual authentication between the hub and device is established.

Step 14: Elliptic-curve Diffie–Hellman (ECDH) protocol begins at this step [4]. Shared information: $E_q(a, b)$ with a point $P = (x_1, y_1)$ with large order $nP = 0$. The device selects an ephemeral private key n_{D_j} and computes $P_{D_j} = n_{D_j}P$. It sends the identity of the user ID_{U_i}, token received from the hub Z, ephemeral public key P_{D_j}, nonce N_{D2}, current timestamp T_{D2}, and signature SI_{U_i}, encrypted using the public key K_{U_i} to the user.

Step 15: User verifies the received token Z by computing $Z = h(h(N_{U_1} \oplus N_{G1})||ID_{U_i})$ and comparing it with the received value. On successful verification, user selects an ephemeral private key n_{U_i} and computes ephemeral public key P_{U_i} where $P_{U_i} = n_{U_i}P$. At this step, the device is authenticated to the user since the verification process reveals the presence of nonces shared by the hub and the user in previous steps 1 and 4. This ensures that the token was indeed issued by the hub. In addition, the user computes the session key K_S where $K_S = P_{D_j}.n_{U_i}$ and signature $SI_{U_i} = Sig_{U_i}(ID_{U_i}, ID_{D_j}, N_{G1}, P_{U_i})$.

Step 16: The user sends the ephemeral public key P_{U_i} along with the identity of the user ID_{U_i}, the identity of the device ID_{D_j}, nonce N_{G1}, newly generated nonce N_{U3}, current timestamp T_{U3}, and signature SI_{U_i}, encrypted using the public key of the device K_{D_j} to the device.

Step 17: The device verifies the presence of nonce N_{G_1} in the message. If the verification succeeds, it proceeds to compute the session key K_S where $K_S = P_{U_i}n_{D_j}$. At this step, the user is authenticated to the device and mutual authentication between the user and the device is established.

Step 18: The user U_i and the device D_j communicate using the established session key K_S where $K_S = n_{U_i}n_{D_j}P$.

3.3 PRNU Update Phase

If the user U_i has lost the smartphone or would like to log in from a different smartphone, the user can use this phase to update the PRNU.

Step 1: User captures photo of her face using the new smartphone and sends a message, $E_{K_G}\{ID_{U_i}, ID_G, REG, I, T_U, N_U, SI_{U_i}\}$.

Step 2: The hub G verifies the time stamp and the signature, SI_{U_i}. Upon successful verification, G performs face recognition of the user. The hub then performs image analysis. Upon verifying the freshness of the image, the hub extracts the PRNU of the received image and stores the information. Otherwise, the user will be prompted to resend the image.

The rest of the steps are similar to the registration phase. Users follow the steps 4–7 in the registration phase to proceed with the PRNU update phase.

4 Security Analysis

In this section, we analyze the security features of the proposed protocol by performing the formal and informal security analysis.

4.1 Formal Security Verification Using AVISPA Tool

We simulate the proposed protocol using extensively-applied SPAN+AVISPA for the formal security verification. This tool contains four backends for verification of Internet security-sensitive protocols: 1. On-the-fly Model-Checker (OFMC), 2. Constraint Logic based Attack Searcher (CL-AtSe), 3. SAT- based Model-Checker (SATMC) and 4. Tree Automata based on Automatic Approximations for the Analysis of Security Protocols (TA4SP).

We translate the proposed protocol in High-Level Protocol Specification Language used in AVISPA. The basic roles are used to represent each entity. The entities of the proposed protocol include user U, hub G and smart device D. The role of the user is as shown in Fig. 4. Composed roles instantiate one or more basic roles as shown in Fig. 5. The participating entities communicate through two different channels: SND and RCV. The session role declares all the channels used by the basic role as shown in Fig. 6. The intruder is modeled using the Dolev-Yao model in which the active intruder can modify, delete or change the contents of the messages being exchanged. The analysis results of the proposed protocol using OFMC and CL-AtSe is as shown in Fig. 7. We can see that OFMC and CL-AtSe find no attacks. In other words, the stated security goals are satisfied for a bounded number of sessions as specified in environment role. Thus, we conclude that the proposed protocol is resilient to MITM and replay attacks.

```
role
role_U(U:agent,G:agent,Ku:public_key,Kg:public_key,Su:text,D:agen
t,SND,RCV:channel(dy))
played_by U
def=
      local

          State:nat,Tu1:text,Im:text,Tg1:text,Sg:text,Sug:text,Nu1:tex
t,Sdg:text,Nd1:text,Kd:public_key,Tu2:text,Nu2:text,F:hash_func,N
g1:text,Pd:text,Pu:text,Secret:text
          init
              State := 0
          transition
              1. State=0 /\ RCV(start) =|> State':=1 /\ Im':=new() /
\ witness(U,G,auth_1,Im') /\ Tu1':=new() /\ Nu1':=new() /\
SND({U.G.Im'.Nu1'.Tu1'.{F(U.G.Im')}_inv(Ku)}_Kg)
              2. State=1 /\
RCV({G.U.Ng1'.Tg1'.Sg'.{F(G.U.Sg'.Ng1')}_inv(Kg)}_Ku) =|> State':
=2 /\ witness(U,D,auth_4,Ng1') /\ Sug':=new() /\ Nu2':=new() /\
Tu2':=new() /\
SND({U.G.D.F(F(Sug'.U).Ng1').Tu2'.Nu2'.{F(U.G.F(F(F(Sug'.U).Ng1')
))}_inv(Ku)}_Kg)
              7. State=2 /\
RCV({D.U.F(F(xor(Nu1,Ng1)).U).Pd'.{F(D.U.F(F(Sdg'.G).Nd1').Pd')}_
inv(Kd')}_Ku) =|> State':=3 /\
SND({U.D.Ng1.Pd'.Nu2.Tu2.F(U.D.Ng1.Pd')}_Kd')
              9. State=3 /\ RCV({Secret'}_exp(Pu',Pd)) =|> State':=4
end role
```

Fig. 4. The role of the user

```
role
session1(C:text,Sug:text,Sg:text,Im:text,Ku:public_key,U:agent
,Su:text,D:agent,G:agent,Kd:public_key,Res:text,Sdg:text,Kg:pu
blic_key)
def=
      local
              SND3,RCV3,SND2,RCV2,SND1,RCV1:channel(dy)
      composition
              role_D(D,G,Kd,Res,Sdg,Kg,SND3,RCV3) /\
role_G(U,G,Kg,Ku,Kd,Im,Sg,Sug,Sdg,C,Res,SND2,RCV2) /\
role_U(U,G,Ku,Kg,Su,D,SND1,RCV1)
end role

role
session2(C:text,Sug:text,Sg:text,Im:text,Ku:public_key,U:agent
,Su:text,D:agent,G:agent,Kd:public_key,Res:text,Sdg:text,Kg:pu
blic_key)
def=
      local
              SND3,RCV3,SND2,RCV2,SND1,RCV1:channel(dy)
      composition
              role_D(D,G,Kd,Res,Sdg,Kg,SND3,RCV3) /\
role_G(U,G,Kg,Ku,Kd,Im,Sg,Sug,Sdg,C,Res,SND2,RCV2) /\
role_U(U,G,Ku,Kg,Su,D,SND1,RCV1)
end role
```

Fig. 5. The session among participants

4.2   Informal Security Analysis

Man in the Middle Attack (MITM). In MITM, an adversary A intercepts user's requests and sends forged messages. This can occur due to the following reasons. In the first scenario, A uses an image I' captured using the user's camera and sends a message encrypted using the public key of hub represented as $E_{K_G}\{ID_{U_i}, ID_G, I', T_A, N_A, SI_{U_i}\}$. Upon receiving the message, the hub verifies

```
role environment()
def=
      const
      sdg:text,kd:public_key,device:agent,ki:public_key,sug:text,k
u:public_key,const_1:text,alice:agent,hash_
0:hash_func,c:text,sg:text,su:text,hub:agent,res:text,kg:public_k
ey,auth_1:protocol_id,auth_2:protocol_id,auth_3:protocol_id,auth_
4:protocol_id,sec_5:protocol_id
            intruder_knowledge = {alice,hub,ku,kg,ki,inv(ki)}
            composition
            session2(c,sug,sg,const_
1,ki,i,su,device,hub,kd,res,sdg,kg) /\ session1(c,sug,sg,const_
1,ku,alice,su,device,hub,kd,res,sdg,kg)
      end role

goal
      authentication_on auth_1
      authentication_on auth_2
      authentication_on auth_3
      authentication_on auth_4
      secrecy_of sec_5
end goal
environment()
```

Fig. 6. The environment and goal

```
SUMMARY                                          % OFMC
   SAFE                                          % Version of 2006/02/13
                                                 SUMMARY
DETAILS                                             SAFE
   BOUNDED_NUMBER_OF_SESSIONS                    DETAILS
   TYPED_MODEL                                      BOUNDED_NUMBER_OF_SESSIONS
                                                 PROTOCOL
PROTOCOL                                            /home/span/span/testsuite/results/mutualauthentication.if
   /home/span/span/testsuite/results/mutualauthentication.if   GOAL
                                                    as_specified
GOAL                                             BACKEND
   As Specified                                     OFMC
                                                 COMMENTS
BACKEND                                          STATISTICS
   CL-AtSe                                          parseTime: 0.00s
                                                    searchTime: 0.02s
STATISTICS                                          visitedNodes: 2 nodes
                                                    depth: 1 plies
   Analysed    : 29 states
   Reachable   : 3 states
   Translation: 0.06 seconds
   Computation: 0.00 seconds
```

Fig. 7. The results of analysis using CL-AtSe and OFMC backends

the freshness of the image. Since the timestamp of the image does not lie within the threshold, hub aborts the execution of the protocol. In the second scenario, A sends a fresh image I'' and uses an earlier signature of the user SI_{U_i} to send the message. Since the signatures do not match, hub does not proceed further. Thus, the proposed protocol is resilient to MITM attacks.

Replay Attack. In replay attack, adversary A replays old messages containing stale information which may have a negative impact on the protocol. Various measures to defend against replay attacks include timestamps, nonces and counters. The presence of nonces and timestamps in messages ensures the freshness of messages. For instance, A resends an image of the user I' and signature $SI_{U_i} = Sig_{U_i}(ID_{U_i}, ID_G, I')$. Upon receiving the message, the hub aborts the authentication phase as the timestamp of the image does not lie within the threshold. Hence, images captured within an allowable window are further processed to extract the PRNU. In addition, the presence of signature makes it difficult for A to produce a signature for a chosen image. Thus, the proposed protocol is resilient to replay attacks.

Denial of Service Attack (DoS). In a denial of service attack, adversary A prevents legitimate users from executing the protocol. There are two types of DoS attacks such as resource depletion attacks and connection depletion attacks [4]. Authentication is one of the methods to prevent connection depletion attacks. Digital signatures present in all the messages provide authentication, integrity and non-repudiation. Moreover, mutual authentication is established based on values reconstructed using the shares. Hence, A will not be able to provide these values. Thus, the proposed protocol is secure against DoS attacks.

Key Compromise Impersonation Attack. Suppose adversary A obtains the long-term secret key K_{U_i-} of the user, A can masquerade as a legitimate user to the hub. If A obtains a face image from social media, which is captured using the same smartphone, hub aborts the authentication process as the timestamp of the image does not lie within the threshold. Assume that adversary A obtains an image whose timestamp is within the threshold, A will not be able to perform the mutual authentication since A does not possess the share s_i. In addition to the impersonation attack that involves users, we consider smart device spoofing attacks. Suppose A obtains the private key K_{D_j-} of the device. A can intercept the messages sent by the device. In both, the above scenarios, the compromise of secret keys will not lead to the compromise of session keys as the session keys are computed using the ephemeral private keys of the user and the device. Hence the proposed protocol provides key forward secrecy. Thus, the proposed protocol is secure against impersonation attacks.

Unknown Key Share Attack. In unknown key share attack, adversary A intercepts the message by providing the ephemeral public key P_A. However, signatures in the message prevent the adversary from launching an unknown key share attack, since they include the identities of the sender and the receiver. Hence, the proposed protocol is secure against unknown key share attacks.

Fingerprint Forgery Attack. In this attack, adversary A fabricates forged images using the PRNU estimates of publicly available images. Image analysis will reveal a forged image and the hub aborts the execution of the protocol. Hence, we can conclude that the protocol is secure against the fingerprint forgery attacks.

Stolen Device Attack. Consider a scenario where adversary A obtains physical access to a smartphone and generates a login request using a recently captured face image of the user. Authentication will not succeed as the timestamp

Table 3. Comparison of security features

Security features	[30]	[18]	[5]	[25]	Proposed
Mutual authentication between hub and smart device	Y	Y	N	N	Y
Mutual authentication between user and smart device	Y	N	Y	Y	Y
Mutual authentication between user and hub	Y	N	N	N	Y
Resilience to user impersonation attack	Y	NA	Y	N	Y
Resilience to device impersonation attack	Y	Y	Y	Y	Y
Resilience to MITM attack	Y	Y	Y	Y	Y
Resilience to replay attack	Y	Y	Y	N	Y
Resilience to DoS attack	Y	Y	N	Y	Y
Resilience to stolen smartphone/smartcard attack	Y	NA	Y	N	Y
Resilience to smart device capture attack	N	N	Y	Y	Y
Forward secrecy	N	N	N	Y	Y

of the image does not lie within a threshold. Moreover, A cannot acquire a face image of the legitimate user as the device is in A's possession for more than an allowed time period. Thus, the proposed protocol is secure against stolen smartphone attack. In the second scenario, A physically captures a smart device. This can be considered as an insider attack. In both scenarios, physical capture of a device does not lead to compromise of previously established session keys because of the security provided by ECDH. Hence the proposed protocol is secure against smart device capture attacks.

5 Performance Comparison

In this section, we compare the proposed protocol with existing user authentication protocols for IoT, particularly for smart homes. Existing protocols include schemes of Wazid [30], Kumar [18], Challa [5] and Santoso [25].

5.1 Security Features Comparison

The comparison of security features among the proposed protocol and other schemes is shown in Table 3.

The scheme of Wazid lacks forward secrecy and thereby vulnerable to smart device capture attack as the session key can be compromised when an adversary captures the device. In Kumar's scheme, a session key generated at the hub is sent encrypted using the long term shared key to the device. If the long term shared key is compromised, the session keys will also be compromised. Hence, this scheme lacks forward secrecy and thereby vulnerable to smart device capture attack. Moreover, the scheme does not achieve mutual authentication among all participating entities. Challa's scheme does not provide mutual authentication among all participating entities. The stored session keys can be easily compromised. Hence the scheme lacks forward secrecy. In addition, lack of mutual and message authentication can lead to DoS attacks. Santoso's scheme provides forward secrecy since it uses the DH Key agreement but fails to provide mutual authentication among all participating entities. In addition, the absence of timestamps, counters or nonces makes it vulnerable to replay attacks. In contrast, based on the security analysis we conclude that our scheme provides all the security features listed in the table. Hence, the proposed protocol provides significantly better security compared to other existing schemes.

5.2 Computation Overhead Comparison

The estimated time for ECC operations on an image is given in Table 4. The drawback of this proposed protocol is the computation overhead at the hub and smartphone. It is recommended to use a small image size to reduce the computation overhead and the transmission delay. We can infer that the step 1 of the authentication phase will incur high computation overhead. Whereas, the rest of the steps in both phases will incur less computation overhead compared to step 1. The approximate time required for performing various cryptographic operations and the notations are listed in Table 5. The comparison of computation overhead at the smart device is listed in Table 6.

Table 4. Computation overhead of the cryptographic operations on image [26]

Image size	Encryption time	Decryption time	Signature generation	Signature verification
1024 × 1024	2.47 s	1.58 s	4.37 s	4.38 s
512 × 512	0.79 s	0.60 s	1.39 s	1.37 s
256 × 256	0.29 s	0.30 s	0.48 s	0.44 s

Table 5. Approximate estimation of computation time [15]

Notation	Operations	Approximate time (s)
T_{PM}	Point multiplication	0.0171
T_H	Hash function	0.00032
T_S	Symmetric key operations	0.0056
T_{MI}	Modular inverse	0.00004275
T_M	Modular multiplication	0.00001425

We compare the computation overhead at the smart device during the authentication phase of the proposed protocol with related protocols. Total computation time for our proposed protocol is slightly higher than the protocols that we have considered for comparison. The digital signature we use, to combat unknown key share attack, man in the middle attack and denial of service attack, contribute more to the computation overhead. Also, the number of messages in the protocol is also increased as we ensure the legitimacy of all the participating entities to achieve mutual authentication.

Table 6. Comparison of computation overhead at the smart device

Schemes	Total cost	Estimated time (s)
Wazid [30]	$7T_H + T_S$	0.00784
Kumar [18]	$4T_H + 2T_S + 4T_{PM}$	0.08088
Challa [5]	$5T_H$	0.0016
Santoso [25]	$3T_H + 5T_{PM}$	0.08646
Proposed	$5T_H + 5T_{MI} + 5T_M + 8T_{PM}$	0.13872

6 Conclusion

In this paper, we explore the idea of leveraging the face biometric and PRNU to securely authenticate users to smart home environments. We design an attack resilient and usable user authentication protocol that identifies the smartphones of users. The users need to take a photo of their face to authenticate to the hub which reduces the authentication overhead from the users' perspective. Our security analysis of the protocol shows that it is resilient to common attacks in smart homes. Performance comparison with other existing protocols shows that the proposed protocol provides significantly better security with a reasonable overhead.

Acknowledgment. We thank Dr. Atul Prakash, Professor, University of Michigan, for his valuable comments and suggestions on this work.

References

1. Ali, B., Awad, A.I.: Cyber and physical security vulnerability assessment for IoT-based smart homes. Sensors **18**(3), 817 (2018). https://doi.org/10.3390/s18030817
2. Armando, A., et al.: The AVISPA tool for the automated validation of internet security protocols and applications. In: Etessami, K., Rajamani, S.K. (eds.) CAV 2005. LNCS, vol. 3576, pp. 281–285. Springer, Heidelberg (2005). https://doi.org/10.1007/11513988_27
3. Ba, Z., Piao, S., Fu, X., Koutsonikolas, D., Mohaisen, A., Ren, K.: ABC: enabling smartphone authentication with built-in camera. In: Network and Distributed System Security Symposium, pp. 18–21 (2018)
4. Boyd, C., Mathuria, A.: Protocols for Authentication and Key Establishment. Springer, Heidelberg (2013). https://doi.org/10.1007/978-3-662-09527-0

5. Challa, S., et al.: An efficient ECC-based provably secure three-factor user authentication and key agreement protocol for wireless healthcare sensor networks. Comput. Electr. Eng. **69**, 534–554 (2018). https://doi.org/10.1016/j.compeleceng.2017.08.003
6. Chen, E.Y., Pei, Y., Chen, S., Tian, Y., Kotcher, R., Tague, P.: OAuth demystified for mobile application developers. In: Proceedings of the 2014 ACM SIGSAC Conference on Computer and Communications Security, pp. 892–903. ACM (2014)
7. Chen, M., Fridrich, J., Goljan, M.: Digital imaging sensor identification (further study). In: Security, Steganography, and Watermarking of Multimedia Contents IX, vol. 6505, p. 65050P. International Society for Optics and Photonics (2007). https://doi.org/10.1117/12.703370
8. Chifor, B.C., Bica, I., Patriciu, V.V., Pop, F.: A security authorization scheme for smart home internet of things devices. Future Gener. Comput. Syst. **86**, 740–749 (2018)
9. Cooijmans, T., de Ruiter, J., Poll, E.: Analysis of secure key storage solutions on android. In: Proceedings of the 4th ACM Workshop on Security and Privacy in Smartphones & Mobile Devices, pp. 11–20. ACM (2014)
10. Dabov, K., Foi, A., Katkovnik, V., Egiazarian, K.: BM3D image denoising with shape-adaptive principal component analysis. In: Signal Processing with Adaptive Sparse Structured Representations, SPARS 2009 (2009)
11. Dolev, D., Yao, A.: On the security of public key protocols. IEEE Trans. Inf. Theory **29**(2), 198–208 (1983)
12. Fernandes, E., Jung, J., Prakash, A.: Security analysis of emerging smart home applications. In: 2016 IEEE Symposium on Security and Privacy (SP), pp. 636–654. IEEE (2016)
13. Fouladi, B., Ghanoun, S.: Honey, i'm home!!, hacking zwave home automation systems. Black Hat USA (2013)
14. Genet, T.: A short SPAN+ AVISPA tutorial. Ph.D. thesis, IRISA (2015)
15. He, D., Kumar, N., Lee, J.H., Sherratt, R.S.: Enhanced three-factor security protocol for consumer usb mass storage devices. IEEE Trans. Consum. Electron. **60**(1), 30–37 (2014). https://doi.org/10.1109/TCE.2014.6780922
16. Jeong, J., Chung, M.Y., Choo, H.: Integrated OTP-based user authentication scheme using smart cards in home networks. In: Proceedings of the 41st Annual Hawaii International Conference on System Sciences, pp. 294–294. IEEE (2008)
17. Koblitz, N.: Elliptic curve cryptosystems. Math. Comput. **48**(177), 203–209 (1987)
18. Kumar, P., Gurtov, A., Iinatti, J., Ylianttila, M., Sain, M.: Lightweight and secure session-key establishment scheme in smart home environments. IEEE Sens. J. **16**(1), 254–264 (2016)
19. Lomas, N.: Critical flaw identified in zigbee smart home devices (2015)
20. Lukas, J., Fridrich, J., Goljan, M.: Digital camera identification from sensor pattern noise. IEEE Trans. Inf. Forensics Secur. **1**(2), 205–214 (2006). https://doi.org/10.1109/TIFS.2006.873602
21. Miller, V.S.: Use of elliptic curves in cryptography. In: Williams, H.C. (ed.) CRYPTO 1985. LNCS, vol. 218, pp. 417–426. Springer, Heidelberg (1986). https://doi.org/10.1007/3-540-39799-X_31
22. Nimmy, K., Sethumadhavan, M.: Novel mutual authentication protocol for cloud computing using secret sharing and steganography. In: ICADIWT, pp. 101–106 (2014). https://doi.org/10.1109/ICADIWT.2014.6814685
23. Rahmati, A., Fernandes, E., Eykholt, K., Prakash, A.: Tyche: risk-based permissions for smart home platforms. arXiv preprint arXiv:1801.04609 (2018)

24. Sankaran, S.: Lightweight security framework for IoTs using identity based cryptography. In: 2016 International Conference on Advances in Computing, Communications and Informatics (ICACCI), pp. 880–886. IEEE (2016)
25. Santoso, F.K., Vun, N.C.: Securing IoT for smart home system. In: 2015 IEEE International Symposium on Consumer Electronics (ISCE), pp. 1–2. IEEE (2015)
26. Singh, L.D., Singh, K.M.: Image encryption using elliptic curve cryptography. Procedia Comput. Sci. **54**, 472–481 (2015). https://doi.org/10.1016/j.procs.2015.06.054
27. Tewari, A., Gupta, B.: A lightweight mutual authentication protocol based on elliptic curve cryptography for IoT devices. Int. J. Adv. Intell. Paradigms **9**(2–3), 111–121 (2017)
28. UC-Denver: Secret sharing schemes. http://www-math.ucdenver.edu/wcherowi/courses/m5410/ctcsss.html. Accessed 2 Jan 2018
29. Vaidya, B., Park, J.H., Yeo, S.S., Rodrigues, J.J.: Robust one-time password authentication scheme using smart card for home network environment. Comput. Commun. **34**(3), 326–336 (2011)
30. Wazid, M., Das, A.K., Odelu, V., Kumar, N., Susilo, W.: Secure remote user authenticated key establishment protocol for smart home environment. IEEE Trans. Dependable Secure Comput. (2017). https://doi.org/10.1109/TDSC.2017.2764083
31. Zhang, Y., Xiang, Y., Huang, X., Chen, X., Alelaiwi, A.: A matrix-based cross-layer key establishment protocol for smart homes. Inf. Sci. **429**, 390–405 (2018)

Modeling and Analysis of Attacks

Modeling and Analyzing Multistage Attacks Using Recursive Composition Algebra

Ghanshyam S. Bopche[1]([✉])[ID], Gopal N. Rai[2][ID], B. M. Mehtre[3][ID],
and G. R. Gangadharan[4][ID]

[1] Madanpalle Institute of Technology and Science (MITS),
Madanapalle, Andhra Pradesh, India
ghanshyambopche.mca@gmail.com
[2] Rockwell Collins, Cedar Rapids, USA
gopalnrai@gmail.com
[3] Centre of Excellence in Cyber Security, IDRBT, Hyderabad, India
mehtre@gmail.com
[4] National Institute of Technology, Tiruchirappalli, Tiruchirappalli, India
geeyaar@gmail.com
https://www.mits.ac.in/, https://www.rockwellcollins.com/,
http://www.idrbt.ac.in, https://www.nitt.edu/

Abstract. This paper proposes a multistage attack modeling technique based on the recursive composition algebra (RCA_{MA}). For a given vulnerable network configuration, the RCA_{MA} generates recursive composition graph (RCG) which depicts all possible multistage attack scenarios. The prime advantages of the RCG is that it is free from cycles, therefore, does not require computation intensive cycle detection algorithms. Further, the canonical sets obtained from the RCG classifies network vulnerabilities into five classes: (i) isolated, (ii) strict igniter (entry point), (iii) strict terminator (dead end) (iv) overlapping, and (v) mutually exclusive. These classes (logical inferences) provide better insight into the logical correlation among existing vulnerabilities in a given network and hence in prioritizing vulnerability remediation activities accordingly. The efficacy and applicability of our proposition is validated by means of a case study.

Keywords: Threat modeling · Vulnerability · Exploit
Recursive composition algebra · Recursive composition graph
Network hardening

1 Introduction

In this paper, we model and analyze the multistage attacks using a recursive composition based algebra. To the best of our knowledge, no prior work exist for algebraic modeling of vulnerability composition. Originally, the *recursive composition algebra* (RCA) [30], [31] was proposed for the modeling and verification

© Springer Nature Switzerland AG 2018
V. Ganapathy et al. (Eds.): ICISS 2018, LNCS 11281, pp. 67–87, 2018.
https://doi.org/10.1007/978-3-030-05171-6_4

of Web service composition. In the domain of Cyber security, similar kind of scenarios arise as an adversary combines multiple vulnerabilities to gain incremental access to enterprise critical resources. The underlying idea behind using recursive composition based algebra for multistage attack modeling is that the composed vulnerabilities can participate in further composition process as a single vulnerability. In order to completely suite our requirements, we slightly modify the RCA [30], [31] and name it as RCA_{MA} (recursive composition algebra for multistage attack). Adopting the recursive composition in the modeling process reduces the computational complexity of determining all possible attack paths and facilitates hierarchical aggregation of vulnerabilities [24] at different levels.

RCA_{MA} incorporates mainly three operators: successor ($\succ$), composition ($\oplus$), and recursive composition ($\circledast$). For a given network, entry point vulnerabilities in an Internet facing (or client-side) application are directly exploitable by the adversary. Application of recursive composition operation ($\circledast$) on an entry point vulnerability generates a *recursive composition graph* (RCG). The RCG, topologically sorted directed acyclic graph (DAG), depicts all possible multistage attack scenarios in a given network. The RCG differs from the attack graph in that it is free from cycles. Detection and removal of a cycle in an attack graph is a computation intensive process. Canonical sets of the vulnerabilities, derived from the RCG, classifies the network vulnerabilities into: (1) isolated, (2) strict igniter (entry point), and (3) strict terminator (dead end). An administrator can prioritize vulnerability remediation activities based on the above stated classification. Though, cycles does not appear in the RCG, the presence of a cycle in a network can be detected using the concept of canonical set.

2   Related Work

In order to get knowledge of all plausible multistage attacks in an enterprise network, the formal models based on the vulnerability composition have been widely studied. In particular, the formal models allow inexpensive security analysis without real experiments [15] and offer elegant solutions for network vulnerability assessment and hardening. In the context of multistage attack, fault trees [14], privilege graph [8,9], attack graphs [13,18,36,39], and vulnerability graphs [1,16] are the most appropriate modeling methodologies. Kordy et al. [21] presented a complete overview of such modeling techniques. Most of these models are the natural extension of the *Threat Logic Tree* [42] in one or several dimensions. Each model has different features, goals, advantages, and disadvantages.

In reliability engineering, fault trees [14] are primarily proposed for system failure analysis. Even though fault trees are well suitable for modeling conjunction (AND logic) and disjunction (OR logic) of faults, they are not expressive enough to capture all possible system failure scenarios. On the other hand, attack trees [10,17,22,32,34,35] were proposed to find out likely attack scenarios which can result in a violation of the network security policy. As attack trees are the scenario based approaches, it is impossible to cover all likely attack scenarios with few numbers of attack trees if there are several potential targets in a given network. Further, an attack tree contains more subjective nodes and the amount of information it requires is not available in practice. Therefore, the attack tree is expert-specific and applicable only to completely known scenarios. In addition to the above mentioned limitations, the attack tree does not capture an attack scenario where one node having multiple parents (that is, one initial condition can invoke multiple exploits).

The privilege graph [8,9] depicts the adversaries privilege escalation in a target network. In a privilege graph, a node represents a set of privileges on a set of network resources and an edge represents the privilege escalation through successful execution of one or more exploits. Attack graphs [18,26,29,36,39] are obtained from privilege graphs by exploring various ways an adversary may obtain the required privileges. Essentially, the attack graphs capture the computational environment and ease the vulnerability analysis of a network. It establishes the cause-consequence relationship between the adversarial actions. Initially, the attack graphs used to be constructed manually by red teams [19]. However, manual construction of an attack graph is tedious, error-prone, and impractical for moderate size networks. Phillips and Swiler [29] proposed an attack graph model, where a node represents state of the network and an edge represent the actions taken by an adversary during the attack. However, the approach in [29] suffers from similar kind of limitations as in the manual construction of attack graphs.

In order to alleviate the problem of manual construction of an attack graph, Sheyner et al. [36] used a model checking based technique. The usefulness of the model checking based attack graph generation technique depends on the granularity of the input specification. The finer the granularity is, better will be the coverage, but it introduces a large number of states and hence the well-known state explosion problem. Finally, the vulnerability graphs (exploit-dependency attack graphs) [1,16] depicts the cause-consequence relationship between exploitable network vulnerabilities and the privileges that are required for an adversary to incrementally compromise the target network. In contrast to the model checking based approach [36], the vulnerability graphs are more popular for their improved scalability and granularity [16,27]. In spite of all these proposals, the presence of a cycle in the attack graph complicates quantitative and qualitative analysis. To ease the analysis, administrator has to apply computation intensive cycle detection algorithms. Similar to the attack graph, our proposition generates recursive composition graph (RCG), however, the RCG is free from the cycles.

Templeton and Levitt [40] proposed the require/provide model for logical correlation of different kinds of atomic attacks. The require/provide model states that a multistage attack comprises of a sequence of attacks and the early stages of an attack prepares for the later stages. Authors in [40] defined system states using simple predicates and devised JIGSAW language for the attack correlation. However, the approach of developing predicates in [40] is not systematic.

Pandey et al. [28] proposed an algebra for capability based attack correlation and discussed algebraic operations and relations between the capabilities. A new service dependency model for attack response evaluation is proposed by Kheir et al. [20] that enables the evaluation of intrusion and response impact. The ultimate goal of above stated approaches [20,28,40] is IDS alert correlation, whereas our approach deals with vulnerability composition. Our proposed algebra make use of the require/provide model proposed in [28,40]. At the core of our exploit composition process, capabilities (privileges) obtained by an adversary from the successful exploitation of previous vulnerability are used to satisfy a prerequisite (one of the enabling preconditions) of subsequent vulnerabilities. Moreover, expressiveness of our proposed algebra subsumes the expressiveness of require/provide model.

3 Running Example

We consider a test network (similar to [6]) whose topology is shown in Fig. 1. There are six machines located within two subnets. A Web Server and a Mail Server are located inside the demilitarized zone (DMZ), and are separated from the local network by a Tri-homed DMZ firewall. The firewall has a strong set of connectivity-limiting policies (as shown in Table 1) to prevent an adversary from gaining remote access to the internal hosts. All service requests (coming from outside of the network) are fulfilled through the machines in the DMZ. In the

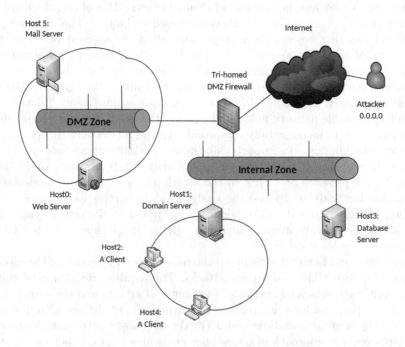

Fig. 1. Test network (adapted from [6])

Table 1, *ALL* specifies that a source host may access all services running over the destination host and *NONE* specifies that a source host is prevented from having access to any service running over the destination host.

Table 1. Connectivity-limiting firewall policies

Host	adversary	$Host_0$	$Host_1$	$Host_2$	$Host_3$	$Host_4$	$Host_5$
adversary	Local-host	ALL	NONE	NONE	NONE	NONE	SMTP
$Host_0$	ALL	Local-host	ALL	Netbios-ssn OpenSSH	Squid LICQ	Squid LICQ	NONE
$Host_1$	ALL	IIS	Local-host	Netbios-ssn	Squid LICQ	NONE	NONE
$Host_2$	ALL	IIS	ALL	Local-host	Squid, LICQ MS SMV	ssh	SMTP
$Host_3$	ALL	IIS	ALL	ALL	Local-host	NONE	NONE
$Host_4$	ALL	NONE	NONE	NONE	NONE	Local-host	NONE
$Host_5$	ALL	NONE	NONE	NONE	NONE	NONE	Local-host

$Host_3$ is the adversary's target machine and *MySQL* is the critical resource running over it. The adversary is an malicious entity and her goal is to obtain root-level privileges on $Host_3$. Table 2 shows the system characteristics for the hosts available in the network. Such kind of information is available in public vulnerability databases viz. Bugtraq [4], NVD [25], etc.

Table 2. System characteristics for the test network

Host	Services	Ports	Vulnerabilities	CVE IDs
$Host_0$	IIS web service	80	IIS buffer overflow	CVE-2010-2370
	ftp	21	ftp buffer overflow	CVE-2009-3023
$Host_1$	ftp	21	ftp rhost overwrite	CVE-2008-1396
	ssh	22	ssh buffer overflow	CVE-2002-1359
	rsh	514	rsh login	CVE-1999-0180
$Host_2$	netbios-ssn	139	netbios-ssn nullsession	CVE-2003-0661
	rsh	514	rsh login	CVE-1999-0180
	OpenSSH	22	Heap Corruption in OpenSSH	CVE-2003-0693
$Host_3$	LICQ	5190	LICQ-remote-to-user	CVE-2001-0439
	Squid proxy	80	squid-port-scan	CVE-2001-1030
	MySQL DB	3306	local-setuid-bof	CVE-2006-3368
	MS SMV Service	445	MS SMV Service Stack BoF	CVE-2008-4050
$Host_4$	LICQ	5190	LICQ-remote-to-user	CVE-2001-0439
	Squid proxy	80	squid-port-scan	CVE-2001-1030
	ssh	22	ssh buffer overflow	CVE-2002-1359
$Host_5$	SMTP	25, 143	SMTP Remote Code Execution	CVE-2004-0840
	Squid proxy	80	squid-port-scan	CVE-2001-1030

The attack graph, generated for the running example using MulVAL tool [27], is shown in the Fig. 2, where an exploit is shown by an oval, an initial condition by a box, and a postcondition by a simple plaintext. There are many cycles in the attack graph, but for easier illustration we consider only two: $node37 \rightarrow node29 \rightarrow node35 \rightarrow node32 \rightarrow node37$ and $node19 \rightarrow node37 \rightarrow node29 \rightarrow node27 \rightarrow node25 \rightarrow node19$. These two cycles in the attack graph are depicted using bold arrows.

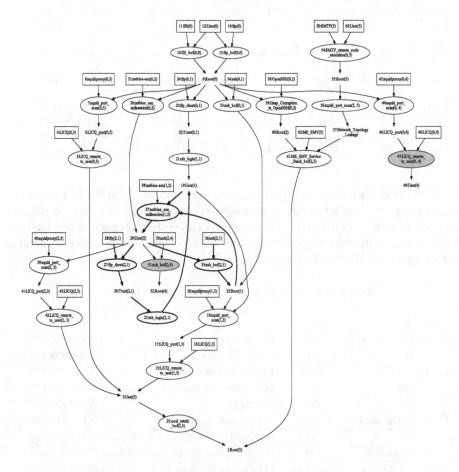

Fig. 2. Goal-oriented attack graph for the test network

As per the monotonicity assumption [1], the adversary never relinquishes her privileges on the previously compromised hosts. Therefore, in a realistic scenario, the adversary does not follow loop attack paths as she does not strive for already acquired privileges. Being aware of this point, an administrator makes effort to find all non-loop attack paths to a target resource. Since the presence of a cycle in the attack graph complicates quantitative analysis, existing multistage attack modeling techniques [1,5,16,27] apply cycle detection algorithms. However, detection of a cycle in a large attack graph is computationally expensive.

4 Recursive Composition Algebra for Multistage Attack Modeling (RCA_{MA})

In this section, we present the complete description of recursive composition algebra for multistage attack modeling (RCA_{MA}) with its algebraic properties. In comparison to the previously proposed RCA [30], [31], RCA_{MA} consists of three key modifications: (1) exploits are the operands for RCA_{MA} instead of Web services and (2) introduction of a term *exploit-preconditions* tuple and based on it, (3) we redefine the operators: conditional successor, restrictive successor, and recursive composition.

In order to build intuition about the RCA_{MA}, we make the following assumptions:

1. An adversary is a skilled intruder, external to the network, whose goal is to gain illegitimate access to the enterprise resources. Moreover, we assume that she is able to successfully exploit all the vulnerabilities present in the network.
2. Since the adversary does not gain any sort of direct access into the network by performing a *Denial of service* (DoS) attack, we do not consider the vulnerabilities related to the attacks on availability.

4.1 The Exploit

Let $\mathbb{H} = \{h_1, h_2, \cdots, h_m\}$ be a finite set of hosts in an enterprise network that can be potential targets for the adversary and let $\mathbb{V} = \{v_1, v_2, v_3, \cdots, v_n\}$ be a finite set of vulnerabilities present on the vulnerable hosts. Let $\mathbb{E} = \{e_1, e_2, \cdots, e_n, \epsilon\}$ be the finite set of exploits that can take advantage of vulnerabilities in the set $\mathbb{V}$. An empty exploit ϵ never exploits any of the vulnerability present in $\mathbb{V}$ and can not be invokable from any other exploit. We define an exploit $e_i \in \mathbb{E}$ as follows:

Definition 1 (Exploit). *The exploit $e_i \in \mathbb{E}$ is a 3-tuple $\langle I, O, Rl \rangle$, where $I = \{I_1, \cdots I_p\}$, $p \in \mathbb{N}$ is a finite set of preconditions, that e_i requires in order to be executed successfully. $O = \{O_1, \cdots, O_q\}$, $q \in \mathbb{N}$ is a finite set of postconditions, that e_i produces once executed successfully. Rl is a relation that maps preconditions from I to postconditions in O ($Rl \subset 2^I \times O$). $e_i.I$ and $e_i.O$ are referred as the set of preconditions and the set of postconditions for exploit e_i.*

With the perception of relation between security conditions (preconditions and postconditions) and exploits, the relation Rl can be splitted into two namely, *require relation* and *imply relation*. In general, a precondition represents the property of the system (or network) for successful execution of an exploit. An exploit and its preconditions are related by *require relation* which states that for successful execution of an exploit, all of its preconditions need to be satisfied conjunctively. Given an exploit e_i, let $e_i.I = \{pre_1, pre_2, pre_3\}$ and $e_i.O = \{post_1, post_2, post_3\}$ be the sets of preconditions and postconditions, respectively. Then $e_i.Rl$ is the relation that maps all the preconditions from $e_i.I$ to one of the postconditions in $e_i.O$, i.e. $e_i.Rl = \langle pre_1 \wedge pre_2 \wedge pre_3, post_1 \rangle$ or $\langle pre_1 \wedge pre_2 \wedge pre_3, post_2 \rangle$ or $\langle pre_1 \wedge pre_2 \wedge pre_3, post_3 \rangle$.

Example 1. In our running example (Fig. 2), $IIS(0)$ and $User(0)$ are the two preconditions for the exploit $IIS\_bof(0, 0)$ (node no. 10) and $Root(0)$ is the implied postcondition.

$$IIS\_bof(0, 0).I = (IIS(0), User(0))$$
$$IIS\_bof(0, 0).O = (Root(0))$$
$$IIS\_bof(0, 0).Rl = \langle IIS(0) \wedge User(0), Root(0) \rangle$$

An exploit can be engineered in many different ways to get the advantage of an exposed vulnerability. Therefore, based on the goal of the adversary, consequences of successful exploitation of a particular vulnerability could be many ranging from accidental disclosure of non-relevant information to fully privileged remote access to critical system. The consequences may be in the terms of any of the following: increased connectivity, escalated privileges, and increased vulnerabilities. One of the ultimate goal of an expert adversary is to establish a foothold in order to maintain control of the compromised hosts even if the user logs off or the computer reboots. This type of maintaining *persistence control* can be achieved by installing rootkits/backdoors, creating new services, new scheduled tasks, modifying registry keys, so the malicious service starts at next boot. An *imply relation* exists between an exploit and its postconditions. Successful exploitation of a vulnerability leads to the generation of any of the above mentioned postconditions disjunctively. Further, the implied postconditions may act as preconditions for other exploits.

4.2   Operators

Definition 2 (Absolute Successor). *Let '$\succ$' be a symbol to represent the successor operator. $\succ$ maps an element of the $\mathbb{E}$ to an element of the power set of the set $\mathbb{E}$ ($\succ: \mathbb{E} \to 2^{\mathbb{E}}$). Let $S \subset \mathbb{E}, e_i \in \mathbb{E}$, and $e_j \in S$ then $\succ (e_i) = S$ if and only if $\forall e_j \in S : e_i.O \cap e_j.I \neq \emptyset$.*

In other words, the absolute successor operator ($\succ$) is an unary operator that provides exploit(s) directly invokable by a given exploit. Such invoked exploit(s) are called as successor exploit(s). The successor operator captures the dependency among exploits. The dependency between two exploits is satisfied if all the initial conditions vital for the successful exploitation of dependent (invoked) exploit are satisfied by the dependee. Exploit dependencies are made explicit by invoking other exploit(s) from the given exploit. Such dependency is possible when a postcondition of an exploit is proved to be one of the necessary preconditions for other exploit(s) provided that the remaining preconditions are already satisfied.

Consider that the exploit $e_i \in \mathbb{E}$ invokes exploit $e_j \in \mathbb{E}$. Then $\succ (e_i) = e_j$. If e_j is not known in advance, we write $\succ (e_i) = e_{i+1}$ unless stated otherwise. If the exploit e_i directly invokes a set of exploits $(e_1, \cdots, e_l) \subset \mathbb{E}$ then $\succ (e_i) = \{e_1, \cdots, e_l\}$. If the exploit e_i does not invoke any exploit from the set $\mathbb{E}$ then $\succ (e_i) = \epsilon$.

Nowadays, Cyber attacks combine multiple exploits in order to get incremental access to network resources. The composition of exploits (say $n \in \mathbb{N}$, number of exploits) is the combination of multiple host-only exploits into a meta exploit based on their require/imply relationship. The exploits can be composed either sequentially or parallely. Let '$\oplus_s$' and '$\oplus_p$' be two symbols that represent the sequential composition and parallel composition, respectively. We define sequential and parallel composition as follows.

Definition 3 (Sequential composition). *Given two exploits $e_i, e_j \in \mathbb{E} : e_j \in (\succ e_i)$, sequential composition of e_i and e_j (represented as $e_i \oplus_s e_j$) yields a meta-exploit e_k such that the preconditions of e_k matches with the preconditions of e_i and the postcondition of e_k matches with the postcondition of e_j.*

$$e_i \oplus_s e_j \triangleq \{e_k : (e_k.I = e_i.I) \wedge (e_k.O = e_j.O)\} \tag{1}$$

Figure 3(a) depicts a scenario (from the running example) that composes exploits $IIS\_bof(0,0)$ and $ssh\_bof(0,1)$ sequentially.

Definition 4 (Parallel composition). *Given two exploits $e_i, e_j \in \mathbb{E} : e_j \notin (\succ e_i) \wedge e_i \notin (\succ e_j)$, parallel composition of e_i and e_j (represented as $e_i \oplus_p e_j$) yields a composite exploit e_k such that the preconditions of e_k is consolidation of the preconditions of e_i and e_j and the postcondition of e_k is consolidation of the postconditions of e_i and e_j.*

$$e_i \oplus_p e_j \triangleq \{e_k : (e_k.I = (e_i.I \cup e_j.I)) \wedge (e_k.O = (e_i.O \cup e_j.O))\} \tag{2}$$

Parallel composition of exploits in multistage attack points towards the possibility of coordinated attack. In order to improve the chances of successful attack, two or more attackers controlling different hosts (in a target network) may collude and cooperate towards achieving a common goal [3].

Example 2. If exploit e_i implies the postcondition o_1 and exploit e_j implies the postcondition o_2, and both o_1 and o_2 are required by exploit e_s, then e_s can not be executed before e_i and e_j are executed. More than one adversary could coordinate to execute e_i and e_j at a time.

In a case of parallel composition, an adversary has to compulsorily execute all of the participating exploits. The postconditions generated by the participating exploits becomes the preconditions for the successor exploit. Figure 3(b) depicts a parallel composition scenario for the running example.

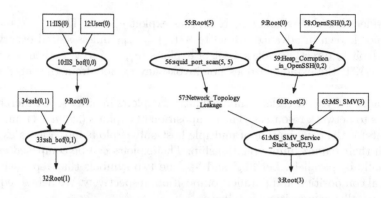

a: Sequential composition of exploits   b: Parallel composition of exploits

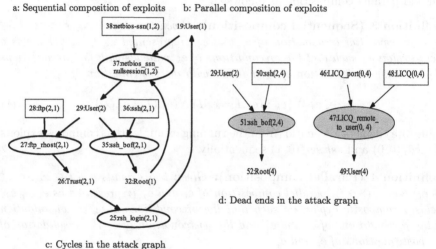

c: Cycles in the attack graph

d: Dead ends in the attack graph

Fig. 3. Various constructs in the attack graph (depicted in the Fig. 2)

Let symbol '$\oplus$' be a common representation for both sequential composition operator and parallel composition operator (removing the suffixes s and p from $\oplus_s$ and $\oplus_p$). Let $e_i, e_j \in \mathbb{E}$ be two exploits such that their composition $(e_i \oplus e_j)$ is possible. However, the resultant exploit (e_k) for the composition does not exist in the set $\mathbb{E}$. Then, '$e_i \oplus e_j$' itself represents a composite exploit that is able to participate in further composition processes as a single exploit. However, composition of an exploit with an empty exploit results in the exploit itself. $(e_i \oplus \epsilon = e_i)$.

Definition 5 (Conditional Successor). *A conditional successor operator (represented as '$\succ_C$') accepts the input and produces the output in the form of a tuple $\langle e_i, I_p \rangle$, where $e_i \in \mathbb{E}$ and I_p is a set of preconditions for e_i. Given a tuple $\langle e_i, I_p \rangle$, $\langle e_j, I_r \rangle$ is a conditional successor of $\langle e_i, I_p \rangle$ (written as: $\langle e_j, I_r \rangle \in (\succ_C \langle e_i, I_p \rangle))$ if and only if $e_j \in (\succ e_i)$ and $I_r \in e_i.Rl(I_p)$.*

Here, $\succ_C$ operator accepts input in the form of pair $\langle e_i, I_p \rangle$, where e_i is the exploit and I_p is the set of preconditions required for successful exploitation of e_i. All the preconditions must have to be conjunctively satisfied for e_i to be executed successfully. The notion of $\succ_C$ arise from the AND relationship between preconditions of an exploit e_i. Conditional successor of e_i produces an output pair $\langle e_j, I_r \rangle$ where I_r is the (set of) postcondition(s) generated by e_i. There is a disjunctive OR relationship between the generated postconditions and they act as one of the preconditions required for successful exploitation of e_j.

Restrictive successor operator ($\succ_R$) is a conditional successor operator such that $Domain(\succ_R) = Domain(\succ)$ and $Range(\succ_R) \subseteq Range(\succ_C)$. The rational behind using $\succ_R$ operator is to realize the notion of monotonicity [1] in the multistage attacks which states that adversary's control over the network increases monotonically. In other words, the adversary need not relinquish her privileges on the already compromised resources while advancing further in the network. The notion of monotonicity allows all potential network attacks to be represented as a sequence of dependencies among exploits and security conditions, rather than as an enumeration of states. We formally define restrictive successor operator as follows:

Definition 6 (Restrictive successor). *Let* $\langle e_i, I_p \rangle \oplus \langle e_j, I_q \rangle \oplus \cdots \oplus \langle e_n, I_s \rangle$ *be an exploit composition chain and* $\langle e_x, I_x \rangle$ *be an exploit-precondition tuple, then* $\langle e_x, I_x \rangle \in \Big(\succ_R \langle e_i, I_p \rangle \oplus \langle e_j, I_q \rangle \oplus \cdots \oplus \langle e_n, I_s \rangle \Big)$ *if and only if* $\langle e_x, I_x \rangle \in \Big(\succ_C \langle e_i, I_p \rangle \oplus \langle e_j, I_q \rangle \oplus \cdots \oplus \langle e_n, I_s \rangle \Big)$ *and* $\langle e_x, I_x \rangle \notin \{\langle e_i, I_p \rangle, \langle e_j, I_q \rangle, \cdots, \langle e_n, I_s \rangle\}$.

The advantage of $\succ_R$ is that it eliminates the cycles in the resulting multigraph. Algorithm 1 presents the process for computation of restrictive successor.

Algorithm 1. ResSuc($\langle e_i, I_p \rangle \oplus \langle e_j, I_q \rangle \oplus \cdots \oplus \langle e_n, I_s \rangle, \mathbb{E}$)

Input: $\langle e_i, I_p \rangle \oplus \langle e_j, I_q \rangle \oplus \cdots \oplus \langle e_n, I_s \rangle, \mathbb{E}$
Output: Restrictive successors of $\langle e_i, I_p \rangle \oplus \langle e_j, I_q \rangle \oplus \cdots \oplus \langle e_n, I_s \rangle$
1: **for all** $e_j \in e_i \oplus \cdots \oplus e_n$ **do**
2:   $\mathbb{E} \leftarrow \mathbb{E} - \{e_j\}$
3: **end for**
4: **for all** $e_k \in \mathbb{E}$ **do**
5:   **if** $e_n.Rl(I_s) \in e_k.I$ **then**
6:     $\langle e_k, (e_n.Rl(I_s)) \rangle \in \big(\succ_R (\langle e_i, I_p \rangle \oplus \langle e_j, I_q \rangle \oplus \cdots \oplus \langle e_n, I_s \rangle) \big)$
7:   **end if**
8: **end for**

Let '$\circledast$' be a symbol to represent recursive composition. To define recursive composition, we incorporate restrictive successor operator ($\succ_R$) and composition operator ($\oplus$) as supplementary operators (defined earlier in this section).

Definition 7 (Recursive composition). *Recursive composition for a given exploit-precondition tuple* $\langle e_i, I_p \rangle$ *is defined as follows:*

$$\circledast \langle e_i, I_p \rangle \triangleq \begin{cases} \epsilon & ; if \langle e_i, I_p \rangle = \epsilon \\ \langle e_i, I_p \rangle & ; if \succ_R \langle e_i, I_p \rangle = \epsilon \\ \langle e_i, I_p \rangle \oplus \left\{ \circledast \left(\succ_R \langle e_i, I_p \rangle \right) \right\}; otherwise \end{cases} \quad (3)$$

Algorithm 2 presents the process for computation of recursive composition.

Algorithm 2. RecComp($\langle e_i, I_p \rangle, \mathbb{E}$)

    Input: $\langle e_i, I_p \rangle, \mathbb{E}$
    Output: RCG with $\langle e_i, I_p \rangle$ as root
 1: make $\langle e_i, I_p \rangle$ as root node
 2: $ParentNode \leftarrow \langle e_i, I_p \rangle$
 3: $\mathbb{E} \leftarrow \mathbb{E} - \{e_i\}$
 4: $S \leftarrow \emptyset$
 5: **for all** $e_j \in \mathbb{E}$ **do**
 6:    $\mathcal{R} \leftarrow ResSuc(\langle e_i, I_p \rangle, \mathbb{E})$
 7:    **if** $\langle e_j, I_x \rangle \in \mathcal{R}$ **then**
 8:      $e_i \oplus e_j$
 9:      $ParentNode.Child \leftarrow \langle e_j, I_x \rangle$
10:      $S \leftarrow (\langle e_i, I_p \rangle \oplus \langle e_j, I_x \rangle)$
11:      $\mathbb{E} \leftarrow \mathbb{E} - \{e_j\}$
12:    **end if**
13: **end for**
14: **while** $S \neq \emptyset$ **do**
15:    **for all** $\langle e_i, I_p \rangle \in S$ **do**
16:      RecComp($\langle e_i, I_p \rangle, \mathbb{E}$)
17:    **end for**
18: **end while**

Recursive composition on e_i generates a topologically sorted directed acyclic graph with e_i as a root node. We call every path (from the root to the sink node) in the graph as a *attack trace*. Let e_i be an exploit then $\mathcal{T}_{e_i}$ represents a set which contains all the attack traces generated by applying the recursive composition on e_i. Figure 4 represents a recursive composition graph (RCG) corresponding to the running example.

5   Logical Inferences

Once we have the RCG for a network under consideration, we can perform further analysis of it to extract security relevant information for proactive network hardening. For doing this, we make use of canonical sets of exploits derived from the RCG. The term *canonical* is not an absolute one. It gives meaning to the word adjoining it. The use of the word *canonical set* varies from context to context in mathematics, logic, and algebra. We redefine the term *canonical set* in the context of our proposed algebra (RCA_{MA}) as follows:

Definition 8 (Canonical set of Exploit e_i). *Given the set $\mathbb{E}$, a canonical set $\mathcal{C}_i$ for an exploit $e_i \in \mathbb{E}$ is a subset of $\mathbb{E}$ such that it consists of all sink nodes (other than the root node) of a RCG generated from the application of the recursive composition operation ($\circledast$) on the exploit e_i.*

Let $\mathcal{C}_i$ be a canonical set for exploit e_i and '$\rightsquigarrow$' be a symbol to represent '*leads to*'. Then, $\circledast e_i \rightsquigarrow \mathcal{C}_i$. Even if an exploit does not invoke any other exploit, an empty canonical set exists for it. For instance, if $\circledast e_i = \epsilon$ then $\circledast e_i \rightsquigarrow \mathcal{C}_i = \emptyset$. The computation of canonical sets for all the exploits yields a set $\mathbb{C}$ of the set $\mathbb{E}$. The partition set $\mathbb{C}$ (may be non-disjoint) consists 'n' number of sets $\mathbb{C} = (\mathcal{C}_1, \ldots, \mathcal{C}_n)$. $\mathcal{C}_i$ is the canonical set generated by e_i where $0 < i \leq n$.

Let S_{is}, S_{ig}, and S_{tm} be the sets of isolated, strict igniter, and strict terminator exploits, respectively. Several logical interpretations based on the canonical sets are deduced and discussed with their significance as follows:

Isolated Exploit: A non-trivial isolated exploit is one that cannot be invoked by any other exploit as well as it cannot invoke other exploits. Excluding isolated exploits (vulnerabilities) out from $\mathbb{E}$ is mandatory as their presence in the exploit set $\mathbb{E}$ increases the computational overhead during exploit composition. On the basis of recursive composition operator and canonical sets, isolated exploits can be recognized automatically as follows:

$$(\exists e_i \in \mathbb{E}) \left[(\nexists e_j \in \mathbb{E}) \left((\circledast e_i \rightsquigarrow \mathcal{C}_i = \emptyset) \wedge (\circledast e_j \rightsquigarrow \mathcal{C}_j) \wedge (e_i \in \mathcal{C}_j) \right) \right] \Leftrightarrow e_i \in S_{is} \quad (4)$$

In practice, for a computer network of reasonable size, vulnerability scanners generate an overwhelming amount of data in the form of laundry list of vulnerabilities. Patching all reported vulnerabilities in a network is mission impossible for the administrator as it costs money, time, resources, etc., so where does an administrator start? If there are so many vulnerabilities to fix, the administrator needs to identify the vulnerabilities that really matter most in securing the network. Due to the absence of one or more enabling conditions, some of the vulnerabilities in a network are not exploitable. Therefore, in today's resource-constrained network environment, patching of such temporarily inactive vulnerabilities is of no value. One needs to focus on a group of exploitable vulnerabilities that endangers the network security. Identification of isolated vulnerabilities (temporarily inactive) reduces administrator search space and thereby help in cost-effective network hardening. For running example (shown in Fig. 1), the vulnerability *CVE-1999-0180* in *rsh* service running over the $Host_2$ is the isolated vulnerability. Even though the *rsh* service is vulnerable, the vulnerability is not exploitable. It is because the service is not accessible to any other hosts.

Algorithm 3. Computing Logical Inferences from Canonical Sets

---
Input: $\mathbb{E} = \{e_1, \cdots, e_n, \epsilon\}, \succ, \oplus, \circledast$
Output: Logical inferences
1: let $\mathbb{C} = \emptyset$ be a set
2: **for all** $e_i \in \mathbb{E}$ **do**
3:    $\circledast e_i \rightsquigarrow \mathcal{C}_i$ ▷ Derive canonical set for each exploit in the network.
4:    $\mathbb{C} \leftarrow \mathcal{C}_i$
5: **end for**
6: let $S_{tm} = \emptyset$, $S_{is} = \emptyset$, $S_{ig} = \emptyset$ be the sets of strict terminator exploits, isolated exploits and strict igniter exploits, respectively.
7: **for all** $\mathcal{C}_i \in \mathbb{C}$ **do**
8:    **if** $\mathcal{C}_i = \emptyset$ **then**
9:        **for all** $\mathcal{C}_j \in \mathbb{C}$ **do**
10:            **if** $e_i \in \mathcal{C}_j$ **then**
11:                $S_{tm} \leftarrow e_i$ ▷ Strict terminator exploit
12:            **else**
13:                $S_{is} \leftarrow e_i$ ▷ Isolated exploit (non-exploitable vulnerability)
14:            **end if**
15:        **end for**
16:    **else if** $\nexists \mathcal{C}_j \in \mathbb{C}$ *such that* $e_i \in \mathcal{C}_j$ **then**
17:        $S_{ig} \leftarrow e_i$ ▷ Strict igniter exploit (entry-point vulnerability)
18:    **end if**
19: **end for**
20: $\mathbb{E} \leftarrow \mathbb{E} \backslash S_{is}$ ▷ Exclude non-exploitable vulnerabilities
21: **for all** $e_i \in S_{is}$ **do**
22:    $\circledast e_i \rightsquigarrow \mathcal{C}_i$ ▷ Derive canonical set for non-exploitable vulnerabilities
23:    $\mathbb{C} \leftarrow \mathbb{C} \backslash \mathcal{C}_i$
24: **end for**
25: **for all** $\mathcal{C}_i \in \mathbb{C}$ **do**
26:    **for all** $\mathcal{C}_j \in \mathbb{C}$ **do**
27:        **if** $\mathcal{C}_i = \mathcal{C}_j$ **then**
28:            $\mathcal{T}_{e_i}$ and $\mathcal{T}_{e_j}$ behave alike (i.e. attack traces from e_i and e_j end up in the same set of resources)
29:        **else if** $\mathcal{C}_i \subset \mathcal{C}_j$ **then**
30:            **if** e_i is a successor of e_j **then**
31:                preventing e_j from execution also prevents e_i
32:            **else**
33:                both e_i and e_j needs to be prevented from execution
34:            **end if**
35:        **end if**
36:    **end for**
37: **end for**

Strict Igniter Exploit: A strict igniter exploit is one that cannot be invoked by other exploit but can invoke other exploits.

$$(\exists e_i \in \mathbb{E}) \left[(\nexists e_j \in \mathbb{E}) \left((\circledast e_i \rightsquigarrow \mathcal{C}_i \neq \emptyset) \wedge (\circledast e_j \rightsquigarrow \mathcal{C}_j) \wedge (e_i \in \mathcal{C}_j) \right) \right] \Leftrightarrow e_i \in S_{ig} \quad (5)$$

Adversary performs reconnaissance of the Internet facing hosts/servers in a target network and collect information about the entry point vulnerabilities. The adversary can enter into the network by exploiting entry point vulnerabilities where the exploited vulnerability lays the groundwork for the exploitation of subsequent vulnerabilities. Identification of such entry point vulnerabilities (or strict igniter exploits) helps administrator in closing all required doors leading to mission critical resources/assets.

Strict Terminator Exploit: A strict terminator exploit is one which does not invoke any exploit but can be invoked by other exploits.

$$(\exists e_i \in \mathbb{E}) \left[(\exists e_j \in \mathbb{E}) \left((\circledast e_i \rightsquigarrow \mathcal{C}_i = \emptyset) \wedge (\circledast e_j \rightsquigarrow \mathcal{C}_j) \wedge (e_i \in \mathcal{C}_j) \right) \right] \Leftrightarrow e_i \in S_{tm}$$
$$(6)$$

Classifying exploits into separate sets, namely, strict igniter and strict terminator exploits reduces the search space while analyzing exploit composition. By leveraging the condition $(\nexists e_j \in \mathbb{E})[e_i \in \mathcal{C}_j]$ and $(\exists e_j \in \mathbb{E})[e_i \in \mathcal{C}_j]$, strict igniter and strict terminator exploits can be computed.

Each attack trace starts from the adversary's initial position (i.e. the Internet) and ends up with either the target (i.e. critical resource of highest importance) or with the intermediate resource of less importance. Similar to [37], we define a dead end to be an exploit postcondition (adversary state) from which there is no attack path to the goal that the adversary wants to compromise. If the adversary follows the path that ends up with dead ends, then she will not be able to reach the desired target resource. Dead ends arise in the network because some host configurations cannot be penetrated, leaving no opportunity to the adversary to reach her goal.

Nowadays, it may not be possible for an adversary to reach the goal in all cases, because the adversary may get hold of the intermediate machines from which the target machine simply cannot be reached. Further, a dead end may arise if no exploit is applicable for the target machine. Therefore, if an adversary encounters a dead end along a attack path, she has to backtrack. As per the monotonicity assumption [1], adversary never relinquishes obtained privileges on the compromised machines. After backtracking, the adversary needs to scan other reachable hosts for vulnerabilities. Once found, she may exploit the newly discovered vulnerabilities. In the process, the adversary spends significant amount of effort and time in exploiting dead end vulnerabilities. Maintaining more number of dead end vulnerabilities distract adversary from reaching the target. Consequently, the ongoing attack will be slowed down and an administrator will get enough time to take preventive measures. Sun and Jajodia [38] proposed an attack surface expansion (ASE) mechanism that focuses on increasing the number of vulnerabilities (entry-point vulnerabilities, in particular) visible to an adversary so that she cannot easily identify the real internal attack surface. Similar to [38], an administrator can increase number of dead end vulnerabilities from where the adversary cannot reach the desired target resource. Since the administrator has a direct access to all of the network components, she can discover all the dead end vulnerabilities through internal scanning. Therefore, instead of patching the dead end vulnerabilities, it is desirable to increase them. An administrator can selectively patch the most critical vulnerabilities in the network in a cost effective manner. Figure 3(d) depicts the dead ends in the RCG generated for the running example.

Relations: As an added advantage of the canonical sets, an administrator can compare two exploits in terms of their attack propagation. The canonical set for an exploit e_i indicates how deeper (sphere of attack propagation) the adversary can penetrate the network, considering e_i as the first exploit. In the resource-constrained environment where patching of all the vulnerabilities is not possible, an administrator prioritize the exploitable vulnerabilities and patches the most pressing ones. For finding most pressing vulnerabilities, she has to derive a relation between exploitable vulnerabilities. A relation represents a logical association between two or more vulnerabilities. The relation between vulnerabilities is of two types: (i) overlapping relation and (ii) mutually exclusive relation.

(I) Overlap. Two exploits (exploitable vulnerabilities) overlap if there exists common exploit(s) between their canonical sets. Two exploits e_i and e_j are said to be overlapping if Eq. 7 is satisfied.

$$(\exists e_i \in \mathbb{E}) \left[(\exists e_j \in \mathbb{E}) \left((\circledast e_i \rightsquigarrow \mathcal{C}_i) \wedge (\circledast e_j \rightsquigarrow \mathcal{C}_j) \wedge (\mathcal{C}_i \cap \mathcal{C}_j \neq \emptyset) \right) \right] \quad (7)$$

Two possible cases of the overlapping relation are discussed as follows:

- **Case I.** e_i and e_j are two overlapping exploits such that e_i is a successor (need not be immediate successor) of e_j. In this case, preventing e_j from execution (i.e. patching of respective vulnerability) automatically stops e_i, whereas converse is not true in general.
- **Case II.** e_i and e_j are two overlapping exploits such that no successor-predecessor relationship exists between e_i and e_j. In this case, preventing e_i from execution does not affect the adversary's capability in reaching the target resources. Therefore, an administrator must prevent (stop) both the exploits from execution.

(II) Mutually Exclusive. Two exploits e_i and e_j are said to be mutually exclusive if $\mathcal{C}_i \cap \mathcal{C}_j = \emptyset$ in Eq. 7. That is, the sphere of influence of one exploit is independent of the other and vice versa. Therefore, an administrator must focus on both the exploits while designing the security remediation plan. Existence of the mutually exclusive relation between exploitable vulnerabilities assist administrator in understanding the number of independent vulnerabilities present in the network.

Identification of the above mentioned relationships between exploits, helps administrator in reducing the vulnerability search space and hence results in efficient hardening of the network.

Algorithm 3 presents the process for deriving the logical inferences from the generated RCG using the notion of canonical set.

Cycle Detection in Attack Graph: If an administrator wants to know about the cycles, if any, present in the network, she can obtain such knowledge based on the notion of canonical set. Exploits in an attack cycle states that one exploit is reachable from the other and vice versa. The fulfillment of the following condition infers that the attack traces generated by e_i ($\mathcal{T}_{e_i}$) and e_j ($\mathcal{T}_{e_j}$) lead to a cycle in the network.

$$(\exists e_i \in \mathbb{E}) \left[(\exists e_j \in \mathbb{E}) \left((((\circledast e_i \rightsquigarrow \mathcal{C}_i) \land (e_j \in \mathcal{C}_i)) \land ((\circledast e_j \rightsquigarrow \mathcal{C}_j) \land (e_i \in \mathcal{C}_j)) \right) \right] \quad (8)$$

Figure 3(c) depicts the scenarios where cycles exist in the network.

6   Case Study

We have applied RCA_{MA} to a test network shown in Fig. 1. For our test network, we assume that the adversary is the skilled malicious entity on the Internet, capable of successfully exploiting all the vulnerabilities present in the network, and her goal is to obtain root privilege on the database server (i.e. Host 3). Initially, the adversary has an access to the services running over the Web Server hosted in the DMZ. Host(s) and network description captures information about the network hosts, services running over them, service connectivity between hosts, and vulnerabilities present in the network. Service connectivity information is obtained from the firewall rules (access control policies). Vulnerability scanners such as GFI Languard [11], Nessus [23], Retina [33] etc., can be used to obtain information about the vulnerabilities present in the network. The proposed algebra leverages XML specification for the modeling substrates such as threat agent (adversary), vulnerable host(s), and exploits for exploit composition.

Recursive composition yields exhaustive recursive composition graph (RCG) as shown in the Fig. 4. The RCG enumerates all potential multistage attack scenarios for the test network and is free from the cycles. Each attack trace is a series of exploits that leads to an undesirable state (i.e. the state where an adversary can obtain user/root level privileges). Once we have a RCG for a specific network, we can utilize it for further analysis.

Similar to the attack graphs, the generated RCG can be used for (i) attack forecasting [12] (ii) cost-benefit security hardening [41] (iii) evaluating the impact of network infrastructure factors such as network segregation/partitioning, defense-in- depth, service connectivity, etc., on the network security risk [7], and (iv) measuring the temporal variation in the network security risk [2]. The logical inferences derived from the RCA_{MA} help administrators to take proactive actions against the possible attacks.

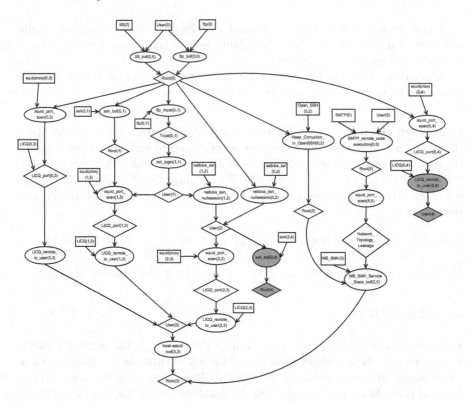

Fig. 4. RCG for the test network

7 Conclusions

In this paper, a recursive composition based algebra RCA_{MA} is presented for multistage attack modeling. The RCA_{MA} generates recursive composition graph (RCG) which depicts all possible multistage attack scenarios. RCA_{MA} supports the systematic analysis of multistage attacks. The logical inferences deduced from the canonical sets helps administrator in extracting security relevant information for proactive network hardening.

There are a number of directions for extending the research presented in this paper. RCA_{MA} can be extended to: (i) capture distributed kind of attacks where multiple attack sources (i.e. multiple colluding attackers) and multiple targets are involved, (ii) investigate the effect of increasing dead end vulnerabilities on the robustness of a given network under cost constraint, and (iii) aggregate vulnerabilities at the different level for improving visual complexity of the multistage attacks in a RCG.

References

1. Ammann, P.: Scalable, graph-based network vulnerability analysis. In: Proceedings of the 9th ACM Conference on Computer and Communications Security, pp. 217–224. ACM Press (2002)
2. Awan, M.S.K., Burnap, P., Rana, O.: Identifying cyber risk hotspots: a framework for measuring temporal variance in computer network risk. Comput. Secur. **57**, 31–46 (2016)
3. Braynov, S., Jadliwala, M.: Representation and analysis of coordinated attacks. In: Proceedings of the ACM Workshop on Formal Methods in Security Engineering, pp. 43–51. ACM (2003)
4. Bugtraq. http://www.securityfocus.com/archive/1
5. Chen, F., Liu, D., Zhang, Y., Su, J.: A scalable approach to analyzing network security using compact attack graphs. J. Netw. **5**(5), 543–550 (2010)
6. Chung, C.J., Khatkar, P., Xing, T., Lee, J., Huang, D.: Nice: network intrusion detection and countermeasure selection in virtual network systems. IEEE Trans. Depend. Secure Comput. **10**(4), 198–211 (2013)
7. Cowley, J.A., Greitzer, F.L., Woods, B.: Effect of network infrastructure factors on information system risk judgments. Comput. Secur. **52**, 142–158 (2015)
8. Dacier, M.: Towards quantitative evaluation of computer security. Ph.D. thesis, Institut National Polytechnique de Toulouse - INPT, December 1994
9. Dacier, M., Deswarte, Y.: Privilege graph: an extension to the typed access matrix model. In: Gollmann, D. (ed.) ESORICS 1994. LNCS, vol. 875, pp. 319–334. Springer, Heidelberg (1994). https://doi.org/10.1007/3-540-58618-0_72
10. Dawkins, J., Campbell, C., Hale, J.: Modeling network attacks: extending the attack tree paradigm. In: Proceedings of the Workshop Statistical Machine Learning Techniques in Computer Intrusion Detection (2002)
11. GFILanguard. http://www.gfi.com
12. GhasemiGol, M., Ghaemi-Bafghi, A., Takabi, H.: A comprehensive approach for network attack forecasting. Comput. Secur. **58**, 83–105 (2016)
13. Ghosh, N., Ghosh, S.: A planner-based approach to generate and analyze minimal attack graph. Appl. Intell. **36**(2), 369–390 (2012)
14. Gorski, J., Wardziński, A.: Formalising fault trees. In: Redmill, F., Anderson, T. (eds.) Proceedings of the Achievement and Assurance of Safety, pp. 311–327. Springer, London (1995). https://doi.org/10.1007/978-1-4471-3003-1_18
15. Iyer, A., Ngo, H.Q.: Towards a theory of insider threat assessment. In: Proceedings of the International Conference on Dependable Systems and Networks, DSN 2005, pp. 108–117. IEEE Computer Society, Washington, DC (2005)
16. Jajodia, S., Noel, S.: Topological vulnerability analysis: a powerful new approach for network attack prevention, detection, and response. In: Proceedings of the Algorithms, Architectures, and Information System Security. Indian Statistical Institute Platinum Jubilee Series, pp. 285–305 (2009)
17. Jauhar, S., et al.: Model-based cybersecurity assessment with NESCOR smart grid failure scenarios. In: Proceedings of the IEEE 21st Pacific Rim International Symposium on Dependable Computing (PRDC), pp. 319–324 (2015)
18. Jha, S., Sheyner, O., Wing, J.: Two formal analysis of attack graphs. In: Proceedings of the 15th IEEE Workshop on Computer Security Foundations, CSFW 2002, pp. 49–57. IEEE Computer Society, Washington, DC 2002)
19. Jha, S., Sheyner, O., Wing, J.M.: Minimization and reliability analyses of attack graphs. Technical report, CMU, USA, February 2002

20. Kheir, N., Cuppens-Boulahia, N., Cuppens, F., Debar, H.: A service dependency model for cost-sensitive intrusion response. In: Gritzalis, D., Preneel, B., Theoharidou, M. (eds.) ESORICS 2010. LNCS, vol. 6345, pp. 626–642. Springer, Heidelberg (2010). https://doi.org/10.1007/978-3-642-15497-3_38

21. Kordy, B., Piètre-Cambacédès, L., Schweitzer, P.: DAG-based attack and defense modeling: don't miss the forest for the attack trees. Comput. Sci. Rev. **13–14**, 1–38 (2014)

22. Moore, A., Ellison, R., Linger, R.: Attack modeling for information security and survivability. Technical report, CMU/SEI-2001-TN-001, Software Engineeing Institute, Carnegie Mellon University, Pittsburgh (2001)

23. Nessus. http://www.tenable.com/products/nessus

24. Noel, S., Jajodia, S.: Managing attack graph complexity through visual hierarchical aggregation. In: Proceedings of the ACM Workshop on Visualization and Data Mining for Computer Security, pp. 109–118. ACM (2004)

25. NVD. https://nvd.nist.gov/

26. Ortalo, R., Deswarte, Y., Kaaniche, M.: Experimenting with quantitative evaluation tools for monitoring operational security. IEEE Trans. Softw. Eng. **25**(5), 633–650 (1999)

27. Ou, X., Boyer, W.F.: A scalable approach to attack graph generation. In: Proceedings of 13th ACM Conference on Computer and Communications Security (CCS), pp. 336–345. ACM Press (2006)

28. Pandey, N.K., Gupta, S.K., Leekha, S.: Algebra for capability based attack correlation. In: Onieva, J.A., Sauveron, D., Chaumette, S., Gollmann, D., Markantonakis, K. (eds.) WISTP 2008. LNCS, vol. 5019, pp. 117–135. Springer, Heidelberg (2008). https://doi.org/10.1007/978-3-540-79966-5_9

29. Phillips, C., Swiler, L.P.: A graph-based system for network-vulnerability analysis. In: Proceedings of the Workshop on New Security Paradigms, NSPW 1998, pp. 71–79. ACM, New York (1998)

30. Rai, G.N., Gangadharan, G.R., Padmanabhan, V.: Algebraic modeling and verification of web service composition. In: Proceedings of the 6th International Conference on Ambient Systems, Networks and Technologies (ANT), pp. 675–679 (2015)

31. Rai, G.N., Gangadharan, G., Padmanabhan, V., Buyya, R.: Web service interaction modeling and verification using recursive composition algebra. IEEE Trans. Serv. Comput. (2018)

32. Ray, I., Poolsapassit, N.: Using attack trees to identify malicious attacks from authorized insiders. In: di Vimercati, S.C., Syverson, P., Gollmann, D. (eds.) ESORICS 2005. LNCS, vol. 3679, pp. 231–246. Springer, Heidelberg (2005). https://doi.org/10.1007/11555827_14

33. Retina. http://www.amtsoft.com/retina/

34. Schneier, B.: Attack trees. https://www.schneier.com/paper-attacktrees-ddj-ft.html

35. SecurelTree: Amenaza technologies. http://www.amenaza.com/

36. Sheyner, O., Haines, J., Jha, S., Lippmann, R., Wing, J.: Automated generation and analysis of attack graphs. In: Proceedings of the IEEE Symposium on Security and Privacy, pp. 273–284 (2002)

37. Shmaryahu, D.: Constructing plan trees for simulated penetration testing. In: The 26th International Conference on Automated Planning and Scheduling, vol. 121 (2016)

38. Sun, K., Jajodia, S.: Protecting enterprise networks through attack surface expansion. In: Proceedings of the Workshop on Cyber Security Analytics, Intelligence and Automation, pp. 29–32. ACM (2014)

39. Swiler, L., Phillips, C., Ellis, D., Chakerian, S.: Computer-attack graph generation tool. In: Proceedings of the DARPA Information Survivability Conference and Exposition II, DISCEX 2001, vol. 2, pp. 307–321 (2001)
40. Templeton, S.J., Levitt, K.: A requires/provides model for computer attacks. In: Proceedings of the Workshop on New Security Paradigms, NSPW 2000, pp. 31–38. ACM, New York (2001)
41. Wang, S., Zhang, Z., Kadobayashi, Y.: Exploring attack graph for cost-benefit security hardening: a probabilistic approach. Comput. Secur. **32**, 158–169 (2013)
42. Weiss, J.: A system security engineering process. In: Proceedings of the 14th National Computer Security Conference, vol. 249, pp. 572–581 (1991)

RiskWriter: Predicting Cyber Risk of an Enterprise

K. Aditya[1,2(✉)], Slawomir Grzonkowski[2], and Nhien-An Le-Khac[3]

[1] UCD School of Computing, Dublin, Ireland
aditya_kuppa@ucdconnect.ie
[2] Symantec Corporation, Mountain View, USA
slawomir_grzonkowski@symantec.com
[3] University College Dublin, Dublin, Ireland
an.lekhac@ucd.ie

Abstract. Empirically measuring security posture of an enterprise is a challenging problem. One has to thoroughly understand external and, internal exposure for a given firm to assess security posture at a given time. Various security metrics are used to model each type of security exposure. Due to the lack of data on internal security metrics for a broad sample of firms, the research community has relied on external, proxy data points to assess the cyber risk of a firm. Recent studies, which attempted to solve this problem either used a small set of enterprises or used artificial datasets. Moreover, we are not aware of any existing approach to assess the security posture of an enterprise using only external and business data. In this paper, we present *RiskWriter*, a framework to assess the internal security posture of an enterprise using only external and business data. In our study, we measure a set of internal, external and business attributes of around 200,000 firms of different sizes, line of business, locations and security profiles for a period of 12 months. Prediction models were built by deriving, for each company, a comprehensive set of metrics using novel filtering and, normalizing techniques and then building machine learning models to assess the internal security posture of a company using only external and business data. We also evaluate *RiskWriter* with 2000 enterprises, with a variety of metrics and show that prediction is stable with high accuracy. Specifically for this work, the longitudinal study a broad sample of firms and for a period of one year is done for the first time.

1 Introduction

The cyber insurance market has been growing rapidly over the past decade. Experts estimate that it will reach $10 billion by 2020 [1]. Despite the strong growth over the past decade, insurance carriers are still faced with one key challenge: how to assess and predict the risks most accurately across potential insureds. A key challenge in quantifying cyber risk is lack of reliable, near real-time data for risk quantification. This impacts every aspect of cover including the pricing of premiums, limits of cover and exclusions. Typically, risk assessment in cyber insurance is done using underwriting tools which use questionnaires to

© Springer Nature Switzerland AG 2018
V. Ganapathy et al. (Eds.): ICISS 2018, LNCS 11281, pp. 88–106, 2018.
https://doi.org/10.1007/978-3-030-05171-6_5

assess the risk of a company. The application questionnaires provide insights into the security technologies and management practices of a company. Despite these lengthy questionnaires, there are still gaps to be addressed [2]. Normally, underwriting tools complement the questionnaires with external data collected using passive scans of IP Space and domains owned by an enterprise to assess the risk of a company.

Ideally, underwriting platforms [3] will be in a better position to assess and predict cyber risk if they have information about actual security incidents seen inside the enterprise, but due to regulatory and privacy reasons, this information is unavailable. Lately, insurance companies have been seeking to leverage information obtained from the insured entities by voluntary disclosure (e.g., fitness tracking data for health insurance, driving habits data collected through special hardware for car insurance, etc.). However, in case of cyber insurance obtaining data for a varied set of portfolio companies and quantifying risk from collected data is an open problem for underwriters.

We present *RiskWriter*, a machine learning approach to assess the internal security posture of an enterprise by using external and business attributes. The data was collected for a period of 12 months for around 200k enterprises of different sizes, locations, industries and, both internal and external security profiles. For measuring internal exposure, we use data from six million endpoints to measure blocking effectiveness of enterprise to attacks, readiness to security incidents relevant to cyber insurance, average remediation time of company to attacks, general hygiene to malware and web-based attacks, vulnerabilities found in client software and, presence of multi-purpose tools which are used by attackers. External security posture of a company is derived from first, establishing IP and domain ownership for a given firm from 9 million domains and around 2000 million IP address found in passive scans, and then measuring port, vulnerability, blacklists, end of life product, source code exposure, password leak, profiles are derived. Business attributes like size, revenue and, line of business are derived using various databases.

We implemented a two-stage process in *RiskWriter*. Stage one groups companies with similar security posture using an unsupervised method with external, internal and, business metrics as features. Next, we calculate and store the statistics for each internal metric per cluster - mean, median, standard deviation, outlier score and probability of particular data point being part of that cluster. In stage two, using cluster labels as classification labels and external and business metrics as features we train a classification model. This process is repeated every month, as security posture of firms keeps changing every day. Monthly scans recorded observable change points in data. Once models are created, given external and business metrics of a company for a given month - we run prediction per month to assess internal security metrics for the given firm.

The presented method solves multiple problems faced by underwriting platforms: (a) Quantifying security risk of an enterprise by comparing it with its peers. (b) Empirically, verifying answers provided by potential insureds in the questionnaires and, (c) Statistics of internal metrics can be directly consumed into actuarial models.

In summary, the contributions of our paper are as follows:

- We propose *RiskWriter*, a framework that leverages both supervised and semi-supervised learning methodologies to assess the internal security posture of a given firm using data from 200k enterprises.
- We use novel filtering, normalizing techniques to handle Internet scan and attack datasets.
- Using data from 2000 enterprises of different sizes, line of business and, internal security profiles we perform a comprehensive evaluation of *RiskWriter* and show that *RiskWriter* can assess internal security posture of firm with high precision and stable across a period of one year.
- Finally, longitudinal study of this size was never done before and this is first time using external and business metrics internal security posture of firm is assessed.

2   Security Metrics

Metric refers to assigning a value to an entity while the measurement is the process of estimating attributes of an entity. Attributes of an entity should be measured by certain scales, and frequency. Choice of scale may influence accuracy, statistical inference, leading to a different degree of understanding in a given value as a metric [4]. The frequency of measurement plays a vital role in security due to dynamic nature of threat landscape.

One way to understand security posture of an enterprise is by quantitative measuring [4]: (a) efforts of a defender to prevent attacks, (b) Opportunity of an attacker and, real attacks, (c) Security habits of users, and (d) Security decisions made by stakeholders. In *RiskWriter* we define 3 categories of metrics to measure (a), (b) and (d) (Table 1).

Table 1. Measurement frequencies of different metrics

Type	Measurement	Data collection frequency	Aggregation
Defender efforts	Internal metrics	Daily	Monthly
Opportunity of an attacker and real attacks	Internal and External Metrics	Daily and Monthly	Monthly
Security decisions made by stake holders	Internal and Business Metrics	Daily and Adhoc	Monthly

Internal Metrics. This category of metrics aims to measure the effort of the defender made to secure a system, and actions performed by an adversary inside the enterprise. These can be measured by a sensor which records security incidents and attack attempts seen inside the enterprise. For this study, we use following internal metrics, though *RiskWriter* is not limited to only these:

Remediation Efficiency: It is the percentage of infections or threats deleted from the network on the first day of detection. Difference between the first seen time of the infection on a computer and the last seen time of that infection in the period of aggregation gives the time taken to remove an infection or threat from an endpoint.

Readiness to Security Incidents: Presence of set of protection, configuration and backup tools on the endpoint and version change of those tools over time gives a strong indication of a firm's readiness towards security incidents. This is measured by the presence of tools across endpoints for a given month.

Hygiene and Blocking Effectiveness: These measures give a general indication of how for a given month the malware and web-based attacks are removed and blocked on endpoints and also give insight into the type of attacks being targeted towards an enterprise. These are measured by the total number of blocks and removals per endpoint.

Patch Profile: Measuring how firms internally patch software is important for security posture assessment. As each firm has unique software usage profile, we need to assess patch levels per firm separately. We also need to prioritize unpatched software list w.r.t. exploit code availability or exploit found in the wild.

- Collect top 100 common files found in a given enterprise, then extract respective software name, version and signer using clean file database shared by AV company.
- Next, using software name and version, National Vulnerability Database(NVD)[1] and, exploit databases e.g., [2] create the list of vulnerabilities w.r.t. each software, version, and exploit code availability. Counting number of endpoints with vulnerable software using the list which gives a measure of patching profile inside the firm.

Presence of Multipurpose Tools: Multi-purpose tools are programs that may not be malicious in their origin but can be exploited by hackers to attack computer systems and networks. Presence or usage of these tools on endpoints gives insight into understanding attacker activity inside an enterprise. This is measured by counting the number of endpoints executing and hosting these tools in the enterprise. In *RiskWriter* we use following categories:

- General purpose tools: Tools which are found on endpoints can be used by an attacker for malicious activity.
- Research and help desk tools: Tools which are generally used by an administrator, analyst, developer or help desk. We focus on these (legitimate) applications due to a growing number of advanced threats that incorporate system administration or diagnostic tools in various stages of their attacks.

---

[1] https://nvd.nist.gov/.
[2] https://www.exploit-db.com/.

– Suspicious and Penetration testing tools: Tools which are generally used by pen testers and attackers. These include applications that are either directly attack-related or can help the attacker achieve more than the previous two categories of tools.

External Metrics. This category of metrics aims to measure mainly, attacker opportunity and attack surface of an enterprise from outside of an enterprise. These metrics are collected by passive scans of IPv4 space and establishing IP and domain ownership of an enterprise.

Servers Hosting End of Life Products: Count of 'End of Life' products hosted by enterprise IP space and domains. When a product has reached the 'End of Life' cycle, manufacturers no longer offer updates or support. The presence of legacy and End of Life systems within an enterprise network allows for vulnerabilities to accumulate over time, creating a larger attack surface for potential exploitation.

Vulnerable Services: Count of Vulnerabilities found in services hosted by enterprise IP Space. Vulnerabilities for which an exploit code or POC released are only considered for measurement.

Password Leaks: Count of enterprise owned domain specific email addresses found in password leaked database circulating within the public realm and/or within the hacker underground. The data sources consist of forums, pastebin-style websites, and archives of leaked/breached public databases. Attackers can use cracked passwords or enterprise email from these databases for phishing campaigns.

Source Code Exposure: Crawling public code repositories for the presence of leaked credentials, source code, API keys, or other data of value. Count of artifacts specific to the impacted enterprise.

Blacklist Profile: Count of IP Addresses owned by the enterprise, found in different blacklisted IP and domain lists. Different categories include- Malware, Spam, Phishing, Fraud and, Command and Control servers.

Business Metrics. This category of metrics aims to measure how size, revenue, and line of business influence security practices internally and attacker choice of targets. A single firm can operate in different sectors, industries, and have multiple subsidiaries.

Subsidiaries Count: Count of the number of subsidiaries owned by a firm.
Revenue: Total revenue of a firm including its subsidiaries.
Industry of Operation: Industry in which the firm operates.

Table 2 shows the distribution of various external and, internal metrics over a period of 1 year.

Table 2. Empirical cumulative distribution functions (ECDFs) of metrics over 3 month interval for 200 randomly sampled enterprises.

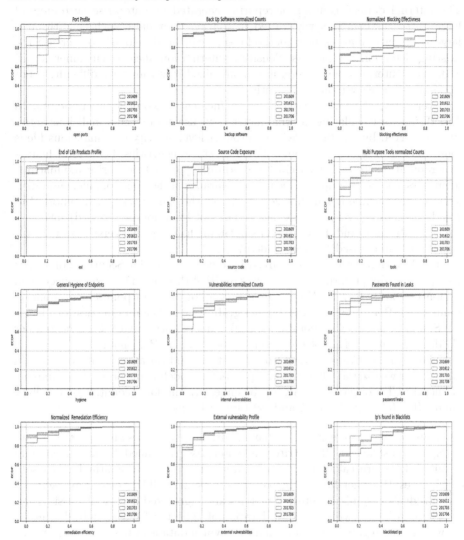

3   Datasets and Processing

In this section, we describe various datasets used in *RiskWriter* and methodology used in for preprocessing and cleaning of data, to make sure we are collecting and comparing right data for underlying models.

3.1 Data Sets

The internal dataset consists of reports generated by enterprise customers of large anti-virus company who opted in sharing their data, such that through large-scale data analysis new methodologies can be developed to increase the existing detection capabilities. Sensitive information such as customer id, IP addresses, enterprise names etc. are anonymized it is thus very difficult, if not impossible, to recover the real identities.

Every day, the data centers receive incidents recorded on endpoints. In *RiskWriter* for calculating internal metrics, we use data when a malicious activity is observed by a network level or browser level activity or a malicious file is found on a user system (through blocking, static heuristics, behavioral heuristics, reputation etc.). The data include: (a) (anonymized) enterprise and machine identifiers, (b) timestamps for the first appearance of the infection, file, and intrusion on the machine (local time zone) and for the time when it was reported to the data centers (PST), (c) Signature name of Intrusion or virus (d) intrusion URL (e) file name and directory, (f) sha256 file hash, (g) file version and (h) file signer (i) (anonymized) customer identifier.

The External datasets are sourced by outside-in vendor SecurityScoreCard[3] who periodically performs passive scans on IPv4 IP space. Data was collected on a monthly basis. In *RiskWriter* we extract following data points from monthly dumps: (a) IP address, (b) Raw banner grab, (c) emails found in password leaks, (d) Source code exposure per domain, (e) Vulnerability service, CVE hosted per IP/domain, and (f) End of Life products hosted per IP/Domain.

The business data is sourced from Avention[4] and Datanyze[5] data vendors. In *RiskWriter* we use the following data points for modeling purposes: (a) Company Name, (b) URL of the company, (c) Revenue, (d) Employee count, (e) Subsidiary count, (f) SIC/NIACS Code, and (g) Line of business.

- *Enterprise:* An enterprise can have multiple subsidiaries and operate in multiple industries. In *RiskWriter* an enterprise is defined by its parent and all metrics are calculated, w.r.t. parent. For example, a firm has 10 subsidiaries, IP ownership for the parent is the sum of all IP's owned by itself and subsidiaries, similarly internal metrics are aggregated across all subsidiaries. There are cases when internal data is not collected from all subsidiaries, so we only aggregate across subsidiary for which data is available and assign the same value to parent, the rationale being generally security decisions in a firm are centralized and insights into one subsidiary or site of operation gives fair measure of overall security posture of the parent.
- *Data normalization:* One of the main goals for *RiskWriter* is to find firms with similar security posture and normalization of data plays an important role in achieving this goal. We apply a density-based technique to bring all measured attributes on to the same scale. For IP and domain-based measurement: first,

---

[3] https://securityscorecard.com/.

[4] http://www.hoovers.com/.

[5] https://www.datanyze.com/.

we count the total number of IP's owned by a given firm, next we normalize all IP based measurements by dividing the total number of IP's. This method makes sure all data points are in the range of [0,1] in *RiskWriter*. Let's say a large firm A has 50 IP's hosting vulnerable services with IP Ownership 1000 IP's vs a small firm B which has 50 IP's hosting vulnerable services with IP ownership 100 IP's. When we compare Firm A and Firm B vulnerability profiles without normalization we get same profile as vulnerable IP count is same, but with normalization, they are different *i.e.,* 0.05, 0.5 respectively. A similar technique is used for the domain based measurements. For internal data, we normalize with the total count of endpoints which are active in an enterprise for the given period of aggregation.

- *Missing values:* Real life datasets without missing values are rare. Missing values occur due to collectors not configured correctly, data not available from enrichment databases, data corruption in transit, and passive scan errors. For external data, any IP or domain not found in external data set is not considered for analysis. Attributing an IP with multiple scan sources is left for future work. For internal data, we consider only those endpoints on which sensor was active, there may be cases due to misconfiguration of the sensor, data is never sent back to collector gateways. We drop these endpoints for the analysis for that month. An enterprise can operate in multiple industries, sectors and can have many subsidiaries. In *RiskWriter* we only look for parent companies *i.e.,* for example, company B is a subsidiary of company A for analysis, we only consider company A. Since we have multiple sources to fill in missing values for business data, we use a heuristics approach: (a) If two or more sources agree on the same data point we use that data point with high confidence, and (b) Freshness of data- the source with the latest data is given more preference over another source. For smaller companies, the dataset has still missing values. To solve this we use website content classification provided by the anti-virus company to map back content hosted by the website to line of business.

- *Filtering outliers:* Outliers are part of dataset we collect. Identifying and removing outliers is an important step in *RiskWriter* as the output is based on heuristics generated by a group of firms. Outliers in measurements can skew the heuristics.

  Internal data: Endpoints owned by researchers and analysts which trigger a large number of diversified incidents in a day, week. As these incidents are raised by intentional triggers so these attacks do not contribute to the security posture of the firm. We filter research endpoints by heuristics- grouping machines by different profiles, and filtering machines which don't fit normal profiles. In multiple cases, analysts tag machines as researcher machines by manual inspection and these machines are filtered from datasets.

  External data: Some Enterprises host public facing honeypots to record and understand the different type of attack activity on firms IP space. Similar to internal data, these servers which host vulnerable services are intentional and need to be removed from the dataset for correct measurements. Using features for a set of IP's of a given firm, and Shodan honey score[6] as ground truth, we trained a binary classifier to identify honeypots in the IP space of a firm.

– *Customer of Customer:* A firm can rely on multiple services for DNS, hosting, Cloud services, and content delivery networks. IP and domain attribution is harder when IP is shared among service providers and firm. In *RiskWriter* we attribute all IP to a child firm instead of a service provider. We use data from sub-domains owned by the firm, firmographics data (See footnote 5) and certificate subject data to understand customer of customer relationship.

3.2 IP and Domain Attribution

IP and domain attribution play a key role in measuring external metrics. We use Whois, Internet Router Registry (IRR), weekly passive DNS scans and, business domain datasets to establish IP and domain ownership for a given firm.

Domain Attribution:

– Get business domains of a firm from business datasets for seeding. Query Whois data to get ownership, contact information and technical organization and email address.
– Using seed domain Whois information - Query all other domains owned by with similar information. Filter only those domains which match the business name of the firm.
– Finally, extract all subdomains owned for all the domains found in the previous step.

IP Attribution:

– Process DNS, IRR, Whois and business domains dataset to extract- Whois domain, Whois email domain, DNS domain, IRR domain, business domain, DNS IP, IRR iprange, business name, Whois org info.
– Match DNS domain with Whois email domain, whois domain, business domains and subdomains.
– For each matched IP in DNS dataset, search in IRR range tree and extract start range and end range for matched IP addresses to create dataset in the format of - IP, DNS domain, IRR domain, Whois domain, max_ip_dns ,min_ip_dns, count of IP's, irr_range
– Allocate all IP addresses in the IRR range to the domain which have same domain across all datasets.
– Filter common mail, Whois and, hosting service providers domains.
– Finally, run IP attribution process daily and update the dataset.

---

[6] https://securityonline.info/shodan-check-ip-address-whether-honeypot-real-control-system/.

4 Methodology

In this section, we provide a detailed description of our methodology (see, Fig. 1). First, we explain the model creation phase and the query phase. Next, we describe the motivation of algorithms used in *RiskWriter*. Finally, we provide a set of evaluation metrics for *RiskWriter*.

Internal security metrics can not be shared directly with underwriting platforms for regulatory and privacy reasons. When assessing risk posture of a company underwriters compare security metrics of a firm with similar firms. Thus, instead of predicting the exact values of internal security metrics *RiskWriter* predicts a set of statistical measures for a group of similar companies. Given a set of external and business metrics of a *single* firm, *RiskWriter* predicts: (a) Mean, (b) Median, (c) Value Quantiles - 10%, 25%, 50%, 75%, 90%, 95%, (d) Standard deviation and, (e) Count of firms with **similar** overall security posture *external, internal and business metrics*.

RiskWriter operates in two phases, in model creation phase monthly metrics are collected from different data sources, and models are created. In query phase or new assessment, an underwriter queries for risk assessment of a firm with external and business data; and then *RiskWriter* returns statistical measures for a set of firms with similar internal, external and business metrics. Models are created for every new month and queried through out the month.

Unsupervised Stage: Clustering is a process of finding subsets of the data points which group "naturally", without necessarily assigning a cluster for all points. In *RiskWriter* we are interested in finding enterprises which have **similar**: (a) Industry of operation, (b) External security profiles and, (c) Internal security profile. The similarity of a set of enterprises can be defined by a density function f, defined on a metric space $(\mathcal{X}, d)$. One can construct a hierarchical cluster structure, where a cluster is a connected subset of an f-level set $\{x \in (\mathcal{X}, d) \mid f(x) \geq \lambda\}$. As $\lambda \geq 0$ varies these f-level sets nest in such a way as to construct an infinite tree, which is referred to as the *cluster tree*. Each cluster is a branch of this tree, extending over the range of λ values for which it is distinct.

Among clustering methods [5], we use Hierarchical Density-Based Spatial Clustering (HDBSCAN) [6,7] algorithm for clustering to the following merits:

– Easier parameter selection and tuning.
– Robustness to noise in the data.
– No implicit assumption about the distribution of data in the clusters.
– It is scalable on large data sets like ours.

Supervised Stage: The general aim of supervised models is to reduce error which is the sum of bias and variance. Random Forest Classifier (RFC) are ensemble machines with decision trees [8,9] which output a weighted vote of the decision output of each individual tree. They aim at reducing the variance of the learning model through the bias-variance trade-off.

We use RFCs due to the following merits:

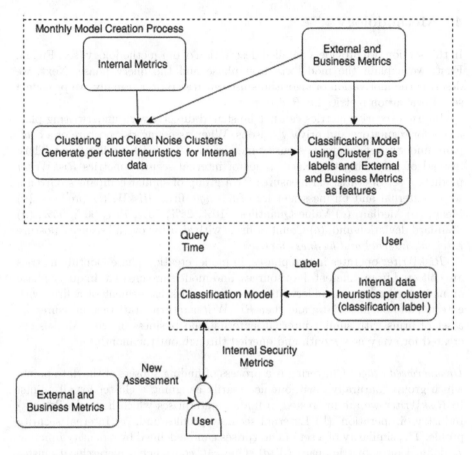

Fig. 1. *RiskWriter* Framework - Model Creation Process - (a) Using internal, external and business metrics run clustering and classification for a given month. (b) New Assessment - Query time an underwriter queries for internal metrics of a given company by sending external and business metrics. (process enclosed in dotted line is private and underwriter has no access to the actual internal data)

- They behave well with new and previously unseen testing data, providing unbiased estimates of the generalization. error; hence, they give a good approximation to the true classification boundary.
- RFCs are intrinsically scalable and run very efficiently on large-scale datasets similar to ours. [10]

Model Creation:

- Cluster **internal, external and business metrics** data using the HDBScan algorithm for a given month.
- Filter out noise clusters and data points which have outlier score below for a given threshold for example <0.1.

- For each Cluster, record statistical measures of the metrics and number of clusters.
- Evaluate resulting cluster metrics.
- Train Random Forest classification model using **external and business metrics** as features and cluster id as labels.
- Save the model for query phase.

Model Query Phase: For a given firm - when queried with external and, business metrics, the model returns statistical measures of internal metrics for a similar set of firms.

4.1   Evaluation

The unsupervised stage is validated on two criteria: (a) Enterprise clusters are well formed with no noise data points in each cluster. (b) Clusters formed, truly represent internal metrics of the set of firms in the group.

For (a) we use silhouette coefficient which is mean of intra-cluster distance m and the distance between a sample and the nearest cluster that the sample is not a part n of, for each sample. The best value is 1 and the worst value is -1. Values near 0 indicate overlapping clusters. Negative values generally indicate that a sample has been assigned to the wrong cluster, as a different cluster is more similar.

For (b) we run a K-means clustering using **only internal metrics**, with input k (n - number of clusters found using unsupervised step). Using the k-means labels, and labels from unsupervised step we measure homogeneity score(all of its clusters contain only data points which are members of a single class) and, completeness score(all the data points that are members of a given class are elements of the same cluster). As these metrics are independent of the absolute values of the labels, a permutation of the class or cluster label values won't change the score value in any way. For Supervised step, we measure accuracy, with 10-fold cross-validation process with train and test split of 0.7.

For testing *RiskWriter* on unseen data, we set aside 2000 enterprises with similar internal metrics which are not part of the modeling process, and use them as test data.

5   Results

We run unsupervised, and supervised methods on monthly data, using HDB-SCAN clustering and random forest classifiers. Parameter tuning is done for the month of September 2016 and same parameters were used for remaining months. Parameters used for HDBSCAN: (a) minimum cluster size = 220, (b) minimum samples in each cluster = 10, (c) cluster selection method = leaf and, (d) metric = correlation. Random forest is run with a set of 600 trees as larger sizes improved neither the stability nor the quality of results. For K-means clustering,

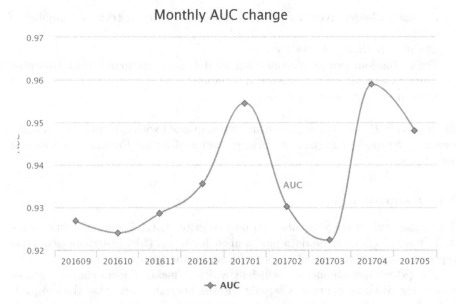

Fig. 2. Classifier accuracy change with monthly Data

input k *i.e.,* number of clusters derived from HDBSCAN output. For calculating completeness and homogeneity metrics we use cluster labels from k-means and HDBSCAN. For silhouette coefficient, we use labels from HDBSCAN and input data set. We set aside 2000 enterprises every month, with similar internal metrics to test *RiskWriter* performance on unseen data. These enterprises were only used in model query phase.

The quality of classifier accuracy is dependent on cluster performance metrics making preprocessing and normalizing datasets important in *RiskWriter*. Table 3 summarizes the results for each month runs. As noted in Fig. 2 *RiskWriter* results are stable between 0.92 and 0.95 on multiple runs across year long datasets.

Feature Significance

To list the most discriminative features, we employ the mean decrease impurity methodology provided by the random forest classifiers. When training the trees in Random Forest(RF), we compute how much each feature decreases the weighted impurity in the trees. Once the forest is built, we average the impurity decrease from each feature and rank them to identify the features that contribute the most to the classification accuracy. In Fig. 3 we present the monthly feature importance of external and business metrics contribution to overall accuracy in *RiskWriter*.

It demonstrates that, business metrics have contributed the most significantly to classification results consistently for each month followed by end of life products profiles, vulnerability profiles, and private information exposure. Sur-

Table 3. A summary of evaluation results for each month.

Completeness	Homogeneity	Silhouette coefficient	Accuracy	Month
0.836263	0.917876	0.874967	0.926735	201609
0.829313	0.905183	0.862023	0.923986	201610
0.848347	0.919319	0.885415	0.928571	201611
0.875359	0.921377	0.889607	0.935553	201612
0.885378	0.967493	0.892456	0.954544	201701
0.873135	0.920462	0.884967	0.930190	201702
0.821259	0.910491	0.856297	0.922249	201703
0.896181	0.969299	0.925180	0.958935	201704
0.883139	0.946989	0.905561	0.948109	201705

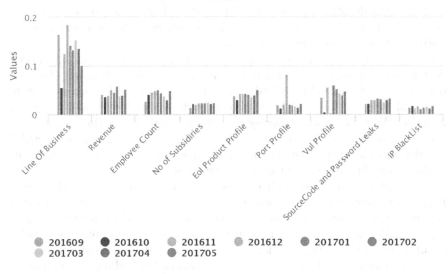

Fig. 3. Feature importance per month

prisingly, port profiles [11] and, blacklist profile [12] which have been significant in other studies, have a less importance factor. We think the presence of exploit code or proof of concept in the wild as one of our filtering step is reflected in the feature importance.

One possible way to explain results is by the analogy of intrusion kill chain in which adversaries execute intrusions in discernible stages or steps. External metrics influence reconnaissance stage in which attacker is researching, identifying the targets, for the opportunity and for attackers, not all services are important. Objective stage in kill chain is driven by business metrics *i.e.,* selection of the target. Internal metrics record attacker actions for other stages - delivery, exploitation, installation and, command and control. The implicit assumption of the density function in clustering algorithm can be mapped to set of attack stages grouped for a set of enterprises. So, we think for measuring security posture of a firm one has to use all the three metrics.

6 Related Work

In cyber insurance, researchers used analytical modeling [13,14] or study the actions of security professionals within the firms [15] or use data based on publicly disclosed attacks [12,17,18] to assess and predict the security posture of the firm. Other studies focused on understanding security investment [16] of firms by interviewing Chief Information Security Officer (CISO) level executives.

One study [11] used internal security information and vulnerable services(hosted on firm IP space) of 480 Fortune 500 enterprises, to link internal security posture to external observable attributes. Our work extends on this idea in a boarder scale with large set of diverse firms, different set of security metrics instead of two data point and, creating a framework for assessing internal security posture of a firm with high confidence.

Security metrics is one of the most important open problems in security research and received wide attention not only from research community but also from government and industry bodies. Large body of work focused on how to define and measure vulnerabilities, threats, defenses and situations inside an enterprise. We refer to recent survey for detailed analysis [4]. Rarely, measurements are done both inside and outside of an enterprise for a similar metric which we address in this work. We also use the derived metrics to create a machine learning model for risk assessment of an enterprise.

In computer security, the body of work done on risk prediction inside a set of enterprises is limited. Researchers used machine learning to identify and predict risky users, events, and risky security events from historical incidents [19], risky endpoints [20] using endpoint data. Our work uses similar end point datasets for measuring internal security metrics but our goal is find similar enterprises with similar internal, external and business metrics instead of finding risky endpoints inside an enterprise.

7 Conclusions and Future Work

As threat landscape evolves, more enterprises are investing in purchasing cyber insurance packages so that when the incident happens, a part of their loss can be covered. Though application questionnaires provide insights into the security technologies and management practices of a company, underwriters have limited scope to verify answers empirically. For privacy and regulatory reasons, companies can not share real security incidents to third-party underwriting platforms. In this work, we particularly focused on addressing this gap in the cyber ecosystem by proposing a framework, *RiskWriter*, that can predict the internal security posture of enterprises with externally observable attributes with reasonably high accuracy. To date, none of the previous works attempted to address this problem at this scale and achieve this level of accuracy.

Despite the impressive results of *RiskWriter* to predict the internal security posture, we want to highlight its inherent limitations and subjects for future work:

- Datasets: Our internal datasets suffer from biases, *i.e.,* we assume that at least one security control already installed inside the enterprise which may not be the case for small companies. We only use one source for collecting external data and are limited by the correctness of the source.
- IP and domain attribution: Establishing IP and domain ownership is key to *RiskWriter* measurements. The process we followed is still evolving and may result in attribution errors. Also, we have not measured anything hosted on IPV6 due to non-availability of scanned data.

In the future, we also plan to extend the work we have done to be able to address the highlighted limitations by (a) Using multiple datasets for measurement and for modeling; (b) improving accuracy, IP attribution process and use SSL and mail server misconfiguration datasets to external metrics; (c) applying deep-learning methods [21] in the prediction. We will also take into account IPv6 security [22] in our future work. In addition, there are multiple internal metrics which are missing in *RiskWriter* and are relevant to cyber insurance-like protection towards breaches, attacks coming from third-party vendors etc. we plan to include them in future.

A   Appendix

See Tables 4 and 5.

Table 4. Datasets - multi purpose tools, infections and attack categories, and vulnerabilities and EOL found in scans

Pen Test Tools	– maltego, nemesis, konboot, nessus,ollydbg
	– burpsuite, aircrack, metasploit, acunetix
	– beefproje, fiddler, immunitycanvas
	– immunitydebug, firesheep
	– kismac, kismet, qualysguard
General Tools	– ping, nmap, ftp, netstat, traceroute, putty
	– winscp, nbtstat, cURL, plink, realvnc
	– wireshark, pscp, whois

(continued)

Table 4. (*continued*)

Research/HelpDesk Tools	– ntop, superscan, hijackthis, nbtscan, dig
	– inssider, rkill, netcat, bootdefrag, encase
	– tcpview, volatility, tcpdump, ngrep
Suspicious Tools	– grabitall, netstumbler, sqlping, pwdump7
	– gsecdump, winfo, ettercap, skipfish, netscan, dumpsec
	– dsniff, pmdump, snmpgetif, abelcain, ShareEnum
	– webscarab browselist, thchydra, sqldict, pshtoolkit
	– smbgetserverinfo, mcafeefport, nbdecode, rpcscan
	– nbnamequery,x-deep32, passwordcrack, sqlninja
	– boottime, diskinfo, wpscan, smbexec, pstools
	– lsasecretsdump, sqlmap, angryscanner, p0f, languard
	– ikescan, johntheripper, telnet, smbserverscan, crackme
	– ntpasswd, parosproxy, arpsniffer, openvas, langaurd
	– sniff, l0phtcrack, smbbf, cmsexplorer, trinityrescue
	– dumpusers,getifsnmp, remoxec, ophcrack, smbdumpusers
	– grendelscan, incognito, cachedump, rainbowcrack
Infection and Attack Category	– Misleading Application, Trojan, Ransomware, Attack
	– Backdoor, Java/SWF/JS/Suspicious Download, Fake Scan
	– Macro, Exploit, Malvertisement
	– Malicious redirections, Exploit kit, Adware, Infostealer
	– Bot, VBS, RAT, Malicious Site, FTP Attack, Worm, DDOS
	– MS Attack, Web Attack, DNS Attack, TCP Attack
	– MSRPC Attack, Spyware, Dropper, MSIE Attack, HackTool
	– Fake App Attack, Malicious Cookie, HTTP, Suspicious
	– Android, .NET Malware,OS Attack, Trojan
	– Adware, Trackware, Dialer, Spyware, Security Risk,
	– HackTool, Dropper, Remote Access
	– Keylogger, Potentially Unwanted App,
End of Life Product (Vendors) from external scans	– Cisco, Citrix, Huawei
	– Microsoft, Netgear
Vulnerabilities found from external scans(Exploits Code Found in the Wild or POC Released for # of CVE ID's)	– CentOS(11), Debian(65), Fedoraproject(28), HP(11), IBM(13)
	– Mandriva(22), Oracle(13), Redhat(16), Ubuntu(14), WordPress(174)

Table 5. End of life products used for measurement

Name	Vendor
ATA 186 Analog Telephone Adaptor, 4402 Wireless LAN Controller, ASA 5510 Adaptive Security Appliance, AP541N Wireless Access Point, WAP4410N Wireless-N Access Point - PoE Advanced Security, PIX 500 Series Security Appliances, SRW2016 16-port Gigabit Switch - WebView, RV220W Wireless Network Security Firewall, 4400 Series Wireless LAN Controllers, VG248 48-Port Analog Voice Gateway, RV120W Wireless-N VPN Firewall, WAP2000 Wireless-G Access Point - PoE, Unified IP Phone 7912G	Cisco
XenServer 5.6	Citrix
S5000 Series Switches S5624P-PWR, Core Network MGW Products A8010, S8500 Series Ethernet Switches S8500, Quidway AR Series Partial Routers AR28-09	Huawei
SQL Server 2000, Windows Server 2003, Exchange 2003, Internet Information Services 7.0, Windows 2000, SQL Server 2008, Internet Information Services 5.0 (via ftp), Windows CE 5.0, Internet Information Services 5.1, Windows XP, Internet Information Services 5.0, Internet Information Services 3.0, Internet Information Services 4.0, SQL Server 2005, Internet Information Services 6.0, Internet Information Services 7.5, Internet Information Services 2.0, Windows CE 5.0 (via ChipPC)	Microsoft
FVX538 ProSafe VPN Firewall Dual WAN with 8-Port 10/100 and 1 Gigabit LAN Port Switch	Netgear

References

1. ABI Research: Cyber insurance market to reach \$10B by 2020. https://www.advisenltd.com/2015/07/30/abi-research-cyber-insurance-market-to-reach-10b-by-2020/
2. Romanosky, S., Ablon, L., Kuehn, A., Jones, RT.: Content Analysis of Cyber Insurance Policies: How Do Carriers Write Policies and Price Cyber Risk? RAND Corporation, Santa Monica (2017). https://www.rand.org/pubs/working_papers/WR1208.html
3. Bogomolniy, O.: Cyber insurance conundrum: using CIS critical security controls for underwriting cyber risk (2017). https://www.sans.org/reading-room/whitepapers/legal/cyber-insurance-conundrum-cis-critical-security-controls-underwriting-cyber-risk-37572
4. Pendleton, M., Garcia-Lebron, R., Cho, J.-H., Xu, S.: A survey on systems security metrics. In: ACM Computing Survey, February 2017
5. Cai, F., Le-Khac, N.-A., Kechadi, M.-T.: Clustering approaches for financial data analysis: a survey. In: Proceeding of the 8th International Conference on Data Mining (DMIN 2012), NE, USA, July 2012
6. McInnes, L., Healy, J.: Accelerated hierarchical density based clustering. In: 2017 IEEE International Conference on Data Mining Workshops (ICDMW), pp 33–42. IEEE (2017)

7. Campello, R.J.G.B., Moulavi, D., Sander, J.: Density-based clustering based on hierarchical density estimates. In: Pei, J., Tseng, V.S., Cao, L., Motoda, H., Xu, G. (eds.) PAKDD 2013. LNCS (LNAI), vol. 7819, pp. 160–172. Springer, Heidelberg (2013). https://doi.org/10.1007/978-3-642-37456-2_14

8. Ho, T.K.: Random decision forest. In: Proceedings of the 3rd International Conference on Document Analysis and Recognition, pp. 278–282 (1995)

9. Breiman, L.: Random forests. Mach. Learn. **45**(1), 5–32 (1995)

10. Liaw, A., Wiener, M.: Classification and regression by randomForest. R News **2**(3), 18–22 (2002)

11. Nagle, F., Ransbotham, S., Westerman, G.: The effects of security management on security events. In: Annual Workshop on the Economics of Information Security (2017)

12. Liu, Y., et al.: Cloudy with a chance of breach: forecasting cyber security incidents. In: USENIX Security, 1009–1024 (2015)

13. Kannan, K., Telang, R.: Market for software vulnerabilities? Think again. Manag. Sci. **51**(5), 726–740 (2005)

14. Gupta, A., Zhdanov, D.: Growth and sustainability of managed security services networks: an economic perspective. MIS Q. **36**(4), 1109–1130 (2012)

15. Mahmood, M.A., Siponen, M., Straub, D., Rao, H.R., Raghu, T.S.: Moving toward black hat research in information systems security: an editorial introduction to the special issue. MIS Q. **34**(3), 431–433 (2002)

16. Moore, T., Dynes, S., Chang, F.R.: Identifying how firms manage cybersecurity investment. Southern Methodist University (2015). http://blog.smu.edu/research/files/2015/10/SMU-IBM.pdf

17. Sarabi, A., Naghizadeh, P., Liu, Y., Liu, M.: Risky business: fine-grained data breach prediction using business profiles. J. Cybersecur. **2**(1), 15–28 (2016)

18. Edwards, B., Hofmeyr, S., Stephanie, F.: Hype and heavy tails: a closer look at data breaches. In: Workshop on the Economics of Information Security, vol. 14 (2015)

19. Veeramachaneni, K., Arnaldo, I., Cuesta-Infante, A., Korrapati, V., Basslas, C., Li, K.: AI^2: training a big data machine to defend. In Proceedings of the 2nd IEEE International Conference on Big Data Security (2016)

20. Bilge, L., Han, Y., Dell'Amico, M.: RiskTeller: predicting the risk of cyber incidents. In: Proceedings of the 2017 ACM SIGSAC Conference on Computer and Communications Security (2017)

21. Kuppa, A., Grzonkowski, S., Le-Khac, N.-A.: Enabling trust in deep learning models: a digital forensics case study. In: Proceeding of the 17th IEEE International Conference on Trust, Security and Privacy in Computing and Communications (IEEE TrustCom-18), NY, USA, 1–3 August 2018

22. Nicolls, V., Chen, L., Scanlon, M., Le-Khac, N.-A.: IPv6 security and forensics. In: Proceeding of the 6th IEEE International Conference on Innovative Computing Technology (INTECH 2016), Dublin, Ireland, August 2016

ProPatrol: Attack Investigation via Extracted High-Level Tasks

Sadegh M. Milajerdi[1]([✉]), Birhanu Eshete[2], Rigel Gjomemo[1], and Venkat N. Venkatakrishnan[1]

[1] University of Illinois at Chicago, Chicago, IL 60607, USA
{smomen2,rgjome1,venkat}@uic.edu
[2] University of Michigan-Dearborn, Dearborn, MI 48128, USA
birhanu@umich.edu

Abstract. Kernel audit logs are an invaluable source of information in the forensic investigation of a cyber-attack. However, the coarse granularity of dependency information in audit logs leads to the construction of huge attack graphs which contain false or inaccurate dependencies. To overcome this problem, we propose a system, called PROPATROL, which leverages the open compartmentalized design in families of enterprise applications used in security-sensitive contexts (e.g., browser, chat client, email client). To achieve its goal, PROPATROL infers a model for an application's high-level tasks as input-processing compartments using purely the audit log events generated by that application. The main benefit of this approach is that it does not rely on source code or binary instrumentation, but only on a preliminary and general knowledge of an application's architecture to bootstrap the analysis. Our experiments with enterprise-level attacks demonstrate that PROPATROL significantly cuts down the forensic investigation effort and quickly pinpoints the root-cause of attacks. PROPATROL incurs less than 2% runtime overhead on a commodity operating system.

1 Introduction

Targeted and stealthy cyberattacks (referred to as Advanced Persistent Threats (APTs)) follow a multi-stage threat workflow [5] to break into an enterprise network with the goal of harvesting invaluable information. APTs often utilize spear phishing and drive-by download to gain a foothold in an enterprise (initial compromise). After this step, APTs propagate to enterprise targets (e.g., Intranet servers) in pursuit of high-value assets such as confidential information.

Once APTs are detected, it is crucial to track the causal linkage between events in a timely manner to find out the attack provenance. Consequently, attack provenance may be used to detect affected entities within a host or across multiple hosts. As soon as an attack provenance is uncovered, a system analyst

---

The second author performed this work as a postdoctoral associate at the University of Illinois at Chicago.

V. Ganapathy et al. (Eds.): ICISS 2018, LNCS 11281, pp. 107–126, 2018.
https://doi.org/10.1007/978-3-030-05171-6_6

can take immediate damage control measures, use it to make sense of past attacks or to prevent future attacks.

The state-of-the-art technique for provenance tracking is to use *kernel audit logs* to record information flow between system entities [7,15] and then correlate these entities for forensic analysis. In particular, after an attack is detected, system analysts use the detection point as a seed to initiate *backward tracking* strategies to determine the root-cause of that attack, and *forward tracking* methods to find out the impacts of the attack.

Kernel auditing techniques interpose at the system call layer; therefore, they have acceptable runtime overheads but suffer from the *dependency explosion* problem. In particular, due to coarse nature of dependencies that manifest in audit logs, an entity may *falsely* appear to be causally dependent on many other entities. For instance, consider a browser process that has multiple tabs open, each receiving data from different socket connections. If the browser process writes to a file, then during forensic analysis, that file will look causally dependent on all the socket connections the browser has accessed up to the write operation. In case of a drive-by-download attack that exploits that browser, it becomes challenging for system analysts to pinpoint the origin of the attack among all the accessed sockets.

To mitigate the dependency explosion problem, researchers have proposed compartmentalization techniques to partition the execution of a long-running process to smaller units [18,20,21]. BEEP [18] and ProTracer [21] compartmentalize processes to low-level units based on iterations of event handling loops. MPI [20] compartmentalizes processes to high-level tasks based on source code annotations manually performed by developers. Unfortunately, these techniques rely on source code or binary instrumentation.

Our Work. In this paper, we present an approach (called PROPATROL), aimed at high-level activity compartmentalization to address the dependence explosion problem and to provide *units of execution boundaries* to aid forensic attack investigation. One of the main benefits of our approach is that does not require application source/binary instrumentation. The key insight in our approach is to leverage the execution compartments that are inherent to the design of certain Internet-facing applications (e.g., browsers, chat clients, email clients) in order to mitigate the dependence explosion problem during forensic analysis and are able to pinpoint true dependencies. Through a *combination of execution compartments and provenance*, we demonstrate how a cyber-analyst can perform precise forensic attack investigation. Starting with the choice of compartmentalized applications, our approach also includes an inference mechanism to identify the execution compartments implemented in these applications directly from their audit log traces.

Our approach does require enterprise users to be restricted to the use of compartmentalized Internet-facing applications. While this may seem stringent, recent trends [13] towards locked-down enterprise software (e.g., Windows 10 S) suggest that enterprises and software vendors desire this direction. In addition, modern applications are moving to a sandboxing-based architecture both for security and performance purposes. Google Chrome, for instance, is a relevant example of such an application, while Firefox is moving in the same direction [1].

Results Overview. Using APT scenarios as case studies, we evaluated the effectiveness and efficiency of PROPATROL on five attack scenarios in an enterprise setting. PROPATROL successfully constructed forensic graphs on five distinct lateral movement attempts that target high-value assets in Intranet servers. We note that these attacks cover a broad surface of the APT landscape. More precisely, our evaluation covers the major APT attack vectors such as spear phishing, drive-by downloads, and classic web-based attack vectors such as CSRF and DNS rebinding. In all the attacks, lateral movement is attempted by initiating a connection to an Intranet server. In addition to covering a wide space of APT vectors, our evaluation also spans web browsers, email clients, and instant messaging clients—which are the common classes of applications targeted by APTs. Measured on the five attack scenarios for its runtime, on average, PROPATROL operates with an overhead of less than 2%. Most importantly, PROPATROL is able to detect the execution compartments responsible for the attacks correctly in all the cases, thus efficiently addressing the *dependency explosion* problem.

Outline. The remainder of this paper is organized as follows. In Sect. 2 we motivate the problem by showing the importance of execution partitioning for better forensic analysis and describe details of Provenance Monitoring techniques that are required for log collection. Section 3 discusses the details of our compartmentalization approach. In Sect. 4, we highlight implementation details. Evaluation of our approach appears in Sect. 5. Section 6 discusses related work. Finally, Sect. 7 concludes the paper.

2 Background

2.1 Motivating Example

An enterprise network is typically composed of several employee machines and Intranet servers that host high confidentiality and high integrity assets. The network is often protected by a defensive perimeter consisting of firewalls and IDSs. In a typical setting, the employee machines may interact with external machines on the Internet, while the Intranet servers may receive connections only from inside the enterprise network. APTs typically exploit such connectivity of the employee machines to gain an initial foothold in the enterprise and subsequently perform lateral movement to reach high-value assets.

The most widely used APT attack vectors include sophisticated social engineering (e.g., spear phishing), browser compromises (e.g., via drive-by downloads), and web attacks (e.g., session riding) [12] that impersonate legitimate users of an enterprise host and connect to Intranet servers. Consider the following APT attack vector that highlights the need for precise provenance tracking.

Alice, an employee of an enterprise, has several tabs open on her browser. In one of the tabs, she is lured to a malicious website that contains a 0-day Java exploit that targets an unpatched Java plugin inside her browser. The exploit instantaneously drops an executable file, which is executed and spawns a shell where the attacker can remotely enter commands. Using this shell, the attacker reads Alice's recent activities from her command history and notices a series of *git* commands to an internal GIT server. Next, the attacker executes a *git pull* command to retrieve the most recent documents and proceeds to slowly exfiltrate them to a C&C server that he controls. Alice is unaware of any of these actions.

This example showcases a drive-by-download APT attack vector [22], a common method used to gain an initial foothold in an enterprise. The next step is typically gaining control of the compromised local machine followed by further connections to other internal machines. When a step of this attack is detected, it is crucial to causally link it with the events of the initial infection and ultimately with the provenance of the input that causes the initial infection. For doing so, we need to deal with several challenges pertinent to provenance tracking, dependence explosion, abstraction of input/output, dynamics of applications, and performance issues for timely analysis. In particular, *dependency explosion* is one of the major hurdles to a fast and effective forensic investigation. This problem arises when a process receives several inputs from different sources within a short amount of time, while at the same time producing several outputs. In this context, the primary challenge is to associate the provenance of each input to the correct outputs. For instance, the average number of records generated by the audit logs is typically between 5,000–500,000 records per minute, only a minuscule portion of which is related to the attack [9].

2.2 Provenance Monitoring

In this section, we describe details of a provenance monitoring system which produces logs required for building a dependency graph that is used for post-attack forensics analysis. As the dependency graph is built based on information flow among system entities, we do not need to log all the system calls. Table 1 shows a summary of the most important system calls that are required for information flow tracking and provenance identification. In the table, we show different categories of system calls according to their purpose. Some system calls are responsible for the actual information flow between objects. For instance, when a new process is created via a `clone` system call, it inherits the file descriptors of its parent. Therefore, there is information flow from the parent to the child process.

A subset of the system calls (third row of Table 1) is responsible for initializing and setting up data structures rather than dealing with information flow directly. For example, the *socketpair* system call creates two sockets. *Preparatory* system calls initialize data structures, and in certain cases provide the provenance of the subsequent data. For example, by checking the *lseek* system call and considering file offsets, we only track specific offsets of a file to prevent unnecessary dependencies. *Termination* system calls deal with the destruction of objects.

Flow Types. Table 2 shows the details of information flow sources, destinations, and events. We summarize these details in the table by using only three types of

Table 1. System event types.

Purpose	Relevant system calls
Information flow	*clone* (process), *fork, msgsnd, msgrcv, write, send, read, recv, exec*
Creation	*open, creat, dup, link, socket, socketpair*
Preparatory	*lseek, connect, listen, accept, bind, clone* (thread), *link, sendto*
Termination	*close, exit, exit_group, unlink, kill*

Table 2. Information flow events.

From	To	Relevant system calls	Source	Destination
Process	Process	*clone* (process), *fork, vfork, rfork, msgsnd*	event caller	arg(s)
Process	Process	*wait, msgrcv*	arg(s)	event caller
Process	File/Socket	*write, pwrite, writev, pwritev, send, sendto, sendmsg*	event caller	arg(s)
File/Socket	Process	*read, recv, recvfrom, recvmsg, execl, execv, execle, execve, execlp, execvp*	arg(s)	event caller

objects (File, socket, process). As shown in the table, there are different kinds of information flow between system objects. These include: (*i*) from a process to another process initiated by events like *fork* and *clone*, (*ii*) from a process to a file/socket initiated by events like *write* and *send*, and (*iii*) from a file/socket to a process initiated by events such as *read*, and *receive*. In the last two columns of Table 2, we use *arg(s)* to indicate the argument(s) of system calls to refer to the object(s) that the *caller process* manipulates. In particular, depending on the system call, the argument type may be the *id* of a process, the *name* of a file, or a *descriptor* referring to a file/socket.

3   Approach

Approach in a Nutshell. The goal of PROPATROL is to compartmentalize execution of long-running processes to smaller partitions by leveraging the high-level tasks extracted from audit logs. More precisely, after traces of an attack are detected, we want to perform forensic analysis and identify *who* initiated the connection (untrusted source versus legitimate local user), *how* it happened (history of the connection), and *what* system entities (processes, files, etc.) are affected. To answer these questions, we systematically follow the dependency between *system entities* (e.g., files, sockets, processes), which is constructed based on a system-wide provenance monitoring. This provenance monitoring is transparent to users, incurs negligible overhead, and does not require application instrumentation (details are discussed in Sect. 2.2). An overview of PROPATROL is shown in Fig. 1. The provenance monitoring module constructs a dependency graph based on audit logs coming from enterprise hosts. Once an attack is detected, the compartmentalization module partitions long-running processes to smaller parts called Active Execution Units, where each Active Execution Unit relates inputs to outputs that are *truly dependent on those inputs*. For instance, in the case of a browser such as Google Chrome, each Active Execution Unit represents a single user-supplied URL. Once the Active Execution Units are determined, PROPATROL detects the root cause of the attack by performing a backward traversal from an attack point. In addition, it detects the affected objects by performing a forward traversal from the root cause. Thus, system analysts can quickly pinpoint the attack source and the affected system entities, which minimizes manual investigation efforts.

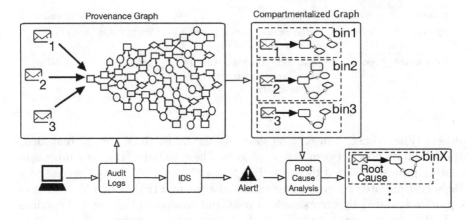

Fig. 1. Approach overview.

3.1   Attack Investigation

Solving the Dependency Explosion Challenge. In prior approaches dealing with *dependency explosion*, a process is partitioned into smaller units of execution based on performing heavy code instrumentation or assuming that source code is available and software developers annotate it [18,20,21]. They use each unit to next correlate the provenance of received inputs to the produced outputs. On the contrary, we propose an approach that takes advantage of application compartments to learn a model through the analysis of the sequence of system calls it generates. Using this model, we define a partitioning scheme for applications, which assigns the provenance to the output objects of each Active Execution Unit.

In particular, we define an *active execution unit* as the segment of an application that processes an input or a set of inputs as a result of user activity. Examples of such activities include reading a new email, browsing on a new website, and so on. We note that for the attacks that we deal with in this paper (e.g., drive-by download) we assume that such user activity is always present.

To use Active Execution Units to assign provenance, we need to be able to identify them from the system call traces when an Active Execution Unit starts and when it ends. Besides, for every system call that interacts with an object (e.g., a file or a process) and that appears between that start and that end, we associate the provenance related to the Active Execution Unit to that object. For instance, the *Active Execution Unit* of a browser such as Chrome is the website instance sending a request to Chrome's kernel process, while for an email client, the Active Execution Unit is the email that the user is currently reading.

3.2   Active Execution Unit Identification

Our methodology is based on an initial guided inference phase which exercises different applications with a variety of inputs. The inference is guided by an intuitive knowledge of what represents an active execution unit that might get compromised. For instance, for Google Chrome, active execution units are represented by visited websites, while for Thunderbird by the single emails. Such inference can be made with a high degree of certainty for several applications whose design and architecture are public knowledge, either because they are open source, or because of developer documentation.

When a new Active Execution Unit starts, some system events are generated by the part of application that is responsible for handling a new Active Execution Unit while others are commonly generated as a result of other application logic unrelated to this. Based on our observations, the latter represents a significant portion of the system calls and, during the inference phase, a source of 'noise' for correctly deriving the boundaries between Active-Execution-Units. Next, we propose a method to extract a sequence of system calls responsible for handling Active Execution Unit.

Using our previous definition, we can partition an application into several Active Execution Units, only one of which is active at any given time. To assign a system call to the correct Active Execution Unit, we must, however, be able to identify which Active Execution Unit is active when the system call is generated.

In general, the problem can be defined as follows: Given a stream of system calls arriving one at a time, and given a set of bins, each representing an Active Execution Unit, which is the active bin (that is the current active Active Execution Unit), to which a system call belongs?

We tackle this problem by creating an inference procedure, which exercises different activities to switch among Active Execution Units and user actions that cause new input to be received. More formally, for each application, we want to derive the following rules during such inference phase:

- Rule 1: $if(isObserved(S_k) \Rightarrow Bin_k = newBin();)$
- Rule 2: $if(isObserved(S_i) \Rightarrow \{k = non\_active; i = active; \})$
- Rule 3: $if(isActive(i))) \Rightarrow Bin_i = Bin_i \cup s_j$

Rule 1 deals with the creation of a new Active Execution Unit (e.g., a new tab, or a new email which comes under the user's focus). In this rule, S_k is a commonly observed sequence of system calls and their arguments when a new Active Execution Unit is created, and Bin_k represents a new empty bin. This sequence is typically manifested during the initialization of a new Active Execution Unit. Rule 2 deals with the switching tasks among different Active Execution Units. In this rule, S_i represents a commonly observed sequence of system calls when the user switches among Active Execution Unit, k and i represent the previous Active Execution Unit, which becomes inactive, and the newly activated Active Execution Unit, respectively. Rule 3 deals with assigning the current system call s_j to the currently active bin.

These rules are based on the key intuition that activities such as the creation of new Active Execution Unit or switching among existing ones are executions of the same code in an application and they usually manifest in the same system call sequences.

To derive the sequences S_k and S_i for each application, we run that application under different scenarios (e.g., open a tab, click on a link in an existing tab or open the link in a new tab, or check an email or open an email in a new window, etc.), with different actions and user inputs. For each creation or switching, we record its start by introducing a special event (e.g., a mouse click) and collect the traces of system calls and their arguments, together with additional information such as PIDs and TIDs (thread ids). Next, we compare the sequences and extract the longest common subsequence among all the traces.

More formally, given a set of system call traces, collected for the same type of activity repeated M times:

- $S_1 = (s_{11}, s_{12}, s_{1N})$
- $S_2 = (s_{21}, s_{22}, s_{2N})$
- ...
- $S_M = (s_{M1}, s_{M2}, s_{MN})$

We find the longest subsequence $S_L = (s_{l1}, s_{l2}, s_{lK})$ where each s_{li} is present in all the traces $(S_1, ..., S_M)$, and where for any two consecutive s_{li} and s_{li+1} in S_L, s_{li+1} follows s_{li} in each of the traces $(S_1, ..., S_M)$, possibly with other system calls between them. This subsequence represents a system call signature related to the specific activity, which is always present at the start of that activity. We use such subsequence as the 'boundary' between the different active execution units.

After such subsequences are learned for a number of different activities under different inputs, we introduce them in the rules previously described. In particular, every time a new Active Execution Unit's start is detected, we initiate a new bin. While this Active Execution Unit is active, we assign the connections that are created to receive input to that bin. When a switch to an existing Active Execution Unit is detected, we save the state of the current Active Execution Unit, in order to restore it once it becomes active again. If no subsequences can be identified, we conclude that the application is not suitable to be compartmentalized by our approach.

4   Implementation

4.1   Provenance Monitor

To trace the system calls, PROPATROL makes use of Systemtap [2], a very efficient Linux profiling tool designed to have near zero overhead. For each system call, we collect the timestamps, caller process id, group process id, system call name, and its arguments. We store these logs into a file to be analyzed further by the attack investigation module. Whenever a `fork` or `clone` appears in the logs, the new process or thread is monitored too.

4.2   Compartmentalization

4.2.1   Google Chrome

To isolate websites from each other, Google Chrome consists of multiple renderer processes which communicate with Chrome's kernel process. Google Chrome supports different models of how to allocate websites to the renderer processes [30]. However, by default, it creates a separate renderer process for each web page instance which user visits. Each renderer process communicates the jobs to the kernel process and receives responses via the `recvmsg` system call. Chrome's kernel process is responsible for networking and filesystem I/O tasks. These jobs include DNS requests, content download, reading and writing to the file system and so on. Consequently, PROPATROL associates the provenance of an input with a renderer process which has sent a request to Chrome's kernel process.

Active Execution Unit Selection. An active execution unit includes a renderer process and all the objects and processes initiated by the kernel in response to that renderer's messages. To be able to correctly assign and propagate the provenance, the attack investigation module must, therefore, associate each system call it receives with the correct active execution unit. We do this by taking advantage of the `recvmsg` system calls. In particular, when a `recvmsg` between the kernel and one of the renderer processes is found by the attack investigation module, we associate that system call, and all the subsequent system calls of the kernel and the renderer to the active execution unit related to that renderer. These system calls may include forking of new processes (e.g., plugins), writing to files, and so on. The new objects that are created or modified as a result of these system calls are associated with the provenance of the renderer. When a new `recvmsg` is 'seen' by the attack investigation module from a different renderer process, we switch to the active execution unit corresponding to that renderer.

4.2.2   Thunderbird

In the case of Thunderbird, each received email can be considered as a different sandbox associated with some provenance information related to the sender. Thunderbird stores all emails in a single file called INBOX and when a user opens a specific email, this file is accessed at an offset corresponding to that email using the `read` system call.

Active Execution Unit Selection. An active execution unit in Thunderbird is defined as a set of objects to which information flows from Thunderbird as a result of reading an email. This set may include, files written by Thunderbird to the file system, browser processes forked by Thunderbird as a result of clicking on a link in an email and so on. In Thunderbird, each email is stored at a different offset in a single file, and Thunderbird uses this offset to access emails when prompted by the user. Therefore, when the attack investigation module finds a `read` system call into the INBOX file at a particular offset, it associates all the subsequent system calls with the active execution unit corresponding to the email at that offset.

4.2.3 Pidgin Chat Application

Pidgin is a chat application. Each active execution unit in Pidgin corresponds to a chat window and the objects to which information flows from that window. Similar to Thunderbird, interaction with each chat window corresponds to access to a file. However, Pidgin keeps separate files for each chat window.

Active Execution Unit Selection. *Pidgin*'s screen is separated into different chat windows each of which corresponds to a different file on disk. Therefore, an active execution unit is switched by the attack investigation module when it finds a `read` system call to the file associated with a chat window.

5 Evaluation

5.1 Enterprise Setup

To evaluate the effectiveness of PROPATROL, we simulate a set of attacks on an enterprise testbed of user workstations and Intranet servers. In particular, the Intranet consists of three Ubuntu user workstations and three Intranet servers. The Intranet servers include a GIT server used for collaborative coding within the enterprise, a web-based router, and a web server interfaced with a database that manages employees' personal information.

5.2 Graphs

To facilitate forensic analysis, PROPATROL produces visual graph representations to be used by analysts. In the Linux kernel, threads are implemented as processes that have the same process group. In the graph representation, we cluster the processes with the same process group (the process and its threads) together. The graphs depict processes and threads as ovals, sockets, and files, as well as information flow, labeled by numbers that show the sequence of events as they happened over time. Note that all the graphs we present in this section use these notations.

5.3   Summary of Results

Table 3, summarizes PROPATROL's compartmentalization capability on high-lighting five different classes of attacks that target common applications such as browsers and email clients. These attacks include Remote Administration Tools (RAT) installation via an attachment on a spear-phishing email, drive-by download that exploits a Java plugin vulnerability, social engineering via an IM client, CSRF, and DNS rebinding. After the initial compromise in all these attacks, attackers pivot to one of the intranet machines that contain confidential information. At that point, an attack is detected, and system analysts use PROPATROL to find the root-cause of a connection to the corresponding sockets.

Table 3. Overview of attack investigation results.

Application	Attack	Root-cause detection?
Email Client (Thunderbird)	RAT	✓
Browser (Google-Chrome)	Drive-by download	✓
IM Client (Pidgin)	Social engineering	✓
Browser (Google-Chrome)	CSRF	✓
Browser (Google-Chrome)	DNS Rebinding	✓

5.4   Root-Cause Analysis

Below we present details of the five scenarios on which we evaluated PROPATROL.

5.4.1   Remote Access Trojan (RAT)

Setup. A RAT is a malicious binary that can execute several commands sent by the attacker. In this evaluation, we consider a spear-phishing email containing a RAT as an attachment. We assume that the user that receives this email is tricked into saving and executing the attachment. The attachment performs some malicious activity in the background without the user noticing it. In our evaluation, after it is downloaded to the user workstation, the RAT binary performs network scanning in the background. In this scenario, we used Nmap and a shell script that starts Nmap to mimic a RAT, which after being executed scans an internal IP address.

Attack Investigation. Using PROPATROL, we were able to find the root-cause of this RAT starting from the connections sent to Intranet servers. The sequence of system calls related to the active execution unit is processed by PROPATROL to create a causal graph depicted in Fig. 2. Using this graph, a system administrator can easily infer the machine that has fallen victim to a malicious RAT that scans the network in the background.

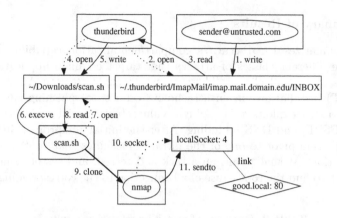

Fig. 2. Provenance graph for RAT detection scenario.

5.4.2 Drive-By Download

Setup. This attack exploits CVE-2012-4681, a vulnerability that allows a Java applet to bypass *SecurityManager* restrictions in Oracle Java Runtime Environment (JRE) version 7. We set up an external malicious web server that hosts a Java applet exploiting this vulnerability. Whenever a victim browser with the Java Plugin connects to the malicious web server, the attacker can execute arbitrary code on the victim's machine. Specifically, we install JRE version 7 on the user workstations inside our network and set up the Java plugin for the Google-Chrome browser. Then we conduct the attack on one of the user's machines. The attack proceeds as follows. The user opens Google-Chrome, and among other benign activities, he opens a tab connecting to a malicious web server. When the user workstation connects to the malicious web server, the attacker notices this event. Then using Metasploit, the attacker opens a remote shell on the user workstation. Next, as a lateral movement for accessing the Intranet servers, the attacker tries to steal the enterprise project's data from the Git Server. Using the remote shell, the attacker performs `git pull` to pull the latest codebase of the project on the Git Server. Finally, the attacker sends the codebase to the attacker's server.

Attack Investigation. A provenance graph generated by PROPATROL, starting from a backward traversal from the `git` connection to the internal git server, is visualized in Fig. 3. The first edge is artificial, and we consider it to show that the socket connection on port 80 of `evil.org` is on a malicious website. `Chrome` is the initial process that is executed by the user opening Google-Chrome. Later, that process clones two threads (`Chrome_IOThread` and `Chrome_ProcesssL`) (edges labeled with 2 and 3). The `Chrome_IOThread` connects to the attacker's site and retrieves some data. The thread (`Chrome_ProcessL`) clones a set of different processes, threads, and applications for getting access to the remote shell (see edges 7–19). These intermediate steps are considered as internal mechanisms of Metasploit and the Java exploit we are using. After accessing the remote shell

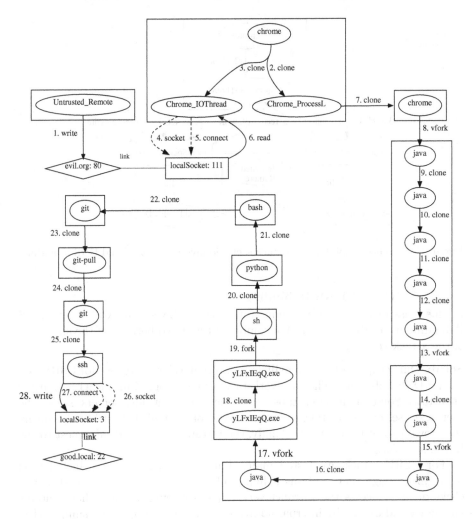

Fig. 3. Provenance graph for drive-by-download attack detection.

at edge 21, the attacker enters a `git` command. As the Git server uses SSH protocol, an SSH process is cloned and connects to port 22 on the Intranet Git server `good.local` (edges 26–28).

For the attack that exfiltrates the code base of the Git server, using the PROPATROL, we were able to identify the root-cause starting from the point that the attacker performs lateral movements to internal servers.

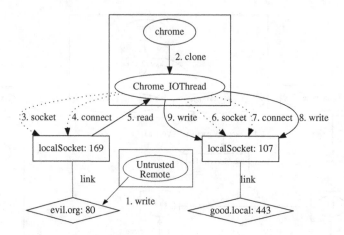

Fig. 4. Provenance graph for web attack scenario involving CSRF and DNS rebinding.

5.4.3   CSRF and DNS Rebinding

In this class of attacks, we demonstrate how we investigate CSRF and DNS Rebinding using PROPATROL. We combined these two because of the similarity of the attack vectors.

Setup. Our setup involves two malicious external web servers, one for CSRF and one for DNS Rebinding. The user workstation runs Google-Chrome with multiple open tabs. Some of the open tabs are connected to Intranet servers' sites. The user next uses one of the tabs to browse to one of the malicious websites, causing the browser to retrieve a page. Finally, the retrieved page sends a request to the Intranet server.

For CSRF attack, we tested many different scenarios. These include: (*i*) retrieving a page that contains a hyperlink to an Intranet server and a user clicks on it to access the Intranet server, (*ii*) retrieving a page that contains an element addressed by internal addresses and a JavaScript code snippet that checks the availability of those elements for port-scanning the enterprise network, and (*iii*) a JavaScript code snippet sending a malicious GET/POST request to the webpage of the internal router having a CSRF vulnerability for changing the password.

To evaluate PROPATROL against DNS Rebinding attacks, we set up a malicious external site containing a web server and a DNS server implemented with *Dnsmasq*. The DNS server has two IP addresses registered for the domain name of the web server, i.e., the IP address of the web server and the IP address of the Intranet server. When the user browser connects to this site and tries to resolve the domain name, the first IP it receives is the IP address of the web server. As a result, the browser connects to the web server and loads a webpage containing a JavaScript code that keeps requesting resources from the Intranet web server. These requests are blocked because Same-Origin-Policy prevents accessing the contents hosted on other origins. After a while, the user's browser connects to the DNS server one more time and tries to resolve the domain name again. This time, it is resolved to the Intranet web server's IP address, and the Same-Origin-Policy is circumvented—enabling the attacker's script to read the response from Intranet server and send it to the attacker's machine.

Attack Investigation. As shown in Fig. 4, PROPATROL has detected the root-cause starting by a backward traversal from the attacker's attempt to send a malicious request to the Intranet server. The first edge is artificial, and we consider it to show that the socket connection on port 80 of evil.org is on an untrusted site. Chrome process is the initial process that is executed by the user opening Google-Chrome. Later that process clones a thread named Chrome_IOThread. This thread creates the local socket 169 and connects to the attacker's site. Then edge numbers 6 to 9 are events related to making a connection to the port 443 of the Intranet server good.local. Event numbers 8 and 9 transfer some untrusted information to the socket on the intranet server. Note that PROPATROL did not correlate the attack to the other valid requests going to Intranet servers in other applications or other tabs of the browser.

5.4.4   Instant Messaging Client

Setup. To demonstrate how PROPATROL forensically investigates attacks targeting Instant messaging clients, we considered the *Pidgin* IM client. Pidgin maintains individual conversation history in separate files for each contact of a user. We add a google account in the Pidgin that contains a list of added buddies. Then we start chatting with some of them. For each buddy, there is a chat communication that is stored in a separate file from the other conversations.

Attack Investigation. The provenance graph for detecting an attack that happens via an IM client is shown in Fig. 5. In the chat communication with username2, username1 receives a chat messages with a link to a vulnerable Intranet server. When username1 clicks on the malicious link, a Google-Chrome process is forked by pidgin, and a connection to the Intranet server is initiated. At this moment, the active execution unit corresponds to the chat window with username2. Therefore, PROPATROL detects username2 as the root-cause of this attack.

5.5   Effectiveness

Table 4 shows the effectiveness of PROPATROL pertaining to event volume reduction. In this table, the second column shows the number of system calls generated by each application for its initialization which is the duration from the start of the application until it loads completely. Execution of each one of these applications could be compartmentalized to smaller bins depending on user activities. For instance, a new bin is created when a user opens a new tab in Chrome, or opens a new chat window in Pidgin, or reads a new email in Thunderbird. The third column shows the number of events assigned to each bin on average.

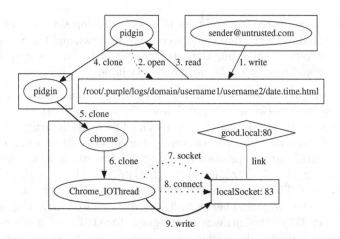

Fig. 5. Provenance graph for an attack scenario that targets an IM client.

For example, in the case of Google Chrome, if a user opens 10 tabs, the size of provenance graph would be about $200K + 10 \times 14K$. In any attack, typically only one bin is responsible for the attack, and PROPATROL successfully identifies it. The fourth column shows the final number of events that PROPATROL shows to the system analyst after detecting the root-cause. As evidenced by this table, PROPATROL can achieve orders of magnitude reduction in event volume.

Table 4. Effectiveness of attack summaries.

Application	Initialization syscalls	Average bin syscalls	Average active execution unit Syscalls
Google-Chrome	200K	14K	<50
Thunderbird	91.5K	8K	<20
Pidgin	20.5K	1K	<15

5.6 Performance Overhead

Table 5 shows the performance overhead introduced by PROPATROL and the time required for generating the attack graphs. As shown in the second column of Table 5, we calculate the average time for a single system call per scenario in microseconds. The third column shows the overhead (in percentage) by the monitoring infrastructure (which includes Systemtap and the provenance graph building module), which on average is 1.1.%. We set up the graph generation module on a 32 bit Ubuntu OS, Quad-Core 2.4 GHz Intel Xeon Processor with 10 GB RAM. The time (in seconds) this module took for highlighting the root-cause of an attack is shown in the fourth column of Table 5 showing a very minimal overhead. Overall, both the graph generation module and Systemtap incur negligible overhead due to the coarse-grained provenance tracking underlying PROPATROL.

Table 5. Overhead for the provenance monitor and graph generation time.

Scenario	Avg event time (μs)	Provenance monitor overhead (%)	Graph generation time (sec)
RAT	8.87	0.72	0.12
Drive-by download	16.37	1.57	0.001
Social engineering	9.87	0.16	0.0004
CSRF	8.10	1.14	0.03
DNS rebinding	15.71	1.88	0.08

6   Related Work

6.1   System-Wide Provenance Collection

SPADE [6] and PASS [25] are operating system level provenance systems. SPADE hooks into the audit subsystem in the Linux kernel to observe program actions whereas PASS intercepts system calls made by a program. Both of these systems observe application events such as process creation and input/output, which is then used to find out the relationship between data sets. LineageFS [28] modifies the Linux kernel to log process creation and file-related system calls in *printk* buffer. A user-level process reads this buffer periodically to generate lineage records. Similar approaches to collect provenance are Hi-Fi [27] and LPM [3]—these are kernel level systems that track the provenance of system objects. While they provide a secure and application-transparent way of collecting provenance, they do need provenance awareness at the application level in order to counter the dependence explosion problem. Moreover, SLEUTH [9] and HOLMES [23] use kernel audit logs for real-time attack detection and forensics, which could benefit from the light-weight compartmentalization approaches such as PROPATROL to improve accuracy.

6.2   Information Flow Tracking

Some past work (such as [29,33]) proposed information flow tracking at processor-level with manufacturer support. Some others (e.g., [14,26] perform binary rewriting at runtime to instrument machine code with additional instructions that update shadow memory. Xu et al. [31] employ source code transformation by instrumenting C code with additional code that can handle flow tracking. Being fine-grained techniques, they offer good precision in tracking the source of enterprise activity. However, all these approaches impose a high overhead. For instance, [14] imposes a 3.65x slowdown factor. Another line of work also uses techniques to decouple taint tracking from program execution [4,11,17,24].

In the coarse-grained tracking front, Backtracker by King et al. [15] is one of the first works in this area that introduced the notion of dependency graphs. The same authors extended Backtracker in [16] with support for multi-host dependencies, forward tracking and correlating disconnected IDS alerts. To reduce the size of audit logs, different methods [8,10,19,32] are proposed leveraging graph abstraction, garbage collection, or compactness techniques.

6.3   Execution Partitioning

Execution partitioning techniques are proposed for dividing the execution of long-running programs into smaller units, resulting in a better forensic analysis. BEEP is a closely related approach to PROPATROL. BEEP is based on the notion of independent units whereby a long-running program is partitioned into individual units by monitoring the execution of the program's event-handling loops, with each iteration corresponding to the processing of an independent input/request. An essentially backward forensic tracing system, BEEP, is suitable for programs that tend to have independent loop iterations. Ma et al. [21] introduced ProTracer, a lightweight provenance tracing system that only captures system calls related to taint propagation. ProTracer records the history of objects by logging important events. It utilizes an instrumentation technique called BEEP [18] for partitioning an execution into smaller units. BEEP [18] and ProTracer [21] use training and code instrumentation to divide execution to multiple iterations of the main loop in a program. Another related work, MPI [20] relies on users to annotate the application's high-level task structures to enable semantic-aware execution partitioning.

7   Conclusions

In this paper, we presented PROPATROL, as a compartmentalization approach for doing more accurate and timely root-cause analysis. PROPATROL uses a lightweight provenance monitoring system to effectively perform forward/backward tracking. Our evaluation shows that the tracking system operates with a very minimal overhead of less than 2%. We demonstrated in an enterprise setting that PROPATROL is able to detect the root-cause of a broad class of APT vectors such as spear phishing, drive-by downloads, RATs, CSRF, and DNS Rebinding attacks.

Acknowledgements. This work was primarily supported by DARPA (under AFOSR contract FA8650-15-C-7561) and in part by SPAWAR (N6600118C4035), and NSF (CNS-1514472, and DGE-1069311). The views, opinions, and/or findings expressed are those of the authors and should not be interpreted as representing the official views or policies of the Department of Defense, National Science Foundation or the U.S. Government.

References

1. Multiprocess firefox. https://developer.mozilla.org/en-US/Firefox/Multiprocess_Firefox
2. Systemtap. https://sourceware.org/systemtap/
3. Bates, A., Tian, D.J., Butler, K.R., Moyer, T.: Trustworthy whole-system provenance for the Linux kernel. In: 24th USENIX Security Symposium (USENIX Security 2015), pp. 319–334 (2015)
4. Chow, J., Garfinkel, T., Chen, P.M.: Decoupling dynamic program analysis from execution in virtual environments. In: USENIX 2008 Annual Technical Conference on Annual Technical Conference, pp. 1–14 (2008)
5. Corporation, M.: Apt1: exposing one of china's cyber espionage units. Technical report (2013)
6. Gehani, A., Tariq, D.: SPADE: support for provenance auditing in distributed environments. In: Narasimhan, P., Triantafillou, P. (eds.) Middleware 2012. LNCS, vol. 7662, pp. 101–120. Springer, Heidelberg (2012). https://doi.org/10.1007/978-3-642-35170-9_6
7. Goel, A., Po, K., Farhadi, K., Li, Z., De Lara, E.: The taser intrusion recovery system. In: ACM SIGOPS Operating Systems Review, vol. 39, pp. 163–176. ACM (2005)
8. Hassan, W.U., Lemay, M., Aguse, N., Bates, A., Moyer, T.: Towards scalable cluster auditing through grammatical inference over provenance graphs. In: Network and Distributed Systems Security Symposium (2018)
9. Hossain, M.N., et al.: SLEUTH: real-time attack scenario reconstruction from COTS audit data. In: 26th USENIX Security Symposium (USENIX Security 2017), pp. 487–504. USENIX Association, Vancouver (2017)
10. Hossain, M.N., Wang, J., Sekar, R., Stoller, S.D.: Dependence-preserving data compaction for scalable forensic analysis. In: 27th USENIX Security Symposium (USENIX Security 18), pp. 1723–1740. USENIX Association, Baltimore (2018)
11. Ji, Y., et al.: Rain: refinable attack investigation with on-demand inter-process information flow tracking. In: Proceedings of the 2017 ACM SIGSAC Conference on Computer and Communications Security, pp. 377–390. ACM (2017)
12. Johns, M., Winter, J.: Protecting the intranet against "JavaScript Malware" and related attacks. In: M. Hämmerli, B., Sommer, R. (eds.) DIMVA 2007. LNCS, vol. 4579, pp. 40–59. Springer, Heidelberg (2007). https://doi.org/10.1007/978-3-540-73614-1_3
13. Keizer, G.: Enterprises to get locked-down Windows 10 in six months. https://www.computerworld.com/article/3232749/microsoft-windows/enterprises-to-get-locked-down-windows-10-in-six-months.html. Accessed 08 Oct 2018
14. Kemerlis, V.P., Portokalidis, G., Jee, K., Keromytis, A.D.: libdft: practical dynamic data flow tracking for commodity systems. ACM SIGPLAN Not. **47**, 121–132 (2012)
15. King, S.T., Chen, P.M.: Backtracking intrusions. ACM SIGOPS Oper. Syst. Rev. **37**, 223–236 (2003)
16. King, S.T., Mao, Z.M., Lucchetti, D.G., Chen, P.M.: Enriching intrusion alerts through multi-host causality. In: NDSS (2005)
17. Kwon, Y., et al.: MCI: modeling-based causality inference in audit logging for attack investigation. In: Proceedings of the 25th Network and Distributed System Security Symposium (NDSS) (2018)

18. Lee, K.H., Zhang, X., Xu, D.: High accuracy attack provenance via binary-based execution partition. In: NDSS (2013)
19. Lee, K.H., Zhang, X., Xu, D.: Loggc: garbage collecting audit log. In: Proceedings of the 2013 ACM SIGSAC Conference on Computer & Communications Security, pp. 1005–1016. ACM (2013)
20. Ma, S., Zhai, J., Wang, F., Lee, K.H., Zhang, X., Xu, D.: MPI: multiple perspective attack investigation with semantics aware execution partitioning. In: USENIX Security (2017)
21. Ma, S., Zhang, X., Xu, D.: Protracer: towards practical provenance tracing by alternating between logging and tainting (2016)
22. Mathew, S.J.: Social engineering leads apt attack vectors. http://www. darkreading.com/vulnerabilities-and-threats/social-engineering-leads-apt-attack-vectors/d/d-id/1100142?
23. Milajerdi, S.M., Gjomemo, R., Eshete, B., Sekar, R., Venkatakrishnan, V.: HOLMES: real-time APT detection through correlation of suspicious information flows. In: Proceedings of the IEEE Symposium on Security and Privacy. IEEE (2019)
24. Ming, J., Wu, D., Wang, J., Xiao, G., Liu, P.: Straight taint: decoupled offline symbolic taint analysis. In: Proceedings of the 31st IEEE/ACM International Conference on Automated Software Engineering, pp. 308–319. ACM (2016)
25. Muniswamy-Reddy, K.K., Holland, D.A., Braun, U., Seltzer, M.I.: Provenance-aware storage systems. In: USENIX Annual Technical Conference, General Track, pp. 43–56 (2006)
26. Newsome, J., Song, D.: Dynamic taint analysis for automatic detection, analysis, and signature generation of exploits on commodity software (2005)
27. Pohly, D.J., McLaughlin, S., McDaniel, P., Butler, K.: Hi-fi: collecting high-fidelity whole-system provenance. In: Proceedings of the 28th Annual Computer Security Applications Conference, pp. 259–268. ACM (2012)
28. Sar, C., Cao, P.: Lineage file system. http://crypto.stanford.edu/cao/lineage.html (2005)
29. Suh, G.E., Lee, J.W., Zhang, D., Devadas, S.: Secure program execution via dynamic information flow tracking. ACM Sigplan Not. **39**, 85–96 (2004)
30. Team, T.C.: Chromium Project Process Model. https://www.chromium.org/developers/design-documents/process-models. Accessed 05 Oct 2018
31. Xu, W., Bhatkar, S., Sekar, R.: Taint-enhanced policy enforcement: a practical approach to defeat a wide range of attacks. In: USENIX Security, pp. 121–136 (2006)
32. Xu, Z., et al.: High fidelity data reduction for big data security dependency analyses. In: Proceedings of the 2016 ACM SIGSAC Conference on Computer and Communications Security, pp. 504–516. ACM (2016)
33. Yin, H., Song, D., Egele, M., Kruegel, C., Kirda, E.: Panorama: capturing system-wide information flow for malware detection and analysis. In: Proceedings of the 14th ACM Conference on Computer and Communications Security, pp. 116–127. ACM (2007)

Smartphone Security

SGP: A Safe Graphical Password System Resisting Shoulder-Surfing Attack on Smartphones

Suryakanta Panda[1]($\boxtimes$), Madhu Kumari[2], and Samrat Mondal[1]

[1] Indian Institute of Technology Patna, Patna, India
{suryakanta.pcs15,samrat}@iitp.ac.in
[2] National Institute of Technology Patna, Patna, India
madhu98710@gmail.com

Abstract. Graphical passwords have been taken as a potential alternative to alphanumeric passwords. Graphical password based authentication is widely used in many applications for system security and privacy. It increases ease of password use i.e., memorability of the password. With the rapid development of mobile devices, graphical passwords have already been implemented on smartphones. However, shoulder-surfing attack is a major threat to the security of graphical password systems. To overcome this problem, we proposed a novel graphical password authentication system, SGP. SGP uses a pattern of digits for the input of graphical password images. This pattern changes the position of input images in each authentication session. SGP prevents shoulder-surfing attacker to derive which password images are used by the user, even if the attacker records a complete login process. SGP does not use any secondary channels to resist shoulder-surfing attack.

Keywords: Graphical password · Shoulder-surfing attack
Authentication

1 Introduction

The advancement of mobile technology and its continuous evolve, makes smartphones an alternative to personal computers. Consumers are using smartphones more than personal computers to access the internet. According to mobile marketing statistics the smartphone had overtaken personal computer shipments in 2011, and also the number of smartphone users exceeds desktop users in 2014, which is closed to 2 billion [4]. So, companies are making their websites mobile friendly and more and more mobile applications (apps) are created to meet the needs of end users. We can verify our bank account while rock climbing, we can do shopping while eating, we can book movie tickets while traveling and many more things with the help of these apps. There is an app for each service which makes our life easy and effective. To access these personalized remote

© Springer Nature Switzerland AG 2018
V. Ganapathy et al. (Eds.): ICISS 2018, LNCS 11281, pp. 129–145, 2018.
https://doi.org/10.1007/978-3-030-05171-6_7

services, users need to be authenticated. In general, alphanumeric passwords comprised of numbers, upper-case letters, lower-case letters, and special characters are used for the authentication purpose. However, due to the physical constraint of smartphones, typing of alphanumeric passwords is not an easy task and leads to frustration.

A potential alternative to address the problems and weaknesses associated with alphanumeric passwords in smartphones is the use of Personal Identification Numbers or PINs. User authentication through PINs is used because of its simplicity, deployability and maturity. From the security point of view, authentication through PIN is susceptible to brute force attacks or guessing attacks by exploiting the circumstances of human password generation process [5,13].

To mitigate the limitations of PINs, authenticating users through graphical password is one of the promising alternative. Because, human brain is better at remembering and recognizing images than text [15]. Hence, many researchers have proposed graphical password schemes for smartphones to overcome the limitations of alphanumeric passwords and PINs [12,16,19].

However, a simple but very dangerous attack on graphical password systems that is still hard to counter is shoulder-surfing [6,11]. In shoulder-surfing, an attacker compromises the password by looking or surfing behind a legitimate user during the login process. Here, the attacker either physically present in the user's vicinity or can see the login process through vision enhancing devices like binoculars. In public places, the attacker can get the video recording of complete authentication process from the security cameras or using his own recording device.

The motivation behind this work relies on the hypothesis that, graphical password authentication schemes could be highly accepted in user community by preventing shoulder-surfing and guessing attack without a significant overhead on its usability. Usability overhead includes issues like time requirement for login and the complicated method of authentication that requires training and practice. Although a significant number of shoulder-surfing resistant graphical password systems exist in the literature, that are not feasible to implement in smartphones. Small screen size of smartphones is a major constraint in implementing them. Moreover, the existing schemes can prevent shoulder-surfing attacker with naked eye but vulnerable to use in public places. The goal of this work is to create an shoulder-surfing resistance graphical password system that can be used in public places i.e., resistant to recording of some sessions. The proposed approach is resistant to shoulder-surfing and guessing attack without any usability overhead. Our approach does not require any hardware change for the existing system, so it is cost effective. Moreover, we do not use any secondary channel to protect the challenge-response pair from adversaries. A layman can use our approach without any difficulty or rigorous training.

2   Related Work

From the past decades many researchers have presented their research results in the literature on graphical password authentication techniques. In this section, we are going to discuss some recent works that are mostly related to our proposed approach.

Wu et al. [18] proposed a graphical password authentication scheme using convex-hull graphical algorithm. To reduce shoulder-surfing attack, they added dynamic moving color balls on the screen. When one ball corresponding to the password color moves into the authentication region, the user enters the space key to confirm it. Although this scheme resists shoulder-surfing attack, cannot be implemented on smartphones due to small screen size.

Passmatrix [16] proposed by Sun et al., resists multiple camera based attack using a one-time login indicator per image. With a login indicator and circulative horizontal and vertical bars covering the entire pass-images, Passmatrix does not leak any information to narrow down the password space. It is based on the assumption that a small area (login indicator) of the mobile screen is easy to protect from the attackers. The security of the Passmatrix depends on the user activity (to secure a small portion of the mobile device) but human users are considered as the weakest link in the computer security system [14,17].

Meng et al., developed click-draw based graphical password CD-GPS [12], using multi-touch actions on smartphones. It combines three traditional graphical password input types such as clicking, selecting, and drawing. According to the usability study done by the authors, it has a positive influence on user's performance. However, it is not effective to resist the shoulder-surfing attack.

Yu et al. proposed Evopass [19], an evolvable graphical password system for mobile devices. It transforms password images to pass sketches as user credentials. It improves the password strength gradually by degrading the pass sketches. The continuous degradation of pass sketches increases the difficulty of shoulder-surfing attackers. But the number of evolved versions of pass sketches is limited and to balance usability the default evolving period is 2 week. If the shoulder-surfing attacker tries to authenticate within the evolving period, then the difficulty is reduced. It is also vulnerable to a single session recording attack i.e., after recording one session the attackers can easily authenticate.

Our work is very much similar to [14] which uses digraph substitution rules to prevent shoulder-surfing attack. Here, two password images are used and indirect user input (pass-image) from the password images are generated using digraph substitution. There are three different cases exist for the digraph substitution rules i.e.

- When both password images appear diagonal to each other, first password image is used to determine the row of the pass-image and second password is used to determine the column of the pass-image. Thus, the intersection is the required pass-image.
- When both the password images appear in the same row, then the image just right to the first password image is the required pass-image.
- When both the password images appear in the same column, then the image just below the first password image is the required pass-image.

It uses a 5 × 5 image grid and three challenge-response pairs in each session to authenticate a user. From the digraph substitution rules it is pretty clear that the password images sit on the row and column of pass-image. The above discussed three cases of digraph substitution states that the clicked pass-image is not the password image in any of the three cases. So, when user clicks on the pass-image in the first response, attacker filters 8 images from the grid of 25 images as possible password images. Thus, a memory bounded shoulder-surfing attacker with memory capacity m = 8 can easily get the password image in one session as a single session consists of three rounds of challenge-response pairs [9]. In addition to this, this is also vulnerable to single session recording attack.

In a nutshell, we can conclude that the above literature survey brings us three requirements for the design of a password entry method, that are (i) security, (ii) usability, (iii) cost-effectiveness.

3   Definition and Threat Model

3.1   Definition

Definition 1. *Let 'M' be a graphical password system employed in mobile devices and 'SS' represents a shoulder-surfing attacker without any recording devices. The probability that the attacker extracts the correct password is denoted by $P_{SS,n}(M)$ where 'n' represents number of times the attacker shoulder surfs the password entry process.*

Definition 2. *Like the success probability of shoulder-surfing attack, the success probability for recording attack can also be defined. Let 'M' be a graphical password system employed in mobile devices and 'RA' represents a recording attacker capable of recording the whole login process. The probability that the attacker extracts correct password is denoted by $P_{RA,n}(M)$ where 'n' represents the number of times the attacker records the password entry process.*

Definition 3. *Password images: A set of 4 images chosen by the user from 9 images in the registration phase of SGP.*

Definition 4. *Pass-images: A set of 4 images clicked by the user in the login phase of SGP.*

3.2   Threat Model

Shoulder Surfing Attack. Based on existing literature [8] and from the discussion in previous section (Sect. 1) we concluded that, the users may reveal their secret credentials to the people with bad intention while giving input in public. Based on the means of the attackers behavior and capacity, we categorize shoulder-surfing attack into four types such as:

1. Type-I: Attacker with naked eye.
2. Type-II: Attacker capable of capturing video of entire authentication process exactly once.

3. Type-III: Attacker capable of capturing video of entire authentication process twice or thrice.
4. Type-IV: Attacker capable of capturing video of entire authentication process more than thrice.

If an authentication scheme is able to resist against the later types of attacks then it is also secured against previous types of attacks. In a similar manner, if any scheme is vulnerable to former types of attacks then it is also unsafe to later types of attacks.

Following the theorem proposed in [10], we can conclude that it is impossible to design a secure password entry method where the attacker is allowed to observe all the challenge-response pairs. Therefore, except the attack Type-IV our focus is on the other categories, that is Type-I, Type-II, Type-III.

Smudge Attack. Oily residues remaining on the touch screen during the login phase can be exploited in smudge attack. The smudge attack is a matter of great concern regarding privacy of password entry.

4   Proposed Method

In this section, we present a system which satisfies all the derived requirements from the literature survey. In our proposed method to avoid the direct input of password images some kind of detour is used which provides resistance to shoulder-surfing attack.

Our proposed password method consists of the following components:

1. Image grid display module
2. Password verification module
3. Password database

Image Grid Display Module: This module displays the image grid to users as a challenge. As shown in Fig. 1 the image grid contains nine images from which users would identify four password images and find the respective pass-images. Image grid is displayed in such a way that an image is not repeated in the same position upto next six continuous challenges. Thus, with a recording of six continuous challenge-response pairs attacker fails to extract the genuine password images using intersection analysis. Image grid display module follows the algorithm below to display all the images in a challenge.

Algorithm 1. image grid formation

    Input   : Set T containing nine images
    Output: Image grid without position repetition of any image in last six
                 challenges

1 **while** *T is not empty* **do**
2   select one image from T & place it in the grid,
3   remove that image from T
4   **if** *conflict* **then**
5   backtrack, try in other position of the grid
6   **end**
7 **end**
8 **return** *Success, display image grid*

Fig. 1. Image grid

Password Verification Module: This module verifies the user's password in the authentication phase. The user is authenticated only if the image input correctly matches with the corresponding pass-image. The details of the login and verification process will be described in the next section.

Password Database: The database server contains tables that stores user accounts, patterns, password images.

The proposed method consists of two phases: registration phase and authentication phase.

4.1   Registration Phase

In the registration phase a new user is required to register a userid and selects four images from the image grid as her password images. In addition to this the user has to arrange nine digits in a 3 × 3 grid excluding one digit from the available set of ten decimal digits like shown in the Fig. 2. Users can follow a pattern to easily remember the arrangements of the digits. The user needs to remember the pattern and password images.

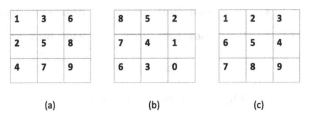

(a)   (b)   (c)

Fig. 2. Pattern of digits

4.2   Authentication Phase

In the authentication phase, the image grid containing same set of images but randomly permuted is displayed to the user. The same set of images are used in the image grid to prevent frequency of analysis attack [7]. To login, the user has to identify the pre-registered password images and click on the respective pass-images. The pass-images are determined from the password images and pattern, using the proposed algorithm. Then, the authentication server verifies whether the clicked images are exactly matching with the pass-images or not. If correctly matched then, the user is authenticated successfully.

4.3   Proposed Algorithm

The core idea of the proposed algorithm is inspired from the shift cipher, a well known encryption technique. Let p1, p2, p3, p4 are the positions of the first password image, second password image, third password image, and fourth password image in the pattern respectively.

Algorithm 2. pass-image determination

Input : position(p1, p2, p3, p4) derived from the pattern,
              password image (I1, I2, I3, I4)
    Output: pass-image $(I1', I2', I3', I4')$

1   $I1' = (I1 + p1) \% 9;$
2   $I2' = (I2 + p2) \% 9;$
3   $I3' = (I3 + p3) \% 9;$
4   $I4' = (I4 + p4) \% 9;$

Consider the Fig. 3 for a detail explanation of our proposed scheme. Assume that a user selects all the digits from 1 to 9 excluding the digit 0. Then, the user follows a pattern as shown in the Fig. 3(a). After that, the user selects four images from a grid of nine images as password images. Let the selected password images are IMG1, IMG2, IMG3, IMG4 respectively. The user needs to remember the pattern along the selected password images.

1	3	6
2	5	8
4	7	9

IMG3	IMG8	IMG7
IMG1	IMG2	IMG4
IMG6	IMG5	IMG9

IMG3	IMG8	IMG7
IMG1	IMG2	IMG4
IMG6	IMG5	IMG9

     (a)   (b)   (c)

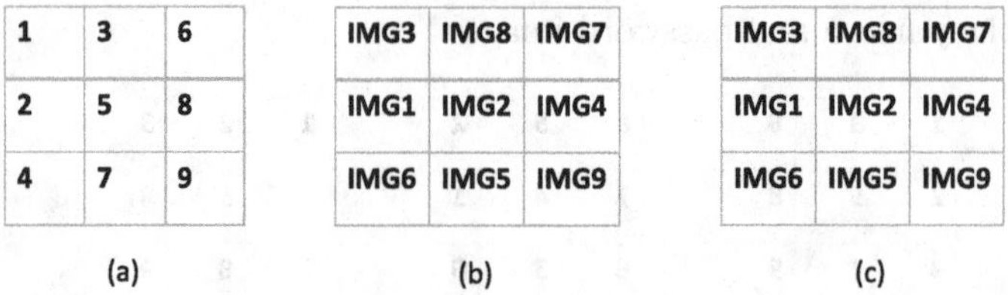

Fig. 3. Authentication processes

In the authentication phase, the system throws a set of images and asks the user to click on the correct pass-images. Note that, the system does not display the pre-registered pattern in authentication phase, the user needs to remember the pattern. Assume that, the system displays a grid of images as shown in Fig. 3(b). Then, the user identifies the password images i.e., IMG1, IMG2, IMG3, IMG4 along with their position according to the pattern. Here, the position for IMG1, IMG2, IMG3, IMG4 are 2, 5, 1 and 8 respectively. Thus, p1 = 2, p2 = 5, p3 = 1, p4 = 8. Hence, password image IMG1 shifts 2 positions following the pattern to get the first pass-image $I1'$ i.e., $I1' = (I1 + 2)\%9 =$ Image at position 4 = IMG6. Password image IMG2 shifts 5 positions following the pattern to get the second pass-image $I2'$ i.e., $I2' = (I2 + 5)\%9 =$ Image at position 1 = IMG3. In a similar manner, password image IMG3 shifts 1 position and password image IMG4 shifts 8 position to get the respective pass-images. Thus, the pass-images are $I1' = IMG6$, $I2' = IMG3$, $I3' = IMG1$ and $I4' = IMG5$.

5   Prototype Implementation

We have designed a prototype of SGP using android studio 3.1.3 [2] and 000webhost [1] server for its generality and popularity. We have selected 9 animal images for the image grid as shown in the Fig. 1.

6   Security Analysis

6.1   Resistance to Shoulder-Surfing

The login process neither reflects actual password images nor the pattern. In each session the position of images in the grid are randomly permuted i.e., one image will not appear in the same position upto six sessions. Thus, the password images and pass-images also changed accordingly. This prevents shoulder-surfing attack because of the limited human cognitive memory.

The other way to extract the pattern and password images is to record the whole login process. Following the theorem proposed in [10], we can conclude that it is impossible to design a secure password entry method where the attacker is allowed to observe all the challenge-response pairs. However, there is a need for a graphical password entry system which maintains a high probability of resistance upto some session recordings i.e., at least $P_{RA,0}(M) = P_{RA,1}(M)$ and the existing schemes in the literature without any secondary channel fails in this respect.

The method proposed by Por et al. [14], which uses digraph rules in 5×5 grid of images have $P_{RA,0}(M) = 0.003$. But with the recording of one challenge-response pair the probability reduces to $1/28$ from $1/300$. Thus, after recording one session (three challenge response pairs are used in one session) and using the intersection analysis the attacker can extract the password images easily.

However, in our proposed scheme recording of only one session do not leak any information to the attacker that reduces the probability of guessing.

Consider the example shown in the Fig. 4. In this example, the red color represents the clicks of the user. The pass-images are obtained from both combinations of password images and position of the key on the respective password images. The pass-image may be the password image itself, if the key is 0. Otherwise, it can be a one distant shift from the password image, two distant shift from the password image and so on. Thus, the attacker do not get any information

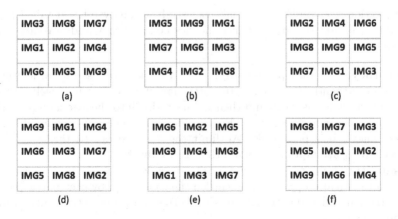

Fig. 4. Recordings of login processes

and the probability remains same after recording one session. In a formal manner we can say that $P_{RA,0}(M) = P_{RA,1}(M) = 0.008$. Ordinary human attackers frequently fail to do the correct click.

Thus, indirect input using both the image grid and pattern, makes security of the system independent of the user upto some extent. Even if an attacker records the complete authentication process the real password remains hidden. In addition to this, proposed system is resistant to other spy attacks that captures the input because each time the input will be different.

6.2 Resistance to Guessing Attack

In SGP, the number of images in the challenge set is 9 and the user needs to select 4 images as her pass-image. Then, the total possible password space is $C(9,4) = 126$. In Evopass user has to select 3 sketches from 9 available sketches. So, the password space is $C(9,3) = 84$. Similarly, the password space for the most recent Por et al.'s scheme is $C(25,2) = 300$. Thus, the password space of our proposed SGP is within the Evopass and Por et al.'s scheme. Probability of success for a guessing attack is 0.008 in SGP which is within the range of other existing graphical password schemes for smartphones. Guessing probability is 0.003 for Por et al.'s scheme and 0.012 for Evopass.

6.3 Resistance to Smudge Attack

In our system, the position of password images are randomly permuted in the grid (without repeating same position upto six continuous sessions). Hence, the pass-image positions varies from session to session, so the smudge left by the users provides no useful information about the password images.

7 User Study

In this section, we conduct an in-lab user study to analyze the detailed procedure that evaluates two performance metrics i.e., accuracy and usability of our proposed system.

- **Accuracy:** Accuracy perspective focuses with the success rate of legitimate users in authentication phase. In particular, it describes how well do users remember their password and their ability to log into the system after a time interval since registration. It also considers the successful login rate when users know their passwords. We limit the login retries to thrice i.e., after three wrong attempts we marked that as a failure.
- **Usability:** Usability measures the total time consumed in both registration and authentication phase. We recorded the time spent by each participant on registration and authentication to see whether our proposed system consumes more time or not.

Twenty participants (6 females and 14 males) including university students, technical staff, and non-technical staff took part in the evaluation process. All participants are regular smart phone users and also familiar with graphical password authentication schemes. The average age of participants are 26.5 years at the time of study. All participants came voluntarily for their participation in the user study.

First, we provide an introduction about the study to the participants. Then, they were explained the concept and purpose of the proposed system with a presentation. With the help of some simple animations, we showed the procedure they should use in order to use our system for login. All the participants then underwent a demo before doing their job.

In the registration phase, all the participants were required to select four images from the image grid. For easy memorization the participants can remember these images using a story. The selected four images are password images. Then, the participants arranged nine digits in a pattern as shown in Fig. 5. Participants need to remember both the password images and pattern of digits. The whole process of registration phase is completed in a private place. Otherwise, it does not make any sense to secure the login phase. Then, participants were instructed to log into their account in practice mode. They can repeat this step until they fell complete satisfaction about how to produce pass-images. After

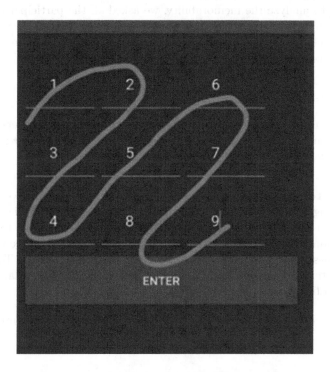

Fig. 5. Example of a pattern

Table 1. Post-test questionnaire. Responses are out of 5. A 5 is most positive

Questions	Mean	σ(standard deviation)
Some information is exposed to shoulder-surfing attacker when authenticating in public	4.05	0.55
The proposed scheme can protect my credential from being attacked by shoulder-surfing attacker	4.29	0.66
The time consumed for using the proposed system is acceptable	3.73	0.78
In general, this is a user-friendly system and is easy to use	3.89	0.85
I am likely to choose this method for security-sensitive applications in public places	3.85	0.69

thorough practice, participants were requested to log into their accounts formally in login mode. All users were instructed to complete five successful logins. After this, participants were asked to answer a short questionnaire about their experience as summarized in Table 1.

In order to analyze the memorability, we asked all the participants to come back again one week later to log into their account. In the session which took place one week later, participants were asked to log into the system repeatedly until five successful logins.

7.1   Results

In this section, we discuss and analyze the collected data and users feedback obtained from experiments. We employ success rate and average completion time to evaluate the accuracy and usability, respectively.

Success Rate: As defined in the previous section, participants were allowed to keep trying to log into their account until they have failed thrice. In other words we can say, a successful attempt means that a user is able to pass the authentication with a correct password in less than or equal to three tries. If all the three tries failed, then this attempt will be marked as failure. To measure accuracy in terms of success rate two terms 'first accuracy' and 'total accuracy' were defined below:

$$first\ accuracy = successful\ attempts\ in\ first\ try/total\ attempts \qquad (1)$$

$$total\ accuracy = successful\ attempts/total\ attempts \qquad (2)$$

Table 2. Accuracy of authentication in two sessions

Session	First accuracy	Total accuracy
First	85%	100%
Second	74%	95%

Table 2 presents the first accuracy and total accuracy of login phase in both sessions. We found that both the first accuracy and total accuracy in the first session are higher than those in the second session that occurred one week later. In the first session, 17 out of 20 participants were able to login successfully in their first attempt and the rest 3 participants were also logged in within the allowed attempts i.e., three attempts. Thus, our proposed system gives a total accuracy of 100 percent. In the second session, we found some decrements in both first accuracy and total accuracy. After one week of time interval, 14 out of 19 participants were able to login successfully in the first attempt. However, only one participant could not able to login within three attempts and fails. To know the reason behind the decrements in the percentage of first accuracy and total accuracy, we interacted with all the participants and specially with more cares those failed in their first attempts. From the interaction we found that the participants did not forget their password images but face some difficulties to shift the password image into its proper position. In summary, we can conclude that password images and patterns in our system is easy to memorize. The total accuracy is 95% even after one week time.

Average Completion Time. We have used human performance modeling tool CPM-GOMS, for theoretically measuring the execution time [3]. In CPM-GOMS every operator is represented with a predetermined time duration. The order of activities along with their time duration is represented in Table 3 and Fig. 6 illustrates the CPM-GOMS modeling of a pass-image entry. Thus, a single pass-image entry requires 8.5 s of time and the complete login process (four pass-image entry) requires 34 s.

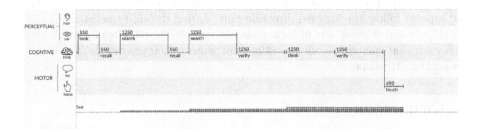

Fig. 6. Modeling of SGP. (First pass-image entry is 8.5 s)

Table 3. Order of CPM-GOMS operators used in SGP

Operator	Time (in milliseconds)
Attend password image	50
Look image grid	550
Recall password image	550
Search password image	1250
Recall pattern	550
Search pin	1250
Verify pin	1250
Store pin	50
Think for pass-image	1250
Verify pass-image	1250
Initiate finger movement	50
Touch	490

Along with theoretical measurement of login time, we verified the time duration experimentally. Table 4 presents the average completion time that participants consumed in the registration phase and authentication phase. The registration time is around 1.5 min on average. This is because in the registration phase participants need more time for selecting password images and to arrange the digits in a pattern. Thus, the time required in the registration phase is acceptable.

The average time each participants spent in the authentication phase is 33 seconds in the first session and 40 s in the second session. We discussed with all participants about the slight increase of the time duration. From their feedback we found the reason for increase in the time duration depends on two factors i.e., password recall and shift direction. In the second session participants needed to recall their password images and pattern. In addition to this, due to the practice before first session, the participants shift the password images in both directions i.e., when a password image is on the digit 7, user can shift 2 places in backward direction instead of 7 forward shifts. However, in the second session maximum participants follow the forward direction only, during the shift operation. A survey [16] showed that 35–40 s of login time is acceptable to 83.33% of participants if they felt that spending little more time can protect their passwords from shoulder surfing attackers.

8   Comparison

In Sect. 2, we have discussed the recent graphical password systems in the literature that are related to our proposed SGP. In our study of Por et al. [14] system, we have found that after observing one challenge-response pair attacker can get 8

Table 4. Average completion time in two sessions

Session	Registration time	Login time
First	92 s	33 s
Second	–	40 s

possible password images. To distribute images in the challenge they have used uniform randomization algorithm. Thus, after observing one more challenge-response pair, in best case attacker may get the two password images and in worst case attacker can reduce the possible password image set to 6. In their system one session consists of 3 rounds of challenge-response pair, so an attacker can easily derive the password images by observing one session only. However, in SGP observation of a single session does not reduce the possible password image set. Although Passmatrix [16] performs better than SGP, it's security strength based on the assumption on secure user activity. But, researchers have been considering that human users are the weakest link in the computer security system [14,17]. Wu et al.'s system [18] provides the same level of security as SGP however, it couldn't be implemented in smartphones due to the small screen size. Table 5 summarizes the detail comparison of SGP with other related and recent schemes in the literature.

Table 5. Comparison with other related schemes

Scheme	Password space	Resistant to SSA with naked eye	Resistant to RA of a single session	Resistant to RA of two sessions	Memory load
Wu et al. [18]	Depends on the number of icons & color balls	Yes	Yes	Yes	At least 3 icons, at least one color ball
Passmatrix [16]	$(7 \times 11)^N$	Partial	Partial	Partial	N Pass-squares
CD-GPS [12]	5.34×10^{18}	No	No	No	4 images in an ordered sequence, 6 clicks on a image
Evopass [19]	C(9,3)	Yes	No	No	3 images
Por et al. [14]	C(25,2)	Yes	No	No	2 images
Proposed SGP	C(9,4)	Yes	Yes	Yes	4 images, a pattern

9   Conclusion

With the fast development of the internet technology, there is an exponential growth in web services and apps across the globe. In order to protect user's privacy, authentication has received maximum attention in recent times. However, conducting the authentication process in public places might attract potential shoulder-surfing attackers. Now-a-days, public places are under surveillance for security reasons. Due to the presence of high definition video surveillance cameras attacker tries to extract the password directly or using hand gestures from the recorded footage. In addition to this, in crowded places attacker can also record the user's complete login process with smart phones or other recording devices. Authentication using graphical passwords can be revealed easily to the shoulder-surfing attackers. To overcome these problems, in this work we have proposed a secure graphical password system that can easily prevent one session recording attack and also resists upto six session recording attacks with high probability. Using a pattern and password images user can provide the indirect input for authentication in our system. From the user study, we have verified that our proposed system balances the security and usability unlike other existing schemes.

References

1. 000webhost. https://in.000webhost.com/
2. Android studio. https://developer.android.com/studio/
3. Human performance calculator. http://cogulator.io/index.html
4. Mobile marketing statistics compilation. https://www.smartinsights.com/mobile-marketing/mobile-marketing-analytics/mobile-marketing-statistics/
5. Bonneau, J., Preibusch, S., Anderson, R.: A birthday present every eleven wallets? The security of customer-chosen banking PINs. In: Keromytis, A.D. (ed.) FC 2012. LNCS, vol. 7397, pp. 25–40. Springer, Heidelberg (2012). https://doi.org/10.1007/978-3-642-32946-3_3
6. Chakraborty, N., Mondal, S.: An improved methodology towards providing immunity against weak shoulder surfing attack. In: Prakash, A., Shyamasundar, R. (eds.) ICISS 2014. LNCS, vol. 8880, pp. 298–317. Springer, Cham (2014). https://doi.org/10.1007/978-3-319-13841-1_17
7. Davis, D., Monrose, F., Reiter, M.K.: On user choice in graphical password schemes. In: USENIX Security Symposium, vol. 13, p. 11 (2004)
8. Kwon, T., Hong, J.: Analysis and improvement of a pin-entry method resilient to shoulder-surfing and recording attacks. IEEE Trans. Inf. Forensics Secur. 10(2), 278–292 (2015)
9. Kwon, T., Shin, S., Na, S.: Covert attentional shoulder surfing: human adversaries are more powerful than expected. IEEE Trans. Syst. Man Cybern.: Syst. 44(6), 716–727 (2014)
10. Lee, M.-K.: Security notions and advanced method for human shoulder-surfing resistant pin-entry. IEEE Trans. Inf. Forensics Secur. 9(4), 695–708 (2014)
11. Maheshwari, A., Mondal, S.: SPOSS: secure pin-based-authentication obviating shoulder surfing. In: Ray, I., Gaur, M.S., Conti, M., Sanghi, D., Kamakoti, V. (eds.) ICISS 2016. LNCS, vol. 10063, pp. 66–86. Springer, Cham (2016). https://doi.org/10.1007/978-3-319-49806-5_4
12. Meng, W., Li, W., Choo, K.-K.R., et al.: Towards enhancing click-draw based graphical passwords using multi-touch behaviours on smartphones. Comput. Secur. 65, 213–229 (2017)
13. Narayanan, A., Shmatikov, V.: Fast dictionary attacks on passwords using time-space tradeoff. In: Proceedings of the 12th ACM Conference on Computer and Communications Security, pp. 364–372. ACM (2005)
14. Por, L.Y., Ku, C.S., Islam, A., Ang, T.F.: Graphical password: prevent shoulder-surfing attack using digraph substitution rules. Frontiers Comput. Sci. 11(6), 1098–1108 (2017)

15. Shepard, R.N.: Recognition memory for words, sentences, and pictures. J. Verbal Learn. Verbal Behav. **6**(1), 156–163 (1967)
16. Sun, H.-M., Chen, S.-T., Yeh, J.-H., Cheng, C.-Y.: A shoulder surfing resistant graphical authentication system. IEEE Trans. Dependable Secure Comput. (2016)
17. Suo, X., Zhu, Y., Owen, G.S.: Graphical passwords: a survey. In: 21st Annual Computer Security Applications Conference, p. 10. IEEE (2005)
18. Wu, T.-S., Lee, M.-L., Lin, H.-Y., Wang, C.-Y.: Shoulder-surfing-proof graphical password authentication scheme. Int. J. Inf. Secur. **13**(3), 245–254 (2014)
19. Yu, X., Wang, Z., Li, Y., Li, L., Zhu, W.T., Song, L.: Evopass: evolvable graphical password against shoulder-surfing attacks. Comput. Secur. **70**, 179–198 (2017)

Towards Accuracy in Similarity Analysis of Android Applications

Sreesh Kishore[(✉)], Renuka Kumar[(✉)], and Sreeranga Rajan

Amrita Center for Cybersecurity Systems and Networks,
Amrita School of Engineering, Amritapuri Campus, Amrita Vishwa Vidyapeetham,
Kollam, India
ksreesh28@gmail.com, renukak@gmail.com

Abstract. Android malware is most commonly delivered to a user through the many open app marketplaces. Several recent attacks have shown that the same malware infects different apps in the app market. Automated triaging by computing similarity of apps to known software components can help learn the evolution and propagation of malware. While the emphasis of existing research is on detecting repackaged apps, a similarity analysis system that can identify similar portions of code in dissimilar apps, is important. Only few public tools exist that furnish these details accurately. In this paper, we present a proof-of-concept of an analysis system that compares Android apps using a technique that combines class and method features of an app. We use a two-step process that first compute similar classes and then compute similar methods of those classes. To identify similar classes, we propose a novel set of software birthmarks. We use Normalized Compression Distance to compute similar methods. The birthmarks are evaluated on a set of over 65,000 classes from 60 APKs. To evaluate the performance of our tool, we establish ground truth by manually reverse engineering each app. The proposed system is compared with Google's *androsim*, the only open-source tool for similarity analysis that also uses NCD. Our approach shows an improvement in accuracy in the worst-case when comapred to *androsim*. Finally, we furnish a case-study of our system to detect fake and repackaged apps by analyzing 1470 Android apps from various sources.

Keywords: Android · Similarity analysis
Normalized compression distance · Androguard

1 Introduction

Malware authors typically re-use code from existing apps, third party libraries or existing malware components to generate malware variants. Prior research on characterizing malicious Android apps has indicated that of the 1260 malware samples that were studied, 86% of them are repackaged variants of legitimate applications [50]. Research has also shown that several apps carry one or more ad libraries or backdoor components that leak information [49]. Recently, Google

© Springer Nature Switzerland AG 2018
V. Ganapathy et al. (Eds.): ICISS 2018, LNCS 11281, pp. 146–167, 2018.
https://doi.org/10.1007/978-3-030-05171-6_8

removed 500 different apps from the Play store that contained the same spyware [37]. Sophos detected thousands of apps in Play store that contained the same aggressive adware, banking bots and spyware [37] that has infected millions of users. Distinguishing a new malware or a variant (or clone) of an existing strain is crucial for timely incident response and containment.

To prevent a malware from being published, Google Play and certain third-party app markets provide automated scanning of apps. For instance, Bouncer, is a cloud-based security service offered by Google that performs static and dynamic analysis on a new app before they publish it. However, despite such application scanners, many malicious apps have gained entry into app markets [12].

Prior research on similarity analysis uses syntactic, semantic, GUI-based, graph-based or machine learning based approaches to detect code clones. GUI based approaches are suitable only to detect repackaged apps. Semantics analysis that use solvers or symbolic execution engines are time-consuming and not scalable. Fuzzy hashing [26] fails when the size of apps are not comparable. Juxtapp [18] is a well-known framework that computes similarity using k-grams. They remove third-party libraries from the apps and limits the size of the apps analyzed to 724 KB. Their approach is also vulnerable to lexical obfuscation. *Androsim* is a similarity analyzer that uses Normalized Compression Distance (NCD) as the distance metric. However, they abstract away classes and pairwise compare methods of all classes. This introduces additional computational overhead and results in the comparison of methods with similar structure from different classes. This affects the similarity value computed and generates spurious results. This drawback exists for any technique that compares methods of all classes of an app to arrive at a similarity score [1,18,38].

In this work, we design and implement a proof-of-concept of a two-step analysis system that computes similarity of two Android apps. In contrast to existing research, the similarity is computed only of methods of similar classes. This optimizes on the number of pairwise comparisons made. To do this, we propose a set of birthmarks that can identify similar classes. Methods of similar classes are compared using NCD as the distance metric. We use the research by Google's *androsim's* [1] as the foundation for NCD-based comparison. NCD is measured on signature strings extracted from the syntactic features of methods from an app's bytecode. To uniquely characterize methods of a class, we augment *androsim's* grammar to generates method signatures that also include features such as method descriptor, exceptions and annotations. We include third-party libraries in our analysis and do not limit the size of the apps analyzed. The focal points of our research is outlined below.

- We present the design and implementation of a two-step analysis system that computes similarity of apps by comparing methods of similar classes. Unlike existing literature where the atomic unit of comparison is a method, we propose to compare methods belonging to similar (identical implied) classes.
- We evaluate some existing birthmarks proposed for Java applications and expound why those birthmarks are inadequate for similarity analysis. We

propose two novel class birthmarks that can be used to identify similar classes. We evaluate the birthmarks on 65,000 classes from 60 APKs and demonstrate the precision of our birthmarks.

- We furnish a comparative study of our system with *androsim* that also uses NCD as the distance metric. We establish ground truth by manually reverse engineering applications to determine similar classes and similar methods of those classes. We obtain the results of similarity analysis using *androsim* and compute the number of false positives obtained. We discuss the reasons for the failures. Overall, using our proposed approach, we achieve a substantial improvement over *androsim* when comparing different apps.
- We analyze a total of 1470 apps from various sources such as app market places, devices and malware repositories. We present a case-study of our system to detect fake and repackaged apps by correlating the results of similarity with meta-information extracted from the apps. The case-study is conducted on 1000 apps. We do not attempt to classify or detect malware; the case study is just an application of this research.

The rest of the paper is organised as follows: Sect. 2 presents the background required for this study and Sect. 3 discusses related work. The design and implementation of our system is elaborated in Sect. 4. The results of experimental evaluation is presented in Sect. 5. Section 6 concludes our research.

2   Background

2.1   Overview of an Android App

The compiled code, data and resources required to run an Android program is packaged into an archive file called Android Package that ends with .apk extension. The contents of an APK file include - application code as .dex files, resources, assets and a manifest file. Dalvik executable (.dex) files are the compiled classes in the Dalvik bytecode format and is executed on the Android run-time. The manifest file is an XML file that describes permissions required by an app, package name of the application, minimum Android API version, a list of imported libraries, components, etc. Resources of an app include icons, drawable files, strings, etc., and assets include files such as textures and gaming data that are compiled into the APK. Finally, meta-information such as developer name and affiliated organization, contact information and app certificate (or signature) is stored in a directory called META-INF.

2.2   Normalized Compression Distance

Normalized Compression Distance (NCD) is the computable form of Kolmogorov complexity and lies in $[0, 1]$ [6]. Kolmogorov complexity $K(x)$ of an object(string) is defined as the length of the shortest program that represents the object [34]. For two complex sequences x, y, $K(x|y)$ is the shortest program that can generate

x from y. In practice, $K(x|y)$ is non-computable. Compression algorithms are used to compute NCD.

$$NCD(x,y) = \frac{C(xy) - min(C_x, C_y)}{max(C_x, C_y)} \qquad (1)$$

where $C(xy)$ = compressed size(x+y), $C(x)$ and $C(y)$ are compressed sizes of x & y. Intuitively, the complexity of a string is reduced by applying a compression algorithm. For example, if x and y are two strings to be compared, then when applying a compressing transformation on (xy), if nothing is compressed, then x & y are dissimilar.

2.3 Similarity

Similarity is defined as the amount of shared information between two objects. To state formally [6]:

Definition 1: Given a set X, a real-valued function (x, y) on $X \times X$ is a similarity metric if, for a given $x, y, z \in X$ the similarity $s(x, y)$ should satisfy

1. $s(x, y) = s(y, x)$,
2. $s(x, x) > 0$,
3. $s(x, x) > s(x, y)$, $x \neq y$,
4. $s(x, y) + s(y, z) \leq s(x, z) + s(y, y)$,
5. $s(x, x) = s(y, y) = s(x, y)$, if and only $x = y$.

Intuitively, (1) states that similarity is symmetric, i.e. comparing two objects in any permutation must yield the same similarity. (2) states that similarity of an object to itself is always nonnegative. (3) states that similarity of an object to itself is always greater than the similarity between two different objects. (4) is equivalent to the triangular inequality property of distance. (5) is equivalent to the identity of indiscernibles, which implies that two objects share the same properties only when they are the same.

Similarity and distance is correlated as [6]:

$$Similarity = 1 - Distance \qquad (2)$$

2.4 Software Birthmark

Software birthmark is a set of intrinsic characteristics of an application that is used to uniquely identify it. Tamada et al. [41] formally defines a birthmark for two programs x and y that are bound by a copy relation denoted by $\equiv$, i.e. $x \equiv y$:

Definition 2: If $f(x)$ is the set of characteristics identified in x by f, then $f(x)$ is called the birthmark of x if and only if:

1. $f(x)$ is obtained from x without any additional information.

2. If x is copied from y, then $f(x) = f(y)$

Three types of copy relations can be defined on programs x and y: (a) duplicates (b) variants obtained by renaming identifiers in the source code (c) variant obtained by removing comments. A birthmark must satisfy the following properties.

Property 1: For a program x, $f(x) = f(t(x))$ i.e., the birthmarks must be preserved even if x is modified.

Property 2: If x and y are two independently written programs then $f(x) \neq f(y)$ i.e., birthmarks of two independently written programs must be non-identical.

Prior research on birthmarking Java classes has proposed four birthmarks [41]:

1. Used Classes (UC): They are classes used within a class to implement a functionality.
2. Constant Values in Field Variables (CVFV): These are the constant values that have been assigned to field variables of a class.
3. Sequence of Method Calls (SMC): These are the sequence of invocations of methods of well-known classes.
4. Inheritance Structure (IS): They are a hierarchy of classes from which a class has been derived.

3   Related Work

Summary. Syntactic analysis based on code structure has been widely employed to gauge similarity between apps [9,10,17,18,26,29,44,49]. Graph based approaches to similarity analysis has been experimented in [4,11,15, 38,48]. GUI-based approaches to detect repackaged apps are studied in [5, 14,21,33,36,39,47]. Semantic analysis based techniques have been proposed in [16,32,43]. Other approaches include Shannon entropy [13], frequency analysis [45], meta-information [24], dynamic birthmarks [25], UI views, machine learning approaches [28,35] and traffic analysis [19].

Syntactic Analysis. DroidMoss [49] is a similarity analysis system that uses context triggered piecewise fuzzy hashing [26] to detect repackaged APKs. Code blocks are chunked based on some reset points, and a traditional hash of the chunks is concatenated to form the final hash of the APK. The distance between hashes is measured using edit distance. A threshold of 70% is applied to detect repackaged APKs. However, fuzzy hashing [26] fails when the sizes of the APKs are not comparable or when there is a change in the code layout [26,44]. Also, DroidMoss assumes that the apps in Google Play is legitimate.

Juxtapp [18] uses k-grams to find buggy code, pirated applications and known malware components in APKs. Prior to construction of a feature matrix, Juxtapp groups basic blocks based on package information. This makes their approach vulnerable to lexical obfuscation. K-grams are also susceptible to code transformations [12]. The scalability of their approach for large APKs is not known as the average size of the apps they have analyzed is 724 KB. They exclude common third-party libraries from their analysis. Research has shown that use of common third-party libraries boosts false positives and false negatives by a small margin, and can impact similarity assessment [27]. [27] also creates a white list of ad libraries. However, white-listing or excluding third-party libraries from analysis discounts the possibility of them being an attack vector.

Androsim uses Normalized Compression Distance (NCD) [7,9,30,34] for finding the similarity of two applications. They use a grammar [34] to represent instructions of a method as a string, which we leverage in our work. Even though Androsim overcomes the limitations of fuzzy hashing [26] technique, they compare methods of an app to obtained the similarity score [20].

In [10], authors use a three-fold approach to detect plagiarism. Here, both *.smali* code and Java byte code is compared using a popular plagiarism detection tool called MOSS. Additionally, they apply k-gram over the set of instruction opcodes with operands excluded. Here too, methods are the unit of comparison and excluding operands will induce numerous false positives. [29] locates malicious packages in Android apps without the use of a baseline app. It identifies code junctions where the switch to the malicious code happens. [17] information from the app such as its name and icon and compares it with a database of trusted applications to detect repackaged apps.

Semantic Analysis. CLANdroid [32] uses semantic features such as identifiers, Android APIs, Intents, permissions and sensors to detect similar apps. These features are too vague to be used for similarity analysis. In [43], code base of the application is partitioned based on multiple dependence relations, where each region represents a different behavior. [16] computes both function similarity and app similarity. They use an SMT solver to determine function similarity.

Graph-Based Approaches. Dendroid [38] is a tool that classifies Android malware families based on the control flow graph(CFG) of methods of an app. They also use *androsim's* grammar to extract the CFG of a program, and models it as a vector space model to study the frequency of occurrence of common code chunks in malware. In [4], authors use a geometric property of dependency graphs called centroid to detect similarity between methods. [11] computes static call graphs with sensitive APIs as its nodes. They compute a sensitivity coefficient by assessing the frequency of occurrence of sensitive API calls.

PiggyApp [48] is a system designed to detect repackaged apps by decoupling the repackaged code from the host app. They use agglomerative clustering on a program dependency graph (PDG) of the packages to do this. The decoupled module is then semantically analyzed to find similarities by using features such as APK signatures, used Android APIs, requested permissions, intents, etc. A linearithmetic search is employed to detect similar apps. Constructing PDGs at the granularity of the packages will fail to detect cases where malicious classes have been added to existing packages. Their approach is also not resilient to lexical obfuscation.

GUI-Based Approaches. UI based detection approaches though computationally intensive will provide the best accuracy in case of repackaged apps. However, they are not suitable to detect variants of malware when the only common component is the malicious code snippet that may or may not have a GUI component. In [5,36], the UI views of apps are compared to detect repackaged apps. [33] discusses a two-phase clone detection technique specifically for packed apps. In the first phase, they use a function-based fast selection to select suspicious apps. Subsequently, a schema layout of each app is matched for similarity. In a similar work, DroidEagle [39] extracts the layout resources of an app to detect visually similar apps. [14,21,47] use similar techniques that compare resource, assets and libs of apps to determine repackaged apps. [46] collects the run-time trace of an app and draws a layout group graph from the traces. The graph is used as the birthmark for analysis.

Other Approaches. Androsimilar [13] uses Shannon entropy to compare APKs with known malicious samples. The signatures of the malicious samples are computed apriori. In [45] authors develop a system to detect app clones using a two phase technique. In the first phase, suitable clone candidates are selected based on frequency of Android API calls and in the second phase they count the number of times each variable occurs in a code segment. [25] uses dynamic birthmarks by gathering API call traces of applications, which is compared using Jacquard similarity. The API call traces are obtained using the Monkey tool packaged with Android. Traces thus obtained will not have sufficient coverage to determine birthmarks accurately. AppIs [31] protects apps against run-time repackaging attacks by inserting guards into the app at sensitive points of an application. Hashes are used to detect a breach of the guards. [28,35] uses a machine learning classifier detect repackaged apps. [22] performs similarity analysis on the source code using b-bit min-wise hashing. [19] detects repackaged apps by monitor HTTP communication made to the server where in the app sends its information to the server.

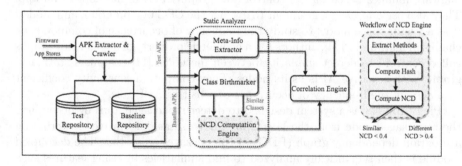

Fig. 1. System architecture

4 System Design and Implementation

4.1 Threat Model

We assume that the malicious actor has the ability to (a) access APKs in any of the Android market places (b) tamper and upload an APK to any market place (c) influence Android device makers to disseminate malicious updates or install malicious apps on his behalf (d) clone APKs and (e) tamper any one of the common third-party libraries.

4.2 Design Overview

The architecture of our proposed framework is shown in Fig. 1. We want our analysis system to have the following capabilities:

- *Resilience to lexical obfuscation*: Lexical obfuscation must have no impact on analysis. Common control flow obfuscation constructs may have an impact as the control flow of a code program is modified.
- *Detecting plausible attack through third-party libraries*: We conservatively include third-party libraries in our analysis since the libraries may themselves be an attack vector. This could however boost similarity values.
- *Resilience to mutable elements*: System must be resilient to changes to values of variables (for example, hard-coded strings) across app revisions.
- *Neutrality to the order of inputs*: The results of analysis must be independent of the order of inputs of the APKs.

The following are not goals of our prototype system:

- *Analysis of native code:* Native code is excluded from our analysis. Datasets collected from prior research show that only a very small percentage of apps contain native code [8].
- *Analysis of Multiple DEX files:* There may be more than one DEX file packaged into an APK as a work-around to a hard-limit of 64 K methods allowed in a DEX file [2]. In this case, only one DEX file is analyzed. We believe that this is the case even with existing systems. Optimized DEX files (ODEX files) are also excluded from the scope of our analysis.
- *Detecting or Reversing Obfuscation:* Comparing two similar APKs that are obfuscated differently may result in a low similarity value. Though we are yet to see this case, we do not discount the possibility. Yet, detecting or reversing obfuscation is not a goal of this research.

4.3 APK Extractor

APK extractor is an amalgamation of a *Python* script, a custom Android app and a crawler. The script extracts APKs from various downloaded custom firmwares, the Android app extracts privileged (or pre-installed) and secondary (or user) APKs from any Android device and the crawler downloads APKs from app market places. Privileged apps are extracted from *dir/priv-app* of the firmware, and secondary apps from *dir/apps*.

Table 1. Class and .smali code example

```
public class HelloWorld
{
    public static String VERSION="1.0";
    void HelloWorld()
    {}

    public void print_available() {
        Toast.makeText(this,
            "Folder exists!!..", 0).show
                ();
    }
}
```

```
.method public print_available()V
const-string v20, "Folder exist!!.."}}
const/16 v21, 0x0
move-object/from16 v0, p0
move-object/from16 v1, v20
move/from16 v2, v21
invoke-static {v0, v1, v2},Landroid/
    widget/Toast;->makeText(Landroid/
    content/Context;
  Ljava/lang/CharSequence;I)Landroid/
    widget/Toast
move-result-object v20
invoke-virtual/range {v20 .. v20},
    Landroid/widget/Toast;->show()V
return-void
.end method
```

4.4 Repositories

They are centralized databases where APKs are stored for analysis. There are two types of repositories - baseline and test. The baseline repo contains APKs used as baselines for analysis (called baseline APKs) and test repo maintains APKs that are to be evaluated (called test APKs).

Baseline repo includes apps downloaded from Google Play, official app websites and Nexus devices. Apps from Nexus devices serve as baselines to analyze system apps such as Contacts, Dialer, etc. The usefulness of using Nexus apps as baseline is unknown, yet we use them for system apps, for lack of other baselines. Prior research has also shown that Nexus apps are comparatively the safest based on three metrics- proportion of devices free from known critical vulnerabilities, proportion of devices updated to the most recent version, the number of vulnerabilities the manufacturer has not yet fixed on any device [42].

4.5 Static Analyzer

4.5.1 Notation

The notations used in the paper is outlined here. S_b is the similarity value when the first input is the baseline app (and second is the test app), S_t is the similarity value when the first input is the test app (and second is the baseline), V_b & V_t are version numbers of baseline and test apps, S_{zb} & S_{zt} are their sizes, Avg_s is the average similarity expressed as percentage, S_g is a boolean that indicates a match in the signature of the apps. M_i is the number of identical methods, M_s is the number of similar methods, M_d is the number of different methods, M_{new} is the number of new methods, M_{del} is the number of deleted methods, M_T is the total number of methods.

The static analysis engine is a toolkit written in *Python* and consists of three components - Meta-info extractor, Class birthmarker and NCD computation engine.

4.5.2   Meta-Info Extractor

Data that describes an APK is called its meta-information. This includes details such as developer information, version number, public key signature, size and permissions of the apps. The primary use of this component is to extract meta-information for use in our case-study. The module uses a tool called Android Asset Packaging Tool (*aapt*), to extract version and permissions of an APK. The developer signature is extracted using *openssl* command.

4.5.3   Class Birthmarker

This component categorizes classes as similar or different based on their birthmarks. Class birthmarks are properties of a class that are invariant across any transformation applied to it. The transformation may be in the form of obfuscation, incremental updates or augmented functionality. These classes need not be identical and a hash of the two classes will yield different values.

Section 2.4 identifies three types of transformations for a copy relation based on which existing research defines birthmarks. We define a stronger notion of copy relation based on which the birthmarks are evaluated and new ones proposed. Two programs x and y maybe - (a) variants obtained by redefining constants (b) variants obtained by reordering methods or instructions (c) variants obtained by adding new methods or deleting existing methods from a class.

4.5.3.1 Discussion on Existing Birthmarks

Of the existing birthmarks proposed from Sect. 2.4, we exclude Inheritance Structure due to the overhead in state and computation required to calculate it. The feasibility of the other birthmarks for similarity is discussed below.

(a) Used Classes (UC): The disassembled output of an APK reveal four types of used classes - new instances of a class (eg. *new-instance v0, Landroid/content/Intent;*), objects as method parameters (eg.*install(Ljava/lang/String;)V*), objects whose methods are invoked (eg., *invoke-virtual v0, Ljava/lang/Thread;->start()V*) and field variable objects (eg.,.*field public codes:Ljava/util/Vector;*). Of the four, we extract used classes from invoke instructions such as *invoke-virtual, invoke-direct,invoke-static,invoke-super* and *invoke-interface*.

(b) Constant Values of Field Variables: Constant values are developer specified and are susceptible to changes across app revisions. For instance, in a Google Chrome update, the only change to a particular constants class was a change in the constant *.field static final PRODUCT_VERSION:Ljava/lang/String; = "49.0.2623.91"* to *.field static final PRODUCT_VERSION:Ljava/lang/String; = "49.0.2623.105"*. Comparison of the classes using Stigmata [40], a birthmarking tool, showed a similarity of 99.5378%. This birthmark is excluded since it does not satisfy the copy relation proposed by our design.

(c) Sequence of Method Calls: Table 1 shows a classfile that contains 2 methods- a constructor and a function *print_available()*. In a comparison of the class with a transformed version containing reordered methods, the similarity computes to 88.847%. Reordering method calls is a commonly applied obfuscation transformation. We exclude this birthmark too from our design.

4.5.3.2 Discussion on Proposed Birthmarks

We propose two birthmarks for this research - Field Variable Type and Method Descriptor.

(a) Field Variable Type (FVT): For a class c, let $v_1, v_2, \ldots, v_n$ be the field variables declared in c. Then $\{t_i\}$ $(1 \leq i \leq n)$ is the type of the variable that forms the birthmark. The basic premise of this birthmark is that similar classes will retain a majority of the field variables even if their values are changed or undefined. The FVT birthmark for the class in Table 1 is *[static string]*.

(b) Method Descriptor (MD): It is a string that represents the parameters and return type of a method. For a method m of the form t_r $m(t_1 p_1, t_2 p_2, \ldots, t_n p_n)$ a string that concatenates $(t_1, t_2, \ldots, t_n)t_r$ forms a descriptor. This birthmark is resilient to reordering obfuscation. The MD birthmark for the class in Table 1 is *[() V, () V]*.

A match percentage of each birthmark is computed. If B_f, B_m and B_c is the set of all FVT, MD and UC birthmarks, then the generic equation for match percentage of any birthmark B_i is computed as:

$$MP(B_i) = \frac{2 \times |B_i|}{Total\#B_i} \tag{3}$$

where Total $\#B_i$ is the combined total of the number of birthmarks of type i present in both classes. We start with a fuzzy match threshold of 50% for each birthmark to determine similarity of classes. We do not use set intersection to compute the match percent since taking an intersection will remove repeated birthmarks.

Premise 1: Two classes are similar (identical is contained), if

$$(MP(B_f) > 0.5) \wedge (MP(B_m) > 0.5) \wedge (MP(B_c) > 0.5)$$

4.5.4   NCD Computation Engine

Figure 1 shows the work-flow of the NCD computation engine. It computes NCD of methods of similar classes on a signature string Sig_2 that describes a method. We use *androsim's* grammar [34] as the foundation for our research. Listing 4.5.4 shows the modified grammar. We augment the method features to include additional information such as method descriptor, types of invoke instructions, return values and exceptions.

```
Procedure ::=  MethodSignature | AnnotationList | BasicBlock
MethodSignature ::= AccessSpecifier | ExceptionList |
                    MethodDescriptor
MethodDescriptor ::= ParameterList ReturnType
ParameterList ::= Type ParameterList | Type
ReturnType ::=Type
Type ::='B' | 'C' | 'D' | 'F' | 'I' | 'J' | 'L' Id |
        'S' | 'Z' | '['
AccessSpecifer ::= Id
BasicBlock ::= Epsilon | StatementList
StatementList := Statement | Statement StatementList
Statement ::= Return | Goto | If | Field | Invoke | New
Return ::= 'R' | 'RV' | 'RW' | 'RO'
Goto ::='G'
If ::= 'I'
Field ::= 'put' | 'get'
Invoke ::= 'invoke-virtual'|'invoke-super'|'invoke-direct'|
           'invoke-static'|'invoke-interface'|
           'invoke-virtual/range'|'invoke-super/range'|
           'invoke-direct/range'|'invoke-static/range'|
           'invoke-interface/range'
New ::= 'new-' Id
Number ::= \d+
Id ::= [a-zA-Z]\w+
```

Let Ω be a non-empty set of methods and $\mathbb{R}^+$ be a set of non-negative real numbers. The NCD function on Ω is a function $D : \Omega \times \Omega \to \mathbb{R}^+$, where $\mathbb{R}^+ \in [0,1]$. Prior experiments and our findings have confirmed that the NCD of two identical strings is never zero [3]. The NCD value is influenced by the length of string to be compressed and the window size of the compressor used for compression. The question then arises as to how to determine methods that are identical to each other since the NCD of two identical methods is always non-zero. A pair-wise comparison of the SHA-256 hash of a method's signature (Sig_1), obtained by concatenating its method descriptor, opcode sequence and constant values, is performed to filter out identical methods.

$$Sig_1 = Hash(method\ descriptor + opcode\ sequence + constant\ value) \quad (4)$$

Premise 2: Matching Sig_1 is a sufficient condition for methods of similar classes to be identical i.e., $Sig_1(x) = Sig_1(y) \Rightarrow x = y$

Similar methods are identified by computing the NCD between the Sig_2 signature strings. The distance between two strings x and y is:

$$D(x,y) = \begin{cases} 0 \leq d \leq 0.4, & S \\ 0.4 \leq d \leq 1, & Diff \end{cases}$$

Final similarity is computed as the weighted average of the similarity of identical, similar and different methods.

$$Similarity = \frac{(M_i \times 1) + (M_s \times (1 - NCD_m)) + (M_d \times 0)}{M_T} \quad (5)$$

where NCD_m = the average NCD of similar methods, and M_T = total number of methods. The average NCD of similar methods is computed as:

$$NCD_m = \frac{\sum_{j=1}^{M_s} NCD(M_j)}{M_s} \quad (6)$$

Premise 3: $NCD_m < 0.4$ is a sufficient condition for two methods to be similar i.e., $NCD(Sig_2(x), Sig_2(y)) < 0.4 \Rightarrow x \sim y$

The final similarity value, Avg_s, is the average of S_b and S_t.

4.6 Correlation Engine

Correlation Engine is a complex event processing engine developed using a tool called *ESPER* that triggers an alert when a fake or repackaged app has been spotted. This is done by correlating the meta-information of apps with similarity metric. The engine was implemented solely for the case-study on detection of fake and repackaged apps.

5 Experimental Evaluation

For evaluation, we compute similarity in two different ways for both the proposed system and *androsim* (a total of four ways): (1) with respect to the baseline APK as the first input (2) with respect to test APK as the first input. We evaluate a total of 1470 APKs on standard desktop systems with 16 GB RAM and 4 cores. For some APKs whose sizes were of the order of 60 MB or more, analysis using *andorsim* took over a 72 h. Memory turned out to be a huge bottle-neck. We furnish - (a) evaluation of proposed system (b) comparative study of the system with *androsim* (c) a case study of the proposed system to detect fake and repackaged apps.

5.1 Dataset

For similarity analysis, we have used apps from the official websites of apps and Google Play as the baseline. We include widely adopted apps such as Whatsapp and Facebook that has over a billion installs, system apps and other apps obtained from the Androtracker [23] dataset. For system apps, we extract apps from the following custom firmwares- Cyanogenmod (versions 11, 12 & 13), AOSP-based ROM (versions 4.4, 5.1), Resurrection Remix (versions 4.4, 5.1), Euphoria, Cosmic ROM and from the following Android smartphones- Lenovo, Nexus 4, Nexus 5, Nexus 6, Xiaomi, Asus Zenfone, MI3, Lenovo A7000, Samsung Grand, Samsung J5. The following third-party app market places were crawled for test APKs: APKPure, Evozi, Mumayi and Anzhi. We also include 30 known fake app samples of popular apps such as Whatsapp, Microsoft Word, Google Chrome, Pokemon Go, etc. These apps were previously found on Google Play and other app market places.

5.2 Prelimnary Analysis Using Androsim

Below is a sample output of comparing WhatsApp *ver* 6.9 from a third party app store, with a baseline WhatsApp(*ver* 2.16.88) from their official website.

The size of the third-party APK is 199 KB and that of the baseline is 29.3 MB. This suggests that the third-party APK is a fake. The result of the aforesaid analysis was counter-intuitive in two different ways:

1. *Androsim* returns a similarity of 64.13% which is impossible since the size of the fake APK is not even 1% of the baseline. In this case, the baseline APK was supplied as the first input.
2. In another comparison that reverses the order of inputs, the similarity obtained changes drastically to 0.37%, with $M_i = 41$, $M_s = 98$, $M_{new} = 19122$ and $M_{del} = 59$. The drastic difference is due to how *androsim* computes similarity. It is computed as $\dfrac{(M_i \times 1) + (M_s \times (1 - NCD_m))}{M_i + M_s + M_{new}}$, where $NCD_m =$ the average NCD of similar methods. The similarity is a function of NCD, identical, similar and new methods. New methods are those methods that are not in the baseline app but is present in the test app. On reversing the order of inputs, methods that were previously included in the deleted list, is now considered new. Thus $M_{new} = 19122$ drastically reduces the similarity value and violates the symmetry property of similarity. Additionally, *androsim* determines M_i by computing the set intersection of the methods. This is done to retain the same value of M_i even when the order of inputs is reversed.

Table 2. Comparison with adware called ad.notify1

Package name	Androsim			Manual		# Total class
	M_i	M_s	M_T	M_i	M_s	
aimoxiu.theme.bnbszksi	2	7	26	0	0	13
co.lvdou.livewallpaper.ld81155	19	48	6233	2	0	1063
com.appbyme.app54117	21	63	21581	1	0	3326
com.cnmkmj.bookshelf	17	49	3706	1	0	596

We manually reversed many synthetic and third-party APKs to confirm our findings on the results of *androsim*. Table 2 shows examples of comparing some third-party APKs with an adware. The columns show M_i and M_s as computed by *androsim* and the true positives determined by manually reverse engineering the apps. There are two key observations on the results of *androsim*: (a) majority of the methods flagged similar/identical were false positives (b) they belonged to different classes (e.g. for the APK *aimoxiu.theme.bnbszksi*, all 9 methods belonged to different classes).

5.3   Evaluation of Proposed System for Similarity

Accuracy of the proposed system is contingent on the accuracy of two components - Class Birthmarker and NCD Computation Engine. Two types of false positives can occur in our system - (1) Dissimilar classes that are falsely labeled similar (2) Dissimilar methods that are falsely labeled similar. False negatives occurs when similar classes are labeled dissimilar.

5.3.1   Evaluation of Class Birthmarker

We measure the precision of Class Birthmarker as:

$$Precision = \frac{Correctly\ classified\ similar\ classes}{Total\ number\ of\ similar\ classes} \tag{7}$$

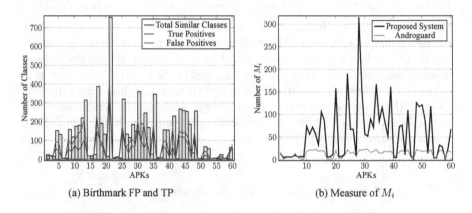

(a) Birthmark FP and TP   (b) Measure of M_i

Fig. 2. Evaluation of class birthmarker

The proposed birthmarks are evaluated using 60 APKs whose sizes ranged from 11 KB-8 MB, obtained from a third-party app store called Anzhi. These APKs were compared with malicious apps from the Androtracker repository. From a total of 65155 classes of the 60 APKs, 3544 classes were classified as similar. Since the proposed birthmarks are novel, we were unable to use Stigmata [40] to verify the results and resorted to manual reversing to assess the ground truth. We use the *JEB* decompiler to decompile the classes and *Apktool* to disassemble the APK. We restrict the number of APKs analyzed to 60 due to the difficulty entailed in manually reversing each APK.

5.3.1.1 Discussion on False Positives

Of the 3544 classes that were flagged similar, 1933 were false positives. The Class Birthmarker thus has a precision of 45.45%. Based on Premise 1, false positives occur when each individual birthmark incurs a match of over 50%. Figure 2a shows the graph of true positives and false positives of classes labeled similar. For some APKs with large number of classes, the false positives were more than true positives.

The birthmarks *Used Classes* and *Method Descriptor* contributed to false positives. First, recall that only one of the 4 types of used classes was implemented for this study. In addition, we count only one occurrence of a used class, even if the class is used several times. For instance in a comparison of two classes with one having a single occurrence of *Ljava/lang/System*, and another having 10, the match percentage is 100. Second, we excluded methods that did not contain a body, for instance compiler generated default constructor. As a result, this also eliminates abstract methods and interfaces. Lastly, a specific case of false positives occur for classes that statistically contain less number of methods. For instance, in a comparison of two classes with one containing 1 method, another with 3, and 1 similar method, the match percentage for method descriptor, $\mathrm{MP}(B_m) = (2 * 1)/4 = 50\%$.

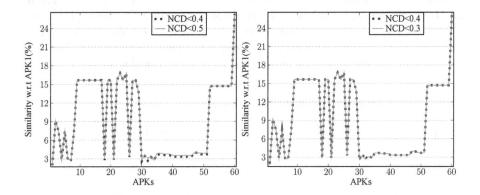

Fig. 3. Effect of NCD values on similarity

5.3.1.2 Discussion on False Negatives

We identified two corner conditions that result in false negatives. When comparing resource classes that contain no fields, the match percent of *Field Variable Type* is computed as 0. We deem this as an anomaly since when both the classes do not contain a specific birthmark, then the classes match for that birthmark. In a similar case, when the classes contain only constant definitions and no methods, the match percent of *Method Descriptor* is also 0. This we fixed by strengthening the match rule (Premise 1), to state that the match percentage is a 100, if the birthmarks do not exist in the classes being compared.

Despite the false reports, the results are encouraging. The failures identified can be rectified by improving the birthmarks. The threshold of 50% for match percent is more an intuitive threshold, the empirical evaluation for which is pending for future work.

5.3.1.3 Precision of M_i

We manually verify the precision of the number of identical methods for the 60 APKs reported by both the tools.

$$Precision = \frac{Correctly\ classified\ identical\ methods}{Total\ number\ of\ identical\ methods} \qquad (8)$$

Of the 837 methods reported as identical by *androsim*, only 279 were correctly classified as identical, which is a precision of 33%. Of the 3521 methods identified as identical by the proposed system, all of them were correctly classified. Figure 2b shows the results of our analysis. Based on the reported M_i, our system identifies more identical methods than *androsim* and have observed no false positives or false negatives.

5.3.2 Evaluation of NCD Computation

We use a threshold of 0.4, the same as *androsim*, to allow for a fair evaluation between the two systems. *Androsim* does not justify its use of 0.4 as the threshold. Hence we conduct a quick comparative study using NCD thresholds of 0.3 and 0.5 for the 60 APKs. Figure 3 plots the similarity obtained using 0.4 as the baseline. For the 60 APKs, there is only a marginal difference. A thorough evaluation of the threshold is a subject for further empirical study.

Table 3. Examples Proposed system vs Androsim

SL.#	APK name	Baseline ver	Test ver	Szb(MB)	Szt(MB)	Avg_s(%)	Proposed system (S_b, S_t)(%)	Androsim (S_b, S_t)(%)	Sig
1	Facebook	77.0.0.20.66 (Google Play)	77.0.0.20.66 (APKPure)	45.6	38.4	99.99	(99.99, 99.99)	(99.99, 99.99)	Y
2	Chrome	50.0.2661.89 (Google Play)	50.0.2661.89 (APKPure)	59.1	59.1	100	(100, 100)	(100, 100)	Y
3	Chrome	49.0.2623.105 (Nexus)	49.0.2623.91 (MotoG)	59.1	59.2	99.97	(99.98, 99.97)	(99.98, 99.97)	Y
4	Wallpaper	5.1.1-2237560 (Nexus4)	6.0-24 (MotoG)	1.67	0.09	1.31	(0.38, 2.24)	(69.45, 3.91)	N
5	Wallpaper	5.1.1-2237560 (Nexus4)	6.0-2343511 (Nexus6)	1.67	1.92	99.14	(99.55, 98.73)	(99.43, 97.81)	Y
6	Clock	4.3(2552012) (Nexus4)	4.3(2552012) (MotoG)	7.1	7.1	100	(100, 100)	(100, 100)	Y
7	Calculator	6.0(2715628) (Nexus4)	6-1.0(Mi3)	.953	.203	2.99	(3.24, 2.75)	(42.21, 8.23)	N

Table 4. Fake apps (from malware repo) - Proposed system vs. Androsim

SL.#	APK name	Baseline ver	Test ver	Szb(MB)	Szt(MB)	Avg_s(%)	Proposed system (S_b, S_t)(%)	Androsim (S_b, S_t)(%)	Sig
1	Whatsapp	2.16.88 (Official)	6.9	29.3	.199	3.98	(0.96,7.002)	(64.13,0.37)	N
2	MS Word	16.0.7030.101 (Google Play)	1.0	64.2	.38	2.34	(3.76, 0.93)	(59.96, 3.48)	N
3	Whatsapp	2.16.88 (Official)	2.16.235	29.3	32.42	79.57	(72.99, 86.15)	(80.92, 89.45)	N
4	Pokemon Go	0.29.0 (Google Play)	0.29.0	60.9	61	97.65	(95.30, 100)	(94, 100)	N

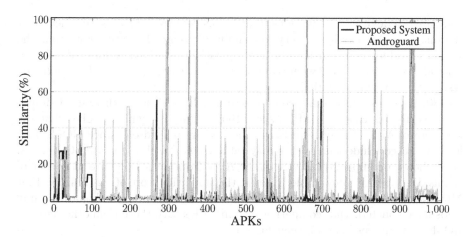

Fig. 4. Analysis of 1000 apps

5.3.3   Evaluation of Proposed System

The baselines for comparing user apps are obtained from Google Play. For system apps, the apps from Nexus devices are used as a baseline. We compare 470 apps-popular apps with their similar variants, popular apps with known fake variants and system apps with apps from other phones. For each comparison, we manually confirm the results of analysis. Table 3 shows select results for this discussion. Subsequently, we analyze a mix of 1000 apps both benign and malicious for our case study.

(#1) is a comparison of Facebook APKs of the same version from different app markets. Despite a 7MB difference in sizes, both the tools report 99.99% similarity on the apps. However, while *androsim* reported 4627 identical methods, 1 similar method and no new or deleted methods, the proposed system reported 7355 identical methods (the remaining numbers are the same). Our system detects more identical methods due to the class birthmarking feature. The difference is sizes is due to additional resource files in the larger APK.

(#2) shows a comparison of identical versions of Chrome APKs from different app stores. In this case, both the tools report a 100% similarity. (#3) is a comparison of Chrome extracted from a Nexus device with another extracted from MotoG. The APKs are of different versions and approximately the same size yielding an average similarity of 99.97%. For APKs that are similar, we make two observations (a) both *androsim* and the proposed system yields comparable results (b) reversing the order of inputs changes similarity only by a nominal amount.

From a total of 83 system APKs extracted from several Android devices, 51 did not contain a DEX file. This is because DEX files of those APKs were moved to a cache folder */data/dalvik-cache* for optimization. These APKs are only extractable from rooted phones. (#4& #5) are examples of a Wallpaper app (a system app) from Nexus 4, compared with versions extracted from MotoG and Nexus 6 devices. The versions from Nexus devices are almost identical, and the one from MotoG has a very low similarity score. However, note that the similarity values reported for #4 show a marked discrepancy for *androsim*. In general, we observe that when comparing apps that are dissimilar, *androsim* results show a wide variation.

(#6) is an example of a system app, from MotoG and Nexus, but of similar versions. In this case, the APKs show 100% similarity, which implies that the firmware of MotoG may have been inherited from Android stock ROM. This leads us to conclude that Nexus may be a viable baseline for MotoG devices. (#7) shows a comparison of Calculator APK from an MI3 device with that of Nexus. Despite the comparable versions, the similarity score of 3.24% shows that MI3 apps may have no bearing on the apps on Nexus devices. Thus, this study leads us to conclude that comparing system APKs with those from other custom ROMs may give us clues on their lineage.

Table 5. Summary of evaluation of 1000 APKs

App Category	Total	Anomalies	
		Proposed system	Androguard
Fake	30	0	30
Repackaged	2	0	0
System	144	3	57
Others	848	41	113

Table 4 shows select results of comparing different apps. #1 shows the results of comparing a version of Whatsapp from Google Play with a fake version (discussed in Sect. 5.2). Using the proposed system, $M_i = 415$, $M_s = 3$ and $M_d = 42617$ when the baseline is the first app and *androsim* shows $M_i = 41$, $M_s = 8$, $M_n = 7$, $M_del = 45$. This demonstrates that androsim results are not dependable when apps are different. The proposed system shows a similarity of 0.96% when the first input is the baseline. The 0.96% similarity is contributed by common Android libraries. The average similarity value when compared both ways is 3.98%. Overall, our tools yields better accuracy when compared to *androsim* even when the apps are not similar as demonstrated in #2 & #3. #4 is a comparison of PokemonGo with its repackaged variant. Both the tools show comparable results since the apps are actually similar.

5.4   Case Study of Proposed System

In this section, we perform a case study to assess the efficacy of the similarity analysis engine to detect repackaged and fake apps. We analyze 1000 APKs the summary of which is in Table 5 and Fig. 4. For all the comparisons, the baseline APK is the first. We manually examine the results of analysis to determine spurious results.

The proposed system identifies all fake apps, while *androguard* showed >50% similarity values in all the cases. The results are tricky for repackaged apps. While both the systems do not show anomalies, it is hard to identify a repackaged app purely based on similarity values alone. In our case, the correlation engine, correctly flags this as a repackaged app based on the app's signatures. One strategy to detect repackaged apps without using app signatures maybe to introspect into the differences in components rather than similarity.

From a total of 1000 apps, 200 apps showed spurious results using *androsim*, while the proposed system only generated 44 anomalies. The results of the proposed system can be further improved by augmenting the class birthmarks.

6   Conclusion

In this paper, we have presented an analysis system to accurately compute similarity of Android apps even when the apps are disparate. The proposed analysis is two fold- first we identify similar classes and then we identify methods of similar classes. Similar classes are determined using class birthmarks and methods of similar classes are compared using Normalized Compression Distance applied on signature strings generated using a grammar. An evaluation of the birthmarks show a precision of 45.5% in detecting similar classes. Our proposed system shows 100% precision in detecting identical methods of similar classes. This is a substantial improvement in the worst-case over Google's *androsim*, the state-of-the-art. The proposed work can be used to study the lineage of apps or detect malicious components in apps. A case study of the system to detect fake apps achieved a success rate of 100%. However, additional features such as serialized signatures of the apps may be required to detect repackaged apps. Overall for 1000 apps, the proposed system produced 0.4% anomalies in the computed similarity, which can be improved further by enhancing the class birthmarker.

References

1. Androguard (2016). https://code.google.com/p/androguard/
2. Android: Configure Apps With Over 64K Methods (2016). https://developer. android.com/studio/build/multidex.html
3. Cebrián, M., Alfonseca, M., Ortega, A.: Common pitfalls using the normalized compression distance: what to watch out for in a compressor. Commun. Inf. Syst. **5**, 367–384 (2005)
4. Chen, K., Liu, P., Zhang, Y.: Achieving accuracy and scalability simultaneously in detecting application clones on Android markets. In: ICSE (2014)
5. Chen, K., et al.: Finding unknown malice in 10 seconds: massing vetting for new threats at Google-pay scale. USENIX (2015)
6. Chen, S., Ma, B., Zhang, K.: On the similarity metric and the distance metric. Theor. Comput. Sci. **410**, 2365–2376 (2009)
7. Chen, X., Francia, B., Li, M., McKinnon, B., Seker, A.: Shared information and program plagiarism detection. IEEE Trans. Inf. Theory **50**, 1545–1551 (2004)

8. Crussell, J., Gibler, C., Chen, H.: Attack of the clones: detecting cloned applications on Android markets. In: Foresti, S., Yung, M., Martinelli, F. (eds.) ESORICS 2012. LNCS, vol. 7459, pp. 37–54. Springer, Heidelberg (2012). https://doi.org/10.1007/978-3-642-33167-1_3

9. Desnos, A.: Android: static analysis using similarity distance. In: AusPDC (2010)

10. Desnos, A.: Measuring similarity of Android applications via reversing and k-gram birthmarking. In: AusPDC (2010)

11. Fan, M., Liu, J., Wang, W., Li, H., Tian, Z., Liu, T.: DAPASA: detecting Android piggybacked apps through sensitive subgraph analysis. IEEE Trans. Inf. Forensics Secur. **12**, 1772–1785 (2017)

12. Faruki, P., et al.: Android security: a survey of issues, malware penetration, and defenses. IEEE Commun. Surv. Tutor. **17**, 998–1022 (2015)

13. Faruki, P., Ganmoor, V., Laxmi, V., Gaur, M., Bharmal, A.: AndroSimilar: robust statistical feature signature for Android malware detection. In: AusPDC (2010)

14. Gadyatskaya, O., Lezza, A.-L., Zhauniarovich, Y.: Evaluation of resource-based app repackaging detection in Android. In: Brumley, B.B., Röning, J. (eds.) NordSec 2016. LNCS, vol. 10014, pp. 135–151. Springer, Cham (2016). https://doi.org/10.1007/978-3-319-47560-8_9

15. Gascon, H., Yamaguchi, F., Arp, D.: Structural detection of Android malware using embedded call graphs (2018)

16. Guan, Q., Huang, H., Luo, W., Zhu, S.: Semantics-based repackaging detection for mobile apps. In: Caballero, J., Bodden, E., Athanasopoulos, E. (eds.) ESSoS 2016. LNCS, vol. 9639, pp. 89–105. Springer, Cham (2016). https://doi.org/10.1007/978-3-319-30806-7_6

17. Gurulian, I., Markantonakis, K., Cavallaro, L., Mayes, K.: You can't touch this: consumer-centric Android application repackaging detection. Future Gener. Comput. Syst. **65**, 1–9 (2016)

18. Hanna, S., Huang, L., Wu, E., Li, S., Chen, C., Song, D.: Juxtapp: a scalable system for detecting code reuse among Android applications. In: Flegel, U., Markatos, E., Robertson, W. (eds.) DIMVA 2012. LNCS, vol. 7591, pp. 62–81. Springer, Heidelberg (2013). https://doi.org/10.1007/978-3-642-37300-8_4

19. Haoshi, H.: Detecting repackaged Android apps using server-side analysis. Master's thesis, Eindhoven University of Technology (2016)

20. Huang, H., Zhu, S., Liu, P., Wu, D.: A framework for evaluating mobile app repackaging detection algorithms. In: Huth, M., Asokan, N., Čapkun, S., Flechais, I., Coles-Kemp, L. (eds.) Trust 2013. LNCS, vol. 7904, pp. 169–186. Springer, Heidelberg (2013). https://doi.org/10.1007/978-3-642-38908-5_13

21. Ishii, Y., Watanabe, T., Akiyama, M., Mori, T.: Clone or relative?: understanding the origins of similar Android apps. In: IWSPA (2016)

22. Ishio, T., Sakaguchi, Y., Ito, K., Inoue, K.: Source file set search for clone-and-own reuse analysis. In: ICSE (2017)

23. Kang, H., Jang, J., Mohaisen, A., Kim, H.K.: Detecting and classifying Android malware using static analysis along with creator information. IJDSN **11**, 479174 (2015)

24. Kang, S., Shim, H., Cho, S., Park, M., Han, S.: A robust and efficient birthmark-based Android application filtering system. In: RACS (2014)

25. Kim, D., Gokhale, A., Ganapathy, V., Srivastava, A.: Detecting plagiarized mobile apps using API birthmarks. Autom. Softw. Eng. **23**, 591–618 (2016)

26. Kornblum, J.D.: Identifying almost identical files using context triggered piece-wise hashing. Digit. Invest. **3**, 91–97 (2006)

27. Li, L., Bissyande, T.F., Klein, J., Traon, Y.L.: An investigation into the use of common libraries in Android apps. CoRR (2015)
28. Li, L., et al.: On locating malicious code in piggybacked Android apps. J. Comput. Sci. Technol. **32**, 1108–1124 (2017)
29. Li, L., et al.: Automatically locating malicious packages in piggybacked Android apps. In: MOBILESoft (2017)
30. Li, M., Chen, X., Li, X., Ma, B., Vitányi, P.M.B.: The similarity metric. IEEE Trans. Inf. Theory **50**, 3250–3264 (2004)
31. Lina, S., et al.: AppIS: protect Android apps against runtime repackaging attacks. In: ICPADS (2017)
32. Linares-Vásquez, M., Holtzhauer, A., Poshyvanyk, D.: On automatically detecting similar Android apps. In: IEEE ICPC (2016)
33. Lyu, F., Lin, Y., Yang, J.: An efficient and packing-resilient two-phase Android cloned application detection approach. Mob. Inf. Syst. **2017**, 12 p. (2017). https:// doi.org/10.1155/2017/6958698. Article ID 6958698
34. Pouik, G.: Phrack (2016). http://phrack.org/issues/68/15.html#article
35. Salem, A.: Stimulation and detection of Android repackaged malware with active learning. arXiv (2018)
36. Soh, C., Tan, H.B.K., Arnatovich, Y.L., Wang, L.: Detecting clones in Android applications through analyzing user interfaces. In: ICSE (2015)
37. Sophos (2018). https://nakedsecurity.sophos.com/2017/08/24/malware-rains-on-googles-android-oreo-parade/
38. Suarezl, G., Tapiador, J.E., Peris-Lopez, P., Blasco, J.: Dendroid: a text mining approach to analyzing and classifying code structures in Android malware families. Expert Syst. Appl. **41**, 1104–1117 (2014)
39. Sun, M., Li, M., Lui, J.C.S.: DroidEagle: seamless detection of visually similar Android apps. In: ACM WiSec (2015)
40. Tamada, H.: (2016). http://stigmata.osdn.jp/
41. Tamada, H., Nakamura, M., Monden, A., Matsumoto, K.I.: Java birthmarks - detecting the software theft. IEICE Trans. **88**, 2148–2158 (2005)
42. Thomas, D.R., Beresford, A.R., Rice, A.C.: Security metrics for the Android ecosystem. In: SPSMCCS. ACM (2015)
43. Tian, K., Yao, D., Ryder, B.G., Tan, G.: Analysis of code heterogeneity for high-precision classification of repackaged malware. In: SPW (2016)
44. Gayoso Martínez, V., Hernández Álvarez, F., Hernández Encinas, L.: State of the art in similarity preserving hashing functions. SAM (2014)
45. Wang, H., Guo, Y., Ma, Z., Chen, X.: WuKong: a scalable and accurate two-phase approach to Android app clone detection. In: ISSTA. ACM SIGSOFT (2015)
46. Yue, S., et al.: RepDroid: an automated tool for Android application repackaging detection. In: ICPC (2017)
47. Zhauniarovich, Y., Gadyatskaya, O., Crispo, B., La Spina, F., Moser, E.: FSquaDRA: fast detection of repackaged applications. In: Atluri, V., Pernul, G. (eds.) DBSec 2014. LNCS, vol. 8566, pp. 130–145. Springer, Heidelberg (2014). https://doi.org/10.1007/978-3-662-43936-4_9
48. Zhou, W., Zhou, Y., Grace, M., Jiang, X., Zou, S.: Fast, scalable detection of "piggybacked" mobile applications. In: CODASPY. ACM (2013)
49. Zhou, W., Zhou, Y., Jiang, X., Ning, P.: Detecting repackaged smartphone applications in third-party Android marketplaces. In: CODASPY. ACM (2013)
50. Zhou, Y., Jiang, X.: Dissecting Android malware: characterization and evolution. In: IEEE Symposium on S&P. IEEE (2012)

Cryptography and Theory

Secret Sharing Schemes on Compartmental Access Structure in Presence of Cheaters

Jyotirmoy Pramanik[1], Partha Sarathi Roy[2(✉)], Sabyasachi Dutta[3], Avishek Adhikari[1], and Kouichi Sakurai[3]

[1] Department of Pure Mathematics, University of Calcutta, Kolkata, India
jyotirmoy.pramanik2@gmail.com, avishek.adh@gmail.com
[2] Information Security Laboratory, KDDI Research, Inc., Fujimino, Japan
pa-roy@kddi-research.jp
[3] Faculty of Information Science and Electrical Engineering, Kyushu University, Fukuoka, Japan
saby.math@gmail.com, sakurai@inf.kyushu-u.ac.jp

Abstract. Various adversarial scenarios have been considered in secret sharing for threshold access structure. However, threshold access structure can not provide efficient solution when participants are classified in different compartments. Of many access structures for which ideal secret sharing schemes can be realized, compartmental access structure is an important one. This paper is targeted to initiate the study of secret sharing schemes for compartmental access structure secure against malicious adversary. This paper presents definitions of cheating detectable, cheater identifiable and robust secret sharing schemes in compartmental access structure and their realization through five different constructions in the information-theoretic setting. Moreover in case of cheater identification and robustness, proposed protocols are secure against rushing adversary who are allowed to submit (possibly forged) shares after observing shares of the honest participants in the reconstruction phase.

Keywords: Compartmental access structure
Multi-receiver authentication code · Cheating detection
Cheater identification · Robustness

1 Introduction

Secret sharing is a mechanism, which allows the data owner to store the data in a distributed manner on a number of storage providers, such that only specific subsets of them are able to recover the data. Cloud storage is a natural

J. Pramanik—Research is supported by Council of Scientific & Industrial Research (CSIR), India (Grant no. 09/028(961)2015-EMR-1).
S. Dutta—Research is supported by National Institute of Information and Communications Technology (NICT), Japan under the NICT International Invitation Program.

V. Ganapathy et al. (Eds.): ICISS 2018, LNCS 11281, pp. 171–188, 2018.
https://doi.org/10.1007/978-3-030-05171-6_9

application of this mechanism in which we can think of storage providers as participants. In traditional threshold secret sharing schemes all the participants are treated equally. However, it might be possible that the participants are classified in different compartments based on their power and/or attributes.

For motivation let us consider a scenario where one fixed participant is "essential" in the sense that without him no final decision can be made. However, the *essential* participant cannot take any decision at his whim - he must have support of say, any k "ordinary" parties other than him. This scenario when translated into the realm of secret sharing simply says that along with any k ordinary parties the *essential* party can recover the secret. No other conglomeration of parties will be able to recover the secret entity. A closer look reveals that the set of parties are partitioned into two disjoint compartments - first compartment contains only the *essential* party and the second compartment contains rest of the parties. To recover the secret, agreement has to be made between the levels to satisfy certain *threshold* conditions in the number of parties - 1 from the first level and k from the second level. A natural extension gives the idea of compartmental access structure where there are say, l many compartments and from each level at least a threshold number of parties are required to retrieve the secret. The studies of such access structure was initiated by Simmons in 1988 [22]. There are many follow up works with the aim to construct efficient *ideal* scheme, where ideal means that the size of shares and secret are the same. The first follow up work by Brickell [5] demonstrated two ideal schemes, however both of them are inefficient. Towards this direction, we can find notable contributions in [10,23–25,27]. But, all of the studies, till now, consider only *semi-honest* adversaries who do not deviate from the protocol but are interested in gathering more information than they are supposed to. In order to encompass more realistic scenarios, it is of paramount importance to consider *malicious* adversaries who can deviate from the protocol in an arbitrary way. Moreover, most schemes known so far implicitly assume existence of *synchronous network*, and they do not deal with cheating by *rushing* cheaters who may submit their shares *after* observing shares of honest users. In presence of malicious participants - also called *cheaters* - it is *not guaranteed* that all the shares submitted in the reconstruction phase are correct. At the end of the reconstruction phase, several issues may occur, in particular: an incorrect secret may be reconstructed or the secret may not be reconstructed at all. Therefore, it is an important issue to safeguard the interest of honest participants in presence of malicious participants. There are cheating detectable schemes for threshold access structure, e.g., [2–4,14–17]. *But, none of them initiated studies for compartmental access structure.* In some situation, it is required to identify the cheaters. Many cheater identifiable schemes for threshold access structure are proposed, e.g., [2,7,12,13,20,26]. *However, none of these approaches provide cheater identification for compartmental access structure.* Note that cheater identifiable schemes do not guarantee recovery of the secret, focusing - as the name suggests - on exposure of malicious participants. On the contrary, robust secret sharing schemes do guarantee reconstruction of the secret. During the last three decades, many results on robust secret sharing have been published, e.g., [1,6,8,13,18,19] in case of threshold access structure. *None of these approaches deal with robustness for compartmental access structure.*

Our Contribution: In this paper, for the first time, we propose definition as well as *constructions* of *cheating detectable, cheater identifiable* and *robust* secret sharing schemes realizing compartmental access structure secure against malicious adversary. In case of *cheater identifiable* and *robust* scheme, we consider *rushing* nature of malicious adversary. Our methodology is generic in the sense that it does not depend upon the underlying compartmental secret sharing scheme. We provide constructions of one cheating detectable, two cheater identifiable and two robust compartmental secret sharing schemes. We provide an estimation of the share sizes of the proposed schemes.

2   Preliminaries

2.1   Secret Sharing

In the model of secret sharing schemes, there is set $\mathcal{P} = \{P_1, \ldots, P_n\}$ of n parties and a dealer $\mathcal{D}$. The set of parties who are allowed to reconstruct the secret is characterized by an *access structure* $\Gamma \subseteq 2^{\mathcal{P}}$; that is, parties $P_{i_1}, \ldots, P_{i_k}$ are allowed to reconstruct the secret if and only if $\{P_{i_1}, \ldots, P_{i_k}\} \in \Gamma$. The model consists of two algorithms: a share generation algorithm ShareGen and a secret reconstruction algorithm Reconst. The share generation algorithm ShareGen takes a secret $s \in \mathcal{S}$ as input and outputs a list $(v_1, v_2, \ldots, v_n)$. Each $v_i \in \mathcal{V}_i$ is called a *share* and is given to a party P_i. In a usual setting, ShareGen is invoked by the dealer. The secret reconstruction algorithm Reconst takes a list of shares and outputs a secret $s \in \mathcal{S}$.

A secret sharing scheme **SS** = (ShareGen, Reconst) is called *perfect* if the following two conditions are satisfied for the output $(v_1, \ldots, v_n)$ of ShareGen(s) where the probabilities are taken over the random tape of ShareGen.

1. if $\{P_{i_1}, \ldots, P_{i_k}\} \in \Gamma$ then $\Pr[\mathsf{Reconst}(v_{i_1}, \ldots, v_{i_k}) = s] = 1$,
2. if $\{P_{i_1}, \ldots, P_{i_k}\} \notin \Gamma$ then $\Pr[\mathcal{S} = s \mid \mathcal{V}_{i_1} = v_{i_1}, \ldots, \mathcal{V}_{i_k} = v_{i_k}] = \Pr[\mathcal{S} = s]$ for any $s \in \mathcal{S}$.

Conditions 1 and 2 are called the *correctness* and *perfect secrecy* respectively.

A *threshold access structure* denotes the case where the access structure is defined as $\Gamma = \{A \subseteq \mathcal{P} \mid |A| \geq t + 1\}$. A secret sharing realizing this access structure is called (t, n) *threshold secret sharing*.

2.2   Secret Sharing in Compartmental Access Structure

Let $\mathcal{P}$ denote a collection of n participants who are so compartmented into l levels, namely, $\mathcal{L}_1, \mathcal{L}_2, \ldots, \mathcal{L}_l$ that $|\mathcal{L}_i| = n_i$ for $i = 1, 2, \ldots, l$.

Definition 1 (Compartmental Access Structure [5]). *The compartmental access structure Γ on $\mathcal{P}$ is defined as follows:*

$$\Gamma = \{A \subseteq \mathcal{P} : |A \cap \mathcal{L}_i| \geq t_i + 1 \, for \, i = 1, 2, \ldots, l \wedge |A| = t \geq (\sum_{i=1}^{l} t_i) + l\}$$

Let us denote such an access structure explicitly as $\Gamma(n, l, \{n_i\}, t, \{t_i\})$, or Γ in short and a secret sharing scheme realizing this access structure by Π_Γ.

2.3 (t, n)-Multi Receiver Authentication (MRA) Codes

Traditional unconditional message authentication codes consist of three participants: a transmitter, a receiver and an opponent. To send message to multiple receivers a trivial solution is to generate point-to-point secure information theoretically secure signatures for every message which however leads to heavy overhead and computations. Desmedt, Frankel and Yung introduced multi receiver authentication (MRA) codes in [9] which reduced this overhead. Naini and Wang [21] gave construction of (t,n) MRA code to allow 'w' multiple messages to be authenticated with the same key. Here, we briefly describe the construction by Naini and Wang.

1. **Key Distribution Centre:**
   (a) Generates $(w + 1)$-random polynomials $g_0(x), g_1(x), \ldots, g_w(x)$ of degree at most t each over $\mathcal{GF}(q)$, where q is a prime power.
   (b) Chooses n distinct points $x_1, x_2, \ldots, x_n$ uniformly at random from $\mathcal{GF}(q)$ and makes them public.
   (c) Sends $e = (g_0(x), g_1(x), \ldots, g_w(x))$ to the Sender.
   (d) Sends
       - $e_1 = (g_0(x_1), g_1(x_1), \ldots, g_w(x_1))$ to the receiver R_1.
       - $e_2 = (g_0(x_2), g_1(x_2), \ldots, g_w(x_2))$ to the receiver R_2.
       - $\ldots \ldots$
       - $e_n = (g_0(x_n), g_1(x_n), \ldots, g_w(x_n))$ to the receiver R_n.

2. **Sender:**
   (a) Wishes to send a message s.
   (b) Evaluates $A_s(x) = g_0(x) + sg_1(x) + s^2g_2(x) + \cdots + s^wg_w(x)$.
   (c) Broadcasts $(s, A_s(x))$.

3. **i-th Receiver R_i:**
   (a) Verifies if $A_{s'}(x_i) = g_0(x_i) + s'g_1(x_i) + s'^2g_2(x_i) + \cdots + s'^wg_w(x_i)$.
   (b) Accepts s' if and only if the above equality holds.

Proposition 1. *[21] The (t, n)-MRA Code described in Sect. 2.3 can authenticate up to w messages with the same key with impersonation and substitution probabilities $1/q$.*

Before going into any formal discussion, let us fix the communication model to be used throughout the paper.

Communication Model: We assume all the participants and the dealer are connected by pairwise private and authenticated channel. We also assume a common broadcast channel available to all.

3   Secret Sharing with Cheating Detection (CDSS) for Compartmental Access Structure

In this section, we, for the first time in literature, define cheating model for secret sharing in Compartmental Access Structure with cheating detectability. We provide an information theoretically secure secret sharing scheme with such properties in Sect. 3.2.

3.1   Cheating Model and Setup

We assume the strongest possible centralized adversary $\mathcal{A} = (\mathcal{A}_1, \mathcal{A}_2)$ who can choose and corrupt upto $n - 1$ out of n participants, where $\mathcal{A}_1$ and $\mathcal{A}_2$ denote two Turing machines who choose participants to corrupt them and modify their shares respectively. More precisely, $\mathcal{A}_1$ chooses T ($\leq n - 1$) participants and $\mathcal{A}_2$ modifies their shares after viewing that of all $n - 1$ participants under his ($\mathcal{A}$) influence. We define the game $\mathsf{Game}(\mathsf{CDSS}, \mathcal{A})$ to describe the nature of corruption in Fig. 1.

$\mathsf{Game}(\mathsf{CDSS}, \mathcal{A})$

$\quad s \leftarrow \mathcal{S} \qquad$ (according to the probability distribution over $\mathcal{S}$)

$\quad (v_1, \ldots, v_n) \leftarrow \mathsf{ShareGen}_{\mathsf{CDSS}}(s)$

$\quad ((i_1, \ldots, i_T), (i_{T+1}, \ldots, i_m), \mathsf{state}_C) \leftarrow \mathcal{A}_1(s)^*$

$\quad \mathsf{state}_R \leftarrow \emptyset$

$\quad \textbf{for } rid = 1 \textbf{ to } \mathtt{RidMax}^{**} \textbf{ do}$

$\quad\quad \textbf{for } \ell = T + 1 \textbf{ to } m \textbf{ do}$

$\quad\quad\quad \mathsf{state}_R \leftarrow \mathsf{Reconst}_{\mathsf{CDSS}}(rid, P_{i_\ell}, v_{i_\ell}^{(rid)}, \mathsf{state}_R)$

$\quad\quad \textbf{done}$

$\quad\quad ((v_{i_1}'^{(rid)}, \ldots, v_{i_T}'^{(rid)}), \mathsf{state}_C) \leftarrow \mathcal{A}_2(rid, (v_{i_{T+1}}^{(rid)}, \ldots, v_{i_m}^{(rid)}), (v_{i_1}, \ldots, v_{i_T}), \mathsf{state}_C)$

$\quad\quad \textbf{for } \ell = 1 \textbf{ to } T \textbf{ do}$

$\quad\quad\quad \mathsf{state}_R \leftarrow \mathsf{Reconst}_{\mathsf{CDSS}}(rid, P_{i_\ell}, v_{i_\ell}'^{(rid)}, \mathsf{state}_R)$

$\quad\quad \textbf{done}$

$\quad \textbf{done}$

$\quad \mathsf{output} \leftarrow \mathsf{Reconst}_{\mathsf{CDSS}}(\cdot, \cdot, \cdot, \mathsf{state}_R)$

$^{*}m = \#(\text{reconstructing participants})$ and $T \leq n - 1$

** $\mathtt{RidMax}$ denotes the maximum number of rounds in the reconstruction phase.

Fig. 1. Game between CDSS and $\mathcal{A}$.

A CDSS for Compartmental Access Structure consists of a share generation algorithm $\mathsf{ShareGen}_{\mathsf{CDSS}}$ and a secret reconstruction algorithm $\mathsf{Reconst}_{\mathsf{CDSS}}$. $\mathsf{ShareGen}_{\mathsf{CDSS}}$ takes as input a secret s and outputs a list of shares $(v_1, v_2, \ldots, v_n)$ and $\mathsf{Reconst}_{\mathsf{CDSS}}$ is considered as an interactive Turing machine that interacts with the participants multiple times and they release a part of their shares to $\mathsf{Reconst}_{\mathsf{CDSS}}$ in each round. $\mathsf{Reconst}_{\mathsf{CDSS}}$ takes round identifier rid, user identifier P_i, and part of share $v_i^{(rid)}$ and state information state_R as input and outputs either the secret or the special symbol $\perp$ ($\perp \notin \mathcal{S}$). $\mathsf{Reconst}_{\mathsf{CDSS}}$ outputs $\perp$, if and only if cheating has been detected. It is convenient to assume that $\mathcal{A}$ knows the secret (possibly from other sources) before $\mathsf{Reconst}_{CDSS}$ takes place.

The successful cheating probability $\epsilon(CDSS, \mathcal{A})$ of cheaters $\mathcal{A}$ against $CDSS = (\mathsf{ShareGen}_{CDSS}, \mathsf{Reconst}_{CDSS})$ is defined as

$$\epsilon(CDSS, \mathcal{A}) = Pr[s' \leftarrow \mathsf{Reconst}_{CDSS} | s' \in \mathcal{S} \wedge s' \neq s],$$

where the probability is taken over the distribution of the secret space $\mathcal{S}$, and the random tapes of $\mathsf{ShareGen}_{CDSS}$ and $\mathcal{A}$. The security of cheating detectable secret sharing schemes in Compartmental Access Structure is defined as follows:

Definition 2. *A secret sharing scheme* $CDSS = (\mathsf{ShareGen}_{CDSS}, \mathsf{Reconst}_{CDSS})$ *realizing the Compartmental Access Structure* $\Gamma(n, l, \{n_i\}, t, \{t_i\})$ *with cheating detection is called ε-secure if, $\epsilon(CDSS, \mathcal{A}) \leq \varepsilon$ for any adversary $\mathcal{A}$ controlling $n - 1$ cheaters.*

3.2 A Construction for CDSS in Compartmental Access Structure

Let $\Gamma(n, l, \{n_i\}, t, \{t_i\})$ denote a Compartmental Access Structure as defined in Definition 1. We represent the secret space $\mathcal{S}$ as an embedding in a finite field $\mathcal{GF}(q)$. Let s be the secret to be shared among the collection of participants $\mathcal{P} = \{P_1, \ldots, P_n\}$ which is parted into l compartments $\mathcal{L}_1, \mathcal{L}_2, \ldots, \mathcal{L}_l$ with $|\mathcal{L}_i| = n_i$ and corresponding level reconstruction threshold t_i, $i = 1, 2, \ldots, l$.

$\mathsf{ShareGen}_{CDSS}$: On input a secret $s \in \mathcal{GF}(q)$, $\mathsf{ShareGen}_{CDSS}$ outputs a list of shares $(v_1, v_2, \ldots, v_n)$ as follows:

1. The Dealer $\mathcal{D}$ chooses $l - 1$ elements $u_1, u_2, \ldots, u_{l-1}$ uniformly at random from $\mathcal{GF}(q)$. $\mathcal{D}$ computes $u_l = s - \sum_{i=1}^{l-1} u_i$. Let us call u_i, the 'level-share' for $\mathcal{L}_i$.
2. $\mathcal{D}$ so generates l random polynomials $a_i(x)$, $i = 1, 2, \ldots, l$, over $\mathcal{GF}(q)$ of degrees t_i, $i = 1, 2, \ldots, l$ respectively that $a_i(0) = u_i$. He further computes $w_j = a_i(j)$ for $j = 1, 2, \ldots, n$, when the jth participant P_j belongs to the ith compartment $\mathcal{L}_i$.
3. $\mathcal{D}$ generates n distinct field elements $x_1, x_2, \ldots, x_n$ uniformly at random from $\mathcal{GF}(q) - \{0\}$. Finally, $\mathcal{D}$ generates a random polynomial $g(x)$ of degree $(t_1 + t_2 + \cdots + t_l)$ passing through $(0, s)$ and evaluates $c_i = g(x_i)$, for $i = 1, 2, \ldots, n$.

$\mathsf{ShareGen}_{CDSS}$ outputs $(v_1, v_2, \ldots, v_n)$, where $v_i = (w_i, x_i, c_i)$, $i = 1, 2, \ldots, n$.

$\mathsf{Reconst}_{CDSS}$: $\mathsf{Reconst}_{CDSS}$ takes a set of 'm' shares as input and outputs s or a special symbol $\perp$.

1. Broadcast w_i, x_i, c_i.
2. [Local Computation] Interpolate the polynomials $a_i(x)$, $i = 1, 2, \ldots, l$ and $g(x)$. Further compute $s' = \sum_{i=1}^{l} a_i(0)$.

3. [Cheating Detection] If $s' = g(0)$ output s', else output $\perp$.

Theorem 1. *The secret sharing scheme* CDSS *described in Sect. 3.2 realizing the Compartmental Access Structure $\Gamma(n, l, \{n_i\}, t, \{t_i\})$ is ε-secure against up to $n - 1$ cheaters who may know the secret beforehand. Moreover the share size is*

$$|V_i| = q^3 = |\mathcal{S}| \left(n + \frac{t_1 + t_2 + \cdots + t_l}{\epsilon} \right)^2, \text{ where } \varepsilon = \frac{t_1 + t_2 + \cdots + t_l}{q - n} \text{ and } V_i$$

denotes the share space of the ith participant P_i.

Proof. Suppose, an honest participant P_h having the share $v_h = (a_k(h), x_h, g(x_h))$ belongs to the kth compartment $\mathcal{L}_k$. For a valid but incorrect secret $s' \in \mathcal{S}$ to be accepted by P_h, after parsing another check polynomial, say, $g'(x)$ of degree $t_1 + t_2 + \cdots + t_l$ with $g'(0) = s'$, the point $(x_h, g(h_h))$ should lie on the polynomial $g'(x)$. So,

$$\epsilon(\text{CDSS}, \mathcal{A}) = Pr[g'(x) \text{ passes through a point } (x_h, g(x_h)) \text{ unknown to } \mathcal{A}].$$

Since, both $g(x)$ and $g'(x)$ are two polynomials of degree $t_1 + t_2 + \cdots + t_l$ with a different constant term, both of them can intersect at (at most) $t_1 + t_2 + \cdots + t_l$ points. Hence, $\epsilon(\text{CDSS}, \mathcal{A}) = \dfrac{t_1 + t_2 + \cdots + t_l}{q - n}$. ∎

4   Secret Sharing with Cheater Identification (CISS) for Compartmental Access Structure

In this section, we, for the first time in literature, define cheating model for secret sharing in Compartmental Access Structure with cheater identification. We provide two information theoretically secure secret sharing schemes with such properties in Sects. 4.2 and 4.3 respectively. The first scheme uses MRA codes and the latter is a generic construction from existing threshold cheater identifiable secret sharing schemes.

4.1   Cheating Model and Setup

We assume a centralized adversary $\mathcal{B} = (\mathcal{B}_1, \mathcal{B}_2)$ who can choose and corrupt upto $T \le \lfloor t_1/2 \rfloor + \lfloor t_2/2 \rfloor + \cdots + \lfloor t_l/2 \rfloor$ out of n participants, with the restriction that the set of cheaters contains at most $\lfloor t_i/2 \rfloor$ participants from the ith compartment. Here $\mathcal{B}_1$ and $\mathcal{B}_2$ denote two Turing machines who choose participants to corrupt them and modify their shares respectively. We define the game Game(CISS, $\mathcal{B}$) to describe the nature of corruption in Fig. 2.

A CISS for Compartmental Access Structure also consists of a share generation algorithm ShareGen$_{\text{CISS}}$ and a secret reconstruction algorithm Reconst$_{\text{CISS}}$. ShareGen$_{\text{CISS}}$ takes as input a secret s and outputs a list of shares $(v_1, v_2, \ldots, v_n)$ and Reconst$_{\text{CISS}}$ is considered as an interactive Turing machine that interacts with the participants multiple times and they release a part of their shares to Reconst$_{\text{CISS}}$ in each round. Reconst$_{\text{CISS}}$ takes round identifier rid, user identifier

P_i, and part of share $v_i^{(rid)}$ and state information $state_R$ as input and outputs (s', L), where L is a list of cheaters ($L = \phi$ if no cheater is identified), if Reconst$_{\text{CISS}}$ detects cheating and honest participants do not form a qualified set, it outputs $(\bot, L)$, where "$\bot$" is a special symbol indicating failure of secret reconstruction.

The successful cheating probability $\epsilon(\text{CISS}, \mathcal{B}, P_j)$ of P_j against CISS = (ShareGen$_{\text{CISS}}$, Reconst$_{\text{CISS}}$) is defined as

$$\epsilon(\text{CISS}, \mathcal{B}, P_j) = Pr[(s', L) \leftarrow \text{Reconst}_{\text{CISS}} | P_j \notin L]$$

where the probability is taken over the distribution of the secret space $\mathcal{S}$, and the random tapes of ShareGen$_{\text{CISS}}$ and $\mathcal{B}$. The security of cheater identifiable secret sharing schemes in Compartmental Access Structure is defined as follows:

Definition 3. *A secret sharing scheme* CISS = (*ShareGen*$_{\text{CISS}}$, *Reconst*$_{\text{CISS}}$) *realizing the Compartmental Access Structure* $\Gamma(n, l, \{n_i\}, t, \{t_i\})$ *with cheater identification is called* (T, ε)-*secure if,*

1. $\epsilon(\text{CISS}, \mathcal{B}, P_j) \leq \varepsilon$ *for any adversary* $\mathcal{B}$ *controlling* T *or less rushing cheaters* L *and for any cheater* $P_j \in L$ *who submits forged share* $v'_j \neq v_j$.
2. $P_j \notin L$ *for any party* P_j *who does not forge its share.*

Game(CISS, $\mathcal{B}$)

$\quad s \leftarrow \mathcal{S}$ *(according to the probability distribution over $\mathcal{S}$)*
$\quad (v_1, \ldots, v_n) \leftarrow$ ShareGen$_{\text{CISS}}(s)$
$\quad ((i_1, \ldots, i_T), (i_{T+1}, \ldots, i_m), \text{state}_C) \leftarrow \mathcal{B}_1()^*$
$\quad \text{state}_R \leftarrow \emptyset$
$\quad$ **for** $rid = 1$ **to** RidMax** **do**
$\quad\quad$ **for** $\ell = T + 1$ **to** m **do**
$\quad\quad\quad \text{state}_R \leftarrow$ Reconst$_{\text{CISS}}(rid, P_{i_\ell}, v_{i_\ell}^{(rid)}, \text{state}_R)$
$\quad\quad$ **done**
$\quad\quad ((v_{i_1}'^{(rid)}, \ldots, v_{i_T}'^{(rid)}), \text{state}_C) \leftarrow \mathcal{B}_2(rid, (v_{i_{T+1}}^{(rid)}, \ldots, v_{i_m}^{(rid)}), (v_{i_1}, \ldots, v_{i_T}), \text{state}_C)$
$\quad\quad$ **for** $\ell = 1$ **to** T **do**
$\quad\quad\quad \text{state}_R \leftarrow$ Reconst$_{\text{CISS}}(rid, P_{i_\ell}, v_{i_\ell}'^{(rid)}, \text{state}_R)$
$\quad\quad$ **done**
$\quad$ **done**
$\quad$ output $\leftarrow$ Reconst$_{\text{CISS}}(\cdot, \cdot, \cdot, \text{state}_R)$

---

*$m =$ #(reconstructing participants) and $T = \lfloor t_1/2 \rfloor + \lfloor t_2/2 \rfloor + \cdots + \lfloor t_l/2 \rfloor$
** RidMax denotes the maximum number of rounds in the reconstruction phase.

Fig. 2. Game between CISS and $\mathcal{B}$.

4.2 A Construction for CISS in Compartmental Access Structure Using (T, n)-MRA Codes

Let $\Gamma(n, l, \{n_i\}, t, \{t_i\})$ denote a Compartmental Access Structure as defined in Definition 1. We represent the secret space $\mathcal{S}$ as an embedding in a finite field

$\mathcal{GF}(q)$. Let s be the secret to be shared among the collection of participants $\mathcal{P} = \{P_1, \ldots, P_n\}$ which is parted into l compartments $\mathcal{L}_1, \mathcal{L}_2, \ldots, \mathcal{L}_l$ with $|\mathcal{L}_i| = n_i$ and corresponding level reconstruction threshold t_i, $i = 1, 2, \ldots, l$.

ShareGen$_{\mathsf{CISS}}$: Suppose $(\overline{\mathsf{ShareGen}}, \overline{\mathsf{Reconst}})$ be an ideal secret sharing scheme realizing the access structure $\Gamma(n, l, \{n_i\}, t, \{t_i\})$ (without cheater identification), e.g. [11]. On input a secret $s \in \mathcal{GF}(q)$, the share generation algorithm ShareGen$_{\mathsf{CISS}}$ outputs a list of shares $(v_1, \ldots, v_n)$, where $n = n_1 + \cdots + n_l$, as follows:

1. The dealer $\mathcal{D}$ first runs the protocol
   $\overline{\mathsf{ShareGen}}(s) \rightarrow (s_1, \ldots, s_n) \in \mathcal{GF}(q)^n$.
2. Generate random polynomials $g_0(x), g_1(x), \ldots, g_n(x)$ from $\mathcal{GF}(q)[x]$ each of degree at most T for a (T, n) MRA code with n messages, where $T = \lfloor t_1/2 \rfloor + \lfloor t_2/2 \rfloor + \cdots + \lfloor t_l/2 \rfloor$ is the total number of cheaters involved.
3. Compute $a_i(x) = g_0(x) + s_i g_1(x) + \ldots + s_i^n g_n(x)$ for $i = 1, 2, \ldots, n$ as the authentication tag for s_i.
4. Compute $v_i = (s_i, a_i(x), e_i)$ where $e_i = (g_0(i), \cdots, g_n(i))$ is verification key of the i-th participant.

Reconst$_{\mathsf{CISS}}$: On input a list of m shares, the secret reconstruction algorithm Reconst$_{\mathsf{CISS}}$ outputs either (s', L) or $(\perp, L)$ as follows:

1. [Round 1] Broadcast $s_i', a_i'(x)$ by each $P_i \in core$, where $core$ denotes the collection of m reconstructing participants.
2. [Round 2] Broadcast e_i' by each $P_i \in core$.
3. **Local Computation:** Every party in $core$ for each $P_i \in core$, computes
   $support_i = \{P_j : a_i'(j) = g_0(j) + s_i' g_1(j) + \cdots + s_i'^n g_n(j)\} \cup \{P_i\}$.
   If $|support_i| < T + 1$, then put P_i in L, where L is the list of the cheaters.
4. – If $core \backslash L$ **is a qualified set:** Using s_i' for all $P_i \in core \backslash L$, run $\overline{\mathsf{Reconst}}\{s_i' : P_i \in core \backslash L\}$ to output (s', L).
   – If $core \backslash L$ **is a forbidden set:** Output $(\perp, L)$.

Theorem 2. *The secret sharing scheme CISS described in Sect. 4.2 is (T, ε)-secure against rushing cheaters under the influence of a centralized adversary $\mathcal{B}$ corrupting up to $T = \lfloor t_1/2 \rfloor + \lfloor t_2/2 \rfloor + \cdots + \lfloor t_l/2 \rfloor$ participants ($\lfloor t_j/2 \rfloor$ from the jth compartment), where $\varepsilon = \dfrac{1}{q}$. Moreover, $|V_i| = q^{n+T+3} = \dfrac{|S|^{n+T+2}}{\varepsilon}$, where $|S| = q$ and V_i denotes the share space of the ith participant P_i.*

Proof. Suppose P_c submits forged share $v_c' = (s_c', a_c'(x), e_c')$, where $s_c' \neq s_c$. We calculate the maximum probability of this cheating going undetected, i.e. $\epsilon(\mathsf{CISS}, \mathcal{B}, P_c)$. For this cheating to go undetected (i.e. $P_c \notin L$), we must have $|support_c| \geq T + 1$, which means that there is at least one honest participant $P_h \in support_c$. Now, this would be possible only if

$$a_c'(h) = g_0(h) + s_c' g_1(h) + \ldots + s_c'^n g_n(h) \ldots\ldots\ldots (\star)$$

Now, note that, s'_c and $a'_c(x)$ are broadcast in Round-1, whereas e'_c is broadcast in Round-2. This means that, even for rushing cheaters who might want to delay their responses within a round, s'_c and $a'_c(x)$ are announced by P_c without knowledge of $e_h = (g_0(h), \cdots, g_n(h))$. Still for $(\star)$ to pan out, P_c has to make a 'good enough' guess for e_h for which P_c will have a probability $\dfrac{1}{q}$ [refer Proposition 1]. ∎

4.3   Another Construction for CISS in Compartmental Access Structure Using Composition of Threshold CISS Schemes

Let $\Gamma(n, l, \{n_i\}, t, \{t_i\})$ denote a Compartmental Access Structure as defined in Definition 1. We represent the secret space $\mathcal{S}$ as an embedding in a finite field $\mathcal{GF}(q)$. Let s be the secret to be shared among the collection of participants $\mathcal{P} = \{P_1, \ldots, P_n\}$ which is parted into l compartments $\mathcal{L}_1, \mathcal{L}_2, \ldots, \mathcal{L}_l$ with $|\mathcal{L}_i| = n_i$ and corresponding level reconstruction threshold t_i, $i = 1, 2, \ldots, l$.

We present another CISS scheme for compartmental access structure using other cheater identifiable secret sharing schemes for compartmental access structures. Let $\{\Omega_i = (\mathsf{ShareGen}_i, \mathsf{Reconst}_i)\}$ denote a sequence of $(\lfloor t_i/2 \rfloor, t_i, n_i)$, $i = 1, 2, \ldots, l$, cheater identifiable secret sharing schemes.

$\mathsf{ShareGen}_{\mathsf{CISS}}$: On input a secret $s \in \mathcal{GF}(q)$, $\mathsf{ShareGen}_{\mathsf{CISS}}$ outputs a list of shares $(v_1, v_2, \ldots, v_n)$ as follows:

1. The Dealer $\mathcal{D}$ chooses $l - 1$ elements $u_1, u_2, \ldots, u_{l-1}$ uniformly at random from $\mathcal{GF}(q)$. $\mathcal{D}$ computes $u_l = s - \sum\limits_{i=1}^{l-1} u_i$. Let us call u_i, the 'level-share' for $\mathcal{L}_i$.
2. $\mathcal{D}$ runs $\mathsf{ShareGen}_i(u_i)$ to generate shares v_j for P_j, if $P_j \in \mathcal{L}_i$ for $j = 1, 2, \ldots, n$ and $i = 1, 2, \ldots, l$.

$\mathsf{Reconst}_{\mathsf{CISS}}$: On input a list of m shares by the reconstructing subset $core$ of $\mathcal{P}$, the secret reconstruction algorithm $\mathsf{Reconst}_{\mathsf{CISS}}$ outputs either (s', L) or $(\bot, L)$ as follows:

1. For $i = 1, 2, \ldots, l$, within the ith compartment $\mathcal{L}_i$, on input a list of $m_i = |core \cap \mathcal{L}_i|$ shares v'_i, $\mathsf{Reconst}_i$ outputs either $(u'_i, \overline{L}_i)$ or $(\bot, \overline{L}_i)$, where $\overline{L}_i$ denotes the list of cheaters from $\mathcal{L}_i$.
2. Evaluate $L = \bigcup\limits_{i=1}^{l} \overline{L}_i$,
3. – If **for** $i = 1$ **to** l: $\mathsf{Reconst}_i \to (\bot, \overline{L}_i)$
      - Break
      - Output $(\bot, L)$.
   – Else
      - If $core \setminus L$ **is a qualified set**: Compute $s' = \sum\limits_{i=1}^{l} u'_i$ to output (s', L).

- If $core \setminus L$ **is a forbidden set:** Output $(\perp, L)$.

Theorem 3. *The secret sharing scheme* CISS *described in Sect. 4.3 is* (T, ε)-*secure against cheaters under the influence of a centralized adversary* $\mathcal{B}$ *corrupting up to* $T = \lfloor t_1/2 \rfloor + \lfloor t_2/2 \rfloor + \cdots + \lfloor t_l/2 \rfloor$ *participants* $(\lfloor t_j/2 \rfloor$ *from the* j*th compartment), where* $\varepsilon = \sum\limits_{j=1}^{l} \varepsilon_j$, *where* ε_j *is the error probability for* Ω_j, $j = 1, 2 \ldots, l$. *Moreover,* $|V_i| = |\overline{V_j}|$, *where* $|\mathcal{S}| = q$ *and* $\overline{V_j}$ *denotes the share space of the* i*th participant* P_i *in* Ω_j *if* $P_i \in \mathcal{L}_j$, $i = 1, 2, \ldots, n$ *and* $j = 1, 2, \ldots, l$. *Finally, if all the schemes* Ω_i *are secure against rushing cheaters,* Reconst$_{\text{CISS}}$ *can be so modified that* CISS *described in Sect. 4.3 becomes secure against rushing cheaters.*

Proof. The proof is obvious, however, the following comment may be made. The error probability ε described here is a loose one (occurs due to union bound). The scheme described in Sect. 4.3 is actually (T, ε')-secure with $\varepsilon' = \sum\limits_{j=1}^{l} \varepsilon_j - \sum\limits_{\substack{j=1 \\ j \neq k}}^{l} \varepsilon_j \varepsilon_k + \sum\limits_{\substack{j=1 \\ j \neq k \neq m}}^{l} \varepsilon_j \varepsilon_k \varepsilon_m - \cdots .$ ∎

Remark 1. In Table 1, we compare between the two proposed CISS schemes in Sects. 4.2 and 4.3. We call the scheme *flexible*, when the security level (i.e. a success probability of the cheater(s)) can be set independently of the secret size. Use of cheater identifiable threshold secret sharing scheme described in [2] as the base threshold schemes (Ω_is) in Sect. 4.3, yields flexibility. Use of (T, n)-MRA codes in Sect. 4.2 provides re-usability of the keys whereas in Sect. 4.3, one shall obtain the share size of cheater identifiable threshold secret sharing, even in compartmental setup. For example, on use of base cheater identifiable threshold schemes from [2] in Sect. 4.3, the share size for $P_i \in \mathcal{L}_j$ is $q^{n_j + t_j}$ which is much improvement from that obtained in Sect. 4.2 as q^{n+T+3}.

5 Robust Secret Sharing (RSS) for Compartmental Access Structure

In this section, we, for the first time in literature, define cheating model for secret sharing in Compartmental Access Structure with robustness. We provide two information theoretically secure secret sharing schemes with such property in Sects. 5.2 and 5.3 respectively. The first scheme uses MRA codes and the latter is a generic construction from existing threshold robust secret sharing schemes.

5.1 Cheating Model and Setup

We assume a centralized adversary $\mathcal{C} = (\mathcal{C}_1, \mathcal{C}_2)$ who can choose and corrupt upto $T \leq \lfloor n_1/2 \rfloor + \lfloor n_2/2 \rfloor + \cdots + \lfloor n_l/2 \rfloor$ out of n participants, with the restriction

Table 1. Comparison between two proposed CISS.

Scheme	#Cheaters	Share size	Error	Efficiency*	Rushing	Flexible
CISS using MRA codes	T^{**}	$\dfrac{|S|^{n+T+2}}{\varepsilon}$	$\dfrac{1}{q}$	Yes	Yes	No
CISS as comp. of other thr. CISS	T	$|\overline{V_j}|^{***}$	ε'^{****}	Yes	Yes, if $\{\Omega_i\}$ are so	Yes, if $\{\Omega_i\}$ are so

* This column indicates, whether computational complexity of the reconstruction phase is polynomial in the number of participants n or not.

** $T = \lfloor t_1/2 \rfloor + \lfloor t_2/2 \rfloor + \cdots + \lfloor t_l/2 \rfloor$

*** $\overline{V_j}$ denotes the share space of the ith participant P_i in Ω_j if $P_i \in \mathcal{L}_j$, $i = 1, 2, \ldots, n$ and $j = 1, 2, \ldots, l$

**** $\varepsilon' = \sum\limits_{j=1}^{l} \varepsilon_j - \sum\limits_{\substack{j=1 \\ j \neq k}}^{l} \varepsilon_j \varepsilon_k + \sum\limits_{\substack{j=1 \\ j \neq k \neq m}}^{l} \varepsilon_j \varepsilon_k \varepsilon_m - \cdots$

that the set of cheaters contains at most $\lfloor n_i/2 \rfloor$ participants from the ith compartment. In other words, every compartment has honest majority. Here $\mathcal{C}_1$ and $\mathcal{C}_2$ denote two Turing machines who choose participants to corrupt them and modify their shares respectively. We define the game Game(RSS, $\mathcal{C}$) to describe the nature of corruption in Fig. 3.

An RSS for Compartmental Access Structure also consists of a share generation algorithm ShareGen$_{RSS}$ and a secret reconstruction algorithm Reconst$_{RSS}$. ShareGen$_{RSS}$ takes as input a secret s and outputs a list of shares $(v_1, v_2, \ldots, v_n)$ and Reconst$_{RSS}$ is considered as an interactive Turing machine that interacts with the participants multiple times and they release a part of their shares to Reconst$_{RSS}$ in each round. Reconst$_{RSS}$ takes round identifier rid, user identifier P_i, and part of share $v_i^{(rid)}$ and state information $state_R$ as input and outputs updated state information. When interactions with users are finished, Reconst$_{RSS}$ outputs the secret.

The successful cheating probability $\epsilon(RSS, \mathcal{C})$ against RSS = (ShareGen$_{RSS}$, Reconst$_{RSS}$) is defined as

$$\epsilon(RSS, \mathcal{C}) = Pr[s' \leftarrow \text{Reconst}_{RSS} | s' \in \mathcal{S} \wedge s' \neq s]$$

where the probability is taken over the distribution of the secret space $\mathcal{S}$, and the random tapes of ShareGen$_{RSS}$ and $\mathcal{C}$. The security of robust secret sharing schemes in Compartmental Access Structure is defined as follows:

Definition 4. *A secret sharing scheme RSS = (ShareGen$_{RSS}$, Reconst$_{RSS}$) realizing the Compartmental Access Structure $\Gamma(n, l, \{n_i\}, t, \{t_i\})$ is called (T, δ)-robust if, $\epsilon(RSS, \mathcal{C}) \leq \delta$ for any adversary $\mathcal{C}$ controlling up to T rushing cheaters as a minority of participants from every compartment.*

Game(RSS, $\mathcal{C}$)

$s \leftarrow \mathcal{S}$ (according to the probability distribution over $\mathcal{S}$)

$(v_1, \ldots, v_n) \leftarrow \mathsf{ShareGen}_{\mathsf{RSS}}(s)$

$((i_1, \ldots, i_T), (i_{T+1}, \ldots, i_n), \mathsf{state}_\mathcal{C}) \leftarrow \mathcal{C}_1()^*$

$\mathsf{state}_R \leftarrow \emptyset$

for $rid = 1$ **to** $\mathtt{RidMax}^{**}$ **do**

  for $\ell = T + 1$ **to** n **do**

    $\mathsf{state}_R \leftarrow \mathsf{Reconst}_{\mathsf{RSS}}(rid, P_{i_\ell}, v_{i_\ell}^{(rid)}, \mathsf{state}_R)$

  done

  $((v_{i_1}^{\prime(rid)}, \ldots, v_{i_T}^{\prime(rid)}), \mathsf{state}_\mathcal{C}) \leftarrow \mathcal{C}_2(rid, (v_{i_{T+1}}^{(rid)}, \ldots, v_{i_n}^{(rid)}), (v_{i_1}, \ldots, v_{i_T}), \mathsf{state}_\mathcal{C})$

  for $\ell = 1$ **to** T **do**

    $\mathsf{state}_R \leftarrow \mathsf{Reconst}_{\mathsf{RSS}}(rid, P_{i_\ell}, v_{i_\ell}^{\prime(rid)}, \mathsf{state}_R)$

  done

done

output $\leftarrow \mathsf{Reconst}_{\mathsf{RSS}}(\cdot, \cdot, \cdot, \mathsf{state}_R)$

$^*T = \lfloor n_1/2 \rfloor + \lfloor n_2/2 \rfloor + \cdots + \lfloor n_l/2 \rfloor$

** $\mathtt{RidMax}$ denotes the maximum number of rounds in the reconstruction phase.

Fig. 3. Game between RSS and $\mathcal{C}$.

5.2 A Construction for RSS in Compartmental Access Structure Using (T, n)-MRA Codes

Let $\Gamma(n, l, \{n_i\}, t, \{t_i\})$ denote a Compartmental Access Structure as defined in Definition 1. We represent the secret space $\mathcal{S}$ as an embedding in a finite field $\mathcal{GF}(q)$. Let s be the secret to be shared among the collection of participants $\mathcal{P} = \{P_1, \ldots, P_n\}$ which is parted into l compartments $\mathcal{L}_1, \mathcal{L}_2, \ldots, \mathcal{L}_l$ with $|\mathcal{L}_i| = n_i$ and corresponding level reconstruction threshold t_i, $i = 1, 2, \ldots, l$.

ShareGen$_{\mathsf{RSS}}$: Suppose $(\overline{\mathsf{ShareGen}}, \overline{\mathsf{Reconst}})$ be an ideal secret sharing scheme realizing the access structure $\Gamma(n, l, \{n_i\}, t, \{t_i\})$ (without robustness), e.g. [11]. On input a secret $s \in \mathcal{GF}(q)$, the share generation algorithm $\mathsf{ShareGen}_{\mathsf{RSS}}$ outputs a list of shares $(v_1, \ldots, v_n)$, where $n = n_1 + \cdots + n_l$, as follows:

1. The dealer $\mathcal{D}$ first runs the protocol
   $\overline{\mathsf{ShareGen}}(s) \rightarrow (s_1, \ldots, s_n) \in \mathcal{GF}(q)^n$.
2. Generate random polynomials $g_0(x), g_1(x), \ldots, g_n(x)$ from $\mathcal{GF}(q)[x]$ each of degree at most T for a (T, n) MRA code with n messages, where $T = \lfloor n_1/2 \rfloor + \lfloor n_2/2 \rfloor + \cdots + \lfloor n_l/2 \rfloor$ is the total number of cheaters involved.
3. Compute $a_i(x) = g_0(x) + s_i g_1(x) + \ldots + s_i^n g_n(x)$ for $i = 1, 2, \ldots, n$ as the authentication tag for s_i.
4. Compute $v_i = (s_i, a_i(x), e_i)$ where $e_i = (g_0(i), \cdots, g_n(i))$ is verification key of the i-th participant.

Reconst$_{\mathsf{CISS}}$: On input a list of n shares, the secret reconstruction algorithm $\mathsf{Reconst}_{\mathsf{RSS}}$ outputs either s' or $(\perp, L)$ as follows:

1. [Round 1] Broadcast $s'_i, a'_i(x)$.
2. [Round 2] Broadcast e'_i.
3. **Local Computation:**
   - Compute the largest self consistent subset *core* of participants who are 'happy' with each other's shares. i.e. for all $P_i, P_j \in core$, $a'_i(j) = g_0(j) + s'_i g_1(j) + \ldots + s'^n_i g_n(j)$.
   - Clearly, *core* contains all the honest participants. Run $\overline{\text{Reconst}}\{s'_i : P_i \in core\}$ to output s'. If no such secret exists in $\mathcal{S}$, then output $\perp$.

Theorem 4. *The secret sharing scheme RSS described in Sect. 5.2 is (T, δ)-robust against rushing cheaters under the influence of a centralized adversary $\mathcal{C}$ corrupting up to $T = \lfloor n_1/2 \rfloor + \lfloor n_2/2 \rfloor + \cdots + \lfloor n_l/2 \rfloor$ participants ($\lfloor n_j/2 \rfloor$ from the jth compartment), where $\delta = \dfrac{1}{q}$. Moreover, $|V_i| = q^{n+T+3} = \dfrac{|\mathcal{S}|^{n+T+2}}{\delta}$, where $|\mathcal{S}| = q$ and V_i denotes the share space of the ith participant P_i.*

Proof. We need to show that $\epsilon(\text{RSS}, \mathcal{C}) = \dfrac{1}{q}$. The rest is obvious.

Now $\epsilon(\text{RSS}, \mathcal{C})$ denotes the probability that a different secret $s'(\neq s)$ is reconstructed. Suppose some cheating participant, say P_c, submits forged share $v'_c = (s'_c, a'_c(x), e'_c)$ where $s'_c \neq s_c$. Now for this cheating to work out in favour of the cheaters, there must exist one honest participant P_h who authenticates P_c's share, i.e. $a'_c(h) = g_0(h) + s'_c g_1(h) + \ldots + s'^n_c g_n(h)$. Now, this happens with a nominal probability $\dfrac{1}{q}$, due to the error probability of the underlying (T, n)-MRA code (refer Proposition 1).

Altogether, this implies that $\epsilon(\text{RSS}, \mathcal{C}) = \dfrac{1}{q}$. ∎

5.3   Another Construction for RSS in Compartmental Access Structure Using Composition of Threshold RSS Schemes

We present another RSS scheme for compartmental access structure using other robust secret sharing schemes for threshold access structures. Let $\{\Omega_i = (\text{ShareGen}_i, \text{Reconst}_i)\}$ denote a sequence of $(\lfloor n_i/2 \rfloor, \delta_i)$, $i = 1, 2, \ldots, l$, robust secret sharing schemes respectively.

ShareGen$_\text{RSS}$: On input a secret $s \in \mathcal{GF}(q)$, ShareGen$_\text{RSS}$ outputs a list of shares $(v_1, v_2, \ldots, v_n)$ as follows:

1. The Dealer $\mathcal{D}$ chooses $l - 1$ elements $u_1, u_2, \ldots, u_{l-1}$ uniformly at random from $\mathcal{GF}(q)$. $\mathcal{D}$ computes $u_l = s - \sum_{i=1}^{l-1} u_i$. Let us call u_i, the 'level-share' for $\mathcal{L}_i$.
2. $\mathcal{D}$ runs ShareGen$_i(u_i)$ to generate shares v_j for P_j, if $P_j \in \mathcal{L}_i$ for $j = 1, 2, \ldots, n$ and $i = 1, 2, \ldots, l$.

Reconst$_{\text{CISS}}$: On input a list of n shares by the reconstructing the largest self-consistent subset *core* of $\mathcal{P}$, the secret reconstruction algorithm Reconst$_{\text{RSS}}$ outputs either s' or $\perp$ as follows:

1. For $i = 1, 2, \ldots, l$, within the ith compartment $\mathcal{L}_i$, on input a list of n_i shares v'_i, Reconst$_i$ outputs either u'_i or $\perp$.
2. $\quad$ – If **for** $i = 1$ **to** l: Reconst$_i \to \perp$
   - Break
   - Output $\perp$.
   – Else
   - If *core* **is a qualified set:** Compute $s' = \sum_{i=1}^{l} u'_i$ to output s'.
   - If *core* **is a forbidden set:** Output $\perp$.

Theorem 5. *The secret sharing scheme RSS described in Sect. 5.3 is (T, δ)-secure against cheaters under the influence of a centralized adversary $\mathcal{C}$ corrupting up to $T = \lfloor n_1/2 \rfloor + \lfloor n_2/2 \rfloor + \cdots + \lfloor n_l/2 \rfloor$ participants ($\lfloor n_j/2 \rfloor$ from the jth compartment), where $\delta = \sum_{j=1}^{l} \delta_j$, where δ_j is the error probability for Ω_j, $j = 1, 2 \ldots, l$. Moreover, $|V_i| = |\overline{V_j}|$, where $|\mathcal{S}| = q$ and $\overline{V_j}$ denotes the share space of the ith participant P_i in Ω_j if $P_i \in \mathcal{L}_j$, $i = 1, 2, \ldots, n$ and $j = 1, 2, \ldots, l$. Finally, if all the schemes Ω_i are robust against rushing cheaters, Reconst$_{\text{RSS}}$ can be so modified that RSS described in Sect. 5.3 becomes robust against rushing cheaters.*

Proof. The proof is obvious. In addition, it should be mentioned that the scheme is actually (T, δ')-secure where $\delta' = \sum_{j=1}^{l} \delta_j - \sum_{\substack{j=1 \\ j \neq k}}^{l} \delta_j \delta_k + \sum_{\substack{j=1 \\ j \neq k \neq m}}^{l} \delta_j \delta_k \delta_m - \cdots$ and δ_j denotes the error probablity of the scheme Ω_j, $j = 1, 2, 3, \ldots, l$. $\blacksquare$

Table 2. Comparison between two proposed RSS.

Scheme	#Cheaters	Share size	Error	Efficiency*	Rushing	Flexible
RSS using MRA codes	T**	$\dfrac{|\mathcal{S}|^{n+T+2}}{\varepsilon}$	$\dfrac{1}{q}$	Yes	Yes	No
RSS as comp. of other thr. RSS	T	$|\overline{V_j}|$***	δ'****	Yes	Yes, if $\{\Omega_i\}$ are so	Yes, if $\{\Omega_i\}$ are so

* This column indicates, whether computational complexity of the reconstruction phase is polynomial in the number of participants n or not.

** $T = \lfloor n_1/2 \rfloor + \lfloor n_2/2 \rfloor + \cdots + \lfloor n_l/2 \rfloor$

*** $\overline{V_j}$ denotes the share space of the ith participant P_i in Ω_j if $P_i \in \mathcal{L}_j$, $i = 1, 2, \ldots, n$ and $j = 1, 2, \ldots, l$

**** $\delta' = \sum_{j=1}^{l} \delta_j - \sum_{\substack{j=1 \\ j \neq k}}^{l} \delta_j \delta_k + \sum_{\substack{j=1 \\ j \neq k \neq m}}^{l} \delta_j \delta_k \delta_m - \cdots$

Remark 2. In Table 2, we compare between the two proposed RSS schemes in Sects. 5.2 and 5.3. Use of robust threshold secret sharing scheme described in [19] as the base threshold schemes (Ω_i) in Sect. 5.3, yields flexibility. Note that, use of (T, n)-MRA codes in Sect. 5.2 inherits the property of re-usability of the keys whereas in Sect. 5.3, one shall obtain the share size of robust threshold secret sharing, even in compartmental setup. For example, on use of base robust threshold schemes from [19] (with slight modification to suit to our context) in Sect. 5.3, the share size for $P_i \in \mathcal{L}_j$ is $q^{2n_j + \lfloor n_j/2 \rfloor - 1}$ which is much improvement from that obtained in Sect. 5.2 as q^{n+T+3}.

6   Conclusion

We provided definitions for cheating detectable, cheater identifiable and robust secret sharing schemes on compartmental access structure and constructed schemes which are information theoretically secure against malicious adversary. In case of cheater identification and robustness, we consider *rushing* adversary. Studying the lower bounds of share sizes is an interesting problem for future work.

References

1. Adhikari, A., Morozov, K., Obana, S., Roy, P.S., Sakurai, K., Xu, R.: Efficient threshold secret sharing schemes secure against rushing cheaters. IACR Cryptology ePrint Archive 2015, 23 (2015)
2. Adhikari, A., Morozov, K., Obana, S., Roy, P.S., Sakurai, K., Xu, R.: Efficient threshold secret sharing schemes secure against rushing cheaters. In: Nascimento, A.C.A., Barreto, P. (eds.) ICITS 2016. LNCS, vol. 10015, pp. 3–23. Springer, Cham (2016). https://doi.org/10.1007/978-3-319-49175-2_1
3. Araki, T.: Efficient (k, n) threshold secret sharing schemes secure against cheating from $n - 1$ cheaters. In: Pieprzyk, J., Ghodosi, H., Dawson, E. (eds.) ACISP 2007. LNCS, vol. 4586, pp. 133–142. Springer, Heidelberg (2007). https://doi.org/10.1007/978-3-540-73458-1_11
4. Araki, T., Ogata, W.: A simple and efficient secret sharing scheme secure against cheating. IEICE Trans. Fundam. Electron. Commun. Comput. Sci. **94**(6), 1338–1345 (2011)
5. Brickell, E.F.: Some ideal secret sharing schemes. In: Quisquater, J.-J., Vandewalle, J. (eds.) EUROCRYPT 1989. LNCS, vol. 434, pp. 468–475. Springer, Heidelberg (1990). https://doi.org/10.1007/3-540-46885-4_45
6. Cevallos, A., Fehr, S., Ostrovsky, R., Rabani, Y.: Unconditionally-secure robust secret sharing with compact shares. In: Pointcheval, D., Johansson, T. (eds.) EUROCRYPT 2012. LNCS, vol. 7237, pp. 195–208. Springer, Heidelberg (2012). https://doi.org/10.1007/978-3-642-29011-4_13
7. Choudhury, A.: Brief announcement: optimal amortized secret sharing with cheater identification. In: Proceedings of the 2012 ACM Symposium on Principles of Distributed Computing, pp. 101–102. ACM (2012)

8. Cramer, R., Damgård, I., Fehr, S.: On the cost of reconstructing a secret, or VSS with optimal reconstruction phase. In: Kilian, J. (ed.) CRYPTO 2001. LNCS, vol. 2139, pp. 503–523. Springer, Heidelberg (2001). https://doi.org/10.1007/3-540-44647-8_30

9. Desmedt, Y., Frankel, Y., Yung, M.: Multi-receiver/multi-sender network security: efficient authenticated multicast/feedback. In: Eleventh Annual Joint Conference of the IEEE Computer and Communications Societies, INFOCOM 1992, pp. 2045–2054. IEEE (1992)

10. Farràs, O., Martí-Farré, J., Padró, C.: Ideal multipartite secret sharing schemes. J. Cryptol. **25**(3), 434–463 (2012)

11. Ghodosi, H., Pieprzyk, J., Safavi-Naini, R.: Secret sharing in multilevel and compartmented groups. In: Boyd, C., Dawson, E. (eds.) ACISP 1998. LNCS, vol. 1438, pp. 367–378. Springer, Heidelberg (1998). https://doi.org/10.1007/BFb0053748

12. Kurosawa, K., Obana, S., Ogata, W.: t-Cheater identifiable (k, n) threshold secret sharing schemes. In: Coppersmith, D. (ed.) CRYPTO 1995. LNCS, vol. 963, pp. 410–423. Springer, Heidelberg (1995). https://doi.org/10.1007/3-540-44750-4_33

13. McEliece, R.J., Sarwate, D.V.: On sharing secrets and reed-solomon codes. Commun. ACM **24**(9), 583–584 (1981)

14. Obana, S., Tsuchida, K.: Cheating detectable secret sharing schemes supporting an arbitrary finite field. In: Yoshida, M., Mouri, K. (eds.) IWSEC 2014. LNCS, vol. 8639, pp. 88–97. Springer, Cham (2014). https://doi.org/10.1007/978-3-319-09843-2_7

15. Ogata, W., Araki, T.: Cheating detectable secret sharing schemes for random bit strings. IEICE Trans. Fundam. Electron. Commun. Comput. Sci. **96**(11), 2230–2234 (2013)

16. Ogata, W., Eguchi, H.: Cheating detectable threshold scheme against most powerful cheaters for long secrets. Des. Codes Cryptogr. **71**(3), 527–539 (2014)

17. Ogata, W., Kurosawa, K., Stinson, D.R.: Optimum secret sharing scheme secure against cheating. SIAM J. Discret. Math. **20**(1), 79–95 (2006)

18. Rabin, T., Ben-Or, M.: Verifiable secret sharing and multiparty protocols with honest majority. In: Proceedings of the Twenty-First Annual ACM Symposium on Theory of Computing, pp. 73–85. ACM (1989)

19. Roy, P.S., Adhikari, A., Xu, R., Morozov, K., Sakurai, K.: An efficient robust secret sharing scheme with optimal cheater resiliency. In: Chakraborty, R.S., Matyas, V., Schaumont, P. (eds.) SPACE 2014. LNCS, vol. 8804, pp. 47–58. Springer, Cham (2014). https://doi.org/10.1007/978-3-319-12060-7_4

20. Roy, P.S., Adhikari, A., Xu, R., Morozov, K., Sakurai, K.: An efficient t-cheater identifiable secret sharing scheme with optimal cheater resiliency. IACR Cryptology ePrint Archive 2014, 628 (2014)

21. Safavi-Naini, R., Wang, H.: New results on multi-receiver authentication codes. In: Nyberg, K. (ed.) EUROCRYPT 1998. LNCS, vol. 1403, pp. 527–541. Springer, Heidelberg (1998). https://doi.org/10.1007/BFb0054151

22. Simmons, G.J.: How to (really) share a secret. In: Goldwasser, S. (ed.) CRYPTO 1988. LNCS, vol. 403, pp. 390–448. Springer, New York (1990). https://doi.org/10.1007/0-387-34799-2_30

23. Tassa, T., Dyn, N.: Multipartite secret sharing by bivariate interpolation. J. Cryptol. **22**(2), 227–258 (2009)

24. Wang, X., Fu, F.W., Guang, X.: Probabilistic secret sharing schemes for multipartite access structures. IEICE Trans. Fundam. Electron. Commun. Comput. Sci. **99**(4), 856–862 (2016)

25. Wang, Y., Wu, Q., Wong, D.S., Qin, B., Mu, Y., Liu, J.: Further ideal multipartite access structures from integer polymatroids. Sci. China Inf. Sci. **58**(7), 1–13 (2015)
26. Xu, R., Morozov, K., Takagi, T.: Cheater identifiable secret sharing schemes via multi-receiver authentication. In: Yoshida, M., Mouri, K. (eds.) IWSEC 2014. LNCS, vol. 8639, pp. 72–87. Springer, Cham (2014). https://doi.org/10.1007/978-3-319-09843-2_6
27. Yu, Y., Wang, M.: A probabilistic secret sharing scheme for a compartmented access structure. In: Qing, S., Susilo, W., Wang, G., Liu, D. (eds.) ICICS 2011. LNCS, vol. 7043, pp. 136–142. Springer, Heidelberg (2011). https://doi.org/10.1007/978-3-642-25243-3_11

Privacy Preserving Multi-server k-means Computation over Horizontally Partitioned Data

Riddhi Ghosal[1]([✉]) and Sanjit Chatterjee[2]([✉])

[1] Indian Statistical Institute, Kolkata, India
postboxriddhi@gmail.com
[2] Department of Computer Science and Automation, Indian Institute of Science,
Bengaluru, India
sanjit@iisc.ac.in

Abstract. The k-means clustering is one of the most popular clustering algorithms in data mining. Recently a lot of research has been concentrated on the algorithm when the data-set is divided into multiple parties or when the data-set is too large to be handled by the data owner. In the latter case, usually some servers are hired to perform the task of clustering. The data set is divided by the data owner among the servers who together compute the k-means and return the cluster labels to the owner. The major challenge in this method is to prevent the servers from gaining substantial information about the actual data of the owner. Several algorithms have been designed in the past that provide cryptographic solutions to perform privacy preserving k-means. We propose a new method to perform k-means over a large set of data using multiple servers. Our technique avoids heavy cryptographic computations and instead we use a simple randomization technique to preserve the privacy of the data. The k-means computed has essentially the same efficiency and accuracy as the k-means computed over the original data-set without any randomization. We argue that our algorithm is secure against honest-but-curious and non-colluding adversary.

Keywords: Privacy preserving computation · k-Means
Multiple servers · Horizontal partition

1 Introduction

The k-means clustering is one of the most widely used techniques in data mining [2,11,15,16,20]. The k-means clustering algorithm is used to find groups which have not been explicitly labeled in the data. This can be used to confirm business assumptions about what types of groups exist or to identify unknown groups in complex data sets. It has been successfully used in various domains including market segmentation, computer vision, geostatistics, astronomy and agriculture [6,27,29]. k-means clustering is rather easy to implement and apply even on

© Springer Nature Switzerland AG 2018
V. Ganapathy et al. (Eds.): ICISS 2018, LNCS 11281, pp. 189–208, 2018.
https://doi.org/10.1007/978-3-030-05171-6_10

large data sets, particularly when using heuristics such as Lloyd's algorithm. However, sometimes the data-set contains private information that cannot be made available to the party who is computing the k-means for a user [1,8]. There are times when the data is huge and the data owner does not have the computational capability to do clustering on his/her own. In our work we deal with this particular case. Another scenario may be a few independent parties contain parts of data on whom clustering has to be performed as a whole [5,13, 32].

The privacy and secrecy considerations can prohibit the parties from sharing their data with each other. The solution should not just provide the required privacy assurance but should also minimize the additional overheads in terms of communication and computation costs required to introduce privacy. Solutions proposed in the works such as [5,9,13,32] compute k-means by making the participating parties compute common functions, without having to actually reveal their individual data to any other party. Such algorithms face a lot of challenges because it is not very easy to reach an optimal point that will provide a perfect balance for security, accuracy and efficiency.

One of the most common approaches to solve this issue is using data perturbation to preserve the privacy of the data. Some of the common techniques are using additive noise [18], multiplicative noise [22], geometric perturbation, or rotational perturbation [7], all of which have the "Distance Preservation Property". Some works use secure multiparty computation [28], and homomorphic encryptions [3,14] to safeguard the data. But these schemes are generally computationally costly and reduce the performance of the clustering algorithm significantly. The latter approaches provide more protection to the data than the former at the cost of efficiency and sometimes their application becomes practically infeasible.

The setup we consider in this work is somewhat similar to [31] in which *Upmanyu et al.* use a so-called shatter function (a function described [31] to divide a value into many secret shares keeping the privacy of the data intact) and the Chinese Remainder theorem [10,25] to encrypt and reconstruct respectively. They propose a 'cloud computing' based solution that utilizes the services of non-colluding servers. Each of the users, is required to compute the secret shares of its private data using a shatter function. Each share is then sent over to a specific server for processing. The cloud of employed servers, now runs the k-means algorithm using just the secret shares. The protocol ensures that none of the users/servers have sufficient information to reconstruct the original data, thus ensuring privacy.

1.1 Our Contribution

We use the concept of outsourcing [21] the data to third parties who will do the computation for the data provider. These third parties are considered as adversarial, hence the data needs to be protected from them. Though [31] is fairly efficient, our protocol is better because we avoid any cryptographic overheads and use multiplicative data perturbation. Since our protocol divides the data into parts and every server works in parallel, it boosts the performance in comparison to a single server performing the whole algorithm [33]. We argue that our protocol is secure against attacks on data perturbations because of the introduction of a noise term. Keeping the noise under a certain limit, we have been able to provide a clustering algorithm that achieves the same accuracy as the iterative k-means over non-randomized data.

2 Proposed Solution

2.1 Problem Setup

In our setting, there is one data owner who holds a large dataset $\mathcal{D}$ containing n data points each having d attributes. All the attributes are considered to be floating point parameters. Hence $\mathcal{D}$ can be thought as containing n points in $\mathcal{R}^d$. Let these points be labeled as $X_1, X_2, ..., X_n$.

The data owner wishes to use t servers to compute the k-means. In this work we consider horizontal partitioning of the data, which means dividing the entire dataset into subsets based on tuples. Each tuple contains all the attributes involved. Let m be the number of iterations needed for the k-means to converge where k represents the number of clusters we want to form. The problem is computing the k-means on the entire dataset securely, efficiently and accurately by dividing the dataset horizontally among the servers without revealing any information about the original data points and any of the attributes to the servers.

2.2 Our Protocol

- The data provider generates $2d$ random numbers $r_i, i \in 1, 2, ..., 2d$ from a large set $\mathbb{R}$. A lower bound for the value of r_i will be discussed in a later section.
- The data provider selects a small enough $\epsilon > 0$ and then chooses n many ϵ_i, $i \in 1, 2, ..., n$ uniformly from $(0, \epsilon)$. They will behave as noise added to the data to improve the security. A detailed analysis of the upper bound of ϵ has been provided later.
- Let us denote $X_i = (x_{i1}, x_{i2}, ..., x_{id})$.
  Randomize the data by the following computation:

$$X_i' = ((r_1 + \epsilon_i) * x_{i1} + r_2, (r_3 + \epsilon_i) * x_{i2} + r_4, ..., (r_{2d-1} + \epsilon_i) * x_{id} + r_{2d}). \quad (1)$$

Hence the jth attribute of X_i is transformed to:

$$(r_{2j-1} + \epsilon_i) * x_{ij} + r_{2j}. \quad (2)$$

- The data owner then locally partitions the transformed data horizontally into $t - 1$ parts and sends it to $t - 1$ servers, which means the tth server does not receive any data. The work of the tth server shall be to perform certain calculations using the data provided to it by the remaining servers. The details of which shall be discussed below.

The k-mean Computation

Initialization Step. The data provider picks k many transformed data points at random.[1] These points will act as the initial cluster centers. These points say, $c_1, c_2, ..., c_k$ shall be sent to all the $t - 1$ servers who have some part of the transformed data points.

Lloyd's Step

1. Each server computes the Euclidean distance of its share of data from the initial centers and assigns cluster labels to the points locally.
2. Every server finds the number of points allotted to each center among their share of the data. Suppose for server s_i, m_{ij} denotes the number of data points belonging to cluster c_j. Here $i \in \{1, 2, ..., (t - 1)\}, j \in \{1, 2, ..., k\}$.
3. Each server computes the sum of the points belonging to each center. Let us denote it by d_{ij}, which denotes the sum of the points belonging to cluster j for server i.
4. Next step involves the generation and sharing of two secret keys x and y among the $t - 1$ servers. For this purpose, the data owner may generate two random numbers and transfer them to the $t - 1$ servers alongside the transformed data set that is being transferred. The key sharing will be performed only for the first iteration. From the next iteration onwards we can use a cryptographically secure hash function to get modified values of x and y for every step. The hash function used will be a common function known to each of the first $t - 1$ servers. The key generation procedure and hash function will be discussed in details in Sect. 2.3.
5. Each server computes

$$x * d_{ij} \tag{3}$$

and

$$y * m_{ij} \tag{4}$$

for each center j, $1 \leq j \leq k$ and sends it to the tth server.
6. Server t calculates:

$$\frac{\sum_{i=1}^{t-1}(x * d_{ij})}{\sum_{i=1}^{t-i}(y * m_{ij})} \tag{5}$$

for $1 \leq j \leq k$ centers and returns this result to the other servers. This value shall work as the centroid i.e. the new centers for the subsequent iteration of the Lloyd's step.

Let the centroid be denoted by $\nu_1, \nu_2, ..., \nu_k$.

Re-initialization. Repeat Lloyd's step till convergence. If the new centroids computed are not equal to the centroids computed in the previous iteration, i.e. $\{c_1, c_2, ..., c_k\} \neq \{\nu_1, \nu_2, ..., \nu_k\}$ then reassign $c_1, c_2, ..., c_k = \nu_1, \nu_2, ..., \nu_k$. These shall be the updated centroid values.

---

[1] We are aware of several other methods to select the initial centers which may make the k-means work more efficiently. But in this work we do not concentrate on assignment of initial clusters too much.

Output. After the iterations are complete, the $t - 1$ servers send the cluster centers and cluster assignments of their share of data to the data provider. The data owner now possesses the cluster labelling of all the data and the final cluster centers. Hence, the algorithm terminates at this step.

2.3   Group Key Sharing and Hash Function

As previously mentioned, the initial set of x and y will be provided to the $t - 1$ servers by the data provider. Alternatively the $t - 1$ servers may indulge in a group key sharing algorithm [4] to generate the first pair of random numbers. But this would lead to additional computational costs which we are compensating for, by a little bit of additional communication that is involved in transferring two random numbers from the data owner to servers. For the subsequent iterations, we use a publicly available hash function. This function will take as input the output of the previous iteration and the round number. This will allow only the parties that have access to the group key to generate random numbers using the hash iteratively. The hash function used should be a one way function, i.e. computation of the inverse of the hash function should be computationally hard.

2.4   Dynamic Setting

In our protocol, we have only talked about static data. In case, the data provider gets access to more data that it wishes to include in the k-means calculation, the data provider does the randomization as Eq. (1) over the new data points. The new points will then be partitioned and sent to the servers. These servers will just include these new points during the assignment of clusters and finding of centroids from the subsequent iteration and proceed as before till convergence.

3   Analysis

In this section, we will be performing a detailed analysis of the correctness of our protocol. We will inspect the accuracy and show how we handle error in our protocol by providing an upper bound for the noise element. Further we will scrutinize our protocol from the security point of view, where we will talk about leakage of information and conclude how such a leakage does not compromise the privacy. Lastly we will provide a brief account of the efficiency of our algorithm.

3.1   Correctness

Since iterative k-means guarantees convergence, our protocol will be deemed correct if we can prove convergence of our algorithm over the transformed data and if we can show that the error involved in clustering the transformed data is acceptable when compared to the clustering of the original data.

Without loss of generality, we have made the assumption that all data points have non negative attributes. This assumption can be made because all points can easily be translated such that all their coordinates become positive. This is done without distorting the geometry at all, hence it does not affect the clustering algorithm.

Necessarily the main operations in the k-means computation are the following steps.

1. Find Distance: Computing distance between points and the centroids.
2. Compare Distance: Find which centroid is nearest to a point.
3. Find new centroid: Re-initialize the centers.

For two data points X_1, X_2 and the corresponding transformed data points X_1', X_2' we can express the respective distances as follows.

$$\text{Distance}(X_1, X_2) := \sqrt[2]{\sum_{i=1}^{d}(x_{1i} - x_{2i})^2} \tag{6}$$

$$\text{Distance}(X_1', X_2') := \sqrt[2]{\sum_{i=1}^{d}(r_{2i-1}(x_{1i} - x_{2i}) + \epsilon_1 x_{1i} - \epsilon_2 x_{2i})^2} \tag{7}$$

$$= \sqrt[2]{\sum_{i=1}^{d}(r_{2i-1}^2(x_{1i} - x_{2i})^2 + (\epsilon_1 x_{1i} - \epsilon_2 x_{2i})^2 + 2r_{2i-1}(x_{1i} - x_{2i})(\epsilon_1 x_{1i} - \epsilon_2 x_{2i}))}.$$

In order to make our calculations and analysis simpler, the above expression under the root maybe looked upon as a quadratic polynomial in ϵ. Assuming ϵ to be sufficiently small (say ≤ 0.1), the polynomial will be dominated by the lower order and the constant terms, hence the quadratic term of ϵ can be neglected. Thus, the final expression takes the form:

$$\sqrt[2]{\sum_{i=1}^{d}(r_{2i-1}^2(x_{1i} - x_{2i})^2 + 2r_{2i-1}(x_{1i} - x_{2i})(\epsilon_1 x_{1i} - \epsilon_2 x_{2i})}. \tag{8}$$

In some places we will use expression (8) instead of (7) and will provide proper justification for its usage. We introduce an error term λ where $\lambda_1 = (\epsilon_1 x_{1i} - \epsilon_2 x_{2i})^2 + 2r_{2i-1}(x_{1i} - x_{2i})(\epsilon_1 x_{1i} - \epsilon_2 x_{2i})$ and $\lambda_2 = 2r_{2i-1}(x_{1i} - x_{2i})(\epsilon_1 x_{1i} - \epsilon_2 x_{2i})$ shall be considered to be the error terms for (7) and (8) respectively added to the distance due to inclusion of noise. Note that the error terms λ_1, λ_2 are directly proportional to ϵ and the difference in co-ordinates of the two points (X_1, X_2). Given a sufficiently small ϵ, the error can be easily bounded by an acceptable threshold. This will be made clearer shortly when we discuss the bound of ϵ and r_is. We emphasise that the distance between the transformed points (X_1', X_2') is nothing but the scaled distance between the original points (X_1, X_2) with some error term added to it. The scaling is done uniformly for all data points X_i, $1 \leq i \leq n$.

It is evident that k-means converges when the distance between the new and original centroid becomes 0. Expression (6) becomes 0 when $x_{1i} - x_{2i} = 0, \forall i \in 1, ..., d$. Given that each $r_i > 0$, it will be evident that (8) will become 0 if and only if the above condition holds. Since our exact distance form is described by (7), (8) becoming 0 implies an error element may prevail in (7) that may not become 0, but we can neglect that error under the above assumption of sufficiently small ϵ.

Hence, we can claim that the k-means on the transformed data shall converge at the same time when the k-means on the plain text converges. So, the number of iterations required for convergence is exactly the same.

Lower Bound of r_i. We need to specify a range of r_is for which the error term involved in the above expression can be acceptable. We can say that the error term will not influence our clustering if it does not alter our Compare Distance method. Hence, if

$$\sqrt[2]{\sum_{i=1}^{d} (x_{1i} - x_{2i})^2} < \sqrt[2]{\sum_{i=1}^{d} (x_{1i} - x_{3i})^2} \tag{9}$$

then,

$$\sqrt[2]{\sum_{i=1}^{d} (r_{2i-1}^2 (x_{1i} - x_{2i})^2 + (\epsilon_1 x_{1i} - \epsilon_2 x_{2i})^2 + 2r_{2i-1}(x_{1i} - x_{2i})(\epsilon_1 x_{1i} - \epsilon_2 x_{2i}))}$$

$$< \sqrt[2]{\sum_{i=1}^{d} (r_{2i-1}^2 (x_{1i} - x_{3i})^2 + (\epsilon_1 x_{1i} - \epsilon_3 x_{3i})^2 + 2r_{2i-1}(x_{1i} - x_{3i})(\epsilon_1 x_{1i} - \epsilon_3 x_{3i}))} \tag{10}$$

for all possible values of i, which means,

$$\max \sqrt[2]{\sum_{i=1}^{d} (r_{2i-1}^2 (x_{1i} - x_{2i})^2 + (\epsilon_1 x_{1i} - \epsilon_2 x_{2i})^2 + 2r_{2i-1}(x_{1i} - x_{2i})(\epsilon_1 x_{1i} - \epsilon_2 x_{2i}))}$$

$$< \min \sqrt[2]{\sum_{i=1}^{d} (r_{2i-1}^2 (x_{1i} - x_{3i})^2 + (\epsilon_1 x_{1i} - \epsilon_3 x_{3i})^2 + 2r_{2i-1}(x_{1i} - x_{3i})(\epsilon_1 x_{1i} - \epsilon_3 x_{3i}))}$$

Solving the above equation with proper bounds and using the expression (10) we get a lower bound for r_is.

$$r > max \frac{\sum_{l=1}^{d} (x_{il}^2 - (x_{il} - x_{kl})^2)}{2 \sum_{l=1}^{d} (x_{il} - x_{kl})^2 - x_{il}(x_{il} - x_{jl})}, \forall i, j, k \tag{11}$$

where r=$\min(r_i), \forall i$. Refer to Appendix A.1 for detailed calculation.

Upper Bound on ϵ. The requirement that the term inside the root in expression (8) must be non-negative, gives us an upper bound for ϵ. A sufficient condition to achieve it is, $r_{2i-1}^2(x_{1i} - x_{2i})^2 > \lambda_2$. Substituting for the value of λ_2 we get, $r_{2i-1}(x_{1i} - x_{2i}) > 2(\epsilon_1 x_{1i} - \epsilon_2 x_{2i})$ over all possible values of i. Hence, $r_{2i-1}(x_{1i} - x_{2i}) > \max(2(\epsilon_1 x_{1i} - \epsilon_2 x_{2i}))$. Upon simplification, we get

$$\epsilon < \min \frac{r_{2k-1}(x_{ik} - x_{jk})}{2x_{ik}}, \forall i, j, k. \tag{12}$$

If we use (7) as our parent equation then (9) remains unchanged. This is so because λ_1 is greater than λ_2. So using the latter provides us a stronger upper bound for ϵ.

Equations (11) and (12) show the bound of r and ϵ. Combining the two relations, we will get a common expression for the relation between ϵ and r that shall ensure correctness. Thus if ϵ and r_is lie in this range then the output of Compare Distance function will not be altered for the transformed data.

It is guaranteed that assignment of intermediate clusters for the points remain consistent with the assignment without the transformation. That is so because the centroids are found by taking the average over the points in a particular cluster, hence the distance between a centroid and a data point will be less than the global maximum and more than the global minimum as described in the derivation of (11) and (12) respectively. These conditions will ensure that the clustering over the randomized data points is same as the clustering over the original data. This way we ensure the accuracy of our clustering technique.

3.2   Security

We consider the adversarial servers to be honest-but-curious.

Adversarial Power:

1. Every server tries to obtain maximum information about the original data without deviating from the protocol.
2. Every server would like to gain knowledge about the data possessed by the other servers.
3. Servers record and store all intermediate information made available to them and use it to find out more information about the data.
4. Collusion among servers is not allowed.

Information available to servers 1 to $t-1$:

1. Randomized data points.
2. Intermediate cluster assignments of their own data only.
3. Intermediate cluster centers.
4. Number of iterations needed to converge.

Information available to t^{th} server:

1. A scaled version of the intermediate centers.
2. Randomized sum of coordinates of the data points that belong to a particular cluster at each iteration.
3. Randomized value for the number of data points belonging to every cluster for each server at every iteration.
4. Randomized value of intermediate centers.
5. Number of iterations needed to converge.

Security Against Existing Attack Scenarios. Recall that the information initially available to the first $t - 1$ servers is of the form of Eq. (1). Various algebraic methods have been discussed in [19, 23, 24] to design attacks on data perturbation techniques. But most of the attacks described so far in the above works are applicable for additive noise. In [23], Liu et al. have discussed in detail the security in random perturbation from the attackers point of view. Their model deals with known sample or known input-output models in case of Distance Preserving Transformations. Liu et al. [22] talked about attacks on multiplicative data perturbation. Their approach uses Independent Component Analysis to remove the randomization and gain information about the data. Given that Principle Component Analysis (PCA) works successfully only when the perturbation matrix is orthogonal, so if the transformation is not distance preserving as in our case, PCA is unsuccessful to gain any significant information about the original data.

The crux of all these attack approaches is the fact that that distance preserving transformation in a vector space over a real field is an orthogonal transformation. The advantage of our technique is that the data transformation does not preserve the distance hence making the transformation a non-orthogonal one. This fact appears to make it more secure than the Distance Preserving transformations.

A recent work [17] has devised an attack on Relation Preserving Transformation (RPT). Since RPT is the basis of our transformation, it may be open to breach by [17]. Assuming that such an attack is implemented, we analyze the feasibility of it in detail.

We first recall the salient features of the attack proposed in [17]. It is assumed that there exists a third party malicious adversary and the attacker has knowledge about some original data points. The attack reveals which side of the hyperplane does the point lie. No information is found about the exact location of the point. A major assumption is that the search space is discrete. It has been stated that the algorithm is useful for data set that is usually low dimensional. The main basis of a successful attack is that probability of choosing a point inside a bounded area is non negligible which again goes back to the assumption of a discrete search space.

As per [17], the complexity of their algorithm is $O(\binom{|K|}{2}(\frac{R}{c})^d \mathcal{I})$. In the above expression, $|K|$ is the size of known sample, R is the range of data points, c the length of a cell into which the entire space is divided and $\mathcal{I}$ is the complexity of finding Intersection.

We argue why such an attack is not practically applicable in our case. The attacker has no knowledge about any of the original data and all communication channels are assumed to be secure and the servers have no information about any data point. We are working with high dimensional data sets where, usually $d \geq 8$. We consider the best case scenario for the attacker and take $|K| = 2$. In the following table, we tabulate complexity of the attack for different choices of R, c and d (Table 1).

Table 1. Complexity of the attack $(O(x\mathcal{I}))$, where $x = \binom{|K|}{2}(\frac{R}{c})^d$ from [17] in our setting.

R	c	d	x in $O(x\mathcal{I})$
1000	0.01	2	2^{33}
1000	0.01	3	2^{49}
1000	0.01	4	2^{66}
10	0.001	5	2^{66}
10	0.001	6	2^{79}
10	0.001	8	2^{105}
100	0.01	9	2^{118}
10	0.001	10	2^{132}
10	0.001	12	2^{158}
1000	0.01	11	2^{181}

In the current computational power, around 2^{64} steps is considered barely feasible. To compute k-means, let's assume we require precision of at least 3 digits for accuracy. Since we are dealing with large values of d, even in the best case for the attacker where $R = 10$, the complexity can be seen to be much larger than 2^{64}. While dealing with large datasets, it is not a practical assumption that the data points are dispersed over a range of just 10 units. It will be much more than this in most cases and $d \geq 8$ in most cases where cloud computing is used. We can thus conclude from the above table that this attack cannot be practically implemented whenever the dimension is more than 5 because of the extremely high complexity. Since the attack is exponential in d, the attack becomes extremely inefficient for large and high dimensional data sets making it infeasible to implement in real life.

Security Against Data Leakage. Our technique allows certain information leakage to the servers. After convergence, servers 1 to $(t - 1)$ will get to know information about the final cluster allotments for every data-point that they have access to. They also learn which points belong to the same cluster. The

t^{th} servers knows the intermediate as well as the final cluster centres. This leakage allows the servers to gain information about the transformed points only. Knowing about the cluster assignments of the randomized points does not help the adversary gain any significant information about the original points or their cluster assignments. We shall now justify this statement with concrete analysis.

The adversarial servers may try to remove the randomness from the data they have and retrieve maximum information about the original data. If they take the attribute wise quotient of their data then they get the following:

$$\frac{r_1(x_{11} - x_{21}) + \epsilon_1 x_{11} - \epsilon_2 x_{21}}{r_1(x_{41} - x_{31}) + \epsilon_4 x_{41} - \epsilon_3 x_{31}}. \tag{13}$$

If the servers wish to use the entire data points instead of the attributes, then the one possible method to proceed will be to compute the generalized inverse [26] by treating the vectors as column matrix. Finding the g-inverse of a point and multiplying it with another data point can be interpreted as a quotient between two vectors. This calculation leads us back to a form of the above expression (13).

We next analyse the effectiveness of a probabilistic approach to see if there is some significant leakage of data. We want to ensure that the above expression (13) reveals no significant information about

$$\frac{x_{11} - x_{21}}{x_{41} - x_{31}}. \tag{14}$$

We assume probability distributions over expression (13) and (14) and proceed to check how similar are these two distributions. If the distributions are not similar then we can claim the expression (13) does not reveal anything significant about expression (14).

We use the Kullback-Leibler Divergence function [12] as a metric to compare the two distributions. Kullback-Leibler divergence is a bounded function between 0 and 1. The further the value is from 0, the less similar are the two distributions. With the help of proper upper and lower bounds, simplification of the divergence functions gives us a lower bound on the metric. Let us denote KD as the output of the divergence function. Then,

$$KD \geq d\frac{x_{11} - x_{21}}{x_{41} - x_{31}} \log \frac{r_1 + \frac{\epsilon x_{41}}{x_{41} - x_{31}}}{r_1 - \frac{\epsilon x_{11}}{x_{11} - x_{21}}}. \tag{15}$$

Refer to Appendix A.2 for details.

The definition of Kullback-Leibler guarantees the value of (15) to be non negative. Since (15) is an increasing function of ϵ, the greater the value of ϵ, more is the deviation of the function from 0. We can increase ϵ till the upper bounds to ensure that the Kullback-Leibler distance moves away from 0. Hence, by regulating ϵ, the probability distributions can be made dissimilar.

Finally, we discuss the leakage of information to server t. Server t receives information in the form of Eqs. (3) and (4). Its aim again will be to remove the randomization and get information about the original values. It can try the following two divisions to extract out the randomness. Compute

$$\frac{(x * d_{ij})}{(y * m_{ij})} \tag{16}$$

or compute using only (3)

$$\frac{(x_1 * d_{ij})}{(x_2 * d_{ij})} \tag{17}$$

and do similar with the use of (4) alone. Again, using the same techniques as before of assuming probability distributions and finding the Kullback-Leibler divergence function between the randomized and the non-randomized values, it can be shown that KD for (16) is:

$$-\log \frac{x}{y} \sum \frac{d_{ij}}{m_{ij}} \tag{18}$$

while KD for (17) is:

$$-\log \frac{x_1}{x_2} z \tag{19}$$

where z denotes the number of points taken into consideration while computing KD.

Thus we see that as long as x and y are not same, the occurrence of which has negligible probability as the numbers are generated randomly, the Kullback-Leibler divergence function will give an output that will be away from 0.

There is no interaction between servers $1, ..., (t - 1)$ other than the key exchange, so a server cannot gain any information about the data of the other servers when collusion is disallowed. The other leakage of information that we compromise with is the number of iterations needed to converge, but we can accommodate this because it does not give up on the privacy of the data which is our primary goal.

3.3   Efficiency

In analyzing the performance of our algorithm on the basis of the total communication and computational cost, we discuss the complexity of the entire process by dividing it into three different stages: the data provider, the first $t - 1$ servers and the tth server.

Data Provider Computation: The only computation done here is the randomization of the data where the computation cost is dominated by the number of multiplications.

Communication: There shall be a one time communication necessary to send the randomized data to the respective servers. Without loss of generality, we may assume that the data provider divides the data set into $t - 1$ parts each of size $n_1, n_2, ..., n_{t-1}$. The communication cost will depend on the size of the data transferred. In this and all further cases that we discuss, we will deal with the worst case, i.e. we assume that the size of the data is the upper bound for all the possible values. Say this upper bound is U.

Servers 1 *to* $(t-1)$ Computation: The main computations being done here are finding distance and comparing distance before assigning the necessary clusters. Here the operations that dominate the performance are performing squares and doing comparisons to find which cluster a point should belong to.

Communication: Sending $x * d_{i,j}$ and $y * m_{i,j}$ (see expressions (3) and (4) respectively) to server t uses up some bandwidth. Here consider that all values sent by a server i in the form of (3) and (4) shall have an upper bound N_i and M_i. This communication cost will be accounted for m number of times where m is the number of iterations needed for the algorithm to converge.

Server t Computation: Computing the intermediate cluster centres (see (5)) requires division operation that will be the main computational cost in this case.

Communication: Returns k many values of intermediate cluster centres to each server m number of times. Assumption is that the value of those centres will always be less than C, where C is the upper bound of all values to be returned by server t.

Comparison with [31]. Since our model is closest to the one proposed by Upmanyu et al., it is fair to compare the efficiency of both the approaches. Instead of using three layers of interaction like us, they use only two levels of interaction. Their communication cost for sending data from data owner to servers is same as ours because they have to send secret shares of each data point to the servers similar to our sharing of data points to servers. Computationally, our algorithm beats theirs because of the following. (i) In [31], the data owner needs to shatter the data points leading to performing t modulo operations for each data point. Hence, nt modulo operations are to be performed, whose computation cost is similar to inversion that is heavier than multiplication. (ii) At the server level, in order to assign clusters, the servers need to merge their share of secrets together and then proceed with distance computation and comparison. This process in whole involves two main operations, sharing common secret keys using group key sharing and merging the shared secrets. The merging operation uses Chinese Remainder Theorem (CRT), which has a complexity of $O(N^2)$, where N is the modulus in CRT. Repeating this for all n data points and for m many rounds makes the complexity $O(nN^2m)$. In addition to this, the usage of a common group key sharing algorithm further increases the computation cost significantly. Thus the amount of computations to be done by [31] is much heavier than in our case. We summarize in the tables below, the comparison between computation cost of the two algorithms.

Performance Comparison When Data Owner Locally Compute k-means. If the data provider did not outsource the computation of k-means and instead did the entire process on his/her own, the complexity would be $O(nkdm)$. The performance would be dominated by multiplications and inversions. Whenever the number of clusters to be formed becomes large, the efficiency would

Table 2. Our algorithm

	Computational	Communication
Data provider	$O(nd)$(Multiplication)	$O(nU)$
Servers 1 to $(t-1)$	$O(kn_i dm)$(Multiplication)	$O(m(N_i + M_i))$
Server t	$O(mk)$(Inversion)	$O(mkC)$

Table 3. Algorithm in [31]

	Computational	Communication
Data provider	$O(nt)$ (Inversion)	$O(nU)$
Servers	$O(nN^2 m)$ (Chinese Remainder Theorem)	$O(n_i N_i)$

be affected. By outsourcing, one will also be relieved of performing numerous inversions and comparisons that will be taken care of by the servers. Moreover, along with time complexity, another constraint might be space complexity as well. If the entire algorithm is performed locally, then the data owner needs storage space in order to keep all the intermediate information recorded at every round of iteration. In this case, all that the data provider needs is storage for the data set for only the first round (Tables 2 and 3).

4   Choice of Parameters for Practical Implementation

It may seem that pre-processing the data for randomization will require a significant amount of computation. Following the naive approach, the first step would be selecting values of r_i and ϵ. Following (11), to find the strict bound of r shall take $O(n^3)$ many inversions. This would go against our claim of having a very efficient algorithm. However, the problem can be easily solved by using a weaker bound instead of using the strict bound that we have derived in (11) and (12). From (11) we have,

$$r > \max \frac{\sum_{l=1}^{d} (x_{il}^2 - (x_{il} - x_{kl})^2)}{2 \sum_{l=1}^{d} (x_{il} - x_{kl})^2 - x_{il}(x_{il} - x_{jl})}, \forall i, j, k.$$

Note that,

$$\max \frac{\sum_{l=1}^{d} (x_{il}^2 - (x_{il} - x_{kl})^2)}{2 \sum_{l=1}^{d} 0(x_{il} - x_{kl})^2 - x_{il}(x_{il} - x_{jl})} \leq \max \frac{\sum_{l=1}^{d} (x_{il}^2 - (x_{il} - x_{kl})^2)}{2 \sum_{l=1}^{d} (x_{il} - x_{kl})^2 - x_{il}^2} \leq -\frac{1}{2}.$$

Since (11) gives the range for correctness, $r > -\frac{1}{2}$ will retain the correctness. From (12), we have,

$$\min \frac{r_{2k-1}(x_{ik} - x_{jk})}{2 x_{ik}} \geq \min \frac{r_{2k-1}}{2}.$$

Since we are dealing with only positive values of ϵ, one can choose any non-negative real number w. Then choosing $r > w$ and $\epsilon < \frac{w}{2}$ will ensure correctness.

This process helps us get the value of the parameters in constant time. The next step would be performing multiplications to randomize the data. Our aim is to optimize security and efficiency. We use the bit length of r_i and ϵ_i to analyze the efficiency and the security. The efficiency is dominated by the multiplications to be performed. Multiplying two numbers of ℓ-bits has a complexity of $O(\ell^2)$. Total nd many multiplications are needed to be performed that will be a complexity of $O(nd\ell^2)$. Let the bit length of the maximum value of r_i be ℓ_1 and that of the maximum value of ϵ_i be ℓ_2. We assume that our algorithm is deemed secure if the adversary cannot guess the random numbers with probability more that 2^{-80}. We analyze the security of two expressions. In the first, the adversary needs to guess two values of r_is and one value of ϵ_i to get to know about one of the coordinates of a data point from expression 1:

$$X_i' = ((r_1 + \epsilon_i) * x_{i1} + r_2, (r_3 + \epsilon_i) * x_{i2} + r_4, ..., (r_{2d-1} + \epsilon_i) * x_{id} + r_{2d}).$$

For the second case, the adversary has to guess one value of r_i and three values of ϵ_is with non negligible probability from Eq. 13 as reproduced below:

$$\frac{r_1(x_{11} - x_{21}) + \epsilon_1 x_{11} - \epsilon_2 x_{21}}{r_1(x_{41} - x_{31}) + \epsilon_4 x_{41} - \epsilon_3 x_{31}}.$$

In the following table we demonstrate some plausible values of ℓ_1, ℓ_2 that will optimize security along with correctness. The way of choosing ℓ_1 and ℓ_2 has been talked about in details in Appendix B.

We consider $n = 2^{16}$ and $d = 2^4$. One assumption is that $\ell_1 > \ell_2$ as we do not want the noise to surpass the scaling factor (Table 4).

Table 4. Parameters for practical implementation

ℓ_1	ℓ_2	Probability of guessing (1)	Probability of guessing (13)	$O(nd\ell_1^2)$
34	32	2^{-77}	2^{-80}	2^{30}
40	32	2^{-89}	2^{-82}	2^{31}
64	32	2^{-137}	2^{-110}	2^{32}
128	8	2^{-241}	2^{-102}	2^{34}

5   Conclusion

In this work, we have proposed a solution to perform cloud-based k-means clustering in the multi-server setting. The main aim was to perform clustering as efficiently as possible without compromising with the privacy of the data to the extent possible. We have provided a technique that is easy to understand and implement along with being robust. In our work, we have analyzed the correctness and security of the algorithm in details. Our analysis shows that the proposed technique is secure against a passive adversary. Our method is very efficient as it does not include any heavy cryptographic computation. The k-means process we have described is similar to the iterative k-means used over original data set. Hence the efficiency of both the algorithms is comparable. We also discussed practical parameter choices for our algorithm. One interesting future work would be to extend the perturbation based approach to allow partial collusion among the servers.

A   Detailed Computations

A.1   Lower Bound for r_i, $1 \le i \le 2d$

$$\max {}^2\sqrt{\sum_{i=1}^{d}(r_{2i-1}^2(x_{1i}-x_{2i})^2 + (\epsilon_1 x_{1i} - \epsilon_2 x_{2i})^2 + 2r_{2i-1}(x_{1i}-x_{2i})(\epsilon_1 x_{1i} - \epsilon_2 x_{2i}))}$$

$$< \min {}^2\sqrt{\sum_{i=1}^{d}(r_{2i-1}^2(x_{1i}-x_{3i})^2 + (\epsilon_1 x_{1i} - \epsilon_3 x_{3i})^2 + 2r_{2i-1}(x_{1i}-x_{3i})(\epsilon_1 x_{1i} - \epsilon_3 x_{3i}))}$$

To maximize LHS and minimize RHS, we take $\epsilon_1=\epsilon$, $\epsilon_2=0$, $\epsilon_3 = \epsilon$ and thus,

$$\sum_{i=1}^{d}(r_{2i-1}^2(x_{1i}-x_{2i})^2 + (\epsilon^2 x_{1i}^2 + 2r_{2i-1}(x_{1i}-x_{2i})(\epsilon x_{1i}))$$

$$< \sum_{i=1}^{d}(r_{2i-1}^2(x_{1i}-x_{3i})^2 + (\epsilon^2 (x_{1i}-x_{3i})^2 + 2r_{2i-1}\epsilon(x_{1i}-x_{3i})^2)$$

Using (10), we further get,

$$\epsilon \sum_{i=1}^{d}[x_{1i}^2 - (x_{1i}-x_{3i})^2] + 2\sum_{i=1}^{d} r_{2i-1}[x_{1i}(x_{1i}-x_{2i}) - (x_{1i}-x_{3i})^2] < 0$$

$$\Rightarrow 2\sum_{i=1}^{d} r_{2i-1}[(x_{1i}-x_{3i})^2 - x_{1i}(x_{1i}-x_{2i})] > \epsilon \sum_{i=1}^{d}[x_{1i}^2 - (x_{1i}-x_{3i})^2]$$

$$\Rightarrow r > \max(\epsilon \frac{\sum_{l=1}^{d}(x_{il}^2 - (x_{il}-x_{kl})^2)}{2\sum_{l=1}^{d}(x_{il}-x_{kl})^2 - x_{il}(x_{ik}-x_{jl})}), \forall i,j,k. \tag{20}$$

Given that ϵ is sufficiently small, it can be safely assumed to be less than 1. Hence if (12) is satisfied, (20) is satisfied as well. Although (20) is a better bound, we use (12) to make it independent of ϵ.

A.2   Kullback Leibler Distance

The Kullback Leibler Distance (KD) is defined to be $-\sum_i P(i) \log \frac{Q(i)}{P(i)}$ where

$$P(i) = \frac{x_{1i} - x_{2i}}{x_{4i} - x_{3i}} \quad \text{and} Q(i) = \frac{r_{2i-1}(x_{1i} - x_{2i}) + \epsilon_1 x_{1i} - \epsilon_2 x_{2i}}{r_{2i-1}(x_{4i} - x_{3i}) + \epsilon_4 x_{4i} - \epsilon_3 x_{3i}}.$$

$$KD = -\sum_i \frac{x_{1i} - x_{2i}}{x_{4i} - x_{3i}} \log \frac{r_{2i-1} + \frac{\epsilon_1 x_{1i} - \epsilon_2 x_{2i}}{x_{1i} - x_{2i}}}{r_{2i-1} + \frac{\epsilon_4 x_{4i} - \epsilon_3 x_{3i}}{x_{4i} - x_{3i}}}$$

$$= \sum_i \frac{x_{2i} - x_{1i}}{x_{4i} - x_{3i}} \log \frac{r_{2i-1} + \frac{\epsilon_1 x_{1i} - \epsilon_2 x_{2i}}{x_{1i} - x_{2i}}}{r_{2i-1} + \frac{\epsilon_4 x_{4i} - \epsilon_3 x_{3i}}{x_{4i} - x_{3i}}}. \tag{21}$$

Without loss of generality, we assume that for $i = 1$, the above expression attains minima,

$$\geq d \frac{x_{21} - x_{11}}{x_{41} - x_{31}} \log \frac{r_1 + \frac{\epsilon_1 x_{11} - \epsilon_2 x_{21}}{x_{11} - x_{21}}}{r_1 + \frac{\epsilon_4 x_{41} - \epsilon_3 x_{31}}{x_{41} - x_{31}}}$$

Let,

$$D_1 = \frac{KD}{d \frac{x_{21} - x_{11}}{x_{41} - x_{31}}} \geq \log \frac{r_1 + \frac{\epsilon_1 x_{11} - \epsilon_2 x_{21}}{x_{11} - x_{21}}}{r_1 + \frac{\epsilon_4 x_{41} - \epsilon_3 x_{31}}{x_{41} - x_{31}}}.$$

Hence,

$$e^{D_1} \geq \frac{r_1 + \frac{\epsilon_1 x_{11} - \epsilon_2 x_{21}}{x_{11} - x_{21}}}{r_1 + \frac{\epsilon_4 x_{41} - \epsilon_3 x_{31}}{x_{41} - x_{31}}} \geq \frac{r_1 - \frac{\epsilon x_{21}}{x_{11} - x_{21}}}{r_1 + \frac{\epsilon x_{41}}{x_{41} - x_{31}}}.$$

Finally,

$$KD \geq d \frac{x_{11} - x_{21}}{x_{41} - x_{31}} \log \frac{r_1 + \frac{\epsilon x_{41}}{x_{41} - x_{31}}}{r_1 - \frac{\epsilon x_{21}}{x_{11} - x_{21}}}.$$

B   Range of Bit Length of the Parameters

The probability of correctly guessing the random numbers from Eq. (1) is computed as follows. The adversary may arbitrarily fix the choice of two indices from $\{1, \ldots, 2d\}$ for the r_is and the corresponding index from $\{1, \ldots, n\}$ for the choice of ϵ. Fixing the two r_i from $2d$ many r_i's can be done in $\binom{2d}{2}$ ways. Similarly choosing one ϵ_i from n many ϵ_i's can be done in n ways. Hence the probability is:

$$\binom{2d}{2}\binom{n}{1} \frac{1}{2^{2\ell_1}} \frac{1}{2^{\ell_2}}.$$

Similarly, the probability of correctly guessing from Eq. (13) is:

$$\binom{2d}{1}\binom{n}{3} \frac{1}{2^{\ell_1}} \frac{1}{2^{3\ell_2}}.$$

Fixing n and d as chosen, for the probability to be less than 2^{-80}, the following two equations must be satisfied,

$$2\ell_1 + \ell_2 \geq 103, \tag{22}$$

and

$$\ell_1 + 3\ell_2 \geq 130. \tag{23}$$

Hence the above two equations give us the range for the bit length of the parameters.

References

1. Agrawal, R., Srikant, R: Privacy-preserving data mining, vol. 29. ACM (2000)
2. Alsabti, K., Ranka, S., Singh, V.: An efficient k-means clustering algorithm (1997)
3. Beye, M., Erkin, Z., Lagendijk, R.L.: Efficient privacy preserving k-means clustering in a three-party setting. In: 2011 IEEE International Workshop on Information Forensics and Security, pp. 1–6 (2011)
4. Boyd, C., Davies, G.T., Gjøsteen, K., Jiang, Y.: Offline assisted group key exchange. Cryptology ePrint Archive, Report 2018/114 (2018). https://eprint.iacr.org/2018/114
5. Bunn, P., Ostrovsky, R.: Secure two-party k-means clustering. In: Proceedings of the 14th ACM Conference on Computer and Communications Security, CCS 2007, pp. 486–497, ACM, New York (2007)
6. Celik, T.: Unsupervised change detection in satellite images using principal component analysis and k-means clustering. IEEE Geosci. Remote Sens. Lett. **6**(4), 772–776 (2009)
7. Chen, K., Liu, L.: Privacy preserving data classification with rotation perturbation. In: Fifth IEEE International Conference on Data Mining (ICDM 2005), 4 p. (2005)
8. Cranor, L.F.: Internet privacy. Commun. ACM **42**(2), 28–38 (1999)
9. Doganay, M.C., Pedersen, T.B., Saygin, Y., Savaş, E., Levi, A.: Distributed privacy preserving k-means clustering with additive secret sharing. In: Proceedings of the 2008 International Workshop on Privacy and Anonymity in Information Society, PAIS 2008, pp. 3–11. ACM, New York (2008)
10. Goldreich, O., Ron, D., Sudan, M.: Chinese remaindering with errors. In: Proceedings of the Thirty-First Annual ACM Symposium on Theory of Computing, pp. 225–234. ACM (1999)
11. Hartigan, J.A., Wong, M.A.: Algorithm as 136: a k-means clustering algorithm. J. R. Stat. Soc. Ser. C (Appl. Stat.) **28**(1), 100–108 (1979)
12. Hershey, J.R., Olsen, P.A.: Approximating the Kullback Leibler divergence between Gaussian mixture models. In: IEEE International Conference on Acoustics, Speech and Signal Processing, ICASSP 2007, vol. 4, p. IV–317. IEEE (2007)
13. Jagannathan, G., Pillaipakkamnatt, K., Wright, R.N.: A new privacy-preserving distributed k-clustering algorithm. In: Proceedings of the 2006 SIAM International Conference on Data Mining, pp. 494–498. SIAM (2006)
14. Jagannathan, G., Wright, R.N.: Privacy-preserving distributed k-means clustering over arbitrarily partitioned data. In: Proceedings of the Eleventh ACM SIGKDD International Conference on Knowledge Discovery in Data Mining, KDD 2005, pp. 593–599. ACM, New York (2005)

15. Jain, A.K.: Data clustering: 50 years beyond k-means. Pattern Recogn. Lett. **31**(8), 651–666 (2010)
16. Kanungo, T., Mount, D.M., Netanyahu, N.S., Piatko, C.D., Silverman, R., Wu, A.Y.: An efficient k-means clustering algorithm: analysis and implementation. IEEE Trans. Pattern Anal. Mach. Intell. (7), 881–892 (2002)
17. Kaplan, E., Gursoy, M.E., Nergiz, M.E., Saygin, Y.: Known sample attacks on relation preserving data transformations. IEEE Trans. Dependable Secure Comput. (2017)
18. Kargupta, H., Datta, S., Wang, Q., Sivakumar, K.: On the privacy preserving properties of random data perturbation techniques. In: Third IEEE International Conference on Data Mining, ICDM 2003, pp. 99–106. IEEE (2003)
19. Kargupta, H., Datta, S., Wang, Q., Sivakumar, K.: Random-data perturbation techniques and privacy-preserving data mining. Knowl. Inf. Syst. **7**(4), 387–414 (2005)
20. Likas, A., Vlassis, N., Verbeek, J.J.: The global k-means clustering algorithm. Pattern Recogn. **36**(2), 451–461 (2003)
21. Liu, D., Bertino, E., Yi, X.: Privacy of outsourced k-means clustering. In: Proceedings of the 9th ACM Symposium on Information, Computer and Communications Security, ASIA CCS 2014, pp. 123–134. ACM, New York (2014)
22. Liu, K.: Random projection-based multiplicative data perturbation for privacy preserving distributed data mining. IEEE Trans. Knowl. Data Eng. **18**(1), 92–106 (2006)
23. Liu, K., Giannella, C., Kargupta, H.: An attacker's view of distance preserving maps for privacy preserving data mining. In: Fürnkranz, J., Scheffer, T., Spiliopoulou, M. (eds.) PKDD 2006. LNCS (LNAI), vol. 4213, pp. 297–308. Springer, Heidelberg (2006). https://doi.org/10.1007/11871637_30
24. Liu, K., Kargupta, H., Ryan, J.: Random projection-based multiplicative data perturbation for privacy preserving distributed data mining. IEEE Trans. Knowl. Data Eng. **18**, 92–106 (2006)
25. Mignotte, M.: How to share a secret. In: Beth, T. (ed.) EUROCRYPT 1982. LNCS, vol. 149, pp. 371–375. Springer, Heidelberg (1983). https://doi.org/10.1007/3-540-39466-4_27
26. Mitra, S.K.: On a generalised inverse of a matrix and applications. Sankhyā: Indian J. Stat. Ser. A, 107–114 (1968)
27. Oyelade, O.J., Oladipupo, O.O., Obagbuwa, I.C.: Application of k means clustering algorithm for prediction of students academic performance. arXiv preprint arXiv:1002.2425 (2010)
28. Samet, S., Miri, A., Orozco-Barbosa, L.: Privacy preserving k-means clustering in multi-party environment. In: SECRYPT (2007)
29. Tellaeche, A., BurgosArtizzu, X.-P., Pajares, G., Ribeiro, A.: A vision-based hybrid classifier for weeds detection in precision agriculture through the Bayesian and fuzzy k-means paradigms. In: Corchado, E., Corchado, J.M., Abraham, A. (eds.) Innovations in Hybrid Intelligent Systems. AINSC, vol. 44, pp. 72–79. Springer, Heidelberg (2007). https://doi.org/10.1007/978-3-540-74972-1_11
30. Turow, J.: Americans online privacy: the system is broken (2003)
31. Upmanyu, M., Namboodiri, A.M., Srinathan, K., Jawahar, C.V.: Efficient privacy preserving k-means clustering. In: Chen, H., Chau, M., Li, S., Urs, S., Srinivasa, S., Wang, G.A. (eds.) PAISI 2010. LNCS, vol. 6122, pp. 154–166. Springer, Heidelberg (2010). https://doi.org/10.1007/978-3-642-13601-6_17

32. Vaidya, J., Clifton, C.: Privacy-preserving k-means clustering over vertically parti-
    tioned data. In: Proceedings of the Ninth ACM SIGKDD International Conference
    on Knowledge Discovery and Data Mining, KDD 2003, pp. 206–215. ACM, New
    York (2003)
33. Yu, T.-K., Lee, D.T., Chang, S.-M., Zhan, J.Z.: Multi-party k-means clustering
    with privacy consideration. In: International Symposium on Parallel and Dis-
    tributed Processing with Applications, pp. 200–207 (2010)

Secure Moderated Bargaining Game

Sumanta Chatterjee[(⊠)] [iD]

Microsoft India Private Limited, Hyderabad, India
sumanta.chatterjee.nitk@gmail.com

Abstract. Bargaining problem is one of the oldest problems in economics to explain the interaction between traders in variable pricing model. Many game theory approaches are used as solution over years. With proliferation of world wide web bargaining game is gaining relevance in online market places. Formal definition of an honest but curious mediator, in a three-party bargaining game is discussed in this paper. An honest but curious moderator facilitates the interaction between interested parties, but also wishes to learn information about the trade for his own benefit. An approach is also proposed to secure the bargain in the presence of an active adversary and honest but curious mediator, using Oblivious commitment based envelop protocol. It is shown that the protocol is IND-CCA secure and moderator cannot infer additional information of the trade except knowing the parties involved.

Keywords: Bargaining game · Multiparty computation
Oblivious commitment based envelop · Profit model

1 Introduction

Asset distribution is one of the oldest economic problems. Bargaining is a strategy most frequently used to achieve reasonable and fair division of resources that satisfies each participating party based on its satisfaction criteria. Example of such interaction includes purchase of a product, wage negotiation between workers and contractor or direct sales between customer and seller, shared resources allocation by third party resource provider. Bargaining creates a different selling experience of the seller where instead of selling objects at fixed prices, and earning a fixed profit, he can sell the object at variable prices to different buyers based on their risk tolerance and cost allocation. In a variable pricing model, profit earned by the seller is not fixed and often lies in a range over different object sold.

During the process, two- parties attempt to come to a consensus in distributing some quantifiable components between them, so that each party can achieve its desired benefit. The interaction or game is a failure if none of the parties accept the distribution result. If a game is concluded as failure, participating parties gets only disagreement values, thus, concluding the game is rational for better benefit.

© Springer Nature Switzerland AG 2018
V. Ganapathy et al. (Eds.): ICISS 2018, LNCS 11281, pp. 209–227, 2018.
https://doi.org/10.1007/978-3-030-05171-6_11

Before the bargaining game begins, both parties agree on a disagreement value which is the minimum amount each party is going to receive if they do not come to an agreement. There are many ways bargaining game can be conducted. In 'Take it or leave it' approach, one party offer certain distribution of his own choice to the other party and second party can choose to agree on that distribution or reject it. If the second party accepts the offer the game is a success and he gets the proposed amount otherwise the game fails [2]. 'Take it or leave it approach' is a onetime negotiation and often considered aggressive bargaining strategy. The fairness of the game in this strategy is skewed towards the player who proposes first as he will try to achieve the maximum for himself. To increase fairness, another variation of 'Take-it-or-leave-it' strategy was given where first player proposes more than one possible distribution to the second player and the second player has options to agree upon any of the proposed distribution [18].

Alternatively, two parties can negotiate in a limited offer model or an unlimited offer model over a specific time duration. In this approach, all players are aware of the moves available to other player and sequentially takes turn in proposing his distribution offer. If both the player agrees, the deal is struck, and both gets the proposed amount. Otherwise the negotiation continues for a limited time or round. It is also considered that delay in achieving negotiation is associated with the risk and cost of the parties involved [16]. So, the longer the bargain continues the less each player gets out of the trade. Decrease in gain from the trade depends on time value of money and the risk-taking attribute of each player. After each round the amount to distribute is decreased by a constant factor. Each player is also associated with a discount factor, i.e. the factor by which the player is accepting the future amount of the bargain compared to the current amount. Player with higher discount factor tends to close the negotiation in lesser rounds.

With the proliferation of the world wide web a different version of bargain game is also prevalent now. In this model the bargaining is moderated by a third-party mediator, who for a short amount of time possess the information of the object or quantifiable component being bargained upon. Example of such model includes online host of bargaining site, online peer to peer market places. This gives flexibility to the parties involve proposing their distribution without being present together but also exposes the risk of third-party manipulation by the mediator. it is of paramount importance that information shared with third party should not be tampered with or shared to an unintended recipient. In our paper we

- Provide a formal definition of the third-party mediator in bargaining game and establish constraints and restrictions of such entity defining the boundary of operation. Also, we establish the information flow in and out of a moderator entity. An honest but curious moderator model is proposed for n-party bargaining game.
- Propose a secure 2-object 2-party bargaining model in the presence of an honest but curious moderator. We also prove that the model is a generic model suitable for n-object 2-party bargaining game with one moderator.

– Provide an analysis of the security of the protocol. The protocol is not only secure against moderator model defined but also secure against IND-CCA model of attacker with access to historical records of bargaining game.

The paper is organized as follows, in Sect. 2 we review earlier works in proposed concept and protocols and present a brief overview of the perquisites required. In Sect. 3 we introduce the framework of secure bargaining game in the presence of an honest but curious moderator. In Sect. 3 also we propose implementation of the proposed framework and proved that the protocol is secure against probabilistic polynomial time adversary. Implementation of the protocol is discussed in Sect. 4. Conclusion and scope of future work in given in Sect. 5.

2   Literature Review

Zeuthen proposed bargaining problem in the context of labor-management wage negotiations [22]. During negotiation, it is assumed that each party is capable of rational calculation of the cost-of-conflict, and the risk associated with non-negotiation and utility achieved after the negotiation. Avoidance of this conflict is assumed to be the motivation for consensus in such negotiations. In this model negotiating parties agrees to a minimum concession and both parties propose a concession based on his risk profile. If the other party does not agree, the game continues. The game terminates on an agreement of concession proposed in subsequent steps. It was noted that modeling traders only by their initial endowments and indifference curves, while often adequate to determine a unique competitive equilibrium in a market, would nevertheless leave indeterminate the outcome of bargaining, although it could determine a "contract curve" in which the outcomes of successful bargaining might be found.

Von Neumann and Morgenstern extended the bargaining problem to game theoretic approach. Although Neumann and Morgenstern did not identify a unique solution of the bargaining problem, their theory of games presented a framework which has been used for most subsequent analyses in this and closely related areas [20].

Nash in his paper extended the game theoretic approach to introduce utility function as the gain of each party and disagreement values that the parties get if no negotiation take place [12,13]. Nash product is an inter-operation between utility and disjoint value and each party attempt to maximize the value while reaching the equilibrium state. Nash solution for bargaining game have certain properties like assumption of in-variance, assumption of independence of irrelevant alternative. It satisfies the assumption of in-variance with respect to utility transformations. This holds that a solution for one bargaining game should also be the solution for any other game in which the utilities of either player (or both) are changed by a direct linear transformation of those of the original game.

The assumption of independence of irrelevant alternative states that when a solution for one game is also a feasible outcome of a second game, then the solution also applies to the second game. Nash solution provides symmetry, i.e.

if the positions of the players are symmetrical then the solution will provide and equal payoff to each player. It is Pareto optimal i.e. there exists no other solution that can provide better utility to one player without affecting other players. However it does not support resource monotonicity axiom as proposed by Kalai [5]. Resource monotonicity states that if, for every utility level, that player 1 may demand, the maximum feasible utility level, that player 2 can simultaneously achieve is increased, then the utility level assigned to player 2 according to the solution should also be increased. New solutions are proposed to support this new axiom in [4,5].

Rubinstein proposed the idea of Perfect Equilibrium partition while distributing a surplus in two player bargaining game where each bargain cost a fixed amount to the players or their exists a fixed discounting factor. Discounting factor is a function of risk taking ability of the player. It was shown that there exists an equilibrium for an in finitely repeated game [16]. In this model first player has an advantage over second player during first proposal however the advantage reduces with successive iteration. Baron and Ferejohn in their work "Bargaining in Legislatures" extended Rubinstein model for more than two players [1]. In N player model, negotiation can be achieved in closed rule or an open rule. In closed rule one acting party proposes a split while others vote on the split immediately. If the bargain is approved the legislation closes or the motion moves on to next stage with discounted payoffs. in open rule once a slice of the resource is proposed one among the remaining actors can propose an alternative distribution. Final pay off is selected through vote after considering discounting factor for each round of indifference. Analysis of N person model is evaluated in [3,10,11]. A comprehensive survey of bargaining game is given by Schellenberg in [19].

Online bargaining model is discussed in [9,17]. In [9] the author primarily focuses on dynamic pricing model, in multi-agent environment, based on seller and buyer price series to optimize the chance of negotiation. Tuomas Sandholm in his paper [17] introduced the concept of third-party mediator to perform game theoretic incentive distribution. This paper mostly focuses on implementing enhancement of computational and combinatorial bidding. However, in each case exchange of information is fully visible to intermediate agent and they are susceptible to tamper by dishonest third party. Negotiation between security agents on behalf of a user to mediate strangers' access to local resources is discussed in [21]. In this paper the author implemented a policy checker component model tightly coupled with the user exchanging local resources.

Oblivious commitment based envelop protocol (OCBE) was discussed as access control by Li in their paper Oblivious Attribute Certificate [6,7]. Provably secure and efficient OCBE protocols for the Pendersen commitment scheme and comparison predicates as well as logical combinations of them was explained in the paper. OCBE is a protocol used to construct certificate to obtain access control using predicate based construction. One of the draw backs of OCBE is that each party must disclose his identity to other to exchange the information. That limitation is eliminated in Oblivious Signature Based Envelop(OSBE) where before information exchange each party ensures that their message can only be decrypted by recipient who has certain agreed upon permission without disclosing their identities [8,14]. In [8] author introduced OSBE over RSA and identity based encryption which is further extended to include El-Gamal family of encryption in [14].

Not much research was conducted to secure bargaining game between concerned parties in the presence of an adversary with malicious intent. An adversary can alter the content of the bargain proposed to establish a false bargain commitment for his own advantage. Similarly, when the bargain is conducted in the presence of a third party. Third party mediator can gain business advantage by relaying the conversation of the bargain to an unintended recipient. In this paper, we establish a framework for secure bargain system and proposed implementation using oblivious commitment based envelop protocol.

In following section we introduce some essential primitives.

2.1 Prerequisite

Definition 1. *Bargaining Game [13]: Bargaining game between two players $i = 1, 2$ is a pair $\mathcal{B} = \{\mathcal{U}, d\}$ where $\mathcal{U}$ consists of all possible agreements between two players in terms of utilities (u_1, u_2) and disagreement point d contains the values $\{d_1, d_2\}$ that the players will receive if they do not reach consensus. For a successful bargaining game $u_1 + u_2 \leq M$ where $M > 0$ is the surplus that is distributed and it reaches the equilibrium if $u_1, u_2 > 0$.*

Oblivious commitment based envelop protocol (OCBE) is a cryptography primitive that enables oblivious access control. It enables attribute-based access control without revealing any information about the attributes. Informally, in an OCBE scheme, the receiver has a private attribute value a which has been committed to the sender; the sender has a public predicate b and a private message M. The sender and receiver engage in interactive protocol and finally the receiver receives the message M if the predicate holds for the private attribute i.e. $b(a) = true$ and the sender learns nothing about the receivers private value.

Definition 2. *Oblivious Commitment Based Envelop protocol [7]: An OCBE scheme received a parameter of commitment scheme **commit**. An OCBE scheme involves a sender, a receiver, and a trusted third party, and has the following five phases:*

- **Setup:** *The trusted third party provider, for a security parameter k produce a tuple $<P, S, V>$ where P is the public parameter for **commit**, S is a set of possible values and V is a collection of predicates. For each $v \in V$ maps to each element of S as either true or false, i.e. $\forall v \in V \; v(s) = b; b \in \{0, 1\} \wedge s \in S$. The domain of **commit** contains B as a subset. The third party sends $<P, S, V>$ to sender and receiver.*
- **Receiver Commit:** *The receiver chose a value $a \in S$ and commit to the value by a random parameter r and send the commitment $c = \mathbf{commit}(a, r)$ to the sender.*

– **Sender Initialization**: *The sender chose a message $M \in \{0,1\}^*$ and a predicate $v \in V$ and disclose the predicate to the receiver. After this step the sender has c, M, v and receiver has c, v, a, r.*
– **Interaction**: *The sender and the receiver run an interactive protocol, during which an envelope containing an encryption of M is delivered to the receiver.*
– **Open**: *After the interaction phase, if $v(a)$ is true, the receiver outputs the message M. Otherwise, the receiver does nothing*

An OCBE protocol should satisfy the following properties

1. **Soundness**: *A protocol is sound if for any chosen predicate $v \in V$, the receiver can output the message M with overwhelming probability only if the condition is satisfied.*
2. **Oblivious**: *The OCBE scheme is oblivious when a polynomial adversary does not have more than negligible advantage in learning $a_b \in \{a_0, a_1\} \subset S$ given $M \in \{0,1\}^*, v \in V$ while running an interactive game with sender.*
3. **Secure Against Receiver**: *The OCBE scheme is secure against receiver when a polynomial adversary (Receiver) can have not more than negligible advantage in learning $a \in S$ for a given $v(a) = false$ and $M_0, M_1 \in \{0,1\}^*$ while running an interactive game with Sender.*

3   Secure Bargaining Game Framework

In this section we explain the model of secure bargaining game between seller $\mathcal{S}$ and customer $\mathcal{C}$ in the presence of a third party moderator $\mathcal{M}$. We consider a simple 2-person bargain game between seller and customer. A seller places objects in market place and a customer proposes price of the object. The seller accepts the bargain if the profit obtained by him by selling the object at the proposed price satisfies his criteria of profitability. Similarly the customer agrees to pay the prices if he finds the discount received on market prices acceptable. There are many proven approaches for selling consumer and retails goods in bargaining model. Table 1 contains the definitions and symbols used in this paper.

Portfolio Profitability
This is one of most commonly observed profit model for the seller.

– Seller $\mathcal{S}$ wishes to place places N objects in marketplace with maximum discount estimated per object as a collection $\{d_{a_0}, \ldots, d_{a_n}\}$. He releases the list of objects in the marketplace without disclosing the maximum allowed discount value.
– Customer $\mathcal{C}$ who wishes to purchase a set of object places his choice of discount claim for those objects as $\{d_{c_i}, \ldots d_{c_j}\}; 1 \leq i < j \leq n$.
– Seller $\mathcal{S}$ accepts the transaction if for each object in the list of transaction either $d_{a_i} \geq d_{c_i}$ or even if $d_{a_i} < d_{c_i}$ the seller gets an over all profit in the entire transaction i.e. $\sum_{k=i}^{j} d_{a_k} \geq \sum_{k=i}^{j} d_{c_k}$.

Table 1. Nomenclature

Symbol	Description
$\mathcal{S}$	Seller
$\mathcal{C}$	Customer
$\mathcal{M}$	Moderator
d_{a_i}	Acceptable discount on i-th object
d_{c_i}	Discount claimed on i-th object
$e : G \times G \to G_T$	Bi-linear map defined over cyclic group G, G_T
g, h	Generators of Groups G
r	Random number selected from Z
$\mathcal{D}$	Set of all objects available for bargaining
Υ	Predicate Criteria
I	Index of objects being bargained

it can be easily seen that portfolio profitability in favor of seller satisfies Nash's equilibrium condition.

Lemma 1. *Given* $\{d_{a_0}, \ldots, d_{a_n}\}$ *and* $\{d_{a_0}, \ldots, d_{a_n}\}$ *if* $\sum_{k=i}^{j} d_{a_k} \geq \sum_{k=i}^{j} d_{c_k}$ *the bargaining game always reaches an equilibrium.*

Proof. Assume that For a given ith object market Price as MP_i, and cost of the object is CP_i. $\{u_a\}$ is a set of choices as profit earned by the seller S and $\{u_c\}$ is a set of choices as the profit earned by Customer. Clearly $u_{c_i} = d_{c_i} \forall i \leq n$ as profit earned by the customer is equivalent to the profit claimed by him, and expected profit by Seller for ith object is $u_{a_i} = MP_i - CP_i - d_{a_i}$. The value of payoff to be shared between seller and customer for each object, is equal to the gain of marked price over cost of the object. Maximum achievable profit margin achievable per object is MP-CP. Thus if both Seller and Customer starts with a joint disagreement value of $(0, 0)$ the bargaining game for n objects is essentially reduced to

$$\mathcal{B} = \sum_{i}^{n}(u_{a_i} + u_{c_i}) \leq \sum_{i}^{n}(MP_i - CP_i)$$

where $u_{a_i} \geq 0 \forall i \leq n : \{u_a, u_c\} \in \mathcal{U}, \{0,0\} \in d$.

Now,

$$\sum_{i}^{n}(u_{c_i} + u_{a_i}) = \sum_{i}^{n}(MP_i - CP_i + (d_{a_i} - d_{c_i}))$$

$$if d_a \geq d_c \Rightarrow u_a + u_c = MP - CP + \delta$$

$$\Rightarrow u_a + u_c \leq MP - CP : \delta \geq 0$$

$$\sum_{i}^{n} d_{a_i} \geq \sum_{i}^{n} d_{c_i} \Rightarrow \sum_{i}^{n}(u_{a_i} + u_{c_i}) \leq \sum_{i}^{n}(MP_i - CP_i)$$

$$d_{a_i} < d_{c_i}, \sum_i^n d_{a_i} \geq \sum_i^n d_{c_i}$$

$$\Rightarrow \sum_i^n d_{a_i} - \sum_i^n d_{c_i} \geq \sum(\delta) \geq 0$$

$$\sum_i^n d_{a_i} \geq \sum_i^n d_{c_i} \Rightarrow \sum_i^n (u_{a_i} + u_{c_i}) \leq \sum_i^n (MP_i - CP_i)$$

And the bargaining game reaches equilibrium.

Discounting Model

Another alternating approach a seller can chose for bargaining is discounting model on portfolio. In this model the seller focuses on amplifying the product sell rather than optimizing the profit. Discounting model is more applicable during new product launch or clearance sell. In this model

- Seller S wishes to place places N objects in marketplace with maximum discount estimated per object as a collection $\{d_{a_0}, \ldots, d_{a_n}\}$ and min product sale quota value Q and historical record of sales N. He releases the list of objects in the marketplace without disclosing the maximum allowed discount.
- Customer C who wishes to purchase a set of object places his choice of discount claim for those objects as $\{d_{c_i}, \ldots d_{c_j}\}; 1 \leq i < j \leq n$.
- Seller S accepts the transaction if for each object in the list of transaction either $d_{a_i} \geq d_{c_i}$ or even if $d_{a_i} < d_{c_i}$ the seller gets an over all profit in the entire transaction i.e. $\sum_{k=i}^j d_{a_k} \geq \sum_{k=i}^j d_{c_k}$.
- In discounting model the seller can chose to accept the transaction if the sales value of the transaction assists in reaching quota set by him i.e. if $\sum_{k=i}^j d_{a_k} \leq \sum_{k=i}^j d_{c_k} \wedge N + j \geq Q$.

We propose a framework for **Secure Bargaining Game** between a seller and consumer. The framework consists of following polynomial time algorithms in probabilistic polynomial adversary model as a collection of polynomial time algorithm (**Initialize, Set Up, Evaluation**).

- **Initialize**: During initialization phase Seller S and Customer C agree on a set of object $\mathcal{D}$ with security parameter κ. S chooses a predicate Υ as bargaining criteria over $\mathcal{D}$.

$$(\mathcal{D}, \Upsilon) \leftarrow \textbf{Initialize}(S, C, \kappa) \tag{1}$$

- **Set Up**: During set up phase S chose a function $f_S()$ to commit on maximum allowed discount $\{d_{a_0}, \ldots, d_{a_n}\} \in \mathcal{D}$ and shares committed value. Similarly C chooses function $f_C()$ to commit on his discount claims $\{d_{c_i}, \ldots d_{c_j}\} \in \mathcal{D}; 1 \leq i < j \leq n$.

$$(f_S(.), f_C(.)) = \textbf{Set Up}(S, C, \mathcal{D}) \tag{2}$$

- **Evaluation**: During evaluation phase, $f_C()$ and $f_S()$ is evaluated against Υ. Evaluation function is a polynomial time function $\mathcal{M}$ is given as

$$\mathcal{M}(f_S(), f_C(), \Upsilon) = \begin{cases} 1 & if\ \Upsilon \\ 0 & \text{otherwise} \end{cases} \tag{3}$$

We restrict the scope of the bargaining criteria to portfolio model. However the framework proposed is generic and can be adopted to any bargaining criteria that satisfies Nash equilibrium. In this paper we adopt the following

$$\Upsilon : \sum_{k=i}^{j} d_{a_k} \geq \sum_{k=i}^{j} d_{c_k} \tag{4}$$

The bargain system described above can have a third party mediator. This third party provides necessary platform and computation capabilities for the seller to host the bargain. A mediator received the commitment $f_S()$ from seller, claims from the customer $f_C()$ and conclude the bargaining is a valid one by computing $\mathcal{M}$. So with out loss of information we can consider moderator as synonymous to **Evaluation** as $\mathcal{M}$.

To simulate real life scenario, we assume that $\mathcal{M}$ is honest-but-curious i.e. he correctly computes the functionality, but also has business interest in knowing details of a bargaining transaction. He can perform some additional computation on the data input and result, to obtain information regarding the discount obtained by the customer or profit gained by the seller. If the mediator gain access to this information, he can distribute it to his favorable seller who is also using the same platform to aid him in business. With additional knowledge of transactions the moderator might promote sellers of its own choice, giving away certain discount to the customer. Therefore, using extended knowledge of a bargaining game the mediator can disrupt a fair business system.

We propose limitations of an honest but curious moderator $\mathcal{M}$ defined over security parameter κ as

- $\mathcal{M}$ computes the decision correctly i.e.

$$Pr[f_S(d_a) \leftarrow \mathcal{S}; f_C(d_c) \leftarrow \mathcal{C}; \mathcal{M}(f_S(d_a), f_C(d_c)) = 1]_{d_a \geq d_c} = 1 \tag{5}$$

- $\mathcal{M}$ can not derive any information regarding d_a and d_c. For a negligible function $\eta(\kappa)$ for a security parameter κ.

$$Pr[f_S(d_a) \leftarrow \mathcal{S}; f_C(d_c) \leftarrow \mathcal{C};$$
$$\mathcal{M}(f_S(d_a), f_C(d_c)) = 1]_{d_a \geq d_c} - Pr[r_s \leftarrow Z; r_c \leftarrow Z; \mathcal{M}(r_s, r_c) = 1]_{r_s \geq r_c} \leq \eta(\kappa) \tag{6}$$

- Weaker assumption of $\mathcal{M}$ is that, it can derive some information regarding d_c but no information of d_a is available to $\mathcal{M}$ i.e.

$$Pr[f_S(d_a) \leftarrow \mathcal{S}; f_C(d_c) \leftarrow \mathcal{C};$$
$$\mathcal{M}(f_S(d_a), f_C(d_c)) = 1]_{d_a \geq d_c} - Pr[r_s \leftarrow Z; \mathcal{M}(r_s, d_c) = 1]_{r_s \geq d_c} \leq \eta(\kappa) \tag{7}$$

The algorithm for secure bargaining game in the presence of an honest but curious moderator with above limitations uses a variation of oblivious commitment based envelop protocol (OCBE) for inequality check.

OCBE is used to provide secure interaction between Seller $\mathcal{S}$. Customer $\mathcal{C}$, and mediator $\mathcal{M}$ to achieve a bargaining game between seller and buyer in the presence of a third party facilitator. The seller $\mathcal{S}$ commits on maximum allowed discount d_a on the object using Pendersen commitment scheme and attach the proof of commitment. $\mathcal{M}$ validates the proof and displays the object and its market price to the viewer. $\mathcal{C}$ chose a discount d_a and commit the discount claimed to $\mathcal{M}$. $\mathcal{M}$ compares two commitment using OCBE with a chosen predicate to verify as $d_a \geq d_c$ and returns the result to the customer.

3.1   1-Object Secure Bargain System

In this section we describe a secure bargaining system with three parties, i.e. seller, customer and mediator. Only one object is available for bargaining from a seller and the customer claims discount on the same object. The entire operation is hosted by the moderator that performs the decision whether the bargain should be concluded based on the committed maximum discount allowed by the seller for the object. 1-Object secure bargain system is described as

- The seller $\mathcal{S}$ places an object in marketplace with maximum discount allowed on the object as d_a. The seller releases a commitment on d_a with disclosing the value and eligible maximum market price of the object.
- The customer $\mathcal{C}$ wishes to purchase the object claim a discount d_c for the object and commits to it.
- The Seller accept he transaction only if $\Upsilon : d_a \geq d_c$.

An algorithm for 1-Object secure bargain system that is executed among the seller $\mathcal{S}$, the customer $\mathcal{C}$ and the mediator $\mathcal{M}$ is given in Algorithm 3.1.

Theorem 1. *The mediator is correctly able to compute the protocol.*

Proof. Given idea is correct if it correctly proofs the acceptability of a valid bargain transaction and rejects an invalid one. For any maximum acceptable discount d_a and discount claim by the user d_c it can be observed that,

$$e(\alpha * \alpha^c, h) = e(g^{d_a} h^{r^2} * g^{-d_c} h^{-r_c^2}, h)$$
$$= e(g^{(d_a - d_c)} h^{(r^2 - r_c^2)}, h)$$
$$= e(g^{d_a - d_c} h^{r^2 - r_c^2}, h)$$
$$= e(g^{(d_a - d_c)}, h).e(h, h)^{(r^2 - r_c^2)}$$
$$e(\beta^c * \beta, \beta^c * \beta^{-1}) = e(h^{r_c + r}, h^{r_c - r}) = e(h, h)^{r_c^2 - r^2}$$
$$e(\alpha * \alpha^c, h).e(\beta^c * \beta, \beta^c * \beta^{-1}) = e(g^{(d_a - d_c)}, h).e(h, h)^{(r^2 - r_c^2)}.e(h, h)^{(r_c^2 - r^2)}$$
$$= e(g^{(d_a - d_c)}, h)$$

Algorithm 3.1. 1-Object Secure Bargaining Game

Require: Cyclic group G of prime order p, G_T as an extension group of G, a bi-linear map $e : G \times G \to G_T$, Maximum discount allowed for the object d_a, Discount claimed by the customer C as d_c, predicate Υ for validating the result.

Ensure: Claim for a discount is accepted or declined by the mediator $\mathcal{M}$.

1. Initialize: S, C agree on Group G, G_T and a bi-linear map e, g, h are generators of a cyclic group G and h
2. STEP 1: Seller compute commitment on the element d_a as $\alpha = g^{d_a} h^{r^2}, \beta = h^r$
3. The seller computes $f_S(d_a, r) = \{\alpha, \beta\}$ for $r \in Z$.
4. STEP 2: The seller S shared the commitment $\{\alpha, \beta\}$ with $\mathcal{M}$ with aggregated proof of commitment π and listed market price of the objects.
5. STEP 3: $\mathcal{M}$ verifies the proof of commitment and make the object available for bargain in the market.
6. STEP 3: Customer C commits the discount claim d_c and computes

$$\alpha^c = g^{-d_c} h^{-r_c^2}, \beta^c = h^{r_c}$$

   for $r_c \in Z$.
7. STEP 4: Customer C sends the claim $f_C(d_c, r_c) = \{\alpha^c, \beta^c d_c\}$ to $\mathcal{M}$.
8. STEP 5: $\mathcal{M}$ computes

$$l = f_\mathcal{M}(f_S(d_a, r), f_C(d_c, r_c))$$
$$= e(\alpha * \alpha^c, h).e(\beta^c * \beta, \beta^c * \beta^{-1})$$

   where $*, .$ are multiplication operations defined in G and G_T respectively
9. STEP 6: $\mathcal{M}$ sends $\{l, d_c\}$ to Seller S and inform the predicate parameter d_c
10. STEP 7: Seller validates $l = e(g, h)^{[(d_a - d_c) mod p]}$
11. STEP 8: Then if $\Upsilon : d_a - d_c < 0$ the transaction is rejected by Seller otherwise the transaction is accepted.

Now Seller can easily validate if information provided by the moderator is correct by checking

$$l = e(g, h)^{[(d_a - d_c) mod p]}$$

and successively take decision on whether to accept or reject the transaction based on Υ.

Theorem 2. *Proposed algorithm is IND-CCA secure in OCBE assumption.*

Proof. To proof that bargaining system is secure against indistinguishability chosen cipher text attack (IND-CCA) and also preserve the indistinguishability property described in Eq. 7, we propose a security games. In this game a probabilistic polynomial time adversary $\mathcal{A}$ wishes to challenge an honest mediator $f_\mathcal{M}$ over a set of distinct allowed discount and claim discount pairs. Adversary has access to n previous set of decisions namely a collection of tuples $H = \{\{d_{a_1}, d_{c_1}, l_1\} \ldots, \{d_{a_n}, d_{c_n}, l_n\}\} \forall 1 \leq i \leq n$

$$\mathcal{M}(f_S(d_{a_i}, r), f_C(d_{c_i}, r_c)) = \begin{cases} 1 = 1 & if\, d_a \geq d_c \\ 0 & otherwise \end{cases} \qquad (8)$$

Adversary $\mathcal{A}$ wished to be challenged on a pair of accepted discount and claimed discount tuple $t_0 = \{d_{a_0}, d_{c_0}\}, t_1 = \{d_{a_1}, d_{c_1}\}$. He can generate the tuple with the help of the history H but should satisfy the following conditions to eliminate obvious cases.

- $t_0 \notin H \wedge t_1 \notin H$
- if $d_{a_0} \geq d_{c_0}$ then $d_{a_1} \geq d_{c_1}$.

Adversary has black box access to the polynomial time algorithm $\mathcal{S}$ and $\mathcal{C}$ that simulates the algorithm f_C and f_S over d_a and d_c.

For each tuple he generates $T_0 = \{\mathcal{S}(d_{a_0}), \mathcal{C}(d_{c_0})\}, T_1 = \{\mathcal{S}(d_{a_1}), \mathcal{C}(d_{c_1})\}$ and sends to the mediator $\mathcal{M}$. After receiving T_0 and T_1, $\mathcal{M}$ tosses a fair, unbiased coin to chose $b \in \{0, 1\}$ and return $l_b = f_{\mathcal{M}}(T_b)$ to the adversary.

Adversary computes $\mathcal{A}(l_b, T_0, T_1) = b\prime$, Adversary wins the challenge if he is successfully able to predict $b\prime = b$.

For a given distinguisher

$$D(b, b\prime) = \begin{cases} 1 : if b = b\prime \\ 0 : \quad \text{otherwise} \end{cases}, \tag{9}$$

$$Pr[D(b, b\prime) = 1] = Pr[\mathcal{A}(l_b, T_0, T_1) = b] = \frac{1}{2} + Pr[f_{\mathcal{M}}(T_0) = 1] - Pr[f_{\mathcal{M}}(T_1) = 1]$$

$$= \frac{1}{2} + Pr[f_{\mathcal{M}}(\mathcal{S}(d_{a_0}), \mathcal{C}(d_{c_0})) = 1] - Pr[f_{\mathcal{M}}(\mathcal{S}(d_{a_1}), \mathcal{C}(d_{c_1})) = 1]$$

$$= \frac{1}{2} + Pr[e(g^{d_{a_0} - d_{c_0}}, h) \in G_T] - Pr[e(g^{d_{a_1} - d_{c_1}}, h) \in G_T]$$

$$\leq \frac{1}{2} + \alpha(\kappa)$$

By Oblivious assumption of OCBE in a cyclic group and by the choice restriction of the adversary given in Subsect. 3.1, where $\alpha(\kappa)$ is the negligible function defined over the security parameter κ. Thus, by definition advantage of the adversary

$$Adv_{\mathcal{A}} = |Pr[D(b, b\prime) = 1] - \frac{1}{2}| \leq \alpha(\kappa) \tag{10}$$

Thus a polynomial adversary does not gain any advantage in identifying the allowed discount and claim discount pair from the response of $\mathcal{M}$.

Theorem 3. *Honest but curious mediator cannot extract any information about the maximum discount allowed by seller.*

Proof. To prove that mediator can not infer any knowledge about the discount allowed, it is sufficient to prove that commitment is zero knowledge in the presence of a honest verifier. We now describe the honest verifier zero knowledge proof of the given protocol with minor change to the zero knowledge proof proposed by Okamoto [15]. The conversation between a seller $\mathcal{S}$ as prover and honest verifier is given as $\mathcal{V}$.

Prover	**Verifier**

$$f_S(d_a, r) = \{\alpha, \beta, \beta^{-1}\}$$

$$a = g^u h^{r_a^2} \quad u, r_a \in_R \mathbb{Z}$$

$$c \in_R \{0, 1\}$$

$$\xrightarrow{\quad a \quad}$$

$$\xleftarrow{\quad c \quad}$$

$$\{r_0 = u + cd_a, r_1 = r_a^2 + cr^2\}$$

$$\xrightarrow{\quad r_0 \quad r_1 \quad}$$

$$\alpha^c . a? = g_0^r h_1^r$$

- Prover and verifier agree on a group G with generator g, h of prime modulo q.
- prover commit on maximum discount allowed as $f_S(d_a, r) = \{\alpha, \beta, \beta^{-1}\}; d_a, r \in \mathbb{Z}$
- Prover shares $a = g^u h^{r_a^2}; u, r_a \in_R \mathbb{Z}$.
- Verifier tosses an unbiased coin to send a challenge $c \in \{0, 1\}$.
- On receiving the challenge the prover send response as $r = \{r_0 = u + cd_a, r_1 = r_a^2 + cr^2\}$.
- Verifier verifies $\alpha^c . a? = g_0^r h_1^r$.

By Okamoto ID proof it is apparent that given scheme is honest verifier zero knowledge. In a simulated conversation

$$\mathcal{V}^* = \{a, c, r; c \in_R \{0, 1\}; r_0, r_1 \in \mathbb{Z}; a = \alpha^{-c} g_0^r h_1^r\} \tag{11}$$

it can be observed that $Pr[\mathcal{V}] - Pr[\mathcal{V}^*] \le \eta(\kappa)$ where $\eta(\kappa)$ is a negligible function defined over the negligible parameter κ as probability of success of both conversations is $\frac{1}{n^2}$. It can directly infer that for any random r_s, and r_c

$$Pr[f_S(d_a, r) \leftarrow S] - Pr[r_s \in \mathbb{Z}] = \eta(\kappa)$$
$$Pr[f_C(d_c, r) \leftarrow S] - Pr[r_c \in \mathbb{Z}] = \eta(\kappa)$$

$$Pr[f_S(d_a) \leftarrow S; f_C(d_c) \leftarrow C;$$
$$\mathcal{M}(f_S(d_a), f_C(d_c)) = 1]_{d_a \ge d_c} - Pr[r_s \leftarrow Z; r_c \leftarrow Z; \mathcal{M}(r_s, r_c) = 1]_{r_s \ge r_c} \le \eta(\kappa) \tag{12}$$

3.2 N-Object Secure Bargain System

In this section we extend the idea of a single object bargain system to meet the requirement of another real world scenario. In most practical cases, the seller who intends to sell multiple objects may not get a hard profit margin for individual objects, rather he would chose to have an affordable profit margin over the entire lot. In a scenario closely resembling real life example, the seller might sell something even if the claim of a discount is more than maximum allowed discount on the object as long as the seller can get a net profit out of the entire lot. The seller tends to achieve an overall profit from the lot. Following implementation emulated portfolio bargaining model as described in

- The seller S places a set of objects in marketplace with maximum discount allowed on the object as $D_a = \{d_{a_0}, \ldots, d_{a_n}\}$. The seller releases a commitment on D_a without disclosing the value and eligible maximum market price of the object.
- The customer C wishes to purchase the object claim a discount $D_c = \{d_{c_i}, \ldots d_{c_j}\}$ for the object and commits to it.
- The mediator M can compute the and send necessary information to the seller so that the Seller chose to accept or reject a bargain based on the acceptance criteria. But M should not know any formation regarding maximum discount allowed and discount claim in the process.
- The seller accept or reject the transaction based on acceptance criteria Υ.

In this model of bargaining system, the decision to complete the transaction is chosen based on total profit obtained from the entire transaction. To illustrate the scenario, let us assume a seller places a set of 3 object at a maximum discount claim cut off as 25 each on marked prices. Now if a customer claims discount of 20, 30 and 15 respectively on three objects, then even if claim discount of 30 is more than maximum discount claim of individual object, the seller still chose to allow the transaction as total discount claim in three objects $30 + 15 + 20 = 65$ is less than total maximum discount allowed as $25 \times 3 = 75$. Though the seller is loosing the bargain on any one object he is gaining in totality thus winning the over all game.

We propose the algorithm for N-Object Secure Bargain System as an extension of the algorithm proposed in Algorithm 3.2. In this algorithm as well it is trivial that honest but curious moderator can not derive any further information of the trade except knowing the parties involved. Similar to the security prove discussed in Theorem 2, we can also show that advantage of a polynomial time active adversary A with access to historical bargaining transactions and black box access to polynomial function S and C, is negligible.

Theorem 4. *The mediator is correctly able to compute the bargaining game.*

Proof. Given idea is correct if it correctly proofs the acceptability of a valid bargain transaction and rejects an invalid one. For any maximum acceptable discount $D_a = \{d_{a_0}, \ldots, d_{a_n}\}$ and discount claim by the user $D_c = \{d_{c_i}, \ldots d_{c_j}\}; 1 \leq i < j \leq n, |D_c| \leq |D_a| = n$ it can be observed that,

---

Algorithm 3.2. N-Object Secure Bargaining Game

Require: Cyclic group G or prime order p, G_T as an extension group, a bi-linear map $e : G \times G \to G_T$, Maximum discount allowed for N objects in the system $D_a = \{d_{a_0}, \ldots, d_{a_n}\}$, Discount claimed by the customer $\mathcal{C}$ as $D_c = \{d_{c_i}, \ldots d_{c_j}\}; 1 \leq i < j \leq n, |D_c| \leq |D_a| = n$, Predicate to verify as Υ

Ensure: Claim for a discount is accepted or declined by the mediator $\mathcal{M}$.

1. Initialize: $\mathcal{S}, \mathcal{C}$ agrees on Group G, G_T and a bi-linear map e
2. STEP 1: Seller computes commitment on each element in D_a as

$$\alpha_i = g^{d_{a_i}} h^{r_i^2}, \beta = h^{r_i} \forall d_{a_i} \in D_a; 1 \leq i \leq n$$

where g, h are generators of a cyclic group G. The seller computes

$$f_S(D_a, \{r_1, \ldots, r_n\}) = \{\{\alpha_1, \beta_1\} \ldots, \{\alpha_n, \beta_n\}\}$$

for all $r_i \in Z$.

3. STEP 2: The seller $\mathcal{S}$ shared the commitment $\{\{\alpha_1, \beta_1\} \ldots, \{\alpha_n, \beta_n\}\}$ with $\mathcal{M}$ with aggregated proof of commitment Π and listed market price of the objects.
4. STEP 3: $\mathcal{M}$ verifies the proof of commitment and make the object available for bargain in the market.
5. STEP 3: Customer $\mathcal{C}$ commits the discount claim D_c on a set of objects $\{i, j\} : 1 \leq i < j \leq n$ and computes

$$\alpha_k^c = g^{-d_{c_k}} h^{-r_{c_k}^2}, \beta^c = h^{r_{c_k}} \forall d_{c_k} \in D_c \ r_{c_k} \in \mathbb{Z}; i \leq k \leq j, \gamma = \sum_{k=i}^{j} d_{c_k}$$

6. STEP 4: Customer $\mathcal{C}$ sends the claim to $\mathcal{M}$.

$$f_C(D_c, \{r_{c_i}, \ldots, r_{c_j}\}) = \{\{\alpha_i^c, \beta_i^c\}, \ldots, \{\alpha_j^c, \beta_j^c\}, \gamma\}$$

7. STEP 5: $\mathcal{M}$ computes

$$l = f_\mathcal{M}(f_S(D_a, \{r_1, \ldots, r_n\}), f_C(D_c, \{r_i^c, \ldots, r_j^c\}))$$

$$= e(\prod_{k=i}^{j} \alpha_k * \alpha_k^c, h). \prod_{k=i}^{j} e(\beta_k^c * \beta_k, \beta_k^c * \beta_k^{-1})$$

where "$*, .$" are multiplication operations defined in G and G_T respectively.

8. STEP 6: $\mathcal{M}$ sends $\{l, \gamma, I\}$ to Seller $\mathcal{S}$ with information the predicate parameter γ and $I = \{i, \ldots, j\} : i \leq k \leq j$ for all k objects in bargain
9. STEP 7: Seller validates

$$l = e(g, h)^{[(\sum_{k \in I} d_{a_k} - \gamma) mod p]}$$

for all k objects in bargaining

10. STEP 8: If $\sum_{k \in I} d_{a_k} - \gamma < 0$ the transaction is rejected otherwise the transaction is accepted.

$$e(\prod_{k=i}^{j} \alpha_k * \alpha_k^c, h) = e(\prod_{k=i}^{j} g^{da_k} h^{r_k^2} * g^{-dc_k} h^{-r_{c_k}^2}, h)$$

$$= e(\prod_{k=i}^{j} g^{(da_k - dc_k)} h^{(r_k^2 - r_{c_k}^2)}, h)$$

$$= e(g^{\sum_{k=i}^{j}(da_k - dc_k)} h^{\sum_{k=i}^{j}(r_k^2 - r_{c_k}^2)}, h)$$

$$= e(g^{\sum_{k=i}^{j}(da_k - dc_k)}, h).e(h, h)^{\sum_{k=i}^{j}(r_k^2 - r_{c_k}^2)}$$

$$\prod_{k=i}^{j} e(\beta_k^c * \beta_k, \beta_k^c * \beta_k^{-1}) = \prod_{k=i}^{j} e(h^{r_{c_k} + r_k}, h^{r_{c_k} - r_k})$$

$$= \prod_{k=i}^{j} e(h, h)^{(r_{c_k}^2 - r_k^2)}$$

$$= e(h, h)^{\sum_{k=i}^{j}(r_{c_k}^2 - r_k^2)}$$

$$e(\prod_{k=i}^{j} \alpha_k * \alpha_k^c, h). \prod_{k=i}^{j} e(\beta_k^c * \beta_k, \beta_k^c * \beta_k^{-1}) = e(g^{\sum_{k=i}^{j}(da_k - dc_k)}, h).e(h, h)^{\sum_{k=i}^{j}(r_k^2 - r_{c_k}^2)}.e(h, h)^{\sum_{k=i}^{j}(r_{c_k}^2 - r_k^2)}$$

$$= e(g^{\sum_{k=i}^{j}(da_k - dc_k)}, h) = l$$

Now the seller validates the commitment of the client with given predicate as

$$l = e(g, h)^{[(\sum_{k \in I} da_k - \gamma)]}$$

and rejects the transaction if

$$\Upsilon : \sum_{k \in I} da_k - \gamma = \sum_{k=i}^{j} da_k - \sum_{k=i}^{j} dc_k < 0$$

Theorem 5. *N-Object bargaining model is secure with OCBE assumptions.*

Proof. To prove that N-Object bargaining model is secure against polynomial adversary in OCBE assumption; it is sufficient to prove if a polynomial algorithm can break N-Object model, same can be used by another polynomial algorithm to break 1-Object bargaining model construction and in turn OCBE. Assume that there exists a polynomial adversary $\mathcal{A}^N$ that runs the following game with Moderator $\mathcal{M}$.

- $\mathcal{A}^N$ chose item collection $\{d_a, d_c\}, \{d_a', d_c'\}$ such that

$$d_a = \{d_{a_i}, \ldots, d_{a_j}\} \in D_a \forall 1 \leq i < j \leq n, |D_a| = n$$
$$d_a' = \{d_{a_k}, \ldots, d_{a_l}\} \in D_a \forall 1 \leq k < l \leq n, |D_a| = n, i \neq k, j \neq l$$
$$d_c = \{d_{c_i}, \ldots, d_{c_j}\} \in D_c \forall 1 \leq i < j \leq n, |D_c| \leq |D_a|$$
$$d_c' = \{d_{c_k}, \ldots, d_{c_l}\} \in D_c \forall 1 \leq k < l \leq n, |D_a| = n, i \neq k, j \neq l$$

- For each elements in d_a and d_c he invokes Seller oracle $\mathcal{S}$ to simulated $f_{\mathcal{S}}$ and computes $\mathcal{S}(d_a) = \{\mathcal{S}(d_{a_i}), \ldots, \mathcal{S}(d_{a_j})\}$ and $\mathcal{S}(d_a') = \{\mathcal{S}(d_{a_k}), \ldots, \mathcal{S}(d_{a_l})\}$.
- For each elements in d_c and d_c' he invokes Customer oracle $\mathcal{C}$ to simulate $f_{\mathcal{C}}$ and compute $\mathcal{C}(d_a) = \{\mathcal{C}(d_{a_i}), \ldots, \mathcal{C}(d_{a_j})\}$ and $\mathcal{C}(d_a') = \{\mathcal{C}(d_{a_k}), \ldots, \mathcal{C}(d_{a_l})\}$.
- $\mathcal{A}^N$ generate pair of tuples $T_0 = \{\mathcal{S}(d_a), \mathcal{C}(d_c)\}$ and $T_01 = \{\mathcal{S}(d_a'), \mathcal{C}(d_c')\}$ to challenge the moderator $\mathcal{M}$.
- After receiving T_0 and T_1, $\mathcal{M}$ tosses a fair, unbiased coin to chose $b \in \{0, 1\}$ and return $l_b = f_{\mathcal{M}}(T_b)$ to the adversary.

– Adversary computes $\mathcal{A}^N(l_b, T_0, T_1) = b\prime$, Adversary wins the challenge if he is successfully able to predict $b\prime = b$.

For a non-negligible function defined over a security parameter κ i.e. $\mu(\kappa)$ assume that $Pr[\mathcal{A}^N(T_0, T_1, l_b) = b] \geq \mu(\kappa)$ i.e. Adversary can break N-Object bargaining protocol with overwhelming probability. We define another poly time algorithm $\mathcal{A}$ that invokes $\mathcal{A}^N$ as follows

– $\mathcal{A}$ chose $T_0 = \{d_a, d_c\} = \{\{d_{a_i}, d_{a_j}\}, \{d_{a_i}, d_{c_j}\}\}$
– $\mathcal{A}$ chose $T_1 = \{d_a', d_c'\} = \{\{d_{a_k}, d_{a_l}\}, \{d_{a_k}, d_{c_l}\}\}$
– It invokes $\mathcal{A}^N$ with $\{T_0, T_1\}$ and outputs l_b.

If $Pr[\mathcal{A}^N(T_0, T_1, l_b) = b] \geq \mu(\kappa)$ then

$$Pr[\mathcal{A}(T_0, T_1, l_b) = b] = Pr[\mathcal{A}^N(T_0, T_1, l_b) = b] \geq \mu(\kappa)$$

$$\frac{1}{2} + Pr[f_\mathcal{M}(\mathcal{S}(d_a), \mathcal{C}(d_c)) = 1] - Pr[f_\mathcal{M}(\mathcal{S}(d_a'), \mathcal{C}(d_c')) = 1] \geq \mu(\kappa)$$

$$\frac{1}{2} + Pr[e(g^{d_{a_i} - d_{c_j}}, h) \in G_T] - Pr[e(g^{d_{a_l} - d_{c_l}}, h) \in G_T] \geq \mu(\kappa)$$

Hence, the polynomial time algorithm $\mathcal{A}$ is successfully able to break 1-Object bargaining game with moderator $\mathcal{M}$ with tuple set $\{d_{a_j}, d_{c_j}\}, \{d_{a_l}, d_{c_l}\}$ using $\mathcal{A}^N$ as a subroutine. This contradicts Theorem 2 as it is secure against OCBE assumption. Thus our initial assumption $Pr[\mathcal{A}^N(T_0, T_1, l_b) = b] \geq \mu(\kappa)$ is also incorrect. Probability that a polynomial adversary can break N-Object bargaining system can not be overwhelming.

4   Implementation

We implemented a simple application to demonstrate the claim in python using charm crypto library v 0.50. Charm crypto is a rapid prototyping tool written in python that supports many pairing groups. In out implementation, we used pairing group defined over super singular curve of 512 bits. We bench mark the performance of 1-Object 2-Player bargaining game and n-object 2-player bargaining game using time taken in seconds. We implemented the algorithm in UNIX environment running standard A1 Azure Virtual Machine with 1 core and 1.75 GiB memory. We capture time taken to perform the operation on 2, 5, 13, 55, 144 233, 377, 610, 987, 2784, 4534, 6535 objects and used standard time function in python to capture the time. Figure 1 shows the computation results. We observe that time taken is almost linear to number of objects considered.

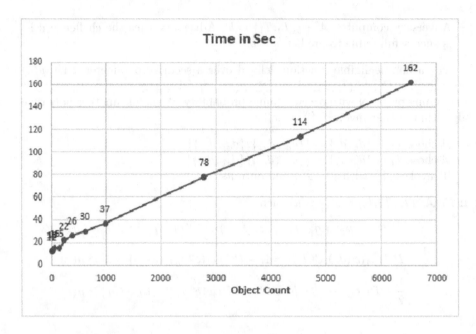

Fig. 1. Time requirement with object count in n-Object 2-Person model

5   Conclusion

In this paper, we established the idea of an honest but curious mediator in the bargaining game between seller and customer and also proposed a mechanism to achieve the secure bargaining game. Though we consider that the mediator is computing the OCBE calculation correctly, there can exist dishonest mediator in the system. Further studies need to be conducted to analyze the impact of a dishonest third party mediator. In our bargain system model, we concluded that the seller is not at a loss for any game with the customer. But there also exists another form of bargaining where a seller might want to sell a few objects at a loss to a customer to achieve overall sales volume benchmark. This scenario opens up another opportunity to make the model proposed in this paper more versatile and robust.

References

1. Baron, D.P., Ferejohn, J.A.: Bargaining in legislatures. Am. Polit. Sci. Rev. **83**(4), 1181–1206 (1989). http://www.jstor.org/stable/1961664
2. Bulow, J., Klempere, P.: Auctions vs. negotiations. Working Paper 4608, National Bureau of Economic Research, January 1996
3. Fréchette, G.R., Kagel, J.H., Lehrer, S.F.: Bargaining in legislatures: an experimental investigation of open versus closed amendment rules. Am. Polit. Sci. Rev. **97**(2), 221–232 (2003). https://doi.org/10.1017/S0003055403000637

4. Kalai, E.: Proportional solutions to bargaining situations: interpersonal utility comparisons. Econometrica **45**(7), 1623–1630 (1977). http://www.jstor.org/stable/1913954

5. Kalai, E., Smorodinsky, M.: Other solutions to Nash's bargaining problem. Econometrica **43**(3), 513–518 (1975). http://www.jstor.org/stable/1914280

6. Li, J., Li, N.: A construction for general and efficient oblivious commitment based envelope protocols. In: Ning, P., Qing, S., Li, N. (eds.) ICICS 2006. LNCS, vol. 4307, pp. 122–138. Springer, Heidelberg (2006). https://doi.org/10.1007/11935308_10

7. Li, J., Li, N.: OACerts: oblivious attribute certificates. IEEE Trans. Dependable Secure Comput. **3**(4), 340–352 (2006). https://doi.org/10.1109/TDSC.2006.54. http://ieeexplore.ieee.org/document/4012646/

8. Li, N., Du, W., Boneh, D.: Oblivious signature-based envelope. Distrib. Comput. **17**(4), 293–302 (2005). https://doi.org/10.1007/s00446-004-0116-1

9. Lin, F.R., Chang, K.Y.: A multiagent framework for automated online bargaining. IEEE Intell. Syst. **16**(4), 41–47 (2001). https://doi.org/10.1109/5254.941356

10. McKelvey, R.D.: An experimental test of a stochastic game model of committee bargaining. Laboratory Research in Political Economy, pp. 139–168 (1991)

11. Miller, L., Vanberg, C.: Decision costs in legislative bargaining: an experimental analysis. Public Choice **155**(3), 373–394 (2013). https://doi.org/10.1007/s11127-011-9866-z

12. Nash, J.: Two-person cooperative games. Econometrica **21**(1), 128–140 (1953). http://www.jstor.org/stable/1906951

13. Nash, J.F.: The bargaining problem. Econometrica **18**(2), 155–162 (1950). http://www.jstor.org/stable/1907266

14. Nasserian, S., Tsudik, G.: Revisiting oblivious signature-based envelopes. In: Di Crescenzo, G., Rubin, A. (eds.) FC 2006. LNCS, vol. 4107, pp. 221–235. Springer, Heidelberg (2006). https://doi.org/10.1007/11889663_19

15. Okamoto, T.: Provably secure and practical identification schemes and corresponding signature schemes. In: Brickell, E.F. (ed.) CRYPTO 1992. LNCS, vol. 740, pp. 31–53. Springer, Heidelberg (1993). https://doi.org/10.1007/3-540-48071-4_3

16. Rubinstein, A.: Perfect equilibrium in a bargaining model. Econometrica **50**(1), 97–109 (1982). http://www.jstor.org/stable/1912531

17. Sandholm, T.: eMediator: a next generation electronic commerce server. Comput. Intell. **18**(4), 656–676 (2002)

18. Sanfey, A.G., Rilling, J.K., Aronson, J.A., Nystrom, L.E., Cohen, J.D.: The neural basis of economic decision-making in the ultimatum game. Science **300**(5626), 1755–1758 (2003). http://www.jstor.org/stable/3834595

19. Schellenberg, J.A.: 'Solving' the bargaining problem. Mid-Am. Rev. Soc. **14**(1/2), 77–88 (1990). http://www.jstor.org/stable/23252907

20. Von Neumann, J., Morgenstern, O.: Theory of Games and Economic Behavior. Princeton University Press, Princeton (1947). https://books.google.co.in/books?id=AUDPAAAAMAAJ

21. Winslett, M., et al.: Negotiating trust in the web. IEEE Internet Comput. **6**(6), 30–37 (2002)

22. Zeuthen, F.: Problems of monopoly and economic warfare. Routledge and K. Paul, London (1967). By F. Zeuthen; with a preface by Joseph A. Schumpeter

Enterprise and Cloud Security

SONICS: A Segmentation Method for Integrated ICS and Corporate System

Khaoula Es-Salhi[1]([✉]), David Espes[2]([✉]), and Nora Cuppens[1]([✉])

[1] IMT Atlantique - LabSTICC, Cesson Sevigne, France
{khaoula.es-salhi,nora.cuppens}@imt-atlantique.fr
[2] University of Western Brittany - LabSTICC, Brest, France
david.espes@univ-brest.fr

Abstract. Integrating Industrial Control Systems (ICS) with Corporate System (IT) is one of the most important industrial orientations. With recent cybersecurity attacks, the security of integrated ICS systems has become the priority of industrial world. *Defense-in-depth* is one of the most important security measures that should be applied to integrated ICS systems. This security technique consists essentially of *"Segmentation"* and *"Segregation"*. Segmentation of an integrated ICS may be based on various types of characteristics such as functional characteristics, business impact, risk levels or other requirements defined by the organization. Although the research conducted so far on this subject has suggested some segmentation solutions, these solutions are unfortunately not generic enough and do not take sufficient account of all the specificities of integrated ICS systems such as their technical and functional heterogeneity. This paper presents SONICS (Segmentation On iNtegrated ICS systems) a new segmentation method that aims to simplify security zones identification by focusing on systems characteristics that are really relevant for segmentation.

Keywords: ICS integration · Industrial control system
Corporate system · Defense-in-depth · Security · Segmentation

1 Introduction

The integration of industrial control systems and corporate systems has become one of the most important orientations of today's industrial world [1,3,5,13,14]. This integration presents multiple advantages but introduces many security problems [20] because industrial systems have always been designed without taking security into account [2,4–6,8].

Defense-in-depth is a highly recommended security measure for Integrated ICS [2,5]. It protects against security problems by dividing the system into encapsulated security zones to create multiple layers of defense. Defence In-depth mainly uses segmentation and segregation techniques. Segmentation involves creating multiple security zones that are controlled, monitored and protected separately. A security zone is a set of *Components* or subsystems connected within a

© Springer Nature Switzerland AG 2018
V. Ganapathy et al. (Eds.): ICISS 2018, LNCS 11281, pp. 231–250, 2018.
https://doi.org/10.1007/978-3-030-05171-6_12

sub-network governed by the same authority and security policy [16]. Integrated ICS segmentation is not easy because they are heavily heterogeneous. Characteristics on which security zones identification should be based may include functional characteristics, business impact, risk levels, or other requirements defined by the organization, but they remain complex and ambiguous. Besides, performing segmentation in large-scale networks taking into account architecture changes and configuration updates is another difficulty with Integrated ICS segmentation. Engineering expertise and intuition are not enough to perform segmentation because it may be error-prone and produce inaccurate results. The work may take more time than necessary while some important aspects may be neglected. Using a framework or a working method is always very useful because it guarantees more accurate results more quickly. Unfortunately, there is currently no method that straightforwardly drives this operation.

For the rest of this document, we will use the abbreviation IICS to refer to "Integrated ICS".

Several research works have studied IICS segmentation. For most of them (NIST [2], ISA [6,8,9] and ANSSI [4] guides ...), segmentation should be done on a case by case basis [10]. However, they do not provide sufficient guidance. Some others [5,15] have an example oriented approach and try to perform segmentation on a well defined reference architecture. They recommend adopting the Purdue Model for Control Hierarchy logical framework (IEC 62264) [6] to delineate security zones.

Few research works [5,14,18] propose a generic solution to the problem. They provide generic rules and guidance to identify security zones while still adopting the IEC 62264 (ISA95) hierarchical model. We believe that this approach can lead to great results if conducted with deep focus on aspects that are relevant for IICS segmentation. Therefore, we propose SONICS, a new generic IICS segmentation method that aims at simplifying IICS security zones identification by focusing on relevant aspects and taking industrial specificity into account. This method uses a simple meta-model to describe IICS systems and allows to identify new potential security zones throughout multiple steps. The new identified potential zones are kept or not based on a constraints analysis.

The paper is structured as follows. Section 2 presents SONICS, our new IICS segmentation method. In this Section we present our IICS meta-model (Sect. 2.2), the system's constraints taken into account by SONICS (Sect. 2.3) and the potential zones identification the constraints analysis process (Sect. 2.4). The fourth part outlines our test plan for validating the method. It explains the test methodology and presents the results we obtained. The latest section discusses the tests results as well as possible improvements.

2 SONICS: The IICS Segmentation Method

2.1 The Principle

The segmentation is done in two phases. The first phase consists of modeling the system to be segmented using the meta-model (Fig. 2) presented in Sect. 2.2. The

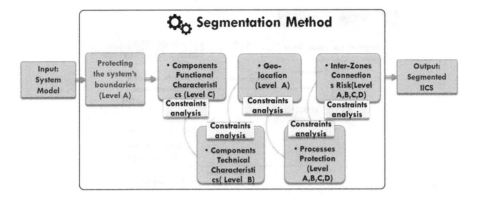

Fig. 1. The segmentation method

system's model is the main input of the second phase. This later consists of segmenting the system through six cycles. At the first cycle, the system's boundaries are protected. This is the first security zone of the system. Next the system's *Components* are grouped cycle after cycle based on only one aspect (Functional, Technical, Geographical, Processes, and Inter-Zones Connections Risk) per cycle to constitute potential security zones. More details about *Components* grouping are provided in the next sections. The identified security zones at each cycle, are kept according to a constraints analysis conducted on the *Components* involved in the new identified zones. Constraints analysis is explained in Sect. 2.3. The principle of SONICS is illustrated in Fig. 1.

2.2 The IICS Meta-model

Our IICS meta-model (Fig. 2) allows to model an IICS as a set of *"Components"*, *"Connections"* and *"Processes"*.

Components

A ***Component*** is any device capable of communicating through the network of the system regardless of its functions and the technologies it uses. A Component is characterized by its functional level, its technical type and the geographical site to which it belongs.

– **Functional levels**

   Components can be grouped according to their function in the system [7,11]. We use an extended model of the IEC 62264 functional hierarchical model (ISA 95) that defines the different functional levels within IICS (see Table 1). Each component of the system belongs to only one functional group. Segmentation based on this aspect is recommended by multiple research studies [5,6,14] because *Components* with different functions usually have different security characteristics.

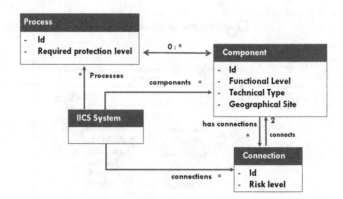

Fig. 2. IICS meta-model

Table 1. Functional levels

Group	Name	Definition
FL-0	Process	This level includes sensors and actuators directly connected to the production process
FL-1	Local or Basic Control	It includes the functions involved in collecting data and manipulating the physical processes
FL-2	Supervisory Control	It includes the functions involved in monitoring and controlling the physical process
FL-3	Operations Management	This level includes the functions involved in managing and optimizing the production work flows
FL-4	Enterprise Business Systems	It includes the functions involved in the business-related activities
FL-ST	Support	It includes *Components* that do not belong to any of the other levels

– **Technical types**
  The technical nature of the *Components* is another key aspect to consider for segmentation. There are many security guides and standards [2,4,6,8,9,12] that state that components of different technical nature must be separated into different security zones because they have different security requirements. A *Component* can be an information technology (IT), Operation Technology (OT) *Component* or an IT-OT *Component*. The latter type is introduced by the method to discern components that are designed to use both types of technologies (IT and OT) such as workstations.
– **Geographical location**
  Components' geographical location is also relevant for segmentation [2]. Two physically distant sites systematically constitute two different security zones. "Physically distant" sites are sites that are either connected by wireless *Connection* or non physically protected wired *Connection*.

Processes

Segmentation should also take into account the organisational aspects of the organisation. This can be achieved with system processes.

A *"Process"* is a set of interrelated interacting activities that transform inputs into outputs. A system is organized into multiple processes. Each component belongs to one or more processes. Process identification should be done by the company. In general, an organizational standard such as ISO9001 is applied to organize the system into processes.

Each process is characterized by its "required protection level" and represents a potential security zone. The "required protection level" of a process can have one of the following values:

- **Level A:** Ultimate protection level
- **Level B:** High protection level
- **Level C:** Medium protection level
- **Level D:** Weak protection level

The level of protection required depends on the risk level of the process and should be evaluated using a risk analysis. We propose a simple risk analysis method based on EBIOS [17] and adapted to the specificity of IICS. The risk level is a function of the gravity of the feared events and their likelihood. It can be evaluated as follows:

1. **Identify the feared events and estimate their gravity:** Feared events gravity is the extent of their impact on one or more of the organization's assets. It can have one of the gravity scale values from Table 2. Estimating the gravity is performed through a qualitative approach that requires a good knowledge of the system and the organization's activity. It should therefore be done in collaboration with the organization's staff. In case a feared event has more than one gravity level from the Table (for example, significant gravity in terms of security aspects but critical financial loss), the worst case is assumed.
2. **Analyze Threat Sources and estimate the likelihood of the attack:** There is one threat source that can affect an IICS process security: the compromise of one of its components or a component that is connected to it. In this case, the whole process can be compromised. The likelihood of such an attack should be estimated using the qualitative scale presented in Table 3, taking into account the system's technical and organizational context, the attack's difficulty as well as the existing solutions.
3. **Evaluate the risk level:** The risk level associated to the process is calculated based on the related gravity and the likelihood of the attack. The risk levels grid in Fig. 3 assists in calculating it.

The required protection level of a process is proportional to its risk level. Table 4 presents how risk levels match "required protection levels".

Table 2. The gravity scale

1. Low	**Safety:** No threat to safety **Regulatory/Legal:** Internal sanction at the most **Company's image:** No impact **Financial:** Low potential financial low (e.g., few dozens of dollars) **Business:** Loss of some few prospects
2. Considerable	**Safety:** Small material damage **Regulatory/Legal:** Small Contractual penalties with some small clients **Company's image:** Local impact, limited number of actors **Financial:** e.g., some thousands of dollars **Business:** Loss of small clients
3. Critical	**Safety:** Considerable material damage **Regulatory/Legal:** Strong contractual penalties with major clients, civil or criminal cases, non-compliance with law or regulation **Company's image:** Wide perimeter impact **Financial:** Dozens of thousands of dollars annually **Business:** Loss of important clients
4. Major	**Safety:** Big material damage, Danger on Human safety **Regulatory/Legal:** Major non-compliance with the law or regulation, massive invasion of privacy, criminal conviction, contractual penalties with multiple actors. **Company's image:** Scandal **Financial:** Hundreds of thousands of dollars annually **Business:** Loss of partnership, Massive loss of clients

Table 3. The likelihood scale

Liklihood	Definition
1. Low	This is unlikely to happen
2. Probable	This may happen
3. Significant	There is a significant risk that this will occur
4. Strong	This should happen one day

Table 4. Risk level/required protection level

Risk level	Required protection level
Extreme risk	Level A (Ultimate)
Critical risk	Level B (High)
Considerable risk	Level C (Medium)
Negligible risk	Level D (Low)

Connections

A "*Connection*" is any channel that can be used by two (or more) *Components* to communicate with each others. It can be physical, where the *Components* are directly linked by a physical (wired or a wireless) connection, or logical, where

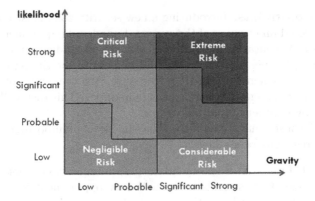

Fig. 3. Risk levels grid

the *Components* are linked through a succession of physical *Connections*. A Connection may be characterized by its risk level. *Connections* impact segmentation especially when they connect *Components* from different zones. This is why we pay special attention to inter-zones *Connections*. These connections emerge at the end of each cycle of the segmentation method, as we progressively create new security zones. Therefore, they can only be modeled when all the *Components* security zones are identified.

Inter-zones *Connections* may connect security zones that have different security levels or contain *Components* of different risk levels. This may introduce security issues. Therefore, these zones should be protected by introducing a new security zone [11] that stages and secure communication through their boundaries.

The risk level of each inter-zone connection of the system should be evaluated based on a risk analysis of the *Connections* and *Components* they connect. We use the same risk analysis method presented in Sect. 2.2. For a given inter-zone connection, all the **Services** exposed by the Components of the zones it connects as well as all the manipulated **Data** should be analyzed in order to perform a more accurate qualitative assessment of the risk associated to these components.

Note that each inter-zone connection is bidirectional. This implies that the risk analysis should be performed on the two interconnected zones components.

2.3 IICS Segmentation Constraints

The addition of a new security zone can sometimes be subject to application difficulties related to the state of the system or its specific requirements. Our segmentation method takes this into account by requiring a constraints analysis at the end of each cycle. The constraints analysis helps to decide whether the identified zones are to be retained or not. There are two generic types of IICS constraints that we focus on:

Functional Constraints. Introducing a new security zone must not adversely affect the expected functioning of the system. Functional requirements that may be sensitive to segmentation should be identified and studied on a case-by-case basis. For example, special attention should be paid to the timing requirements of the critical components of the IICS to ensure that they will not be affected by the flows filtering across security zones boundaries. This task will have to be taken care of by the security administrator.

Functional constraints are not all on the same level of importance. Therefore, we defined three Constraints Levels:

- **Constraint Level A:** Some mandatory requirements can not be satisfied if the new boundary is created. A mandatory requirement is a requirement that can not be dropped out. For example: in a very critical industrial infrastructure, timing requirements of the communication between a PLC and the physical process it controls can be so strict that the response time must not be beyond some milliseconds. This is a mandatory requirement that should not be impacted by the creation of a new security zone. When such a requirement can not be respected, the constraint level is then at Level A.
- **Constraint Level B:** Some important requirements can not be satisfied if the new boundary is created. An important requirement is a requirement that can hardly be dropped out.
- **Constraint Level C:** Some optional requirements can not be satisfied if the new boundary is created. An optional requirement is a requirement that should preferably be satisfied but can be dropped out.

The system administrator has to do a qualitative evaluation of the constraint's level of all the constraints he/she identifies in the system.

Technical Constraints. Creating new security zones and filtering communication through their boundaries can sometimes be very difficult when the system's technologies (protocols, servers, techniques...) lack adapted zoning and filtering (firewalls, IDS,...) security solutions. This is a common issue of industrial systems where legacy and proprietary industrial technologies continue to exist whereas no segmentation product support them. It is all a matter of cost. Theoretically, it is always possible to build custom solutions on demand to meet the specific needs. However, cost can be so high that the return on investment is not interesting. In such a case, adding a new security boundary is simply not worth it. Technical constraints can have one of the following Constraint Levels:

- **Constraint Level A:** Adding the new security boundary has a Very High Cost.
- **Constraint Level B:** Adding the new security boundary has a High Cost.
- **Constraint Level C:** Adding the new security boundary has a Medium Cost.

2.4   Selecting the Potential Zones to Keep

The potential security zones that are progressively identified are kept or not based on a constraints analysis performed on those new zones. Retaining an identified zone is a decision to make by comparing the **Necessity** of this new zone to the **Constraint level** of its elements. We defined, therefore, a **Grading System** that helps to evaluate the **Necessity** of adding a new zone, evaluate the **Constraint's Level** of its elements and compare these two "grades" in order to decide whether or not to keep the new zone. It is composed of the two Necessity and Constraints scales (Tables 5 and 6).

Table 5. Segmentation necessity levels

Necessity Level	Definition
Level A	Non-Negotiable
Level B	Necessary
Level C	Mildly Necessary
Level D	Optional

Table 6. Constraints level scale

Constraint Level	Definition
Level A	Zoning is inconceivable
Level B	Zoning is almost inconceivable
Level C	Zoning is conceivable with difficulty

Segmentation Necessity Grading System

The **Necessity** of a zone represents how important this zone is to ensure the security needs of the system. This depends on the cycle (Functional, Technical ...) in which the zone was identified. For example, functional based zones are not as necessary as geo-location based zones. We therefore estimated the **Necessity** associated to each cycle. All the **Necessity** levels are listed by Table 7. These values were preset based on our knowledge of IICS systems.

Table 7. Segmentation necessity level scale

Meta-characteristic	Segmentation necessity
Functional grouping	Level C
Technical grouping	Level B
Geographical grouping	Level A
Process grouping	Equals the required protection level (A, B, C, D)
Inter-zone staging	Equals the connection risk level (A, B, C, D)

Segmentation Constraints Grading System

The level of a given constraint is its impact on the feasibility of adding a new potential security zone. Each known constraint must be assigned a grade from

Table 6. The company has to evaluate the system's constraint's impact based on their knowledge of the technical and functional context of the system. Constraints levels for functional and technical constraints were presented in Sect. 2.3.

Grades Comparison

The ultimate objective of our two grading systems is to compare a new zone's necessity to its constraints in order to decide if the new zone should be created or rejected. The comparison should be done as follows: Let us assume that we identified a new potential zone based on a given meta-characteristic. We will call this zone **Zone A** for simplicity. Let us also assume that:

- L_{seg}: is the **Necessity Level** of creating the **Zone A**.
- L_{cs}: is the greatest grade of the grades assigned to the constraints that are relevant for **Zone A**.

Then:

- if $L_{seg} \geq L_{cs}$: Creating the new zone is conceivable and it is as necessary as its necessity level grade is great.
- if $L_{seg} < L_{cs}$: Creating the new zone is inconceivable.

2.5   The Method Formalization

The formalization below of the SONICS method using mathematical objects summarizes the method and provides a useful starting point for the implementation.

Preliminary:

Let S an IICS system, $S = <C, X, P, Ge>$ where:

  - C is the set of components of S,
  - X is the set of connections of S, where:
$\forall x \in X, \exists\, c_1, c_2 \in C \text{ where } x = <c_1, c_2>$.
  - P is the set of processes of S.
  - Ge is the set of all the geographical sites of S.

Notations:

- $\forall c \in C$,
  - $fl_c \in \{FL0, FL1, FL2, FL3, FL4, FLST\}$ is the functional level of c.
  - $tt_c \in \{TI, TO, TIO\}$ is the technical type of c.
  - $site_c \in Ge$ is the site to which c belongs.
  - $proc_c \subset P$ is the set of processes to which c belongs.
- $\forall x \in X$,
  - $cl_x \in \{LEVEL\_A, LEVEL\_B, LEVEL\_C, LEVEL\_D\}$ is the constraint level of x.
  - $risk_x \in \{LEVEL\_A, LEVEL\_B, LEVEL\_C, LEVEL\_D, \emptyset\}$ is the risk level of x.

<u>Definitions:</u>

1. The function constraints level cl is defined as follows:

$$cl : X \rightarrow \{LEVEL\_A, LEVEL\_B, LEVEL\_C, LEVEL\_D\}$$
$$x \mapsto cl(x) = cl_x$$

2. The function risk level $risk$ is defined as follows:

$$risk : X \rightarrow \{LEVEL\_A, LEVEL\_B, LEVEL\_C, LEVEL\_D, \emptyset\}$$
$$x \mapsto risk(x) = risk_x$$

3. We define the inter-components connection function as:

$$cx : C \times C \rightarrow X \cup \{\emptyset\}$$
$$(c, d) \mapsto cx(c, d) = \begin{cases} < c, d > : \text{if } c \text{ and } d \text{ are connected} \\ \emptyset \quad\quad : \text{if } c \text{ and } d \text{ are not connected} \end{cases}$$

when c and d are not connected, $cx(c, d) = \emptyset$.

4. *Let $\Sigma_{(S)}$ the set of all possible segmentations of the system S,*
$\Sigma_{(S)} = \{ \sigma/\sigma$ is a partition of C $\}$
σ is a partition of C if:
   - $\emptyset \notin \sigma$
   - $\bigcup_{A \in \sigma} A = C$
   - $\forall A, B \in \sigma, A \neq B \Rightarrow A \cap B = \emptyset$

5. For each cycle of the method, we define the cycle's processor function as:

$$Pr_g : \Sigma_{(S)} \rightarrow \Sigma_{(S)}$$
$$\sigma \mapsto Pr_g(\sigma)$$

$$Pr_g(\sigma) =$$
$$\{$$
$$\quad A' \subset C/\forall c, d \in A',$$
$$\quad\quad (\exists A \in \sigma \text{ where } c, d \in A \text{ and}$$
$$\quad\quad\quad ($$
$$\quad\quad\quad\quad g(c) = g(d)$$
$$\quad\quad\quad\quad or$$
$$\quad\quad\quad\quad cl(cx(c, d)) > necessity_g(c, d)$$
$$\quad\quad\quad))$$
$$\}$$

where $necessity_g$ is the cycle's necessity function of creating a boundary between two components, and g is the cycle's grouping function. The definition of grouping functions is:

$$g : C \rightarrow G$$
$$c \mapsto g(c)$$

G is a set of grouping values (such as functional levels, technical types ...).
Thus:

– The functional grouping function is:

$$func : C \to \{FL0, FL1, FL2, FL3, FL4, FLST\}$$
$$c \mapsto \qquad func(c) = fl_c$$

– The technical grouping function is:

$$tech : C \to \{TI, TO, TIO\}$$
$$c \mapsto \quad tech(c) = tt_c$$

– The geolocation grouping function is:

$$geo : C \to \qquad Ge$$
$$c \mapsto geo(c) = site_c$$

– The processes grouping function is:

$$proc : C \to \qquad P$$
$$c \mapsto proc(c) = proc_c$$

6. The intern-connection-risk grouping function is:

$$IZX : \Sigma_{(S)} \to \quad \Sigma_{(S)}$$
$$c \quad \mapsto IZX(\sigma)$$

$$IZX(\sigma) =$$
$$\{$$

$\quad$ A' $\subset C / \forall \; c \in A', \exists A, B \in \sigma, \exists d \in B$ where :
$\quad$ (

$\qquad A \neq B$ and
$\qquad c \in A$ and
$\qquad cx(c, d) \neq \emptyset$ and
$\qquad cl(cx(c, d)) \leq risk(cx(c, d))$

$\quad$)
$$\}$$

7. We finally define SONICS as:

$$SONICS_{(S)} : \Sigma_{(S)} \qquad\qquad\qquad \to \qquad\qquad \Sigma_{(S)}$$
$$\sigma \mapsto \; IZX \circ Pr_{proc} \circ Pr_{geo} \circ Pr_{tech} \circ Pr_{func}(\sigma)$$

Let us assume that $\sigma_{initial}$, is the initial segmentation of the system S,
$\sigma_{result} = SONICS_{(S)}(\sigma_{initial})$, is the result of the application of SONICS on
the system S.

2.6   SONICS Tool

We have developed a tool that implements our method (Fig. 4). This tool allows
to create system models and run the segmentation steps on a model to obtain a
segmented system.

Creating a model using the tool is fairly simple but requires good knowledge
and prior preparation. It is necessary that the tool's user knows sufficiently
well the architecture of the system, its processes, its risks, and its constraints.
The system's modeling consists, as depicted in Fig. 4, of creating components,
specifying their characteristics and adding connections and processes.

Once the model is created, the tool allows to roll out the steps of the method one after another allowing to assign constraint levels to inter-zones connections. For example, for the first segmentation step, namely functional segmentation, the tools calculates the cycle's new potential zones (differentiating them using different colors) as illustrated by Fig. 5. It outlines the inter-zones connections of these potential zones allowing to set their constraints levels (Fig. 6). The security zones are then recalculated based on the newly set constraints levels values. The next cycles are processed (by pressing the "Next Step" button) in a similar way until we get the final result.

Moreover, the tool is completely recursive. Any value set by the user, no matter whether it is a characteristic of a component, of a connection, or of a process, is included in the system's model and reused through the various steps. For example, if a connection's constraint level is set during some cycle, is does not need to be reset at other cycles as it becomes a characteristic of that connection. This ensures that the segmentation result is automatically recalculated any time the system's model evolves by adding, modifying or deleting components, connections or processes.

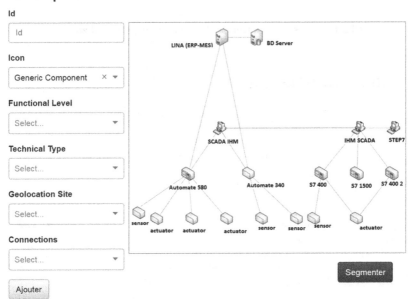

Fig. 4. Our segmentation tool - modeling

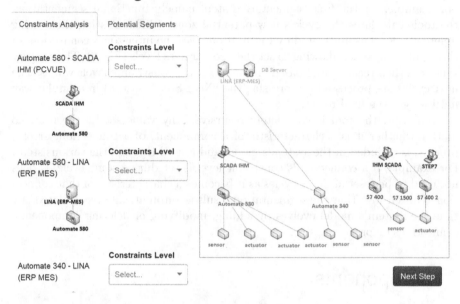

Fig. 5. Our segmentation tool - functional potential zones

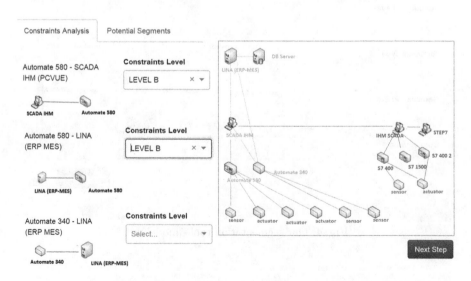

Fig. 6. Our segmentation tool - constraints levels attribution

3   Application and Results

3.1   Test Methodology

SONICS is the result of a rather deep and complex analysis of the segmentation problem. Our approach to design SONICS is completely based on our understanding of industrial systems, and the aspects recommended for segmentation by the standards and research works we have studied. It is very difficult to explain how the different parts of this method were built because it is the result of a very complex process of brainstorming, improvement, refinement and reworking that took a long time. This is not very important in determining the value of our method. The only important thing is to prove that the results of the method are correct. Most, if not all, paradigms and methods introduce new theoretical concepts to try to model a problem or phenomenon without explaining the why and how. They are nonetheless approved when they prove their accuracy. This is done in perfect respect of the modern scientific experimental approach.

Therefore, we designed a validation test method in order to evaluate our segmentation method. This test method is based on the comparison of the result of SONICS to segmentations that are made over time by expertise (without a method) and are assumed to be accurate. Given a test system with an existing accurate segmentation, the validation test consists of applying SONICS on this system and comparing the results with the existing segmentation as explained in Fig. 7. For more readability, we will use the term *Ex-Segmentation* to refer to any "existing accurate segmentation".

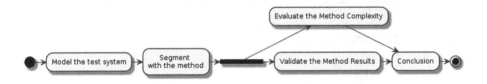

Fig. 7. Test methodology

The comparison of SONICS result with an *Ex-Segmentation* is done using the new concept of segmentation efficiency and accuracy presented below.

Segmentation Efficiency and Accuracy

We define the efficiency of a method on a set of test systems as the mean of the accuracy of the results obtained for each system. A result's accuracy depends on how much the result is similar to the expected one. In our case, a segmentation's result's accuracy is a function of the distance between the segmentation obtained using SONICS and the *Ex-Segmentation*. The distance between two segmentations of a same system is the minimum cost to transform a segmentation into the other one by performing a set of only the following actions:

– Move only one component at a time from one segment to another.

– Remove one segment
– Merge two segments

Each action has a cost of 1. For example, the distance between two segmentations, where it is necessary to move two components of their segments, is equal to 2. Accuracy is calculated based on the distance using the following formula:

$$accuracy = \frac{1}{1 + distance}$$

When two segmentations are the same, the distance between them equals 0, the accuracy then equals 1 (the maximum value). On the other hand, when the distance increases, the accuracy decreases towards 0.

3.2   Test Systems

A test system can only be used in our validation test if it incorporates an *Ex-Segmentation* that has been verified over time. This allows to validate segmentation results on real systems with effective segmentation under real conditions and on a long term basis. However, this approach has the disadvantage of being very expensive and inflexible because creating a good test system is time-consuming and finding existing test systems is not easy.

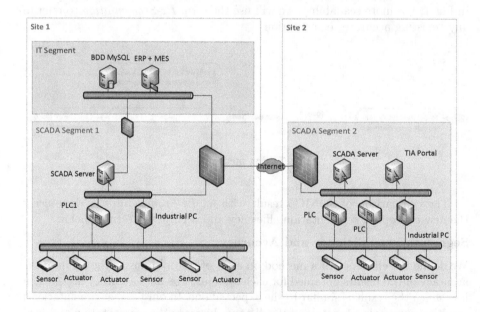

Fig. 8. The IIC test system

We have tested our method on only one test system (Fig. 8). This is the only system available to us that fulfills the criteria of test systems selection. It is based on a real system in production with an *Ex-Segmentation*. It consists of two geographically separate sites and includes the following components

- An ERP/MES - LINA: that manages all the company's resources.
- A CRM Web server: that manages orders, validates them, and launches industrial processes.
- MySQL database: that Contains all the business data. It is shared by the CRM and the ERP-MES.
- SCADA (PCView and WinCC): that controls PLCs, such as loading new programs, retrieving and displaying information...
- The ICS part of the system consists of two field sites.
  1. A main field site where a SCADA network and a set of industrial production devices are deployed.
  2. A remote secondary field site where a remote production unit is deployed.

For simplicity, we suppose that the system does not have any specific legal, organizational or responsibilities grouping requirements.

The system is segmented into 3 segments as illustrated by the figure. This is the *Ex-Segmentation* for our test. It has been made only by skills and security knowledge but has also proven its effectiveness over time. It is also reliable because the test system is not very complex.

3.3   Results and Discussion

The application of our segmentation method on our test system has resulted in the segmented system illustrated by Fig. 9.

By comparing the segmentation result with the *Ex-Segmentation*, the method allowed us to obtain a segmentation rather close to the *Ex-Segmentation*. The distance between the two segmentations remains quite small (equal to 3). We noticed that this distance was mainly due to the division of existing segments into several segments. This means that the method generated a segmentation that are too restrictive and too demanding in terms of securing inter-component flows. This impacted the accuracy but does not mean that the result is completely incorrect. In fact, two unnecessary security zones was added introducing a gap with the *Ex-Segmentation*.

The study of the causes that led to the identification of these additional segments revealed that these segments were useful for flows controls without needing firewalls. That led us to an important conclusion that all the new identified zones do not necessarily have to represent a network segment with a firewall. Other segregation techniques may be used as appropriate to the security characteristics of the identified zone. Incorporating these segregation techniques into the method would be a possible improvement to our method. On the other hand, the method takes into account industrial systems specificities. Nevertheless, we believe that it may also be possible to rely the method a little more on security characteristics (such as Risk and Security Level).

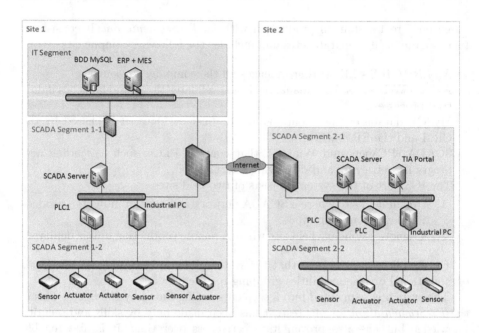

Fig. 9. The segmented IIC test system

In general, the first results support our conviction that SONICS is a valuable solution that provides satisfying and realistic answers to an unresolved problem namely IICS systems segmentation. It is a generic solution that can be applied to different types of IICS. It supplies efficient guidance and allows to be focused only on aspects that are significant for segmentation by using a simple meta-model. It considers multiple aspects in order to ensure that IICS systems heterogeneity is taken into account. Another advantage of our method is its constraints based zoning decision making. This makes the method very pragmatic and ensures more accurate results. In addition, the application of the method remains affordable, especially when using the tool we developed.

4   Conclusion

This paper presents SONICS, a new IICS segmentation method that aims to ensure efficient zoning to meet actual security needs of IICS. It is based on a meta-model that helps to model systems. System models are used by the method to identify potential security zones. These are kept or dropped out based on a constraints analysis.

We designed and carried out a validation test to evaluate the method. This helped us to identify the limitations and difficulties associated with the method and to identify possible improvements. The first test results was acceptable. However, we admit that the method's application is not simple enough without using the tool we developed. That said, our test method is by itself a standalone scientific contribution that can be reused or adapted for other scientific works.

SONICS has a lot of advantages. It is a generic solution that can be applied to different types of IICS. It keeps the focus only on aspects that are really relevant for segmentation. It is a fairly pragmatic method that takes into account IICS constraints and specificity. Note that the method uses industrial systems concepts (Operation functional levels, IT and OT technical types), but it can be applied to a non integrated Corporate system (IT) as well as to a non integrated ICS. This is mandatory and consistent because both are subsystems of an integrated ICS.

However, we agree that the method could be improved by taking more security characteristics (such as Risk and Security Level) into account. The method could also incorporate more segregation concepts to provide more guidance for inter-zones flows protection in order to optimize the Segmentation/Segregation cost.

References

1. Cai, N., Wang, J., Yu, X.: SCADA system security: complexity, history and new developments. In: 6th IEEE International Conference on Industrial Informatics (2008)
2. Stouffer, K., Lightman, S., Pillitteri, V., Abrams, M., Hahn, A.: Guide to industrial control systems (ICS) security. In: NIST Special Publication, vol. 800, no. 82 (2015)
3. Pires, P.S.M., Oliveira, L.A.H.G.: Security aspects of SCADA and corporate network interconnection: an overview. In: IEEE International Conference on Dependability of Computer Systems, pp. 127–134 (2006)
4. ANSSI: Detailed Measures (2013)
5. CSSP, DHS: Recommended proctice: improving industrial control systems cybersecurity with defense-in-depth strategies. US-CERT Defense in Depth, October 2009
6. Security for Industrial Automation and Control Systems: Terminology, Concepts, and Models: Howpublished. ISA-99 Standard 62443-1-1 (Draft2, Edit4) (2013)
7. Enterprise - Control system integration. Part 2: object model attributes. ISA-95 Standard 95.00.02 (Draft 9) (2001)
8. Enterprise - Control system integration Part 3: activity models of manufacturing operations management: Howpublished. ISA-95 Standard 95.00.03 (Draft 16) (2004)
9. Enterprise - Control system integration Part 1: models and terminology: Howpublished. ISA-dS95 Standard (Draft 14) (1999)
10. Es-Salhi, K., Cuppens-Boulahia, N., Espes, D., Cuppens, F.: Analysis of ICS and corporate system integration vulnerabilities. In: The 14th International Conference on Embedded Systems, Cyber-Physical Systems, and Applications (ESCS'2016) (2016)
11. Obregon, L.: Secure architecture for industrial control systems. SANS Institute, InfoSec Reading Room (2015)
12. Zerbst, J.-T., Hjelmvik, E., Rinta-Jouppi, I.: Zoning principles in electricity distribution and energy production environments. In: 20th International Conference on Electricity Distribution (2009)

13. Galloway, B., Hancke, G.P.: Introduction to industrial control networks. IEEE Commun. Surv. Tutor. **15**, 860–880 (2013)
14. Network Segmentation for Industrial Control Environments. Wurldtech, A GE (2016)
15. Network Perimeter Defense: Best Practices in Network Segmentation. Energy ESC, November 2014
16. Mahan, R.E., et al.: Secure data transfer guidance for industrial control and SCADA systems. Report to US Department of Energy, PNNL-20776 (2011)
17. Mcdonald, J., Oualha, N., Puccetti, A., Hecker, A., Planchon, F.: Application of EBIOS for the risk assessment of ICT use in electrical distribution sub-stations. IEEE PowerTech (POWERTECH). IEEE Grenoble (2013)
18. Jonathan, P.: Innovative defense strategies for securing SCADA and control systems. PlantData Technologies (2006)
19. Foley, S.N.: The specification and implementation of "Commercial" security requirements including dynamic segregation of duties. In: Proceedings of the 4th ACM Conference on Computer and Communications Security, Zurich, Switzerland, 1–4 April 1997
20. Johnson, R.E: Survey of SCADA security challenges and potential attack vectors: In. IEEE International Conference for Internet Technology and Secured Transactions (ICITST) (2010)

Proxy Re-Encryption Scheme for Access Control Enforcement Delegation on Outsourced Data in Public Cloud

Gaurav Pareek$^{(\boxtimes)}$ⓘ and B. R. Purushothamaⓘ

Department of Computer Science and Engineering, National Institute of Technology
Goa, Farmagudi, Ponda 403401, Goa, India
{gpareek,puru}@nitgoa.ac.in

Abstract. We consider a model where large number of data items, each with different access privileges for a set of users, is outsourced and access is to be granted according to the access control policy specified by the data owner. Given this scenario and security goals, we highlight severe trust issue in existing proxy re-encryption schemes that are extensively used for access control in cloud computing. Typically, using proxy re-encryption schemes, access is managed through delegation of decryption rights from data owner to a user. In traditional proxy re-encryption schemes, availability of a re-encryption key from a delegator to a delegatee guarantees access delegation irrespective of delegatee's access privileges for different data items encrypted under the delegator's public key. So, employing a re-encryption scheme trivially for access control on outsourced data demands questionable amount of trust on the re-encrypting proxy for not carrying out unauthorized delegations. In this paper, we propose a proxy re-encryption scheme that takes into account the access control policy associated with data item(s) and despite the availability of re-encryption key(s), generates a valid re-encrypted ciphertext only if the delegatee is authorized for the data item being re-encrypted. We also propose an access control enforcement delegation scheme for outsourced data in public Cloud based on the proposed proxy re-encryption scheme. The task of enforcing access control according to the data owner's policy itself is securely outsourced to the semi-trusted cloud service provider. The Cloud service provider is unable to learn anything about the underlying plaintext data item or the secrets of the data owner or the access control policy associated with any data item. The data owner and delegatee users store only their secret keys. The proposed access control enforcement delegation scheme supports dynamic access control policies and preserves forward and backward secrecy following any dynamic updates in the access policies. We prove security of the proposed proxy re-encryption scheme and access control scheme in standard model. The accompanying performance analysis further confirms the applicability of the proposed scheme in real-world setting.

Keywords: Proxy re-encryption · Access control
Public cloud computing

ⓒ Springer Nature Switzerland AG 2018
V. Ganapathy et al. (Eds.): ICISS 2018, LNCS 11281, pp. 251–271, 2018.
https://doi.org/10.1007/978-3-030-05171-6_13

1   Introduction

Storing of data by the clients or data owners, who do not wish purchase and maintain expensive storage servers, on any third-party cloud service provider (CSP) is referred to as data storage outsourcing or simply data outsourcing. While data outsourcing relaxes the burden on data owners of purchasing expensive hardware, critical privacy concerns arise because of an honest-but-curious nature of the CSP in a practical setting. An honest-but-curious CSP is interested in breaching privacy of the stored data or violating access control policy or both given that its action are unnoticeable for the data owner [17]. To achieve privacy, data is encrypted under symmetric secret content keys before outsourcing. Access of outsourced data is granted to authorized users through secure transfer of these content keys to only authorized users using key management techniques. In recent times, proxy re-encryption (PRE) [2,3] has gathered high attention as an efficient tool for managing keys for authorized users in a variety of access control scenarios. PRE allows transformation of ciphertext under delegator's public key (pk_A) into a ciphertext under delegatee's public key (pk_B) using a re-encryption key $(rk_{A \rightarrow B})$. During the re-encryption process, the re-encrypting proxy cannot learn the underlying plaintext or the secret keys of the parties A and B.

Consider a scenario where a data owner wishes a set of data items $\mathcal{D}$ to be outsourced to an honest-but-curious CSP and to manage access of $\mathcal{D}$ for a set of users $\mathcal{U}$. Consider that $\mathcal{D}$ is divided into data partitions, $\mathcal{D} = \{d_1, d_2, \ldots, d_m\}$ with each $d_j \in \mathcal{D}$ having a different access policy for each of the individual users u_i in the set $\mathcal{U} = \{u_1, u_2, \ldots, u_n\}$. The data owner encrypts each data item with a different content key from the set $\mathcal{K} = \{k_1, k_2, \ldots, k_m\}$ and stores the encrypted data set $\mathcal{C} = \{C_1, C_2, \ldots, C_m\}$ on the cloud. For simplicity, consider d_i be symmetric encrypted using k_i. Consider also that each of the individual users $u_i \in \mathcal{U}$ has the public-private key-pairs (pk_i, sk_i) initialized beforehand. Different access policies for a data item d_j means that a set $\mathcal{U}_j \subseteq \mathcal{U}$ is authorized for d_j according to the access control policy. The set $\mathcal{U}_j$ is called authorized set or an Access Control List (ACL). A collection of these ACLs constitutes the access control policy on $\mathcal{D}$. Another way of specifying access control policy on $\mathcal{D}$ is to organize the ACLs to form an $n \times m$ matrix of bits called Access Control Matrix (ACM) defined as:

$$\text{ACM}[i, j] = \begin{cases} 1 & \text{if } u_i \text{ is authorized to access } d_j, \\ 0 & \text{otherwise.} \end{cases}$$

Without loss of generality, suppose that a user u_1 is authorized by the owner of $\mathcal{D}$ to access $\{d_1, d_2, d_3\}$. To manage access according to this "policy", the data owner has to delegate the keys $\{k_1, k_2, k_3\}$ to u_1 using a potentially insecure channel. For managing access control in this case and a more general one, we discuss: (1) a trivial method and (2) a method employing traditional PRE schemes in a straightforward manner and (3) the motivation for a new PRE scheme that fulfills all the functional, security and performance requirements of a secure access control enforcement delegation scheme in a public cloud scenario.

The trivial method [8] is to individually encrypt symmetric secret keys $\{k_1, k_2, k_3\}$ with public key pk_1 of u_1 and store these encrypted content keys on the CSP for u_1 to access. User u_1 can decrypt and obtain these symmetric secret keys using his individual secret key sk_1. So, if user u_i is authorized by the data owner to access $m_1 \leq m$ data items from $\mathcal{D}$, the number of encryptions required to be done by the data owner would be $m_1 n$. The symmetric content keys may have to be updated following any kind of key leakage or data/policy update. In such a case, these $m_1 n = \mathcal{O}(mn)$ encryptions have to be carried out again by the data owner. This leads to both computation and storage overhead on the data owner. A PRE performs better in this scenario. This is because in the trivial method explained above, there are exactly n different asymmetric encryptions of the same symmetric encryption key, one per authorized individual user in $\mathcal{U}$. In PRE, a single encrypted copy of the symmetric encryption key is kept on the CSP. This encrypted copy can be re-encrypted for every user using appropriate re-encryption keys. This approach is particularly efficient when any content key is updated. Only one public key encryption is required to be performed after updating one content key.

More formally, consider that data owner encrypts each symmetric secret key $k_i \in \mathcal{K}$ under its public key pk_O to produce a set of encrypted content keys $\mathcal{C}_\mathcal{K} = \{C_{k_1}, C_{k_2}, \ldots, C_{k_m}\}$. The sets $\mathcal{C}_\mathcal{K}$ and $\mathcal{C}$ (symmetric encryptions of data items in $\mathcal{D}$) are stored on the CSP and the pair (C_i, C_{k_i}) is the outsourced form of the data item d_i. A set $\mathcal{RK} = \{rk_{O \to u_1}, rk_{O \to u_2}, \ldots, rk_{O \to u_n}\}$ contains re-encryption keys corresponding to the delegations from the data owner to each of the individual users in $\mathcal{U}$. Also, an $n \times m$ access control matrix (ACM) is given to the CSP each of whose entries is 1 for authorized delegations and 0 for an unauthorized one. Whenever CSP receives a request from user $u_i \in \mathcal{U}$ for a data item $d_j \in \mathcal{D}$, CSP checks if the entry $\text{ACM}[i, j] = 1$. If yes, then CSP picks $C_{k_j} \in \mathcal{C}_\mathcal{K}$ and re-encrypts it using $rk_{O \to u_i} \in \mathcal{RK}$, otherwise, the CSP ignores the request. This re-encryption produces a ciphertext under pk_i which can be decrypted by u_i using sk_i to obtain k_j. This method is better than the trivial method discussed earlier because it unlike the trivial method, it requires the data owner to perform only m asymmetric encryptions. However, it is possible that CSP re-encrypts C_{k_j} despite the condition $\text{ACM}[i, j] = 0$. This is possible because availability of the re-encryption key $rk_{O \to u_i}$ itself is a guarantee that the valid re-encrypted ciphertext can be produced as the existing notion of proxy re-encryption does not take into consideration the access control policy associated with the data item d_j.

Thus, while trivially applying a PRE scheme solves majority of our problems, this method requires questionable amount of trust to be placed in the CSP. This is because with all the re-encryption keys available, it is possible for the CSP to delegate decryption rights to an unauthorized user without the data owner being aware of the delegation. Such unauthorized delegations do not come to data owner's notice especially when the delegatee users are dishonest as well.

Thus, a new PRE scheme is required that, given a re-encryption key from a data owner to a delegatee user, produces a valid re-encrypted ciphertext selectively corresponding to only those data items that the delegatee user is authorized to access.

In this paper, we propose a PRE scheme that despite the re-encryption key available, produces a valid re-encrypted ciphertext for an individual user only if the user is authorized to access the data item. We also propose an access control enforcement delegation scheme on outsourced data using the proposed PRE scheme. The proposed scheme supports a dynamic ACM. That is, at any given point of time, if an entry $ACM[i, j]$ changes from 0 to 1, the access rights of a user can be re-instated while preserving backward secrecy. Similarly if $ACM[i, j]$ changes from 1 to 0, procedure for revoking access of d_j for u_i preserves forward secrecy. The CSP that acts as a re-encrypting proxy, despite collusion with a subset of individual users is unable to learn anything about the underlying plaintext data item; not even the corresponding access control policy. The proposed PRE scheme is secure under standard model assumption.

Our Contributions

1. We propose a secure data outsourcing and access control enforcement delegation scheme with the two-fold objective of preserving privacy of the outsourced data and enforcing access control on the same according to an access control matrix specified by the data owner. While the data owner goes off-line after outsourcing data, CSP manages access for a set of users on data owner's behalf without being able to carry out any malicious delegations.
2. For achieving the above, we propose a proxy re-encryption scheme where even if a re-encryption key from the data owner (delegator) to individual user (delegatee) is available, re-encryption produces a valid ciphertext if and only if the delegatee user is authorized for the data item. The proposed proxy re-encryption scheme is certificate-less and requires the users in the system and the data owner to store just their respective individual secret keys on their private storage.
3. We define the security notions of the proposed proxy re-encryption scheme and prove that the proposed access control enforcement delegation scheme is secure under these security definitions.
4. In case access rights of a user are to be re-instated or revoked, the owner can do so with limited overhead while preserving forward and backward secrecy.
5. The existing proxy re-encryption schemes require the re-encrypting proxy to be trusted for re-encryption for authorized users only. The proposed scheme circumvents the need to trust the re-encrypting proxy for re-encryption. The proposed scheme forces the re-encryption procedure to consider access control policy along with the re-encryption key(s) for valid delegation of decryption rights.

Paper Organization

Section 2 summarizes literature of related research on access control schemes using PRE and some of the PRE schemes aimed at achieving selective delegation of decryption rights. Section 3 defines abstract system model, its security goals and the definitions of procedures involved and formal definition of security of the proposed proxy re-encryption scheme. The concrete construction of the proposed proxy re-encryption based access control enforcement delegation scheme is presented in Sect. 4. Correctness, security and performance analysis of the proposed scheme are presented in Sect. 5. The paper concludes in Sect. 6.

2   Related Work

We review some of the related research on access control systems that utilize PRE as a core primitive. Also, we survey some of the existing variations of PRE primitive that are proposed aiming the controlled delegation of decryption rights based on some condition.

2.1   Access Control Schemes Using Proxy Re-Encryption

Ateniese et al. [2] employed their proxy re-encryption scheme and proposed an access control scheme for providing access to encrypted files stored on untrusted distributed blocks. The content owner encrypts the files to be outsourced with symmetric content keys which in turn are encrypted with a master public key using a unidirectional proxy re-encryption scheme, forming a lockbox. To grant access to the file the access control server re-encrypts the lock-box such that it can be decrypted by the user. Before re-encryption, it is the job of the access control server to check whether the user is authorized to access the data item present with the lock-box. On similar lines, in the schemes proposed by Tang et al. [18] and Ren et al. [14], Digital Envelope [15] has been used to address this issue. These schemes also require the third party to encrypt for a user only when the user is authorized as in [2].

Yu et al. [27] proposed a scheme for achieving secure, scalable and fine-grained access control in Cloud computing. To achieve this, they combine key policy attribute based encryption [9], proxy re-encryption [3] and lazy re-encryption. Data owner encrypts the data file using a random symmetric encryption key which is encrypted with the corresponding data file attributes using key policy attribute based encryption. When there is a data file access request from a user, the Cloud server re-encrypts the data file using the re-encryption key, and also re-encrypts the requesting user's secret key components. In this scheme, a single user revocation implies that every other user's secret key components have to be updated. Also, all the secret key components of every user are made available to the Cloud server, thus disclosing information about the users to the Cloud server.

Tysowski et al. [20] proposed two models for providing access control; a manager-based model and a Cloud based model. The former consists of a trusted manager, an untrusted Cloud provider, a data owner and users. The manager generates users' secret and public keys, the public and secret keys of the data partitions. Data items in a partition are encrypted under the corresponding partition's public key. When the Cloud receives a data access request from a user, the Cloud sends the requested data item to the manager. The manager generates a re-encryption key to re-encrypt the encrypted data for the user if the user is authorized to access the data item. The manager is responsible for storing all the user secret keys and performing all the re-encryption operations. Thus, the manager has to be completely trusted and is a point of vulnerability.

To improve on this, a Cloud-based model [20] is also proposed in which responsibility of re-encryption is delegated to the Cloud. In this method, every user is in possession of the secret keys used for encrypting the data. This introduces the key management problem. Tysowski et al. address this problem by updating the partition keys at every user in the group following a user join or leave activity in the group of authorized users for that data partition. Also, every user is required to store as many partition secret keys as the number of partitions to which it has authorized access.

The works of Tran et al. [19] and Jia et al. [10] assume that the Cloud servers should be trusted completely. If not, then the Cloud servers can collude with the leaving members and gain information about the encrypted data stored on the Cloud.

On the similar lines many schemes have been proposed [1,12,22,24,29] which address access control in cloud computing using proxy re-encryption. Scheme due to Ali et al. [1] requires the cloud server to be fully trusted for encryption and decryption. Zhou et al. [29] propose a key derivation based access control. A user is assigned to a class in hierarchy. In case of access revocation, re-encryption is done by the cloud server which requires the data owner to trust cloud server. Wang et al. [22] proposed to use public proxies to outsource the data to cloud in a controlled manner. Further, the data outsourced by the outsourcing proxies can be audited at any time for their malicious behavior. A certificate-less proxy re-encryption is proposed by Xu et al. [24] for access control after outsourcing to cloud. The scheme solves the basic key escrow problem in identity based cloud environment. Feng et al. [7] propose to use proxy re-encryption scheme for transferring digital copyrights from one right holder to another using a delegation key. Their scheme also requires the delegating entity to be trusted for carrying out only authorized delegation.

2.2   Proxy Re-Encryption Schemes for Controlled Delegations

Conditional Proxy Re-Encryption(CPRE) [4,23], Fuzzy Conditional Proxy Re-Encryption (FC-PRE) [6] and Proxy Re-encryption with keyword search (PRES) [4,5,21] are the three proxy re-encryption primitives proposed to control delegations that can be allowed with a given re-encryption key. In CPRE, delegation of a ciphertext is valid only when the condition specified (inseparably) in the proxy re-encryption key matches that of the ciphertext. The notion however, cannot be used in a straightforward manner in the access control scenario we consider in the paper. This is because there is exactly one property associated with a user and if n users are to access a data item, n different second-level ciphertexts corresponding to a single data item have to be produced. Revocation and reinstating access rights of an existing user is also costly as it would require the property to be revoked leading to the change in either re-encryption keys of all the users or all the second-level ciphertexts corresponding to the property of the revoked user. FC-PRE schemes, a PRE analogue of the *fuzzy identity-based encryption* [16] includes delegating decryption rights of a data item to a user only if a certain number of properties from the re-encryption key are present in the second-level ciphertext of the data item. This approach requires components of the second-level ciphertext to be equal to the number of users and components of re-encryption keys to be equal to the number of data items to be shared. This makes the process of revoking and reinstating the access rights of a particular user for a data item computationally very costly.

3 Definitions

We express the system model assumptions in terms of procedures involved in the overall system operation. The definitions of all these procedures constitutes the system model. The definition of the proposed PRE scheme is also presented in the form of syntax of the procedures involved. We present the abstract security expectations from the system model under the given access control scenario. We capture these security expectations through formal security definitions of the proposed PRE scheme. In this section, we present all these definitions to capture of the abstraction of the proposed access control enforcement delegation and the proposed PRE scheme.

3.1 Proposed Access Control Enforcement Delegation Scheme

We define the system model for the proposed access control enforcement delegation scheme in the form of construction syntax of the procedures $\Gamma = ($**Set, Out, Delegate, Read, ACM-update**$)$ and abstract security goals. We assume the existence of a CSP, a storage service provider, on which the data owner partitions the storage space available into data labels $\mathcal{D} = \{d_1, d_2, \ldots, d_m\}$. Each data partition d_i is "locked" using symmetric encryption of the partition under a content key k_i. This symmetric key k_i is to be delegated securely to only the users authorized for d_i. The task of delegation of decryption rights itself is to be securely delegated to the semi-trusted CSP. We denote re-encryption keys to transform any message under public key of data owner such that it becomes ciphertext under public key of an individual user $u_i \in \mathcal{U} = \{u_1, u_2, \ldots, u_n\}$, the set of individual users, as $rk_{O \to u_i}$.

1. **Set:** This procedure takes the security parameter and produces global system parameters and delegation parameters. Users in the system are registered by the data owner for access management. Delegation parameters for each authorized delegation are also produced.

2. **Out:** Executed by the data owner, this procedure outsources the data items to the CSP by encrypting each data item d_j under symmetric encryption key k_j to obtain C_j. Each k_j is encrypted under public key pk_O of the data owner to obtain C_{k_j} so that the collection $\{\forall d_j \in \mathcal{D}, (C_j, C_{k_j})\}$ forms a digital envelop. Note that the data owner can open the digital envelop easily through asymmetric decryption using it secret key sk_O. However, each individual user u_i may be granted access to a content key k_j through re-encryption using re-encryption key $rk_{O \rightarrow u_i}$.

3. **Delegate:** Whenever request for a data item, say $d_j \in \mathcal{D}$ arrives from the individual user, say $u_i \in \mathcal{U}$, CSP executes this procedure. The CSP serves each request by executing the following activities:

   (a) Re-encrypt the output of **Out** that is, C_{k_j} using re-encryption key $rk_{O \rightarrow u_i}$.

   (b) Sending this re-encrypted symmetric content key with the encrypted data file over the communication channel.

4. **Read:** A user $u_i \in \mathcal{U}$ can request any data item $d_j \in \mathcal{D}$. After initiating the read request, the user waits for the CSP to execute **Delegate**. The user can decrypt to obtain the correct underlying plaintext d_j only if the user is authorized for d_j. Otherwise, the result of decryption produces a meaningless random-looking quantity $\perp$. The activities involved in this procedure are:

   (a) Decryption of the re-encrypted ciphertext to obtain the symmetric secret key k_j and

   (b) Using k_j to obtain d_j using symmetric decryption.

   At the end of this procedure, a user u_i is able to obtain the correct symmetric secret key k_j and consequently obtain the underlying plaintext data file only if $\mathrm{ACM}[i, j] = 1$.

   $$\mathbf{Read} = \begin{cases} d_j & \text{if } \mathrm{ACM}[i, j] = 1, \\ \perp & \text{otherwise.} \end{cases}$$

5. **ACM-update:** For enforcing dynamic access control, it is must be possible to re-instate and/or revoke access rights of any individual user for any data item. Also, it must be possible to add/remove any row/column in the ACM. In other words, it must be possible to update any entry of the ACM from 0 to 1 and vice versa and to add/remove a row or a column of the ACM. The procedure ACM-update carries out the necessary updates in the system and delegation parameters such that all these changes in the ACM are supported efficiently while preserving forward and backward secrecy, defined in abstract security requirements next.

Abstract Security Requirements

(i) *Strong access control* The CSP must not be able to delegate decryption rights of any data item to a user deemed "unauthorized" by the data owner. This is subject to the condition that no authorized user surrenders its secret key to the CSP or any other colluding user.

(ii) *Collusion resistance* In case of collusion between the CSP and unauthorized user(s), secret keys (including that of owner's and any of the non-colluding users') can not be compromised. Moreover, no information about the data item can be recovered upon collusion between any number of unauthorized users and the CSP.

(iii) *Policy privacy* Access control policy associated with data item(s) must not be disclosed to any of the participating entities (CSP, individual users etc.).

(iv) *Forward/Backward secrecy* Generally speaking, if the ACM is updated, access rights of individual user(s) for data item(s) are either revoked or re-instated. In case the access rights of d_j are to be revoked for user u_i. For preserving *forward secrecy* it must be ensured that no future copies of d_j after access revocation is accessible to u_i. Similarly, *backward secrecy* must be preserved in case access rights of a user u_i are re-instated for a data item d_j which means that not only the current copy, but all the past copies of d_j should be made accessible to u_i.

Note that definition of forward and backward secrecy as in [11,25,26] and adopted in this work are significantly different from that in Secure Group Communication schemes [28].

3.2 Underlying Proposed Proxy Re-Encryption Scheme

As mentioned earlier, data outsourcing and access control scheme proposed in this paper is based on a PRE scheme that allows delegation of decryption rights of a data item for only authorized users. We present definitions of the proposed PRE scheme consistent with the system model defined above. That is, the construction syntax presented here takes the encryption key k_i corresponding to a data item d_i as a plaintext message.

The proposed proxy re-encryption scheme Π to achieve security goals discussed in Sect. 3 is defined as Π = (**Setup, KeyGen, Enc$_1$, Dec$_1$, Enc$_2$, Dec$_2$, ReKeyGen, ReEnc**).

- **Setup(1^λ):** This procedure takes security parameter λ as input to produce *par*, the collection of global system parameters.
- **KeyGen(i, par):** This procedure generates public-secret key-pairs (pk_i, sk_i) corresponding to every individual user $u_i \in \mathcal{U}$ and (pk_O, sk_O) corresponding the data owner. This procedure also generates the set of delegation parameters *delpar* that designate each delegation as either authorized or unauthorized.
- **Enc$_1$(pk_i, k_j):** This procedure takes public key pk_i of the user u_i to encrypt symmetric encryption key k_j corresponding to d_j, to produce first-level ciphertext $C^i_{k_j}$. A first-level ciphertext under pk_i cannot be re-encrypted but can be decrypted using secret key sk_i.
- **Dec$_1$($sk_i, C^i_{k_j}$):** Given a secret key sk_i of a user u_i, this procedure decrypts the first-level ciphertext $C^i_{k_j}$ corresponding to any symmetric encryption key k_j under public key pk_i to obtain k_j in plaintext form.
- **Enc$_2$($pk_O, k_j, delpar$):** This procedure is used to produce second level encryption C_{k_j} corresponding to the symmetric encryption key k_j given the public

key pk_O of the owner and delegation parameter(s) *delpar*. This ciphertext, in addition to decryption by the data owner, may be re-encrypted for any individual user u_i using $rk_{O \to u_i}$.

- **Dec$_2$**(sk_O, C_{k_j}): The data owner can use this procedure to decrypt the second-level encryptions using its secret key sk_O to obtain the symmetric encryption key k_j in plaintext form.
- **ReKeyGen**$(sk_O, pk_i, delpar)$: This procedure is executed by the data owner to generate re-encryption key $(rk_{O \to u_i})$ which enables delegation of decryption rights from the data owner to a user u_i. Input to this procedure is the public key pk_i of the user u_i, secret key sk_O of the data owner and the delegation parameters *delpar*.
- **ReEnc**$(rk_{O \to u_i}, C_{k_j}, delpar)$: This procedure produces a valid re-encrypted ciphertext $C_{k_j}^i$ for a user u_i only if u_i is authorized to access d_j. The inputs to this procedure are the re-encryption key $rk_{O \to u_i}$, second-level ciphertext C_{k_j} and delegation parameters *delpar*. The output, if a valid re-encrypted ciphertext, can be decrypted using **Dec$_1$** with sk_i to obtain the encryption key k_j in plaintext form.

$$\textbf{ReEnc}(rk_{O \to u_i}, C_{k_j}, delpar) = \begin{cases} C_{k_j}^i & \text{if ACM}[i,j] = 1, \\ \perp & \text{otherwise.} \end{cases}$$

Security Definition. The security definition of the proposed PRE scheme captures indistinguishability of the ciphertext produced by direct encryption (**Enc$_1$** and **Enc$_2$**) and re-encryption (**ReEnc**) procedures. We call security of the proposed PRE scheme "target partition and chosen plaintext attack (IND-TP-CPA) security". The target user usually selected in the beginning for defining security in a PRE world is the data owner in the proposed scheme. Additionally, a target data item or data partition d_{j*} is selected that has a specific access control policy associated with it. There can be multiple encryptions and re-encryptions corresponding to the access policy of the target data partition. A probabilistic polynomial time (PPT) adversary $\mathcal{A}$ can collude with any number of individual users of its choice with only one constraint that $\mathcal{A}$ cannot collude with any user authorized for d_{j*}. The goal of $\mathcal{A}$ is/are either one or both of the following:

1. To distinguish two second-level encryptions under the data owner's public key and access policy corresponding to the target data partition d_{j*}.
2. To select a target delegatee u_{i*} and distinguish two re-encrypted ciphertexts corresponding to d_{j*} and intended for u_{i*}

We consider the existence of the following oracles for $\mathcal{A}$ to query and obtain the corruption and other public information:

- $\mathcal{K}_{hon}$, that returns the public key of an honest user.
- $\mathcal{K}_{corr}$, that returns public-secret key pair of a corrupted user.
- $\mathcal{RK}$, that returns a re-encryption key with no corrupted delegator.

As will be discussed later, the output of **ReEnc** reveals strictly more information compared to that of **Enc$_2$**. Consider the following game between a challenger $\mathbb{C}$ and adversary $\mathcal{A}$:

1. *Game-Setup:* The challenger $\mathbb{C}$ outputs all the public system parameters par and delegation parameters, one for each of the $m \times n$ delegation.
2. *Game-Query-1:* In this phase, $\mathcal{A}$ adaptively queries the oracles $\mathcal{K}_{hon}$, $\mathcal{K}_{corr}$ and $\mathcal{RK}$ to obtain public key of the honest users, public-secret key-pair of the corrupted users and all the re-encryption keys with data owner as delegator and any of the individual users as delegatee.
3. *Game-Challenge:* $\mathcal{A}$ selects a target data partition d_{j^*}, a target user u_{i^*} authorized for d_{j^*} and submits two plaintext messages (m_0, m_1) of same length. $\mathbb{C}$ chooses a random bit $s \in_R \{0,1\}$ and encrypts and re-encrypts m_s under the same access policy as that of target data partition d_{j^*} and sends the resulting re-encrypted output intended for target user u_{i^*} as $C_{k_{j^*}}^{i^*}$ to $\mathcal{A}$.
4. *Game-Query-2:* $\mathcal{A}$ continues querying the oracles $\mathcal{K}_{hon}$, $\mathcal{K}_{corr}$ and $\mathcal{RK}$ as in *Game-Query-1* phase under the same constraints.
5. *Game-Guess:* Finally, $\mathcal{A}$ has to output a bit s' and $\mathcal{A}$ wins the game if $s = s'$.

The advantage of $\mathcal{A}$ in the game defined above is $|Pr[s = s'] - \frac{1}{2}|$.

Definition 1. *The proposed proxy re-encryption scheme is Π considered "secure" if $\mathcal{A}$ wins the above game against $\mathbb{C}$ with negligible advantage. That is, $|Pr[s = s'] - \frac{1}{2}| = negl(\lambda)$.*

4   Proposed Proxy Re-Encryption Based Access Control Enforcement Delegation Scheme

The definitions and construction syntax of the proposed access control enforcement delegation scheme and the proposed PRE scheme are concretely described in this section. The proposed PRE scheme is constructed inside the proposed access control enforcement delegation scheme. We first present the preliminaries that constitute the terminology and the standard cryptographic and complexity assumptions used for construction. Then we construct the proposed schemes by describing concretely the procedures involved.

4.1   Preliminaries

Preliminaries of the proposed scheme include the definitions of notations used in the construction, cryptographic primitives and complexity assumptions.

Terminology and Notations. The terminology and notations used through the rest of the paper, also summarized in Table 1, are explained. There is an access control matrix ACM, symmetric content keys k_j, key-pair of individual users (pk_i, sk_i) and re-encryption keys $rk_{O \to u_i}$. Additionally, we have data public and secret key-pairs (R_{d_j}, r_{d_j}) for each data item d_j and a set of delegation

Table 1. Notations for the proposed system with n users and m data items.

Notation	Description
k_i	Symmetric content keys for symmetric encryption of data file $\forall d_i \in \mathcal{D}$
(pk_i, sk_i)	Individual public-secret key pair of users $u_i \in \mathcal{U}$
$rk_{O \rightarrow u_i}$	Re-encryption key from owner to the user u_i
(R_{d_i}, r_{d_i})	Data Public and secret keys (DPK, DSK) $\forall d_i \in \mathcal{D}$
r_{u_i}	Random Key Component (URK) for each user $u_i \in \mathcal{U}$
$DP_{i,j}$	Public delegation parameter for authorized delegations $\forall u_i \in \mathcal{U}, \forall d_j \in \mathcal{D}$
$[T]_{m \times n}$	$n \times m$ matrix of delegation parameter for all the delegations

parameters $DP_{i,j}$ for delegation of d_j for u_i. The matrix $[T]_{n \times m}$ is used for storing these delegation parameters for n users and m data items. For a finite set of values S, the expression $t \in_R S$ denotes that t has been selected uniformly at random from the set S.

Primitives and Complexity Assumptions. Mappings and computational assumptions used for construction are defined.

Definition 2 (Bilinear Maps). *Consider $\mathbb{G}_1$ and $\mathbb{G}_2$ as cyclic groups each with order p for some prime p. If $g \in \mathbb{G}_1$ is a generator, a bilinear map $e : \mathbb{G}_1 \times \mathbb{G}_1 \rightarrow \mathbb{G}_2$ has following properties:*

   i. Bilinearity: $e(g^l, g^k) = e(g,g)^{lk}, \forall \ g \in \mathbb{G}_1, l, k \in \mathbb{Z}_p^*$.
  ii. Non-degeneracy: $e(g,g) \neq 1$.
 iii. Symmetric: $e(g^l, g^k) = e(g^k, g^l) = e(g,g)^{lk}, \forall \ g \in \mathbb{G}_1, l, k \in \mathbb{Z}_p^*$.
  iv. Computability: For computing the bilinear map, an efficient algorithm exists.

Definition 3 (Decisional Bilinear Diffie-Hellman (DBDH) Assumption). *Given two distributions $(g, g^r, g^s, g^t, e(g,g)^{rst})$ and $(g, g^r, g^s, g^t, e(g,g)^W)$ such that $r, s, t, W \in_R \mathbb{Z}_p^*$, according to the **DBDH** assumption, any PPT algorithm $\mathcal{A}$ is able to distinguish the two tuples with only a negligible advantage ϵ that is,*

$$|Pr[\mathcal{A}(g, g^r, g^s, g^t, e(g,g)^{rst}) = 0] - Pr[\mathcal{A}(g, g^r, g^s, g^t, e(g,g)^W) = 0]| \leq \epsilon.$$

4.2 Concrete Construction

The definition of the proposed access control enforcement delegation scheme Γ is presented in Sect. 3.1 and underlying proxy re-encryption scheme Π is defined in Sect. 3.2. Here, we present concrete description of the procedures of Γ in terms of the procedures of Π. Alongside their usage, we also provide the concrete construction of each of the procedures in Π.

1. **Set:** This algorithm uses **Setup** of the proposed proxy re-encryption scheme for initial system set-up, **KeyGen** to generate key-pairs of individual users as

well as the delegation parameters for all the authorized delegations. Procedure **ReKeyGen** is also used for generating re-encryption keys from the owner to each of the system users. Following are the descriptions of procedures **Setup**, **KeyGen** and **ReKeyGen** of the proposed proxy re-encryption scheme:

- **Setup**$(1^k) \rightarrow params$: Determines $params = (\mathbb{G}_1, \mathbb{G}_2, g, Z, e)$ such that $\mathbb{G}_1$ and $\mathbb{G}_2$ are distinct cyclic groups each of which are of prime order p, $g \in \mathbb{G}_1$ the generator of $\mathbb{G}_1$, a public component called group public key $Z = g^{k_g}$ where $k_g \in_R \mathbb{Z}_p^*$ is the group secret key and a bilinear map $e : \mathbb{G}_1 \times \mathbb{G}_1 \rightarrow \mathbb{G}_2$. All these are made public except the group secret key (k_g) which is kept secret by the data owner.

- **KeyGen**$(i, par) \rightarrow \{(sk_O, pk_O), (sk_i, pk_i), \{(r_{d_j}, R_{d_j}), [T]_{n \times m}, r_{u_i}\}\}$: This procedure generates key pair (pk_O, sk_O) of the data owner, key-pair (pk_i, sk_i) for each user $u_i \in \mathcal{U}$, (r_{d_i}, R_{d_i}) pairs for each data item $d_i \in \mathcal{D}$ and r_{u_i} corresponding to each user $u_i \in \mathcal{U}$:
  - Select $sk_O \in_R \mathbb{Z}_p^*$ and compute $pk_O = Z^{sk_O}$,
  - Select $sk_i \in_R \mathbb{Z}_p^*$ and compute $pk_i = g^{sk_i}$,
  - Select $r_{d_i} \in_R \mathbb{Z}_p$ and compute $R_{d_i} = Z^{r_{d_i}}$ and
  - Select $r_{u_i} \in_R \mathbb{Z}_p$ and keep them secret as a reference to each of the users.

  After this, $DP_{i,j}$ corresponding to each valid delegation of d_j for u_i are computed and stored in the matrix T as under:

$$T[i,j] = \begin{cases} r_{i,j} = g^{r_{u_i} r_{d_j}}, & \text{if } ACM[i,j] = 1, \\ \in_R \mathbb{G}_1, & \text{otherwise.} \end{cases}$$

  After the end of the above process, secret keys $sk_i \ \forall u_i \in \mathcal{U}$ are assigned to the respective users while pk_i is published along with $\forall d_j \in \mathcal{D}, R_{d_j}$ and the matrix $[T]_{n \times m}$. The public key pk_O of the data owner is also published.

- **ReKeyGen**$(pk_i, sk_O, r_{u_i}) \rightarrow rk_{O \rightarrow u_i}$: Delegation key $rk_{O \rightarrow u_i}$ for transforming second-level encryptions under pk_O into those under pk_i is computed as:
  - $rk_{O \rightarrow u_i} = g^{-sk_O} . pk_i^{r_{u_i}} = g^{-sk_O + sk_i r_{u_i}}$.

2. **Out:** This algorithm first produces symmetric encryption of each data item $d_j \in \mathcal{D}$ under a symmetric key $k_j \in_R \mathbb{G}_2$ selected at random to produce C_j. Now k_j is encrypted under pk_O and using the data secret key d_j using the procedure **Enc₂** described as follows:

- **Enc₂**$(pk_O, k_g, R_{d_j}, k_j) \rightarrow C_{k_j}$: To produce second-level encryption of k_j under pk_O, the procedure works as under:
  - Select $s \in_R \mathbb{Z}_p$,
  - Compute $\overline{C_1} = k_j . e(pk_O^s, R_{d_j})^{k_g^{-1}} = k_j . e(g, Z)^{sk_O r_{d_j} s}$.
  - Compute $\overline{C_2} = (R_{d_j})^s = Z^{r_{d_j} s}$, and $\overline{C_3} = Z^s$.
  - Output second-level encryption $C_{k_j} = (\overline{C_1}, \overline{C_2}, \overline{C_3})$.

  C_{k_j} produced above can be decrypted using sk_O. The data file d_j is outsourced on the CSP in the form of the pair (C_j, C_{k_j}).

3. **Delegate:** This procedure enables the CSP to delegate decryption rights of d_j to u_i if and only if $ACM[i,j] = 1$. This requires re-encryption of C_{k_j} produced in the previous step to produce $C_{k_j}^i$ using $rk_{O\to u_i}$ and sending it along with the C_j. The procedure used is **ReEnc** which is described as follows:

   - **ReEnc**$(rk_{O\to u_i}, C_{k_j}) \to C_{k_j}^i$: To produce re-encrypted ciphertext given the second-level encryption and a re-encryption key, the following steps are executed:
     - $C_1 = \overline{C_1}.e(\overline{C_2}, rk_{O\to u_i}) = k_j.e(Z^{r_{d_j} r_{u_i}}, pk_i^s) = k_j.e(T[i,j], Z^{sk_i s})$,
     - $C_2 = \overline{C_2}$, $C_3 = \overline{C_3}$, $C_4 = T[i,j]$ and
     - Output re-encrypted ciphertext under pk_i as $C_{k_j}^i = (C_1, C_2, C_3, C_4)$.

   At the end of this procedure, the CSP sends the pair $(C_j, C_{k_j}^i)$ to the user u_i.

4. **Read:** To obtain the requested data item d_j, the user u_i first performs decryption of $C_{k_j}^i$ to obtain k_j which can be used for symmetric decryption of C_j to obtain d_j. The key k_j and consequently the message d_j is correctly obtained only if u_i is authorized to access d_j. Otherwise, a meaningless random-looking quantity is produced which does not reveal any information to obtain either d_j or any other secrets in the system.

   For this, the procedure starts by using **Dec₁** procedure described below to obtain k_j from $C_{k_j}^i$ and decrypting C_j using k_j to obtain d_j the underlying data item. In case the requesting entity is the data owner himself, the CSP does not need to carry out re-encryption, because C_{k_j} can be decrypted using **Dec₂**(sk_O, C_{k_j}). In the following we describe the procedures **Dec₁** and **Dec₂**:

   - **Dec₁**$(sk_i, C_{k_j}^i) \to k_j$: Ciphertext $C_{k_j}^i$ which is the re-encrypted output such that it is now a ciphertext under pk_i is decrypted by u_i as follows:
     - Compute $k_j = C_1.e(C_4, C_3)^{-sk_i}$.
   - **Dec₂**$(sk_O, C_{k_j}) \to k_j$: A second-level encryption C_{k_j} can be decrypted by the data owner using this procedure as under:
     - Compute $k_j = \overline{C_1}.e(\overline{C_2}, g)^{-sk_O}$.

   To access the underlying plaintext message d_j, **Dec**(k_j, C_j) which is symmetric decryption of C_j using k_j, is performed.

5. **ACM-update:** Consider a user u_l whose access for d_j is to be revoked. The entry $ACM[l,j]$ must be changed from 1 to 0 and the value $T[l,j]$ must be invalidated. By invalidation of the delegation parameter value $T[l,j]$ it is meant that delegation of decryption rights of a data item must not be possible even if the previous value of the (valid) delegation parameter is recorded. For achieving this, the value r_{d_j} is updated by the data owner to r'_{d_j} and the value R'_{d_j} is computed. Now the values of the delegation parameter $T[i,j] = (R_{d'_j})^{r_{u_i} k_g^{-1}}$, $\forall u_i \in \mathcal{U}$ such that $ACM[i,j] = 1$ are also updated. The current and all future copies of the data item under label d_j are encrypted using the updated symmetric secret key k'_j. This would prevent u_l from accessing the current and any future copies d_j. The old delegation parameters $T[i,j]$, $\forall u_i \in \mathcal{U}$ such that $ACM[i,j] = 1$ are archived by the CSP so that the previous copies of d_j are still accessible. However, $T[l,j]$ is deleted after revocation which is the delegation parameter corresponding to u_l for d_j. For re-instating

the access rights of a user u_r for d_j, data owner computes the delegation parameter $T[r, j] = (R_{d_j})^{r_{u_r} k_g^{-1}}$. As a result, the re-instated user u_r can have access to not only the current copy of the outsourced data d_j but also to all its previous copies. The users' secret keys and that of the data owner need not be changed in this process.

5   Analysis of the Proposed Proxy Re-Encryption Scheme

The proposed access control enforcement delegation scheme defined in Sect. 3.1 is realized through the concrete construction of the proposed PRE scheme defined in Sect. 3.2. In this section, we analyze security and performance of the proposed access control enforcement delegation scheme through analysis of the proposed PRE scheme. In particular, we present formal security analysis of the proposed PRE scheme and performance analysis of the procedures involved in the resulting access control enforcement delegation scheme.

5.1   Correctness Analysis

A valid first-level ciphertext may arrive at the user u_i from the CSP after re-encryption of a second-level encryption using $rk_{O \rightarrow u_i}$. If the re-encryption procedure is correct, following equalities hold:

1. $\forall u_i \in \mathcal{U}, \forall k_j \in \mathcal{K}$, $\mathbf{Dec_2}(sk_i, \mathbf{Enc_2}(pk_O, k_g, R_{d_j}, k_j))) = k_j$.
2. $\forall u_i \in \mathcal{U}, \forall k_j \in \mathcal{K}$ such that $ACM[i, j] = 1$, $\mathbf{Dec_1}(sk_i, \mathbf{ReEnc}(rk_{O \rightarrow u_i}, \mathbf{Enc_2}(pk_O, k_g, R_{d_j}, k_j))) = k_j$.

The output of $\mathbf{Enc_2}$ has $\overline{C}_1 = k_j.e(g, Z)^{sk_O r_{d_j} s}$, $\overline{C}_2 = Z^{r_{d_j} s}$ and $\overline{C}_3 = Z^s$.

$$
\begin{aligned}
\mathbf{Dec_2}(sk_i, \mathbf{Enc_2}(pk_O, k_g, R_{d_j}, k_j))) &= \overline{C}_1.e(\overline{C}_2, g)^{-sk_O} \\
&= k_j.e(g, Z)^{sk_O r_{d_j} s}.e(Z^{r_{d_j} s}, g)^{-sk_O} \\
&= k_j.e(g, Z)^{sk_O r_{d_j} s}.e(g, Z)^{-sk_O r_{d_j} s} \\
&= k_j.
\end{aligned}
$$

Also,

$$
\begin{aligned}
\mathbf{Dec_1}(sk_i, \mathbf{ReEnc}(rk_{O \rightarrow u_i}, \\
\mathbf{Enc_2}(pk_O, k_g, R_{d_j}, k_j))) &= k_j.e(Z^{r_{d_j} r_{u_i}}, pk_i^s).e(g^{r_{d_j} r_{u_i}}, Z^s)^{-sk_i} \\
&= k_j.e(g, Z)^{r_{d_j} r_{u_i} sk_i s}.e(g, Z)^{-r_{d_j} r_{u_i} sk_i s} \\
&= k_j.
\end{aligned}
$$

A re-encrypted ciphertext with $rk_{O \rightarrow u_i}$ has $C_1 = k_j.e(Z^{r_{d_j} r_{u_i}}, pk_i^s)$ and $C_3 = Z^{r_{d_j} r_{u_i}}$ only if u_i has authorization for d_j. However, if u_i cannot access d_j then C_1 of the re-encrypted ciphertext takes the form $C_1 = k_j.e(Z^x, pk_i^s)$ where $x \in_R \mathbb{Z}_p$

is a random number. So, since the ciphertext component C_3 and Z^x do not match, the decryption using the procedure $\mathbf{Enc_1}$ does not produce the correct plaintext output. If the CSP wants to maliciously grant access to the data item to a user, it must compute $Z^{r_{d_j} r_{u_i}}$ but this value is given to the CSP by the owner only when $ACM[i,j] = 1$ i.e., when u_i can access d_j. So, it is impossible for the CSP to grant access to u_i for the data item d_j.

5.2   Security Analysis

In this section, the proposed PRE scheme is proved secure under IND-TP-CPA of Definition 1. Security of the proposed PRE scheme establishes the ciphertext indistinguishability of procedure $\mathbf{Enc_2}$ and $\mathbf{ReEnc}$ for a target delegatee user.

Theorem 1. *The proposed proxy re-encryption scheme defined in Sect. 3.2 and constructed in Sect. 4.2 is secure under IND-TP-CPA of Definition 1 assuming that DBDH (see Definition 3) is hard in $\mathbb{G}_1, \mathbb{G}_2$.*

Proof. We reduce the capability of $\mathcal{A}$ for distinguishing two re-encrypted ciphertexts to deciding the DBDH tuple over $\mathbb{G}_1, \mathbb{G}_2$. We first consider, for contradiction, the existence of a simulator (PPT algorithm) $\mathcal{B}$ that can be used by $\mathcal{A}$ and that can decide a DBDH tuple. Afterwards, we argue that the only way $\mathcal{A}$ can distinguish two re-encryptions is by using $\mathcal{B}$. Following are the steps of the security game between the challenger $\mathbb{C}$ and adversary $\mathcal{A}$:

1. *Game-Setup:* The challenger $\mathbb{C}$ sends the global public parameters $g, Z = g^c, e(g_1, g)$ for $c \in \mathbb{Z}_p$. Here, $g_1 = g^t$ for some random unknown $t \in_R \mathbb{Z}_p$. Data public keys $R_{d_j} = g^{c.r_{d_j}}$ corresponding to each d_j and each of the $n \times m$ delegation parameters $\forall u_i \in \mathcal{U}, d_j \in \mathcal{D}, DP_{i,j} = g^{r_{u_i} r_{d_j}}$ are given to $\mathcal{A}$.
2. *Game-Query-1:* $\mathcal{A}$ adaptively queries the oracles $\mathcal{K}_{hon}$, $\mathcal{K}_{corr}$ and $\mathcal{RK}$ for number of times polynomial in λ as under:
   (a) $pk_i \leftarrow \mathcal{K}_{hon}(i), \forall u_i \in \mathcal{U}$, such that u_i is an uncorrupted user. Here, $pk_i = g^{s_i}$ for some random unknown $s_i \in_R \mathbb{Z}_p$, the secret key of an honest user u_i.
   (b) $pk_O \leftarrow \mathcal{K}_{hon}(O)$ public key of the data owner. $pk_O = g^{c.sk_O}$ for random $sk_O \in_R \mathbb{Z}_p$, the secret key of the data owner.
   (c) $(pk_x, sk_x) \leftarrow \mathcal{K}_{corr}(x), \forall u_x \in \mathcal{U}$, an unauthorized corrupted user. Here, $sk_x \in \mathbb{Z}_p$ is the secret key of corrupted user and $pk_x = g^{sk_x}$.
   (d) $rk_{O \rightarrow u_i} \leftarrow \mathcal{RK}(pk_O, pk_i)$, re-encryption keys required for delegation from data owner u_O to uncorrupted users u_i. $rk_{O \rightarrow u_i} = g^{sk_O + r_i}$ for some random unknown $r_i \in \mathbb{Z}_p$.
   (e) $rk_{O \rightarrow u_x} \leftarrow \mathcal{RK}(pk_O, pk_x)$, re-encryption keys required for delegation from data owner u_O to u_x, a set of corrupted users. $rk_{O \rightarrow u_x} = g^{sk_O + sk_x r_{u_x}}$ for some random unknown $r_{u_x} \in_R \mathbb{Z}_p$.
3. *Game-Challenge:* $\mathcal{A}$ selects a target data partition d_{j*} subject to the condition that no user corrupted in the previous phase is authorized for d_{j*}. $\mathcal{A}$ further chooses the target individual user u_{i*} which happens to be uncorrupted and has access to d_{j*}. $\mathcal{A}$ now submits two plaintext messages (m_0, m_1) of same

length. $\mathbb{C}$ outputs $C^{i^*}_{m_s} = (g_1^{c.r_{d_{j^*}}}, g_1^c, g^{r_i^*}, m_s.e(g_1,g)^W)$ for $r_{d_{j^*}} \in \mathbb{Z}_p$, the data secret key corresponding to d_{j^*}, delegation parameter $DP_{i,j^*} = g^{r_i}$ and $r_i^* \in \mathbb{Z}_p$.

4. *Game-Query-2:* $\mathcal{A}$ continues querying the oracles $\mathcal{K}_{hon}$, $\mathcal{K}_{corr}$ and $\mathcal{RK}$ as in *Game-Query-1* phase under the same constraints.

5. *Game-Guess:* Adversary utilizes all the queried information α in the previous *Game-Setup*, *Game-Query-1* and *Game-Query-2* phases to output its best guess s'. We denote the relevant information from the collection $(C^{i^*}_{m_s}, \alpha)$, where α is the information queried above, as $(C^{i^*}_{m_s}, \alpha^*)$

$(C^{i^*}_{m_s}, \alpha^*) = (g^c, g_1^{c.r_{d_{j^*}}}, g^{r^*}, g^{sk_{i^*}}, g_1^c, m_s.e(g_1,g)^W)$ for some $W \in_R \mathbb{Z}_p$ and $DP_{i^*,j^*} = g^{r^*}$, the valid delegation parameter for u_{i^*} to access d_{j^*}.

$$(C^{i^*}_{m_s}, \alpha^*) = (g^c, g_1^{c.r_{d_{j^*}}}, g^{r^*}, g^{sk_{i^*}}, g_1^c, m_s.e(g_1,g)^W)$$
$$= (g^c, g^{c.t.r_{d_{j^*}}}, g^{r^*}, g^{sk_{i^*}}, g^{c.t}, m_s.e(g,g)^{t.W})$$

Now the collection $(g^{c.t}, g^{r^*}, g^{sk_{i^*}}, m_s.e(g,g)^{tW})$. If $W = c.r^*.sk_{i^*}$, the collection becomes $(g^{c.t}, g^{r^*}, g^{sk_{i^*}}, m_s.e(g,g)^{(c.t).(r^*).(sk_{i^*})})$.

This forms a perfect DBDH tuple. Thus $\mathcal{A}$ now uses $\mathcal{B}$ to decide this tuple which outputs the bit $b = 1$ to indicate that it was given a valid DBDH tuple and $b = 0$ to indicate that the tuple given was not a valid DBDH tuple. $\mathcal{A}$ wins the game if $s = s'$. However, according to Definition 3, there does not exist a PPT algorithm that can distinguish two DBDH tuples with non-negligible advantage. That is, $Pr[s = s'|b = 1] = 1/2 + negl(\lambda)$. Therefore, $\mathcal{A}$ can break the security of the proposed proxy re-encryption scheme using a simulator $\mathcal{B}$ that breaks the DBDH assumption. But this is in contradiction with the DBDH assumption of Definition 3. Thus, the proposed proxy re-encryption scheme is secure under IND-TP-CPA security given the DBDH is hard in $\mathbb{G}_1, \mathbb{G}_2$.

5.3   Performance Analysis

We analyze storage and computation overhead on the individual users and the data owner. The proposed proxy re-encryption scheme is efficient as it requires only one encryption per data item by the data owner and generation of one proxy re-encryption key per user. Also, it requires the data owner to store none of the encryption keys, re-encryption keys or secret keys of any user. The users need to store nothing except their secret keys as the scheme is proxy invisible. One-time cost of system setup incurred at the data owner includes generating n secret keys and n re-encryption keys (one per user), m data secret keys where m is the number of data items to be shared. Another one-time computation includes computing $\mathcal{O}(n \times m)$ modular exponentiations corresponding to all the authorized delegations to compute one delegation parameter per delegation.

Table 2 shows the computation overhead on data owner, the CSP and the individual users in the proposed access control enforcement delegation scheme

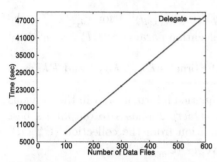
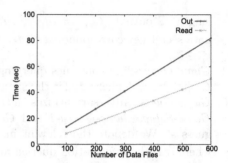
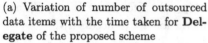

(a) Variation of number of outsourced data items with the time taken for **Delegate** of the proposed scheme

(b) Variation of number of outsourced data items with the time taken for **Read** and **Out** of the proposed scheme

Fig. 1. Comparison of the time taken for different number of outsourced data items for procedures **Read, Out** and **Delegate** of the proposed scheme

Table 2. Processing cost for owner, CSP and users in the proposed scheme apart from symmetric encryption/decryption. Operations include Multiplications (M), modular Exponentiation (E) and Bilinear pairing (B).

Procedure	Data owner	CSP	Individual user
Out	$3t_E + t_M + t_B$	—	—
Delegate	—	$t_B + t_M$	—
Read	—	—	$t_M + t_E$
ACM-update[†]	$t_B + (3 + n_1)t_E + 2t_M$	—	—

[†] cost of revoking the access rights of a user for a particular data item because it is higher than the cost of re-instating the access rights.

in terms of the number of various cryptographic operations namely bilinear pairing, modular exponentiation, multiplication etc. We implemented the proposed scheme using the Pairing-based Cryptography library [13] on a system supporting 4 GB RAM, Intel Core i3 processor, having 64 bit Ubuntu 16.04 LTS. Both data owner and the individual user clients have same configuration. The number of users in the system has been fixed to 100. The number of data files to be shared by the data owner are on the x-axis and computation overhead on the y-axis. The overall computation cost of the procedures **Out, Delegate** and **Read** of the proposed data outsourcing and access control scheme are compared in Fig. 1. The curve for the procedure **Delegate** is shown in Fig. 1a and that of the **Out** an **Read** of the proposed scheme in Fig. 1b. This clearly indicates that the cost of data outsourcing for the data owner and that of access by the users in the system are far less than cost of access delegation. Since the access delegation is carried out by the CSP without any intervention of data owner or delegatee users, the scheme successfully delegates the access control to the CSP in an efficient manner.

6 Conclusion

In this paper, a proxy re-encryption based data outsourcing and access control enforcement delegation scheme has been proposed using which a data owner can securely and efficiently delegate the task of access control enforcement to semi-trusted cloud service provider. The underlying proposed proxy re-encryption scheme is unique as it allows only authorized delegations despite the re-encryption key from the data owner to an individual user being available. The proposed access control enforcement delegation scheme subjects the data owner and individual users to a constant storage and computation overhead. It has been shown that the proposed scheme satisfies forward and backward secrecy in case of change in access rights of an individual user. The proposed scheme has been proved secure against an adversary that colludes with individual users in the system and tries to either learn the underlying plaintext or achieve unauthorized delegations.

References

1. Ali, M., et al.: SeDaSC: secure data sharing in clouds. IEEE Syst. J. **11**(2), 395–404 (2017)
2. Ateniese, G., Fu, K., Green, M., Hohenberger, S.: Improved proxy re-encryption schemes with applications to secure distributed storage. ACM Trans. Inf. Syst. Secur. **9**(1), 1–30 (2006)
3. Blaze, M., Bleumer, G., Strauss, M.: Divertible protocols and atomic proxy cryptography. In: Nyberg, K. (ed.) EUROCRYPT 1998. LNCS, vol. 1403, pp. 127–144. Springer, Heidelberg (1998). https://doi.org/10.1007/BFb0054122
4. Fang, L., Susilo, W., Ge, C., Wang, J.: Interactive conditional proxy re-encryption with fine grain policy. J. Syst. Softw. **84**(12), 2293–2302 (2011)
5. Fang, L., Susilo, W., Ge, C., Wang, J.: Chosen-ciphertext secure anonymous conditional proxy re-encryption with keyword search. Theor. Comput. Sci. **462**, 39–58 (2012)
6. Fang, L., Wang, J., Ge, C., Ren, Y.: Fuzzy conditional proxy re-encryption. Sci. China Inf. Sci. **56**(5), 1–13 (2013)
7. Feng, W., Zhang, Z., Wang, J., Han, L.: A novel authorization delegation scheme for multimedia social networks by using proxy re-encryption. Multimed. Tools Appl. **75**(21), 13995–14014 (2016)
8. Goh, E.J., Shacham, H., Modadugu, N., Boneh, D.: SiRiUS: securing remote untrusted storage. In: NDSS, pp. 131–145 (2003)
9. Goyal, V., Pandey, O., Sahai, A., Waters, B.: Attribute-based encryption for fine-grained access control of encrypted data. In: Proceedings of the 13th ACM Conference on Computer and Communications Security. CCS 2006, pp. 89–98. ACM (2006). https://doi.org/10.1145/1180405.1180418
10. Jia, W., Zhu, H., Cao, Z., Wei, L., Lin, X.: SDSM: a secure data service mechanism in mobile cloud computing. In: 2011 IEEE Conference on Computer Communications Workshops (INFOCOM WKSHPS), pp. 1060–1065, April 2011. https://doi.org/10.1109/INFCOMW.2011.5928784
11. Jung, T., Li, X., Wan, Z., Wan, M.: Privacy preserving cloud data access with multi-authorities. In: 2013 Proceedings of the IEEE INFOCOM, pp. 2625–2633, April 2013. https://doi.org/10.1109/INFCOM.2013.6567070

12. Khan, A.N., Mat Kiah, M.L., Ali, M., Shamshirband, S., Khan, A.u.R.: A cloud-manager-based re-encryption scheme for mobile users in cloud environment: a hybrid approach. J. Grid Comput. **13**(4), 651–675 (2015)

13. Library, P.: The pairing-based cryptography library. https://crypto.stanford.edu/pbc/. Accessed on 02 Feb 2018

14. Ren, K., Wang, C., Wang, Q.: Security challenges for the public cloud. IEEE Internet Comput. **16**(1), 69–73 (2012)

15. RFC2315: Pkcs #7: Cryptographic message syntax (version 1.5). http://www.ietf.org/rfc/rfc2315.txt. Accessed on 28 Apr 2016

16. Sahai, A., Waters, B.: Fuzzy identity-based encryption. In: Cramer, R. (ed.) EURO-CRYPT 2005. LNCS, vol. 3494, pp. 457–473. Springer, Heidelberg (2005). https://doi.org/10.1007/11426639_27

17. Subashini, S., Kavitha, V.: A survey on security issues in service delivery models of cloud computing. J. Netw. Comput. Appl. **34**(1), 1–11 (2011)

18. Tang, Y., Lee, P.P.C., Lui, J.C.S., Perlman, R.J.: Secure overlay cloud storage with access control and assured deletion. IEEE Trans. Dependable Secure Comput. **9**(6), 903–916 (2012)

19. Tran, D.H., Nguyen, H., Zha, W., Ng, W.K.: Towards security in sharing data on cloud-based social networks. In: 2011 8th International Conference on Information, Communications Signal Processing, pp. 1–5, December 2011. https://doi.org/10.1109/ICICS.2011.6173582

20. Tysowski, P.K., Hasan, M.A.: Re-encryption-based key management towards secure and scalable mobile applications in clouds. IACR Cryptology ePrint Archive, 668 (2011)

21. Wang, X.A., Huang, X., Yang, X., Liu, L., Wu, X.: Further observation on proxy re-encryption with keyword search. J. Syst. Softw. **85**(3), 643–654 (2012). Novel approaches in the design and implementation of systems/software architecture

22. Wang, Y., Wu, Q., Qin, B., Shi, W., Deng, R.H., Hu, J.: Identity-based data outsourcing with comprehensive auditing in clouds. IEEE Trans. Inf. Forensics Secur. **12**(4), 940–952 (2017). https://doi.org/10.1109/TIFS.2016.2646913

23. Weng, J., Yang, Y., Tang, Q., Deng, R.H., Bao, F.: Efficient conditional proxy re-encryption with chosen-ciphertext security. In: Samarati, P., Yung, M., Martinelli, F., Ardagna, C.A. (eds.) ISC 2009. LNCS, vol. 5735, pp. 151–166. Springer, Heidelberg (2009). https://doi.org/10.1007/978-3-642-04474-8_13

24. Xu, L., Wu, X., Zhang, X.: CL-PRE: a certificateless proxy re-encryption scheme for secure data sharing with public cloud. In: Proceedings of the 7th ACM Symposium on Information, Computer and Communications Security. ASIACCS 2012, pp. 87–88. ACM, New York (2012). https://doi.org/10.1145/2414456.2414507

25. Xue, K., Hong, P.: A dynamic secure group sharing framework in public cloud computing. IEEE Trans. Cloud Comput. **2**(4), 459–470 (2014)

26. Yang, K., Jia, X., Ren, K., Zhang, B.: DAC-MACS: effective data access control for multi-authority cloud storage systems. In: 2013 Proceedings IEEE INFOCOM, pp. 2895–2903, April 2013. https://doi.org/10.1109/TIFS.2013.2279531

27. Yu, S., Wang, C., Ren, K., Lou, W.: Achieving secure, scalable, and fine-grained data access control in cloud computing. In: Proceedings of the IEEE INFOCOM 2010, pp. 1–9. IEEE (2010). https://doi.org/10.1109/INFCOM.2010.5462174

28. Yu, W., Sun, Y., Liu, K.J.R.: Optimizing rekeying cost for contributory group key agreement schemes. IEEE Trans. Dependable Secure Comput. **4**(3), 228–242 (2007)
29. Zhou, M., Mu, Y., Susilo, W., Yan, J., Dong, L.: Privacy enhanced data outsourcing in the cloud. J. Netw. Comput. Appl. **35**(4), 1367–1373 (2012). Intelligent Algorithms for Data-Centric Sensor Networks

From Cyber Security Activities to Collaborative Virtual Environments Practices Through the 3D CyberCOP Platform

Alexandre Kabil[1]([✉]), Thierry Duval[1], Nora Cuppens[1], Gérard Le Comte[2], Yoran Halgand[3], and Christophe Ponchel[4]

[1] IMT Atlantique, UBL, Lab-STICC, UMR CNRS 6285, Plouzané, France
{alexandre.kabil,thierry.duval,nora.cuppens}@imt-atlantique.fr
[2] Societe Generale, Paris, France
gerard.le-comte@socgen.com
[3] EDF, Paris, France
yoran.halgand@edf.fr
[4] AIRBUS Defence and Space, Toulouse, France
christophe.ponchel@airbus.com

Abstract. Although collaborative practices between cyber organizations are well documented, managing activities within these organizations is still challenging as cyber operators tasks are very demanding and usually done individually. As human factors studies in cyber environments are still difficult to perform, tools and collaborative practices are evolving slowly and training is always required to increase teamwork efficiency. Contrary to other research fields, cyber security is not harnessing yet the capabilities of Collaborative Virtual Environments (CVE) which can be used both for immersive and interactive data visualization and serious gaming for training. In order to tackle cyber security teamwork issues, we propose a 3D CVE called the 3D Cyber Common Operational Picture, which aims at taking advantage of CVE practices to enhance cyber collaborative activities.

Based on four Security Operations Centers (SOCs) visits we have made in different organizations, we have designed a cyber collaborative activity model which has been used as a reference to design our 3D CyberCOP platform features, such as asymetrical collaboration, mutual awareness and roles specialization. Our approach can be adapted to several use cases, and we are currently developing a cyber incident analysis scenario based on an event-driven architecture, as a proof of concept.

Keywords: Cybersecurity · Collaborative interaction · Virtual reality

1 Introduction

Cybersecurity is the collection of tools, policies, security concepts, security safeguards, guidelines, risk management approaches, actions, training, best practices, assurance and technologies that can be used to protect organizations and

V. Ganapathy et al. (Eds.): ICISS 2018, LNCS 11281, pp. 272–287, 2018.
https://doi.org/10.1007/978-3-030-05171-6_14

users assets [36]. Because every organization, nation and company is subject to cyber threats, collaborative strategies and policies are required to manage effective cyber defence activities, but they are still difficult to develop [16]. Moreover, teamwork within organizations is still challenging, as training sessions are time demanding and cyber security tools and softwares are often made for individual use. Far from pop culture stereotypes, cyber operators use classical Command Line Interfaces (CLI) and Graphical User Interfaces (GUI) to detect incidents and cyber threats such as the ELK stack[1], whereas other domains look at Natural User Interfaces (NUI) or even Immersive Analytics solutions to facilitate information sharing between users and even training practices [9].

In this paper we present a Collaborative Virtual Environment (CVE) called the 3D Cyber Common Operational Picture, which aims at enhancing cyber teamwork by applying design methods derived from CVE usages.

We will put the emphasis on how we have integrated cyber security collaborative practices into our CVE and how this general approach could work for several use cases including cyber incident analysis simulations.

In Sect. 2 we will show that as collaboration between and within organizations is an important topic in cyber security, CVEs could tackle cyber teamwork effectiveness issues by providing shared environments and practices. Then in Sect. 3 we will present the cyber collaborative activity model we have conceived by visiting Security Operations Centers (SOCs) and how we have managed to adapt its features to CVEs design practices through our 3D Cyber Common Operational Picture platform. Finally we will detail in Sect. 4 the cyber incident analysis scenario we are still working on based on an event driven architecture, and we will conclude by perspectives of our approach.

2 Collaborative Practices in Cyber Security

As more and more data are generated and collected on networks and infrastructures, cyber security can not be effective without proper collaboration at different scales, from employees (experts and non-experts) to companies, organizations or even countries. As cyber world is not bounded by geographical limits, productivity and telepresence tools such as visioconference or virtual environments are effective when people need to share knowledge, data or experiences but these tools require specific learning methods and workflows.

2.1 Collaboration Management in Cyber Security Organizations

Cyber collaboration is managed at different scales, from nation to private companies, with respect to threats gravity, strategic implications and trust policies, as shown by Petersen and Tjalve [26]. In order to coordinate cyber actions, specific structures such as Security Operations Centers (SOCs) or Computer Emergency Response Teams (CERTs) are well defined and standardized (such as the MITRE

---

[1] https://www.elastic.co/fr/elk-stack.

guide for example[2]). But even if collaborative strategies exist, communication is still difficult between organizations [39], and at employees level, practices and processes are often individual: analysts get tickets to observe, monitor and report incidents, and if they need to ask advice from others, they forward tickets or they communicate information in a tacit way [2]. Moreover, some structures such as SOCs are considered both organizations and teams, which changes the way of organizing processes and work practices [15].

As Rajivan and Cooke explain [28], teamwork effectiveness evaluation is a challenging task as it is more than the evaluation of each team member's Cyber Situational Awareness (CSA) capabilities. Working efficiently among a team requires specific collaborative tools and training sessions, which are not always available to cyber operators.

To fill this gap between collaborative expectations and cyber operators work-flows, Computer Supported Cooperative Work (CSCW) systems such as Collaborative Virtual Environments (CVE) could be used in order to help users to share knowledge and develop understanding of each others' tasks [7].

2.2 Virtual Environments for Cyber Security

Although there are some research papers about 3D metaphors for data representations in cyber security [12,20] or about the usability of Virtual Environments for cyber teamwork [24,27,31], applying User Experience (UX) design for cyber security is quite recent [29], and the usefulness of 3D representations is just now accepted [1,8] which explains maybe why we have not seen much 3D visualizations for cyber security in reviews of literature [13,34], apart from the 2012 Daedalus-Viz project developed by Inoue et al. [17].

Moreover, experts cyber security tools face a paradox: they need to be simple enough in order to help analysts to understand what is going on on the network and they need to be precise enough to help them investigating incidents. CVEs and Immersive Analytics solutions can help solving these problems by either providing separate views towards different analysts but letting them having a common ground, or proposing aggregated 3D interactive data representations that can give more information [6,14].

Another interesting aspect of CVEs is that they are considered useful for learning [10,33], and they could be used to enhance existing cyber training tools which are still very technical or based on serious-gaming approaches [3,30].

We think that CVEs for cyber security should blend educational or serious-gaming approaches and data analysis visualizations as these points are still difficult to manage in cyber organizations [18]. As shown in the Fig. 1, ouar approach aims at providing both data visualization and training scenarios by immersing cyber operators into environments where they will be able to collaborate with respect to their organizational practices to perform specific activities.

---

[2] https://www.mitre.org/capabilities/cybersecurity/overview/cybersecurity-blog/ten-strategies-for-becoming-a-world-class.

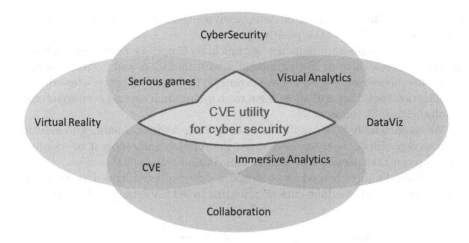

Fig. 1. Venn diagram of our approach combining collaboration, virtual reality and data visualization for cyber security.

3   Collaborative Model and CVE Design

In order to understand cyber security collaborative practices, we have had the opportunity to visit four SOCs of our industrial partners.

We have seen that even if structures' organizations were different, we have been able to define a generic collaborative activity model that can be used to describe and model cyber security practices.

3.1   SOC Activity Analysis

SOCs are structures where networks are constantly monitored in real-time by analysts, who are separated in three technical levels and who investigate incidents either for client companies or for internal security. SOCs practices are studied either from the human factor or the organizational point of view [15,38,39], but as cyber security is by definition a confidential field it is still difficult to record data for making activity analysis. As a consequence, our visits were only one day long and we have not been able to record audio or video, but even with these limitations we were able to get some relevant findings on how SOC operators are working as a team. Day to day SOC's operators work relies on getting aware of alerts from cyber security sensors, suppressing false positive alerts, analyzing network meta-data and application logs, creating incident reports and exchanging information and requests with customer teams (network, security, decision). They need to work quickly, so if they consider that an incident is out of their technical scope, they forward it to an expert (escalation process).

We found out that operators work usually alone by taking tickets from the Security Information and Event Management (SIEM) tool, backbone of SOCs, which collects different kinds of data, analyses them and raises alerts (with a quite significant rate of false positives).

Moreover, collaboration is not so much mediated as operators exchange directly between them or during meetings with managers and decision-makers. As a consequence, some of them have expressed the needs for better user-adapted visualization tools that will allow them to share information and even to interact simultaneously on datasets.

We could classify SOC employees roles by their decision-making and network analysis capabilities: analysts have to get information and report it to coordinators who can take decisions or ask for remediation actions [23].

All these findings helped us to define a cyber collaborative activity model which will be used to adapt current practices to 3D CVE usages (Fig. 2):

Model features	SOC Activities
Roles	Tradeoff between decision and data analysis, hierarchical interactions
Tasks	Ticketing system, specific tasks
Visualizations	Several tools for monitoring, correlation and reporting
Data	Aggregated by SIEMs or from various sources (probes, logs...)
Explicit Collaboration	**Ticketing, processes, messages, reports**
Tacit Collaboration	**Communication, 'over the shoulder' interaction**

Fig. 2. Activity model designed for cyber security practices analysis.

- **Roles:** describes the hierarchical structure and the specific missions of operators.
- **Tasks:** describes how operators are working. Tasks are related to roles and data.
- **Visualizations:** concerns the fact that operators are using plenty of tools to monitor, observe and report cyber events. Objectives or tools are to correlate data in order to get a 'big picture', or Cyber Situational Awareness (CSA).
- **Data:** is available through SIEMs (aggregation of data) or logs from different sensors (raw data). When SIEM's information are insufficient, operators have to dig into specific chunks of data.

– **Explicit Collaboration:** concerns the actual processes of ticketing and reporting. Operators act only if they get a ticket and they coordinate their actions to close this ticket as quickly as possible.
– **Implicit Collaboration:** is effective as operators works in open-space environments and can discuss and ask for help in a informal way.

We have separated collaboration features into explicit and implicit categories as some collaborative activities were not part of operators' tasks but were more 'tacit' [2].

This model does not cover every aspect of tasks, data, roles and features needed for a visualization for cyber security as proposed by EEvi [32], but it will help us to determine our 3D Cyber Common Operational Picture features by taking inspiration from CSA taxonomies and models such as the ones from Evesti, Kanstren and Frantti [11,19].

3.2   3D CyberCOP Platform

As shown in figure Fig. 3, our activity model aims at proposing cyber operators adapted visualizations according to their individual (black arrows) and collaborative (red arrows) practices and interactions: individual interactive systems will be enhanced to make them collaborative and/or more immersive with collaborative interactions mediated by the systems (green arrows), and the level of immersion (Virtual Reality, Windows, Icons, Menu and Pointers (WIMP), post-WIMP interfaces) will be adapted to user's roles (for example an analyst and a coordinator will respectively use a Virtual Reality Headset and tactile wide screen).

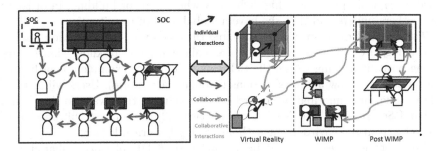

Fig. 3. SOC practices (Left) and their adaptation through the 3D CyberCOP platform (Right). (Color figure online)

Roles will have specific visualizations and interaction capabilities according to their needs and tasks and one user can only have one role at a time (User 1 who plays role A can see only incident information and can only investigate network incidents whereas user 2 in role B has information about risk assessment or regulation policies). Roles will be bounded by hierarchical links, which could be strict (Role A should always wait orders from Role B) or loose (Role A and B should exchange freely information).

Tasks will be coordinated by a ticketing or alerting system: users will have to get tickets in order to execute actions related to their roles (for example an analyst will have to ask permissions for investigating specific assets and coordinator will have to confirm an escalation process). Actions could be defined by experts or more generally by cyber security tasks analysis as [39] or [32].

Visualizations will be 2D, 3D or Immersive, as shown in Fig. 3. These visualizations will get filters with respects to roles and situations. Filters will for example display only network or kinetic related information (for example network topologies and IP addresses, employees' login lists, geographical position of workstations etc..), as in the solution proposed by Zhong et al. [41]. Existing visualization or data analysis tools could be used too if they have a proper communication API.

Data will be for the moment simulated or simplified: is it still cumbersome to represent whole network architectures in 3D or to manage Gigabytes of data so as for the visualizations we will let the opportunity to use existing tools to get realistic data to our platform.

Explicit collaboration will be done by displaying role-related avatars which will not necessarily be on the same scale: real-time analysts will be able to work together in a human-like scale by being immersed in offices whereas a Strategic analyst scale will be much bigger in order to get more high-level information. CVEs allows us to do Asymmetric Collaboration [21] where users could act at different scales from an environment and still get a notion of 'presence' of the others called the 'Mutual Awareness' [21]. Users will be able to share information with different visual feedback, for example analysts will see each other User Interfaces (UIs) and actions because they share the same visual scale whereas a coordinator will appear as a highlight of a whole floor or building, in order to make others understand that she have a global view of the situation.

Tacit collaboration will be available through oral communication and an historic logger of all users' actions: this will allow any user to know what is happening without needing to use the ticketing system (for example a coordinator will be able to follow analysts' actions through the historic). Users will also be able to hide some information, in order to select what they want to share, in a "What I See Is Not What You See" approach [42] (an analyst will be able to interact within the environment without raising historical logger).

Collaborative cues proposed in our 3D CyberCOP platform (shared context, awareness, communication, multiple viewpoints,) are also inspired from [35], from the Information Visualization community. The Fig. 7 'CVE Design solutions' column sums up our design choices for the adaptation of our cyber security activity model into a CVE. We propose simple yet effective features for managing collaboration and we let the opportunity to use existing solutions for the Tasks, Visualization and Data parts as cyber tools are evolving quickly.

In order to instantiate our 3D CyberCOP model and to implement our features, we are developing a collaborative cyber incident analysis simulation based on a malware propagation modelling.

4   3D CyberCOP Use Case: Cyber Incident Analysis Scenario

By considering that incident analysis requires different points of view and specific datasets to evaluate a situation and after discussing with SOCs operators and our industrial partners, we have decided to choose a ransomware propagation analysis scenario as a simple use case to test our approach. We have built this scenario by using an event-driven architecture which have helped us to implement our activity model's features.

4.1   Ransomware Propagation Analysis Scenario

By taking inspiration from the Wannacry[3] attack that occurred in May 2017, we have decided to develop a ransomware propagation scenario by simulating malicious behaviors and investigations activities. Users' objective is to find the vulnerabilities that allow both the file encryption and the propagation through a small office network where workstations have different characteristics (different Operating Systems and known vulnerabilities, different levels of criticity etc.). Ransomware behavior is determined by two simulated metrics, namely the Entropy and the Network Anomaly:

– The **entropy metric** represents the file's system activity of an asset. It increases when files are being encrypted either in a legitimate or malicious way. When this metric reaches a limit, an alert is raised in the system and users will have to investigate to determine the causes of this alert.
– The **network anomaly metric** represents an unusual network activity of an asset which once again can be legitimate or due to a mistake (backup request or peer to peer download) or a malware propagation after a port scan attack (SMB exploit that scans port 445 for example).

With addition to these metrics, ransomware behavior is linked to specific simulated assets vulnerabilitie[4]: the ransomware contaminates assets if and only if they have an old version of Windows (patched before march 2017), no direct access to internet and a SMB exploit available.

At the beginning of the simulation, an asset is infected by the ransomware. As a consequence, an entropy alert is raised while the concerned asset sees its entropy metrics reach a threshold. After a certain amount of time, a network alert is raised due to a high value of the network anomaly metric, as the ransomware

---

[3] http://cert-mu.govmu.org/English/Documents/White%20Papers/White%20Paper%20-%20The%20WannaCry%20Ransomware%20Attack.pdf.

[4] https://www.us-cert.gov/ncas/alerts/TA17-132A.

propagates itself through exploits. If the ransomware successfully propagates, infected assets see their entropy metric increase, and again alerts are raised, and the infection continues until all assets are infected. To add false positive alerts, some assets will perform a daily encryption and backup which will raise entropy and network anomaly levels. Users will have to determine if the raised alerts are from incidents or from false positives. With respect to their roles, they will have various information sources (cyber and kinetic views, alerts information) and collaboration will be necessary in order to characterize the incidents in an efficient way (by crossing information from different sources). To easily implement this scenario, we have used an event-driven architecture that helped us managing ransomware behaviors, users interactions, data visualization and simulation scenario progression.

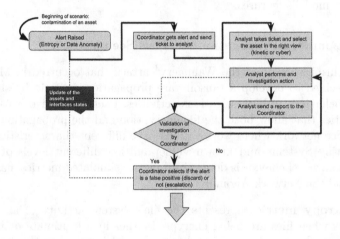

Fig. 4. Alert analysis management from the ticket to escalation.

4.2   Event-Driven Architecture

Event-driven architectures designates an asynchronous programming method where any action of the environment raises events which need to be caught to call functions. Events are not linked to a platform or a user, and the action of catching it (or to listen to it) determines the consequences. For example, clicking on a button could raise a 'Select' event, and according to the system's state, the selection function could be called or not. In our case, we have defined a parameterized event system, and we will give detail about users events (system events works the same).

Users interactions within the simulation (with objects or User Interfaces buttons) raises events like

$$UserEvent(objectId, env, action, userId, alertNumber) \qquad (1)$$

where:

- *objectId* is the object on which the event should occur (e.g. Selection of the asset number three). When a user event is raised, every asset of the simulation gets it and launches actions if it is concerned by this event (for example deactivation of the previously selected asset).
- *env* gives the information on the type of objects this event is related to (for example network nodes and workstations are two different kinds of objects even if they are related to the same asset).
- *action* describes which action was triggered. These tasks (e.g. Selection, Information, Incident Declaration) and modify the scenario progression and the state of the simulation.
- *userId* transmits a reference to the user/role that has launched this event. This parameter allows us to manage the different feedback of actions and to display them with respect to different roles. This parameter can modify the scenario progression.
- *alertNumber* allows users to investigate several tickets at a time and to interact according to specific alerts. A user can get information of any asset for example, but if she is working on a specific ticket, her interaction will have different consequences (scenario update, feedback, and so on).

For example, if user 1 is selecting the cyber object of the asset 3 to investigate the network information required by the ticket 2, user event raised will be:

$$User Event(3, cyber, netinfo, 1, 2) \qquad (2)$$

This event architecture gives us flexibility to manage our 3D CyberCOP features. For example, we can add extra visual feedback if needed or we can control the investigation procedure more strictly by waiting specific actions updating the cyber scenario. Events are not bounded to a specific device and we can trigger them from a 2D tactile display or from a Virtual Reality device. Based on this architecture, we have built the scenario and implemented our activity model features with respect to CVE design features presented before.

4.3   Activity Model Implementation

- We have decided to implement two roles in this simulation:
  - an **analyst** will have to investigate assets and to work on tickets given by a **coordinator**. She is immersed in Virtual Environment but can use a classical dashboard if needed.
  - a **coordinator** will have to transfer tickets to **analysts** and to decide if the alerts should be escalated. She will use a 2D dashboard to do so (but again she can use immersive visualization if needed).

  These roles will have to respect hierarchical interactions: an analyst cannot investigate an asset if she has not get a ticket and a coordinator could not validate an alert if she has not get the analyst's report. Users with same roles will have the same capabilities.

- Users will have to perform tasks in a precise order to progress through the scenario (Fig. 4). First, the coordinator selects an alert and transmits it to an analyst. Then, an analyst who accepts the alert ticket investigates by selecting the concerned asset and the right information (kinetic or cyber) she needs, and then performs an analysis action through a UI. After that, she sends the analysis report to the coordinator via a reporting action on the UI. When the coordinator receives the report, she can validate it or ask for more information. Once she has all information, she escalates the alert to incident or she discards it if it is a false positive. When several assets are compromised (e.g. concerned by incidents), analysts and coordinators could filter assets information in order to find common points or differences between them. These information will be selected on a specific UI to determine if they have found the ransomware attack vectors.
- Users will be able to use 2D, 3D and immersive visualizations according to their roles or needs. Moreover, we will separate the simulation between two environments, the kinetic and the cyber one (Fig. 6 top left and right views).
  - The kinetic environment represents a physical view of the network office, with workstations, office floors and rooms. When users navigate through this environment, they get information about assets entropy level, working processes, login of the last user etc...
  - The cyber environment represents the networked information. Users actions and visualizations will be about network topology, IP Addresses and so on.

  Users will have to get information from these two environments in order to determine the nature of the alert and to have a global view of an asset state.
- Two metrics will be monitored: entropy and network anomalies. Users will get data from assets by selecting them and choosing an action through their graphical interfaces. Assets information are provided by a pre-defined scenario.
- To manage the ticketing feature, an alert list will be provided to the Coordinator who have to transfer them to Analysts. Tickets states allow users to know what others are doing. Coordinator will have a 2D map to follow analysts movements (Fig. 5) and these analysts will have human-like avatars and visible pointers such as feedback and feedforward features. Feedback and feedforward are discrete and continuous interactions cues that allows mutual awareness. Feedback is the information of a consequence of an action (e.g. a visual highlight when a user is selecting an asset as is the right image of the Fig. 5) and feedforward is the information of the action itself (e.g. the view of a users' pointer moving through the environment). These cues are various and with co-presence and the ticketing system they allow users to perform explicit collaboration. Moreover, all users will have information about the scenario's progression.
- Users will be co-located in the same physical area to perform the simulation. They will be allowed to communicate naturally and any role will have an event log where every users' actions will be displayed. Filtering this log will give insights on the actions performed by anyone.

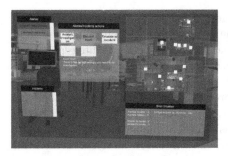
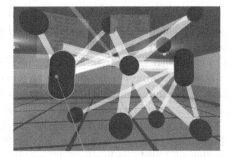

Fig. 5. 2D coordinator dashboard with a map of the environment and a list of current alerts (LEFT) and a selection of an asset from an immersive graph representation of the network (RIGHT).

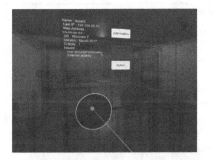
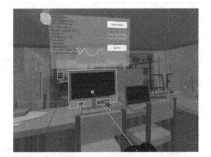

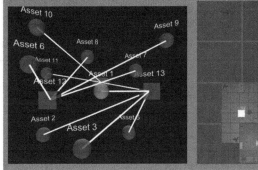

Fig. 6. Cyber (LEFT) and Kinetic (RIGHT) views of the environment, displayed using immersive (TOP) and non-immersive (BOTTOM) setups.

Users will have the opportunity to share or not their UI and their interactions: if a user wants to explain what she has done, she can show her UI to others or she can hide the fact that she is selecting an asset in order to get information.

On the left top of the Fig. 6 a cyber representation of the environment is displayed from an analyst point of view. She has selected an asset which has malicious processes and so she is encouraged to declare the incident to the coordinator that has given her this alert. The right top image represents the same asset but seen from the kinetic environment: information are different and so actions. Both bottom images of the Fig. 6 shows cyber and kinetic 2D views of the environment (respectively a graph representation of the network and a map of the environment). These views provide either topological and network information or IT-oriented data (last user, OS, running processes etc.)

The bottom view of Fig. 6 is a 2D dashboard available for the coordinator: she can select assets from the top left list, she can follow analysts' movements on the map and she has specific actions regarding alerts she has selected.

This simulation is made by using the Unity Game Engine, and is still under development.

FEATURES	SOC	XXXXX Platform	Exemple Scenario
Roles	Tradeoff between decision and data analysis, hierarchical interactions	Users with specific visualizations and actions, Hierarchical interactions	Analyst immersed in VR, Coordinator with 2D Dashboard
Tasks	Ticketing system, specific tasks	Ticketing system, simulated interactions or experts scenarios	Simulated actions for collaborative incident analysis
Visualizations	Several tools for monitoring, correlation and reporting	2D, 3D or Immersive filtered views, integration of existing tools	2D and Immersive views, kinetic and cyber filters
Data	Aggregated by SIEMs or from various sources (probes, logs...)	Simulated data sets, simplified metrics or integration with cyber range tools	Simulated by two metrics, entropy and network anomalies
Explicit Collaboration	Ticketing, processes, e-mails, reports	Ticketing, avatars, mutual awareness, Information sharing	Alerts list, Feedbacks and feedforward, copresence, deterministic scenario
Tacit Collaboration	Communication, 'over the shoulder' interaction	Communication, historic logger, information sharing	Co localisation, events logger, information distribution
FEATURES	Activity Model	CVE Design solutions	Instance of the model

Fig. 7. Features adaptation from cyber security usages to CVE implementation.

5   Conclusion

We have proposed in this paper a 3D CVE model called the 3D Cyber Common Operational Picture, which aims at taking advantage of best CVE practices to enhance cyber collaborative activities. From the cyber collaborative activity model we built, we have selected relevant CVE characteristics that can be used to implement our models features. We are still developing a proof of concept scenario which instantiate these features (last column of figure Fig. 7).

Evaluation of such platforms is complex as it tackles several issues such as cybersecurity skills learning [22], cyber security visualization [37], role adaptation from specifications [25], Computer Supported Collaborative Work (CSCW) [4,5] or Team Cyber Situational Awareness [28] and User Experience [40]. We will evaluate differently our theoretical approach and our proposed simulation in order to get information of future refinements of the cyber or the CVE model.

References

1. Wagner Filho, J.A., Freitas, C.M., Nedel, L.: VirtualDesk: a comfortable and efficient immersive information visualization approach. Comput. Graph. Forum **37**(3), 415–426 (2018). https://doi.org/10.1111/cgf.13430
2. Ahrend, J.M., Jirotka, M., Jones, K.: On the collaborative practices of cyber threat intelligence analysts to develop and utilize tacit threat and defence knowledge. In: 2016 International Conference On Cyber Situational Awareness, Data Analytics And Assessment (CyberSA), pp. 1–10, June 2016. https://doi.org/10.1109/CyberSA.2016.7503279
3. Alotaibi, F., Furnell, S., Stengel, I., Papadaki, M.: A review of using gaming technology for cyber-security awareness. Int. J. Inf. Secur. Res. (IJISR) **6**(2), 660–666 (2016)
4. Antunes, P., Herskovic, V., Ochoa, S.F., Pino, J.A.: Reviewing the quality of awareness support in collaborative applications. J. Syst. Softw. **89**, 146–169 (2014). https://doi.org/10.1016/j.jss.2013.11.1078. https://www.sciencedirect.com/science/article/pii/S0164121213002756
5. Antunes, P., Herskovic, V., Ochoa, S.F., Pino, J.A.: Structuring dimensions for collaborative systems evaluation. ACM Comput. Surv. **44**(2), 8:1–8:28 (2008). https://doi.org/10.1145/2089125.2089128
6. Chandler, T., et al.: Immersive analytics. In: Big Data Visual Analytics (BDVA), pp. 1–8. IEEE (2015)
7. Churchill, E.F., Snowdon, D.: Collaborative virtual environments: an introductory review of issues and systems. Virtual Real. **3**(1), 3–15 (1998). https://doi.org/10.1007/BF01409793
8. Cliquet, G., Perreira, M., Picarougne, F., Prié, Y., Vigier, T.: Towards HMD-based immersive analytics. In: Immersive Analytics Workshop, IEEE VIS 2017, Phoenix, United States, October 2017. https://hal.archives-ouvertes.fr/hal-01631306
9. Donalek, C., et al.: Immersive and collaborative data visualization using virtual reality platforms. In: 2014 IEEE International Conference on Big Data (Big Data), pp. 609–614, October 2014. https://doi.org/10.1109/BigData.2014.7004282
10. Eller, C., Bittner, T., Dombois, M., Rüppel, U.: Collaborative immersive planning and training scenarios in VR. In: Smith, I.F.C., Domer, B. (eds.) Advanced Computing Strategies for Engineering, pp. 164–185. Springer, Cham (2018). https://doi.org/10.1007/978-3-319-91635-4_9
11. Evesti, A., Kanstrn, T., Frantti, T.: Cybersecurity situational awareness taxonomy. In: 2017 International Conference On Cyber Situational Awareness, Data Analytics And Assessment (CyberSA), pp. 1–8, June 2017. https://doi.org/10.1109/CyberSA.2017.8073386
12. Gros, P., Abel, P., Dos Santos, R., Loisel, D., Trichaud, N., Paris, J.: Experimenting service-oriented 3D metaphors for managing networks using virtual reality. In: Laval Virtual-Virtual Reality International Conference, May 2000
13. Guimaraes, V.T., Freitas, C.M.D.S., Sadre, R., Tarouco, L.M.R., Granville, L.Z.: A survey on information visualization for network and service management. IEEE Commun. Surv. Tutor. **18**(1), 285–323 (2016)
14. Hackathorn, R., Margolis, T.: Immersive analytics: building virtual data worlds for collaborative decision support. In: 2016 Workshop on Immersive Analytics (IA), pp. 44–47, March 2016.. https://doi.org/10.1109/IMMERSIVE.2016.7932382
15. Hámornik, B.P., Krasznay, C.: Prerequisites of virtual teamwork in security operations centers: knowledge, skills, abilities and other characteristics. Acad. Appl. Res. Mil. Public Manag. Sci. **16**, 73 (2017)

16. Hui, P., et al.: Towards efficient collaboration in cyber security. In: 2010 International Symposium on Collaborative Technologies and Systems, pp. 489–498, May 2010. https://doi.org/10.1109/CTS.2010.5478473
17. Inoue, D., Eto, M., Suzuki, K., Suzuki, M., Nakao, K.: DAEDALUS-VIZ: novel real-time 3D visualization for darknet monitoring-based alert system, VizSec 2012, pp. 72–79. ACM, New York (2012). https://doi.org/10.1145/2379690.2379700
18. Kabil, A., Thierry, D., Nora, C., Gerard, L., Yoran, H., Christophe, P.: Why should we use 3D collaborative virtual environments (3DCVE) for cyber security? In: 2018 IEEE Third VR International Workshop on Collaborative Virtual Environments (3DCVE), March 2018
19. Kanstrn, T., Evesti, A.: A study on the state of practice in security situational awareness. In: 2016 IEEE International Conference on Software Quality, Reliability and Security Companion (QRS-C), pp. 69–76, August 2016. https://doi.org/10.1109/QRS-C.2016.14
20. Latvala, O.M., et al.: Visualizing network events in a muggle friendly way. In: 2017 International Conference On Cyber Situational Awareness, Data Analytics And Assessment (CyberSA), pp. 1–4, June 2017. https://doi.org/10.1109/CyberSA.2017.8073400
21. Le Chénéchal, M., Chalmé, S., Duval, T., Royan, J., Gouranton, V., Arnaldi, B.: Toward an enhanced mutual awareness in asymmetric CVE. In: Proceedings of International Conference on Collaboration Technologies and Systems (CTS 2015) (2015)
22. Mäses, S., Randmann, L., Maennel, O., Lorenz, B.: Stenmap: framework for evaluating cybersecurity-related skills based on computer simulations. In: Zaphiris, P., Ioannou, A. (eds.) LCT 2018, Part II. LNCS, vol. 10925, pp. 492–504. Springer, Cham (2018). https://doi.org/10.1007/978-3-319-91152-6_38
23. McKenna, S., Staheli, D., Meyer, M.: Unlocking user-centered design methods for building cyber security visualizations. In: 2015 IEEE Symposium on Visualization for Cyber Security (VizSec), pp. 1–8. IEEE (2015)
24. Michel, M.C.K., Helmick, N.P., Mayron, L.M.: Cognitive cyber situational awareness using virtual worlds. In: 2011 IEEE International Multi-Disciplinary Conference on Cognitive Methods in Situation Awareness and Decision Support (CogSIMA), pp. 179–182, February 2011. https://doi.org/10.1109/COGSIMA.2011.5753440
25. Newhouse, W., Keith, S., Scribner, B., Witte, G.: National initiative for cybersecurity education (NICE) cybersecurity workforce framework. NIST Spec. Publ. **800**, 181 (2017)
26. Petersen, K.L., Tjalve, V.S.: Intelligence expertise in the age of information sharing: publicprivate collection and its challenges to democratic control and accountability. Intell. Natl. Secur. **33**(1), 21–35 (2018). https://doi.org/10.1080/02684527.2017.1316956
27. Pirker, J., Gütl, C.: Virtual worlds for 3D visualizations. In: 11th International Conference on Intelligent Environments (Workshop), pp. 265–272 (2015)
28. Rajivan, P., Cooke, N.: Impact of team collaboration on cybersecurity situational awareness. In: Liu, P., Jajodia, S., Wang, C. (eds.) Theory and Models for Cyber Situation Awareness. LNCS, vol. 10030, pp. 203–226. Springer, Cham (2017). https://doi.org/10.1007/978-3-319-61152-5_8
29. Renaud, K., Flowerday, S.: Contemplating human-centred security & privacy research: suggesting future directions. J. Inf. Secur. Appl. **34**, 76–81 (2017). https://doi.org/10.1016/j.jisa.2017.05.006. http://www.sciencedirect.com/science/article/pii/S2214212617302387. Human-Centred Cyber Security

30. Richards, D., Taylor, M.: A comparison of learning gains when using a 2D simulation tool versus a 3D virtual world. Comput. Educ. **86**(1), 157–171 (2015). https://doi.org/10.1016/j.compedu.2015.03.009

31. Robinson, M., Jones, K., Janicke, H., Maglaras, L.: Developing Cyber Peacekeeping: Observation. Monitoring and Reporting, ArXiv e-prints, June 2018

32. Sethi, A., Wills, G.: Expert-interviews led analysis of EEVi - a model for effective visualization in cyber-security. In: 2017 IEEE Symposium on Visualization for Cyber Security (VizSec), pp. 1–8, October 2017. https://doi.org/10.1109/VIZSEC.2017.8062195

33. Shen, C., Ho, J., Ly, P.T.M., Kuo, T.: Behavioural intentions of using virtual reality in learning: perspectives of acceptance of information technology and learning style. Virtual Real. (2018). https://doi.org/10.1007/s10055-018-0348-1

34. Shiravi, H., Shiravi, A., Ghorbani, A.A.: A survey of visualization systems for network security. IEEE Trans. Vis. Comput. Graph. **18**(8), 1313–1329 (2012)

35. Soares, A.G., et al.: A review of ways and strategies on how to collaborate in information visualization applications. In: 2016 20th International Conference Information Visualisation (IV), pp. 81–87, July 2016. https://doi.org/10.1109/IV.2016.69

36. von Solms, R., van Niekerk, J.: From information security to cyber security. Comput. Secur. **38**, 97–102 (2013). Cybercrime in the Digital Economy

37. Staheli, D., et al.: Visualization evaluation for cyber security: trends and future directions, VizSec 2014, pp. 49–56. ACM, New York (2014). https://doi.org/10.1145/2671491.2671492

38. Sundaramurthy, S.C., McHugh, J., Ou, X., Wesch, M., Bardas, A.G., Rajagopalan, S.R.: Turning contradictions into innovations or: How we learned to stop whining and improve security operations. In: Twelfth Symposium on Usable Privacy and Security (SOUPS 2016), Denver, CO, pp. 237–251. USENIX Association (2016). https://www.usenix.org/conference/soups2016/technical-sessions/presentation/sundaramurthy

39. Takahashi, T., Kadobayashi, Y., Nakao, K.: Toward global cybersecurity collaboration: cybersecurity operation activity model. In: Proceedings of ITU Kaleidoscope 2011: The Fully Networked Human? - Innovations for Future Networks and Services (K-2011), pp. 1–8, December 2011

40. Tcha-Tokey, K., Christmann, O., Loup-Escande, E., Richir, S.: Proposition and validation of a questionnaire to measure the user experience in immersive virtual environments. Int. J. Virtual Real. **16**(1), 33–48 (2016). https://hal.archives-ouvertes.fr/hal-01404497

41. Zhong, Z., et al.: A user-centered multi-space collaborative visual analysis for cyber security. Chin. J. Electron. **27**, 910–919 (2018)

42. Zhu, H.: From WYSIWIS to WISINWIS: role-based collaboration. In: 2004 IEEE International Conference on Systems, Man and Cybernetics (IEEE Cat. No. 04CH37583). vol. 6, pp. 5441–5446, October 2004. https://doi.org/10.1109/ICSMC.2004.1401059

Machine Learning and Security

A Deep Learning Based Digital Forensic Solution to Blind Source Identification of Facebook Images

Venkata Udaya Sameer$^{(\boxtimes)}$, Ishaan Dali, and Ruchira Naskar

Department of Computer Science and Engineering, National Institute of Technology, Rourkela 769008, India
{515CS1003,713cs2136,naskarr}@nitrkl.ac.in

Abstract. *Source Camera Identification* is a digital forensic way of attributing a contentious image to its authentic source, especially used in legal application domains involving terrorism, child pornography etc. The state–of–the–art source camera identification techniques, however, are not suitable to work with images downloaded from online social networks. This is because, online social networks impart specific image artefacts, due to proprietary image compression requirements for storage and transmission, which prevents accurate forensic source investigations. Moreover, each social network has its own compression standards, which are never made public due to ethical issues. This makes source identification task even more difficult for forensic analysts. In present day and age, where there is abundant use of social networks for image transmission, it is high time that source camera identification with images downloaded from social networks, be efficiently addressed. In this paper, we propose a *deep learning* based digital forensic technique for source camera identification, on images downloaded from *Facebook*. The proposed deep learning technique is adapted from the popular *ResNet50* network, which majorly consists of convolutional layers and a few pooling layers. Our experimental results prove that the proposed technique outperforms the traditional source camera identification methods.

Keywords: Camera model identification · Classification
Deep learning · Facebook · ResNet · Source camera identification

1 Introduction

Digital Forensics is the science of investigating digital evidences, often related to crime investigations. It involves studying the digital traces remnant in a cyber crime scene, by analysing the digital devices linked to the event. *Source Camera Identification* is a major Image Forensic problem in this domain, wherein the purpose of the analyst is to map an image back to its source device, correctly. In the recent times, easy-to-use and low-cost image editing software and tools have become extensively rampant, which have drastically reduced the credibility

© Springer Nature Switzerland AG 2018
V. Ganapathy et al. (Eds.): ICISS 2018, LNCS 11281, pp. 291–303, 2018.
https://doi.org/10.1007/978-3-030-05171-6_15

of digital images, to serve as source of evidence in legal investigations. Mapping an image to its source device, based on image metadata, is now rendered highly unreliable due to advent of such software, which are capable of altering image metadata information with utmost ease now.

Digital forensic techniques primarily aim to address such security issues, without zero dependency on such pre-processed information (such as, metadata, watermark, fingerprint, hash). Hence such forensic techniques are said to be *blind*, in the sense that they operate without any requirement of a-priori information storage or processing.

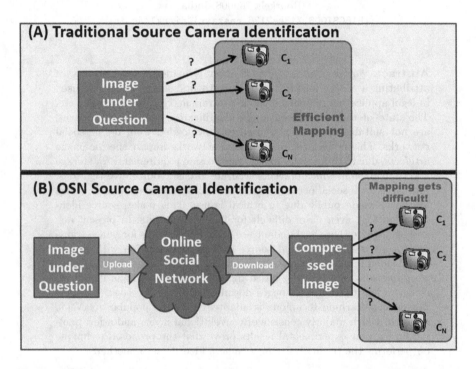

Fig. 1. Traditional source camera identification vs. OSN source camera identification.

A major dimension of today's digital era is constituted of *Online Social Network* (*OSN*) usage. Today, every common man's day-to-day life involves vast amount of information sharing and transmission over the internet, via OSNs, out of which the principle component is *image sharing*. Vast number of images are uploaded and downloaded on a regular basis on every social networking websites, especially the ones popular to the common mass such as Facebook, Twitter, Instagram and Whatsapp. Each OSN has its own proprietary compression features, which are applied to the images before they are uploaded, stored or trans-. mitted. In presence of such inherent image compression features of the OSNs, the existing image source identification techniques fail to provide expected results. Their source identification accuracy drops manifolds, when provided with OSN images. In the current state–of–the–art, source camera identification is performed either by using a fingerprint based technique [1] or a feature based machine learning technique [2]. Both camera fingerprint based techniques, as well the feature based techniques, suffer highly when the test images are compressed by social networks. The traditional source camera identification vs. source identification for Online Social Network images, are depicted in Fig. 1. In the latter case, an image is uploaded and subsequently downloaded from an OSN, hence generating a highly compressed version of the image under question. The traditional camera model identification techniques use many intrinsic properties of the image to map it to its source camera Such properties are lost/destroyed due to high compression impacted by the OSN; hence rendering the existing forensic source camera identification techniques useless in OSN image source identification.

Next, we present a real-life scenario, to depict the necessity of digital forensic techniques for efficient (blind) source identification of OSN images.

"A police complaint is lodged against a subject, who allegedly uploaded obscene photographs of a person on Facebook. The accused claims that his Facebook account is hacked; and hence denies all charges. In this scenario, a feasible solution to establish the claims would be to physically investigate the imaging devices held/owned by the accused, so as to collect useful evidences. The accused would have, without any doubt, deleted all the photos from his own devices. In this case, an efficient forensic technique to map the Facebook image in question, to a device owned by the accused, would be effective enough to establish all claims against the accused to be true."

The key in above solution is to link the culprit's device to the image in question, with sufficient accuracy, so as to establish the findings beyond a reasonable doubt, and hence ascertain the source of the image.

In this paper, we propose a deep learning based forensic solution to perform accurate source identification of Facebook images. In our experimental results, we first demonstrate the accuracy of the state-of-the-art techniques in Facebook images source identification. Next, we present the results obtained with the proposed network model. Our experimental results prove that the proposed model achieves as high as 96% source detection accuracy, even with Facebook images, as compared to the highest accuracy of 82% provided by the state-of-the-art.

Our main contributions in this paper can be summarized as follows:

- We bring to light the necessity of source investigation of OSN images, supported by experimental results showing how far the state-of-the-art forensic techniques fail, when provided with images downloaded from popular OSN, Facebook.
- In this work, we propose a deep learning neural network architecture, which efficiently performs source classification of Facebook images. The proposed network model outperforms the state-of-the-art as proven by our experimental results.
- The proposed forensic technique is robust to common image manipulation operations, such as compression, rotation and noise addition.

The rest of the paper is organised as follows. In Sect. 2, we present an overview of the state–of–the–art researches related to forensic source camera identification. In Sect. 3, we present the proposed deep learning network architecture for source camera identification of Facebook images. Section 4 presents our experimental results and related discussions. Finally, we conclude in Sect. 5 with an insight into future research work in this domain.

2   Related Work

It was discovered in earlier researches such as [1,3], that every camera sensor generates a unique fingerprint in an image, in the form of Photo Response Non–Uniformity (PRNU) noise. It is hypothesized and proved through experiments by Lukas et al. [1] that the PRNU content in an image can be successfully matched against the camera's Sensor Pattern Noise (SPN), for accurate source attribution. Normalized Cross Correlation (NCC) is a metric commonly used to measure the strength of the matching [1]. *Hypothesis Testing* methodology was designed to find camera specific threshold, such that, when NCC of a test image corresponding to a given camera model exceeds the threshold, the image is detected to be generated by the given camera. Later, Goljan et al. [4] identified Peak to Correlation Energy (PCE) as a stable test statistic than NCC, by performing a large scale test for fingerprint based camera identification. Li et al. [5] proposed an *enhancement technique* for extracting camera fingerprints. Here, the authors suggested that the camera fingerprint extracted in earlier methods is contaminated by the scene details. The enhancement was performed by assigning less significant weight factors to strong components in digital wavelet transform domain. *Spectrum Equalization* is a pre–processing mechanism followed by Lin et al. [6] to suppress the non–unique artifacts in an image. The interference of scene content in image source identification using sensor noise, is addressed by Shi et al. [7] and Yang et al. [8], where a local variance based approach was used in the former and a content–adaptive residual network, in the later.

Clustering images based on their sources, also attracted a lot of research attention in the literature due to its practical applications. Majority of the clustering techniques use sensor pattern noise as unique camera fingerprint. A two–step clustering mechanism was proposed by Marra et al. [9,10], where a graph based correlational clustering was performed, and a refinement step was used to find the cluster(s) of images from the same camera(s). A large scale clustering based on image fingerprints is performed by Lin et al. [11] using dimensionality reduction, spectrum equalization and cluster refinement.

Another major approach to camera model identification is through the use of machine learning based classification, by making use of various feature sets. Kharrazi et al. [2] proposed a blind source identification using Image Quality Metrics (IQM) and Higher Order Wavelet Statistics (HOWS) as features. The IQM capture the visual differences in each image and the HOWS capture the underlying color characteristics for different cameras. Apart from IQM and HOWS, Celiktutan et al. [12] proposed Binary Similarity Metrics (BSM) as features to perform source camera identification. Experiments were performed on many mobile devices using IQM, HOWS and BSM as feature sets, and a Sequential Feature Forward Selection (SFFS) was done to achieve a better classification accuracy. Gloe and Böhme [13] published a publicly available dataset (Dresden dataset) for the forensic research community, which they used to benchmark their results. Gloe [14] performed extensive experiments on the Dresden dataset using IQM, HOWS and extended color sets as features. Xu and Shi [15] used local binary patterns as features for source camera identification and achieved considerably better classification results.

Akshatha et al. [16] used higher order statistics on the PRNU of an image, as features, to achieve a considerably high classification accuracy. Tauma et al. [17] extracted three sets of features (co–occurrence matrix, conditional probability based, and color dependencies) on the residual noise of an image. The features are extracted by using a linear pattern calculated from the residual noise. Xu et al. [18] identified image textures such as Local Binary Patterns (LBP) and Local Phase Quantization (LPQ) as suitable features for source camera identification. They achieved great success in terms of classification accuracy and also showed that the image texture features are resilient to various image manipulations such as rotation, scaling, and compression. In [18] the texture feature set is not only extracted from the original image, but also from its noise residual and contourlet decomposition. In our work, we use the LPQ and LBP features extracted from the raw test images, since the noise residual in counter–forensic images is tampered, and cannot be used in feature extraction.

The more recent feature sets proposed are that of residual based local features [19] by Marra et al. and co–occurrence based local features [20] by Marra et al. Both these works were inspired by features used in steganographic applications, and proved to be highly effective in source camera identification. In more recent times, deep learning found to be ubiquitous in image classification systems. Different deep learning based neural network architectures are used for performing source camera identification by Tauma et al. [21] and Bondi et al. [22].

In the next section we present our proposed deep learning solution for source camera identification of facebook images and in the following section we present our experimental findings.

3   Proposed Deep Learning Solution for Camera Model Identification of Facebook Images

3.1   Proposed Workflow

In this work, in order to perform source camera identification of Facebook images, a deep learning based classification model is proposed. Here, we train the deep learning network with images that are uploaded and then downloaded from Facebook. The images are taken from camera models known apriori. The overall workflow is presented in Fig. 2.

With N camera models $(C_1, C_2, \cdots C_N)$ at hand, we first capture and collect sufficiently large number of images from each camera model. Those are then

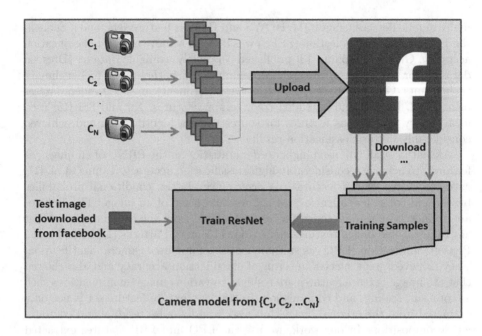

Fig. 2. Proposed workflow

uploaded to Facebook. Subsequently, we download all those images from Facebook, to serve as our training samples. The proposed model is trained so as to predict the source of an unknown Facebook image, with considerably high accuracy, completely based on post-processing analysis, (where it is known that the image comes from one of the N camera models at hand).

3.2 Proposed Deep Network Architecture

Majority of the deep learning architectures are sequential in nature i.e., each layer is connected to the next layer sequentially. ResNet [23] is a form of "exotic" architecture that has micro architecture modules. The micro architectures are "network in a network" type of structures that exist cohesively. The collection of these micro structures leads to the entire network at large. The ResNet [23] architecture is one of the first very deep networks that was able to successfully train using a standard Stochastic Gradient Descent (SGD). Even though ResNet is much deeper than other deep learning networks, the model size is actually substantially smaller due to the usage of global average pooling rather than fully-connected layers, this reduces the model size down to 102MB for ResNet50. In this paper we adapted ResNet50 [23] architecture for classification of source cameras on images from Facebook.

In the proposed network, there is a total of 50 layers, with convolution functions and a few pooling functions. The network architecture is depicted in Fig. 3 and is briefly summarized as follows:

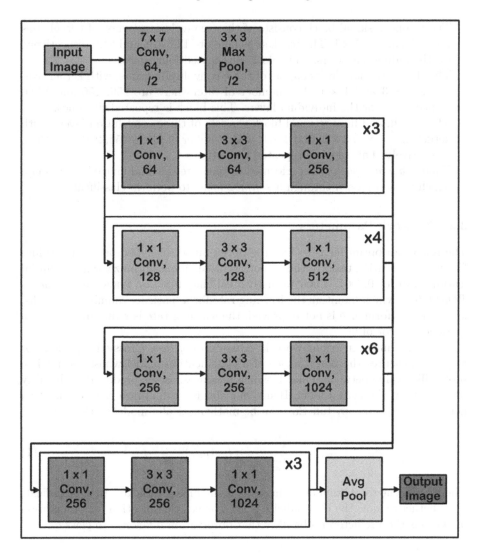

Fig. 3. Proposed deep network architecture

- The input image is passed to a *convolution layer* with a kernel of size 7×7, batch size 64 for number of filters, and a stride of 2.
- A *max pool layer* follows, with a 3×3 kernel, and a stride of 2.
- The first block in the architecture starts next, with three convolution layers having 1×1, 3×3 and 1×1 kernels. The number of filters at the individual layers are 64, 64, and 256, respectively. This block is repeated three times (observe the x3 in Fig. 3)

- The second residual block consists of three convolution layers, of kernel sizes 1×1, 3×3, and 1×1. The block sizes here are 128, 128 and 512, respectively, for the individual layers. This block is repeated four times.
- The third residual block consists of three convolution layers, with kernel sizes 1×1, 3×3 and 1×1. The number of filters here are 256, 256 and 1024, respectively, for the individual layers. This block is repeated six times.
- The fourth, and final residual block consists of three convolution layers, with kernel sizes 1×1, 3×3, and 1×1, with number of filters 256, 256, and 1024, respectively. This block is repeated three times.
- Finally, *average pooling* is performed to generate the final image feature map, which is then passed through a *softmax layer* to perform classification.

3.3   Network Parameters

The role of an optimizer is to find the optimum set of hyper–parameter values for the classification task. In this paper, we used *Adam* optimizer with an initial learning rate of 0.0001. Then we used a callback function known as *ReduceL-ROnPlateau* which monitors the learning rate for a 'patience' number of epochs, and if the performance is not improved, the learning rate is reduced. We used a 'patience' factor of 5.

The loss function in our work is *cross-entropy loss*. Cross-entropy loss, or log loss, measures the performance of a classification model whose output is a probability value between 0 and 1, which increases, as the predicted probability diverges from the actual label. Hence our aim is to minimize the loss function here. The cross-entropy function can be mathematically modelled as follows:

$$- \sum_{c=1}^{M} y_{o,c} \times log(p_{o,c}) \tag{1}$$

where, M is the total number of classes, y is the binary indicator (0 or 1) indicating whether or not, the class label c is the correct classification for observation o, and p is the predicted probability that observation o belongs to class c.

4   Experimental Results and Discussion

In this section we first describe our experimental setup and then we present the performance evaluation results of the proposed approach, along with comparison with the state-of-the-art.

4.1   Experimental Setup

We conduct our experiments using images from the Dresden dataset [13], which is benchmarked dataset used in forensic researches world-wide. The list of cameras used in the experiments are shown in Table 1. It is to be noted from Table 1, how the image resolutions degrade after uploading the images to Facebook, and subsequently downloading those. In this work, we used 100 natural images per camera, listed in Table 1 (a total of 500 images). We used a ratio of 66:34 to divide the train set and validation set. All results presented here, are on the validation set. All the experiments are performed on a computer with 8GB GPU (Geforce GTX1070), 16 GB DDR4 RAM, i7 processor with 3.8 GHz speed. We used the *PyTorch* software library to implement the deep learning API.

Table 1. Cameras used in our experiments.

Camera model	Format	Original image resolution	Facebook downloaded image resolution
Canon A640	JPEG	3648 × 2736	1368 × 1026
Nikon D200	JPEG	3872 × 2592	968 × 648
Nikon D70	JPEG	4352 × 3264	1088 × 816
Sony H50	JPEG	3456 × 2592	1296 × 972
Sony T77	JPEG	3648 × 2736	1368 × 1026

4.2   Performance Evaluation

The experiments are conducted by varying the image block sizes i.e., each input image is divided into non–overlapping blocks of size 64×64, 128×128, 256×256, and 512×512. An epoch represents the time taken for one forward pass and one backward pass of all the training examples. In our work we used a batch size of 50 and hence it takes a total $\frac{N}{50}$ iterations for one epoch (N is the total number of training examples). To find the optimum combination of the number of epochs and the image block size, we varied both of them as listed in Table 2. We observe that for very small image block sizes (such as 64×64), the classification accuracy is not great. For an image block size of 512×512 and for 20 epochs, we obtain the best classification accuracy, i.e., 96%. The confusion matrix for the classification in case of 512×512 block size and for 20 epochs is shown in Table 3. It is the cameras Canon A640 and Sony H50, that cause the majority of mis–classifications, in our experiments.

Table 2. Classification accuracy with varying image block sizes, and varying number of epochs.

Image block size	64 × 64	128 × 128	256 × 256	512 × 512
20 Epochs	85.17%	85.64%	91.29%	**96.00%**
50 Epochs	83.52%	80.94%	87.29%	94.11%
100 Epochs	81.88%	85.41%	90.35%	93.64%
150 Epochs	81.41%	84.94%	86.35%	94.58%

Table 3. Confusion matrix for the case when image block size is 512×512 and the number of epochs is 20.

Actual	Predicted				
	Canon A640	Nikon D200	Nikon D70	Sony H50	Sony T77
Canon A640	67.64%	0.17%	0	0	0.14%
Nikon D200	0	100%	0	0	0
Nikon D70	0	0	100%	0	0
Sony H50	0.02%	0.14%	0	0.82%	0
Sony T77	0	0	0	0	100%

Table 4. Performance comparison of proposed method with state–of–the–art.

Camera model identification method	Detection accuracy (%)
Co–occurrence based features (SRM features) [19]	75
Residual based local features (SPAM features) [20]	76.4
PRNU based technique [4]	78.84
IQM and HOWS features [2]	82.2
Proposed deep learning technique	96

4.3 Comparison with State-of-the-Art

We compare the performance of the proposed deep learning model in Facebook images source classification, with the state–of–the–art. The results of the comparison are presented in Table 4.

We observe that the recently found features (proven to be highly efficient in source camera identification) such as Co–occurrence based features (SRM features) [19] and Residual based local features (SPAM features) [20] are not able to classify the image sources with an accuracy of 75% and 76.4%, respectively. The state–of–the–art PRNU based fingerprinting technique [4] also suffers due to the compression caused by Facebook upload; its source detection accuracy is only 78.84% in this case (we use a PCE threshold of 50 following [4]). The IQM and HOWS features set produced a classification accuracy of 82.2% compared to an accuracy of 96% by the proposed approach.

4.4 Robustness Evaluation

In Sect. 4.3, we showed that the proposed method outperforms the other existing noise residual based and feature based techniques, in source camera identification of Facebook images. In this section, we test the robustness of the proposed source camera identification technique against common image manipulations, viz., *JPEG compression* (we present the results for quality factors 90, 75, and 50), *rotation* (results presented with degrees of rotation 30, 60 and 90), and *addition of noise* (Salt noise and Gaussian noise).

In Table 5, we present the performance of the proposed method under various image manipulations. It is evident from Table 5, that the impact of JPEG compression on camera model identification is more prominent than the other forms of image manipulations (rotation and addition of noise), in case of all state–of–the–art techniques, including the proposed one. The proposed deep learning network is more susceptible to the above image manipulation forms, as compared to the other techniques, as evident from Table 5.

For the proposed technique, the classification accuracy without any image manipulation is 96% (Table 4). The classification accuracy of the proposed approach under JPEG compression is 91.8%, 88.4%, and 86.4% for compression factors of 90, 75, and 50, respectively. The classification accuracy is 93.2%, 94.3%, and 93.2% for rotation with 90, 60, and 30 degrees, respectively. In case of additional noise, the classification accuracy is 94.3% for additional salt noise, and 93.2% for addition of Gaussian noise. Here, we can observe from Table 5, that the effects of various forms of image manipulation on the proposed *camera model identification*, are considerably low. It is also observed that the impact of compression on the proposed classification, is higher compared to other forms of manipulation.

Table 5. Classification accuracy (%) of the proposed method under various image manipulations.

Image manipulations/ Classification accuracy (%)	Jpeg Compression (Quality factor)			Rotation (Degrees)			Additional noise	
	90	75	50	90	60	30	Salt noise	Gaussian noise
Co–occurrence features [19]	62.7	60.8	57.9	74.3	74.2	75.8	73.4	74.3
Residual local features [20]	63.1	61.8	59.6	75.2	74.6	74.2	75.8	74.9
PRNU based technique [4]	75.3	74.6	74.2	76.8	76.2	75.9	77.6	77.2
IQM, HOWS features [2]	78.5	77.4	76.2	79.5	78.6	78.8	81.5	80.9
Proposed technique	91.8	88.4	86.4	93.2	94.3	93.2	94.3	93.2

5   Conclusion

Camera Model Identification on images downloaded from Online Social Networks is a challenging task because of the proprietary compression features of such networks. The state–of–the–art camera model identification techniques fail to successfully perform image source detection in such a scenario. In this paper, we propose a deep learning neural network model for source camera identification of Facebook images. Our experimental results depict a significant performance of the proposed method, in comparison to the state–of–the–art.

In this paper, we have performed camera model identification, where the source camera model of an image under question is identified. A complete analysis of exact device linking (which is to successfully identify the exact camera device out of many camera devices of same make and model) forms the major scope of future work in this direction. Also, we would like to test the robustness of the proposed model to various other Online Social Networks, including Whatsapp, Twitter and Instagram.

Acknowledgement. This work is funded by Council of Scientific and Industrial Research (CSIR), Govt. of India, Grant No. 22(0736)/17/EMR-II, dated: 16/05/2017.

References

1. Lukas, J., Fridrich, J., Goljan, M.: Digital camera identification from sensor pattern noise. IEEE Trans. Inf. Forensics Secur. **1**(2), 205–214 (2006)
2. Kharrazi, M., Sencar, H.T., Memon, N.: Blind source camera identification. In: 2004 International Conference on Image Processing, ICIP 2004, vol. 1, pp. 709–712. IEEE (2004)
3. Chen, M., Fridrich, J., Goljan, M., Lukás, J.: Determining image origin and integrity using sensor noise. IEEE Trans. Inf. Forensics Secur. **3**(1), 74–90 (2008)
4. Goljan, M., Fridrich, J., Filler, T.: Large scale test of sensor fingerprint camera identification. In: Media Forensics and Security, vol. 7254, p. 72540I. International Society for Optics and Photonics (2009)
5. Li, C.-T.: Source camera identification using enhanced sensor pattern noise. IEEE Trans. Inf. Forensics Secur. **5**(2), 280–287 (2010)
6. Lin, X., Li, C.-T.: Preprocessing reference sensor pattern noise via spectrum equalization. IEEE Trans. Inf. Forensics Secur. **11**(1), 126–140 (2016)
7. Shi, C., Law, N.-F., Leung, F.H., Siu, W.-C.: A local variance based approach to alleviate the scene content interference for source camera identification. Digit. Invest. **22**, 74–87 (2017)
8. Yang, P., Ni, R., Zhao, Y., Zhao, W.: Source camera identification based on content-adaptive fusion residual networks. Pattern Recogn. Lett. (2017)
9. Marra, F., Poggi, G., Sansone, C., Verdoliva, L.: Correlation clustering for PRNU-based blind image source identification. In: IEEE International Workshop on Information Forensics and Security (WIFS), vol. 2016, pp. 1–6. IEEE (2016)
10. Marra, F., Poggi, G., Sansone, C., Verdoliva, L.: Blind PRNU-based image clustering for source identification. IEEE Trans. Inf. Forensics Secur. **12**(9), 2197–2211 (2017)
11. Lin, X., Li, C.-T.: Large-scale image clustering based on camera fingerprints. IEEE Trans. Inf. Forensics Secur. **12**(4), 793–808 (2017)
12. Çeliktutan, O., Sankur, B., et al.: Blind identification of source cell-phone model. IEEE Trans. Inf. Forensics Secur. **3**(3), 553–566 (2008)
13. Gloe, T., Böhme, R.: The Dresden image database for benchmarking digital image forensics. J. Digit. Forensic Pract. **3**(2–4), 150–159 (2010)
14. Gloe, T.: Feature-based forensic camera model identification. In: Shi, Y.Q., Katzenbeisser, S. (eds.) Transactions on Data Hiding and Multimedia Security VIII. LNCS, vol. 7228, pp. 42–62. Springer, Heidelberg (2012). https://doi.org/10.1007/978-3-642-31971-6_3

15. Xu, G., Shi, Y.Q.: Camera model identification using local binary patterns. In: 2012 IEEE International Conference on Multimedia and Expo (ICME), pp. 392–397. IEEE (2012)
16. Akshatha, K., Karunakar, A., Anitha, H., Raghavendra, U., Shetty, D.: Digital camera identification using PRNU: a feature based approach. Digit. Invest. **19**, 69–77 (2016)
17. Tuama, A., Comby, F., Chaumont, M.: Camera model identification based machine learning approach with high order statistics features. In: 24th European Signal Processing Conference (EUSIPCO), pp. 1183–1187 . IEEE (2016)
18. Xu, B., Wang, X., Zhou, X., Xi, J., Wang, S.: Source camera identification from image texture features. Neurocomputing **207**, 131–140 (2016)
19. Marra, F., Poggi, G., Sansone, C., Verdoliva, L.: Evaluation of residual-based local features for camera model identification. In: Murino, V., Puppo, E., Sona, D., Cristani, M., Sansone, C. (eds.) ICIAP 2015. LNCS, vol. 9281, pp. 11–18. Springer, Cham (2015). https://doi.org/10.1007/978-3-319-23222-5_2
20. Marra, F., Poggi, G., Sansone, C., Verdoliva, L.: A study of co-occurrence based local features for camera model identification. Multimed. Tools Appl. **76**(4), 4765–4781 (2017)
21. Tuama, A., Comby, F., Chaumont, M.: Camera model identification with the use of deep convolutional neural networks. In: IEEE International Workshop on Information Forensics and Security, 6 p. (2016)
22. Bondi, L., Baroffio, L., Güera, D., Bestagini, P., Delp, E.J., Tubaro, S.: First steps toward camera model identification with convolutional neural networks. IEEE Sig. Process. Lett. **24**(3), 259–263 (2017)
23. He, K., Zhang, X., Ren, S., Sun, J.: Deep residual learning for image recognition. In: Proceedings of the IEEE Conference on Computer Vision and Pattern Recognition, pp. 770–778 (2016)

A Digital Forensic Technique
for Inter–Frame Video Forgery Detection
Based on 3D CNN

Jamimamul Bakas$^{(\boxtimes)}$ and Ruchira Naskar

Department of Computer Science and Engineering, National Institute of Technology,
Rourkela 769008, India
{516cs6008,naskarr}@nitrkl.ac.in

Abstract. With the present-day rapid growth in use of low-cost yet efficient video manipulating software, it has become extremely crucial to authenticate and check the integrity of digital videos, before they are used in sensitive contexts. For example, a CCTV footage acting as the primary source of evidence towards a crime scene. In this paper, we deal with a specific class of video forgery detection, viz., inter-frame forgery detection. We propose a deep learning based digital forensic technique using 3D Convolutional Neural Network (3D-CNN) for detection of the above form of video forgery. In the proposed model, we introduce a *difference layer* in the CNN, which mainly targets to extract the *temporal information* from the videos. This in turn, helps in efficient inter-frame video forgery detection, given the fact that, temporal information constitute the most suitable form of features for inter-frame anomaly detection. Our experimental results prove that the performance efficiency of the proposed deep learning 3D CNN model is 97% on an average, and is applicable to a wide range of video quality.

Keywords: Classification · Convolutional neural network
Deep learning · Inter-frame video forgery · Video forensics

1 Introduction

With present-day rapid evolution of digital technology, the use of digital devices including smart phones, notebooks and digital cameras, has increased massively with each passing day. Today, every common man's day-to-day life encompasses exchange and sharing of digital media in large volumes, especially digital images and videos. Such images and videos, in many cases, serve as the primary sources of legal evidence towards any event or crime, in court rooms. For example, a CCTV footage, produced as major evidence related to a contentious scene in the court of law. However, with the advent of low-cost easy-to-use image and video processing software and desktop tools, manipulation to these forms of multimedia has become an extremely easy task for even a layman. Hence, it

© Springer Nature Switzerland AG 2018
V. Ganapathy et al. (Eds.): ICISS 2018, LNCS 11281, pp. 304–317, 2018.
https://doi.org/10.1007/978-3-030-05171-6_16

has become highly crucial to authenticate and the prove the trust-worthiness of digital multimedia, before being presented/accepted as a court room evidence.

In this paper, we focus on forensic investigation of digital videos. In this work, our main target is the detection of inter-frame video forgeries, whereby, an attacker intelligently introduces/eliminates significant object(s) to/from a video footage, by inserting, deleting or duplicating selected frames of the video maliciously. Subsequently, the attacker produces the tampered video in the court-of-law as an evidence, or shares it over online social sites to spread a fake news. In this work, we deal with the problem of detecting this form of inter-frame forgeries in videos. Specifically, in this work, we aim to detect frame *insertion*, *deletion* and *duplication* types of inter-frame forgeries in digital videos. (The above types of forgeries have been depicted in a schematic diagram in Fig. 1).

Recently, a number of researchers have come up with efficient techniques to detect inter-frame video forgeries based on the followings: (A) Compression artifacts, produced during the video encoding and decoding processes [1–4], (B) Scene dependency, that is to rely on the visual contents of each frame in a video [5–7]. However, all such techniques are unable to perform efficiently, for videos with rapid scene changes, or when the number of forged frames in a video is an integral multiple of its *Group of Pictures* (GOP) length [8].

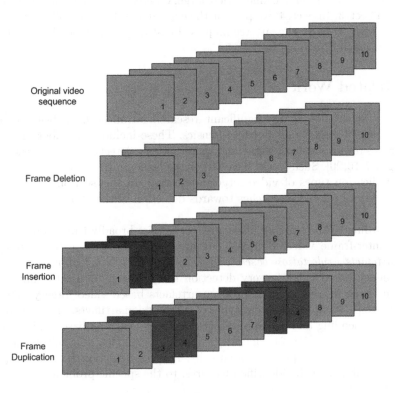

Fig. 1. Types of inter-frame video forgeries [9]

In the recent years, research focus has largely moved to the use of *Deep Learning* in various application domains, including object recognition [10,11], classification [12,13] and action recognition [14,15]. Recently, forensic researchers have also started to explore Deep Learning technique for multimedia forensic applications. For example, the work by Long et al. in 2017 [16], where the authors have succeeded to detect *frame deletion* type of inter-frame forgery in a single video shot[1]

In the proposed work, we use Deep Learning technique based on 3D Convolutional Neural Network (CNN) [17], to detect frame insertion, deletion and duplication types of inter-frame video forgeries in a single video shot. We have demonstrated the tamper detection efficiency of the proposed method through extensive experimentation on a wide range of test videos, irrespective of their compression quality factor. Majority of the state-of-the-art video forensic approaches, such as [2,4,18,19], are limited by fixed length GOP, and the number of frame deletions, being a multiple of GOP length. We aim to overcome this limitation in the proposed scheme. Specifically, the proposed method is completely independent of GOP length, and of its relation to the video compression quality.

The rest of this paper is organized as follows. In Sect. 2, we present an overview of the existing related work. The proposed deep learning technique using 3D CNN for inter-frame video forgery detection has been described in detail in Sect. 3. In Sect. 4, we present the experimental results followed by comparison with state-of-the-art techniques. Finally, we conclude the paper with future research directions in Sect. 5.

2   Related Work

In the past decade, many significant research advances have been made in the domain of digital multimedia forensics. These include a number of notable researches towards video forgery and image forgery detection, such as the works in [1,2,4,7,16,20]. Such works have largely focussed on frame deletion, insertion and duplication types of video forgery detection. In this section, we present a brief review of related researches towards detection of the above types of video forgeries.

According to the existing literature, there exist broadly three approaches to detect inter-frame video forgery. They are, *scene dependency based, compression artefacts exploitation based,* and *Deep Learning based* approaches. Scene dependency based video forgery detection techniques [5–7] use the pixel value of each frame in a video. Compression artefacts based video forgery detection techniques [1–4] exploit different types of compression artifacts, produced during the video encoding and decoding processes. Deep Learning based video forgery detection techniques [16,21], operate by identifying and learning suitable features from the training samples, automatically. Forgery detection accuracy depends on the suitability of the identified features, to the specific problem.

---

[1] A video shot is a sequence of frames, which are captured over an uninterrupted period of time, by a single video recording device.

Next, we present briefly review of related literature in all three above directions.

2.1 Scene Dependency Based Techniques

Recently, Zhao et al. [22] proposed a two step verification method to detect frame insertion, deletion and duplication forgeries in a single shot video. At the first step, the outliers are detected based on *Pearson correlation* [23] distribution over Hue-Saturation (H-S) and Saturation-Value (S-V) color histograms, for every frame. At the second step, *Speed Up Robust Features* (SURF) are extracted from every outlier frames, and then matching with doubtful SURF coded frames using *Fast Library for Approximation Nearest Neighbor* (FLANN) algorithm. If no matching features are found between two adjacent frames at falling peak locations, then frames at those locations are detected to be forged (by frame insertion or deletion operation). And when SURF features of two frames exactly match, those two frames are detected as duplicates of each other.

2.2 Compression Artefacts Based Techniques

To address the issue of inter-frame video forgery detection, Aghamaleki et al. [24] extracted the *DCT coefficients* of all *I-frames*, and used the *first significant digit distribution* of the extracted DCT coefficients, to identify single compressed and double compressed videos in spatial domain. However, double compression detection does not always imply the existence of manipulation in a video. Therefore, a second module was proposed by Aghamaleki et al. [24] to eliminate such false positives. This second module was proposed to detect inter-frame forgeries, based on *time domain analysis* of residual errors of *P-frames*. Here, the authors employ quantization traces in the time domain, to find the forgery locations. In the third module, output of the first module (double compression detection) and output of the second module (inter-frame forgery detection), are fed into a decision fusion box, to classify the tested video into three categories: single compressed videos, forged double compressed videos, and un-forged double compressed videos.

Another recent work for frame insertion, deletion and duplication detection in videos, is proposed by Kingra et al. [25]. Here, the authors have proposed a hybrid model by exploiting optical flow gradient and prediction residual error of P-frames. The authors performed their experiments on CCTV footage videos. This technique performs well for complex scene also. But, the performance of this technique decreases for high illumination videos.

2.3 Deep Learning Based Video Forensics

Noteworthy among the works, in which the authors explored deep learning to detect video forgeries, are the works of [16] and [21]. Long et al. [16] use a 3D CNN for frame deletion detection in a single video shot. At a time, the authors fed 16 consecutive frames, which are extracted from a video sequence, as an input to the CNN. This CNN finally detects whether or not there has been frame deletion operation between the 8th and 9th frames (out of 16). This scheme produced high false alarm rate, especially when the video is captured with camera motion, zoom in or zoom out. To reduce the rate of false alarms, the authors used a post processing method, known as *confidence score*, on the output of the proposed CNN.

In [21], D'Avino et al. proposed an *Autoencoder* with *recurrent neural network* to detect chroma–key composition type of video forgery. In this work, the authors deal with investigation of *video splicing*, which is to copy an object from a green background image, and paste it into a target frame, to manipulate a video. To detect this kind of forgery in videos, the authors divided the frames into patches of size 128×128. From every patch, some handcrafted features using a single high-pass third-order derivative filter, were extracted. The authors use autoencoders to produce an *anomaly score*. The handcrafted features of authentic frames are used to learn the parameters for the autoencoder. In the testing phase, the feature vector generated from the forged frames, do not fit with the intrinsic network model (which was trained with authentic frames), and hence produce large error. The anomaly score is generated based on this error, which is used to produce a "heat" map for detection of forged frames and their locations.

3   Proposed 3D-CNN Based Deep Learning Classification Model for Inter-Frame Video Forgery Detection

The performance of machine learning techniques in a classification problem, depends on the accuracy of features extraction. In other words, features extraction processed directly affect the performance of a machine learning classification. A major challenge here is identification of an efficient feature set. It is not always easy to identify the most suitable features for a particular dataset. For example, when the type of dataset is unknown to the user, i.e., the features are not well-known, or feature selection is computationally heavy. Previously some researchers like [2], extracted hand crafted features with classifiers such as Support Vector Machine (SVM), K-Nearest Neighbor (K-NN) etc., to detect video forgery. The performance of these techniques, based on hand crafted features, was found to be highly dependent on the types of test videos. On the other hand, Deep Learning techniques possess the ability to extract most suitable features from the training dataset, inherently, and hence train the network based on these extracted features. Convolution Neural Networks (CNN) [17] is one class of Deep Learning techniques, especially used for object recognition [10,11], and action recognition [14–16], image classification [12,13] problems.

Since, temporal features are most suited for detection of inter-frame video forgeries (which are a type of temporal domain video forgery), therefore, we propose a 3D-CNN in this work, which generates *spatio-temporal features*, effective for inter-frame video forgery detection. The proposed CNN is inspired by the C3D network [16], which was originally used in action recognition problem.

In general, 3D-CNNs implement Deep Learning technology, using a series of 3D-convolutional layers, 3D-pooling layers and classification layer. The architecture of the proposed 3D-CNN is presented in Fig. 2. From Fig. 2, it can be observed that the proposed 3D-CNN introduces an additional layer, namely *difference layer*, at the beginning. The layers of the proposed network are discussed in detail below:

3.1 Difference Layer

Since, inter-frame forgery is a form of temporal domain forgery in videos, feeding raw image pixels directly as inputs to the CNN did not provide efficient performance. Hence, one additional layer, the *pixel wise difference layer* is introduced into the 3D-CNN model at the beginning, as shown in Fig. 2. Through this pixel difference layer, the pixel-wise difference of adjacent frames, are obtained using the following equation:

$$d(i,j) = P_f(i,j) - P_{f+1}(i,j) \qquad (1)$$

where $P_f(i,j)$ is the pixel value of frame f at location (i,j), and $d(i,j)$ is the pixel difference between two adjacent frames f and $f+1$, at corresponding pixel locations (i,j). This pixel difference $d(i,j)$ provides the temporal information about a video sequence. The output of this layer, $d(i,j)$, is fed into the 3D-CNN.

3.2 Convolution Layer

A *convolution layer* is fully responsible for feature extraction in CNN based Deep Learning. Two operations are performed in this layer: one is convolution and another is activation [26]. The output of a convolution layer is known as *feature map*, which is a representation of features of the input, in a certain region. The convolution operation is performed as follows:

$$I_j^l = \sum_{i=1}^{n} I_j^{l-1} * w_{ij}^{l-1} + b_j^l \qquad (2)$$

where $*$ is the convolution operator, I_j^l is the jth output map at the lth layer. w_{ij}^{l-1} (*weight*) is the trainable convolutional kernel connecting the ith output feature map at $l-1^{th}$ layer, and j^{th} output feature map at l^{th} layer. b_j^l is the trainable bias parameter for the jth output feature map at the lth layer.

After performing convolution operation, an *activation function* (such as tanh, sigmoid, ReLUs etc.) is used on each element of the feature map to achieve *non-linearity*. Without activation function, a neural network acts as a Linear Regression Model, with less power and performance [27]. In this paper, we used *Rectified Linear Units* (ReLUs) activation function, due to its fast convergence characteristics [26]. The ReLUs activation function is defined as follows in Eq. 2:

$$R(I_{m,n}^l) = max(0, I_{m,n}^l) \qquad (3)$$

where $I_{m,n}^l$ denotes the input patch at location (m,n) in layer l.

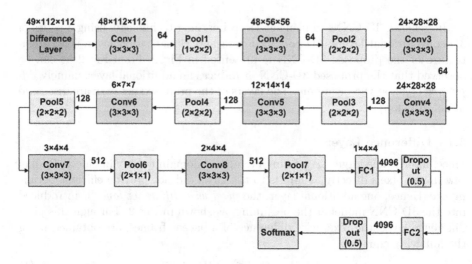

Fig. 2. Pipeline of the proposed CNN

3.3   Pooling Layer

All obtained output feature maps, from the convolution layer, can be used for classification. However, this would lead to high computation cost and would make the system highly prone to over-fitting [26] errors. So, to reduce the computation cost and solve the over-fitting problem, a *pooling operation* is performed. Pooling operation is an aggregation operation, where max (/min/mean) of a particular feature, over a certain region (spatial along with temporal in case of videos) is considered, as a representative of that feature. In this paper, we use the *max pooling layer*, which propagates the maximum value within a certain spatio-temporal region of a video clip, to the next layer of the CNN.

3.4   Classification Layer and Optimizer

The last layer of the CNN is a *classification layer*, which consists of fully con-nected layers (denoted by 'FC1', 'FC2' in Fig. 2), *dropout layer* and *softmax layer*. The learned features, which are extracted through convolution layers, pass thorough fully connected layers, followed by dropout layers and finally fed into the softmax classifier, the top most layer of CNN. The dropout layers [28] are used to reduce over-fitting by dropping some neurons randomly during training phase. Here, softmax layer uses an optimizer algorithm, to update the weight parameters of the training model. We use the Adam optimizer [29] to train our model.

In the next subsection, we elaborate on the parameters of the proposed 3D-CNN for inter-frame video forgery detection.

3.5   Proposed 3D-CNN Network Architecture and Parameters Setting

For ease of understanding, in the rest of this paper, we shall denote a video clip with a size of $c \times f \times h \times w$, where c denotes the number of color channels used to capture the video, f is the number of frames in the video clip, h is the height and w is the width of each frame in terms of pixels. We also denote the kernel size by $d \times k \times k$, where d is the temporal depth of the kernel and k is its spatial size, for 3D convolution and pooling layers.

Network Architecture and Parameter Settings. The proposed 3D-CNN is presented in Fig. 2. Our CNN architecture consists of 8 convolution layers, 7 pooling layers, 2 fully connected layers, two dropout layers and one softmax layer to predict the class labels.

The CNN network takes video clips as inputs. Videos are spit into non-overlapping 49-frames clips, which are used as inputs to the difference layer of the network. The input dimension are $3 \times 49 \times 320 \times 240$. We also perform jittering of the input clips, by using random crops with a size of $3 \times 49 \times 112 \times 112$, during training.

The output of difference layer is fed to the first convolution layer (Conv1) with size $3 \times 48 \times 112 \times 112$. The number of filters for 8 convolution layers from 1 to 8, are 64, 64, 64, 128, 128, 128, 512 and 512, respectively. The kernel size for all convolution layers, is $3 \times 3 \times 3$ and a stride of 1 is used; therefore the input and output sizes of convolution layers are same.

We use the max pooling kernel with size $2 \times 2 \times 2$ and stride 1 in pooling layers 2 to 5. Thus the output sizes of these pooling layers, were reduced by a factor of 8, as compared to the input size. In the first pooling layer, we use a temporal kernel with depth $d = 1$, and spatial kernel with size $k = 2$, because we do not want to merge the temporal signal too early. In last two pooling layers, we use a temporal kernel with depth $d = 2$ and spatial kernel with $k = 1$, so as *not* to merge the spatial signals at the end.

At the end of this series of convolution and pooling layers, the output signal size is $1 \times 4 \times 4 \times 512 = 8192$, which is the input size of the fully connected layer. The output of both the fully connected layers, is 4096. The network starts the learning process with a learning rate of 0.0001, momentum 0.99 and weight decay of 0.0005. In order to avoid over-fitting, we use two dropout layers with probability 0.5 for both. All these are evident from Fig. 2.

In the next section, we present our experimental results pertaining to performance evaluation of the proposed model, along with related discussion, and comparison with state-of-the-art.

4   Experimental Results and Discussion

The proposed 3D-CNN has been implemented in Tensorflow framework, using a 3.3 GHz Intel Xeon processor, 32GB RAM and 4GB GPU (Getforce GTX 970) with 1664 CUDA cores. In this section, we discuss about our experimental data set, followed by our experimental results, related discussion and comparison with state-of-the-art.

4.1 Dataset Description

We have used the UCF101 [30] dataset, which was originally created for human action recognition. The dataset consists of 13320 videos of different time lengths. Out of 13320 videos, we select 9000 video for our experiments, randomly. For the sake of experimentation, we generated our test forged video sequences, from the UCF101 dataset, using the ffmpeg [31] tool. We manually induced different types of inter-frame forgeries into the video sequences, viz., frame insertion, deletion and duplication forgeries. The forged frame sequences were compressed in MP4 format, with H.264 video coding standard. To encode the videos, we used chroma sampling 4:2:2, GOP length 6, and Constant Rate Factor (CRF) 0, 8, 16, 20 and 24.

Hence, for our experiments, we generated three more sets of videos from the original dataset, viz., frame inserted, frame deleted, and frame duplicated video datasets. Our test dataset consists of static and as well as dynamic background videos, with single or multiple foreground objects. Here, we have worked only with single video shots.

In our experiments, we have divided the 9000 authentic videos into three parts: training dataset, validation dataset and test dataset. Training dataset consist of 5000 authentic videos and their corresponding forged videos, used for training the network. Validation dataset contain 2000 authentic videos and their corresponding forged videos, used to validate the network. And test dataset consists of remaining 2000 authentic videos and their corresponding forged videos, used to test the efficiency of the trained network.

4.2 Evaluation Standards

The output of the CNN is a binary probability matrix, used for mapping, to identify the authentic and forged videos. In our experiments, we measure the performance of the proposed model in terms of accuracy, which are defined as follows:

$$Accuracy = \frac{TP + TN}{TP + FP + TN + FN} \times 100\%$$

where TP represents the number of *True Positives* or the number of forged videos correctly detected to be forged, FP represents the number of *False Positives* or the number authentic videos detected as forged, TN represents the number of *True Negatives* or the number of authentic videos correctly detected as authentic, and FN represents the number of *False Negatives*, that is, the number of forged videos falsely detected as authentic.

4.3   Frame Insertion Forgery Detection

In this section, we detect frame insertion type forgery in our test videos. To build the training model, we use 5000 authentic videos, and another corresponding 5000 videos forged by frame insertion operation. Also, for evaluating the performance of the trained model, we used 2000 authentic videos and the corresponding 2000 forged videos by frame insertion. To perform this experiment, we have varied the number of forged frames as 10, 20 30. The results are presented in Table 1.

Table 1. Performance evaluation of the proposed model for frame insertion forgery detection.

#Frames inserted	Accuracy (%)			
	CRF = 0	CRF = 8	CRF = 16	CRF = 24
10	99.12	99.05	98.56	98.95
20	99.2	99.24	99.05	99.1
30	99.35	99.15	99.31	99.25

It is evident from Table 1, that the proposed method performs efficiently for low compressed (CRF = 0), medium compressed (CRF = 8, 16) as well as highly compressed (CRF = 24) videos. The maximum accuracy, we achieved is 99.35%, for video quality factor $CRF = 0$, and number of forged frames 30.

4.4   Frame Deletion Forgery Detection

To test the performance of the proposed method in frame deletion detection, we used the same set of 5000 authentic videos, along with the corresponding 5000 forged video sequences, generated by frame deletion operation, for training the proposed model. We evaluated the efficiency of the proposed CNN with another 2000 authentic and corresponding 2000 forged videos. Similar to the above, we carried out our experiments with low compressed (CRF = 0), medium compressed (CRF = 8, 16) and highly compressed (CRF = 24) videos, with 10, 20 and 30 forged frames. The results are presented in Table 2.

It can be observed from Table 2, that the forgery detection accuracy of the proposed model increases with increase in number of forged frames, for all degrees of compression. Also, it can be also observed that the quality factor (CRF) of the video, does not affect the performance of proposed model significantly. We obtain the maximum accuracy of 95.89%, for 30 forged frames (for CRF = 0).

4.5   Frame Duplication Forgery Detection

To evaluate the proposed model in terms of frame duplication detection, we have used the same set of 5000 authentic videos, and their corresponding frame

Table 2. Performance evaluation of the proposed model for frame deletion forgery detection.

#Frames deleted	Accuracy (%)			
	CRF = 0	CRF = 8	CRF = 16	CRF = 24
10	91.56	91.78	91.1	90.85
20	94.24	94.8	93.55	94.05
30	95.89	95.75	95.1	95.26

duplicated forms, to train our CNN model. To test the proposed model, we use 2000 authentic and corresponding 2000 forged video, generated by frame duplication operation. We carried our experiments with light compressed videos (CRF = 0), medium compressed videos (CRF = 8, 16) and heavy compressed videos (CRF = 24).

We present the frame duplication detection results in Table 3, for CRF = 0, 8, 16, 24. Here, we performed our experiments videos having 10 and 20 forged frames. This is due to the fact that, we used 49 frames at a time to train the network, due to memory constraints. And when we tried to take >= 30 forged frames, the minimum number of input frame requirement, to train the network, was $30 \times 2 = 60$, which exceeded 49.

Table 3. Performance evaluation of the proposed model for frame duplication forgery detection.

#Frames duplicated	Accuracy (%)			
	CRF = 0	CRF = 8	CRF = 16	CRF = 24
10	98.25	98.05	98.34	98.1
20	98.4	98.23	97.7	97.86

It can be noted from Table 3, that the accuracy of the proposed model for frame duplication detection varies between 97.86% to 98.4%. Also, it can be observed that we obtain satisfactory performance results for low, medium, as well as highly compressed videos.

4.6   Comparison with State–of–the–Art

In this section, we present a comprehensive comparison of the proposed model's performance with that of the state–of–the–art, with respect to inter-frame video forgery detection. In this paper, we have compared the proposed method with the works of: (A) Kingra et al. [25], and (B) Long et al. [16], the two note-worthy inter-frame video forgery detection schemes based on Deep Learning, existing in the current literature.

The scheme proposed by Kingra et al. [25], uses optical flow gradient and prediction residual error of In the other scheme proposed by Long et al. [16], the authors have used a C3D CNN with a confidence score, which is a post-processing method, to detect inter-frame forgery in videos. However, this scheme is capable to detect only frame deletion type of forgery in videos, whereas the proposed model detects frame insertion, deletion and duplication forgeries.

The results of this comparison are presented in Table 4. The average accuracy of the proposed method is 97%, and is significantly higher than Kingra et al.'s scheme. Long et al.'s scheme follows our accuracy closely; however it is to be noted here that their accuracy is only for frame deletion detection; whereas the results of the proposed model is the average of frame insertion, deletion and duplication types of forgery detection.

Table 4. Comparison with state-of-the-art.

Scheme	Types of attacks	Accuracy (%)
Kingra et al. [25]	Frame insertion, deletion, duplication	83
Long et al. [16]	Frame deletion	96
Proposed model	Frame insertion, deletion, duplication	97

5 Conclusion and Future Work

In this paper, we present a 3D CNN for inter-frame forgery detection in digital videos. In the proposed CNN, we introduce a pixel difference layer, through which we pass the temporal information related to a video sequence, to the following CNN layer. Since inter-frame forgery in videos is a temporal forgery operation, hence by using this temporal information, the subsequent convolution layers of the CNN are able to learn more suitable features, to detect inter-frame video forgeries. The proposed method is able to detect frame insertion, deletion and duplication types of forgeries, for static as well as dynamic single shot videos, and proves to outperform the state–of–the–art in terms of forgery detection accuracy.

Future research in this direction would include detection as well as frame-wise localization of inter-frame video forgeries. Also, we shall focus on detection and localization of multiple shot video forgeries.

Acknowledgment. This work is funded by Board of Research in Nuclear Sciences (BRNS), Department of Atomic Energy (DAE), Govt. of India, Grant No. 34/20/22/2016-BRNS/34363, dated: 16/11/2016.

References

1. Yu, L., et al.: Exposing frame deletion by detecting abrupt changes in video streams. Neurocomputing **205**, 84–91 (2016)
2. Shanableh, T.: Detection of frame deletion for digital video forensics. Digit. Investig. **10**(4), 350–360 (2013). https://doi.org/10.1016/j.diin.2013.10.004
3. Su, Y., Zhang, J., Liu, J.: Exposing digital video forgery by detecting motion-compensated edge artifact. In: International Conference on Computational Intelligence and Software Engineering, pp. 1–4, December 2009. https://doi.org/10.1109/CISE.2009.5366884
4. Aghamaleki, J.A., Behrad, A.: Inter-frame video forgery detection and localization using intrinsic effects of double compression on quantization errors of video coding. Sig. Process.: Image Commun. **47**, 289–302 (2016)
5. Zhang, Z., Hou, J., Ma, Q., Li, Z.: Efficient video frame insertion and deletion detection based on inconsistency of correlations between local binary pattern coded frames. Secur. Commun. Netw. **8**(2), 311–320 (2015)
6. Li, Z., Zhang, Z., Guo, S., Wang, J.: Video inter-frame forgery identification based on the consistency of quotient of MSSIM. Secur. Commun. Netw. **9**(17), 4548–4556 (2016)
7. Liu, Y., Huang, T.: Exposing video inter-frame forgery by Zernike opponent chromaticity moments and coarseness analysis. Multimed. Syst. **23**(2), 223–238 (2017)
8. Sitara, K., Mehtre, B.: Digital video tampering detection: an overview of passive techniques. Digit. Investig. **18**(Supplement C), 8–22 (2016). https://doi.org/10.1016/j.diin.2016.06.003
9. Bakas, J., Naskar, R., Dixit, R.: Detection and localization of inter-frame video forgeries based on inconsistency in correlation distribution between Haralick coded frames. Multimed. Tools Appl. **2018**, 1–31 (2018). https://doi.org/10.1007/s11042-018-6570-8
10. Sermanet, P., Eigen, D., Zhang, X., Mathieu, M., Fergus, R., LeCun, Y.: Overfeat: integrated recognition, localization and detection using convolutional networks. arXiv preprint arXiv:1312.6229 (2013)
11. Simonyan, K., Zisserman, A.: Very deep convolutional networks for large-scale image recognition. arXiv preprint arXiv:1409.1556 (2014)
12. Krizhevsky, A., Sutskever, I., Hinton, G.E.: Imagenet classification with deep convolutional neural networks. In: Advances in Neural Information Processing Systems, pp. 1097–1105 (2012)
13. Simonyan, K., Vedaldi, A., Zisserman, A.: Deep inside convolutional networks: visualising image classification models and saliency maps. arXiv preprint arXiv:1312.6034 (2013)
14. Ji, S., Xu, W., Yang, M., Yu, K.: 3D convolutional neural networks for human action recognition. IEEE Trans. Pattern Anal. Mach. Intell. **35**(1), 221–231 (2013)
15. Simonyan, K., Zisserman, A.: Two-stream convolutional networks for action recognition in videos. In: Advances in Neural Information Processing Systems, pp. 568–576 (2014)
16. Long, C., Smith, E., Basharat, A., Hoogs, A.: A C3D-based convolutional neural network for frame dropping detection in a single video shot. In: IEEE Conference on Computer Vision and Pattern Recognition Workshops (CVPRW), pp. 1898–1906, July 2017. https://doi.org/10.1109/CVPRW.2017.237

17. Tran, D., Bourdev, L., Fergus, R., Torresani, L., Paluri, M.: Learning spatiotemporal features with 3D convolutional networks. In: Proceedings of the IEEE International Conference on Computer Vision, ICCV 2015, pp. 4489–4497. IEEE Computer Society, Washington (2015). https://doi.org/10.1109/ICCV.2015.510

18. Wu, Y., Jiang, X., Sun, T., Wang, W.: Exposing video inter-frame forgery based on velocity field consistency. In: IEEE International Conference on Acoustics, Speech and Signal Processing (ICASSP), pp. 2674–2678, May 2014. https://doi.org/10.1109/ICASSP.2014.6854085

19. Wang, Q., Li, Z., Zhang, Z., Ma, Q.: Video inter-frame forgery identification based on consistency of correlation coefficients of gray values. J. Comput. Commun. **2**(04), 51 (2014)

20. Su, Y., Nie, W., Zhang, C.: A frame tampering detection algorithm for MPEG videos. In: 6th IEEE Joint International Information Technology and Artificial Intelligence Conference, vol. 2, pp. 461–464 (2011). https://doi.org/10.1109/ITAIC.2011.6030373

21. D'Avino, D., Cozzolino, D., Poggi, G., Verdoliva, L.: Autoencoder with recurrent neural networks for video forgery detection. Electron. Imaging **2017**(7), 92–99 (2017)

22. Zhao, D.N., Wang, R.K., Lu, Z.M.: Inter-frame passive-blind forgery detection for video shot based on similarity analysis. Multimed. Tools Appl. **77**, 1–20 (2018)

23. Hall, G.: Pearson's correlation coefficient. Other Words **1**(9) (2015). http://www.hep.ph.ic.ac.uk/~hallg/UG_2015/Pearsons.pdf. Accessed 3 Oct 2018

24. Aghamaleki, J.A., Behrad, A.: Malicious inter-frame video tampering detection in mpeg videos using time and spatial domain analysis of quantization effects. Multimed. Tools Appl. **76**(20), 20691–20717 (2017)

25. Kingra, S., Aggarwal, N., Singh, R.D.: Inter-frame forgery detection in H. 264 videos using motion and brightness gradients. Multimed. Tools Appl. **76**(24), 25767–25786 (2017)

26. Chen, J., Kang, X., Liu, Y., Wang, Z.J.: Median filtering forensics based on convolutional neural networks. IEEE Sig. Process. Lett. **22**(11), 1849–1853 (2015)

27. Walia, A.S.: Activation functions and it's types-which is better? (2017). https://towardsdatascience.com/activation-functions-and-its-types-which-is-better-a9a5310cc8f. Accessed 13 Aug 2018

28. Srivastava, N., Hinton, G., Krizhevsky, A., Sutskever, I., Salakhutdinov, R.: Dropout: a simple way to prevent neural networks from overfitting. J. Mach. Learn. Res. **15**(1), 1929–1958 (2014)

29. Kingma, D.P., Ba, L.: J., : ADAM: a method for stochastic optimization. In: Learning Representations (2015)

30. Soomro, K., Zamir, A.R., Shah, M.: UCF101: a dataset of 101 human actions classes from videos in the wild. arXiv preprint arXiv:1212.0402 (2012)

31. Developers, F.: FFmpeg tool (Version 3.2.4) [Software] (2017). https://www.ffmpeg.org

Re–compression Based JPEG Tamper Detection and Localization Using Deep Neural Network, Eliminating Compression Factor Dependency

Jamimamul Bakas[(✉)], Praneta Rawat, Kalyan Kokkalla, and Ruchira Naskar

Department of Computer Science and Engineering, National Institute of Technology, Rourkela 769008, India
{516cs6008,naskarr}@nitrkl.ac.in, pranetarawat1994@gmail.com, kalyan.kokkalla@gmail.com

Abstract. In this work, we deal with the problem of re–compression based image forgery detection, where some regions of an image are modified illegitimately, hence giving rise to presence of dual compression characteristics within a single image. There have been some significant researches in this direction, in the last decade. However, almost all existing techniques fail to detect this form of forgery, when the first compression factor is greater than the second. We address this problem in re–compression based forgery detection, here Recently, Machine Learning techniques have started gaining a lot of importance in the domain of digital image forensics. In this work, we propose a Convolution Neural Network based deep learning architecture, which is capable of detecting the presence of re–compression based forgery in JPEG images. The proposed architecture works equally efficiently, even in cases where the first compression ratio is greater than the second. In this work, we also aim to localize the regions of image manipulation based on re–compression features, using the trained neural network. Our experimental results prove that the proposed method outperforms the state–of–the–art, with respect to forgery detection and localization accuracy.

Keywords: Convolution Neural Network · Deep learning
Digital forensics · Double compression · Image forgery
Joint photographic experts group (JPEG)
Re–compression based forgery

1 Introduction

In today's world, majority of day–to–day communication relies on exchange of digital data. Hence, assuring the trustworthiness of their contents is crucial. Images play a very important role in present–day digital world, where they form the primary means of communications, as well as the major sources of

© Springer Nature Switzerland AG 2018
V. Ganapathy et al. (Eds.): ICISS 2018, LNCS 11281, pp. 318–341, 2018.
https://doi.org/10.1007/978-3-030-05171-6_17

evidence towards any event, in legal, media and broadcast industries. Due to the present wide availability of low–cost image processing tools and software, digital images have become highly vulnerable to illegitimate modification attacks. Due to the availability of such tools, *doctored photographs* have become wide–spread, which challenge the forensic analysts and research community greatly. The threat to the integrity and authenticity of digital images, has been further increased by the fact that most image manipulations are indiscernible to human eyes. From the past decade, the field of digital forensics has emerged to protect and restore the integrity and authenticity of digital data. Digital Forensics is the branch of science that deals with the investigation of doctored material found in digital devices related to computer crime. Traditional techniques, such as *Digital Watermarking* and *Digital Signature*, have been very widely adopted till date, for multimedia security and protection. However, a major drawback of these approaches is the requirement of data pre–processing. That is, they involve some precautionary measures, always. This makes such techniques limited to the specially equipped cameras, with specific embedded software and hardware chips. Such security measures are termed *active* techniques [1]. On the contrary, forensic techniques are *passive* (also known as blind) [1]. *Passive techniques* require no a–priori information processing or computation, and are completely based on post–processing of data. This forensics techniques are based on the assumption that digital forgeries alter the underlying statistics of an image, and leave behind *traces*, which may be intelligently exploited in the future to detect the forgeries and their sources.

Joint Photographic Expert Group (JPEG) [2] is the most widely used format for an image data storage, due to its best compression features and optimal space requirement. Substantial research has been carried out in the domain of JPEG forgery detection in the recent years [3–6]. The JPEG attack model considered by the researchers is as follows. A JPEG image is shown in Fig. 1(a). Let QF_1 denotes the initial quality factor, at which this image was JPEG compressed. A region of the image, as shown in Fig. 1(b) has been extracted and re–compressed at a different ratio QF_2, such that $QF_2 \neq QF_1$. The extracted region is put back into the original image, (at the same location), to produce the tampered image, shown in Fig. 1(c). The resultant image is nothing but another JPEG, consisting of two differently compressed regions, one doubly compressed with subsequent quality factors QF_1, QF_2, and the rest of the image singly compressed at QF_1, as shown in Fig. 1(c). It is evident from Fig. 1(c), that the tampered region having a (double) compression ratio, different from the rest of the image, is perceptually indistinguishable.

In this paper, we focus on the detection and localization of double compression based JPEG modification attack, modelled as above. In this work, we model the given challenge as a two–way classification problem. However, conventional machine learning based classifiers are solely based on *feature identification and extraction*. Such conventional classification techniques prove to be inefficient for problems, in which the features are not identified or well–known, or their extraction is difficult. To address this issue, in this work, we develop a *Convolution*

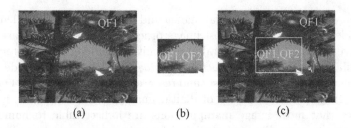

(a)   (b)   (c)

Fig. 1. JPEG attack on image: (a) Original 512 × 512 image; (b) Central region, re–saved at a different compression ratio; (c) Forged image with differently compressed regions

Neural Network (CNN) based *deep learning* network architecture, which would assist in automated feature engineering in classification task. Our first aim is to perform a two–way classification, between (A) unforged (single compressed) JPEG images, and (B) forged (double compressed) JPEG images. Our second aim is localization of forged region(s) in a JPEG image. We achieve this by performing a JPEG block–wise CNN classification, applied to our test images. The performance of the proposed forgery localization method has been improved, by considering vertical and horizontal strides of magnitude, as low as eight pixels. This helped us achieve forgery localization units upto 32 × 32 pixels, hence improving the detection accuracy as compared to the state-of-the-art. This is evident from our experimental results. Additionally, the proposed method successfully addresses those cases of re–compression based JPEG forgeries where the first compression factor is greater than the second ($QF1 > QF2$), unlike other state–of–the–art techniques such as [4,7,8]. Our experimental results prove this.

Rest of the paper is organized as follows. In Sect. 2, we provide an overview of the related background. In Sect. 3, we present the proposed CNN model for JPEG forgery detection and localization, along with the details of its attributes and architecture. In Sect. 4, we present our experimental results and related discussion. Finally, we conclude the paper with future research directions in Sect. 5.

2   Related Work

In this section, we review the existing literature on JPEG image forgery detection and localization. In this paper, we adopt a blind digital forensic approach to address the above problem, and here we present an overview of the related researches in this domain.

A number of significant researches towards double compression based JPEG forgery detection, are based on *Benford's Law* [9–11]. *Benford's law* or *first–digit law*, gives a frequency distribution prediction of the most significant digits in real–life numeric data sets. We focus on detection of image tampering in this paper by checking the DQ effect of the double quantized DCT coefficients. The DQ effect is the exhibition of periodic peaks and valleys in the distributions of the DCT coefficients. Related researches based on exploiting DCT coefficient are listed below.

In [9], the authors had investigated and analyzed the frequency distribution or histogram of DCT coefficients of JPEG images, for re–compression based JPEG forgery detection. Double quantization introduces specific artifacts into a JPEG, which is evident from its DCT coefficients histogram. These artifacts have been exploited in [9], for JPEG forgery detection. In [11], the authors proposed a JPEG forgery detection model, based on statistical analysis of the DCT quantization coefficients distribution, using generalized Benford Distribution Law. Among the other significant works based on Discrete Cosine Transform (DCT) coefficients distribution analysis utilizing generalized Benford's Law, for JPEG double compression detection, are [7,12–14]. The first significant attempt to localize tampered regions in JPEG images, was made by [15], using DCT of overlapping blocks and their lexicographical representations. [9] proposed a *block matching algorithm* to strike a balance between performance and complexity of such methods. Here, the authors adopted Principal Component Analysis (PCA) for image block representation.

Recently, neural networks have started gaining huge popularity in image forgery detection and classification tasks, due to spontaneous feature learning capabilities of such networks, which help to maximize classification accuracy. In [16], Gopi et al. utilized Artificial Neural Network (ANN) based classification and auto regressive image coefficients to generate feature vectors. The authors trained the network with 300 manually tampered training images, and tested the model with a different test set of 300 images. They achieved a forgery detection success rate of 77.67%. In [17], Bayar et al. developed a Convolution Neural Network (CNN) architecture which automatically learns image manipulation features, directly form the training data. In [5], Cozzolino et al. proposed a JPEG forgery detection scheme, which extracts image local residual features by means of a CNN. They fine–tuned the network with the labeled data and performed classification based on the extracted features.

The authors in [6] utilized a CNN to automatically learn hierarchical pattern representations from RGB color images. The pre–trained CNN is used as a patch descriptor to extract dense features from the test images, and to convert it to a more abstract form.

In [18], the authors address the problem of aligned and non–aligned forgery detection in JPEG images. They provided three solutions. The first involving handcrafted features extracted from JPEG, and a feature fusion technique is then adopted to obtain the final discriminative features for SVM classification. In the rest two, the CNN is directly trained with JPEG and with denoised images. CNN based on hand-crafted features allows us to achieve better accuracy than the other two methods, and performs efficiently when the second quality factor is greater than the first.

3   Proposed Deep Learning Model for Double Compression Based JPEG Forgery Detection and Localization

In this section, we present the proposed Convolution Neural Network based model for double–compression based JPEG forgery detection, as well as local-ization. The proposed forgery detection method consists of an initial JPEG pre–processing phase, followed by CNN learning. The trained CNN is later used for forgery localization in tampered JPEG images. For training of the proposed model, we use the following two datasets: (A) A set of images collected from the [19] uncompressed image database, which are subsequently compressed using JPEG with quality factor QF_1 (say); this serves as our authentic singly com-pressed image dataset (S_{SC}). (B) A second set of images which are generated by re–compressing the images in S_{SC}, this time by JPEG quality factor QF_2. This set forms our second training dataset of doubly compressed JPEG images, with quality factor (QF_1, QF_2); we name this dataset as S_{DC}.

In the pre–processing phase of the proposed method, we divide all images in S_{SC} and S_{DC}, into 32 × 32 overlapping blocks, with a stride of 8 pixels. From each such block, a 19 × 7 dimensional feature vector (based on DCT fre-quency histogram [9]) is obtained in this phase; hence generating two sets of features: F_{SC} and F_{DC}, from datasets S_{SC} and S_{DC}, respectively. We label the samples belonging to S_{SC} with 0, and those belonging to S_{DC} with 1, in the pre–processing phase.

The next phase of the proposed method is the CNN learning phase. In this phase, we train the proposed CNN model with F_{SC} and F_{DC}, i.e., the features obtained from singly compressed verses doubly compressed training images. The above features efficiently distinguish between single compressed and double com-pressed JPEG images, as evident from our experimental results in Sect. 4.

By specifying the features in the pre–processing step, we reduce the burden of feature engineering on the proposed CNN, so that it can focus more on dealing with tampered region localization. This considerably helps in complexity opti-mization. For forgery localization, the proposed CNN learns the hidden feature representations of artifacts caused due to tampering. The unit of forgery local-ization in the proposed method, is determined by the magnitude of block stride (used while division of an image into overlapping blocks, in the pre–processing phase), which is 8 × 8 in our work. This maximizes the forgery localization accu-racy of the proposed method. Detailed experimental results are presented in Sect. 4.

Next, we describe the phases of the proposed method in detail, along with description of the proposed CNN architecture.

3.1   Pre–processing and Feature Extraction

The major task in JPEG pre–processing phase of the proposed method is extrac-tion of block–wise features, depending on which we train the proposed CNN model. As stated previously, we divide the image into overlapping $W \times W = 32 \times 32$ blocks, with a stride of $S = 8$. For an $M \times N$ image, we obtain a total of $(\lceil \frac{M-W}{S} \rceil + 1) \times (\lceil \frac{N-W}{S} \rceil + 1)$ blocks of size 32×32 pixels.

For CNN learning, we use distributions of 19 DCT coefficients of each 32×32 image block, starting from second to the twentieth coefficients, in zigzag order, as feature vectors. Since each 32×32 image block consists of 16 8×8 DCT blocks, we have 16 different values of each component (component 2 to component 20). For the i-th component, we find the block where it assumes the highest value as compared to the rest 15 blocks. We consider this block, and its six neighbors: position–wise its three immediate predecessor and three immediate successor blocks, for feature extraction. That is, if the block containing the highest value for component i is indexed 0, we consider blocks indexed $[-3, -2, -1, 0, 1, 2, 3]$, for feature vector generation. This generates a 19×7 feature vector for each

---

Input : Input image I of dimension $M \times N$
Output: Feature matrix F.

Initialize $W \leftarrow blocksize$;
Initialize $S \leftarrow stride$;
Initialize $n\_hor\_blocks \leftarrow (\lceil \frac{M-W}{S} \rceil + 1)$;
Initialize $n\_ver\_blocks \leftarrow (\lceil \frac{N-W}{S} \rceil + 1)$;
Initialize $F\_row \leftarrow 1$ // Row index to feature matrix F, every row of which stores
    19×7 features extracted from each $W \times W$ image block
for i from 1 to $(8 \times n\_hor\_blocks - 7)$ in steps of S **do**
    for j from 1 to $(8 \times n\_ver\_blocks - 7)$ in steps of S **do**
        /* Processing one 32×32 image block   */
        $block \leftarrow I(i : i + W - 1, j : j + W - 1)$;
        Initialize $block\_cnt \leftarrow 0$ // Counter for DCT blocks
        for p from 1 to 4 **do**
            for q from 1 to 4 **do**
                /* Feature extraction from 8×8 DCT blocks   */
                $sub\_block \leftarrow block(8p - 7 : 8p, 8q - 7 : 8q)$;
                $dct\_sub\_block \leftarrow DCT(sub\_block)$;
                $block\_cnt \leftarrow block\_cnt + 1$;
                $f\_vector(block\_cnt, 1 : 19) \leftarrow dct\_sub\_block(2 : 20)$ // store nineteen
                      coefficients for each DCT block
            end
        end
        /* Generating feature matrix for each 32×32 image block   */
        for c from 1 to 19 **do**
            // Computing max value for coefficient c, finding its position, and six
                neighboring DCT blocks
            Initialize $max \leftarrow f\_vector(1, c)$ // Initializing the maximum value with
                value at DCT block 1, for each coefficient c
            Initialize $max\_pos = 1$ // To store block index containing maximum value of
                coefficient c
            for $block\_cnt$ from 1 to 16 **do**
                if $f\_vector(block\_cnt, c) > max$ **then**
                    $max = f\_vector(block\_cnt, c)$;
                    $max\_pos = block\_cnt$;
                end
            end
            $F(F\_row, 7c - 6 : 7c) = f\_vector(max\_pos - 3 : max\_pos + 3, c)^T$;
        end
        $F\_row \leftarrow F\_row + 1$;
    end
end

Algorithm 1: JPEG Pre–processing

32×32 image block, in our work. This abstraction is carried out to reduce computational complexity, without losing any significant block information.

To present the DCT coefficient selection procedure more clearly to the readers, we present an example here, in Fig. 2, which shows a 32×32 image block, consisting of 16 8×8 DCT blocks. In Fig. 2, we can see that the second coefficient assumes values $2.185e^{-16}$, $8.283e^{-16}$ etc. over the different DCT blocks, sequentially. The second coefficient assumes its highest value $9.409e^{-16}$, at the $(4, 1)$–th DCT block. Hence, to generate features corresponding to the second DCT coefficient of the given image block, we consider the $(4,1)$–th DCT block, along with its three preceding and three succeeding neighbours, that is, DCT blocks: $(3, 2)$, $(3, 3)$, $(3, 4)$, $(4, 1)$, $(4, 2)$, $(4, 3)$, $(4, 4)$. The 7–dimensional feature vector, corresponding to the second DCT coefficient of the given image block is: $[2.1852e^{-16}, 2.185e^{-16}, 2.185e^{-16}, 9.409e^{-16}, 4.968e^{-16}, 4.9688e^{-16}, 4.992e^{-16}]$. Similarly, we extract eighteen more 7–dimensional feature vectors from the rest of the coefficients, from third to twentieth; hence generating a 19×7 feature vector for each 32×32 image block, which is fed to the proposed CNN model, described next.

The set of feature vectors, thus obtained from images, belonging to sets S_{SC} and S_{DC}, are denoted as F_{SC} and F_{DC} respectively. The complete pre-processing and feature extraction phase is presented in form of Algorithm 1.

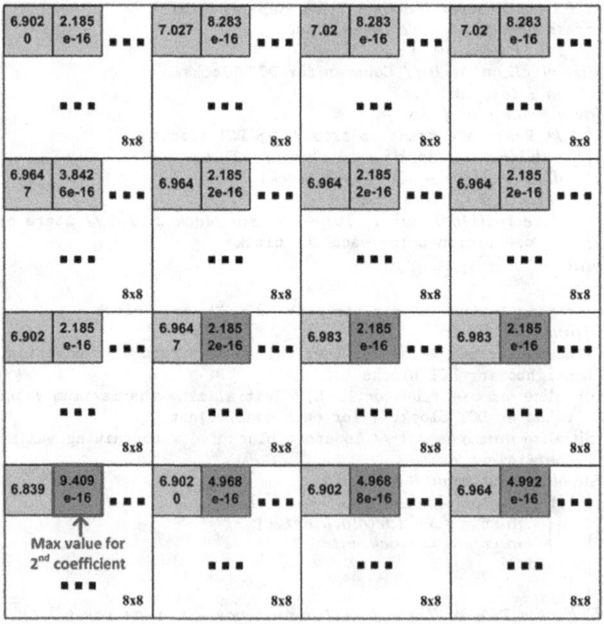

Fig. 2. Example: feature vector generation from DCT coefficients (*second* coefficient shown)

3.2   CNN Architecture

Convolution Neural Networks (CNN) form a variation of Multilayer Perceptrons (MLP), which consist of *neurons*, and *learnable biases* which are dependent on factors including local receptive fields, shared weights, spatial and temporal sub–sampling. CNNs consist of successive Convolution and sub–sampling layers, which are alternated, and finally connected to a Fully–connected layer. Convolution layers are responsible for performing a local feature average, and the sub–sampling layer, also called *Pooling* layer, is responsible for dimensionality reduction of the feature map. The Fully–connected layer implicitly consists of two more layers: *Dense layer* and *Logits layer*. The Dense layer performs classification based on features extracted by the previous convolution/pooling layers. Further, the Logits layer produces the raw prediction values. Each layer of a CNN receives input from the previous layer, multiplied by appropriate learnable weights, and are further added with biases.

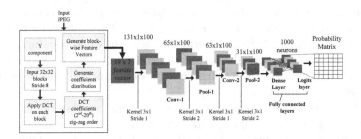

Fig. 3. Convolution Neural Network (CNN) architecture

As discussed in Sect. 3.1, we obtain features F_{SC} and F_{DC}, from our single compressed and double compressed training images, respectively. Each of F_{SC} and F_{DC}, is a matrix where each row consists of 19×7 features, and corresponds to one 32×32 single or double compressed JPEG block, respectively. Next, we shuffle the rows of matrices F_{SC} and F_{DC}, and hence merge those into a single matrix $F_{shuffled}$. Shuffling data serves the purpose of reducing variance in highly correlated examples, and ensuring that the classification model generalizes well and overfits less.

According to Sect. 3.1, we obtain $(\lceil \frac{M-32}{8} \rceil + 1) \times (\lceil \frac{N-32}{8} \rceil + 1)$ 32×32 blocks from an $M \times N$ image. We have used training/test images of size 384×512 pixels in our work, each of which generated 2,745 blocks, according to the above formulation. Our training dataset consists of 480 single and 480 double compressed JPEG images. Therefore, each of F_{SC} and F_{DC} consist of $480 \times 2,745 = 1,317,600$ feature vectors, and $F_{shuffled}$ consists of $1,317,600 \times 2 = 2,635,200$ feature vectors. Summarily, we train the proposed model using $480 \times 2 \times 2,745 = 2,635,200$ image blocks.

In this work, we propose a 2D–Convolution Neural Network architecture as shown in Fig. 3. In the proposed architecture, we adopt a 3×1 kernel at each layer, and vary the stride magnitude according to the required feature dimensionality. The input to the first convolution layer, Conv–1, is a 19×7 pixel matrix. Here we take a stride of 1 pixel, and the number of filters used in this layer is 100. After the first convolution layer, the output obtained is of dimension $131 \times 1 \times 100$, which is fed to the next layer. Here, 100 represents that there are 100 channels, each holding the output from one filter.

Pool–1 layer receives its input from Conv–1, and uses a stride of size 2; the number of filters used is 100. In this layer, our objective is data dimensionality reduction (sub–sampling) Hence, the stride magnitude is increased here to minimize feature dimension. Output of Pool–1 is 65×1 dimensional.

In Conv–2, the input is of dimension 65×1, the stride size and number of filters being exactly same as those in Conv–1. The output of Conv–2 serves as the input to Pool–2, the dimension of which is 63×1. The size of kernel, stride and number of filters in Pool–1 layer, are same as those in Pool–2. The output of Pool–2 layer is 31×1 dimensional.

The final layer is a Fully Connected convolution layer, which consists of the Dense and Logits layers. In the Dense Layer, we use 1000 neurons and the output is fed to a two–way softmax connection. In [20], it has been proven that deep neural networks with ReLUs perform efficiently while training with large databases and faster than tanh and other learning functions. In our network, Rectified Linear Units (ReLUs), with an activation function $f(x) = max(0, x)$, are used for each connection.

The input dimension to this layer is 31×1. To improve the training accuracy of the proposed model, we applied *dropout* regularization to the Dense layer. According to this phenomenon, during the training process, randomly selected neurons are *dropped–out* or ignored. This constraints the learning of the network by reducing dependency between neurons, hence avoiding overfitting. The Logits layer performs the final classification, thus producing the probability of each individual block, of being single compressed or double compressed.

The loss function used in this network, is the *Softmax Cross–Entropy* function at the last layer, which is *back propagated* through the network. We use *Softmax Cross-entropy* here, since a 2–way classification has been performed in this work. To optimize the loss during training, a learning rate of 0.001 and the *Stochastic Gradient Descent* optimizer, have been used.

3.3 Localizing the Tampered Regions

Localization of tampered regions in JPEG images, is accomplished during the testing phase of the proposed model. The model is trained as described in Sect. 3.2, where each 32×32 image block is assigned its class label ('0' for single compressed, and '1' for double compressed). During testing too, we divide an image into 32×32 blocks, using a stride of 8 pixels, similar to the training phase pre–processing. Now, each block is tested using the *trained* CNN model, and the final outcome is block–wise prediction of JPEG forgery (the tampered regions are labelled '1', indicating that the region is double compressed according to our

JPEG attack model discussed in Sect. 1, and the authentic regions are labelled '0').

Although the class prediction is performed by the proposed CNN model for each 32×32 image block, the unit of JPEG forgery localization here, is 8×8 pixels. The reason can be explained following Fig. 4. As evident from Fig. 4, after processing and testing the first 32×32 block (Fig. 4(a)), the stride moves right by 8 pixels, hence targeting the second 32×32 block (Fig. 4(b)). In this situation, after the stride movement towards right by 8 pixels is complete, the previous prediction for the first block, remains preserved only for the first (leftmost) 32×8 pixels. The remaining 32×24 pixels are newly tested and assigned a new class label, same as that of block 2, as they form a part of the second 32×32 block. Similarly, after traversal of one complete row, the stride performs vertical move by 8 pixels, as shown in Fig. 4(c). Hence, effectively, after stride movement of 8 pixels horizontally and vertically, we are left with the old block 1 prediction, only constrained to the top-left 8×8 pixels. This is evident from Fig. 4(d). This mechanism helps us obtain unit of forgery localization in the proposed model, as low as 8×8 image blocks.

Following similar movement/stride pattern, we process each (overlapping) 32×32 JPEG block sequentially, assign its class label using the trained CNN, and move on to the next block. For the last overhead blocks, we pad the image with sufficient number of *zero* rows and columns. This method makes the proposed JPEG forgery localization process considerably accurate, the unit of localization being merely 8×8 image blocks.

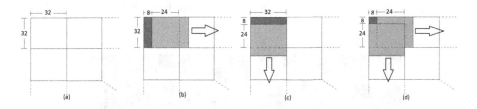

Fig. 4. Stride movement demonstration: (a) top–leftmost 32×32 image block, (b) Stride movement to the second block of the row, (c) First vertical stride movement to the second row, (d) Effective unit of forgery localization: top–leftmost 8×8 image block (in dark shade)

4   Experimental Results and Discussion

In this section, we first describe the dataset and the experimental set–up adopted by us, for performance evaluation of the proposed JPEG forgery detection and localization scheme. Then, we present our detailed experimental results. We compare the proposed method with recent state–of–the–art JPEG compression based forgery detection techniques, and present the relevant analysis results.

4.1 Dataset Generation and Experimental Set–Up

The JPEG pre–processing tasks in the proposed method, have been carried out using *MATLAB Image Processing Toolbox*. The proposed Convolution Neural Network has been implemented in *Tensorflow* parallel processing framework, in a *Python* environment.

In our experiments, we use 500 images collected from the UCID database [19]. All images provided in the UCID database, are in TIFF format, each of dimension 384×512 pixels. For our experiments, we first compress the TIFF images, with JPEG quality factor $QF_1 = 55, 65, 75, 85$ and 95. This way, we produce our single compressed image dataset S_{SC}, (described in Sect. 3). Next, the images in S_{SC} are further re–compressed one more time, with quality factor $QF_2 = 55, 65, \cdots 95$; this time to generate our double compressed image set S_{DC} (described in Sect. 3).

As discussed in Sect. 3.1, the JPEG images undergo a preliminary pre–processing step, before being used for training the CNN.

Out of the 500 images used in our experiment, we used 480 images for training, which generated a total of 1,317,600 blocks for training.

According to the JPEG modification model described in Sect. 1, we tamper our test JPEG images as follows. Some region of an image, compressed with quality factor QF_1 initially, has been modified, and saved at a different quality factor QF_2, to bring about re–compression based JPEG forgery. In particular, for our experiments, we have manually forged the test JPEG images, by replacing some region of a test image, initially compressed with quality factor QF_1, by the corresponding region, extracted from the same image, re–compressed at quality factor QF_2. We have varied the size of forgery as 10%, 30% and 50% of the actual images.

Fig. 5. Forgery detection and localization by the proposed method. Forgery sizes: (a) 10% (b) 30% (c) 50%. (*Top*) Authentic images. (*Middle*) Tampered images: tampered regions highlighted. (*Bottom*) Detected and Localized Forgeries

Forgery detection and localization results of the proposed method have been presented in Fig. 5, for three different forgery sizes.

4.2 Performance Evaluation Metrics

We model the problem of JPEG re–compression based forgery detection and localization, as a two–way classification problem, where we predict block–wise forgery. To evaluate the classification efficiency of the proposed method, we adopt a set of three metrics, viz. *Accuracy, F–measure, Success Rate*. We compare the proposed forgery detection method with con To evaluate the performance of the proposed forgery localization method, we use the following metric: of Forgery Localization, introduced by the authors in [4].

Accuracy of the proposed classification model can be defined as follows:

$$Accuracy = \frac{|TP| + |TN|}{|TP| + |TN| + |FP| + |FN|} \tag{1}$$

where TP, TN, FP and FN represent the sets of True Positive, True Negative, False Positive and False Negative samples, respectively.

The parameter *F–measure*, related to performance of a classification model, is also defined based on TP, TN, FP and FN, as follows:

$$F - measure = \frac{2 \times Precision \times Recall}{Precision + Recall} \tag{2}$$

where,

$$Precision = \frac{|TP|}{|TP| + |FP|}, \; Recall = \frac{|TP|}{|TP| + |FN|} \tag{3}$$

In this paper, we report the F–measure averaged over $N = 20$ test images. Specifically, the reported F–measure is computed as:

$$F - measure = \frac{\sum\limits_{i=1}^{N} F - measure(i)}{N} \tag{4}$$

where *F-measure(i)* gives the test results for the i–th image.

To evaluate the forgery localization efficiency of the proposed method, we follow the parameterization adopted by the authors in [4]. Here, a threshold T_h is chosen, which determines that tampered regions in an image are correctly localized, iff $F - measure \geq T_h$. Similar to [4], we set $T = 2/3$ in this work. So, the third evaluation parameter used in this work, *Success Rate of Localization* is defined as follows:

$$Success \; Rate = \frac{\sum\limits_{i=1}^{N} \delta_{F-measure(i) \geq T_h}}{N} \tag{5}$$

where N is the number of test images, and $\delta_{F-measure(i) \geq T_h}$ for every i–th image is computed as:

$$\delta_{F-measure(i) \geq T_h} = \begin{cases} 1 & \text{if } F - measure(i) \geq T_h, \\ 0 & \text{if others.} \end{cases}$$

Table 1. Performance evaluation and comparison for 10% Forgery: accuracy, F-measure and Success Rate of Localization results.

QF1	QF2		55	65	75	85	95
55	Proposed	Accuracy	**56.683**	**90.833**	93.073	93.073	**95.473**
		F–measure	**29.563**	**73.473**	**82.173**	**86.393**	**90.963**
		Success Rate	0	**100**	**100**	**100**	**100**
	Wang et al. [4]	Accuracy	-	88.37	93.66	95.57	93.59
		F–measure	-	45.87	72.7	81.17	83.85
		Success Rate	-	39.01	70.63	80.19	83.56
	Bianchi et al. [7]	Accuracy	-	90.02	79.53	86.25	74.82
		F–measure	-	67.33	54.17	65.43	50.16
		Success Rate	-	60.09	23.54	50.97	20.4
	Lin et al. [8]	Accuracy	-	87.91	88.21	89.04	94.31
		F–measure	-	1.65	1.95	3.96	68.84
		Success Rate	-	0	0	2.84	70.1
65	Proposed	Accuracy	65.353	**57.643**	83.253	85.193	**96.593**
		F–measure	**44.313**	**36.333**	**75.083**	77.383	**89.823**
		Success Rate	5	0	**90**	**100**	**100**
	Wang et al. [4]	Accuracy	35.39	-	90.06	95.14	93.74
		F–measure	14.02	-	55.12	81.34	84.01
		Success Rate	0	-	49.33	80.57	83.87
	Bianchi et al. [7]	Accuracy	82.87	-	86.1	86.08	65.84
		F–measure	41.02	-	64.16	66.62	40.31
		Success Rate	8.37	-	52.62	55.68	4.78
	Lin et al. [8]	Accuracy	88.53	-	86.59	88.35	93.74
		F–measure	1.12	-	2.29	1.48	60.02
		Success Rate	0	-	0	0	61.41
75	Proposed	Accuracy	74.493	70.843	**58.023**	86.583	**96.573**
		F–measure	**60.793**	**59.363**	**31.123**	76.653	**85.673**
		Success Rate	**35**	**10**	0	**100**	**100**
	Wang et al. [4]	Accuracy	55.19	31.89	-	93.99	94.17
		F–measure	9.11	14.84	-	80.2	84.6
		Success Rate	0	0	-	79.45	83.48
	Bianchi et al. [7]	Accuracy	88.57	88.54	-	64.36	80.22
		F–measure	7.24	24.65	-	43.48	59.52
		Success Rate	0	2.91	-	18.91	41.48
	Lin et al. [8]	Accuracy	88.5	88.5	-	84.33	92.75
		F–measure	1.21	1.99	-	3.62	45.85
		Success Rate	0	0	-	0	47.68

(*continued*)

Table 1. (*continued*)

QF1	QF2		55	65	75	85	95
85	Proposed	Accuracy	80.833	76.563	71.233	**57.693**	**95.693**
		F–measure	**66.393**	**57.403**	**58.753**	37.303	84.653
		Success Rate	**55**	**25**	**20**	0	**100**
	Wang et al. [4]	Accuracy	43.2	24.31	21.94	-	93.02
		F–measure	11.37	15.57	16.02	-	82.9
		Success Rate	0	0	0	-	81.99
	Bianchi et al. [7]	Accuracy	76.42	26.28	87.78	-	44.91
		F–measure	14.59	20.31	19.5	-	28.99
		Success Rate	0	0	0.82	-	0.15
	Lin et al. [8]	Accuracy	88.19	86.65	84.46	-	89.48
		F–measure	1.42	2.47	3.41	-	0.95
		Success Rate	0	0	0	-	0.37
95	Proposed	Accuracy	83.573	81.433	76.903	75.713	**62.323**
		F–measure	**72.033**	**68.363**	**62.603**	**67.633**	**38.533**
		Success Rate	**95**	**65**	**50**	**85**	0
	Wang et al. [4]	Accuracy	37.77	25.43	12.75	34.5	-
		F–measure	12.48	14.75	17.33	12.66	-
		Success Rate	0	0	0	0	-
	Bianchi et al. [7]	Accuracy	73.19	76	65.81	61.5	-
		F–measure	10.32	12.74	14.4	26.16	-
		Success Rate	0	0	0	0	-
	Lin et al. [8]	Accuracy	88.04	86.43	83.26	75.75	-
		F–measure	1.48	2.25	3.67	6.58	-
		Success Rate	0	0	0	0	-

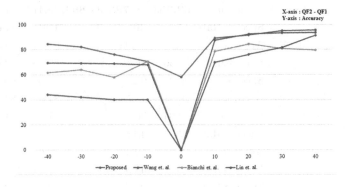

Fig. 6. Average accuracy for varying $QF_2 - QF_1$ values

Table 2. Performance evaluation and comparison for 30% Forgery: accuracy, F-measure and Success Rate of Localization results.

QF1	QF2		55	65	75	85	95
55	Proposed	Accuracy	**55.013**	**91.293**	**92.493**	**93.743**	**95.613**
		F−measure	**31.993**	74.693	82.263	87.373	91.943
		Success Rate	0	**100**	**100**	**100**	**100**
	Wang et al. [4]	Accuracy	-	89.9	91.03	93.65	94.1
		F−measure	-	62.88	87.02	90.3	92.59
		Success Rate	-	55.83	87.37	92.75	94.92
	Bianchi et al. [7]	Accuracy	-	87.86	80.98	87.79	79.68
		F−measure	-	80.87	77.2	84.65	76.31
		Success Rate	-	82.44	81.46	91.7	74.96
	Lin et al. [8]	Accuracy	-	69.62	69.95	73.6	91.46
		F−measure	-	5.56	7.49	18.92	81.96
		Success Rate	-	0.22	2.17	17.64	85.43
65	Proposed	Accuracy	62.033	**57.153**	83.243	85.723	**96.473**
		F−measure	45.243	**35.663**	76.143	78.303	91.283
		Success Rate	5	0	**95**	**100**	**100**
	Wang et al. [4]	Accuracy	43.12	-	85.02	93.62	94.06
		F−measure	36.05	-	73.08	90.61	92.36
		Success Rate	1.72	-	70.4	93.05	94.99
	Bianchi et al. [7]	Accuracy	76.18	-	87.13	87.91	73.01
		F−measure	53.61	-	82.37	84.83	70.3
		Success Rate	33.63	-	84.86	89.31	59.72
	Lin et al. [8]	Accuracy	69.9	-	69.13	69.71	90.75
		F−measure	2.67	-	8.07	10.71	78.79
		Success Rate	0.15	-	0.6	4.33	82.14
75	Proposed	Accuracy	**75.063**	70.903	**55.743**	86.353	**96.723**
		F−measure	**62.253**	**59.793**	**31.863**	76.413	87.363
		Success Rate	**45**	**20**	0	**100**	**100**
	Wang et al. [4]	Accuracy	48.57	40.03	-	92.11	94.57
		F−measure	26.36	36.79	-	89.06	93.09
		Success Rate	0.22	0.22	-	91.55	95.52
	Bianchi et al. [7]	Accuracy	70.21	73.59	-	81	84.09
		F−measure	10.04	30.28	-	77.77	81.38
		Success Rate	0.3	4.11	-	76.31	83.93
	Lin et al. [8]	Accuracy	69.94	69.49	-	67.67	88.53
		F−measure	2.7	4.69	-	12.11	69.66
		Success Rate	0.3	0.22	-	1.2	73.32

(*continued*)

Table 2. (*continued*)

QF1	QF2		55	65	75	85	95
85	Proposed	Accuracy	**82.203**	**77.043**	71.233	**60.343**	**95.503**
		F–measure	**69.143**	**58.413**	**60.323**	**37.763**	84.783
		Success Rate	**75**	**25**	**25**	0	**100**
	Wang et al. [4]	Accuracy	45.92	38.87	33.27	-	93.16
		F–measure	29.66	38.22	43.37	-	91.3
		Success Rate	0.15	0.22	0.22	-	94.62
	Bianchi et al. [7]	Accuracy	64.13	45.45	72.33	-	66.27
		F–measure	23.25	50.65	26.05	-	65.66
		Success Rate	0.37	0.15	1.42	-	45.44
	Lin et al. [8]	Accuracy	69.79	69.12	68.35	-	72.81
		F–measure	3.18	5.23	7.6	-	15.22
		Success Rate	0.15	0.22	0.45	-	13.15
95	Proposed	Accuracy	**84.653**	**82.273**	**75.423**	**76.283**	**64.853**
		F–measure	**74.133**	**69.933**	**64.163**	**68.033**	**37.753**
		Success Rate	**100**	**85**	**65**	**85**	0
	Wang et al. [4]	Accuracy	43.85	37.44	31.26	39.91	-
		F–measure	31.84	38.29	44.67	35.09	-
		Success Rate	0	0.15	0	0	-
	Bianchi et al. [7]	Accuracy	61.87	64.13	59.08	64.54	-
		F–measure	19.18	22.09	28.55	50.8	-
		Success Rate	0.22	0	0.37	1.79	-
	Lin et al. [8]	Accuracy	69.79	69.06	67.93	65.02	-
		F–measure	3.3	4.95	8.39	15.29	-
		Success Rate	0.22	0.22	0.15	0.52	-

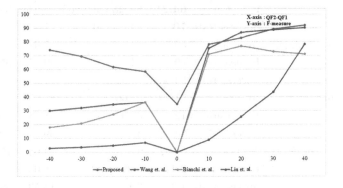

Fig. 7. Average F–measure for varying $QF_2 - QF_1$ values

Table 3. Performance evaluation and comparison for 50% Forgery: accuracy, F-measure and Success Rate of Localization results.

QF1	QF2		55	65	75	85	95
55	Proposed	Accuracy	**56.603**	**90.493**	**93.053**	**94.243**	**96.073**
		F–measure	**32.073**	76.323	83.833	88.103	93.413
		Success Rate	0	100	100	100	100
	Wang et al. [4]	Accuracy	-	67.23	84.83	89.53	93.4
		F–measure	-	62.98	87.27	90.7	94.38
		Success Rate	-	72.27	96.94	97.91	99.48
	Bianchi et al. [7]	Accuracy	-	83.66	83.33	89.85	84.32
		F–measure	-	82.58	86.02	91.2	86.96
		Success Rate	-	89.46	100	100	100
	Lin et al. [8]	Accuracy	-	51.72	52.71	57.38	88.49
		F–measure	-	7.27	10.79	22.45	84.09
		Success Rate	-	3.74	8.15	23.54	89.69
65	Proposed	Accuracy	63.233	**57.783**	84.353	85.233	**96.923**
		F–measure	46.343	**34.413**	76.113	79.373	92.633
		Success Rate	5	0	**95**	100	100
	Wang et al. [4]	Accuracy	51.22	-	77.62	89.31	93.47
		F–measure	50.61	-	77.09	90.74	94.44
		Success Rate	70.4	-	85.35	98.51	99.55
	Bianchi et al. [7]	Accuracy	63.92	-	85.38	89.71	81.49
		F–measure	48.87	-	85.84	91.1	84.86
		Success Rate	27.5	-	94.17	100	100
	Lin et al. [8]	Accuracy	50.81	-	52.45	54.45	85.31
		F–measure	3.38	-	11.1	17.52	77.43
		Success Rate	1.12	-	6.13	15.84	82.51
75	Proposed	Accuracy	**75.523**	71.113	**54.813**	86.443	**97.063**
		F–measure	**64.213**	**62.283**	**31.803**	76.933	88.763
		Success Rate	**70**	50	0	**100**	**100**
	Wang et al. [4]	Accuracy	50.7	50.8	-	87.92	94.51
		F–measure	40.91	54.4	-	89.45	95.26
		Success Rate	54.56	75.34	-	97.83	99.4
	Bianchi et al. [7]	Accuracy	51.99	57.66	-	87.09	88.89
		F–measure	12.96	30.05	-	88.93	90.47
		Success Rate	0.9	3.44	-	99.93	100
	Lin et al. [8]	Accuracy	50.82	51.33	-	53.63	79.44
		F–measure	3.42	6.25	-	18.03	65.19
		Success Rate	1.35	2.17	-	13.53	69.96

(*continued*)

Table 3. (*continued*)

QF1	QF2		55	65	75	85	95
85	Proposed	Accuracy	**82.123**	**76.433**	**72.813**	**59.163**	**95.923**
		F–measure	**70.733**	59.503	61.263	**38.313**	86.203
		Success Rate	**90**	40	40	0	**100**
	Wang et al. [4]	Accuracy	50.86	50.59	50.35	-	93.04
		F–measure	43.72	55.05	64.02	-	93.85
		Success Rate	58.82	77.28	91.63	-	99.55
	Bianchi et al. [7]	Accuracy	51.7	61.79	56.66	-	80.08
		F–measure	26.2	67.93	27.55	-	84.08
		Success Rate	4.33	80.42	1.87	-	99.55
	Lin et al. [8]	Accuracy	50.91	51.4	51.94	-	57.07
		F–measure	3.84	6.54	10.14	-	22
		Success Rate	1.72	2.62	4.48	-	23.84
95	Proposed	Accuracy	**85.213**	**83.263**	**77.033**	**76.223**	**58.713**
		F–measure	**76.213**	**72.033**	**65.853**	**69.583**	**37.133**
		Success Rate	**100**	**100**	70	**85**	0
	Wang et al. [4]	Accuracy	50.68	50.45	50.25	50.3	-
		F–measure	45.74	55.25	65	57.5	-
		Success Rate	60.91	77.58	93.27	82.29	-
	Bianchi et al. [7]	Accuracy	50.33	51.79	51.66	62.89	-
		F–measure	24.15	26.3	34.99	56.25	-
		Success Rate	4.04	3.44	5.68	36.4	-
	Lin et al. [8]	Accuracy	50.95	51.25	51.85	53	-
		F–measure	3.93	6.32	10.71	19.67	-
		Success Rate	1.42	2.84	4.86	11.21	-

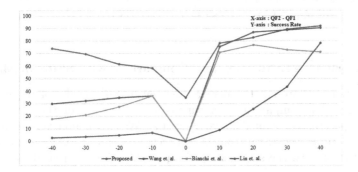

Fig. 8. Average Success Rate of Localization for varying $QF_2 - QF_1$ values

Table 4. Average accuracy, F−measure and Success Rate of Localization results, with varying Q2−Q1 for 10% forgery.

Q2−Q1		Proposed	Wang et al. [4]	Bianchi et al. [7]	Lin et al. [8]
−40	Accuracy	83.573	37.77	73.19	88.04
	F-measure	**72.033**	12.48	10.32	1.48
	Success Rate	**95**	0	0	0
−30	Accuracy	81.133	34.315	76.21	87.31
	F-measure	**67.378**	13.06	13.665	1.835
	Success Rate	**60**	0	0	0
−20	Accuracy	75.98633	30.75	60.22	86.13667
	F-measure	**60.26633**	14.00333	13.98333	2.45
	Success Rate	**36.66667**	0	0	0
−10	Accuracy	70.7855	30.93	80.1725	84.31
	F-measure	**57.5155**	14.385	27.8325	3.275
	Success Rate	**30**	0	3.025	0
0	Accuracy	**58.473**	0	0	0
	F-measure	**34.571**	0	0	0
	Success Rate	0	0	0	0
10	Accuracy	89.0905	91.36	71.3475	87.0775
	F-measure	**77.47**	66.02	50.99	2.13
	Success Rate	**97.50**	62.45	32.94	0.09
20	Accuracy	91.61	94.32	81.94	89.77
	F-measure	**81.74**	79.55	60.10	16.43
	Success Rate	**100.00**	78.23	40.23	15.89
30	Accuracy	**94.83**	94.66	76.05	91.39
	F-measure	**88.11**	82.59	52.87	31.99
	Success Rate	**100.00**	82.03	27.88	32.13
40	Accuracy	95.47	93.59	74.82	94.31
	F-measure	**90.963**	83.85	50.16	68.84
	Success Rate	**100**	83.56	20.4	70.1

4.3 Performance Evaluation and Comparison with State−of−the−Art

In this section, we present the performance evaluation results of the proposed method, as well as compare its performance with the state−of−the−art, in terms of all three parameters defined above (Sect. 4.2). We have compared the proposed method with three recent state−of−the−art techniques for JPEG forgery detection and localization, viz. the schemes of Wang et al. [4], Bianchi et al. [7] and Lin et al. [8].

Tables 1, 2, and 3, show the Forgery detection accuracy, F−measure and Success Rate of Localization results, of the proposed approach, along with the

Table 5. Average accuracy, F–measure and Success Rate of Localization results, with varying Q2–Q1 for 30% forgery.

Q2–Q1		Proposed	Wang et al. [4]	Bianchi et al. [7]	Lin et al. [8]
−40	Accuracy	**84.653**	43.85	61.87	69.79
	F-measure	**74.133**	31.84	19.18	3.3
	Success Rate	**100**	0	0.22	0.22
−30	Accuracy	**82.238**	41.68	64.13	69.425
	F-measure	**69.538**	33.975	22.67	4.065
	Success Rate	**80**	0.15	0.185	0.185
−20	Accuracy	**75.843**	39.56667	58.24667	68.99667
	F-measure	**61.60967**	36.41667	29.74667	5.44
	Success Rate	**45**	0.146667	0.273333	0.223333
−10	Accuracy	**70.113**	39.0825	71.66	68.19
	F-measure	**58.348**	37.825	40.185	7.5625
	Success Rate	**33.75**	0.54	10.2375	0.335
0	Accuracy	**58.621**	0	0	0
	F-measure	**35.007**	0	0	0
	Success Rate	0	0	0	0
10	Accuracy	89.098	90.0475	80.565	69.8075
	F-measure	78.01	79.08	76.67	10.24
	Success Rate	**98.75**	78.10	72.26	3.79
20	Accuracy	91.65	93.07	84.33	76.06
	F-measure	82.64	90.24	81.14	29.29
	Success Rate	**100.00**	91.98	84.90	26.61
30	Accuracy	**95.11**	93.86	80.40	82.18
	F-measure	89.33	91.33	77.48	48.86
	Success Rate	**100.00**	93.87	75.71	49.89
40	Accuracy	**95.61**	94.10	79.68	91.46
	F-measure	91.943	92.59	76.31	81.96
	Success Rate	**100**	94.92	74.96	85.43

methods proposed in [4,7,8]. Tables 1, 2, and 3, present the results for three different forgery sizes: 10%, 30%, 50% respectively, of the actual image, manually forged following the JPEG modification model described in Sect. 1 as well as Sect. 4.1.

As evident from Tables 1, 2, and 3, the diagonal entries, where $QF_1 = QF_2$, that is, the quality factors for the first and second compressions are same, the state–of–the–art methods fail; whereas, the proposed method is able to detect forgery with considerable efficiency. It is also evident that, in most of the cases

Table 6. Average accuracy, F–measure and Success Rate of Localization results, with varying Q2–Q1 for 50% forgery.

Q2–Q1		Proposed	Wang et al. [4]	Bianchi et al. [7]	Lin et al. [8]
−40	Accuracy	**85.213**	50.68	50.33	50.95
	F-measure	**76.213**	45.74	24.15	3.93
	Success Rate	**100**	60.91	4.04	1.42
−30	Accuracy	**82.693**	50.655	51.745	51.08
	F-measure	**71.383**	49.485	26.25	5.08
	Success Rate	**95**	68.2	3.885	2.28
−20	Accuracy	**76.32967**	50.51333	55.14667	51.35667
	F-measure	**63.18967**	53.65333	38.62667	6.89
	Success Rate	60	75.03667	29	2.943333
−10	Accuracy	**70.8455**	50.6675	60.2825	51.77
	F-measure	**59.868**	56.6325	40.68	9.86
	Success Rate	45	79.915	17.3025	4.745
0	Accuracy	**57.415**	0	0	0
	F-measure	**34.747**	0	0	0
	Success Rate	0	0	0	0
10	Accuracy	**89.303**	81.4525	84.0525	53.7175
	F-measure	78.89	80.84	85.36	14.60
	Success Rate	**98.75**	88.75	95.78	11.81
20	Accuracy	**91.78**	89.55	87.31	62.20
	F-measure	83.99	91.09	89.20	31.17
	Success Rate	**100.00**	98.28	100.00	31.32
30	Accuracy	**95.58**	91.50	85.67	71.35
	F-measure	90.37	92.57	88.03	49.94
	Success Rate	**100.00**	98.73	100.00	53.03
40	Accuracy	**96.07**	93.40	84.32	88.49
	F-measure	93.413	94.38	86.96	84.09
	Success Rate	**100**	99.48	100	89.69

the proposed method outperforms the others, specially for those cases where the first compression factor is greater than the second, i.e. $QF_1 > QF_2$.

Existing literature proves that it is challenging to detect the tampered regions when $QF1 > QF2$, as the image behaves more like a single compressed image in this case. In terms of Accuracy, we find that the proposed method performs better than the state–of–the–art techniques, especially when $QF1 > QF2$. This is because, CNNs help to preserve the spatial structured features, and efficiently learn the statistical patterns of JPEG coefficient distribution, hence improving the detection accuracy.

In terms of F–measure, we can observe that the proposed method outperforms the state–of–the–art techniques in most cases even when the forgery size is 10%. It is evident from Tables 1, 2, and 3, that the F–measure results fall, as the forgery size increases.

Also, the proposed method achieves higher Success Rate of Localization, for forgery sizes of 10%, 30% and 50%, specially when $QF_1 > QF_2$. The thresholding on F–measure (in Sect. 4.2) indicates that we consider the successful cases, where 66.66% of the tampered region is correctly located.

Performance with Varying Quality Factors. In Tables 4, 5, and 6, we present the performance evaluation results of the proposed method, with different QF_1 and QF_2 values, specifically, for varying $QF_2 - QF_1$. The evaluation parameters used are the same as above. The results presented in Tables 4, 5, and 6, are the averages over different compression factors, producing a certain $QF_2 - QF_1$ value.

The results are also presented in form of 2D plots in Figs. 6, 7, and 8, for Accuracy, F–measure and Success Rate of Localization, respectively. The above plots are drawn, considering the average of 10%, 30% and 50% forgery sizes (of the entire image). The negative values on the left of the graphs, represent the cases where $QF_1 > QF2$ and the positive values on the right, represent the cases where $QF_1 < QF_2$.

It is evident from Figs. 6, 7, and 8, that for both all three cases, viz. $QF_1 > QF_2$, $QF_1 = QF_2$ and $QF_1 < QF_2$, the proposed JPEG forgery detection technique outperforms the other state–of–the–art methods. However, it performs best in case of $QF1 > QF2$, (left side of origin in the plots); whereas for rest two cases the superiority is marginal. In such cases, the accuracy can be improved further, by considering more (>7) number of blocks in the proposed method. (In this work we have considered only seven neighbouring blocks as described in Sect. 3.1.) But this also increases the training complexity parallely. Our finding is that, seven neighbouring blocks consideration, helps to attain a trade–off between performance efficiency and computational complexity.

5   Conclusion

In this paper, we propose a method to detect re–compression based JPEG image forgery, using deep neural network. We detect the presence of tampering in a JPEG, as well as locate the tampered region(s), based on a proposed CNN model, which is trained with the features of single compressed and double compressed image blocks. The inherent capability of automatic feature learning in deep CNNs, help us to achieve superior performance as compared to the state–of–the–art. Finally, the proposed CNN performs block–wise forgery prediction, for which we have considered nineteen DCT coefficients (second to twentieth in zig–zag order) from each block.

Our experimental results are encouraging and prove that the proposed techniques achieves considerably high forgery detection and localization efficiency, as compared to the state–of–the–art, especially when the first compression ration is greater than the second.

Future research in this direction would involve investigation of triple and higher degrees of JPEG compression based forgeries.

Acknowledgement. This work is partially funded by Board of Research in Nuclear Sciences (BRNS), Department of Atomic Energy (DAE), Govt. of India, Grant No. 34/20/22/2016-BRNS/34363, dated: 16/11/2016.

References

1. Conotter, V.: Active and passive multimedia forensics. Ph.D. thesis, University of Trento (2011)
2. Pennebaker, W.B., Mitchell, J.L.: JPEG: Still Image Data Compression Standard. Springer, Berlin (1992)
3. Birajdar, G.K., Mankar, V.H.: Digital image forgery detection using passive techniques: a survey. Digit. Investig. **10**(3), 226–245 (2013)
4. Wang, W., Dong, J., Tan, T.: Exploring DCT coefficient quantization effects for local tampering detection. IEEE Trans. Inf. Forensics Secur. **9**(10), 1653–1666 (2014)
5. Cozzolino, D., Poggi, G., Verdoliva, L.: Recasting residual-based local descriptors as convolutional neural networks: an application to image forgery detection. In: Proceedings of the 5th ACM Workshop on Information Hiding and Multimedia Security, pp. 159–164. ACM (2017)
6. Rao, Y., Ni, J.: A deep learning approach to detection of splicing and copy-move forgeries in images. In: IEEE International Workshop on Information Forensics and Security (WIFS), pp. 1–6, December 2016. https://doi.org/10.1109/WIFS.2016.7823911
7. Bianchi, T., De Rosa, A., Piva, A.: Improved DCT coefficient analysis for forgery localization in JPEG images. In: IEEE International Conference on Acoustics, Speech and Signal Processing (ICASSP), pp. 2444–2447. IEEE (2011)
8. Lin, Z., Wang, R., Tang, X., Shum, H.Y.: Detecting doctored images using camera response normality and consistency. In: IEEE Computer Society Conference on Computer Vision and Pattern Recognition, vol. 1, pp. 1087–1092. IEEE (2005)
9. Popescu, A., Farid, H.: Exposing digital forgeries by detecting duplicated image regions. Technology report TR2004-515, Department Computer Science, Dartmouth College (2004)
10. Lukáš, J., Fridrich, J., Goljan, M.: Detecting digital image forgeries using sensor pattern noise. In: Electronic Imaging 2006, p. 60720Y. International Society for Optics and Photonics (2006)
11. Fu, D., Shi, Y.Q., Su, W.: A generalized Benford's law for JPEG coefficients and its applications in image forensics. In: Security, Steganography, and Watermarking of Multimedia Contents IX, vol. 6505, p. 65051L. International Society for Optics and Photonics (2007)
12. Li, W., Yuan, Y., Yu, N.: Detecting copy-paste forgery of JPEG image via block artifact grid extraction. In: International Workshop on Local and Non-Local Approximation in Image Processing, pp. 1–6 (2008)
13. Mahdian, B., Saic, S.: Detecting double compressed JPEG images. In: 3rd International Conference on Crime Detection and Prevention (ICDP 2009), pp. 1–6. IET (2009)

14. Malviya, P., Naskar, R.: Digital forensic technique for double compression based JPEG image forgery detection. In: Prakash, A., Shyamasundar, R. (eds.) ICISS 2014. LNCS, vol. 8880, pp. 437–447. Springer, Cham (2014). https://doi.org/10.1007/978-3-319-13841-1_25
15. Fridrich, A.J., Soukal, B.D., Lukáš, A.J.: Detection of copy-move forgery in digital images. In: Proceedings of Digital Forensic Research Workshop. Citeseer (2003)
16. Gopi, E., Lakshmanan, N., Gokul, T., KumaraGanesh, S., et al.: Digital image forgery detection using artificial neural network and auto regressive coefficients. In: Canadian Conference on Electrical and Computer Engineering, (CCECE 2006), pp. 194–197. IEEE (2006)
17. Bayar, B., Stamm, M.C.: A deep learning approach to universal image manipulation detection using a new convolutional layer. In: Proceedings of the 4th ACM Workshop on Information Hiding and Multimedia Security, pp. 5–10. ACM (2016)
18. Barni, M., et al.: Aligned and non-aligned double JPEG detection using convolutional neural networks. J. Vis. Commun. Image Represent. **49**, 153–163 (2017)
19. Schaefer, G., Stich, M.: UCID: an uncompressed color image database. In: Storage and Retrieval Methods and Applications for Multimedia, vol. 5307, pp. 472–481. International Society for Optics and Photonics (2003)
20. Krizhevsky, A., Sutskever, I., Hinton, G.E.: Imagenet classification with deep convolutional neural networks. In: Advances in Neural Information Processing Systems, pp. 1097–1105 (2012)

Privacy

SeDiCom: A Secure Distributed Privacy-Preserving Communication Platform

Alexander Marsalek[1,2(✉)], Bernd Prünster[2], Bojan Suzic[2],
and Thomas Zefferer[3]

[1] Secure Information Technology Center Austria, Graz, Austria
`Alexander.Marsalek@iaik.tugraz.at`
[2] Graz University of Technology, IAIK, Graz, Austria
`{BPruenster,BSuzic}@iaik.tugraz.at`
[3] A-SIT Plus GmbH, Vienna, Austria
`Thomas.Zefferer@a-sit.at`

Abstract. Efficient and secure electronic communication is crucial for successful business-to-business processes. Due to the weaknesses of e-mail communication, a shift towards instant messaging can also be observed in this context. However, reliance on instant-messaging solutions in business processes has its own drawbacks such as the lack of archiving capabilities and unsatisfactory legal compliance. Furthermore, special business scenarios such as bidding processes come with complex security requirements that are not met by current instant-messaging solutions. To also enable efficient and secure electronic communication for these scenarios, we propose a blockchain-based instant-messaging solution under the name SeDiCom. SeDiCom employs the capabilities of the blockchain technology, one-time identities, and the Tor anonymity network to enable confidential instant messaging without leaking any identifying metadata. Our proposed solution provides non-repudiation, censorship resistance, integrated backup facilities, and verifiable notices of receipt, while inherently preventing man-in-the-middle attacks and virtually all other forms of eavesdropping. By this means, SeDiCom enables efficient and secure electronic communication for business scenarios with special security requirements while also catering to today's usage patterns.

Keywords: Blockchain · Messenger · Decentralized
Secure data exchange · Censorship-resistant · Non-repudiation
Privacy preserving

1 Introduction

During the past decades, many workflows and a significant amount of written communication have been migrated from pen-and-paper procedures to e-mail. While person-to-person communication is today typically carried out using

© Springer Nature Switzerland AG 2018
V. Ganapathy et al. (Eds.): ICISS 2018, LNCS 11281, pp. 345–363, 2018.
https://doi.org/10.1007/978-3-030-05171-6_18

instant messengers, with *WhatsApp* having reached over a billion active users [1], business workflows still rely heavily on e-mail. SMTP, the protocol e-mail delivery is based on, was, never designed with confidentiality and authenticity in mind, however, even though it is still heavily used to transport confidential information. In the more recent past, however, this has also begun to change in favor of instant messaging systems. Popular platforms like *Apple's iMessage*[1], *WhatsApp*[2] and *Viber*[3] have recognized the demand for secure and confidential communication and provide (end-to-end) encrypted communication [2–4]. Recently, the need to integrate such messaging solutions into business processes has also been identified [5–7].

Relying on instant messaging in a business context instead of e-mail has its own drawbacks, such as the lack of archiving facilities and increased difficulties when it comes to legal compliance [8,9]. Moreover, certain business processes are subject to specific and complex constraints: Aside from archiving, communication between parties must be kept secret (including metadata) while it happens. At a later point in time, however, any of the involved parties may need or wish to prove to the public not only that a communication took place but also when and about what. Examples include certain bidding processes or tender offers. In such cases, none of the parties involved must be able to repudiate or refute any past statements. More than end-to-end encrypted messaging is required to reach these goals, as encrypting traffic does not prevent third parties from learning about users' communication habits [3,10]. As long as detailed, unaltered metadata of electronic conversations is available, profound conclusions about communicating parties and even the contents of a conversation can be drawn, which enables profiling [11,12] and can serve as a basis for critical decisions [13].

Although increasingly more solutions for encrypted online communication exist [2,14,15], virtually all of them still leak metadata [3]. The factors contributing to this drawback can be traced back to the underlying architecture, centralized designs and the reliance on a single authority. Furthermore, the mechanisms used for key management and the reliance on stable identities of the parties involved may affect the security and privacy of users in numerous ways. In this work, we propose a blockchain-based [16] communication service which not only offers end-to-end encryption, but also guarantees untraceability of all communication. Moreover, our approach inherently supports unforgeable identities, virtually eliminating the risk of man-in-the-middle attacks. Users can therefore be sure about whoever they are communicating with at any time. Our platform also proves whether a particular message has been delivered and read. By relying on the blockchain technology, our design also guarantees immutability of all message contents, non-repudiation and censorship resistance. Essentially, only the parties involved in a conversation know who communicates with whom and about what, moreover nobody can later dispute any statements previously made. Our design is therefore well-suited for transmitting any form of confidential infor-

---

[1]   https://support.apple.com/explore/messages.
[2]   https://www.whatsapp.com/.
[3]   https://www.viber.com/.

mation which might require a notice of receipt and non-repudiation, such as registered electronic mail or legal documents like contracts, for example. While our proposed solution has several advantages, it also comes with some limitations rooted in its blockchain underpinnings such as every participant receiving all (encrypted) messages. However for our envisioned use-cases these drawbacks do not pose an issue.

Our novel approach of relying on one-time addresses, a well-defined address schedule and incorporating the *Tor* [17] anonymity network prevents any and all leaks of conversation metadata. The only detail observable from outside a conversation is the fact that someone is sending something into a blockchain-based network. Due to the nature of blockchain-based systems, it is not even possible to deduce whether someone is receiving any messages at all. At the same time, the most prominent scalability issues associated with blockchain-based designs do not apply, as explained in Sect. 3. To the best of our knowledge, no existing system offers such extensive privacy-preserving mechanisms.

The remainder of this paper is structured as follows. In the next section, we discuss related work and provide the necessary background information. Section 3 presents the architecture of SeDiCom in detail, followed by a performance evaluation in Sect. 4 and an extensive security evaluation in Sect. 5. Finally, we conclude this paper in Sect. 6 and provide an outlook.

2   Background and Related Work

Since we are presenting a blockchain-based communication platform providing an extensive set of security and privacy properties, we first provide some basic background on distributed ledger technologies commonly referred to as blockchain. The blockchain was developed by someone under the pseudonym Satoshi Nakamoto as the decentralized ledger for the cryptocurrency Bitcoin [16] and consists of a list of cryptographically linked blocks. Each block includes the fingerprint of the previous block and a list of transactions. Consensus algorithms are used to agree on which chain of blocks is considered valid. Bitcoin uses a proof-of-work (PoW) consensus algorithm: Network nodes, which want to create new blocks, so-called *miners*, have to solve a cryptographic task (mining). The first one solving the task can create a new block and receives a specified quantity of Bitcoin units as a reward. An attacker willing to delete or modify a block has to redo all the work done by the remaining (honest) network as the network always uses the chain with the highest combined PoW. Later incarnations of blockchain-based systems like *Ethereum* (testnet) [18] do not require computationally intensive tasks to process transactions, but rely on other concepts like proof-of-authority (PoA) as implemented by the *Clique* [19] algorithm. Regardless of the underlying consensus mechanism, a blockchain provides a tamper-proof, trackable, fault-tolerant, DDoS-resistant, censorship-resistant, distributed public ledger, as long as more than half the network's computation power[4] is controlled by honest nodes.

---

[4] In case of a proof-of-work based blockchain.

The advantages of blockchain-based data storage combined with encrypted communication are employed by several privacy-preserving messaging platforms. Systems like the *VooMessenger*[5] or closed-source products like *Echo*[6], *Blokcom*[7] by *Reply S.p.A.*[8] and *CrypViser* [15] are examples for such platforms.

However, all of the above described properties, which are a blockchain-based system's greatest strength can also turn into its greatest weakness from a privacy point of view: When using a blockchain-based system to exchange confidential information, it presents various short-term advantages like tamper-resistance and fault-tolerance. In the long run, however, this can backfire. Considering that all messages ever transmitted using such a system are persistently stored inside a single highly replicated database, which is accessible from anywhere on the Internet, a single flaw in the encryption mechanism can lead to massive data breaches in the future. From this point of view, the utility of blockchain-based messaging platforms for increasing privacy has to be classified as questionable. However, some use cases remain where this is not an issue.

Our system caters to such scenarios where confidentiality (of contents and meta data) is paramount at first, but communication contents are usually divulged at a later point in time. We achieve this by building on the solid foundation of the blockchain and augmenting it to provide extensive guarantees wrt. privacy, non-repudiation, integrity, and availability.

More traditional messaging systems, but also various other blockchain-based messengers, are inherently incapable of achieving these goals due to their architecture [2,14,15].

In the next section we will introduce our proposed solution.

3   SeDiCom

We propose a messaging platform which enables secure and private communication over the Internet without leaking metadata. After all, metadata can be sufficient to severely endanger users' privacy [10–13,20]. Based on the properties of typical messaging solutions and our goals, we can derived the following requirements:

R1 Confidentiality: Only entitled entities may read messages.

R2 Message Authentication: Nobody may alter a message or forge a sender's identity (contrary to what is possible with e-mail addresses [21,22]).

R3 Metadata Protection: It must not be possible to obtain the identities of the communicating parties. At the same time, a user must be able to produce a proof of sending or receiving a message if she chooses to.

R4 Decentralization: There shall be no central instance that can be attacked to obtain unencrypted messages or cryptographic material to decrypt messages. No instance shall be able to collect user-related data, like messages, or metadata.

---

[5] https://faizod.com/blockchain-solutions/business/voomessenger/.

[6] https://my-echo.com/.

[7] http://www.reply.com/en/content/blokcom.

[8] https://reply.com/.

R5 Proof of Existence: The sending time of a message must be provable.

R6 Notice of Receipt: Notices of receipt shall be produced and transmitted automatically entailing a proof of existence (POE).

R7 High Availability, Redundancy: Messages have to be replicated to gain a failure-resistant system. The system should be resistant to denial-of-service (DoS) attacks.

R8 Non-Repudiation: Authors shall not be able to successfully challenge the authorship of a message.

R9 Immutability: Once a message has been sent, it must not be possible to manipulate (e.g. modify or remove) it in any way.

R10 Censorship Resistance: It shall not be possible to block individuals from using the service.

Notably, scalability is not listed as a requirement. The reasons for this apparent lack of an elementary requirement for applications as targeted by our design are threefold: First, current-generation blockchain designs do not suffer from as many scalability issues as Bitcoin. Second, the targeted use case of our design imposes fewer and weaker constraints compared to WhatsApp, for example: Bidding processes and tender offers typically do not require the exchange of millions of messages in a short time frame and the number of participants is typically also lower. Finally, our work focuses on security and privacy and achieves its goals by building upon guarantees provided by blockchain designs (as described in the following section). Advancements made wrt. blockchain scalability thus directly benefits our solution. We therefore expect performance to improve over time.

Our solution proposed in this section meets all identified requirements. We discuss the architecture of this solution in the following section.

3.1 Architecture

Considering the requirements identified in Sect. 3, we have derived a suitable architecture for our secure distributed communication platform, called SeDi-Com. We use a blockchain [16] as the central component. The blockchain provides a highly available, highly redundant, censorship-resistant network communication and storage system, the content of which cannot easily be modified or erased. Figure 1 shows the high-level architecture of our proposed solution. It shows an arbitrary number of clients (nodes) running our software. These clients are connected via the Tor network (visualized as onions) and create a P2P network that maintains and distributes a blockchain. We use transactions to transfer information in this P2P network. These transactions are broadcast through the network. Each transaction contains at least one sender address (input) and one receiver address (output) and is thus ideal for sending content to one or more participants. As every participant can generate addresses on their own and there is no binding to an identity, users remain anonymous. Once a transaction is mined into a block, which is accepted by the network, it can be considered immutable. Therefore, the blockchain provides a highly available, decentralized backup system. The creation time of a block can be used as POE for all included transactions. The sender and receiver addresses are representations of the corresponding public part of the public-private key-pairs. By using the public key of the collocutor, it is possible to encrypt messages. These messages can only be decrypted by the owner of the corresponding private key. Using the private key, it is possible to sign messages and therefore prove key ownership and implicitly prove identity. For the rest of this paper, we will refer to these public-private key pairs as identities. We propose a protocol, where every participant creates a main identity and several one-time identities. The main identity is only used for identity proofs. It will never be used to send or receive messages. Instead, one-time identities are used to send and receive messages. In the next section, we describe a typical process flow between two collocutors.

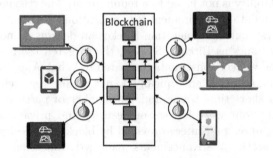

Fig. 1. Proposed solution architecture.

3.2   Generic Process Flow

In this section, we describe a typical process flow between two collocutors who want to securely communicate with each other. The sequence of actions is visualized in Figure 2 for two users, namely Alice and Bob. Initially, both parties create their main identity ID_{AB} and ID_{BA} (1-2). Every identity ID_{XY} consists of a private key ID_{XY}^- and a public key ID_{XY}^+. X denotes the owner of the key, and Y the collocutor. Knowing the public key is equivalent to knowing the corresponding address. Depending on their needs, participants can choose to create several main identities, e.g., one per collocutor. For the protocol it is only important that the same main identity is used for the same collocutor. Otherwise, it would not be possible to verify the message sender's authenticity. The main identity is never used to send or receive transactions, it will only be used to sign messages encoded into transactions. Next, both parties create a one-time send ($IDES_{AB1}$, $IDES_{BA1}$) and receive identity ($IDER_{AB1}$, $IDER_{BA1}$) (3-4) for sending and receiving transactions. These identities will be created for every collocutor individually. Next, the public keys of the main identities ID_{AB}^+, ID_{BA}^+ and the public key (address) of the receiving identity of Bob $IDER_{BA1}^+$

have to be exchanged over an authenticated channel (5), e.g. by digitally signing them using a qualified electronic signature and exchanging the result electronically or by meeting somewhere in person. $IDER$ denotes a one-time, ephemeral identity that is used to receive messages, whereas $IDES$ represents a one-time identity that is used to send messages. The information exchanged in Step 5 is not secret, it is only used to authenticate the other party and to communicate details on how to reach the other party. After the exchange, Alice has all necessary information to communicate securely and anonymously with Bob. Next, Alice sends a message m to Bob and prepends her receiving address $IDER^+_{AB1}$ to the message. The resulting message is signed using Alice's main identity key ID^-_{AB} to prove that the message was indeed sent by her and then signed with $IDES^-_{AB1}$, to prevent replay attacks. From now on we refer to the first signature as inner signature and to the second signature as outer signature. The resulting message is shown in Eq. 1. Note that $Sign(m)$ returns m and the signature over the fingerprint of m.

$$m_{Signed} = \text{Sign}_{IDES^-_{AB1}}(\text{Sign}_{ID^-_{AB}}(IDER^+_{AB1}\|m)) \tag{1}$$

As the message will be sent over the P2P-network, the next step is to encrypt the message, thus preventing unauthorized parties from eavesdropping on it. Next, a shared key is derived using the Diffie–Hellmann key agreement protocol. Both

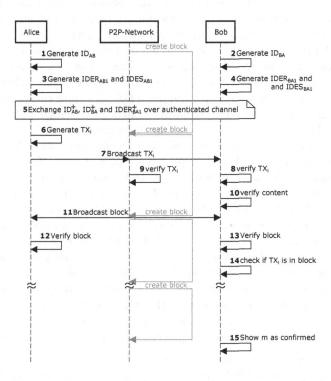

Fig. 2. Exchange of the first message between two parties.

parties can derive the same shared key using their private key and the public key of the collocutor as shown in Eq. 2.

$$SharedSecret = \text{ECDH}(IDES^-_{AB1}, IDER^+_{BA1})$$
$$= \text{ECDH}(IDER^-_{BA1}, IDES^+_{AB1}) \tag{2}$$

Next, the shared secret is hashed using SHA-256 and the resulting fingerprint is used as key for an symmetric cipher as shown in Eqs. 3 and 4.

$$K_{Msg} = \text{SHA-256}(SharedSecret) \tag{3}$$

$$C_{Msg} = \text{E}_{K_{Msg}, IV}(m_{Signed}) \tag{4}$$

Note that neither of the parties has to store the key K_{Msg}. Next, the encrypted message C_{Msg} together with information needed to decrypt the message (depending on the cipher and the chaining mode; e.g. an IV) are packed into a container C as shown in Eq. 5.

$$C = IV||C_{Msg} \tag{5}$$

Next, a new transaction is created, with $IDES^+_{AB1}$ as sender and $IDER^+_{BA1}$ as receiver. This container C is encoded into the transaction's data field. Finally, the transaction will be signed with $IDES^-_{AB1}$ to gain a valid transaction TX_i (6) and broadcast to the network (7). As the transaction is sent from a one-time identity to another one-time identity, no conclusions can be drawn about who communicates with whom. Shortly after sending a message, Bob and other nodes in the network will receive the transaction TX_i and verify it (8-9). Mining nodes will save valid transactions and include them into the next block. Bob will check if the transaction is addressed to him by checking if the receiver address of the transaction matches one of his active ones. If it matches, Bob will decrypt the content using his corresponding private key $IDER^-_{BA1}$ and subsequently verify the outer signature. If the outer signature matches the sender's identity of the transaction, Bob continues to verify the inner signature.

As every receiving address is created for a specific collocutor, Bob can verify whether the signature matches the expected sender's identity. If one of the signatures does not match the expected identity, Bob aborts the process. If the inner signature confirms the expected identity, Bob separates the content m and the reply address $IDER^+_{AB1}$ (10). The reply address $IDER^+_{AB1}$ will be stored for later use and the content m will be shown as *unconfirmed message*. Unconfirmed means that the message is not yet included in a block, thus not all properties (like high availability, for example) hold yet. After the transaction is included in a block by a miner, the block will be broadcast to all network participants (11). Every participant will verify whether the block is valid (12-13). If the block is valid, meaning all transactions are valid and it references the previous valid block, Bob verifies whether TX_i is included (14). To be sure, he will wait until the block's maturity depth[9] is equal or greater than a selected threshold. If the

---

[9] As an example, Bitcoin wallets typically require a maturity depth of six blocks. Meaning six additional blocks need to be created after the block containing the corresponding transaction.

block's maturity depth requirement is fulfilled, the message will be shown to the user as *confirmed message* (15).

If Bob wants to reply to Alice, he generates a new one-time send and receive identity ($IDES_{BA2}$ and $IDER_{BA2}$) and repeats Steps 6 and 7 with opposite roles. Bob will use the saved reply address, extracted from TX_i as target address for his generated transaction. This reply message is simultaneously a proof for Alice that Bob has received the previous message. If one party wants to send another message before a reply is received from the other party, the last receiving identity of the collocutor is used again, but a new sending and receiving identity is created each time, to prevent anyone from concluding anything from it. The new receiving identities are necessary for the read confirmation requirement. Once the other party answers, she will reply to the last received reply address and append all other unused reply addresses to the message. One's one-time identities do not need to be remembered, they can always be derived from the main identity. It is only necessary to remember the number of already used one-time identities. For performance reasons, it makes sense to also remember the unused reply addresses submitted by each collocutor and the unused reply addresses submitted to collocutors.

3.3 Security Features

The blockchain already provides several features, like decentralization, proof of existence high availability, and redundancy. This section highlights two security features of our proposed solution, namely the address schedule used to generate one-time identities, and the proof of receipt feature.

Address Schedule. We describe the process of deriving one-time identities from the main identity. A key requirement for the derivation process is that individual one-time identities can be published without disclosing any information about other identities. We derive our one-time identities based on Eq. 6, where ID_{YZ} is the main identity of user Y used for communicating with user Z. X defines the type of identity (send or receive) to create, i is an integer that is increased every time a new one-time identity of this type is created, H(...) denotes a cryptographic hash function and genKeyPair(...) generates an EC key pair.

$$IDEX_{YZi} = \text{genKeyPair}(\text{H}(ID_{YZ}^- + \text{H}(i||Z||X))) \qquad (6)$$

The security of one-time identities is based on the one-way characteristic (preimage resistance) of the hash function.

Proof - Message Sent/Received. If a party wants to prove that a message was sent by the other party, it needs to publish the corresponding receiving identity. Using this identity, everyone can extract the corresponding transaction from the blockchain and decrypt it. The inner signature of the decrypted content will match the main identity of the other party and thus prove that she signed it.

If Party A wants to prove that she sent a message to B, she has to publish the corresponding sending identity and the receiving identity, on which she received the reply address. Using the sending identity, everyone can extract the corresponding transaction from the blockchain and decrypt it. Thus, it can be shown, that the message was sent and signed by party A. Next, it must be proven that the address the transaction was sent to belongs to Party B. This can be done by publishing the receiving identity on which the reply address from B has been received. The corresponding decrypted message will be signed by Party B and contain the used reply address.

3.4 Implementation

We built a proof-of-concept implementation of the proposed solution based on the Ethereum [18] blockchain. Our implementation relies on Clique [19], instead of a PoW consensus algorithm to improve performance. Furthermore, we reduced the block interval to one minute, to reduce the time until a transaction is included in a block. This also increases the throughput of our solution in terms of messages per time interval[10]. These adjustments remedy virtually all scalability concerns typically associated with blockchain-based systems. We modified our Ethereum implementation, enabling sending transactions for free. Otherwise, every one-time identity would need a balance to pay the fees. This step was necessary, as we currently have no way to send a balance to one-time identities from another identity without leaving metadata, such as which identities belong together. This procedure removes one of Ethereums' main protection mechanisms against attacks that wastes the power of the network or endangers network stability, e.g., endless-loops in smart contracts. We deal with this issue by deactivating Ethereums' smart contract functionality[11]. While this prevents many attacks, spamming the network with useless, but valid, transactions is still possible. These messages will not be shown to the user, but waste space in blocks. We plan to deal with this issue in future work and describe a possible approach in Sect. 6. We implemented our prototype in Java, using the web3j[12] library as connector to a modified version of Geth[13], an Ethereum node implementation written in Go. Our Java application communicates with Geth via JSON-RPC. For simplicity, we tested our approach with a single miner. The implementation demonstrates the feasibility of the proposed solution, which is platform-independent and lightweight enough to be used on desktop systems as well as mobile systems like smartphones.

Ethereum uses the Elliptic Curve SECP-256k1 [23] to generate EC keys for transaction signing. Our proposed one-time identities also rely on this curve. As a consequence, we can use the Elliptic-curve Diffie–Hellmann (ECDH) key

---

[10] Ethereum does not define a maximum block size in contrast to e.g. Bitcoin.
[11] Transactions related to the creation of a smart contracts are ignored and not included into a block.
[12] https://github.com/web3j/web3j.
[13] https://geth.ethereum.org/.

agreement protocol to derive a shared key. This enables the sender and receiver of a transaction to independently calculate a shared secret based on one's private key and the collocutor's public key. Next, the shared secret is hashed using SHA-256 and the resulting fingerprint is used as the key for an AES cipher in counter mode without padding. For the cipher we generate a random initialization vector (IV), which is prepended to the encrypted message C_{Msg}. No other external information, (not available in the transaction) is needed to decrypt the message. Next, we discuss the performance of the proposed solution.

4   Performance Evaluation

This section provides a short overview of the performance impact in terms of size and speed overhead. Note that we did not consider the blockchain performance, as it is independent of our proposed protocol. Instead, we focus on the overhead in size imposed by our protocol and show that the necessary signing, verification, encryption, and decryption steps have no practical consequences in terms of performance.

4.1   Required Overhead

Figure 3 shows the size overhead of the proposed solution for different message lengths, compared to encoding the messages directly into transactions without one-time identities and without signing and encrypting them. As can be seen, the overhead is mainly noticeable for smaller input message sizes since our solution produces a constant overhead independent of the input. In detail, our proposed solution requires 42 bytes for submitting the new receiving address, 65 bytes each for the inner and outer signature, as well as 16 bytes for the IV. This results in 188 bytes overhead. Finally, the payload has to be hex-encoded, which doubles the size. To summarize, our proposed solution produces a per-message overhead of $188 \times 2 = 376$ bytes. Next we discuss the throughput.

4.2   Throughput

We measured how many messages per second can be created and how many received messages per second can be verified. We executed the performance test on a MacBook Air with an Intel Core i7-4650U CPU running at 1.7 GHz using an unoptimized single threaded Java program. The test consists of first signing and encrypting 10,000 messages and then decrypting and verifying 10,000 messages. Based on the time required we calculate the number of messages that can be created and verified every second. We repeated the experiment with different message sizes, namely 1 byte, 1024 bytes, 8192 bytes and 16384 bytes. Note: The test was performed without actually sending the messages, thus ignoring the performance of the Ethereum network. Table 1 shows the results.

The results show that our proposed solution has a small overhead and an minor impact on the performance and is thus well suited for its intended use-cases. Note that the presented solution is not intended to replace a messaging

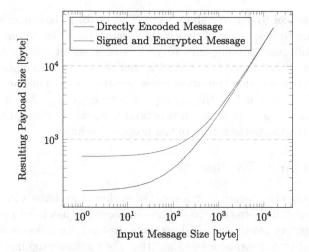

Fig. 3. Comparison of payload sizes of directly encoded messages versus messages sent by the proposed solution. Note the logarithmically scaled x- and y-axes.

Table 1. Throughput of messages per second that can be generated or read for different input sizes.

Size [byte]	Throughput create [Msg/sec]	Throughput read [Msg/sec]
1	810.4	1056.6
1024	827.5	991.4
8192	682.9	833.0
16384	587.8	729.9

platform like Whatsapp. Rather, it aims at specific, but all the more critical use-cases, which require a secret communication process that is likely to be disclosed later on, e.g., a bidding process where all bidders first send their offers without leaking any data and later on the offers can be disclosed to ensure a fair procurement.

5   Security Evaluation

To verify that our proposed approach provides the proclaimed security features, we performed a security evaluation loosely based on the *Common Criteria for Information Technology Security Evaluation* (CC)[14].

We derive security goals and assets from the requirements presented in Sect. 3. Our assumptions rely on the proven security of all underlying technologies and expected secure usage of existing systems. Similarly, the security properties applied in this analysis are derived from our model presented in Sect. 3.

---

[14]   https://iso.org/standard/50341.html.

We further designate the scope of our analysis to the case that provides adequate protection against all but a highly determined attack that requires a tremendous amount of resources and effort.

After elaborating each of these categories in the subsequent sections, we conclude this chapter with the comprehensive overview of threat mitigation mechanisms.

5.1   Assets

A1 Message: Message contents are considered confidential. Only the interlocutors are eligible to read it, unless one involved party wants to publish it.

A2 Main Identity: The private keys belonging to the main identities must not be disclosed. The public part does not need to be protected.

A3 One-time Identities: Private keys of one-time identities are considered confidential until the owner decides to disclose them, e.g. to prove that they sent or received a message.

A4 Metadata: Metadata that can be used to conclude anything about the senders' or receivers' identity, is considered confidential.

5.2   Assumptions

AS1 Secure/Trusted Devices: We assume that users and miners use devices with up-to-date security updates and without malware. Thus, it can be assumed that identities can be securely created and stored on end-user devices and miners can securely use their signing key. In short, we assume that users and miners use secure and trusted systems.

AS2 Confidentiality of Private Keys: Users and miners keep their private keys secret, unless they want to prove the sending or receiving a message. In this case the corresponding one-time identity is disclosed. Note that the private key of the main identity will never be disclosed (A2).

AS3 Secure Cryptographic Primitives: We assume that cryptographic primitives like ciphers, cryptographic hash functions and signature algorithms are practically secure, meaning they cannot be broken in relevant time.

AS4 Global Adversary: We do not consider attackers that can observe or control a large portion of the Internet.

5.3   Security Goals

G1 Confidentiality: The content of the message (R1) as well as the private keys (R2) must be kept confidential (R4).

G2 Anonymity: A key requirement is that parties not involved in a conversation cannot learn anything about the participants nor about the message content itself (R3), except when one of the participants wants to disclose this information.

G3 Non-Repudiation: It is crucial that the author of a message can be identified by the receiving party (R2), and that the author cannot successfully challenge the authorship of a message (R8).

G4 Proof of Existence: The time a message was sent is crucial for certain use cases (R5). Therefore its integrity must be guaranteed.

G5 Immutability: It is important that a message can not be removed or altered after it has been sent (R9) — Neither by the sender nor by anyone else.

G6 Integrity: It must not be possible to tamper with the message or spoof its receiver and sender, without recipients detecting this (R2, R8, R9).

G7 Availability: It must be possible to send and receive messages at any time (R7). Furthermore, old messages need to be available in the network (R4).

G8 Censorship resistance: It is essential that nobody can censor messages without being detected (R9, R10).

G9 Read/Send Confirmation: The sender of a message must be able to prove that it has been sent before a specific point in time (R5). A receiver must be able to prove that she received a message from an individual sender (R8). A sender must be able to prove that a receiver has received an earlier message (R6).

G10 Authentication: The senders' identity must not be forgeable (R2).

5.4 Threats

Analyzing existing approaches and their security analysis targeting relevant problems already yields a baseline for our threat analysis [24–26]. Adapting and extending these analyses for our target domain results in the following threat analysis, also fostering the completeness of the analysis:

T1 Impersonation/Spoofing: An attacker spoofs the senders' identity to impersonate someone else, thus violating G1 and G10.

T2 Message Forgery: An attacker is forging a message, e.g. by encoding random content into transactions, or by modifying an existing transaction. This violates G3, G6, and G10.

T3 Eavesdropping: An attacker eavesdrops on the network communication to learn something, e.g., to get access to the message content or deanonymize a participant. This violates G1 and G2.

T4 Replay Attack: An attacker replays an eavesdropped transaction or extracts its data and encodes it into a new transaction. This violates G3 and G10.

T5 Man-in-the-middle Attack: An attacker actively manipulates the sent transactions or broadcasts faked transactions or blocks. This violates G1, G2, G6, G7, G9, and G10.

T6 Censorship: An attacker deletes transactions from the blockchain or does not forward them, thus violating G4, G7, G8, and G9.

T7 Deanonymization: An attacker deanonymizes a participant by analyzing metadata or by correlation, thus violating G1 and G2.

T8 Denial-of-service Attack: An attacker disrupts the service or attacks individual users, thus violating G7 and G8.

Table 2. Mapping threats to security goals.

	T1	T2	T3	T4	T5	T6	T7	T8	T9	T10	T11
G1	⊗	○	⊗	○	⊗	○	⊗	○	⊗	○	○
G2	○	⊗	⊗	○	⊗	○	⊗	○	⊗	○	○
G3	○	⊗	○	⊗	○	○	○	○	⊗	○	○
G4	○	○	○	○	○	⊗	○	○	○	○	⊗
G5	○	○	○	○	○	○	○	○	⊗	⊗	⊗
G6	○	⊗	○	○	⊗	○	○	○	⊗	⊗	
G7	○	○	○	○	⊗	⊗	○	⊗	○	⊗	⊗
G8	○	○	○	○	○	⊗	○	⊗	○	⊗	⊗
G9	○	○	○	○	⊗	⊗	○	○	○	⊗	○
G10	⊗	⊗	○	⊗	⊗	○	○	○	⊗	○	○

Table 3. Threat mitigation overview.

	T1	T2	T3	T4	T5	T6	T7	T8	T9	T10	T11
SP1	⊘	⊘	○	⊘	⊘	○	○	○	○	○	○
SP2	○	○	⊘	○	○	⊘	⊘	○	○	○	○
SP3	○	○	○	⊘	○	⊘	⊘	⊘	○	⊘	⊘
SP4	○	○	⊘	○	⊘	○	⊘	⊘	○	○	○
SP5	○	○	⊘	○	⊘	○	⊘	⊘	○	○	○
AS1	○	○	○	○	○	○	○	○	○	○	○
AS2	⊘	○	○	○	○	○	○	○	○	○	○
AS3	⊘	○	○	○	○	○	○	⊘	○	○	○
AS4	○	○	○	○	○	○	⊘	○	○	○	○

T9 Key Derivation: An attacker calculates the main identity or a different one-time identity based on a published one-time identity. This attack targets G1, G2, G3, G5, and G10.

T10 Manipulating Blocks: An attacker manipulates or deletes blocks from the blockchain with the goal of disrupting the service or deleting sent or received messages, thus violating G5, G6, G7, G8, and G9.

T11 Untrusted Miner: A miner censors transactions, includes manipulated transactions or stops mining, thus violating G4, G5, G6, G7, and G8. Table 2 visualizes the threat to security goals mapping.

5.5 System Properties

SP1 Signature: Every message and reply address is signed by the main identity. The resulting message is signed again by the one-time send identity to prevent replay attacks. Additionally, all transactions have to be signed.

SP2 Encryption: Every message is encrypted after it has been signed twice. The encryption guarantees confidentiality of the message.

SP3 Decentralization: The P2P-network provides a decentralized infrastructure that replicates the blockchain on every node and forwards transactions.

SP4 One-time Identities: Only anonymous one-time identities are used as the receiving or sending address.

SP5 Network-Layer Anonymity: All parties are connected via the Tor network to the Internet and are thus assigned an anonymous IP-address.

5.6 Threat Mitigation

Preventing T1 Impersonation/Spoofing: Spoofing an identity is prevented by SP1. An attacker has to forge a valid signature thus violating AS2 or AS3.

Preventing T2 Message Forgery: Creating a valid signature without the private key would contradict AS3. An attacker could use a published one-time identity to sign a new transaction and include the data from the published transaction. This attack creates a valid transaction, but the consequences depend on the timing of this attack. If the actual communicating parties have exchanged further messages before the attack, the attack will not have any consequences as no one will be listening to this (old) address anymore. If the published transaction belongs to the most recent exchanged message, the recipient will receive the same message twice, but it will not change any of the security guarantees of the previous message. The attacker cannot change the content of the message (SP1) and its content was already published by one of the collocutors.

Preventing T3 Eavesdropping: An attacker eavesdropping on the communication will see transactions with encrypted content (SP2) being sent from one random address to another random address (SP4). As the message is encrypted, the attacker will not learn anything about its content, except the rough size. The use of one-time identities and anonymized Tor exit-node IP-addresses (SP5) prevent insights for an attacker. An exception is a case where one party sends multiple messages in a sequence. In this case, it will be observable that someone received multiple messages, but not that they originated from the same source.

Preventing T4 Replay Attack: Replay attacks are not feasible, as the same transaction will not be included twice into a blockchain (SP3). As soon as some value of the transaction is changed, the transaction signature breaks (SP1, see T2). If the attacker were to extract the encoded data and include it into a new transaction, she would get a valid transaction, but the recipient will notice the attack as soon as she decrypts the message, as the sending identity and the outer signature of the message do not originate from the same entity (SP1). This attack can be used to unnecessarily increase the size of the blockchain.

Preventing T5 Man-in-the-Middle Attack: The success of this attack depends on where the attacker is located. If she is located directly after the exit-node of the Tor network, she could launch all sorts of attacks, like omitting transactions or blocks or sending forged transactions or blocks to the user. Furthermore, she could use her position to start denial-of-service attacks. In all cases, the user will detect that something is wrong and can simply change the exit-node or wait until it is automatically changed (SP5). Omitted transactions are noticed as soon as the following blocks are appended to the blockchain. Omitted blocks are noticed if the chain is broken (one or several blocks are missing) or if the interval where no new block was found is suspiciously large. Manipulated transactions or blocks are noticed because of the broken signature (SP1).

Preventing T6 Censorship: As the interlocutors and the message contents are not known (SP2, SP4), it is not possible to censor messages based on these attributes. An attacker could try to exclude specific IP-addresses or block the service at all. The decentralized structure of the network (SP3) makes it very hard to censor transactions. Even if one node does not distribute a transaction, other nodes will.

Preventing T7 Deanonymization: As long as the private part of the primary identity is kept confidential (AS2), no connection between one-time identities and the primary identity can be drawn (AS3, SP4). As every message is encrypted (SP2), outsiders can only see one-time identities (SP4) that do not provide any information (SP4). Furthermore, as every node receives all blocks, it is not possible to determine which client received a message (SP3). The IP-address also does not provide any insights, as all nodes are connected over the Tor network (SP5).

Preventing T8 Denial-of-Service (DoS) Attacks: If the attacker controls only some network connections, she cannot harm the network as users can switch their exit node (SP5) and all nodes will forward all valid blocks and transactions (SP3). If the attacker controls the connections of an individual user, this user can be blocked from using the service. An attacker that controls the whole network can block the service, but this attack contradicts AS4.

Preventing T9 Key Derivation: The security of the main identity and the other one-time identities relies on the pre-image resistance feature of the cryptographic hash function (AS3).

Preventing T10 Manipulating Blocks: An attacker would have to delete or manipulate the block on all nodes (SP3), otherwise the network will recover it.

Preventing T11 Untrusted Miner: This attack can be prevented by having a group of miners (SP3), where it is likely that more than half of them are honest. In our scenario, where we likely have only one miner (e.g., the company behind the call for tenders), this attack cannot be prevented, but it will be detected.

All threats except for two — an attacker who controls the Internet connection of the user and an attacker who creates spam messages — are fully mitigated by the design of the proposed solution, as summarized in Table 3.

6   Conclusions and Future Work

In this paper, we have presented a secure and privacy-preserving messaging platform that unifies and improves security and privacy-related features not currently present in any other single messaging solution. The proposed solution is especially designed and suited for business-related scenarios such as bidding processes or tender offers, where data confidentiality is paramount at first, but communication contents are to be divulged at a later point in time. By relying on an adapted Ethereum blockchain and the Clique consensus algorithm, our design scales even beyond the requirements of the targeted use case, since none of the scalability issues typically associated with blockchain-based systems apply. Moreover, advancements made wrt. blockchain scalability also benefit our solution. We therefore expect performance to improve over time.

Our platform relies on two privacy-enhancing pillars which prevent user-profiling, hinder censorship and ensure unlinkable anonymous identities. First, we replace the common centralized service architecture with a distributed architecture based on a blockchain and the Tor network. This allows us to counter a range of issues related to metadata surveillance, eavesdropping, censorship, and control. Second, we separate identities of the parties involved into ephemeral and hidden components, which are derived and associated using a novel address schedule that guarantees their unlinkability for external observers. Using this scheme, all encrypted communication in the network can be traced to the level of ephemeral identities only, which are typically employed only once. When desired, message contents can be published later, including universally verifiable proofs regarding contents and correspondents

We identify two general aspects for further development of our platform. In future work, we first plan to improve platform reliability against spamming and flooding attacks by charging a small amount of currency for every transaction. We also plan to decrease the storage requirements for clients, by allowing them to store only information relevant to them, without losing any security guarantees.

References

1. WhatsApp. One Billion, 1 February 2016. https://blog.whatsapp.com/616/One-billion. Accessed 19 Apr 2017
2. Fiadino, P., Schiavone, M., Casas, P.: Vivisecting WhatsApp in cellular networks: servers, flows, and quality of experience. In: Steiner, M., Barlet-Ros, P., Bonaventure, O. (eds.) TMA 2015. LNCS, vol. 9053, pp. 49–63. Springer, Cham (2015). https://doi.org/10.1007/978-3-319-17172-2_4
3. Coull, S.E., Dyer, K.P.: Traffic analysis of encrypted messaging services: Apple imessage and beyond. ACM SIGCOMM Comput. Commun. Rev. **44**(5), 5–11 (2014)
4. Azfar, A., Choo, K.K.R., Liu, L.: A study of ten popular android mobile voip applications: are the communications encrypted? In: 2014 HICSS-47, pp. 4858-4867 (2014). https://doi.org/10.1109/HICSS.2014.596
5. cnet.com: Instant messaging latest trend in e-commerce software (2009). https://www.cnet.com/news/instant-messaging-latest-trend-in-e-commerce-software/
6. Lawton, G.: Instant messaging puts on a business suit. Computer **36**(3), 14–16 (2003)
7. Doyle, S.: Is instant messaging going to replace SMS and e-mail as the medium of choice for direct customer communications? J. Datab. Mark. Customer Strategy Manag. **11**, 17–182 (2003)
8. Cameron, A.F., Webster, J.: Unintended consequences of emerging communication technologies: instant messaging in the workplace. Comput. Hum. Behav. **21**(1), 85–103 (2005). ISSN 0747–5632
9. Gann, R.: Instant messaging for business (2012). https://www.techradar.com/news/world-of-tech/roundup/instant-messaging-for-business-1075434
10. Schneier, B.: NSA doesn't need to spy on your calls to learn your secrets. Wired (2015)
11. Mayer, J., Mutchler, P., Mitchell, J.C.: Evaluating the privacy properties of telephone metadata. Proc. Nat. Acad. Sci. **113**(20), 5536–5541 (2016). https://doi.org/10.1073/pnas.1508081113

12. Schneier, B.: Metadata = surveillance. IEEE Secur. Priv. **12**(2), 84–84 (2014). https://doi.org/10.1109/MSP.2014.28. ISSN 1540-7993
13. Cole, D.: We kill people based on metadata. N. Y. Rev. Books **10**, 2014 (2014)
14. Goldberg, I., OTR Development Team: Off-the record messaging protocol version 3, 6 January 2016. https://otr.cypherpunks.ca/Protocol-v3-4.0.0.html. Accessed 16 Mar 2017
15. Crypviser GmbH: Crypviser - the most secure solution ever (whitepaper), May 2017. https://ico.crypviser.net/static/docs/CrypViserWhitepaper_en.pdf. Accessed 05 Sept 2017
16. Nakamoto, S.: Bitcoin: a peer-to-peer electronic cash system (2008). eprint: https://bitcoin.org/bitcoin.pdf
17. Dingledine, R., Mathewson, N., Syverson, P.: Tor: the second-generation onion router. In: Proceedings of the 13th USENIX Security Symposium, San Diego, CA, USA, August 2004
18. Buterin, V., et al.: Ethereum white paper (2013). https://github.com/ethereum/wiki/wiki/White-Paper
19. Szilávi, P.: Clique PoA protocol & Rinkeby PoA testnet #225 (2017). https://github.com/ethereum/EIPs/issues/225
20. Greenwald, G.: NSA collecting phone records of millions of Verizon customers daily. The Guardian **6**(5), 13 (2013)
21. Lyon, J., Wong, M.: Sender id: Authenticating e-mail. RFC Editor, RFC 4406, April 2006
22. Carnegie Mellon University: CERT Division: Spoofed/forged email, September 2017. http://cert.org/historical/tech_tips/email_spoofing.cfm. Accessed 05 Sept 2017
23. Brown, D.R.L.: Standards for Efficient Cryptography 2 (SEC 2), January 2010. http://www.secg.org/sec2-v2.pdf. Accessed 27 July 2018
24. Petrlic, R., Sorge, C.: Instant messaging. Datenschutz, pp. 97–108. Springer, Wiesbaden (2017). https://doi.org/10.1007/978-3-658-16839-1_8
25. Schrittwieser, S., et al.: Guess who's texting you. Evaluating the Security of Smartphone Messaging Applications, SBA Research gGmbH (2012)
26. Cohn-Gordon, K., Cremers, C., Dowling, B., Garratt, L., Stebila, D.: A formal security analysis of the signal messaging protocol. In: 2017 IEEE EuroS&P, April 2017, pp. 451–466. https://doi.org/10.1109/EuroSP.2017.27

Efficacy of GDPR's Right-to-be-Forgotten on Facebook

Vishwas T. Patil[✉] and R. K. Shyamasundar

Information Security R&D Center,
Department of Computer Science and Engineering,
Indian Institute of Technology Bombay, Mumbai 400076, India
ivishwas@gmail.com, shyamasundar@gmail.com

Abstract. Online social networks (OSNs) like Facebook witness our online activities either by our consent or by bartering our desire to avail free services. Being a witness, OSNs have access to users' personal data, their social relationships and a continuous flow of their online interactions from various tracking techniques the OSNs deploy in collaboration with the content providers across the Internet. Users' behavioral data critical in predicting their interests, which is not only useful in targeting the users with relevant advertisements but also in clustering them into distinct personality traits that are useful in effective persuasion. Realizing the potential privacy implications of such a collection and usage of personally identifiable data and its potential misuse, the European Union has enacted a law, referred to as GDPR, to regulate the way collection and processing of personal data occurs. One of the core tenets of this regulation is the *right-to-be-forgotten*. In this paper, we analyze the efficacy of this tenet and the challenges when it is invoked by users on online social networks like Facebook. We investigate the reasons behind these challenges and associate their causes to the nature of the communication on social networks in general, the business model of such social platforms, and the design of the platform itself; say for Facebook. In short, in its current form, if the right-to-be-forgotten tenet of GDPR is to be enforced in its *spirit*, it will jeopardize Facebook's business model.

Keywords: Online social network · Privacy · Linkability
Inverse privacy · GDPR

1 Introduction

In the current information age, data is touted as Gold and there is enough evidence (proof) that many of the online services that we use today are found to be coercing users to generate and share data in lieu of monetary fees for those services. Online social networks (OSNs) – a type of service that allows users to represent themselves online and interact with others on the network – is a unique class of services that monetize on the users' data by matching the users with advertisers who pay for a successful match. Therefore, precision in match-making is of paramount importance in the business model of online social networks.

© Springer Nature Switzerland AG 2018
V. Ganapathy et al. (Eds.): ICISS 2018, LNCS 11281, pp. 364–385, 2018.
https://doi.org/10.1007/978-3-030-05171-6_19

Several social networks exist, where each one of them is enticing the same user-base by promising a unique social experience along with certain ancillary services to have a captive user-base. However, the business model across all of these social networks is the same: matching their users with advertisers against a payment [7]. In fact, if two or more, social networks come together and link with each others[1], selectively, it would boost consolidation of clusters of users [9]. Advertisers are motivated to reach to a large user-base at a minimal cost with highest conversion rate (the percentage of users responding to an advertisement) possible. The competition among the OSNs to attract and retain the advertisers, with innovative methods and tools, revolves around not only on the size of the user-base but also on how well the OSNs engage the users and at the same time nudges them to share their data [16,21,26] in exchange of convenience[2] and personalization. For that matter, almost all social networks build an ecosystem of users, service providers or Apps, and advertisers, where each one of them with their intertwined objectives.

Facebook is one such online social network with more than 2 billion monthly active users (out of which 270 million are from India; highest number from any other country where Facebook is available; statista.com) and millions of Apps and advertisers present on its ecosystem. At the time of sign up, users submit their personal data and establish their identity. Users agree to the privacy policy of the platform and allow the platform to use the data they generate during their social interactions with other users, Apps, and also the off-platform interactions with services/websites that rely on Facebook for advertisement revenue. A rich trail of users' online activities and their social relationships to influence each other gives the Facebook a unique insight about its users. The personally identifiable data directly provided by the users, along with the indirectly obtained unique identifiers about the users; like device ID, location, IP address, et al., are used to build dossiers about the users. These dossiers are then compiled using well-known data models [4] in conjunction with the universal facts and knowledge-base to build user profiles. For example, users who are active in the morning and use a health App (Nike, Runtastic) to measure their physical activities are profiled as "healthy" with a high probability; since there are statistical models and empirical evidences to infer so. Such individuals can safely be correlated with healthier food choices, which the platform can reinforce if the user either reacts with healthier-food related posts/pages/events or orders food using one of the Apps associated with the platform. The inference and correlation are done without user's consent/knowledge and sometimes are validated by presenting the user an online experience tailored by Facebook's News Feed[3] algorithm.

The Apps/services/websites act as collaborators of the platform. They not only serve the user but also share the analytics (i.e., the sequence of events and actions) of user interaction with the platform. The platform continuously tracks, collects, stores, and processes user data in order to categorize them in profiles

---

[1] Data Transfer Project, https://datatransferproject.dev.

[2] The tyranny of convenience, Tim Wu, The New York Times, 16/2/2018.

[3] How News Feed Works, https://www.facebook.com/help/1155510281178725.

that are readily useful to other entities of the ecosystem; mainly the advertisers. The portion of data that Facebook collects about its users is also present with the collaborators (e.g., the Apps) of the platform and therefore they too are subject to the same privacy regulations as Facebook. However, since any ordinary user can create an App on the platform, collect user data, and plausibly disappear from the platform without any accountability. This brings us to the issue of governance of user data on OSNs when a user either decides to disassociate herself from a previously installed App or in case of an App turning rouge.

The European Union enacted "General Data Protection Regulation (GDPR)" for governance of users' personal data [8]. This regulation has a tenet called the *right-to-be-forgotten*, when invoked by an user, the user's data controller/processor has to delete all the personal data and any other data pertaining to that user that can potentially identify the user later. However, contrary to the user expectation, users continue to receive quasi-similar experience post invocation of this tenet of GDPR.

Intuitively, assume the user has invoked the right-to-be-forgotten on the health App (assume it is Nike and not Runtastic), the App and the platform have to delete all the personally identifiable information about the user. However, the platform cannot distinguish to the regulator about how the user has been labeled under the "healthy" category, which could be either due to Nike App or the Runtastic App. Assume the user invokes the tenet on Runtastic App also; in which case the platform removes the user from "healthy" category but not from the silo of healthy-food because the platform cannot determine whether it has categorized the users based on the inference/correlation of "healthy" category or based on the users interaction with healthy-food labelled page/event/posts. Assume the user invokes the tenet on the platform itself; in which case the platform and all the Apps installed by the user have to delete the user's data but the desired effects will reflect in the user's experience only until the user stays away from any service/website that is collaborating with the Facebook[4].

In this paper, we investigate the reasons behind the challenges in enforcement of the *right-to-be-forgotten* tenet of the GDPR. In the following section, we elucidate Facebook's data platform ecosystem, its business model and the architectural components. In Sect. 3 we highlight, with the help of prior work, how lack of provenance of user data makes the enforcement of this tenet undecidable. In Sect. 4, we take the reader through the transformation of personal data on the information value chain of Facebook to underline the limitations in governance of data when it is not uniquely identifiable. In Sect. 5, we argue about the efficacy of GDPR's right-to-be-forgotten tenet and list out the challenges in its enforcement. We conclude in Sect. 6.

2 Background

Prior to the era of the online social networks or the era of advertisement-based online service delivery models that emerged during the last decade, we still had

---

[4] https://lifehacker.com/5994380/how-facebook-uses-your-data-to-target-ads-even-offline.

online entities that facilitated online transactions and had access to user data and their activities. For example, DNS, email, digital libraries, directory listings, bulletin boards, IRC, newsgroups, et al. But the data that was being generated at these intermediaries was used only for the purpose of audit, fraud detection, provisioning of services, et al. It is only after the success of advertisement-based service delivery model, the importance of data as digital gold started taking hold. In current era, almost every online service collects user data under the pretext of personalization and/or service measurement and improvement. In the absence of a personal data protection regulation for the collection, storage, processing, and usage of user data, data economy flourished and proliferation of user data continued unchecked. The veracity and volume of collection of user data increased in the advent of OSNs, mobile phones and the issue of user privacy started undermining the trust in online data ecosystem [10].

Among the many services that constitute our new digital economy or data ecosystem, the OSNs require a special consideration because these are the data platforms where users voluntarily divulge their personal data without realizing the potential implications to their privacy. Even before the digital age, user data used to be collected for the purpose of census, credit bureau ratings, election rolls, television viewership, et al., and statistical models were used by firms and governments to make reports about the users for business and government policy making. Data models existed to extract meaningful insights from the data collected from the population of interest. For example, in 1917, Robert Sessions Woodworth of Columbia University and Robert Yerkes, a professor of psychology at Harvard at the time created a model to assess army recruits to decide who should go to the fronts, who was fit to lead and who should stay well behind the lines[5]. Our current data ecosystem, where data is exchanged by users in lieu of free services, has allowed entities like Cambridge Analytica to use such well-known psychometric models on large swaths of population for their personality traits so that personalized persuasion techniques can be used to influence the behavior of this population. Any entity that has access to users' online activity data is processing such data with the help of well-known data models to generate and monetize user profiles. Figure 1 depicts the process these data intermediaries follow to convert raw user data into actionable insights that have many takers in the digital economy.

Myriad of online services collect, analyze, use, and exchange users' personal information either by consent or convoluted opt-in/opt-out schemes with a sole motivation of harvesting user data. Data has indeed become new oil/gold and is been siphoned off wherever possible, with little respect for privacy. More than a thousand companies are now involved in a digital information value chain that harvest data from any online activity and delivers targeted content to online or mobile users within roughly 36 seconds of their entry into the digital realm[6]. The sophistication and ease of targeting users has become so rampant that there is a sense of anxious helplessness. GDPR is devised to specifically address the

---

[5] https://www.nytimes.com/2018/03/22/opinion/democracy-survive-data.html.

[6] https://www.project-syndicate.org/bigpicture/the-privacy-paradox.

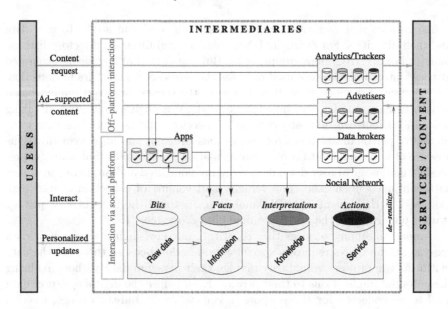

Fig. 1. Business model of data intermediaries (*witness* → *record* → *interpret* → *monetize*)

misuse of personal data and putting the users in control of their personal data. In this paper, we shall analyze its *right-to-be-forgotten* tenet for its efficacy on Facebook's data platform.

Facebook is the epitome of OSNs because it is the most successful network with highest number of users who are not only catered by the platform for their social communication needs but also through ancillary services like WhatsApp, Messenger, Instagram in order to keep them connected with the platform so that their transactional data (also called as metadata) is useful in reinforcing the strength of their social connections, which is an important metric for identifying influential users, clustering users by interests, et al. Facebook's platform has following key entities/stakeholders, apart from the users, that have symbiotic relationship with each other for the sole purpose of collecting, categorizing, and monetizing of user data while keeping users adequately rewarded with convenience, personalization, and social utility.

1. Apps: Act as miniature data platforms that tract, collect, process data of its users. The platform looks at the data collected by the App in the context of the App's category; for example: health, sport, education, etc.
2. Content providers: Act as sensors to the platform by reporting about the users that visit the websites/services. The platform looks at the feed from content providers as users online behavior and interests.
3. Advertisers: Act as consumers of the platform's expertise to compose an audience of interest on payment basis.

4. Trackers: All of the above entities are provided with analytics service by the platform in order to measure their own engagement with the users.

Only a subset of data generated about the users by the entities associated with Facebook platform are available to the user. Facebook provides its users with privacy settings through which the users can control who can access their data. Facebook also provides a log of user activities for amendment to the users, including download and deletion. Facebook acts as a data processor in the scenario of data being collected by an App installed by user and instructs the user to liaise with the App developer in case of access to data and amendments, which is tedious. Any user can become a developer and register an App with the platform. It is important to note that the users may not treat the Apps with same level of trust with which they treat the platform, but the users have no clear idea about the flow of their data on the platform.

Given the state of user data spread across entities of the platform in varying proportion, it is interesting to investigate how those entities adhere to the right-to-be-forgotten tenet of the GDPR.

3 Unauthorized and Unintended Avenues of Data Leakage

It is presumed that when the right-to-be-forgotten is invoked by an user, the data controller will identify the data-set to be deleted from its database. The user has two-fold expectations behind this tenet of the GDPR: (i) the data controller should not be in a position to predict, infer, correlate future events with the user, post deletion; (ii) the user believes that the data that the controller rightfully collected upon consent is deleted and there are no copies of such rightfully deleted data. However, in [20,22] the authors have shown that there are unauthorized avenues of data leakage on Facebook's data platform despite correct policy specifications by its users. We summarize them in this section.

Fig. 2. Hierarchy of access to data by the entities on Facebook platform

Figure 2 depicts the volume of data on the platform and the access hierarchies among the stakeholders of the platform. Since the evolution of data begins with the users creating, sharing, and interacting with the data, users are said to be the primary owners of the data and therefore we list out the data leakages at two layers ("Users" layer and "Apps" layer) despite correct policy specification by the users. The users have no control beyond these two layers on data hierarchy on the platform.

Access Control at User-to-User Level Interactions: Facebook allows its users to specify access policies over their objects using a mix of intensional and extensional labels like "Friends", "Family", "Friend of friends", et al. This type of natural labeling nomenclature allows users to organize their social relationships as they do in offline world. This communicates the affinity/strength of the edge between nodes; thus, inversely a node's ability to influence the node at the other end of the edge. Therefore the list of "Friends" of a user becomes a valuable information and Facebook provides means to protect such objects from unauthorized access. In [22] the authors show that despite correct access control policy specification by the users on their objects, there are instances of leakage of protected data. Their findings are summarized below.

1. Nonrestrictive change in policy of an object risks privacy of others,
2. Restrictive change in policy of an object suspends other's privileges,
3. *"Share"* operation is privacy-preserving,
4. Policy composition using intensional labels is not privacy-preserving,
5. *"Like"* and *"Comment"* operations are not privacy-preserving.

OSNs allow their users to set/specify access policies for their data on the platform such that a certain segment of their social connections can access the data they post. The users trust the platform explicitly but expect protection from unintended users on the platform. The user features/operations like *"Like"*, *"Share"* on the platform diffuse the explicit ownership of user data on OSNs. This is because the resource on which an operation is made is owned by its creator and the state changes due to operations are associated with the resource. If the resource owner deletes the resource, the state changes (Likes, Comments, et al.) also get deleted. However, there are certain sequences of privacy settings and user operations in which the resource restricts undoing of past operations by other users. For example, when a resource's (a post or a photo) access policy is changed from public to private (i.e., only me) all the operations performed on that resource by other users get frozen until the policy is changed by the resource owner. It is an interesting scenario in which the "Superuser" overrides normal users' settings – when a user invokes her right-to-be-forgotten on the platform, the platform has to delete even the frozen Comments of that user.

Access Control at User-to-App Level Interactions: As against the usage of labels are access policies, the Apps get explicit permissions by users upon installation (total 48 such permissions are available in v2.12 of Facebook's graph API). The access control for user data by Apps is designed for facilitating functionalities of the Apps. Users give a set of permissions as requested by an App to obtain the functionality. Whatever transactional/observational data is generated, during the course of App functionality usage, is not controlled by the user. Facebook prompts users that by installing an App, a user abides to the privacy policy of the App. There are 3 broad categories of Apps: (i) Apps that rely on FB for authentication (SSO), (ii) Apps that modify the social graph with consent from user, and (iii) Apps that tailor user experience based on the social graph of its users. The first two categories, by design, shares the user activity with the platform; whereas in the third category the user activity is recorded outside the platform. User's permissions to Apps are perpetual and the data availed by Apps are not governed by FB's privacy policy. Furthermore, the permissions to Apps override the access controls expressed by users in user-to-user layer. For example, an App can access a post by a user with policy "Only Me". In [20] the authors list out scenarios in which Apps either breach users' stated policies or simply undermine user's sensitive information for which the platform does not provide any measure of protection. Their findings are summarized below.

1. App finds out user's friends despite user setting it private.
2. App can access user objects with "Only Me" policy.
3. App can find out what other apps are installed by its users.
4. Linkability: App and advertiser can identify their audience from the analytics data.

In light of the recent Cambridge Analytica [15] revelations, the falsely perceived *status quo* about privacy in social network that existed for past decade, is being questioned widely. This is not a one off scenario of users' privacy breach but it is due to lack of a uniform platform-wide access control model. The access controls are implemented layer-wise, where policies in one layer may contradict with policies in another. As a response to Cambridge Analytica incident, Facebook maintains that it will review and limit Apps' access to user data and also highlights that users are the owners of their content and can control who can access these content. What it is curiously missing is who owns (can access) the meta-data and behavioral data about users. And that is why the enforcement of the right-to-be-forgotten becomes challenging.

Before we get into the analysis of these questions, it would be appropriate to understand the characteristics of information, digital transactions, the life-cycle of personal data, its mutation into other types in presence of auxiliary data, and the risks of de-identification of de-sensitized/anonymized data [19].

4 Does Facebook Have Something the Users Do Not Have Access To?

Personally identifiable information (PII [17]) is "any information about an individual maintained by an agency, including (i) any information that can be used to distinguish or trace an individual's identity, such as name, social security number, date and place of birth, mother's maiden name, or biometric records; and (ii) any other information that is linked or linkable to an individual, such as medical, educational, financial, and employment information." To distinguish an individual is to identify an individual.

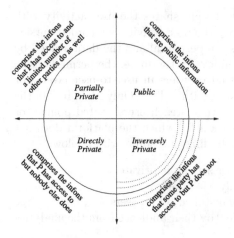

Fig. 3. Classification of PII (infon) of subject P.

Identifiers distinguish a user (or a group of users, or a passive object) from another. Each unique entity that needs to be interacted with has an identifier, e.g., name. Identifiers may have attributes like postal address, city name, date of birth. Attributes are a generic class of identifiers, which do not identify a subject on its own but in presence of its association with a subject improves the uniqueness of subject identification. Observer is an entity that has knowledge of identifiers of subjects and it may assign private attributes to subjects based on their activities under observation. For example, an ISP may legitimately assign attributes like gamer, bankers, student, etc. based on the online activities of its customers. Observer may develop data models based on its customers' online behavior and may devise a method to predict attribute/category for an unknown subject when that subject's log of online activities is fed to the model. Therefore, the potency of an observer is proportional to the volume of data it has access to. When an attribute is unique to a subject then the attribute is equivalent to PII in the given context. For example, if there is only one person with a specific DoB in a database (knowledge-base) then that attribute uniquely identifies the subject it is assigned to. If there are more than two subjects that have same DoB, then the probability of correctly associating a subject to an action reduces to half, and likewise. Whereas instead of one attribute, two attributes of subjects are considered under the same observation model, the probability of subject identification greatly increases. Users neither have knowledge about potency of their observers nor sufficient motivation to judiciously reveal their attributes while online. *Level of privacy is a loose measure of asymmetry of motivation, ability between an observer and the subjects being observed.* An observer (advertiser or its collaborator) is financially motivated to identify its audience and has technical ability (via the platform) to do so; whereas, the users are motivated to get functional benefits of the free service being provided, until and unless adversely affected.

4.1 Coarse Classification of PII

Gurevich et al. classify personal data (infons) of a subject into 4 flat categories as shown in Fig. 3 [11]. Examples of these types of infons are:

1. *Public:* name, email, phone;
2. *Directly Private (secret):* passwords;
3. *Partially Private:* salary, blood group, hobbies, affiliations;

4. *Inversely Private:* mobile location logs.

We termed this classification of PII as coarse because in absence of a context, the above examples will fall in multiple classes: e.g., passwords can also be categorized as partially private, because the validator retains a copy of the password. Likewise, an individual's credit rating can be categorized as inversely private until the individual obtains a copy of her credit rating upon payment. Therefore, context is an important aspect [2] in accurate categorization of PII. Facebook's social graph constantly records all the interactions of its users on the platform and makes use of it to build their respective interests so that the platform introduces the users to the most relevant events in users' social circles. To prioritize the most relevant events it is necessary to know the context. Therefore, we may say that Facebook, with the help of this *inversely private* contextual information about its users, is the best predictor of relevancy: be it for compiling the most important events to a user or be it predicting a relevant advertisement for a user. In other words, with the knowledge of context it is possible to identify a user with the help of non-PII data. So, we add another class of data to the above classification that is called PPII (potentially personally identifiable information). PPII looks innocuous in absence of any context.

In the following, we walk through the process of how users' PII on an OSN platform gets transformed from governable (identifiable, therefore deletable) verbatim strings to ungovernable diffused data in the form of actionable knowledge for monetary benefit. The process is abstracted out in 4-steps and depicted in Figs. 4 and 5.

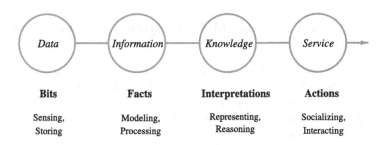

Fig. 4. Abstractions along the information value chain.

4.2 Voluntary Labeling of Data by Users Through Their Interactions

When a user signs-up with the platform by providing her personal details, the platform assigns a 64-bit unique ID (FBID) to the user and is represented as a node on the social graph. FBID acts as a primary identifier on the platform and user fills out various personal details (DoB, affiliation, city, languages) as

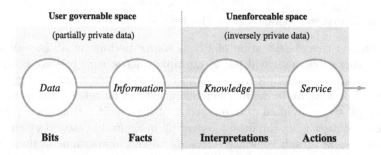

Fig. 5. Information value chain: Scope of governance/regulation.

attributes to the FBID node. User node's edges to other nodes represent relationship of a specific type: social affinity (friends, family, acquaintance, groups, etc.), object ownership (photos, post, video, etc.), actions (check-in, like, comment, tag, events, etc.), and installation of an App. All these possible edge formations by a node is used for labeling the node according to the type of the peer node. For example, user installing a sports App will label the user in "sports" category. The user "like" a post of category "sport" by other user will reinforce the labeling. Thus, a node's category influences the categories of the nodes interacting with it. The platform labels the object nodes (content, location, Apps, groups) to determine interests of its subjects when they voluntarily interact. Apps may have their own private labels, which they may or may not share with the platform.

4.3 Observational Labeling: Linking External Data Points with Local Data

The platform observes and records its users activities on-platform and off-platform (through Pixel, for example). These observations include facts like IP address, type of mobile OS, type of browser [6], active time on platform, active time on other platforms[7], call logs, browser logs, location history, etc [3]. All this factual information along with the voluntary labels/categories form rich profiles about users and also group of users. Further enrichment and fortification of information is done by correlating data from external sources[8] like credit-rating agencies, census data, electoral rolls. Both the Apps and platform track user behavior by modeling events in the interactions of users on/off the platform. This analytics is processed and compiled as formatted information such that it can readily be used to re-target the users towards attending incomplete events; for example, a user added items to shopping basket but did not check-out, so

---

[7] Facebook's Onavo gives social-media firm inside peek at rivals' users, *WSJ*, Aug 2017. https://www.wsj.com/articles/facebooks-onavo-gives-social-media-firm-inside-peek-at-rivals-users-1502622003.

[8] How does Facebook work with data providers?, Facebook. https://www.facebook.com/help/494750870625830.

re-targeting such users to complete payment event is an objective. A user who has history of adding items to basket but not checking-out is not the audience advertisers are interested in.

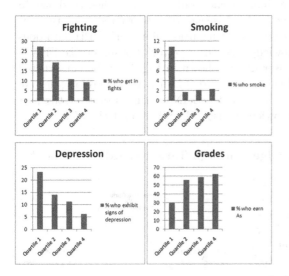

Fig. 6. Multivariate analyses: extrapolating facts into knowledge with the help of empirical evidence.

Figure 6 shows an example of how an observation or a fact (that is, in this case, grades of children) is extrapolated into inferred labels for the children under observation. Empirical statistical evidence models are used to probabilistically infer the likelihood of a subject following the pattern established by empirical statistics. Later, the probabilistic values are reinforced by correlating future interactions of the subject on the platform against the inferred labels (predicted categories). Thus, the facts are voluntarily presented by subjects on the platform (partially private information), on which the platform makes inferences along with the contextual history about the subject available to the platform and builds rich profile for the subject (inversely private information).

4.4 Analytics of Data: Representation and Reasoning of Knowledge

Advertisers are interested in getting a high conversion rate for their advertisement budget, which in turn becomes a competitive criteria for data platform owners like Facebook. Accuracy of identifying relevant audience for an advertisement campaign depends on the platform's ability to predict which users fit into the audience. Since the personality of a user is a strong measure to anticipate her behavior. The user profiles containing rich sets of labels (voluntary, observed, inferred) are synthesized [13,27] by the platform into valuable individual personality traits [12] – which in its abstract form is represented by OCEAN [4] values that constitutes an individual's score (calculated from user's actions: *like, dislike, anger, follow, share, et al.* on the platform) on her Openness, Conscientiousness, Extraversion, Agreeableness, and Neuroticism. Thus the verbatim user profile tuples <FBID, labels> get mutated into <FBID, labels, OCEAN>. Then the users can be de-identified and organized according to their personality traits so that advertisers can rent it out to construct their tailored audience for a specific campaign. Each campaign has a context and FBAN does the placement of advertisement since it has complete knowledge – user profiles, traits, and the context. Expertise from other well-known psychometric models is used to further synthesize the knowledge-base of FBAN to build new reasonings [14] about users' behavior prediction in presence of certain events that are triggered either on the platform or elsewhere. This is how a user's verbatim PII data gets mutated and diffused in the information value chain of Facebook, as knowledge, as shown in Fig. 4. It is possible that same knowledge-base can be constructed using two different datasets. In other words, exclusion or inclusion of a user's PPII data does not substantially change the knowledge-base of a powerful observer like FBAN. That is, personality traits of a user [25] as shown in Fig. 7 can be constructed from several disparate events of the user recorded by FBAN. Therefore, despite forgetting a user by deleting that user's PII, FBAN continues to serve the user as before with the help of the knowledge-base FBAN has built thus far.

4.5   Monetization of Knowledge Through Targeted Advertisement

This knowledge-base (which is built upon users' inversely private information) is not available to users directly but only indirectly in the form of News Feed and targeted advertisements. In other words, the inferred categories[9] that are labelled against users' respective FBIDs are not made available to users but are used in designing advertisement campaigns by the advertisers, who pay for the access to such rich categories. However, post enactment of GDPR, the users are allowed to delete/download their own logs of actions and the data on Facebook.

Facebook's overarching *sensing → recording → processing* platform continuously does 3 tasks in tandem to consolidate its hold on users' information value chain: (i) collect & classify user PII data/actions, (ii) corre-

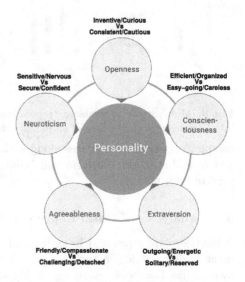

Fig. 7. OCEAN: The 5-factor model (taxonomy of personal traits) used for psychometric profiling.

late data/actions with other facts to build/reinforce profiles, and (iii) dynamically build audiences as per contexts (categories) specified by its customers. In this process, the users' PPII data and actions are constantly transformed through the information value chain and get diffused into actionable knowledge. The omnipresent, overarching data ecosystem of Facebook, through its platform's components and the analytical feedback loops from Internet-wide content collaborators, is a real-time *context delivery service* for the advertisers. FBAN's knowledge-base along with platform's real-time context prediction

---

[9] In 2016, ProPublica collected, through crowd-sourcing, more than 52,000 unique attributes (categories/data points) that Facebook had used to classify users [24].

capability helps Facebook to attract advertisers, governments, and persuaders to build/identify tailored audiences. However, Facebook takes precaution of preventing its customers from tailoring narrow audiences that have sizes smaller than 100. The same knowledge-base is also useful in Facebook's News Feed algorithm, which is famous for its prioritization of relevant updates to a user.

This brings us to the most interesting question in PII's life-cycle: what is the efficacy of the right-to-be-forgotten tenet of GDPR if invoked by an user either on an App associated with the platform or on the platform itself? To answer this question we need to be clear about the expectations a user will have upon the invocation of this legal tenet. It is reasonable to assume that the user will have an expectation to be presented with advertisements as if a previously unknown user is being served and the ecosystem (platform, websites, advertisers) will make use of only the data-points (context) available through that session. In other words, we can also rephrase the question like: is it possible to identify a user with the help of a knowledge-base that is built upon PII, PPII of the user? In the following section, we shall argue about it in affirmation.

5   Challenges in Enforcement of the Right-to-be-Forgotten

GDPR forces the data platforms to explicitly state how users' PII is collected, processed, and disposed off. Under its jurisdiction, the users have to be explicitly consented for PII collection and be informed of its processing for specific purposes. The users are allowed to access their PII and the information attributed to it by the platform when feasible. The users are legally empowered to ask any data handler/processor of their PII to delete their PII and associated information in a reasonable way. Any entity that legally interacts with users across EU are covered under GDPR with certain exceptions[10]. India is formulating its own personal data protection law[11] on similar lines of GDPR and it too has provision for the right-to-be-forgotten. Facebook has its larges user-base in India. Under GDPR, the handlers of the PII are categorized as:

1. *data processors:* entities processing data on behalf of the controller, and
2. *data controllers:* entities deciding what personal data must be processed and how processing will occur.

Facebook acts as both[12] the controller (for its users) and the processor (for its millions of Apps; where Apps act as the controller of user data) of PII. Facebook Apps in their data controller role need to get explicit consent from their users to collect and use the user data, which might directly/indirectly be available to underlying platform of Facebook and thus gets mutated and diffused into FBAN's knowledge-base. Keeping this in mind, let us find out the efficacy of the

---

[10] https://gdpr-info.eu/recitals/no-52/.

[11] A Free and Fair Digital Economy: Protecting Privacy, Empowering Indians. http://meity.gov.in/writereaddata/files/Data_Protection_Committee_Report.pdf.

[12] https://www.facebook.com/business/gdpr.

GDPR's *right-to-be-forgotten*[13] in two scenarios; when a user invokes it on an App and when on the platform itself. Before we analyze the two scenarios, it is important to understand the peculiar nature of information on OSNs.

5.1 Nature of Information on Social Platforms

Social platforms are the intermediaries that facilitate transaction between two or more parties that includes any combination of users, apps, advertisers, and the platform itself. Platforms act as trusted third parties to their constituents – users, apps, advertisers – by facilitating interaction among themselves, via the platform, and are legally bound by their privacy policies towards their respective constituents. However, in [20,22], it is shown that the privacy of Facebook users can be undone beyond the stated privacy policy. One of the reasons behind it, apart from design of the platform and its business model, is the nature of the information in social interactions.

By nature, the information involved in social interactions exist under a *shared ownership* of the *initiator*, the *reciprocator*, and the *facilitator* i.e., the platform. The platform is trusted by its users since they accept the privacy policy that states how it collects, controls, processes, and monetizes their data in order to serve them better. However, the initiator and reciprocator are not bound by any legal statue w.r.t. their privacy protections. For example on Facebook platform, assume that Alice sets her "list of friends" as private in her privacy settings and her friends keep the same setting as public, then Alice's setting has no effect. It is not reasonable for the platform to ensure Alice's privacy setting in this case. In [22], the authors point out several other such scenarios and certain of Facebook's operations that undo users' privacy. We attribute such privacy leakages to the "shared ownership" of data on social platforms.

We coin another term in the context of social platforms – *shared authorship* – signifying the Apps and the platform observing and recording interactions of their users. This is (inversely private) meta-data or analytics of the interactions that users make. When a user installs an app associated with Facebook's platform, she agrees to that App's privacy policy. However, since the App resides on the platform, i.e., it makes use of Facebook's social graph, the platform has access to the data authored by the App as a *processor*. By design, Facebook's role cannot be limited in accessing the data governed by App's privacy policy because both the user and the App exist on the platform and the platform helps the App to generate the analytics. For example, when an App enables its event analytics feature it records the information about its users with the help of the platform (see Figs. 8 and 9). The platform helps the App to identify, track, re-engage its users. Each App on the platform is assigned a category, which in turn is used as a label to indicate the App's users interest. This way the platform has a readymade audience for a category that is shared by many other Apps. Such categories are made available in real-time to the advertisers for composing their advertisement campaigns – *shared viewership*. Advertisers too are provided with analytics

---

[13] https://gdpr-info.eu/art-17-gdpr/.

Fig. 8. Facebook analytics revealing the FBIDs of people who interacted with a promoted page.

feature and such data with shared authorship (in this case, advertisers and the platform) makes its way to shared viewership for monetization purpose.

5.2 Entities and Their Responsibilities in the Enforcement of Right-to-be-forgotten

In the above, we have seen the three distinct data plateaus that are distinguished by the type of data and their controllers/processors. In the following, we list out the roles of each entity in the enforcement of the right-to-be-forgotten.

Shared Ownership (by user/app/platform): The platform and the Apps installed by users handle users' data in the capacity of a data controller and are obliged to comply with GDPR as and when a user invokes her *right-to-be-forgotten*. The data (infons; cf. Fig. 3) at this plateau is *Public* and *Partially Private*, which is identifiable and therefore enforceable.

Shared Authorship (by app/platform): The Apps and the platform observe and profile/label users based on their online interactions. The analytics generated by Apps have the platform as a collaborator. Therefore, the Apps act in the capacity of data controllers and the platform acts in the capacity of a data processor. The data at this plateau is *Inversely Private*, which is identifiable (not by the users, but only by the controller and the processor) and therefore enforceable in good spirit.

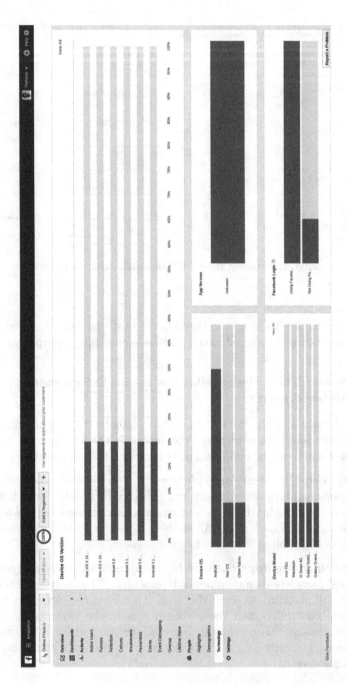

Fig. 9. Facebook analytics showing the PPII of users who interacted with an advertisement.

Shared Viewership (by app/advertiser/platform): The Apps and the advertisers take help of the platform to reach/engage to/with users by building an audience composition request. To do so, they either entirely rely on the platform or upload their own data to the platform in order to get tailored audience. In the former case, the platform makes use of its knowledge-base to identify an audience as per the categories requested by the audience composer. We have discussed earlier about how the knowledge-base is a result of data transformation along the information value chain of the platform, therefore it is *Inversely Private* and only the platform has a direct access to it. As we have discussed about how the user PII gets mutated and diffused along the information value chain, it is difficult to reconstruct the original data from the knowledge-base. In the later case of audience composition, the uploaded data may contain PII (governed by GDPR) or it could be desensitized (such data does not come under the purview of GDPR[14]).

5.3   The Right-to-be-Forgotten: User Expectations and Inherent Limitations

When a user invokes this right, the data controller and processor have to delete all the PII they have collected that can directly or indirectly identify the user. The Recital 26 of the GDPR states:

> *To determine whether a natural person is identifiable, account should be taken of all the means reasonably likely to be used, such as singling out, either by the controller or by another person to identify the natural person directly or indirectly. To ascertain whether means are reasonably likely to be used to identify the natural person, account should be taken of all objective factors, such as the costs of and the amount of time required for identification, taking into consideration the available technology at the time of the processing and technological developments.*

This implies that, post invocation of the right-to-be-forgotten, a user will not be identified and associated with her interests/personality. In the context of this paper, we shall explore the efficacy of right-to-be-forgotten when invoked on (i) the App that is associated with the platform, and (ii) the platform itself. In the following we present a few example scenarios to underline the inherent limitations while enforcing the right-to-be-forgotten.

1. Right-to-be-forgotten invoked on an App: Let us assume that Alice and Bob have installed the "Truecaller" App that helps its users to identify unknown callers. This App has Facebook enabled SSO option for authentication. If opted, user's profile picture, display name and job title (affiliation) are used in building user's profile on the App. When the App is being installed, user's contact list is uploaded to the App's central database in order to extend the database by potential new name:telephone entries fetched from the user's

---

[14] https://gdpr-info.eu/recitals/no-26/.

contact list. Since Alice and Bob have installed this App, their respective contact lists are merged with the App's central database, which in turn is searchable by others who are not related to Alice or Bob. When Alice invokes her right-to-be-forgotten, Truecaller is obliged to delete all the personally identifiable data about Alice that includes Alice:1234567890 entry from the central database of the App. However, post erasure of Alice's data from the database, Bob and others continue to submit Alice:1234567890 entry to the central database without Alice's consent. In order to effectively filter out Alice's entry, the central database has to continuously check all the entries being submitted by its users against the entries that desire to be forgotten, which is a costly operation. Therefore, PII of a user that has shared ownership with other users, cannot be governed efficiently and effectively.

2. Right-to-be-forgotten invoked on the platform: Post invocation of the right-to-be-forgotten by an user, the user continues to get identified by her metadata (IP, locale, time-zone, behavioral fingerprints, hardware fingerprints, et al.) and platform's capability to track[15] non-users [1,23] across the affiliate services/websites that are associated with the platform. This tracking data allows Facebook to determine context of the non-user, which is sufficient to match the non-user's attention to an advertiser with as much relevance as when the user was associated with the platform. And it will be technically not feasible to prove that Facebook has used PII to match the user with an advertiser. In fact, the user will be better off by staying associated with the platform instead of being forgotten by the platform because while associated with the platform the user can at least control her ad preferences.

In order to honor users' right-to-be-forgotten requests, it will have to label and track such users so that FBAN treats them as new users. This could be easily achieved by using a special cookie with "origin policy" set to all of FBAN collaborators. But this will break the business model of Facebook. We have seen the rampant disregard for "Do Not Track" setting in modern browsers[16].

5.4 Targeted Advertisement and Desire to Be Forgotten Are Contradictory Goals

There is a technological imbalance among the stakeholders of our digital economy. The platforms have attained technical superiority in data collection, processing and actively influence the design of fundamental interfaces to Internet (browser, DNS, mobile OS, Apps) to further consolidate[17] their data-driven business model: *record everything → interpret → monetize and persuade.*

Advertisers' primary motivation/aim is to reach their intended audience with minimum expenditure. The expenditure is optimum when there is an exact

---

[15] Facebook admits it does track non-users, for their own good, The Register, Apr 2018. https://www.theregister.co.uk/2018/04/17/facebook_admits_to_track ing_non_users/.

[16] https://www.eff.org/issues/do-not-track.

[17] Net neutrality blocked ISPs from providing services subsidized with advertising.

match, in other words, precision targeting is inevitable. OSNs have created the ability to identify their users for specific criterions that advertisers are interested in. Through OSNs, the *motivation* of advertising industry is easily achieved due to the technical *ability* of OSNs to accurately find the users. On the other hand, users typically lack the motivation and ability to make elaborate privacy decisions. Furthermore, for the platform/advertiser, the cost of making a wrong probabilistic guess about intended target is negligible whereas, for the target/user, it is costly to get identified.

GDPR has stiff financial penalties for laxity in personal data handling. However, provenance is difficult given the fact that a data controller (an App) on Facebook platform, by design interacts with the underlying social graph. Depending on the design of the App, partial or full data of App user is recorded on Facebook's social graph. The data then propagates further in platform's information value chain. It is easy to create an App and start collecting user data without much of practical liabilities. This is because any user can create an App. Facebook has introduced a concept of Scope_ID that issues local identifier to App users such that the identifier can only be valid within the scope of the App. Users cannot be tracked for their activities across the Apps. However, FBAN can resolve the Scope_IDs of all Apps. It will be interesting to see what changes Facebook will usher in to its platform to be compliant with GDPR while acting as a data processor for its Apps. We contend that Facebook's role as a data processor in the context of an App as a data controller is ambiguous. This is because the data under the purview of the data controller seeps into the platform's information value chain by means of analytics and other features the platform provides to the data controller.

In presence of ubiquitous tools like big-data analytics and deep neural networks, preserving privacy appears to be a herculean task [5,18]. To address this challenge coherently, we need to undertake a SoK for identifiers. Because it is their usage beyond the perceived scope of their utility that leads to potential privacy breaches. The SoK should put forward a framework for the use of identifiers in terms of their scope, contextual availability, temporal validity, linkability – and the effects of these parameters on each other. Architects of online services have service functionality and user convenience as primary design criteria. Providing them a methodology to judiciously use the above mentioned parameters with an understanding of their costs and benefits to the system they design.

6   Conclusions

Facebook's data platform is an intertwined ecosystem of collaborators with a fine balance of returns for each stakeholder. The user being the largest stakeholder but ill-informed about the consequences of their personal data's collection, processing, and monetization; are to be protected by data protection laws like GDPR, which have a tenet of the *right-to-be-forgotten*. However, the nature of data in social interactions and the information value chain present on Facebook's platform make it challenging to implement. We showed that lack of provenance

of user data on and off the platform makes the enforcement of this tenet undecidable. The overarching tracking mechanisms deployed by Facebook across the
Internet can quickly identify an erased user from the factual identifiers (like IP
address, browser/phone fingerprint, location, et al.) that the user cannot change
post invocation of the tenet. The success of Facebook's business model is due
to its ability to match an advertiser with its audience with high conversion rate
and to achieve that feat it has developed abilities to track and profile users that
are not registered on its platform – we argued that targeted advertisement and
the right-to-be-forgotten are contradictory goals. In order to enforce this tenet in
spirit on Facebook, each erased user need to be labelled, similar to DNT cookie,
and upon presence of this label Facebook should provide a non-personalized
experience to that user. But this will undermine its ability to provide high conversion rates to the advertisers.

References

1. Acar, G., Eubank, C., Englehardt, S., Juarez, M., Narayanan, A., Diaz, C.: The
   web never forgets: persistent tracking mechanisms in the wild. In: ACM CCS 2014,
   pp. 674–689 (2014)
2. Barth, A., Datta, A., Mitchell, J.C., Nissenbaum, H.: Privacy and contextual
   integrity: framework and applications. In: IEEE S&P 2006, pp. 184–198 (2006)
3. Chaabane, A., Kaafar, M.A., Boreli, R.: Big friend is watching you: analyzing
   online social networks tracking capabilities. In: Proceedings of ACM Workshop on
   Online Social Networks, pp. 7–12. ACM (2012)
4. Costa, P.T., McCrae, R.R.: The Five-Factor Model, Five-Factor Theory, and Interpersonal Psychology, Chap. 6, pp. 91–104. Wiley-Blackwell, Hoboken (2012)
5. De Montjoye, Y.A., Hidalgo, C.A., Verleysen, M., Blondel, V.D.: Unique in the
   crowd: the privacy bounds of human mobility. Sci. Rep. **3**, 1376 (2013)
6. DeKoven, L.F., Savage, S., Voelker, G.M., Leontiadis, N.: Malicious browser extensions at scale: bridging the observability gap between web site and browser. In:
   10th USENIX Workshop on Cyber Security Experimentation and Test (CSET 17)
   (2017)
7. Esteve, A.: The business of personal data: Google, Facebook, and privacy issues in
   the EU and the USA. Int. Data Priv. Law **7**(1), 36–47 (2017)
8. European Union: 2018 reform of EU data protection rules (2018). https://
   ec.europa.eu/commission/priorities/justice-and-fundamental-rights/data-
   protection/2018-reform-eu-data-protection-rulesen
9. Forbrukerrådet: Deceived by Design: how tech companies use dark patterns to
   discourage us from exercising our rights to privacy, Norwegian Consumer Council (2018). https://fil.forbrukerradet.no/wp-content/uploads/2018/06/2018-06-27-
   deceived-by-design-final.pdf
10. FTC: Protecting Consumer Privacy in an Era of Rapid Change: Recommenda-
    tions for Businesses and Policymakers (2012). https://www.ftc.gov/sites/default/
    files/documents/reports/federal-trade-commission-report-protecting-consumer-
    privacy-era-rapid-change-recommendations/120326privacyreport.pdf
11. Gurevich, Y., Hudis, E., Wing, J.M.: Inverse privacy. Commun. ACM **59**(7), 38–42
    (2016)

12. International Personality Item Pool: The 3,320 IPIP Items in Alphabetical Order (2018). https://ipip.ori.org/AlphabeticalItemList.htm
13. Kosinski, M., Stillwell, D., Graepel, T.: Private traits and attributes are predictable from digital records of human behavior. Proc. Natl. Acad. Sci. **110**(15), 5802–5805 (2013)
14. Kristensen, J.B., lbrechtsen, T., Dahl-Nielsen, E., Jensen, M., Skovrind, M., Bornakke, T.: Parsimonious data: how a single Facebook like predicts voting behavior in multiparty systems. PLOS ONE **12**(9), 1–12 (2017)
15. Edwards, L.: Cambridge Analytica and the deeper malaise in the persuasion industry (2018). http://blogs.lse.ac.uk/polis/2018/03/26/cambridge-analytica-a-symptom-of-a-deeper-malaise-in-the-persuasion-industry/
16. Leon, P.G., et al.: What matters to users?: factors that affect users' willingness to share information with online advertisers. In: SOUPS, pp. 7:1–7:12. ACM (2013)
17. McCallister, E., Grance, T., Scarfone, K.A.: SP 800–122. Guide to protecting the confidentiality of personally identifiable information (PII). Technical report, National Institute of Standards and Technology (2010)
18. de Montjoye, Y.A., Radaelli, L., Singh, V.K., Pentland, A.: Unique in the shopping mall: on the reidentifiability of credit card metadata. Science **347**(6221), 536–539 (2015)
19. Ohm, P.: Broken promises of privacy: responding to the surprising failure of anonymization. UCLA Law Rev. **57**, 1701 (2009, 2010)
20. Patil, V.T., Jatain, N., Shyamasundar, R.K.: Role of apps in undoing of privacy policies on facebook. In: Kerschbaum, F., Paraboschi, S. (eds.) DBSec 2018. LNCS, vol. 10980, pp. 85–98. Springer, Cham (2018). https://doi.org/10.1007/978-3-319-95729-6_6
21. Patil, V.T., Shyamasundar, R.K.: Privacy as a currency: un-regulated? In: Proceedings of the 14th International Joint Conference on e-Business and Telecommunications (ICETE 2017). SECRYPT, vol. 4, pp. 586–595. SciTePress (2017)
22. Patil, V.T., Shyamasundar, R.K.: Undoing of privacy policies on Facebook. In: Livraga, G., Zhu, S. (eds.) DBSec 2017. LNCS, vol. 10359, pp. 239–255. Springer, Cham (2017). https://doi.org/10.1007/978-3-319-61176-1_13
23. Portokalidis, G., Polychronakis, M., Keromytis, A.D., Markatos, E.P.: Privacy-preserving social plugins. In: USENIX Security Symposium, pp. 631–646 (2012)
24. ProPublica Data Store: Facebook ad categories (2016). https://www.propublica.org/datastore/dataset/facebook-ad-categories
25. Quercia, D., Lambiotte, R., Stillwell, D., Kosinski, M., Crowcroft, J.: The personality of popular Facebook users. In: Proceedings of the ACM 2012 Conference on Computer Supported Cooperative Work, pp. 955–964 (2012)
26. Schneier, B.: Data and Goliath: The Hidden Battles to Collect Your Data and Control Your World. W. W. Norton & Company, New York City (2015)
27. Youyou, W., Kosinski, M., Stillwell, D.: Computer-based personality judgments are more accurate than those made by humans. Proc. Natl. Acad. Sci. **112**(4), 1036–1040 (2015)

Analysis of Newer Aadhaar Privacy Models

Ajinkya Rajput$^{(\boxtimes)}$ and K. Gopinath

Indian Institute of Science, Banglore, India
{ajinkya,gopi}@iisc.ac.in
http://www.iisc.ac.in

Abstract. Newer protocols for authentication using Aadhaar have been introduced to enhance privacy and security. In this article, we analyze the security and privacy of these new models. We consider the original Aadhaar model [4], the newer VID Aadhaar model [1] introduced by UIDAI, our own CP-UID model [11] and compare them with respect to privacy and scalability. We also introduce and discuss a newer hybrid model based on the VID model that has enhanced privacy. We also present an analysis of the biometric locking feature of Aadhaar.

Keywords: National identities · Privacy

1 Introduction

Aadhaar is national identities project, implemented by the Unique Identities Authority of India (UIDAI) which is a statutory authority of Government of India (GoI). Aadhaar provides digital infrastructure for identity verification of residents of India. Residents are required to verify their identity while availing services from government service providers; for example, for getting subsidies on LPG cylinders. This project also enables the government to make better decisions as it has a deduplicated roster of residents. Aadhaar has been used, for example, for direct benefit transfer to provide various subsidies directly to the bank accounts of the residents, which can reduce fraudulent practices.

Essentially, Aadhaar is a huge database of demographic and biometric information of residents of India. According to UIDAI website [2], more than 1.2 billion residents have been enrolled. The residents get enrolled in the database by providing documents for proof of address and identity to "enrollment centers" in person. Residents' biometrics (all 10 fingerprints, photograph and iris scan of both eyes) and demographic information (name, address, birth year) are recorded during enrollment. After successful verification of provided documents and deduplication, a unique Aadhaar Number or UID is generated for each resident.

Security of such a database is critical as a breach can lead to massive identity thefts. There is a claim of someone having purchased storage space on the Amazon cloud on behalf of someone else using an Aadhaar number [6]. An improper

© Springer Nature Switzerland AG 2018
V. Ganapathy et al. (Eds.): ICISS 2018, LNCS 11281, pp. 386–404, 2018.
https://doi.org/10.1007/978-3-030-05171-6_20

implementation may lead to profiling and tracking of residents through service providers; a good example is the case involving a telecom Payment Bank. Aadhaar enables GoI to deposit various subsidies directly in the bank accounts of the residents linked with their Aadhaar number. The telecom service provider had started an e-Wallet service and wallet accounts were being created for the telecom subscribers. Due to a "click-in" feature not understood by most, the subsidies which were supposed to be deposited in the bank accounts of residents were diverted to wallet account [8]. This was possible because the bank account and the payments bank account were linked to a common Aadhaar number. Such a database can also be used by an unethical government for mass surveillance of its residents. Aadhaar project can definitely be a boon but without sufficient precautionary measures, it might also cause huge losses to the nation.

Aadhaar provides an electronic way for the service providers to verify the information given by the resident. A typical use of Aadhaar is as follows. A resident provides details that are required (name, address, etc.) to a service provider to get services (for e.g., opening a bank account, getting a new telephone connection) along with the Aadhaar number. The service provider uses this Aadhaar number to verify that the information provided by resident is correct. We denote the steps carried out by the service provider for this verification as **"authentication sequence"**. Researchers, such as in [4] and [11], have analyzed the security and privacy of Aadhaar and pointed out various issues. Different authentication sequences provide different degree of security and privacy. For example, in [11], an authentication is presented which provides better security and privacy. UIDAI has also independently rolled out their newer solutions over initial authentication sequence to enhance the privacy and security of Aadhaar.

In this article, we model these authentication sequences formally and represent these different authentication sequences using common notations. Then we compare and contrast these sequences and analyze these sequences in terms of security and privacy. We also propose efficient implementation of some of authentication sequences. We enumerate the authentication sequences that we compare here (their analyses are given in the sections below):

- **Base-Aadhaar**: This is the first authentication sequence introduced by UIDAI. This is however susceptible to profiling and tracking by service providers and enables mass surveillance by government.
- **VID-UIDToken**: This is an upgrade over Base-Aadhaar introduced by UIDAI. This addresses some issues about privacy.
- **CP-UID**: A more general model than VID-UIDToken that has been presented in [11] that provides better privacy guarantees.
- **Offline-KYC**: This is the most recent authentication sequence from UIDAI where UIDAI is not involved in the online verification and is similar to [5].

The rest of the paper is organized as follows. Section 2 provides a summary of components and architecture of Aadhaar infrastructure. In Sect. 3 we provide the notations that we have used. In Sect. 4 we represent different authentication sequences using this notation and present our analysis of these sequences. In

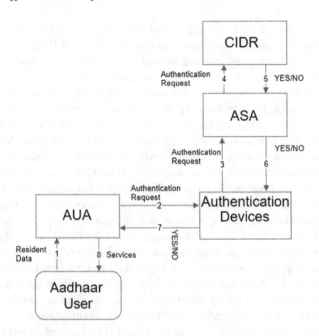

Fig. 1. Architecture of current Aadhaar system (based on figure in [4])

Sect. 5 we discuss the biometric locks solution provided by UIDAI. We present our thoughts on the design of the system and in Sect. 6. In Sect. 7 we provide and compare the models with respect to their scalability and we conclude in Sect. 8.

2   The Aadhaar Architecture

Figure 1 denotes current architecture of Aadhaar system. The following entities are currently part of the Aadhaar system [11]:

- **CIDR:** Central Identities Data Repositories is the central database in which all the electronic records are stored. It is managed by UIDAI and responds to verification request with a Yes/No response.
- **AUA:** Authentication User Agencies (AUAs) are third party service providers who require their clients to be authenticated by the Aadhaar system using the Aadhaar numbers of clients. They, in turn, submit the verification request.
- **ASA:** Authentication Service Agencies (ASA) are connected with CIDR through leased lines and forward authentication requests to CIDR on behalf of one or more AUAs.

- **Aadhaar User:** Aadhaar users are the residents of the country who are issued Aadhaar numbers. Their biometric information is stored in the CIDR.
- **Authentication Devices:** Authentication devices are the devices which are used to read biometrics from the users for authentication.
- **Enrollment Agencies:** Aadhaar users need to go to enrollment agencies to register their biometric information in the CIDR. Enrollment agencies are hired by UIDAI to perform these duties. (These are not shown in the diagram.)
- **eKYC API:** Third-party service providers can get an electronic copy of Aadhaar card of the user by invoking this API. This API returns the user data only if the request is authenticated by the user through biometrics or by OTP on the registered mobile number. This API is gaining popularity as the service provider has to take only a minimum amount of data from the user such as just the Aadhaar number and biometric authentication.

3 Notation

We define following sets and functions to represent authentication sequences.

3.1 Sets

- A set of enrolled residents C
- A set of Aadhaar ids U
- A set of Biometrics B
- A set of Demographics (name, address and birth year) D
- A set of AUAs AUA
- A set of Temporary Ids T
- A set of UID-Tokens (Generation and use explained in further discussion) UT
- A set of Documents $Docs$
- A set of Public Keys $Public\_keys$
- A set of Private Keys $Private\_keys$
- A set of signatures $Signatures$
- A set of bit strings text $Bitstrings$

3.2 Functions

- A biometrics get function given uid: $I_b : U \rightarrow B$
- A demographics get function given uid: $I_d : U \rightarrow D$
- A demographics get function that extracts demographic from document: $doc\_extract\_info : Docs \rightarrow D$
- A UID to Token generation ("1-way") function (hash of uid, specific AUA information and salt): $uid2token : U \times AUA \times Bitstrings \rightarrow UT$
- A function that retrieves uid from UID-Token: $token2uid : UT \rightarrow U$
- A digital signature function: $sign : Bitstrings \times Private\_keys \rightarrow Signatures$
- A one way hash function: $h : Bitstrings \rightarrow Bitstrings$

- A mapping function that maps tempIds to uid: $temp2uid : T \rightarrow U$.
- A verification function that checks if claimed uid matches the resident information (biometrics, etc.): $V : U \times D \times B \rightarrow \{0,1\}$. Here, we represent YES by 1 and No by 0.
- A function that assigns salts to AUAs $salt : AUA \rightarrow Bitstrings$

3.3 Representation

The authentication sequences are represented logically using the functions given above, given along with their function signatures. Each authentication sequence is represented by a verification function V, which is a composition of functions defined above.

4 Authentication Sequences

In this section, we present different authentication sequences. For each sequence, we first give a summary of the authentication sequence. Then we represent the authentication sequence formally using the notation above. Then we present the analysis of the authentication sequence.

4.1 Base-Aadhaar 1: Initial Aadhaar Authentication Sequence Without VIDs

Summary

This is the first authentication sequence introduced by UIDAI. An AUA (service provider) collects the information required according to its policies and Aadhaar number from a resident. The service provider then sends the collected information and Aadhaar number to CIDR. The CIDR replies "YES" which is denoted here by 1, if the information matches the information in CIDR's database and "NO" which is denoted here by 0, otherwise. If the reply is YES, the AUA considers the resident's information correct (Fig. 2).

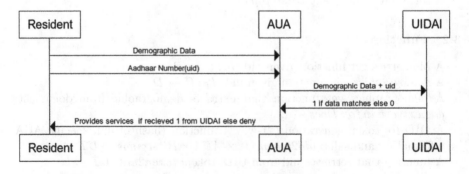

Fig. 2. Summary of Base-Aadhaar

Formal Representation

In this authentication sequence the verification function V is

$$\lambda u, d, b. \text{ if } (b = I_b(u) \text{ and } d = I_d(u)) \text{ then } 1 \text{ else } 0$$

where,

$$u \in U$$
$$b \in B$$
$$d \in D$$

Comments

1. This authentication sequence uses just one Aadhaar number across all AUAs. Because of a single index per person, multiple AUAs can collude and correlate their databases. This allows AUAs to gather more information than they are supposed to.
2. This authentication sequence allows authentication on behalf of a resident without the consent of the resident. This can happen if malicious party knows only the Aadhaar number of the resident. This claim of this happening is provided in [6].

4.2   VID-UIDToken: Aadhaar Authentication Sequence with VIDs

Summary

In this authentication sequence,

1. User requests a virtual id, VID, from UIDAI via a mobile application. UIDAI generates the VID corresponding to UID and sends the VID back. In our notation VID is represented by tempId.
2. User provides VID instead of Aadhaar number to AUA.
3. AUA sends the information that it wants verified, to UIDAI, along with VID.
4. UIDAI then checks the data received from AUA against the data of resident with UID corresponding to VID.
5. If both the data match the UIDAI responds with a YES, here denoted by replying UIDToken, else it replies NO, here denoted by 0.

Formal Representation

In this authentication sequence the verification function V is

$$\lambda t, d, b, a. \text{ if } (b = I_b(temp2uid(t)) \text{ and } d = I_d(temp2uid(t))$$
$$\text{then } uid2token(temp2uid(t), a, salt(a)) \text{ else } 0$$

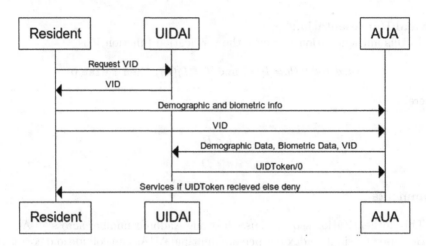

Fig. 3. Summary of VID-UIDToken

where,

$$t \in T$$
$$b \in B$$
$$d \in D$$
$$a \in AUA$$

Note that here the temporary IDs are the VIDs provided by mAadhaar App. The mapping function *temp2uid* here maps the temporary IDs to UIDs. UIDAI assigns AUA specific salts to each AUA. Same salt is used for generating UID-Tokens for that AUA (Fig. 3).

Comments

1. Parameter a can be found from the authentication request. According to UIDAI API specification [3] AUAs have to provide their identifier in their requests. The salts are unique per AUA and are decided by UIDAI.
2. The UID-Tokens solve the problem of collusion between AUAs because UID-Token for a particular resident is different for different AUAs. In this authentication sequence, the UIDAI knows all the UID-Tokens assigned to UIDs and the computation of *temp2uid(t)* can only be done at UIDAI.
3. In all future transactions with UIDAI, AUAs uniquely identify a resident with UID-Tokens. Since the UID-Tokens are generated using a hash of the UID, AUA data and salt, it is computationally hard for the AUAs to extract UIDs from UID-Tokens. This implies that the computation of *token2uid* can only be done at UIDAI.
4. As UIDAI is a part of the (executive) government, the government (if not the UIDAI) can still track the activities of the residents even if temp IDs and UID-Tokens are used as it has access to the critical mapping information *temp2uid* and *token2uid*.

4.3   CP-UID: Proposed Aadhaar Authentication Sequence with Credential Producers

Summary

In this authentication sequence [11], a third party, Credential Producer, is introduced in the authentication sequence. The credential producer provides an anonymization service. The authentication sequence is based on blind signatures [10]. It is similar to the electronic voting: the ballot officer authenticates the "electronic" ballot but is "blind" to the vote that is cast. The steps in this authentication sequence are summarized in Fig. 4.

1. User first registers his Aadhaar number via IVRS or SMS or an application with credential producers.
2. The credential producer generates a temporary identifier, tempId, stores the received Aadhaar number against this tempId and return the tempId.
3. The AUA now collects the data required by him along with tempId.
4. The AUA generates a random number localId.
5. The AUA then creates digest d which is a hash of the concatenation of localId and identifier of AUA.
6. The AUA then sends tempId, data and digest d to CP.
7. CP verifies the data with CIDR using Base-Aadhaar. If data is verified by CIDR then CP signs the digest d and sends it back else it replies with an error.

Formal Representation

In this authentication sequence the verification function V needs to be executed in 2 steps.

1. First the uid u has to be retrieved from the temporary ids i.e. tempIds at the credential provider and then this u has to be sent to UIDAI.
   Therefore the first step in computation will be

$$u = temp2uid(t)$$

   where t is the temporary id that is received from AUA.
2. Let V_b be the verification function of Base-Aadhaar

$$cidr\_response = V_b(u, d, b)$$

   where,

$$u \in U$$

$$b \in B$$

$$d \in D$$

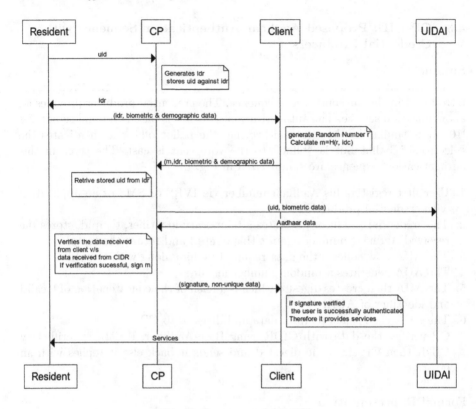

Fig. 4. Summary of CP-UID.

Legend

1. **tempId**: A temporary Identifier randomly generated by Credential Producer for a request generated by the User,
2. **Biometric data**: This is the biometric data provided by User,
3. **Demographic data**: This data is the data that the clients needs to verify before providing services,
4. **clientId**: This is identification of client,
5. **h**: is the hash generated with inputs clientId and localId.

3.

$$\lambda cidr\_response, dig, cp\_private\_key. \textbf{ if } cidr\_response = 1$$
$$\textbf{then } sign(dig, cp\_private\_key) \textbf{ else } 0$$

where,

$$cidr\_response \in \{0, 1\}$$
$$dig \in Bitstrings$$
$$cp\_private\_key \in Private\_Keys$$

4. Note that V is computed at multiple sites. Step one and three above is computed at CP and step two is computed at CIDR.

Comments

1. CP-UID is a generalization of Base-Aadhaar and VID-UIDToken authentication sequences.
   (a) CP-UID authentication sequence is same as the Base-Aadhaar authentication sequence when the mapping function $temp2uid(t)$ is the identity function.
   (b) CP-UID authentication sequence is also the same as the VID-UIDToken authentication sequence if $temp2uid(t)$ returns the UID from the VID provided by the resident. $temp2uid(t)$ retrieves the stored UID corresponding to VID. Also note that another change in CP-UID authentication sequence needed so that it can simulate VID-UIDToken authentication sequence is to ensure that $temp2uid(t)$ is executed at CIDR's site.
   (c) Thus CP-UID authentication sequence is general enough to represent both the authentication sequences Base-Aadhaar and VID-UIDToken.
2. Here the tempIds are chosen randomly, therefore, the AUAs cannot extract UIDs from tempIds. This is guaranteed by the information theoretic hardness. The tempIds behave like one time pads.
3. Details of this authentication sequence are available in [11].

4.4   Offline-KYC: Offline KYC Authentication Sequence

Summary

Whenever a resident authenticates himself at any AUA, UIDAI knows that particular resident is interacting with the AUA which generated the request, at the time of the request. UIDAI also has other information about the AUA like address, domain of service that it provides etc. from the information provided by AUA when it registers with UIDAI. UIDAI can use these pieces of information to track and profile a resident. Offline-KYC has been introduced to facilitate authentication without involving UIDAI in authentication sequence. Offline-KYC is based on an article referred as "document" in following discussions.

The Document

A **Document** is the central entity in offline KYC. The **Document** contains a subset of information stored in Aadhaar database for a particular user. A resident can choose which fields should be present in the document; The document is created by visiting the Aadhaar website. The document is in a non-human-readable format for e.g. QR code.

The Reference Code

Along with every document a **reference code** is generated. The reference code is generated randomly and is guaranteed to be unique. UIDAI has the mapping from reference code to documents and from reference code to Aadhaar number. The reference code is embedded in the document. This **reference code** will be used by AUA in all further transactions with UIDAI regarding that resident. Therefore an AUA can identify a resident uniquely from the reference code. For an AUA, the reference code acts as a handle for the particular resident, in the database of AUA.

The steps involved in offline-KYC are as follows:

1. The resident creates a document d by choosing the fields that he wants in d
2. UIDAI digitally signs the hash of this document to generate a signature with the function $sign : Bitstrings \times Private\_keys \rightarrow Signatures$ according to following function.

$$\lambda d, private\_key.\ encypt(h(d), private\_key)$$

where, $h()$ is any one-way hash function.

$$d \in Docs$$

$$private\_key \in Private\_keys$$

Therefore generating

$$d\_sig = sign(h(d), uidai\_private\_key)$$

3. Resident provides the demographic information required by the AUA and the document to AUA.
4. As document is in machine readable format, AUA scans the document and the software verifies the signature embedded in the document using the public key of UIDAI. AUA verifies the information provided by the resident with the information in the document. Alternatively, if the document contains the photograph, AUA can verify the photograph with the resident present in it and if verified, AUA can directly use demographic information in the document (Fig. 5).

Formal Representation

Therefore the verification function is

$$\lambda d, d\_sig, uidai\_pub\_key, demo\_info.\ \text{if } decrypt(d\_sig, uidai\_public\_key) = h(d) \text{ and}$$
$$demo\_info = doc\_extract\_info(d) \text{ then } 1 \text{ else } 0$$

where,

$$d \in Docs$$

$$d\_sig \in Signatures$$

$$uidai\_pub\_key \in Public\_keys$$

$$demo\_info \in D$$

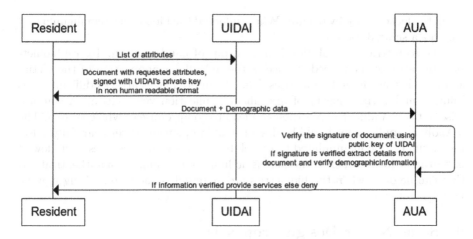

Fig. 5. Summary of Offline-KYC

Comments

1. The reference code is irrevocable. Once a reference code document is created it is valid for life and any resident can be uniquely identified by a reference code. Therefore, the reference code lacks privacy in same way uid lacks privacy in Base-Aadhaar.
2. Assuming we want one time use of reference codes, it must be made easy for residents to use multiple reference codes. Its likely that residents will use the same document at multiple service providers.
3. If certificates of UIDAI are revoked, which happens periodically, the signature embedded in document cannot be verified.

5   UID and Biometric Locks

To prevent authorization without consent, UIDAI has introduced the UID lock: a user can lock it so that no one can authenticate when it is locked. Similarly, UIDAI has provided a biometrics lock because biometrics should not be considered as secret data as there are many techniques for capturing and forging of biometrics [11]. Fingerprints can also be picked up from the smooth surfaces touched by a victim. One can also make use of prosthetic fingers that can provide fingerprints captured from different surfaces. Iris data and fingerprints can also be extracted from high-resolution photographs [7].

UIDAI has introduced "Biometric lock" to take care of this issue. Under this solution, access to biometrics can be one of two states, locked and unlocked. When in the locked state, the UIDAI will not authenticate the resident using biometrics (even if the correct biometrics are provided). To use biometrics, the resident has to unlock the biometrics using mAadhaar application. The biometric authentication will work only when the biometrics are unlocked as the biometrics are in the locked state by default. When unlocked the biometrics remain unlocked only for a short duration.

The biometric lock solution is a good out of band solution. To use biometrics, the attacker now needs to access the mAadhaar application of the victim and need his/her forged biometrics. This definitely makes attacks difficult. This solution makes the security of mAadhaar application very critical. A compromise of the mAadhaar application can lead to compromise of whole system. The mAadhaar application should be designed and implemented very carefully. Also, the victim can be manipulated to unlock biometrics which provides a window of opportunity to an attacker. As there is no limit on the number of authentications that can be done when the biometrics are unlocked; some rate limiting may be useful.

6   Some Newer Design Proposals

6.1   Proposed Adaptations to VID-UIDToken Authentication Sequence for Enhancing Privacy

The VID and UID-Token authentication sequence coupled with biometric locks solves the collusion problem among AUAs with respect to privacy. However, the Government/UIDAI still has data that it can use at its discretion to correlate patterns, so there is no privacy with respect to GoI/UIDAI (an important point in many discussions, including petitions in the Supreme Court recently). The current method of auditing and logging to track accesses to data, if immutable, only ensures that every access, including non-legal ones, can be examined for violations post facto. It cannot prevent the Government or UIDAI to use non-standard ways to access data or destroy or modify the logs if within its powers or exclusive possession.

6.2   Hybrid Authentication Sequence

One small change in VID-UIDToken authentication sequence can solve the above-stated problem of surveillance. The UID-Token generation and management could be offloaded to credential producers as in CP-UID authentication sequence. Some reputed institutions in the country can manage these credential producers; examples could be the election commission or other institutes of national importance and known probity.

Note that the only part offloaded is that of UID-Token generation and request redirection like in CP-UID authentication sequence and not the data management itself. Credential producers can be oblivious to the contents of the messages passed to UIDAI i.e. data of the residents sent for verification by AUA. The whole data stays with the UIDAI. The idea is to separate the data from index (UID-Token) by which the AUAs request the access to user data. The redirection service is similar to credential producers. In this scenario,

1. Credential producers have only the UID to UID-Token mapping. CPs do not have access to user data.

2. UIDAI has only UID to user data mapping. It does not know the UID-Tokens being used. Therefore surveillance is not possible.
3. AUA will only have UID-Token to user data mapping. This is the same as the current VID-UIDToken authentication sequence.

We believe that this is a good hybrid of the CP-UID and VID-UIDToken models.

Security and Privacy Properties of Hybrid Model. We have proved that the above-stated protocol provides privacy of Aadhaar number and correctness of authentication.

Privacy of Aadhaar number. Proverif [12] models an attacker which has access to everything except the things that are explicitly declared as private. We can then query if an attacker can infer the secret from the facts that the attacker knows. Proverif can then be used to prove that the attacker cannot infer the Aadhaar number. Also, it can be shown that the AUAs do not have any more information than the attacker. Therefore, it implies that AUAs cannot infer an Aadhaar number.

Correctness of Authentication. Proverif models the protocol by declaring the actions taken by the parties in the protocol. Proverif supports **events** to signal the progress of the parties in the protocol. We can query the correspondence of events. That is we can check if an event is guaranteed to occur before another event. We use this to prove the correctness of authentication. In Proverif, the events are parameterized so we can make sure that all the events correspond to authentication of the same resident and that there is no interference between two authentication sessions. We define 3 events

1. `aua_considers_verified(vid,data)`: This event is triggered when AUA reaches end of the protocol for a `vid` and `data`.
2. `cp_verified (vid, uid)`: This event is triggered when the CP gets a YES response from CIDR.
3. `cidr_verified(uid, data)`: This event is triggered when CIDR has verified the `data` for a `uid`.

Using Proverif, we prove that `aua_considers_verified` implies `cp_verified` implies `cidr_verified`. This proves the correctness of authentication.

6.3   Proposed Changes to Offline-KYC Authentication Sequence

Note that the **reference code** is valid for life. This code is just like an Aadhaar Number and is irrevocable; unlike VIDs, this identifier does not change. Also, the advantage of offline KYC is that any user can print this information in encoded (non-human-readable, only machine-readable) format and can present to AUAs. AUAs can then verify the information without generating requests to UIDAI. Since this information is printed on paper, it is cumbersome for the resident to create the documents and reference codes, which may lead to usage of the same document and reference code at multiple AUAs.

Let us assume that the document is printed on a paper in form of QR code, which can be read by a machine only. And that AUAs can verify digital signature embedded in this QR code. We recommend that instead of generating only one QR code/reference code, generate and sign n reference codes and provide them on the same page and advise the residents to use one QR code only once and tear of the part of the page after use.

Efficient Implementation of Proposed Changes

If we encourage one time use of reference codes, UIDAI will have to store all the reference codes. This design is not scalable and therefore, we propose a different efficient implementation of the reference codes generation. To generate n different reference codes as described above, the UIDAI has to generate a reference code when the document is generated. Then it should hash the generated reference code, concatenated with some user-specific salt, repeatedly to produce multiple reference codes.

Let $r_1, r_2, ... r_n$ be n reference codes, where r_1 is generated uniquely by UIDAI when document is created.

Let

$$r_2 = h(r_1 || salt)$$
$$r_3 = h(r_2 || salt)$$
$$...$$
$$r_n = h(r_{n-1} || salt)$$

Here, $||$ is the concatenation operator. In this model, UIDAI now has to store n reference codes instead of only one.

Reducing Space Requirement Using Symmetric Encryption

Storing multiple reference codes for a resident is inefficient in terms of storage. This can be handled by placing a backdoor in the reference code. Symmetric key encryption can be used to implement the back door. We propose the following scheme. UIDAI should have a resident specific secret that is only known to UIDAI. Let this secret key be sk. Let $senc$ be a symmetric encryption function.

Let $r_1, r_2, ... r_n$ be n reference codes, where r_1 is generated uniquely by UIDAI when document is created.

Let

$$r_2 = senc(r_1 || 2, sk)$$
$$r_3 = senc(r_1 || 3, sk)$$
$$...$$
$$r_n = senc(r_1 || n, sk)$$

Now, UIDAI does not need to store n reference codes. Instead, it will suffice for UIDAI to store only one reference code and user-specific secret. UIDAI can then retrieve the reference code corresponding to document using sk which acts as a back door. A similar strategy can be devised by the government to implement UID-Tokens.

Enforcing One Time Use

We also propose a scheme to enforce one-time use of each reference code in case of offline KYC. Here the only assumption is that verifying AUA is connected.

We propose change only in the signature scheme that is used. There are various one-time signature schemes; here we describe the use of Lamport's one-time signature scheme. Other more efficient one-time signature schemes can also be used.

Lamport's One Time Signature Scheme

This scheme [9] provides a way to digitally sign a message in a way that the signature can be used only once. The steps of the signature scheme are as follows.

1. Suppose UIDAI wants to sign a document. It hashes the document to n bit digest. Let this digest be dig.
2. UIDAI chooses $2n$ random numbers. Let these numbers be a_n and b_n. These numbers are private key of UIDAI.
3. UIDAI then creates a sequence of n numbers, seq such that if i^{th} bit in dig is 0 then i^{th} number in the sequence is a_i else i^{th} number in sequence is b_i.
4. Along with the document UIDAI also sends seq. This is signature generated by UIDAI for dig.
5. UIDAI also registers hashes of all of a_ns, hashes of all of b_ns and dig with some verifying authority. This authority can be hosted at UIDAI but can be logically separate from UIDAI to make the KYC verification completely separated from UIDAI, thus maintaining the advantage that UIDAI is not involved in the verification process.
6. When an AUA wants to verify a document, it calculates the hash of document to get dig'. It sends digest dig' to verifying authority, which responds with hashes of all a_ns and hashes of all b_ns. AUA can verify the signature by comparing hash of ith element of seq with hash of a_i received from verifying authority if i^{th} bit of dig' is 0. Else comparing hash of ith element of seq with hash of b_i for all i.
7. The verifying authority then de-registers the dig and corresponding seq thereby failing all the authentication requests for dig in future.

7 Scalability Analysis

Aadhaar is a huge database in size therefore, it is very important that the design is scalable. In the following discussion we refer to the CIDR as core of the system and all the AUAs and Credential Producers as the edge of the system. We now present our observations:

7.1 Base-Aadhaar

- This is the most simple model with minimum overheads.
- Most of the computing (for verification) happens at the core.

- It has the least latency for authentication. Let this latency be called t for further discussions below.
- Since it is a highly centralized system, it is the least scalable design.
- This model depends only on one server i.e. CIDR; therefore, this model is more reliable than all except the offline method.

7.2   VID-UIDToken

- Here the computing requirement is higher as compared to Base-Aadhaar because now CIDR also has to compute VID and UIDTokens.
- Storage requirements are higher at the core as compared to Base-Aadhaar because UIDTokens have to be stored for a long time. VIDs have to be stored for a relatively shorter duration.
- The latency of the authentication is $2t$ in the worst case and at least t in this model.
- This model depends only on CIDR but four messages need to exchanged. Therefore availability of this model is relatively less than Base-Aadhaar.

7.3   CP-UID

- In this model the computing is offloaded to edge as tempIds and signatures generated by credential producers.
- Computation at AUAs also increase as AUAs need to verify signatures.
- The number of messages reaching CIDR and computation and storage requirements by CIDR are similar to Base-Aadhaar. This is because Base-Aadhaar is used between credential producers and CIDR.
- This design is scalable because most computation happens at edge.
- In this model six message need to be exchanged and three parties are involved, i.e. CIDR, CP and AUA. Thus the availability of this model is lesser than that of VID-UIDToken.

7.4   Hybrid of VID-UIDToken and CP-UID

- In this model the computing of VIDs and UIDTokens is offloaded to credential producers.
- Computation at AUAs is similar to Base-Aadhaar. This is because AUAs just need to verify if the response is error or UIDToken.
- This is a scalable design because most of the computations happen at the edge.
- The availability of this model is equivalent to CP-UID.

7.5   Offline-KYC

- In this model the only computing requirement at the core of the system is only during the generation of document.

- Almost all of the computation is offloaded to AUAs. AUAs have to verify the signature.
- Computational and network overheads of this method are low.
- The availability of this model is high as it depends only on the certification authority which issued certificate to UIDAI and that the certificate is not revoked.

7.6 Offline-KYC with Repeated Hashing

- In this model the computing requirement at the core of the system is slightly higher during the generation of document.
- Almost all of the computation is offloaded to AUAs. AUAs have to verify the signature.
- Computational overheads of this model are low.
- The storage requirements of this model are high compared to Offline-KYC because this model encourages one time use of reference codes, therefore more reference codes have to be generated as compared to Offline-KYC.
- The availability of this model is equivalent to Offline-KYC.

7.7 Offline-KYC with Backdoor by Encryption

- In this model the computing requirement at the core of the system is high since core has to do repeated encryption.
- But the computing requirement is only during the generation of document.
- Computation for verification is offloaded to AUAs. AUAs have to verify the signatures.
- Computational overheads of this method are more than Offline-KYC and Offline-KYC with repeated hashing.
- Storage overheads of this method are considerably less than Offline-KYC and Offline-KYC with repeated hashing.
- The availability of this model equivalent to Offline-KYC.

7.8 Offline-KYC with One Time Use Enforcement

- In this model the computing requirement at the core are high. If an n bit digest is generated by hashing the document in step one of Offline-KYC with one time use enforcement, the core has to generate n hashes. Thus computational requirements are proportional to size of the digest generated by hashing the document, which is considerably more than Offline-KYC.
- The storage requirements here are similar to Offline-KYC.
- The storage requirements at verifying authority in Offline-KYC with one time use enforcement are proportional to number of documents generated but not verified by AUAs at any given time.
- Efficient implementations of one time signatures can increase the scalability of the system.
- This model depends on CIDR and verifying authority. This reduces the availability of the system as compared to Offline-KYC.

8   Conclusion

The Aadhaar project is likely to have a good cost-benefit ratio; however, good implementation is important. Ideally, all current and likely future threats should be addressed right in the design phase itself. In this paper, we have identified the major Aadhaar authentication sequences currently in practice. We define a formal way to represent these authentications using a common notation so that we can compare and contrast these models. We also highlight some of the problems with some of the authentication sequences. We provide a hybrid model which combines VID-UIDToken and CP-UID authentication sequences. Our solutions are based on the idea of separation of data into smaller components that do not make sense unless the data components are recombined. We also provide suggestions for improving the offline-KYC authentication sequence.

References

1. (2018). https://www.uidai.gov.in/images/resource/UIDAI_Circular_11012018.pdf
2. (2018). https://www.uidai.gov.in/aadhaar_dashboard/india.php
3. (2018). https://uidai.gov.in/images/resource/aadhaar_authentication_api_2_5.pdf
4. Agrawal, S., Banerjee, S., Sharma, S.: Privacy and security of Aadhaar: a computer science perspective. Econ. Polit. Weekly **52**(37), 93–102 (2017)
5. Banerjee, S., Sharma, S.: An offline alternative for Aadhaar-based biometric authentication (2018). http://www.ideasforindia.in/topics/productivity-innovation/an-offline-alternative-for-aadhaar-based-biometric-authentication.html
6. Gupta, K.: Uidai wades in amid twitter row over R.S. Sharma's Aadhaar dare (2018). https://www.livemint.com/Politics/jwcBx4IHN6H5l90O14iRHM/UIDAI-wades-in-amid-Twitter-row-over-RS-Sharmas-Aadhaar-d.html
7. Hern, A.: Hacker fakes German minister's fingerprints using photos of her hands (2018). https://www.theguardian.com/technology/2014/dec/30/hacker-fakes-german-ministers-fingerprints-using-photos-of-her-hands
8. Times of India: LPG subsidy of rs 168 crore sent to Airtel payments bank accounts (2018). https://timesofindia.indiatimes.com/business/india-business/lpg-subsidy-of-rs-168-crore-sent-to-airtel-payments-bank-accounts/articleshow/62120108.cms
9. Lamport, L.: Constructing digital signatures from a one-way function. Technical report, Technical Report CSL-98, SRI International Palo Alto (1979)
10. Maheswaran, J., Wolinsky, D.I., Ford, B.: Crypto-book: an architecture for privacy preserving online identities. In: Proceedings of the Twelfth ACM Workshop on Hot Topics in Networks, p. 14. ACM (2013)
11. Rajput, A., Gopinath, K.: Towards a more secure Aadhaar. In: Shyamasundar, R.K., Singh, V., Vaidya, J. (eds.) ICISS 2017. LNCS, vol. 10717, pp. 283–300. Springer, Cham (2017). https://doi.org/10.1007/978-3-319-72598-7_17
12. Blanchet, B., Cheval, V., Allamigeon, X., Smyth, B.: ProVerif: cryptographic protocol verifier in the formal model (2010). http://prosecco.gforge.inria.fr/personal/bblanche/proverif

Client Security and Authentication

drPass: A Dynamic and Reusable Password Generator Protocol

Suryakanta Panda$^{(\boxtimes)}$ and Samrat Mondal

Indian Institute of Technology Patna, Patna, India
{suryakanta.pcs15,samrat}@iitp.ac.in

Abstract. In general, alphanumeric passwords are used for authentication due to its simplicity and deployability. Strong and distinct alphanumeric passwords are inconvenient to memorize. So, users often pick weak passwords and reuse them. Also, users employ some simple tricks to derive passwords from a basic one. However, such weak and easy to derive passwords could not provide sufficient strength to protect users confidential resources. These passwords reduce the work of attackers to a great extent. Although the strong and distinct passwords reduce brute force attack, they are prone to theft and are often compromised under different vulnerabilities. Thus, by compromising one password, an attacker may gain access to other web-accounts where identical or similar passwords are used by the same user. In this paper, we propose *drPass*, a dynamic and reusable password generating protocol that generates high entropy passwords and thwarts various password stealing attacks. The proposed *drPass* scheme does not require any server-side change of existing websites for its implementation. It reduces the memory burden on users and also helps users to generate and maintain highly secure, distinct passwords for each site.

Keywords: Authentication · Passwords · Security · Reusability

1 Introduction

Authentication using alphanumeric password dominates over all other methods of end-user authentication. People select a userID and password pair during registration and recall that during login, to authenticate to a system. As more and more services are coming to the web, a user has to remember more number of passwords for the identity verification, that is, there is a persistent increase in the number of passwords a user has to memorize. The "password problem" [30] associated with alphanumeric passwords is expected to comply with two conflicting basic requirements: one is associated with usability, and the other is related to security aspects.

1. *Usability aspects:* passwords should be easy to remember and easy to use.

© Springer Nature Switzerland AG 2018
V. Ganapathy et al. (Eds.): ICISS 2018, LNCS 11281, pp. 407–426, 2018.
https://doi.org/10.1007/978-3-030-05171-6_21

2. *Security aspects:* passwords should be secure, should be hard to guess; they should be changed periodically, and should not be same for any two accounts of the same user; they should not be written down or stored in plain text. The authenticity of the site should be verified before logging in.

Meeting both of these requirements is the main challenge in password based authentication system due to the limited cognitive capacity of human memory. So, users tend to reuse passwords across different websites. Florencio et al. [10] found that on average, one user reuses a single password across four different websites.

Another major problem of password reuse is the offline attack or password leak. In recent years an increasing amount of password leaks occurred from major Internet sites [18]. With the advancement of hardware technology and sophisticated password cracking methodologies, attackers can extract the original password from leaked password files and use that password to impersonate a user in other sites where the user is likely to use the same login information [15]. It is estimated that 43–51% of users reuse a single password across multiple sites [9].

Although strong passwords with sufficient entropy can resist guessing, brute force and dictionary attacks, it is not enough to protect against password stealing attacks like phishing, shoulder surfing, and keylogging [11,21]. Phishing is the most common and efficient password stealing attack. According to the report by APWG [4], the total number of phishing sites detected in the second quarter of 2016 was 466,065. This was 61% higher than the previous quarterly record in Q4, 2015.

To address the above discussed problems and enhance password security, a number of techniques have been proposed i.e.

- *Password manager*: It automatically generates strong passwords and fill-in password field on websites. However, using a rogue network, an attacker can extract many passwords from a password manager without user's knowledge. Common users also doubt its security and feel uneasy about using it [20,26].
- *Single sign-on system*: It allows users to log into many sites with a single ID and password which reduces the memory burden of a user to remember many passwords. In this way, single sign-on systems put too much trust in a centralized system and thus vulnerable to single point failure [22,29].
- *Graphical password system*: It makes users to click on images or draw their password on a two-dimensional grid, for authorization. But, almost all graphical password systems are prone to shoulder surfing attack. Although some shoulder surfing resistant graphical password schemes are proposed, that takes more time for authentication and are less accurate as compared to alphanumeric passwords. So, graphical passwords are not matured enough [12].

Despite some limitations in both security and usability context, passwords are highly unlikely to fade away. Reasons are the difficulty to find a better alternative, familiarity in the user community, and the inertia of ubiquitous deployment. The existing alternate techniques offer only minor improvements over passwords and thus have a little chance of displacing it [7,14].

To the best of our knowledge, although many schemes, protocols have been proposed and designed to prevent users from some specific attacks, none of them can defend all the above discussed attacks. Thus, there is a need for a password based authentication system which can defend all these attacks without putting much overhead on the user.

Motivated by the above fact, in this paper, we have proposed a password system, termed as *drPass*, to prevent password stealing attacks and password reuse attacks. Password leakage usually happens when a password is entered during authentication [32]. So, our focus is to avoid the input of a complete static password on an untrusted PC during authentication. We verified that the proposed *drPass* scheme could defend the password threats with no server-side changes and also no change to the user experience.

Overall, our contributions are:

(i) We have proposed a dynamic and reusable password generation scheme *drPass* which is highly secure and user-friendly.
(ii) We have explained that *drPass* reduces the memory burden.
(iii) We have verified that *drPass* is resistant to various password stealing attacks.

The rest of this paper is organized as follows: We describe the existing password schemes in Sect. 2. Section 3 introduces the proposed *drPass* scheme. We present some important design aspects of *drPass* in Sect. 4. The security analysis of *drPass* is in Sect. 5. Section 6 gives the detail about prototype implementation and performance evaluation. We compare the proposed *drPass* with other systems in Sect. 7 and finally conclude in Sect. 8.

2   Related Work

The importance of password has attracted many academic and industrial research. Researchers have proposed many schemes to protect user's secret passwords from adversaries. In this section, we highlight their contributions which are related to our proposed *drPass*.

PwdHash [25] is a browser extension which transparently produces a unique password for each site, improving web password security and defending against phishing and other attacks. Specifically, PwdHash captures the destination domain name and uses it as a salt for sending the hashed password to the remote site. However, PwdHash is vulnerable to dictionary attack as salt is publicly known and advanced phishing attacks using flash objects or focus stealing.

Password Multiplier [13] is also a browser extension technique that uses a strengthened cryptographic hash function to compute secure, distinct, high-entropy passwords for many accounts while requiring the user to memorize a single master password. However, the main limitation of Password Multiplier is that all the derived passwords will be known to adversaries if the master password is stolen. Moreover, changing the master password and the password for a specific site is a complicated task.

Passpet [33], an improvement of Password Multiplier uses petnames to help users recognize phishing attempts. In order to regenerate correct passwords to address roaming users, i.e. on another computer, Passpet relies on a remote server to store site label details. However, Passpet has the same limitation as Password Multiplier regarding master password vulnerability. Changing the master password is also a laborious task because a user needs to migrate passwords for every site. Moreover, its remote server is vulnerable to various malicious attacks.

PasswordAgent [29], a password hashing technique that uses salt repository and a browser plug-in to secure web logins with strong passwords. It provides stronger protection against offline attacks. But, a user must activate password protection by using password prefix or password key which is the main usability limitation. Moreover, it is highly vulnerable to keylogger and other spyware attacks.

Xiao et al. [31] presented a password protection scheme that involves a small amount of human computing to prevent user's passwords from being stolen by attackers. It increases memory burden of a user because user has to remember one virtual password function along with the secret password. Moreover, server side changes are required for its implementation.

MP-Auth [23] protects passwords in untrusted environments through a trusted mobile device. Before sending user's password to a client PC, the password is encrypted by a preinstalled public key of a remote service. Distribution and maintenance of public keys of each website is a practical challenge. A connection between mobile and browser is required every time before login, is also a usability issue.

oPass [27], an improved version of MP-Auth, leverages a user's cellphone and short message service (SMS) to thwart password stealing and password reuse attacks. However, the SMS delay and drop is a major bottleneck in oPass. The average time for registration and login is 21.8 and 21.6 s, respectively. Also, the implementation is costlier enough for the use of SMS and the server side changes.

3   Proposed *drPass* Scheme

To authenticate a user in knowledge based authentication, a system needs to verify a user's identity by operating on the user's ID and the corresponding password which the user provides. It is reasonable that both the user's ID and password are fixed so that it can be easily remembered. However, when passwords are typed, that may be stolen by the adversaries. Protecting a user's password on a kiosk is infeasible when keyloggers are already installed on it [27]. In addition, avoiding shoulder-surfing attacker and identifying phishing websites is a challenging task for a user. We cannot put the password in a randomly variant form as it is beyond our memorability. To address such a challenge, we propose *drPass*, a dynamic password scheme that will prevent users from typing the entire fixed password into kiosks during the login process. Here, we are assuming that the communication link is secure and the attacker can steal the password either from the client side or the server side.

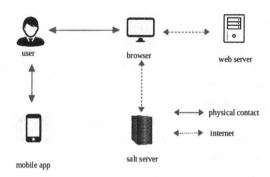

Fig. 1. Architecture of drPass

The goal of *drPass* is two-fold. Firstly, it tries to protect passwords from stealing and leaks. Secondly, it allows users to reuse their password safely. Figure 1 describes the architecture of the *drPass* system. The proposed system consists of various components such as mobile phone, salt server, browser and the web server that user wishes to access. The user operates on her mobile phone and the browser directly to accomplish secure logins to the web server. The communication between the browser and the salt server is through the internet. Similarly, the browser interacts with the web server via the internet. The mobile phone generates a secret key for authentication into the salt server. The salt server stores list of salts and generates site specific passwords. High entropy and distinct site specific passwords are used to login different user accounts. Thus, users get relief from remembering strong passwords for different sites.

The details of different password terms used in this paper are discussed below.

- **application password** (p_a): It is used to authenticate a legitimate user to *drPass* mobile application before secret key generation. Users have to memorize this application password.
- **protected password** (p_p): It is used to generate unique passwords for different sites, that is, the salt server converts the protected password to site-password. From a single protected password, users can generate many distinct site-passwords. To counter against the single point of failure in our protocol, users have to remember this protected password. Thus, the security strength of our protocol depends on both application password and protected password.
- **site-password** (p_{sk}): It is the hashed password generated for a user account based on the stored salt and protected password. It is a high entropy password, and users need not require to remember it.

Table 1. Notations used in drPass protocol

Notation	Description
U	A particular user who wants to login and obtain system resources
uid	userID of user for salt server
SS	Salt server
E	Encryption algorithm (AES)
pep	Pepper value
p_a	User's application password to log into drPass mobile application
r	Random number
p_p	Protected password
S_k	kth site server which offer its resources to the user
sl_k	Salt associated with kth site in the salt server
p_{sk}	Generated site-password for site k
uname	UserID for each domain
$\|\|$	Concatenation
h	Public one-way hash function
$X \rightarrow Y$: (M)	Message M is sent from X to Y through an open channel
$X \Rightarrow Y$: (M)	Message M is sent from X to Y through a closed channel

The various notations used in $drPass$ protocol are presented in Table 1.

3.1 drPass: Registration Phase

The aim of this registration phase is to allow a user and salt server to negotiate some shared secret to authenticate succeeding logins for the user. User begins by installing the $drPass$ application program on a mobile phone. Then, by opening the application, she connects the $drPass$ application to the salt server and goes for the new user registration process.

Like conventional registration process, the user fills the details such as *userID, password (application password), mobile number, email, security question,* etc. Salt server sends an SMS and also an email to the mobile number and email id respectively, provided by the user for verification. After getting a verification response from the user, salt server stows a secret random value(called as pepper) in the verified $drPass$ application which has an important role in the login phase for the secret key generation. At the end of registration process, the salt server stores the user details like userID, stowed pepper value, etc. for future reference and displays a message of registration completion on $drPass$ mobile application.

After the successful registration of $drPass$ mobile application, the individual websites must be registered in the salt server to have a salt associated with the websites. The salt is used to generate distinct site-password for every website. The pictorial representation of registration phase is illustrated in Fig. 2.

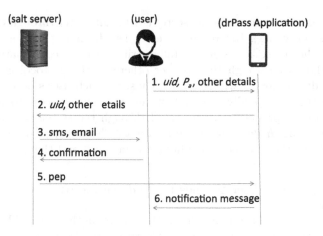

Fig. 2. Procedure of registration phase

3.2   drPass: Login Phase

The user begins the login procedure by sending a request to the salt server to generate a random number. After verifying the request, salt server displays a random number 'r' of five to six digits. Next, the user runs the registered $drPass$ application installed on her phone, login to it with the application password. The $drPass$ mobile application asks for a random number after successful login. The user provides 'r'. Then, $drPass$ application displays a secret key which is valid for one login session. The secret key is computed by using the random number 'r' and pepper. It does not require communication between $drPass$ mobile application and salt server for computing the secret key, i.e., $drPass$ mobile application computes the secret key in offline mode.

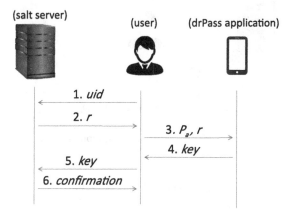

Fig. 3. Login to salt server

In the next step, user sends the secret key to salt server through the browser. The salt server verifies the received secret key from the user and sends its response. If the secret key is successfully verified, then a confirmation message is sent to the user through the browser otherwise the protocol is aborted by throwing a dialog box of wrong input. Thus, for each user's account that has been registered successfully, the salt server will refuse access to the account unless the user is properly authenticated through the secret key generated by the corresponding *drPass* mobile application. The pictorial representation of login process to the salt server is illustrated in Fig. 3 and the details are given as follows:

(i) U $\rightarrow$ SS: (uid), User U sends the *'uid'* with a login request to the salt server *SS*.

(ii) SS $\rightarrow$ U: (r), Salt server SS checks the validity of the received login request. If it is not valid then salt server SS rejects the login request. Otherwise, generates a random number 'r' and sends it to the user U.

(iii) User U runs *drPass* application and provides application password p_a for login.

(iv) *drPass* application verifies the application password and asks for random number 'r'.

(v) User U enters the random number 'r', received from salt server SS.

(vi) *drPass* application uses encryption algorithm to generate a key from the 'r': $key = E_{pep}(r)$. The generated key is displayed on the mobile screen.

(vii) U $\rightarrow$ SS: (key), user U sends the *key* to the salt server SS.

(viii) Salt server SS calculates $key' = E_{pep}(r)$ with the stored pep and 'r'. (r is valid for only one instance).

(xi) Salt server SS compares key' with the received *key* and authenticates the user U.

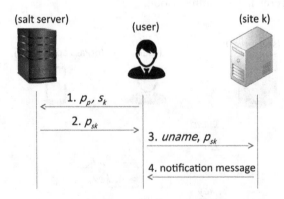

Fig. 4. Login to user accounts

After successful authentication of the user to the salt server, salt server throws a dialog asking for the site name and protected password. After taking the site name and protected password, the salt server generates site-password for the specific site and stores that in a clipboard. The user can copy and paste the site-password into the desired password field. Once, a user is authenticated to the salt server, it can compute multiple site-passwords until logged out from the salt server. The pictorial representation of login phase to different websites is illustrated in Fig. 4 and the details are given as follows:

(i) U $\Rightarrow$ SS: $(p_p,\ s_k)$, User U sends the protected password p_p and site name s_k to the salt sever.

(ii) Salt server calculates site-password: $p_{sk} = h(p_p||sl_k)$ and stores it in a clipboard.

(iii) U $\Rightarrow S_k$: (uname,p_{sk}), User U sends uname and p_{sk} to k^{th} site to access its resources.

3.3   drPass: Recovery Phase

The recovery phase is designed for some specific conditions like when a user forgets $drPass$ application password, loses her mobile phone or replaces an old one with new models. The protocol can recuperate $drPass$ settings on the new mobile phone if the same phone number is used. After installing $drPass$ application program on new mobile phone, the user can launch the application, connects to the salt server. In the next step, a recovery request is required to be sent with $userID$ to the salt server. On receiving it, the salt server sends an OTP to the registered mobile phone number and email. Then, the user has to provide the same OTP to the salt server. Also, some additional security principles like exiting password reset mechanisms are followed. After successful verification, the user can reset the password.

In the present scenario, it is not a difficult task to obtain the lost mobile number. If one registered user loses her mobile number and fails to get the old number, there are no shortcut techniques to regain all the passwords instead of migrating all the passwords manually.

4   Some Important Design Aspects of $drPass$

The two major components of $drPass$ are mobile application and salt server. The mobile application generates the secret key and is used for authentication into the salt server. For each registered user, the salt server securely stores randomly generated salt lists which in turn enables $drPass$ to calculate the site-passwords.

4.1 $drPass$ Mobile Application

The user registration can be done only through the $drPass$ mobile application. In registration phase, the salt server stows a random value (called as pepper) in the $drPass$ mobile application. The pepper has a major role in the login phase. So, an attacker cannot generate the required secret key (used for authentication to the salt server) except the proper $drPass$ mobile application. Thus, one user account in the salt server can be operated only through the corresponding $drPass$ mobile application.

To compute the secret key in the login phase, $drPass$ application asks for the userID (uid) and application password (p_a). A registered user can be authenticated to its corresponding $drPass$ application through p_a. After the successful authentication, $drPass$ application asks for the random number 'r'. Then, the received random number 'r' is encrypted by the $drPass$ mobile application using any standard symmetric encryption technique. It uses the pepper installed by the salt server during registration phase for encryption as shown in Eq. 1.

$$key = E_{pep}(r) \tag{1}$$

Then, it displays the encrypted random number 'r' as a secret key. The secret key should be of sufficient length (e.g., 5–6 characters) to prevent brute-force attack. Here, we are using AES for encryption because of its high resiliency capability against the practical cryptanalytic attack. The installed pepper will act as salt if hash function is used for secret key generation. User may change the installed pepper value of $drPass$ application in a periodic interval through the salt server.

4.2 Salt Server

Before we go into the detailed description of the salt server, in a nutshell, it can be considered as a black box which converts protected password (p_p) into high entropy, distinct site-passwords.

In the login phase, after receiving the secret key from a registered user, the salt server calculates the key for verification following the same method as $drPass$ application. If both the received key and calculated key are same, then the user is allowed to compute the site-password. Otherwise, the protocol is aborted. After successful secret key verification, the salt server asks for website URL and protected password. Then, the salt server generates site-password (p_{sk}) from the website URL, p_p and stores that p_{sk} in a clipboard. Once a user is authenticated to the salt server, then different site-passwords can be generated for different websites associated with the user account.

To create a site-password for a website, user must register the domain name of that site to have a salt associated with it. If a user attempts to generate a site-password for a website that has not been registered, the salt server throws a dialog to warn that the site might be spoofed one from a phishing attacker. After verification of the website URL, the user can go for site registration. By taking the site URL, protected password and retrieving the specific salt of the site for that concerned user, the salt server generates site-password and stores that in the clipboard. The salts are different for different registered sites of a user so that the generated site-passwords are distinct even if the protected password is same.

$$p_{sk} = F \ (\ h \ (\ p_p \ || \ sl_k) \ ) \tag{2}$$

Function 'F' limits the length of p_{sk} to 16 characters and use base85 encoding scheme for the hash output. Base85 encoding scheme covers four types of character sets i.e. uppercase letters, lower case letters, digits and special characters. So, the generated p_{sk} matches the password security requirements of popular consumer websites i.e., minimum length, combining character types, strength assesment [1,5]. We have also tested the p_{sk} with the password meter [3] and yet another password meter [6], both shows p_{sk} achieves highest level of security. Changing the encoding scheme and length of p_{sk} is a trivial work.

Equation-2 clearly shows that p_{sk} depends on both p_p and sl_k. So, one can update the p_{sk} by changing either any one of them or changing both. Only updating the salt, user can change the site-password in a periodic interval. Thus, by memorizing only two passwords (p_a and p_p), a user can generate many distinct site-passwords. The salt server can be publicly accessed via the Internet so that users can retrieve their salt list details from any location.

5   Security Analysis

The goal of an attacker is to masquerade itself as a legitimate user and to access the website without being detected. An attacker can steal user's credentials by various offline and online password stealing techniques like keylogger, phishing, and shoulder-surfing. In this section, we briefly analyze the security features of *drPass* that can resist the effort of an attacker.

5.1   Attacks on Salt Server

Salt server only stores the salt values for computation of site-passwords. It neither stores the protected password (p_p) nor site-password (p_{sk}). So, if the salt server is compromised without being detected, then the attacker only gets some salt values. We know that the site-password is computed from both the salt and protected password as given in Eq. 2. Thus, without p_p, only from salt sl_k the site-password cannot be computed, and the attacker cannot reach the user account by attacking salt server.

5.2   Resistance to Phishing Attack

Our proposed system assists users to distinguish legitimate sites from spoofed sites. Phishing attackers may use a closely similar domain name which directs to a different site. User has to generate site-password from the salt server before logging into any website. For generating site-password, a random salt is required, and it is stored in the salt server associated with the domain name. When a user attempts to generate a site-password for an unregistered spoofed site, the salt server throws a notification. Thus, the salt server provides an early warning against phishing sites. Even after ignoring the warning, when a user wants to generate site-password for this type of spoofed sites he has to register the domain name in the salt server. After successful registration, the salt associated with the legitimate site like *www.somenamebank.com* and the spoofed site *www.somenameb@nk.com* are different. Assume that, the salt for site *www.somenamebank.com* is sl_1 and the salt for *www.somenameb@nk.com* is sl_2. Thus, $p_{s1} = h(p_p||sl_1)$ and $p_{s2} = h(p_p||sl_2)$. As the generation of site-password depends on salt values and when the salt values are different, distinct site-passwords are generated. So, a phishing attacker fails to capture the passwords for legitimate sites using spoofed sites.

5.3   Resistance to Shoulder-Surfing Attack

User copies the site-password from the clipboard, and then paste it into the desired password field and this prevents attackers from reading the password. So, shoulder-surfing attacker cannot succeed to get site-password. Moreover, the application password is used only on the mobile phone, and a user can securely type a password on her mobile phone. Even if an attacker gets both the application password and protected password, she fails to access the salt server without the mobile device. Salt server authenticates the user through the secret key which is generated by the *drPass* application using the equation $key = E_{pep}(r)$. As pepper values are different for different users (mobile devices), the key values are different $key_1 = E_{pep1}(r)$ and $key_2 = E_{pep2}(r)$ for different users with the same r. Thus, it is not an easy task for a shoulder-surfing attacker to capture both the application password and site-password along with victim's mobile phone. In addition, the mobile phones are also protected with screen locks, i.e. patterns, pins, etc. [28].

We conduct a user study to test the resistivity of our proposed method in reducing shoulder-surfing attacks. Twenty participants including university students, technical staff and non-technical staff took part in the evaluation process. First, we provide an introduction about the shoulder-surfing attack to the participants. We divided the participants equally into two groups, i.e. users and attackers. The users were instructed to login in the presence of attackers standing behind them. All users were instructed to complete one successful login, and the attackers instructed to observe that login. Then, the attackers were given three attempts to pass the authentication process. After this, we swapped the role of participants that is, users to attackers and attackers to users. Again the above discussed process is repeated, and the new attackers were given three attempts to pass the authentication process.

In the above user study, none of the attackers were able to find the site-passwords, but most of them got the protected password. Only two of them were able to see the application password due to the carelessness of the user while typing on her mobile phone. However, without that particular mobile phone both the two attackers failed to generate the required site-password. This shows that our scheme is resistant to shoulder-surfing attack.

5.4 Resistance to Keyloggers

Keylogger records all the keys struck on a keyboard. In *drPass*, the application password is typed only in the mobile application, the protected password is typed only in the computer, and the site-password is copied to the password field. Users can access the salt server without entering their password on computers. Clipboard is used to prevent typing of site-password on password fields of different sites. Thus, keyloggers cannot derive user's application password and site-password from untrusted computers by recording the keystrokes. By using keyloggers, an attacker can obtain only protected password. From the Eq. 2, it is clear that site-password cannot be calculated only from p_p without corresponding salt value. To get access to the salt server for the salt value, keylogger attacker needs to calculate the secret key following the equation: $key = E_{pep}(r)$. Thus, protected password is not sufficient to masquerade a user account without the application password and registered mobile phone.

5.5 Resistance to Password Leaks

Most users often use a single password for many different user accounts. Attackers may break a less secure website, retrieve userID-password pair and try those userID-password pairs to access other secure websites. Our proposed *drPass* system prevents this type of attacks by generating high entropy, unique and random site-passwords. Although users can use a single protected password, the salt server generates unique site-passwords for different sites using different salts. For example, using the protected password 'asdfgh' the proposed *drPass* system generates two site-passwords like '48@1DGDCd*UlZcJz' and 'A(KLn@SqzP6CNsqb' which are no way related to each other. Thus, the proposed system is highly resistant to different password-cracking platforms.

5.6 Resistance to Brute-Force Attack

In our prototype, we are using Base85 encoding scheme for computing site-password. The generated site-password is unique and a random one. If we restrict the length of site-password to 16 characters, then the probability of success (per password guess) is 85^{-16}. It will take nearly a year with an effort of 10 million verifications per second. As the generated p_{sk} covers four types of character sets, it can prevent training based password attacks. On the other hand, it is almost impossible for an attacker to guess both application password and protected password after stealing user's mobile phone. Thus, the proposed system has sufficient strength to prevent all the brute-force attacks.

5.7 Resistance to Man-in-the-Middle Attack

We are assuming that the user may try to get access to the salt server through an insecure public desktop PC. If this is the case, such desktop PC might suffer from DNS poisoning: user could be redirected to a fake salt server that can intercept all the communications between the user and original salt server. The web browser has no real way to check if an IP address is associated with the legitimate salt server. However, HTTPS verifies this type of scenario. If a user accessed the salt server from a compromised access point and DNS server returned the address of a fake one, the fake salt server wouldn't be able to display that HTTPS encryption.

5.8 Follows Leakage Resilient Design Criteria

Along with the extension of security strength against various password stealing attacks and password leakage, *drPass* follows all the design criteria discussed in [32].

- *Counter Password Problem*: *drPass* requires only two passwords to memorize which satisfies the usability aspects of the password problem. The generated site-passwords are very strong and distinct. Site-passwords can be changed periodically by updating the associated salts. Thus, the security aspects of password problem can be achieved.
- *Secure Authentication Token*: The protected password is only transferred to site-password, *drPass* does not store the password persistently.
- *Efficient Interaction Channel*: *drPass* uses *vision* for reading random number '*r*' and *motion* for entering secret key, which is the optimal choice.
- *Partial Secure Channel*: In *drPass* the only partial secure channel involved is vision.
- *User Actions*: *drPass* does not require any optional user actions like mental calculations, generating random numbers, etc.
- *Physical Requirement*: The user capabilities required by *drPass* are same as the capabilities required for using conventional passwords.
- *Non-ideal Environment*: The operating environment for *drPass* is also same as conventional passwords.

6 Prototype Implementation and Performance Evaluation

We implemented a prototype of *drPass* to evaluate its performance and usability. The *drPass* mobile application is developed on android operating system using android studio, due to its generality and popularity. An apache server running on a PC works as a salt server for generating site-passwords and PHP is used for server-side operations. For storing the user details we used MYSQL database.

To analyze the usability and effectiveness of *drPass*, we organized a user study with twenty participants (ten male and ten female) including university students (50% of paricipants), technical staff (25% of paricipants), and non-technical staff (25% of paricipants). The age range of participants falls between 20 and 45. All were using computers regularly and previously involved in handling different online accounts. All of them were familiar with the use of smart phones and different mobile applications. Before starting the evaluation process,

Table 2. Participants initial perspective towards password security

Questions	Number of participants	
Do you sometimes reuse passwords in different sites ?	90%	(18)
Are you concerned about the security of passwords ?	65%	(13)
Criteria for choosing passwords:		
Easy to remember	60%	(12)
Difficult for others to guess	40%	(08)
Suggested by the system	5%	(01)
Same as another password	55%	(11)
Other	15%	(03)
Participation in online activities		
Online purchases	90%	(18)
Online banking	90%	(18)
Online bill payments	60%	(12)
Other activities	25%	(05)
Do you use:		
A password manager ?	5%	(01)
A password generation tool ?	0%	(00)

participants were asked for a questionnaire similar to the one in [8, 29] to know their initial perspective towards password security. The details of questions and responses are summarized in Table 2. After that we introduced our proposed system to all the participants with a demo and they are also allowed for one practice test to make sure that they understand the detail operation. Then, all the participants moved to complete a formal test.

Table 3. Post-test questionnaire. Responses are out of 5. A 5 is most positive

Questions	Mean	σ (Standard deviation)
Logging in via drPass was easy.	3.8	0.75
The steps of drPass were complex.	2.05	0.86
Passwords are more secure by using drpass.	4.3	0.78
I am comfortable with not knowing my actual passwords for a website.	3.35	0.90
I need to use drPass to protect my password.	3.1	0.99

For estimating the performance of $drPass$ system, all participants were gone through another post-test questionnaire after the completion of the test as summarized in Table 3.

Most of the participants experienced that the password generation using $drPass$ system is simple and easy. Moreover, they acknowledged that, $drPaas$

is a secure one and easy to remember only two secret passwords (one application password, one protected password) rather than remembering many weak passwords or repeating same password in many user accounts.

To observe the success rate and login time of *drPass* five login instances of *drPass* and password manager (KeePass [2]) were recorded. According to statistical t-tests, the difference in success rate between the *drPass* system and KeePass is acceptable ($t = 0.74, p < 0.05$). However, the login time of *drPass* is statistically greater than KeePass ($t = 5.59, p < 0.05$).

We have used human performance modeling tool CPM-GOMS, for theoretically measuring the execution time [16,17]. In CPM-GOMS every operator is represented as a box with a predetermined time duration [19]. The time duration of each cognitive operator is equal and set to 50 ms. The time of visual perception is set to be 100 ms. The time of motor operator which makes an eye movement is fixed to 30 ms. The motor operator for finger movement is assumed to 300 ms. Figure 5 illustrates the CPM-GOMS modeling of a password character entry and Fig. 6 illustrates the modeling of clipboard button click. Thus, the estimated running time of a single password character entry is 780 ms and coping the password to the clipboard is 730 ms. Except the first instance, KeePass requires 730 ms of login time whereas *drPass* requires $(1460 + 780n)$ ms of login time where 'n' represents the number of characters. Hence, KeePass password manager is faster than the *drPass* system.

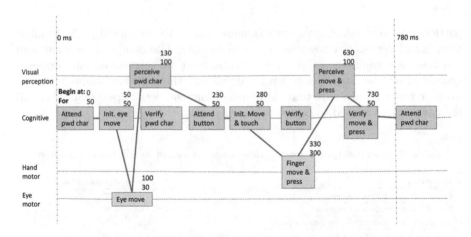

Fig. 5. Modeling of drPass password character entry in CPM-GOMS

From the login phase (Subsect. 3.2), it is pretty clear that before generating site-password salt server needs to authenticate the user. So, for a 12 character length protected password and 6 character length application password, our *drPass* system takes average 55 seconds for first time login (i.e. generating first site-password), after that it takes approximately same amount of time that conventional login systems take. Because *drPass* does not repeat the whole login

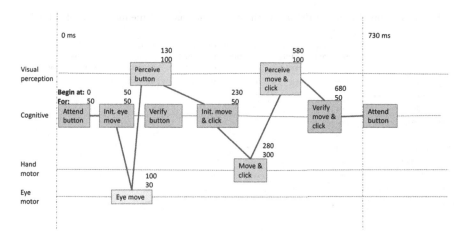

Fig. 6. Modeling of drPass clipboard button click in CPM-GOMS

process each time before generating a site-password. Once, a user is authenticated to the salt server, it can compute different site-passwords until logged out from the salt server.

7 Comparison of *drPass* with Other Systems

Table 4 summarizes a comparison of *drPass* with several other protocols from the literature. Our proposed system is compared with the existing protocols which manage many user accounts (N) using limited number of passwords (say, M where $M < N$). In our proposed, *drPass* system, users can change a site-password either by updating the associated salt or by changing the protected password. This gives an advantage from other password generating protocols like *Password Multiplier* [13] and *Passpet* [33]. *Password Multiplier* and *Passpet* use the website URL as a salt for generating passwords for the corresponding websites. However, our proposed *drPass* system uses a random salt for site-password generation instead of a fixed salt like *Password Multiplier* and *Passpet*. Thus, generating and updating unique password is trivial using *drPass* system.

For implementing Xiao et al. [31], *Phoolproof* [24], *MP-Auth* [23], and *oPass* [27] server side changes are required which is not trivial. However, *drPass* does not need any server side changes. Xiao et al.'s scheme requires a small amount of human computing to generate a virtual password before each login. In addition, users have to remember one virtual password function along with the secret password which increases the memory burden. So, it is not user friendly. The proposed *drPass* scheme does not require any human computing and also, reduces the memory burden.

In *Phoolproof* [24], *MP-Auth* [23] and *oPass* [27] users must connect their mobile phone to a client PC before each login. However, our *drPass* system does not demand any such connection before each login.

Table 4. Comparison of drPass with other systems. ('–' means not applicable)

	phishing resistant	shoulder-surfing resistant	keylogger resistant	unique password for each site	resist offline attack	need server-side change	safe to reuse password
PwdHash [25]	yes	no	no	yes	no	no	no
Password Multiplier [13]	yes	no	no	yes	no	no	no
Passpet [33]	yes	no	no	yes	no	no	no
PasswordAgent [29]	yes	no	no	yes	yes	no	yes
Xiao et al.[31]	yes	no	yes	no	–	yes	yes
Phoolproof [24]	yes	–	yes	no	–	yes	–
MP-Auth [23]	yes	–	yes	no	–	yes	–
oPass [27]	yes	–	yes	no	–	yes	–
Password Manager [26]	no	yes	no	yes	yes	no	yes
drPass	yes	yes	yes	yes	yes	no	yes

oPass [27] uses SMS service which increases the cost of the whole system. It also increases the time for registration and login due to SMS delay and SMS lost. Proposed *drPass* system takes very less amount of time as compared to *oPass*, graphical password schemes and other schemes which require a connection setup between user's mobile phone with client PC.

Unlike password managers and single sign on systems, the security of proposed *drPass* system is not vulnerable to single point of failure. Password manager acts as a database that store user's passwords. Access to this database is controlled by a master password. Password managers also automate the process of retrieving the credentials and logging in to web application. This auto-fill process is also vulnerable to various scripting attacks [20, 26]. All the user accounts linked with a single-sign-on scheme are at risk if the central entity is compromised. However, our proposed system acts like a two factor authentication and the individual user accounts are safe even if security of salt server or mobile application were compromised.

8   Conclusion

Many password security researchers have assumed a necessary trade off between security and usability (e.g. memorability) aspects. However, in this paper, we proposed a password generating protocol named *drPass* which balances the security and memorability nicely. *drPass* prevents various password stealing attacks like phishing attack, shoulder-surfing attack, keylogger attack along with password leaks. Proposed system does not require any server side changes of individual sites for protecting the password. The generated site-passwords are so random and distinct that it assures users from the consequences of password database leaks because database leak of one account cannot affect others. Through *drPass*, each user needs to remember only two passwords i.e., application password and protected password. Application password is used to authenticate securely to the salt server and protected password generates unique passwords for different sites. Based on a very simple idea, our proposed *drPass* system is the first user friendly protocol which simultaneously prevents password stealing and password leaks.

To prevent a single point of failure due to unavailability of salt server because of network problem, server issues or any other reasons, a multiple synchronized salt server can be built in the future. Additionally, we would also like to explore game based approach to login to the salt server instead of the application password.

References

1. Basic password security requirement. https://www.tripwire.com/state-of-security/latest-security-news/nearly-half-popular-consumer-websites-lack-basic-password-security-requirements/
2. Keepass. https://keepass.info/
3. The password meter. http://www.passwordmeter.com
4. Phishing activity trends report, second quarter (2016). http://www.antiphishing.org/
5. Poor password requirements of popular consumer websites. https://betanews.com/2017/08/09/consumer-websites-poor-passwords/
6. Yet another password meter. http://www.yetanotherpasswordmeter.com
7. Bonneau, J., Herley, C., Van Oorschot, P.C., Stajano, F.: The quest to replace passwords: a framework for comparative evaluation of web authentication schemes. In 2012 IEEE Symposium on Security and Privacy, pp. 553–567. IEEE (2012)
8. Chiasson, S., van Oorschot, P.C., Biddle, R.: A usability study and critique of two password managers. In: Usenix Security, vol. 6 (2006)
9. Das, A., Bonneau, J., Caesar, M., Borisov, N., Wang, X.: The tangled web of password reuse. In: NDSS, vol. 14, pp. 23–26 (2014)
10. Florencio, D., Herley, C.: A large-scale study of web password habits. In: Proceedings of the 16th International Conference on World Wide Web, pp. 657–666. ACM (2007)
11. Florêncio, D., Herley, C., Coskun, B.: Do strong web passwords accomplish anything? HotSec, **7**(6) (2007)
12. Gao, H., Jia, W., Ye, F., Ma, L.: A survey on the use of graphical passwords in security. J. Softw. **8**(7), 1678–1698 (2013)
13. Halderman, J.A., Waters, B., Felten, E.W.: A convenient method for securely managing passwords. In: Proceedings of the 14th International Conference On World Wide Web, pp. 471–479. ACM (2005)
14. Herley, C., van Oorschot, P.C., Patrick, A.S.: Passwords: if we're so smart, why are we still using them? In: Dingledine, R., Golle, P. (eds.) FC 2009. LNCS, vol. 5628, pp. 230–237. Springer, Heidelberg (2009). https://doi.org/10.1007/978-3-642-03549-4_14
15. Ives, B., Walsh, K.R., Schneider, H.: The domino effect of password reuse. Commun. ACM **47**(4), 75–78 (2004)
16. John, B.E.: Extensions of GOMS analyses to expert performance requiring perception of dynamic visual and auditory information. In: Proceedings of the SIGCHI conference on Human factors in computing systems, pp. 107–116. ACM (1990)
17. John, B.E., Gray, W.D.: CPM-GOMS: an analysis method for tasks with parallel activities. In: Conference companion on Human factors in computing systems, pp. 393–394. ACM (1995)

426 S. Panda and S. Mondal

18. Kontaxis, G., Athanasopoulos, E., Portokalidis, G., Keromytis, A.D.: Sauth: protecting user accounts from password database leaks. In: Proceedings of the 2013 ACM SIGSAC conference on Computer & communications security, pp. 187–198. ACM (2013)

19. Kwon, T., Shin, S., Na, S.: Covert attentional shoulder surfing: human adversaries are more powerful than expected. IEEE Trans. Systems, Man, Cybern.: Syst. **44**(6), 716–727 (2014)

20. Li, Z., He, W., Akhawe, D., Song, D.: The emperor's new password manager: security analysis of web-based password managers. In: 23rd USENIX Security Symposium (USENIX Security 14), pp. 465–479 (2014)

21. Maheshwari, A., Mondal, S.: SPOSS: secure pin-based-authentication obviating shoulder surfing. In: Ray, I., Gaur, M.S., Conti, M., Sanghi, D., Kamakoti, V. (eds.) ICISS 2016. LNCS, vol. 10063, pp. 66–86. Springer, Cham (2016). https://doi.org/10.1007/978-3-319-49806-5_4

22. Mainka, C., Mladenov, V., Feldmann, F., Krautwald, J., Schwenk, J.: Your software at my service (2014)

23. Mannan, M., van Oorschot, P.C.: Using a personal device to strengthen password authentication from an untrusted computer. In: Dietrich, S., Dhamija, R. (eds.) FC 2007. LNCS, vol. 4886, pp. 88–103. Springer, Heidelberg (2007). https://doi.org/10.1007/978-3-540-77366-5_11

24. Parno, B., Kuo, C., Perrig, A.: Phoolproof phishing prevention. In: Di Crescenzo, G., Rubin, A. (eds.) FC 2006. LNCS, vol. 4107, pp. 1–19. Springer, Heidelberg (2006). https://doi.org/10.1007/11889663_1

25. Ross, B., Jackson, C., Miyake, N., Boneh, D., Mitchell, J.C.: Stronger password authentication using browser extensions. In: Usenix security, pp. 17–32, Baltimore, MD, USA (2005)

26. Silver, D., Jana, S., Boneh, D., Chen, E., Jackson, C.: password managers: attacks and defenses. In: 23rd USENIX Security Symposium (USENIX Security 14), pp. 449–464 (2014)

27. Sun, H.-M., Chen, Y.-H., Lin, Y.-H.: opass: a user authentication protocol resistant to password stealing and password reuse attacks. IEEE Trans. Inf. Forensics Secur. **7**(2), 651–663 (2012)

28. Van Bruggen, D., Liu, S., Kajzer, M., Striegel, A., Crowell, C.R., D'Arcy, J.: Modifying smartphone user locking behavior. In: Proceedings of the Ninth Symposium on Usable Privacy and Security, pp. 10. ACM (2013)

29. Strahs, B., Yue, C., Wang, H.: Secure passwords through enhanced hashing. In: Proceedings of LISA 2009: 23rd Large Installation System Administration Conference, pp. 93 (2009)

30. Wiedenbeck, S., Waters, J., Birget, J.-C. Brodskiy, A., Memon, N.: Passpoints: design and longitudinal evaluation of a graphical password system. In: International Journal of Human-Computer Studies, **63**(1), 102–127 (2005)

31. Xiao, Y., Li, C.-C., Lei, M., Vrbsky, S.V.: Differentiated virtual passwords, secret little functions, and codebooks for protecting users from password theft. IEEE Syst. J. **8**(2), 406–416 (2014)

32. Yan, Q., Han, J., Li, Y., Zhou, J., Deng, R.H.: Leakage-resilient password entry: challenges, design, and evaluation. Comput. Secur. **48**, 196–211 (2015)

33. Yee, K.-P., Sitaker, K.: Passpet: convenient password management and phishing protection. In: Proceedings of the second symposium on Usable privacy and security, pp. 32–43. ACM (2006)

MySecPol: A Client-Side Policy Language for Safe and Secure Browsing

Amit Pathania[✉], B. S. Radhika, and Rudrapatna Shyamasundar

Indian Institute of Technology Bombay, Mumbai, India
sujanian.amit@gmail.com, radhikabs184@gmail.com, shyamasundar@gmail.com

Abstract. Web browsers handle content from different sources making them prone to various attacks. Currently, users rely either on web developers or on different browser extensions for protection against different attacks. In this paper, we propose a simple architecture for defining client-side policy using a policy language `MySecPol`. The client-side policy gives the users control over the content being served to them. Users can define their policy independent of the browser or the Operating System (OS). The policy is then realized by integrating it into the browser with appropriate mechanisms. The policy specification can combine various security mechanisms providing a robust protection. We describe an implementation of `MySecPol` as a Chromium extension. We also show how several of the existing approaches are captured as instances of `MySecPol`. We have further evaluated the system with real-world websites for testing soundness of the approach by checking the functionality of these sites relative to different policies. We have also compared our system with several related works.

Keywords: Browser security · Client-side policies · Web security

1 Introduction

A web browser handles content from different sources based on user's requirement. Modern websites use scripts, images, and objects from third-party servers to make the browsing experience more satisfying and interactive. The third-party content includes social media sharing widgets (e.g. Facebook, Twitter), video player embeds (e.g. YouTube, Vimeo), analytics scripts (e.g. Google Analytics), advertising scripts (e.g. Google Adsense), user commenting systems (e.g. Disqus, IntenseDebate) and so on. This third-party content runs with the same access privileges as the hosting page and poses potential privacy and security risks [1]. Malicious scripts embedded in a web page can leak sensitive user information to third-party servers without user permission. Analytics and advertising scripts can be used to fingerprint users and to create user profiles based on the browsing habits. Information leakage and cross-site scripting (XSS) are the most prevalent vulnerabilities found in Dynamic Application Security Testing (DAST)

© Springer Nature Switzerland AG 2018
V. Ganapathy et al. (Eds.): ICISS 2018, LNCS 11281, pp. 427–447, 2018.
https://doi.org/10.1007/978-3-030-05171-6_22

with 37% and 33% likelihood as per 2017 WhiteHat Security Application Security Statistics Report [24]. Other prevalent attacks include Cross-Site Request Forgery (CSRF), clickjacking, phishing etc.

The existing browser security solutions can be broadly categorized into two categories: server-side, and client-side. The server-side techniques involve either code rewriting using a subset of JavaScript functions like *ECMAScript 5 strict mode* [10] or using newly defined functions that place restrictions on JavaScript code such as JavaScript sandboxing mechanism for *eval()* [9].

ADsafe [5] makes it safe to place third-party advertising scripts or widgets code on a web page. Other measures supported by browsers to reduce risks of third-party contents include creating a Content Security Policy (CSP) [13] and/or to use subresource integrity (SRI) [3]. CSP defines trusted sources of content and SRI helps browsers to check the integrity of received resources.

Client-side solutions can be implemented in two broad categories: browser core modifications and browser extensions/add-ons. The modifications in browser core (like rendering engine, JavaScript Core execution engine) involve enforcing information flow control by tagging security labels to sensitive data and checking third-party script accesses to those sensitive data or DOM elements. *FlowFox* [6] is a modified Firefox browser that implements information flow control for scripts by assigning labels. *ConScript* [22] enables web developers to define policy that is enforced at browser. In some approaches, JavaScripts are executed in a sandboxed or virtualized environment to visualize their interaction with sensitive data in a controlled environment. *Virtual Browser* [2] is one such browser.

Browser extensions or add-ons provide a way to enforce security policies without browser modifications. The browser extensions like *Noscripts* [17] and *Ghostry* [16] provide protection by either creating whitelists or by restricting the execution of third-party scripts. Users can create whitelist and blacklist for different classes of requests using *uMatrix* [14] and enforce HTTPS connections using *HTTPS Everywhere* [11] browser extension.

In this paper, we present a simple architecture for defining and enforcing client-side policy using a policy specification language `MySecPol`. `MySecPol` structurally is comparable to policy specification in CSP or SELinux [19] and can capture security requirements of the user. User can control the information being sent out and the content being served by the browser by specifying the appropriate policy. Note that this could result in loss of functionality or interactivity for some websites but it is the choice of security over interactivity/functionality by the user.

The policy defined by user is independent of the browser/OS and is integrated with appropriate mechanisms into the browser. We have transformed this policy as a Chromium extension and evaluated it against top Alexa sites for soundness, performance overhead, and compatibility for different policies. The advantage of using a client-side policy against server-side mechanisms is that user doesn't have to rely on web developers for defining the security policy. The implementation of client-side policy can use or enhance the already existing client-side mechanisms and combine different existing solutions to create a more robust security framework which can provide protection against a wide range of attacks.

The rest of the paper is organized as follows: Sect. 2 explores the existing security mechanisms and important works on browser security. In Sect. 3, we describe our architecture and `MySecPol`. Section 4 gives an illustration of typical policies in our approach. Section 5, describes our implementation followed by evaluation in Sect. 6. Section 7 concludes the paper.

2   A Brief Survey of Browser Security

In this section, we discuss prominent works on making browsing secure. This includes both server-side and client-side defenses.

2.1   Existing Security Mechanisms

Same Origin Policy (SOP) states that scripts contained in one website are allowed to read and modify only the contents received from the same origin. Here, an origin is defined as a combination of protocol, hostname and port number. If a user has opened a malicious website in one browser tab and accessing email on another tab, then SOP ensures that the malicious website can't access personal information contained in other tabs by reading their cookies or HTTP requests. Content Security Policy (CSP) [13] provides additional HTTP header that allows websites to declare trusted sources of contents (scripts, images, fonts, and so on) that the browser is allowed to load in that page. This helps to reduce XSS risks as browser implementing CSP can execute or render resources only from these trusted sources. So, even if an attacker injects a malicious script in the web page, it won't be executed by the browser. The vulnerabilities arise when CSP policies are misconfigured or are too permissive.

2.2   Other Proposed Solutions

JavaScipt provides a sandboxing mechanism called *evalInSandbox()* [9] to run JavaScript code inside a sandbox with reduced privileges.

ECMAScript 5 strict mode [10] is a standardized subset and restricted variant of JavaScript. *ADsafe* [5] defines a subset of JavaScript that restricts third-party code from doing any malicious activity and thereby, makes it safe to include third-party advertising scripts or widgets on the web page. The *Caja Compiler* [21] is a tool which makes third-party content safe for embedding in the websites.

ConScript [22] provides a client-side implementation of policy defined by the web developer by introducing a new attribute 'policy' to the HTML <script> tag that can store a policy defined by the web developer. Here, a modified Microsoft Internet Explorer 8 parses this new policy attribute and enforces it.

ScriptInspector [27] is a modified version of Firefox browser that is capable of intercepting sensitive API calls from third-party scripts to critical resource and records accesses that violate the policy for a given domain. The solutions based on browser modifications are useful for proof-of-concept evaluation of a security mechanism, however, they don't find widespread implementation since browser developers must be convinced to implement these modifications.

Browser Enforced Authenticity Protection (BEAP) [20] is a browser based solution which provides protection against clickjacking attacks by stripping authorization information from all cross-origin requests after checking referrer header. However, it also affects genuine cross-origin requests. *CsFire* [7] also strips authorization information from cross-origin HTTP requests to mitigate CSRF attacks, except for whitelisted requests. It makes use of either client-defined policy or server-supplied policy to enforce security. However, CsFire can't handle genuine cross-origin requests in the absence of whitelist. Telikicherla et al., defined *Cross-Origin Request Policy* (CORP) [25] that enables a server to control cross-origin requests initiated by a browser. The policy defined by a web developer is sent to user's browser as part of an additional HTTP response header. CORP helps to mitigate attacks which exploit cross-origin requests.

Noscripts [17] is a firefox browser extension that provides anti-XSS and anti-Clickjacking protection using whitelisting mechanisms. It blocks all JavaScript codes, and other executable contents by default and allows users to selectively enable JavaScript and other features on trusted sites. *Ghostery* [16] detects and blocks browser tracking on the websites to protect user's data and privacy. *Abine* [15] helps users to control third-party services which exist on the current page. The users can control their personal information that other people and companies can view online. *uMatrix* [14] is browser extension which works in relaxed block-all/ allow-exceptionally mode. The user can create whitelist/blacklist for one or multiple classes of requests according to the destination and type of data. *HTTPS Everywhere* [11] extension encrypts communications with websites that offer HTTPS by switching connection from insecure 'HTTP' to secure 'HTTPS'. HTTPS Everywhere can protect only when the user is using the sites that support 'HTTPS' and for which HTTPS Everywhere includes a ruleset. The *Chrome Tab Limit* [12] limits the number of the opened tabs in Chrome which provides protection against attacks like tabnabbing.

2.3   Merits of Using Client-Side Policy

Server-side approaches are largely dependent on web developers for security and privacy. Most websites today are vulnerable to different attacks due to bad coding practices, use of unsafe JavaScript functions, lack of input sanitization and unrestricted access to third-party scripts. Hence, we can't completely rely on web developers for securing user data and protecting their privacy.

Table 1. Comparison with other browser extensions

Name of work	Type of Request supported							Set browser settings	Block download	Enforce HTTPS	Set tab limit	Set HttpOnly cookies	Strip cookie	Create blacklist	Block User-agent	Port policies	Set CSP	Remarks
	images	scripts	fonts	iframe	XHR	media	Cross-origin											
uMatrix	Yes	Yes	Yes	Yes	Yes	Yes	Yes	No	No	No	No	No	Yes	Yes	No	No	No	Can't configure privacy settings or port policies.
Ghostery	No	Yes	No	No	No	No	No	No	No	No	No	No	Not known	Yes	No	No	No	Prevents ads and trackers only.
NoScripts	No	Yes	Yes	Yes	Yes	Yes	Yes	No	No	No	No	No	Yes	Yes	No	No	No	Protects against XSS and click-jacking.
CsFire	No	No	No	No	No	No	Yes	No	No	No	No	No	Yes	NA	No	No	No	Protects against CSRF and click-jacking only.
Abine	No	Yes	No	No	No	No	No	No	No	No	No	No	Not known	Yes	No	No	No	Protects user privacy online.
HTTPS Every-where	No*	No	No	No	No	No	No	No	No	Yes	No	No	No	NA	No	No	No	*No selective monitoring.
Chrome Tab Limit	No	No	No	No	No	No	No	No	No	No	Yes	No	No	NA	No	No	No	Limits maximum opened tabs only.
MySecPol	Yes	Yes	Yes	Yes	Yes	Yes	Yes	Yes	Yes	Yes	Yes	Yes	Yes	Yes	Yes	Yes	Yes	Can support other browsers.

Many current browsers support CSP, but most websites still don't include CSP headers. Even in case of the websites which use CSP headers, the policies are too permissive. As per a survey done by Lukas Weichselbaum et al. [26], 94.72% of unique CSP policies are trivially bypassable and 90.63% of them remove XSS protection by allowing the execution of inline scripts or the loading of scripts from arbitrary external hosts. *CORP*, *ScriptInspector*, and *Conscript* require browser modifications and rely on web developer to define security policies and hence, don't find widespread implementation. Most of the existing client-side solutions provide defense against specific attacks and require installation of multiple extensions. *BEAP* and *CsFire* provide defense against CSRF and clickjacking attacks. *NoScripts* and *Ghostery* provide defense against XSS and other privacy violating attacks. *uMatrix* allows user to define policy for different classes of requests but doesn't permit user to configure other browser privacy settings. *HTTPS everywhere* focuses on enforcing HTTPS connections only. The extensions available online provide piece meal solutions and do not provide any formal method to define security policy for the user. They also do not provide flexibility to import the policy either from one browser to another browser or from one machine to another. Table 1 shows the comparison of our proposed solution with a few existing browser extensions.

The proposed client-side policy based architecture helps users to define their security requirements. Our policy language `MySecPol` is simple and easy to understand with limited domain knowledge. The client-defined policy is captured and integrated into the browser without user worrying about the implementation. The same policy can be shared among users of the organization and implemented on different browsers on different Operating Systems. Our approach captures the essence of the existing solutions and provides a more robust security framework which can provide protection against a wide range of security and privacy risks. In next section, we discuss our proposed architecture and describe our client-side policy specification language `MySecPol`.

3   Our Approach via MySecPol

Security policy is a set of rules defining the security requirements of the user. The key idea of MySecPol is to specify a user-controlled, browser-enforced security mechanism. We assume that the user defining the policy is familiar with the basic web concepts and can create a new policy or modify a base policy as per his/her requirements. A client-side policy should satisfy the following requirements:

- The policy *should be **simple*** to define and understand.
- The policy *should be **non-conflicting*** and should be able to resolve conflicts in case of either dependent or conflicting rules.
- The policy *should be **implementable*** in current web context without browser modifications. Current web standards should support the user defined policy.
- The policy *should be **OS and browser independent***.

We propose a simple, policy-based architecture which enables users to harden their browser security. Our policy specification defines the user's security requirements for browsing. As shown in Fig. 1, the user-defined policy is read by a parser and then realized at browser as an extension. The HTTP requests and responses are checked against the rules defined in the security policy and are blocked or modified in case of the violation.

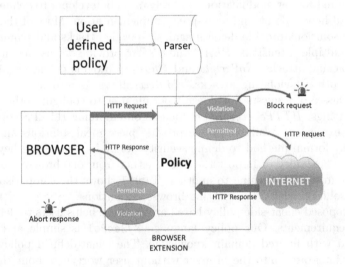

Fig. 1. Proposed architecture for secure browsing

3.1   Specification of Security Policy

Our client-side policy specification language `MySecPol` is browser and platform independent. The abstract syntax of `MySecPol` is defined below:

```
policy ::= rule*
rule ::= action field dstn-domain [host-domain]
action ::= allow | deny
field ::= resource | browser-setting | HTTP-header | property
resource ::= javascript | image | iframe | font | object | XMLHTTPRequest
             | stylesheets | media
browser-setting ::= thirdpartycookies | autofill | safeBrowsingEnabled
             | passwordSavingEnabled | doNotTrackEnabled | webRTC
HTTP-header ::= User-Agent | Referer
property ::= maxtabsN | access | connection-type | downloads | executable
             | HttpOnlycookies | cookies
connection-type ::= https | http
dstn-domain ::= origin+ | crossdomain | crossdomain- | * | *-
host-domain ::= origin+ | *
origin ::= RFC 6454
```

Listing 1.1. Syntax of client side policy

The interpretation of `MySecPol` is given below:

action specifies the permission. It can be either allow or deny.

field represents the resource, property, browser setting or HTTP header field for which rule has been defined. The '**resource**' corresponds to an element in set S = {image, javascript, object, iframe, XMLhttprequest, font, media}. The '**browser-setting**' defines browser privacy and network settings in set B = {thirdpartycookies, autofillEnabled, safeBrowsingEnabled, passwordSavingEnabled, doNotTrackEnabled and webRTC}. The '**HTTP-header**' defines HTTP headers like user-agent or referer. The '**property**' tag corresponds to an element in set P = {maxtabs, access, connection-type, download, executable, HttpOnlycookies, cookie}. The 'maxtabsN' defines the number of maximum opened tabs to be N. The 'access' keyword enforces the specified action to all requests for a given domain. The 'connection-type' specifies type of connection i.e. http or https. The 'downloads' keyword specifies file downloads. The 'executable' keyword denotes executable downloads. The 'HttpOnlycookies' keyword is used to specify the type of cookies. The keyword 'cookie' is used to specify cookie information for requests.

dstn-domain is the address of the target domain. For resources, it is the origin of resource. For example, if we want to block images from domain "www.abc.com", then policy would be: "*deny image* www.abc.com". The wildcard '*****' represents all domains, '***-**' represents all domains except those that are listed in the subsequent rules using 'allow', '**crossdomain**' represents all domains other than current domain, and '**crossdomain-**' represents all cross-origin domains except those listed later in the policy using 'allow'.

By default, the rules defined by a policy are applicable to all domains. However, by using the optional field **host-domain** in the policy, we can define domain-specific rules. For example, if we want to block images from domain "www.abc.com" for "www.xyz.com" only, then policy would be: "*deny image* www.abc.com www.xyz.com".

3.2 Interpretation of Policy Application

The default policy is "allow * *" which allows all resources from all domains. Once the user defines a policy, the corresponding access control rules are implemented by the browser. Let P_U be an user defined policy which contains a set of rules R such that rules R_1, R_2, ... $R_n \in$ R. Let P_E be the policy implemented by the browser containing set of rules R' s.t. rules R'_1, R'_2, ... $R'_n \in$ R'.

Property 1: All rules defined in the user-defined policy P_U will be included in the effective policy P_E if the rules are disjoint. Two rules R_i and R_j are said to be disjoint if they are independent of each other and are non-conflicting. Two rules are said to be conflicting if access to a resource granted by one rule is denied by the other rule. $\forall R_i, R_j \in$ R s.t, $R_i \cap R_j = \emptyset$, then $R_i, R_j \in$ R'. Consider the rules R1 and R2 in the following user policy P_U. Since, these rules are disjoint, both will be included in the effective policy P_E.

R1: deny javascript www.xyz.com	R1: deny javascript www.xyz.com
R2: deny javascript www.abc.com	R2: deny javascript www.abc.com
User defined Policy P_U	Effective Policy P_E

Property 2: If there are two rules such that one rule R_j is a subset of the other rule R_i, then only superset R_i will be included in P_E. $\forall R_i, R_j \in$ R s.t, $R_i \supset R_j$, then $R_i \in$ R' and $R_j \notin$ R'. Consider two rules R1 and R2 in the below policy P_U. R2 is a subset of R1. So, only R1 will be included in the effective policy P_E which will block all scripts including those from "www.abc.com".

R1: deny javascript *	
R2: allow javascript www.abc.com	R1: deny javascript *
User defined Policy P_U	Effective Policy P_E

Property 3: If two rules for a resource or domain are either dependent or conflicting with each other, then the stricter of the two will be taken. Consider the following two rules in P_U. R1 blocks all scripts but R2 permits scripts from domain "www.abc.com" which conflicts with Rule1. So, R1 which enforces stricter security policy will be included in P_E discarding R2.

R1: deny javascript *	
R2: allow javascript www.abc.com	R1: deny javascript *
User defined Policy P_U	Effective Policy P_E

However, if user wants to block all scripts except those from domain www.abc.com, the correct policy would be:

| R1: deny javascript *— |
| R2: allow javascript www.abc.com |

4   Security Policies In MySecPol

In this section, we present several useful policies that can be specified using MySecPol.

4.1   No Scripts

The simplest policy is to disable all scripts. JavaScript is extensively used to dynamically update the page but can also be misused to track or steal user information. All Javascripts can be blocked by using the following policy.

```
deny      javascript   *
```

4.2   Blacklist Scripts

Websites include tracking, advertising and analytic scripts for revenue generation or tracking user behavior. User can blacklist scripts from specific domains.

```
deny      javascript   *://*.tracker.com/*
deny      javascript   *://*.ad.com/*
```

Cross-origin Javascripts are the most common attack vectors. We can block them by using wild-card 'crossdomain'.

```
deny      javascript   crossdomain
```

4.3   Selective Resources

The user can specify rules for HTTP requests for different resources like images, objects, fonts, and so on. Many a times, XSS attacks are carried out by inserting scripts to fetch these resources which in turn carry user information as payload of a request. The below policy specifies rules for these resources:

```
deny      object         *
deny      image          *—
allow     image          *://trusted.com/*
deny      stylesheet     *://evil.com/*
deny      media          *
deny      XMLhttprequest *
```

4.4   Disable IFrame Creation

An IFrame is used to embed another document within a HTML document and can be exploited for clickjacking attacks. User can restrict IFrames by using the following rule.

```
deny      iframe   *
```

4.5 Block Non-HTTPS Connections

User can block unencrypted HTTP connections by using the below rule:

```
deny     http     *
```

4.6 Block User-Agent Headers

User-Agent information in HTTP request helps web server decide how to deliver content best suited for user's browser but this information can be used by websites for user fingerprinting based on user's OS, version number and web browser. This can be thwarted by defining the given rule.

```
deny     user-agent    *://*.sniffer.com/*
```

4.7 Create Whitelist for Cross-Origin Requests

This policy helps to create a whitelist of trusted domains for cross-origin requests. The policy will remove cookie information from all cross-origin requests except from the requests that are intended for whitelisted domains.

```
deny     cookie     crossdomain-
allow    cookie     ://www.abc.com/*
```

4.8 Create Blacklist

User can block access to untrusted websites by creating a blacklist as below:

```
deny     access    *://*.evil.com/*
```

4.9 Create Whitelist

The user can create whitelist of trusted URLs while blocking others. The user can permit the trusted domains exclusively as given in the below policy.

```
deny     access    *-
allow    access    *://*.abc.com/*
```

4.10 Block All Application Downloads

Some websites serve the application data or binary data which can contain malicious code embedded in them. The Content-Type for such HTTP responses can be javascript, octet-stream, zip, pdf etc. User can define policy for such content. Similarly, we can define policy specific for executable downloads.

```
deny downloads *://*.xyz.com/*        deny executable *://*.evil.com/*
```

4.11 Restrict Cookie Type to 'HttpOnly' Cookies

'HttpOnly' cookies cannot be read by scripts running in the page and hence, provide protection against cookie stealing scripts. This policy restricts cookie type to 'HttpOnly'.

allow	HttpOnlycookies	*

4.12 Limit the Number of Opened Tabs

As the number of opened tabs increases, the browsers tend to hide tabs' titles making user susceptible to attacks like tabnabbing [8]. This policy allows clients to define the maximum number of opened tabs.

allow	maxtabs6	*

4.13 Set Browser's Privacy Settings

Users' privacy can be protected by configuring various browser features like auto-fill option for web forms, password saving for different websites, third-party cookies, webRTC traffic handling, safe browsing mechanisms and doNotTrack header for HTTP requests. A sample privacy protection policy is given below.

deny	thirdpartycookies	*
deny	autofill	*
allow	safeBrowsingEnabled	*
deny	passwordSavingEnabled	*
allow	doNotTrackEnabled	*
deny	webRTC	*

4.14 Implement CSP at Browser

As discussed in Sect. 2.3, many web servers either still don't implement CSP or mis-configure CSP with very permissive policies. Using the fourth (optional) field of the MySecPol rule, domain-specific rules that are equivalent to CSP can be configured. (However, our current implementation doesn't support this optional field yet.) The following policy configures CSP for *://abc.com/* domain.

deny	object	*	*://abc.com/*
deny	javascript	*–	*://abc.com/*
allow	javascript	www.xyz.com	*://abc.com/*

The above policy is equivalent to given CSP header for domain *://abc.com/*. If response header from a website contains CSP header, then user can decide either to follow server-side CSP or user-defined CSP or union of both.

Content−Security−Policy: default−src 'self'; object−src 'none';
                          script−src 'www.xyz.com';

As shown in this section, we can address a wide range of client-side security concerns with our succinct policies. The policies are easy to write and understand. As a result, a user can start with a simple base policy, either self-written or an off-the-shelf policy and keep updating and fine-tune it as the security requirements change over the period. Another advantage of using our method is that it is browser/platform independent which enables users to use the same policy on different systems and browsers. MySecPol provides the flexibility to easily add new keywords to protect against common attacks as explained in Sect. 6.4.

5   Implementation of MySecPol

In this section we describe our implementation of the proposed solution as a Chromium extension.

5.1   A Parser for MySecPol

The MySecPol policy parser essentially reads the policy and captures the various field parameters of MySecPol and their corresponding action rules. The fields that are allowed in a rule are given by the set F ={image, javascript, access, XMLhttprequest, http, object, iframe, executable, downloads, user-agent, referer, maxtabs, font, media, Httponlycookies, auth-info, cookies, thirdparty-cookies, autofill, safeBrowsingEnabled, passwordSavingEnabled, doNotTrackEnabled, webRTC}. Each field defined in F has (i) a flag to indicate whether a rule exists for that field, (ii) a whitelist and (iii) a blacklist of domains for that field. The parser first sets the flag, whitelist, and blacklist to default values for all the fields. Then, for each rule, it checks the field and sets its flag to true and adds the domain to whitelist or blacklist as per the action defined in the rule. In the end, parser tries to remove duplicate entries and resolve conflicting rules for a given field based on Property 2 and 3 respectively given in Sect. 4.2. Once the parser has parsed all the rules defined in the user policy, it writes appropriate values in the browser extension.

5.2   Policy Implementation

Once the parser sets the extension parameters for various fields, the extension implements the policy without any user intervention. The chrome.webRequest API is used to intercept and monitor all originating requests and received responses against the user-defined policy. The *onBeforeRequest* event listener monitors requests before any TCP connection is made and the *onHeadersReceived* event listener captures the HTTP response event and these can be used to modify or cancel originating request and response received from the server

Table 2. Summary of policy implementation

Policy	API used	Event handler	Remarks
No scripts	webRequest	onBeforeRequest, onHeadersReceived	Monitoring based on request type 'script', CSP header modified for inline scripts
Blacklisting scripts	webRequest	onBeforeRequest	Monitoring based on request type 'script'
Selective resources	webRequest	onBeforeRequest	Monitoring based on request type "main_frame", "sub_frame", "stylesheet", "script", "image", "font", "object", "xmlhttprequest", "media"
Disable IFrame	webRequest	onBeforeRequest, onHeadersRecieved	Monitoring based on request type 'sub-frame'
Block non-HTTPS connections	webRequest	onBeforeRequest	Cancelling requests for url type 'http://*/*'
Blocking cross origin JavaScript	webRequest	onBeforeRequest	Monitoring based on referer header and request type 'script'
Removing cookie and authorization information from cross origin requests	webRequest	onBeforeRequest	Removing cookie headers for cross origin requests
Creating whitelist and blacklist	webRequest	onBeforeRequest	Monitor outgoing requests for whitelisted or blacklisted domains
Blocking user-agent information	webRequest	onBeforeRequest	Removing user-agent header from requests
Blocking all application downloads	webRequest	onHeadersReceived	Filter responses with header 'content-type' as application
Blocking all executable file downloads	webRequest	onHeadersReceived	Filter responses with header 'content-type' as application/octet-stream
Restricting cookie type to 'HttpOnly'	webRequest	onHeadersReceived	Modify cookie type in response to 'HttpOnly'
Limit number of opened tabs	tabs	onCreated, onRemoved	Keep count of opened tabs using event handlers
Setting browser's privacy settings	privacy	Properties (network, services, websites) used	Objects ('thirdPartyCookiesAllowed', 'autofillEnabled', 'safeBrowsingEnabled', 'passwordSavingEnabled', 'doNotTrackEnabled' and 'webRTCIPHandlingPolicy') used

respectively. We have taken motivation from the existing solutions like Simple-Block [18], CsFire [7], Chrome Tab Limit [12], NoScripts [17] and combined them with our solution to provide a more comprehensive, policy-based enforcement.

The client policies 4.1, 4.2, 4.3 and 4.4 are enforced by monitoring requests for resources like images, scripts, fonts, objects, and IFrames. Policy 4.1 blocks all Javascripts including inline scripts. So all HTTP requests of type 'script' are blocked and 'content-security-policy' header value of response is modified by setting script-src to "none", thereby blocking all scripts including inline scripts.

In case of policy 4.5, all non-secure HTTP requests can be blocked by canceling all requests of type "http://*/*". Similarly, all cross-domain requests are blocked by matching the domain of HTTP request with the domain given in the referrer header of the request. We have considered only domain name to identify the origin and have intentionally left out port number and protocol. The header field 'User-Agent' in HTTP request is blocked for the domains specified in the policy 4.6. The 'cookie' header is stripped for cross-origin domains for policy 4.7. For enforcing policies 4.8 and 4.9, all requests are monitored against the lists of blacklisted and whitelisted domains to permit or deny access.

The HTTP response with 'Content-type' as 'application' will be blocked for policy 4.10. Similarly, the responses with 'Content-type' as 'application/octet-stream' will be blocked to prevent executable file downloads. Sometimes, a response may not contain the 'Content-type' header field. All such responses can be blocked for strict enforcement of the policies. The 'Set-Cookie' response header is modified to set 'HttpOnly Cookies' to implement policy 4.11.

The prototype extension uses chrome.tabs API's tab creation and deletion event listeners to restrict the number of opened tabs to the number specified in policy 4.12. The chrome.privacy API is used to implement policy 4.13 to control browser's privacy settings. The API exposes various objects to control various network, services and websites' properties. The *webRTCIPHandlingPolicy* controls how WebRTC traffic will be routed and how much local address information is exposed to the network. The *passwordSavingEnabled* controls whether password manager will prompt to store user's passwords or not. If *safeBrowsingEnabled* is enabled, the browser uses its inherent protection against phishing attacks. The *autofillEnabled* controls whether Chrome will prompt for autofill options while filling forms. If *doNotTrackEnabled* is enabled, Chrome adds doNotTrack header with outgoing requests. If *thirdPartyCookiesAllowed* is disabled, third-party sites are blocked from setting cookies. We have summarized our implementation details for Chromium extension in Table 2.

6   Experimental Evaluation

As discussed before, the aim of our work is to define client-side policy for safe and secure browsing. In this section, we first discuss how effectively our prototype extension implements different client-side policies and then try to assess the extension overhead in terms of page rendering time or user browsing experience. The browsing experience is a qualitative feature and varies from user to user and website to website. We also try to illustrate flexibility offered by our solution.

6.1   Effectiveness of the Prototype

In order to test whether our prototype can effectively implement the client-side policy, we first tested it for different individual rules followed by various combinations of these rules for a complete solution. We monitored the HTTP requests sent, responses received and the content served by the browser in absence and

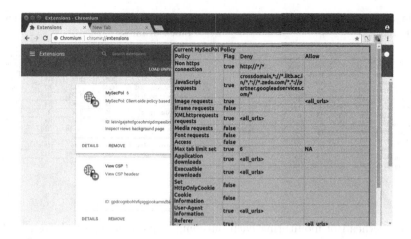

Fig. 2. User defined policy implemented by extension

presence of certain rules in the policy. We also logged the violations of rules reported by the extension and analyzed the logs manually for verification. The effectiveness of the prototype extension in implementing user defined policy is by design, since it intercepts and inspects all incoming and outgoing HTTP requests for possible violations against the policy. Figure 2 shows a user-defined policy being implemented as a Chromium extension.

6.2 Performance

We aim to implement our proposed solution without affecting users' browsing experience. The browsing experience can be defined in terms of page load time and loss of functionality or interactivity of websites after policy implementation. In order to measure the load time performance overhead of our prototype extension, we used an open source Chromium extension 'Performance-Analyser' [23]. This extension helps to measure page load time and other statistics like total requests sorted by type and domain etc. We measured load times of Alexa Top 50 websites with and without our prototype extension for different policies. For each website, we measured load times for five times and computed the average of the same excluding the first access to website to account for caching at local servers (reducing the time for TCP connection and DNS lookup). In subsequent subsections, we discuss the same for a few policies.

Policy to Block All Cross-Origin JavaScripts (Policy 4.2). The results show that there was an increase in average load time for websites. However, the average load time decreased for the websites where the number of blocked third-party scripts was high, thereby reducing the total number of requests and content to be fetched. Table 3 shows the results for Top 10 Alexa sites.

Policy to Block Iframes (Policy 4.4). We tested the policy for Alexa Top 50 sites and found that there was an increase of 26.96% in average page load time

Table 3. Performance with cross origin scripts blocked

Domain	Load time(in ms)			Total requests		JS requests	
	without extension	with extension	% increase	without extension	with extension	without extension	with extension
google.com	312	384.5	23.24	19	14	6	2
youtube.com	5285	1875	-64.52	67	28	10	0
facebook.com	2798	1334	-52.32	313	14	102	0
baidu.com	159	599	276.73	18	6	7	0
wikipedia.org	387	398.5	2.84	6	5	2	2
reddit.com	679.5	1432	110.74	68	31	15	0
yahoo.com	3479	1003	-71.16	150	31	82	0
qq.com	5861.1	1510	-74.24	150	114	26	6
google.co.in	354	376	6.21	18	12	5	2
taobao.com	2744.5	2800	02.02	112	12	29	0

Table 4. Performance with policy to block iframes

Domain	Load time (in ms)			Total requests	
	without extension	with extension	% increase	without extension	with extension
google.com	312	336	7.69	19	19
youtube.com	5285	4200	-20.5	67	56
facebook.com	2798	3884	38.81	313	244
baidu.com	159	538	238.3	18	17
wikipedia.org	387	395	2.06	6	5
reddit.com	679.5	1663	144.6	68	62
yahoo.com	3479	1859	-46.56	150	150
qq.com	5861	6052	3.25	150	150
google.co.in	354	377	6.49	18	16
taobao.com	2744.5	2365	-13.81	112	105

due to overhead of monitoring each outgoing request of type 'sub-frame'. The performance overhead for most websites was found to be less than 10%. We also observed a decrease in average load time of the websites which contain iframes for showing embedded content like ads or videos. The results for top 10 websites are given in Table 4.

Policy to Create the Blacklist (Policy 4.8). The average performance overhead for policy given in the Listing 1.2 was very low. More than 70% of the websites had less than 10% increase in load time as the requests that are not targeted to the blacklisted domains are not passed to the extension. Further, the average load time reduced for the websites loaded with content from the blacklisted domains.

```
deny     access    *://*.zedo.com/*
deny     access    *://*.googleadservices.com/*
deny     access    *://*.doubleclick.net/*
deny     access    *://*.googlesyndication.com/*
deny     access    *://*.google-analytics.com/*
deny     access    *://gstatic.com/*
deny     access    *://*.adbrite.com/*
```

Listing 1.2. Blacklisted advertising and analytic domains

Policy to Block All Executable Downloads (Policy 4.10). This policy checks the response headers for 'Content-type' as 'application/octet-stream', thereby adding additional overhead. For this policy, there was an average increase of 30% in load time. However, this overhead was less than 10% for fifty percent of websites as shown in Table 5.

Policy to Set Browser Privacy Setting (Policy 4.13). We implemented the policy defined in 4.13 for evaluation. This policy adds very insignificant overhead with approximately 80% websites having average increase in page load time of less than 10%.

Overall, the performance overhead of implementing user policy does not affect the user's browsing experience adversely. The delay is very insignificant for most websites. The delay was found to be less than 10% even when multiple rules

Table 5. Performance with policy to block all executable downloads

% increase in load time	% of websites
Less than 10%	50%
10%–50%	31%
50%–90%	8%
More than 90%	11%

were implemented by the policy. There was considerable increase in page load time upto 200% for few websites like www.baidu.com and www.reddit.com for all policies. The Performance-Analyser extension measures page load time from the time when first request is sent to the time when last request is fetched, since these sites wait for content to be fetched by blocked requests, there was considerable increase in page load time but user won't notice any visible delay because rest of the page has been rendered in the browser. We also measured the page load time for such websites with Ghostery chrome extension and found increase comparable to our extension. Moreover, we expect that this overhead can be significantly reduced if we can implement the client-side policy directly within the browser instead of using the browser's extension.

6.3   Compatibility

Compatibility of a policy can be defined in terms of loss of functionality and ease of usage for the given websites. The more restrictive policy means more loss of interactive features of the websites. Here we discuss compatibility of some of the policies from Sect. 4.

Policy to Block All Cross-Origin JavaScripts (Policy 4.2). Manual verification was done to check any loss of functionality. It was found that there was not any degradation of useful web content displayed for sites which use cross-domain scripts for ads, analytics or additional features. However, it was found that there was a complete loss of functionality for a few websites like youtube.com and facebook.com as most of the scripts loaded on these websites are from different domains (https://static.xx.fbcdn.net for facebook.com, https://s.ytimg.com/ for youtube.com). We were able to retrieve most of the functionality on these websites by whitelisting these scripts manually. A future enhancement of the prototype can automate this process.

Policy to Block All Iframes (Policy 4.4). The loss of functionality of websites was either not found or was very limited for most of the websites. However, the websites which use iframes to display site content faced the significant degradation of services. The Fig. 3 shows the implementation of this policy.

Policy to Create Blacklist (Policy 4.8). We found no significant loss of interactivity for most of the websites except for those websites which deny their content when the domains given in the Listing 1.2 are blocked.

(a) Webpage with iframes   (b) Webage without iframes

Fig. 3. Web page with policy to block iframes

Policy to Block Executable Downloads (Policy 4.10). There was no visible loss of functionality with this policy.

Policy to Set Browser Privacy Setting (Policy 4.13). Some websites which require third-party cookies to be enabled give error when we disable these cookies. Currently, chrome.privacy API doesn't support enabling third-party cookies for selected domains. However, user can add these exceptions manually by using Chrome settings when prompted.

The compatibility analysis shows that there was very limited loss of useful functionality for websites which use scripts or other objects for displaying ads or other revenue generating third-party content. The future implementation can automate selective whitelisting of domains, by prompting user to block or permit the requested domain when he/she visits the site for the first time. Recently, the European Union (EU) passed a regulation, General Data Protection Regulation (GDPR)[4] to ensure data protection and privacy for all individuals within the EU. Many websites have since then, decided to run a separate version of their websites for EU users, which don't have any tracking scripts and ads. The user can achieve similar results by defining a policy to block such scripts.

6.4 Flexibility

Another important advantage of `MySecPol` is flexibility to add new keywords. Here, we propose a method to reduce user's vulnerability to phishing using a new field 'sensitive' to mark websites which need protection against phishing. In phishing attack, the attacker tricks a victim into clicking a link to phishing website sent via an email, or text message. The attacker's website looks similar to legitimate websites but have slightly different URLs. The parser was modified to read this new field and extension was modified to implement the same.

```
allow    sensitive    www.onlinesbi.com
```

The extension compares the visited domains against the list of protected domains and calculates percentage of similarity in domain names. If the level of similarity between two domain names is above the specified threshold percentage, user can be alerted for manual verification of the domain name.

Fig. 4. Protection against phishing

The Fig. 4 shows the alert message that is displayed when a user visits 'on1inesbi.com', a phishing website for the user's bank 'onlinesbi.com' (with threshold set to 50% for trials. The value can refined after detialed experimentation). The rate of false positives and false negatives depend upon the threshold value. The number of false positives and false negatives can be reduced by combining URL comparison with other phishing detection techniques such as comparing current page with cached screen-shot of legitimate page of sensitive domain, etc. Similarly, fields like 'popup', 'location', or 'notification' can be easily added to define rules to either block popups, or create whitelist of sites that can push notifications or access user's location.

7   Conclusion

In this paper, we have presented a client-side policy based architecture for secure web browsing using MySecPol. The main advantages of the proposed solution are (i) it is independent of platform/browser - making it easy to port policy from one browser to other, (ii) policy is easy to understand and intuitive to write and (iii) allows integrating several existing solutions. Our experimental results show that MySecPol scores over other approaches like uMatrix, in terms of features that are in demand by the users for configuring web security.

We have implemented it as a browser extension for Chromium. The experimental results show that our solution provides effective security with low-to-moderate overhead for a spectrum of users' applications. We have tested our Chrome extension on Windows 10 and Ubuntu 16.04. Browsers like Mozilla Firefox provide APIs similar to webrequest and privacy APIs of Chrome. The same client policy defined using `MySecPol` can be captured and integrated with other browsers with slight modifications in parser and browser extensions.

In summary, the policy language abstraction is intuitive and it enables organizations to write the specifications and integrate several user requirements based on a trade-off between security vs convenience. `MySecPol` provides flexibility to import existing ad-hoc browser security solutions targeting specific attacks like clickjacking, CSRF, phishing, etc., by adding new fields or keywords.

References

1. Bichhawat, A., Rajani, V., Jain, J., Garg, D., Hammer, C.: WebPol: fine-grained information flow policies for web browsers. CoRR abs/1706.06932 (2017). http://arxiv.org/abs/1706.06932
2. Cao, Y., Li, Z., Rastogi, V., Chen, Y., Wen, X.: Virtual browser: a virtualized browser to sandbox third-party JavaScripts with enhanced security. In: Proceedings of the 7th ACM CCS. ASIACCS 2012, pp. 8–9. ACM, New York (2012). https://doi.org/10.1145/2414456.2414460
3. World Wide Web Consortium: Subresource integrity (2016). https://www.w3.org/TR/SRI/
4. Council of European Union: Council regulation (EU) no 679/2016. In: Official Journal of the European Union, vol. L119 (4 May 2016), pp. 1–88 (2016). https://eur-lex.europa.eu/legal-content/EN/TXT/PDF/?uri=CELEX:32016R0679
5. Crockford, D.: ADsafe: making JavaScript safe for advertising (2008). http://www.adsafe.org/
6. De Groef, W., Devriese, D., Nikiforakis, N., Piessens, F.: FlowFox: a web browser with flexible and precise information flow control. In: Proceedings of the 2012 ACM CCS. CCS 2012, pp. 748–759. ACM, New York (2012). https://doi.org/10.1145/2382196.2382275
7. De Ryck, P., Desmet, L., Heyman, T., Piessens, F., Joosen, W.: CsFire: transparent client-side mitigation of malicious cross-domain requests. In: Massacci, F., Wallach, D., Zannone, N. (eds.) ESSoS 2010. LNCS, vol. 5965, pp. 18–34. Springer, Heidelberg (2010). https://doi.org/10.1007/978-3-642-11747-3_2
8. De Ryck, P., Nikiforakis, N., Desmet, L., Joosen, W.: TabShots: client-side detection of tabnabbing attacks. In: Proceedings of the 8th ACM SIGSAC. ASIA CCS 2013, pp. 447–456. ACM, New York (2013). https://doi.org/10.1145/2484313.2484371
9. MDN Web Docs: EvalInSandbox reference (2017). https://developer.mozilla.org/en-US/docs/Mozilla/Tech/XPCOM/Language_Bindings/Components.utils.evalInSandbox
10. MDN Web Docs: Javascript strict mode reference (2018). https://developer.mozilla.org/en-US/docs/Web/JavaScript/Reference/Strict_mode
11. Electronic Frontier Foundation: HTTPS everywhere, June 2018. https://github.com/efforg/https-everywhere
12. Gallagher, N.: Chrome tab limit (2013). https://github.com/necolas/chrome-tab-limit
13. W3C Working Group: Content security policy (2015). https://www.w3.org/TR/CSP1/
14. Hill, R.: uMatrix, July 2018. https://github.com/gorhill/uMatrix
15. Abine Inc.: Abine blur, May 2018. https://www.abine.com/index.htm

16. Ghostery Inc.: Ghostery, June 2018. https://www.ghostery.com/
17. InformAction: Noscript (2018). https://noscript.net/
18. Lingamneni, S.: Simpleblock (2017). https://github.com/slingamn/simpleblock
19. Loscocco, P., Smalley, S.: Integrating flexible support for security policies into the Linux operating system. In: Proceedings of the FREENIX Track: 2001 USENIX Annual Technical Conference, pp. 29–42. USENIX Association, Berkeley (2001). http://dl.acm.org/citation.cfm?id=647054.715771
20. Mao, Z., Li, N., Molloy, I.: Defeating cross-site request forgery attacks with browser-enforced authenticity protection. In: Dingledine, R., Golle, P. (eds.) FC 2009. LNCS, vol. 5628, pp. 238–255. Springer, Heidelberg (2009). https://doi.org/10.1007/978-3-642-03549-4_15
21. Miller, M.S., Samuel, M., Laurie, B., Awad, I., Stay, M.: Caja: safe active content in sanitized Javascript, 1 June 2017. https://developers.google.com/caja/
22. Meyerovich, L.A., Livshits, B.: ConScript: specifying and enforcing fine-grained security policies for Javascript in the browser. In: Proceedings of the 2010 IEEE Symposium on Security and Privacy. SP 2010, pp. 481–496 (2010)
23. Mrowetz, M.: Performance-analyser, May 2015. https://github.com/micmro/performance-bookmarklet/
24. WhiteHat Security: Application security statistics report 2017 (2017). https://info.whitehatsec.com/rs/675-YBI-674/images/WHS%202017%20Application%20Security%20Report%20FINAL.pdf?
25. Telikicherla, K.C., Agrawall, A., Choppella, V.: A formal model of web security showing malicious cross origin requests and its mitigation using CORP. In: Proceedings of the 3rd ICISSP, pp. 516–523 (2017). https://doi.org/10.5220/0006261105160523
26. Weichselbaum, L., Spagnuolo, M., Lekies, S., Janc, A.: CSP is dead, long live CSP On the insecurity of whitelists and the future of content security policy. In: Proceedings of the 23rd ACM CCS, Vienna, Austria (2016)
27. Zhou, Y., Evans, D.: Understanding and monitoring embedded web scripts. In: Proceedings of the 2015 IEEE Symposium on Security and Privacy. SP 2015, pp. 850–865, IEEE Computer Society, Washington, DC (2015). https://doi.org/10.1109/SP.2015.57

Gaze-Based Graphical Password Using Webcam

Abhishek Tiwari[1,2] and Rajarshi Pal[1(✉)]

[1] Institute for Development and Research in Banking Technology (IDRBT),
Hyderabad, India
abhishektiwari500@gmail.com, iamrajarshi@yahoo.co.in
[2] University of Hyderabad, Hyderabad, India

Abstract. Authentication refers to verification of the identity of an user. There exist various types of authentication techniques, starting from simple password based authentication up to behavior biometric based authentication. In this paper, a new way of authentication is proposed where the user provides her password through eye gaze. It is based on graphical password scheme where she can choose her password from a large image data set. At the time of authentication, she needs to recall it and look at the chosen passcode appearing in a display in correct sequence. The method uses a machine learning technique where a convolutional neural network is used to determine gaze locations using inputs from a simple web camera. It takes her cropped eye as input and provides gaze location as output. Proposed method is cost effective solution as gaze tracking is done through a simple web camera. The proposed method is also free from attacks such as shoulder surfing, smudge, brute-force attacks. Experiments have been carried out to validate the system. It has been observed to perform accurately for all the volunteers.

Keywords: Authentication · Graphical password · Gaze tracking

1 Introduction

Authentication refers to verification of the identity of a subject. User authentication is required in most of human-to-computer interactions. User authentication is a method of deciding whether a user is allowed to get access to a specific resource or not. To authenticate an individual, the credential provided by her are compared to the reference credential which is stored in a file or in a database. If the provided information is matched with stored information, then the user will be granted access to that resource. There are many factors using which an user can provide her credential. An authentication factor is a category of credential being used for identity verification. The three most common categories are often described as something you know (the knowledge factor), something you have (the possession factor), and something you are (the inherence factor).

Knowledge based password can be classified in two categories as textual and graphical password. In graphical password based method, pictures are used as

V. Ganapathy et al. (Eds.): ICISS 2018, LNCS 11281, pp. 448–461, 2018.
https://doi.org/10.1007/978-3-030-05171-6_23

symbols of a password. Graphical password methods are useful when devices do not allow typed input. Graphical password scheme has been proved to be more secure, as they are resistant to phishing/vishing based attempts to steal a password. They are considered easier to use due to the human tendency to remember pictures more comfortably than text. An user is required to select few images or to create a pattern during registration. During authentication, she needs to recognize the chosen images or to re-create the same pattern. For example, in [1], many random objects are displayed on the screen and the user identifies a set of pre-determined objects among them. Subsequently, she imagines a convex hull being formed with those objects and clicks on the imaginary area of the convex hull in order to get authenticated. In the PassPoint technique [2], the user is asked to remember some specific points of a given image. During authentication, she is supposed to click in approximately the same areas with proper sequence. Each point has a specific boundary which is invisible to the user. In another variation of this scheme [3], a personalized physical object (or image) is used for authentication. The user has to display the token on the camera. Simultaneously, the live video is demonstrated in a touch pad enabled screen. Then, the user clicks on specific pre-selected portions of the object (or image) in the video. In [4], the user draws free form signature, which is called as doodle, on the screen to get authenticated. It is matched with the registered signature of the concerned user. In [5], a graphical authentication method for mobile devices has been proposed where user's input generates vibration on the device. It is converted into a code, which is referred as vibration code. It is produced by counting the number of vibration of the device for the specific input. Generation of same vibration code as what has been registered, authenticates the user.

This paper aims to provide gaze-based solution for authentication problem. Some of the existing gaze-based authentication methods are discussed here. These techniques can be grouped into two divisions: gaze movement based biometric and gaze based communication of password. An user's gaze movement while viewing a scene has been considered as a biometric trait for her [6,7]. A low-frequency gaze tracking system is used in [6]. The method is based on saccade analysis, where saccade pattern of each user is presented by gaze movement. Two classification algorithms have been used which are based on k-nearest neighbor and naive Bayes classifiers. Kolmogorov-Smirnov statistics based distance measure is used in this context. In [7], a RGB-D sensor has been used to estimate gaze points. A video based extraction of certain biometric traits has been suggested in [8]. Acceleration, geometric and muscle properties are derived from gaze movement as biometric traits. Multilayer perceptron and support vector machine (SVM) are used as classifier to identify individuals. The method in [9] extracts certain dynamic features of eyes from the sphincter muscles and dilation muscles which are responsible to encircle and to expand the pupil. These features along with velocity and acceleration of gaze movement contribute to identification of an individual. Recently, a review of research progresses in the field of gaze movement biometric has been presented in [10].

On the contrary, in [11], an on-screen keyboard is presented to an user. She communicates her password through a gaze based interaction involving a gaze tracker. Captured gaze points are clustered to draw an inference as where she is looking at. The corresponding symbol from the keyboard is matched with the symbol in the known password. As involvement of any physical contact based input device (key board, mouse or touch screen) is not there, this method is resistant to shoulder surfing, key logger and screen logger based attacks.

In a public crowded area, it is practice by intruders to directly or indirectly looking over an user's shoulder to obtain her personal information. There are several types of attacks possible such as shoulder surfing, smudge attack, key logger attack, social engineering attack, brute force and dictionary attack. To enhance the security of a system, this paper attempts to combine the concept of gaze-based input with graphical password. It develops a user-friendly graphical interface that allows a user to enter her authentication credentials using eye gaze via a normal webcam. The proposed method is cost effective, as it does not require any special hardware to implement. The approach is to detect an eye from a facial image. This image of the eye serves as input to an artificial neural network. The output is the coordinate on the screen. Hence, user can provide her credential through eye by gazing at a graphical user interface (GUI) in order to get authenticated by the system. The proposed method is free from shoulder surfing and key-logger attacks, as the user is not required to have any physical connection with the system. Similarly, the use of graphical password prevents the attempts to steal the password through malware and phishing/vishing attacks.

The organization of the paper is as follows: Sect. 2 outlines the proposed webcam-based graphical password technique. Section 3 discusses each step of the proposed method in detail. Experimental validation of the proposed method is reported in Sect. 4. Section 5 contains concluding remarks of the paper along with possible interesting extensions.

2   Proposed System: Basic Philosophy

This paper proposes a graphical password based user authentication method using gaze based input. The proposed method can be divided into following three modules:

- Image processing for face and eye detection
- Machine learning for understanding gaze input
- Authentication based on graphical password.

In the image processing module, the face of the user and subsequently, one eye is detected which will be sufficient to estimate user's gaze point on the screen. This is done by using various feature detection techniques. This cropped eye portion of the image is given as input to the artificial neural network. This neural network is trained to get the coordinate value of the screen where the user is looking at. A convolution neural network is trained to perform this task. It takes the cropped image of user's eye as input and accordingly, outputs coordinate

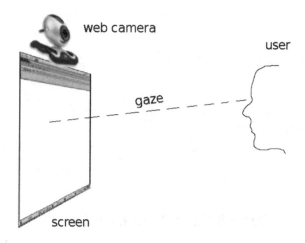

Fig. 1. Experimental setup

value on the screen. For authentication, a graphical password based scheme is developed. The password for authentication is a sequence of pictures. During registration, the user has to select a sequence of any k images as her password from a large pool of n images. The values of n and k are 100 and 4, respectively, for the reported experiments. At the time of authentication, 9 different images are displayed on the screen at a single point of time. One of those 9 images is part of the user's password. Thus, remaining parts of the user's password are also presented to her one by one. The user needs to just look over her pass-codes on each frame in a pre-registered sequence to get herself authenticated.

2.1 Available Resources

Following resources are used to design the authentication system:

- **Web Camera**: To make the system cost-effective, a normal Logitech web camera is used. The resolution of the captured image is 640×480 pixels.
- **Software:** The main implementation (eye detection and GUI for authentication) is done in Matlab 2015a by using image processing tool box. Neural network module (for learning the coordinate of gaze fixation) is implemented in Python by using Keras library.

2.2 Restriction in the Setup

Some restrictions have been imposed in the proposed scheme. The position of web camera is in a fixed place (with respect to the display) for experiment. The user's head is positioned in the same elevation as with the camera. The distance between user's head and camera is approximated between 50 to 60 cm. The user is required to remove her spectacles, unfortunately. The resolution of the screen is fixed to 1450×750 for both enrollment and authentication GUIs. A representative diagram of the setup is given in Fig. 1.

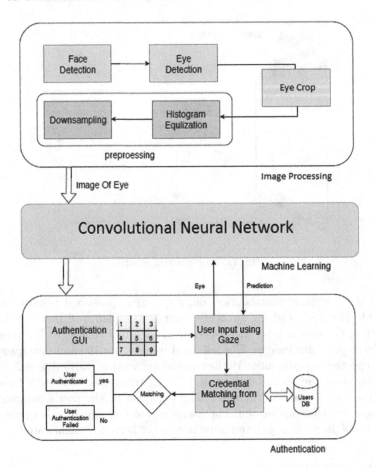

Fig. 2. Workflow diagram

3 Proposed Method: Workflow

Overall workflow can be properly understood with the help of a flow diagram in Fig. 2. Detail of each module along with its algorithm and results is explained in further subsections.

3.1 Face and Eye Detection

This section provides the details about the first module, i.e., image processing for face and eye detection. Face of the user is extracted at first. Subsequently, one eye is detected in the face and cropped.

Face Detection. Detecting face of the user is a key requirement for subsequent detection of eye. Among many available face detection algorithms, Viola-Jones algorithm [12] is the most widely used to detect face. This algorithm uses machine learning technique in which training a classifier is done by giving input of some faces and some non-faces. Once the training is complete, the system is able to identify faces and non-faces. Some key components of this face detection algorithm are:

- **Haar features:** Haar features are like convolution kernels that are used to catch the presence of any specific feature in a given image. Each feature's outcome is a value, which can be calculated by subtracting the sum of white rectangle pixels from the sum of black rectangle pixels (Fig. 3).

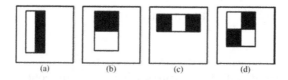

Fig. 3. Haar features used in Viola-Jones [12]

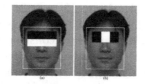

Fig. 4. Application of Haar on a facial image

Every filter is used to extract some properties from the image. For example, Fig. 4(b) shows identification of the eyes. The Haar feature is rolled all over the image from top left to bottom right to generate a value at each point. The highest value will come only on those pixels where the Haar pattern matches exactly. Basically, these Haar features represent some properties of the face. These features with each possible pixel configurations are rolled over the image for detecting any facial feature. But if all possible configurations are considered over the image, then the process becomes complex. For this, the basic idea is to eliminate the redundant features and to calculate only those features which are useful for detecting the interesting features.

- **Integral Image:** In the integral image, the outcome $I(x, y)$ at a pixel (x, y) is the summation of all pixel values at top and left side of it (Eq. 1). This is illustrated in Fig. 5. It represents the summation of intensities of all pixels of any rectangle using the bottom-right corner value. It helps to calculate difference between pixel intensities of a dark and a light region as given in Fig. 3.

$$I(x, y) = \sum_{x' \leq x \; y' \leq y} i(x', y') \tag{1}$$

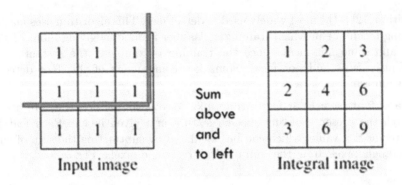

Fig. 5. Integral image

where $i(x, y)$ is the value of the pixel at (x, y).

- **AdaBoost:** To identify the features which are only contributing in distinguishing face and non-face, the Adaboost algorithm is used. It filters out irrelevant features and provides a set of relevant features which are sufficient to identify a face.

- **Cascading:** Viola-Jones algorithm [12] uses 24×24 window for evaluating features on any image. This 24×24 window has to be rolled over an input image for a large number of features to consider a linear combination of all cases in order to decide as face or non-face. This process too seems a bit time consuming. Cascading is used to overcome it. Each stage works upon a subset of all available filters. Each stage decides whether a given sub-window has any chance of containing a face or not. Any input image can pass onto next stage only if it passes previous stage test. Otherwise, it will be discarded immediately.

Eye Detection. The eye detection method in [13] is used for eye pair detection on the detected face image. A classifier has been trained using a collection of over 6000 sample images. It basically makes use of the Viola-Jones algorithm [12] for eye detection. Only few Haar features are required for detection of eyes, as the input is an already detected face. An illustrative result for both face and eye detection is shown in Fig. 6.

Eye Cropping. After detection of pair of eyes, the specific area (which corresponds to the right eye) is cropped out from the face image (Fig. 7). A specific aspect ratio is used for cropping the right eye from the bounding box of detected eye pairs. This aspect ratio of the cropped window is fixed for every user during experiments. This ratio is experimentally set in such a way that any eye feature should not be lost for any user. In the proposed method, only right eye is used for further operation.

Fig. 6. Face and eye detection

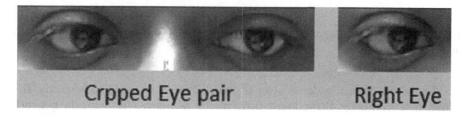

Fig. 7. Eye cropping

Pre-processing of Cropped Image for Classification Module. The image of the cropped right eye is the input to the neural network for identifying where the user is looking at. Following pre-processing is performed on the cropped image before processing it further:

- Histogram equalization: Histogram equalization is performed on the cropped image to adjust the intensity values of pixels. This adjustment of contrast results in brightening the sclera portion and darkening the eye boundary.
- Down sampling: The histogram equalized image is resized to 64×64 dimension. It is basically down sampled to reduce the training time of the neural network. Bicubic interpolation is used here.

Figure 8 shows the effect of histogram equalization and down sampling on the cropped image.

3.2 Neural Network Module

A convolutional neural network is used to determine the portion of the screen where an user is looking at. The authentication GUI, which has been developed, has nine distinct portions. This is because 9 different images will be shown to the user where one of those 9 images is a symbol of her graphical password. Hence, the gaze point estimation has been formulated as a 9-class classification problem. Hence, the output layer of this neural network has 9 neurons. The input layer of the convolutional neural network is of size 64×64. The hidden layers consist of two convolutional layers, one max-pooling layer, and one dense layer. The convolutional layers use a 3×3 kernel. Max-pooling layer uses a

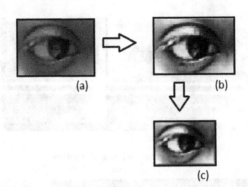

Fig. 8. Pre-processing: (a) cropped image, and the result of (b) histogram equalization and (c) down sampling

2×2 window. At last, a dense layer is used. Dropout is added to overcome the problem of overfitting. It randomly turns off few neurons. This helps the network to remember the training data as all neurons will not be active at the same time. So, the network does not memorize anything from nonactive neurons.

Keras library is used for creating the above neural network, which is written in Python. It is a machine learning library that runs over TensorFlow.

Training the Neural Network. As the authentication GUI displays nine images at a time and the user is asked to look at one of those nine images (which is part of her password), the convolutional neural network is trained to determine which one of the nine locations in the GUI the user is looking at. Hence, the following operations have been carried out to train the network:

- A GUI window is created of fixed size, i.e., 1440×750. This window is divided into 9 non-overlapping sections of size 480×250.
- At the center of each section, a black circular marker of 50-pixel diameter is created with a background of the image being white (Fig. 9(a)).
- System is programmed in such a way that out of those 9 markers, one marker appears on the screen at a time (Fig. 9(b)). The user is asked to look at that marker with fixed head position.
- Three images of the user are captured on the appearance of each marker. These images are processed as per the image pocessing module (Fig. 2). The processed cropped images of the right eye are used to train the neural network.
- 26 volunteers participated to provide the training data. Each volunteer was shown those markers and corresponding eye images were recorded. Three images of the user are captured on the appearance of each marker. Marker at each of those 9 positions appears 5 times during the experiment with a single volunteer.
- 80% of the collected data set were used for training the network, whereas remaining 20% of the data were used to test the network.
- The network was trained for 100 epochs. A batch size of 512 was used.

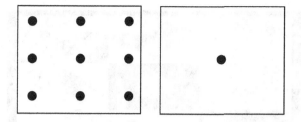

Fig. 9. Training data collection setup: (a) all possible markers, and (b) one marker is displayed at a time to the volunteer

3.3 Authentication

The main purpose of the proposed method is to propose a new way of authentication in which an user is able to provide her credentials into the system via eye gaze. The system compares the user provided inputs with the stored credentials (which have been recorded a priori during registration).

A convolutional neural network takes user's eye image as an input and determines the corresponding block or coordinate on the screen where the user is looking at.

The proposed authentication algorithm is a type of graphical password method. A password consists of a sequence of k images. The value of k is 4 for the experiments. At a time, one of those k images is displayed in the authentication GUI among a set of 9 images. User's gaze is estimated from the captured images using a web camera. This is repeated k times to estimate the user's gaze for each of the symbols (i.e., images) of her password. These k images appear in the same sequence as in the password. The authentication method can be divided into two phases, i.e., registration phase and authentication phase.

Registration Phase. During registration, the user has the independence of creating her password. In the proposed method, for registration, a collection of n (100 for our experiments) images is provided to the user. She can select any k images from that collection in a sequential manner. It forms a graphical password for her. Selected password is stored in the database. The user needs to remember those images in a proper sequence. All the images for password space are collected in such a way that they are different from each other. Hence, the user will not be confused at the time of authentication.

Authentication Phase. A GUI is created for authentication to show the images of the user's password. Each image of her password is displayed along with 8 other randomly selected images. This GUI window is of 1440×750 dimension. The size is same with the window which was used to collect the training data set using markers (Fig. 9). This GUI window is divided into nine non-overlapping blocks of same size. 9 images appear in those 9 blocks. The screenshot of the GUI is presented in Fig. 10. The authentication algorithm is explained with the help of following points:

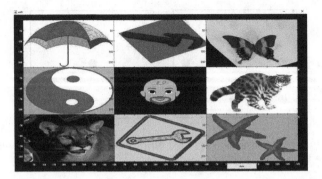

Fig. 10. Authentication GUI

- The first image of the password and 8 other random images from the collection of password space are displayed into a 3 × 3 layout of images. The passcode image can come in any position out of those 9 positions.
- The user looks at her passcode image only. Three images of her face are captured.
- Upon clicking on the next button, another 3 × 3 layout of the images appears. It contains the second passcode image of the user. Once again, three facial images of her are captured. This process is carried out two more times, as the password contains a sequence of 4 images.
- The system is programmed in such a way that it records three images of the user when a new set of images is displayed in the GUI. These captured images are processed according to the methods in Sect. 3.1. The cropped eye images are fed to the neural network. It outputs the corresponding blocks where the user looks at.
- Three images are captured each time with the intention of increasing surety of authentication. When the neural network predicts the output class, the majority of three results is selected as output class for each window.
- After getting class output from the neural network module, it is compared with the registered password of the corresponding user. If the registered password and the predicted password match, then she is declared as a legitimate user.

4   Experimental Results

Results of the experiments are summarized through following points:

1. For training the neural network, the data has been collected from 26 volunteers. The neural network demonstrates 93.14% accuracy on the test data set. Figure 11 shows the accuracy and the loss as functions of epoch on training and test data.

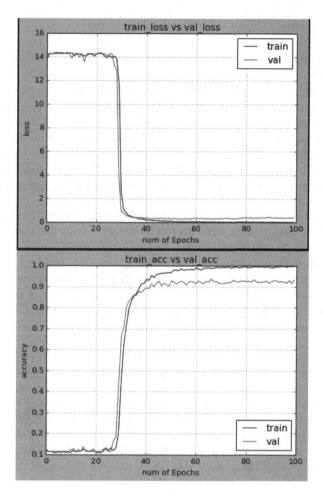

Fig. 11. Loss and accuracy as functions of epoch

2. To test the proposed authentication system, experiments are performed with the same 26 volunteers. They have been asked to use the proposed authentication system with their own created passcode.
3. As explained in Sect. 3.3, the system captures three images to determine each symbol (image) in the password. These images are fed to neural network one at a time. The majority of class predictions as indicated by the neural network is chosen as the result class. All the volunteers were able to successfully authenticate using this method. Successful authentication is considered when all four passcode images are correctly identified.
4. The authentication accuracy decreased to approximately 75% when only one facial image per layout is taken into consideration (instead of three images) for the classification. Hence, the necessity of the majority voting for class label identification using three captured images of the face is established.

5   Conclusion

The paper proposes a new way of user authentication, where the user can use her eye gaze to provide input to the system. It provides a low-cost solution to the problem which is not vulnerable to password compromise attacks. The user provides her credentials via eye gaze only using a simple web camera. Hence, there is no possibility of shoulder surfing or key logger based attacks. The proposed system has been tested by performing an experiment where 26 volunteers participated. They have been asked to perform authentication with their own set of passcode. The system was able to authenticate successfully all of them. The following points about the proposed system can be highlighted:

- The proposed system is a cost-effective solution to the authentication problem. It does not require any specific hardware. Hence, it can be used for several simple domestic purposes.
- The system does not take much processing time for authentication, as the training is performed only once. No calibration is needed afterward.
- User has a large number of choices (i.e., images) to create her passcode. Also the symbols (i.e., images) of the chosen user passcode do not appear at the same place every time. It makes the system more secure against attacks.

The proposed system captures facial images in order to estimate gaze locations. Hence, face biometric can be easily incorporated to make it a multi-factor authentication system. Hence, the graphical password will contribute to the knowledge factor and the face biometric will contribute to the inherence factor to build the multi-factor authentication system. The only limitation of the proposed system is that it imposes restriction on the user in terms of relative positioning of the head with respect to the display. This restriction may be eliminated by training the system with more number of images.

References

1. Sobrado, L., Birget, J.C.: Graphical passwords. The Rutgers Scholar, An Electronic Bulletin for Undergraduate Research, vol. 4 (2002)
2. Wiedenbeck, S., Waters, J., Birget, J., Brodskiy, A., Memon, N.: PassPoints: design and longitudinal evaluation of a graphical password system. Int. J. Hum.-Comput. Stud. Special issue: HCI Res. Priv. Secur. Crit. 63(1–2), 102–127 (2005)
3. Bianchi, A., Oakley, I., Kim, H.: PassBYOP: bring your own picture for securing graphical passwords. IEEE Trans. Hum.-Mach. Syst. 46(3), 380–389 (2016)
4. Diaz, M., Fierrez, J., Galbally, J.: Graphical password-based user authentication with free-form doodles. IEEE Trans. Hum.- Mach. Syst. 46(4), 607–614 (2016)
5. Azad, S., et al.: VAP code: a secure graphical password for smart devices. Comput. Electr. Eng. 59, 99–109 (2017)
6. Cherepovskaya, E.N., Lyamin, A.V.: An evaluation of biometric identification approach on low-frequency eye tracking data. In: Proceeding of IEEE 15th International Symposium on Applied Machine Intelligence and Informatics, January 2017

7. Cazzato, D., Evangelista, A., Leo, M., Carcagni, P., Distante, C.: A low-cost and calibration-free gaze estimator for soft biometrics: an explorative study. Pattern Recognit. Lett. **82**(2), 196–206 (2016)
8. Liang, Z., Tan, F., Chi, Z.: Video-based biometric identification using eye tracking technique. In: Proceeding of IEEE International Conference on Signal Processing, Communication and Computing, August 2012
9. Darwish, A., Pasquier, M.: Biometric identification using the dynamic features of the eyes. In: Proceeding of IEEE Sixth International Conference on Biometrics: Theory, Applications and Systems, September-October 2013
10. Rigas, I., Komogortsev, O.: Current research in eye movement biometrics: an analysis based on BioEye 2015 cometition. Proc. Image Vis. Comput. **58**, 129–141 (2017)
11. Weaver, J., Mock, K., Hoanca, B.: Gaze-based password authentication through automatic clustering of gaze points. IEEE International Conference on Systems, Man, and Cybernetics (2011)
12. Viola, P., Jones, M.: Rapid object detection using a boosted cascade of simple features. In: Proceedings of the 2001 IEEE Computer Society Conference on Computer Vision and Pattern Recognition, vol. 1, pp. 511–518 (2001)
13. Shiqi Yu's Homepage. http://yushiqi.cn/research/eyedetection

Invited Keynote

(Invited Paper) on the Security of Blockchain Consensus Protocols

Sourav Das$^{(\boxtimes)}$, Aashish Kolluri, Prateek Saxena, and Haifeng Yu

Computer Science Department, School of Computing,
National University of Singapore, Singapore, Singapore
souravdas1547@gmail.com, {aashish7,prateeks,haifeng}@comp.nus.edu.sg

Abstract. In the last decade, several permissionless proof-of-work blockchain protocols have focused on scalability. Since these protocols are very difficult to change once deployed, their robustness and security are of paramount importance. This paper summarizes the desired end properties of blockchain consensus protocols and sheds light on the critical role of theoretical analyses of their design. We summarize the major paradigms in prior constructions and discuss open issues in this space.

1 Introduction

Blockchain protocols, which originated in Bitcoin [57], allow a large network of computers to agree on the state of a shared ledger. Applications utilizing blockchains embrace a semantics of immutability: once something is committed to the blockchain, it can not be reversed without extensive effort from a majority of computers connected to it. These protocols embody the vision of a global "consensus computer" to which arbitrary machines with no pre-established identities can connect for offering their computational resources (in return for a fee), without dependence on any centralized authority. Despite this, the computational infrastructure strives to offer failure resistance against arbitrarily malicious actors. Security is at the heart of these protocols and applications built on them, as they now support an economy valued at several hundred billion dollars[1].

Theoretical frameworks should guide the construction of practical systems. The last decade of work on designing blockchain protocols highlights the importance of this interplay. In this paper, we distill the essence of the problem of designing secure blockchain consensus protocols, which are striving towards lower latencies and scalability. Our goal is to present key results that have surfaced in the last decade, offering a retrospective view of how consensus protocols have evolved. We examine a central question: is Bitcoin's original consensus protocol—often called Nakamoto consensus—secure, and if so, under which conditions?

The authors are sorted alphabetically by the last name.

[1] Total market capitalization of cryptocurrencies is $217, 279, 849, 996$ USD at the time of writing [5].

© Springer Nature Switzerland AG 2018
V. Ganapathy et al. (Eds.): ICISS 2018, LNCS 11281, pp. 465–480, 2018.
https://doi.org/10.1007/978-3-030-05171-6_24

There have been many folklore claims, for instance, that Nakamoto consensus is categorically secure up to $\frac{1}{2}$ adversarial power, beyond which "51% attacks" violate its guarantees [57,62]. Careful analysis, however, has dispelled many such claims. The quest for designing more scalable and secure consensus protocols has ensued. We review some of these construction paradigms and open problems. We focus mostly on protocols that are designed to operate in the open or permissionless setting which limit adversaries by computational power only.

2   The Blockchain Consensus Problem

One of the novel algorithmic advances in Bitcoin is its consensus algorithm called Nakamoto consensus. The protocol runs between a set of *miners* (computers), connected via a peer-to-peer (P2P) overlay over the Internet. Miners agree on the state of a globally distributed ledger of *transactions* periodically. Transactions are broken up into sets of constant size called "blocks", and miners broadcast them to other miners continuously. The essence of the blockchain consensus protocol is to reach agreement on the *total order* on a common subset of blocks seen by all the honest miners. The total ordering of blocks is sufficient to achieve a well-defined notion of consistency [43]. With this, for instance in a cryptocurrency application, it is easy to avoid double-spends: the client can always pick the first[2] transaction that spends a coin, ignoring later (conflicting) transactions that spend the same coin.

One way to agree on the total order, as proposed in Nakamoto consensus is to order blocks in a hashchain data structure [2], which coined the term "blockchain". In a blockchain, blocks are chained in a sequence using cryptographic hashes, where one block hash binds it to its predecessor in the total order. Transactions can have any semantics. For instance, in Bitcoin these transactions represent ownership (and payments) of virtual coins. In more recent cryptocurrencies, transactions represent the more traditional notion of atomic state updates for programs called smart contracts [4,68].

2.1   Threat Model and Assumptions

Miners who follow the prescribed protocol are called *honest*. This consensus protocol makes three assumptions, which strikingly differ from prior literature:

(a) honest peers, with no pre-established identities, can broadcast publicly to all other honest nodes a block synchronously, within a delay δ;
(b) the total computational power of the system is approximately known, out of which a known fraction f is assumed malicious (Byzantine [44]);
(c) all peers have an unbiased source of local randomness, and a trusted setup phase creates public parameters in a constant size "genesis block".

---

[2] Earliest one in the total order.

Bitcoin's assumptions, especially the combination of (a) and (b), are novel and minimalistic in a sense. Prior works in the literature study asynchronous networks which can lose connectivity between honest miners in the P2P overlay for indefinite periods of time [10,28,51]. We say that the network is "partitioned" if honest nodes lose connectivity to a significant fraction of other honest miners. Under this asynchronous model, a deterministic consensus is classically impossible [28] and most probabilistic consensus algorithms in the classical model have exponential round complexity [39][3]. This suggests that some more assumptions are necessary to avoid well-known impossibility results and long-standing problems. Assumption (a) of δ-synchronous broadcast is stronger than assuming an arbitrarily asynchronous network, but the protocol designer can estimate an acceptable network delay δ, and the Nakamoto consensus protocol can be instantiated with a block generation time that is large enough to accommodate it [15,56]. Different blockchains use this flexibility of picking different tolerance to network partitions [3,4]. Many prior protocols in the literature have assumed much more complex communication models of strongly synchronized clocks across nodes, pre-established identities attached to each message, global directories of identities participating (e.g. PKI), secret communication channels between peers, and so on [29]. Bitcoin takes a fresh approach assuming none of these.

Some form of sybil resistance is necessary to an open system where any number of computers or miners can connect [23]. Assumption (b) is a form of Sybil resistance, which is substantially different from prior protocols that assume pre-established identities or PKI [52]. For instance, popular Byzantine agreement protocols achieve consensus in a setup that assumes that the set of participants in the protocol are known to each other in advance [19,44]. Bitcoin does not assume that miners know identities of other miners in advance. More recently, many "Proof-of-Stake" (PoS) proposals assume that identities are pre-established and have an agreed upon fractional ownership in virtual coins (or stake) [20,32,38]. Such staking assumptions can be bootstrapped from Assumption (b).

Assumption (c) is assumed only once at the start of the blockchain. However, we believe this assumption is not necessary; it can be constructed directly from assumptions (a) and (b) using recent works as building blocks [7,34]. It is convenient, however, to assume this to avoid complexity of bootstrapping.

Attacking the Assumptions. A number of works have shown direct attacks on these assumptions. Assumption (a) states that all messages from honest nodes reach other honest within time δ; however, partitioning and eclipse attacks subvert these directly [8,33]. In partitioning attacks, malicious nodes aim to disconnect honest miners from each other at the P2P or ISP level. Similarly, eclipse attacks allow certain malicious miners to delay the propagation of network messages selectively to other miners. Protecting against these attacks is directly

---

[3] King at el. have presented the first theoretical result with polynomial round complexity recently in the model where no secret channels are constructed; the construction tolerates less than 1% Byzantine adversary [12,39].

important to fixing the parameters of the consensus algorithms; however, these are outside the scope of the design of the consensus protocol itself. It does motivate building "hard-to-partition" P2P overlays, and defenses to avoid centralization at the ISP-level on the Internet, upon which blockchain overlays operate.

Assumption (b) has been challenged as well. The assumption that the adversary controls no more than fraction f of the compute power has been subject to much debate, since centralization of mining power is an acknowledged concern [25,48]. Mining protocols that force mining pools to run fairly, such as by executing a smart contract, have been investigated as a practical solution [50]. Prior work has proposed dis-incentives against forming mining pools or coalitions through non-outsourceable puzzles [53]. However, recently, there have been reports of real attacks that they require short-lived capital to carry out the attacks on specific public blockchains [14]. Addressing these attacks effectively, through incentives or technical means, is an open problem. Nonetheless, we argue that some forms of Sybil resilience and network delivery guarantees seem necessary; therefore, Bitcoin's assumptions are an acceptable starting point.

2.2   Nakamoto Consensus

Bitcoin's consensus protocol is a concrete example of a blockchain protocol. The protocol uses a specific computational puzzle or "proof-of-work" (PoW) puzzle [2,24]. The puzzle asks miners to find a nonce such that $H(nonce||seed||\dots) < 2^d$, where d is tunable "puzzle difficulty" parameter and H is a cryptographically strong hash function. Anyone with the solution to the puzzle $<nonce, seed, d>$ can verify in one hash evaluation whether the solution is valid. The *seed* serves the role of a randomized value for instantiating new puzzles over time. It is useful to think of PoW puzzles as a procedure to sample from the computational power distribution in the mining network.

Each miner in the protocol keeps minimal state, i.e., the longest chain of blocks in its local view. Each miner solves a PoW puzzle, which is stateless computation. The inputs of a puzzle are taken only from miner's local view, specifically, the latest block hash value serves as *seed* of the PoW puzzle. If a miner receives a block from the network, it inspects the validity of the block. If the block has a valid PoW solution, the miner extends its local view of the blockchain by one block, and the next round of mining starts with this new seed. If the miner receives a valid chain longer than its present chain, the miner switches its local view to it immediately. A block is confirmed after a constant number of blocks (k) extend it in the longest chain. The protocol sets k internally ($k = 6$ in Bitcoin). This consensus protocol is orthogonal to the representations of transaction data (UTXO [57] vs. accounts [72]), DoS-prevention checks on network messages [71], and validity checks (double-spend validation) [17,47,71].

2.3   The Problem

The blockchain consensus protocol allows each miner to periodically output a set of blocks that it deems as *confirmed* or final. The security goal of the consensus protocols is to ensure that honest miners (a) agree on the same total order for all confirmed blocks, and (b) the set of confirmed blocks includes those proposed by all miners fairly, i.e., in proportion to their contributed computation power for mining. We consider a protocol secure up to a fraction f of adversarial power if it can guarantee its security goals with high probability (w.h.p.)[4]. The underlying constraint is δ, the time taken for honest miners to receive a fixed size block, which is pre-determined by the network bandwidth of the miners. The performance criterion is how quickly blocks proposed by miners are agreed upon by the honest network.

Protocols can be compared both on their *block confirmation rate* and their tolerance to adversarial fraction f. If a protocol A includes strictly more blocks in its agreed total order per unit time than protocol B, tolerating the same adversarial power, then A is strictly better in performance. Likewise, if protocol A agrees on the same number of blocks per unit time as B, but tolerates strictly more adversarial power, then A is strictly better in security. One can even compare different configurations of the same protocol. Taking Nakamoto consensus as an example, the parameter k (number of confirmation blocks) offers a tradeoff between security tolerance and confirmation time. If we compare two configurations of Nakamoto consensus, with different values of k, it turns out the configuration with larger values of k offer slower confirmation times but higher security tolerance.

Security Properties of Blockchain consensus Protocols. The foremost question for any blockchain consensus protocol is which security guarantees it provides when a fraction f of power is controlled by a Byzantine adversary. One can think of the blockchain the protocol as a continuous time protocol, where at any time instant, each miner reports a set of blocks as confirmed and a total ordering relation over them. The first security goal is to ensure that an honest miner does not change its set of confirmed blocks over time, captured by a *stability* property:

Stability: For any honest miner, the set of confirmed blocks output at time t_1 is a subset of the set of confirmed blocks at time t_2 w.h.p, if $t_2 > t_1$. The order of confirmed blocks does not change over time w.h.p.

One oft-cited strategy for the attacker to subvert the stability property in Nakamoto consensus is to introduce an alternate longer chain starting at a block that is at least k blocks deep. If successful, this causes honest miners to switch their view on what is confirmed. This strategy was analyzed in the original Bitcoin paper [57]. However, this is not the only strategy to consider; the protocol must remain secure under all adversarial strategies [16].

The second security goal is to prove that miners following the protocol reach *agreement*: for any two honest miners, the confirmed blocks of one are also confirmed by the other, and that the order of the confirmed blocks is identical for both. Specifically, the following agreement property captures this:

---

[4] For any security parameter $\lambda > 0$, an event happening *with high probability* (w.h.p) implies that event happens with probability $1 - O(1/2^\lambda)$.

Agreement: Let C_1 and C_2 be the set of confirmed blocks reported by any two honest miners, then w.h.p:

(A) Either $C_1 \subseteq C_2$ or $C_2 \subseteq C_1$; and
(B) the blocks in $C_1 \cap C_2$ are ordered identically by both miners.

At any time instant, note that requirement (A) above allows one miner to not have confirmed all the blocks of the other honest miner. But, it disallows the case where two honest miners confirm two blocks, each one of which is only confirmed by one miner and not the other. Requirement (B) ensures blocks that are confirmed by both will necessarily be in the same order.

In Nakamoto consensus, satisfying the agreement property implies that the longest chain, discarding the last k blocks, of an honest miner should be a prefix of the longest chain of other honest miners [17]. Ensuring a common prefix satisfies both requirement (A) and (B) above. These properties (and others) are used to prove rigorous analytical bounds on the fraction f tolerated under different attack models by Nakamoto consensus and its variants [30,36,58].

A third critical property of the blockchain protocols is *fairness*. In a fair protocol, if the adversary controls fraction f of the computational power, the expected fraction of blocks contributed by it in the confirmed set blocks should be close to f. However, the adversary can deviate from the honest protocol to mine more blocks [27,31,63]. It may do so to increase its mining rewards, to favor or censor transactions of its choice, or bias the fairness of the application running on top of the blockchain in some way. The following property captures this security notion of fairness:

Fairness: There is a negligible probability that the fraction of blocks proposed by the adversary in the set of confirmed blocks, over any time interval $t > c \cdot \delta$, for some constant c, is more than f.

The constant c in the above definition specifies whether the protocol is fair over a small time windows or larger ones. Protocols that minimize c are desirable, as they sample from the computational power distribution in the mining network frequently. To understand the importance of minimizing this constant, consider the following proposal: one could run any fair consensus protocol to agree on a leader (say) once a week who broadcasts a massive "block" for the rest of the week. This is sufficient to utilize the bandwidth available, and in expectation over a large time window (say 1 year), it would be fair in picking leaders. However, such a protocol is *not* desirable as that leader may favor its own transaction blocks for a week. Further, the leader may be targeted for Denial-of-Service (DoS) or eclipse attacks during its tenure. Therefore, blockchain protocols that agree of (lots of) small blocks, sampling often from the computation power distribution, are better as fairness holds over shorter time windows.

Existing blockchain protocols can be compared directly on the minimum time window (or c) over which their fairness holds. Existing scalable blockchain protocol compete on lowering c for better decentralization and DoS-resilience.

3   Security Analysis of Nakamoto Consensus

Stability & Agreement Properties. Different strategies to subvert the stability and agreement properties of Nakamoto consensus have been studied, both experimentally and analytically, in prior works [30,58,66]. One key observation from these analyses is that Nakamoto consensus protocol exhibits poor tolerance to adversarial power when the block interval reduces significantly, especially as it starts to approach the broadcast latency. Intuitively, at low block intervals, many miners will start to mine blocks nearly simultaneously; these will be received in an unpredictable order by other miners. Consequently, some miners will mine on one block while the others on other blocks. This results having temporary "forks" in the chain. The rate of forks, often measured by the creation rate of "stale blocks" (which do not end up on the longest chain), is measured empirically by Gervais et al. for various configurations of Nakamoto consensus [31].

The security of Nakamoto consensus protocol hinges primarily on the ratio of the block interval to the broadcast latency. Several analyses have shown that there exists a large enough k (number of block confirmations) for which the protocol is secure for some large values of the block interval [30,58,66]. For certain high block interval rates (e.g., 10 min as in Bitcoin) for broadcast delay δ of a few tens of seconds observed empirically [22], prior analysis shows that the agreement property holds close to $f = \frac{1}{2}$ adversarial power fraction. However, this adversarial power tolerated drops as block interval rates reduce. Specific attack strategies have shown that the f drops to well-below 40%, even when the ratio of block interval rate to δ is close to 1, as in Ethereum [36,58]. The theoretical security tolerance thresholds for which security is guaranteed drops quickly as block interval decreases further. These results explain that Nakamoto consensus is not categorically secure under arbitrary block interval rates, unlike what folklore claims portray. More effective attack strategies and models than those proposed in prior works are possible and an open area of investigation.

Fairness Property. The fairness property has been extensively studied as well. The selfish mining and short-term block withholding strategies (c.f. Eyal and Sirer [27]) provide prominent results. This work shows that even a miner with 25% of the computation power can bias the agreed chain with its blocks (gaining more reward than expected). This shows that Nakamoto consensus cannot withstand a $\frac{1}{3}$ or $\frac{1}{2}$ adversarial power, as is assumed by the folklore claims of "51% attacks". This is relevant because a number of works rely on this fairness property for application-specific security guarantees (e.g. beacons [13,16], lotteries [7,13], bounties [18], samplers [6,41,47,73]), assuming that fairness property holds for certain adversarial power.

When studying the fairness property, many works have emphasized a subclass of rational adversaries, i.e., miners incentivized to optimize some utility function (e.g. maximizing their expected profits, maximize blocks mined by it, censor certain transactions, and so on) [27,31,63]. There have been various results showing the coin reward structures are not incentive-compatible, and rational miners can maximize their utility by deviating from the protocol [35,49,69,70,74].

Remarks. We remind readers that assuming that no miners are Byzantine, just that miners are either rational or honest, has some limitations. Rationality arguments are often made in virtual coin incentives and there are real markets today where coins are traded for fiat currencies. An attack may seem irrational (not incentivized) viewed from the objective of an assumed utility function for the attacker, whereas it may be incentivized as it may impact the valuation of virtual coins. Early works on the Goldfinger attacks [42] and feather-forking [1] discuss this issue of how reasonable it is to assume that miners will be rational versus Byzantine. Nakamoto protocol safety merits a study independently of the model of incentives, directly in the threat model of Byzantine adversaries.

4   Scalability Extensions to Nakamoto Consensus

Increasing Block Sizes. One natural way of increasing transaction rates is to have large blocks in Nakamoto consensus that consume all the bandwidth available. In such a design, optimal bandwidth utilization is achieved by picking large block sizes. Therefore, in such a solution, the constant c of the fairness property is directly dependent on the block sizes sufficient to saturate the entire network's bandwidth. As discussed earlier, this may not guarantee fairness in short time windows, and the attacker can target a single block proposer in each epoch. Several proposals utilize this design choice, such as the use of key blocks in Bitcoin-NG [26] and the identity establishment step of [21], implicitly inheriting the issue of ensuring fairness.

Reducing Block Interval. For achieving fairness in shorter intervals, one prominent re-configuration of Nakamoto consensus is to reduce the block interval. In Nakamoto consensus, this is achieved by lowering the puzzle difficulty for the known computational power. This tack is utilized in many cryptocurrencies. Bitcoin fixes the interval to be approximately 10 min, whereas Litecoin reduces it by four times and Ethereum brings it to 10–17 s. The lower the block interval rate, the better the fairness in choosing how many block proposal are generated per unit time. However, as explained in Sect. 2.3, the longest chain rule for selecting the total order does not remain secure. Lowering the block interval lowers the adversarial power f that the protocol tolerates significantly.

When block intervals are reduced in Nakamoto consensus, the open problem is how to order the blocks received by a miner. Various ordering rules have been proposed in the literature, but a solution that provably achieves optimal security and confirmation rate is not yet known. We summarize existing proposals next.

GHOST Rule. Sompolinsky and Zohar proposed the GHOST rule, an alternative to the longest chain rule of counting the number of blocks [66]. In the GHOST rule, miners retain information of all blocks they obtain from the network in their local view. These blocks thus form a block tree-like structure i.e., each block contains a subtree of blocks mined upon it. The weight of a block is the number of blocks in all forks belonging to its subtree. The GHOST rule dictates that heaviest chain consists of the heaviest block, by weight, at each depth in the tree of forks, thus, allowing blocks that are *not* on the heaviest to contribute to the weights of blocks on it. Hence, in essence, it picks the "heaviest" chain (with evidence of the most mining work contributed to it), rather than the longest.

A security analysis of the GHOST rule for certain attack strategies is presented in the proposal of Sompolinsky and Zohar [66]. Kaiyias et al. establish that GHOST rule is secure for certain parameters when block intervals are large [37]. The security analysis of the GHOST rule, especially when the block interval is smaller than the broadcast delay, merits a careful analysis, like in the case of Bitcoin's longest chain rule. Specifically, the security depends on how ties between heaviest blocks of equal weight are resolved. Several tie-breaking rules have been proposed, picking (a) uniformly between candidate blocks, (b) the first one that the miner receives, (c) the one with the smallest timestamp, and (d) the one with the smallest PoW puzzle solution. Different attacker models have been studied showing that GHOST is not unilaterally superior to the long chain rule [37,66]. It has been suggested that strategy (a) is preferred to strategy (b) for certain range of block intervals when the adversary uses a selfish mining strategy for fairness [27]. We conjecture that, in fact, strategy (a) is not universally better because it splits the available honest mining power across various forks. This reduces the power necessary for the adversary to create the heaviest chain by mining selfishly on its own fork, impacting the stability and agreement property.

Much like the longest chain rule, the final selected chain in GHOST discards all blocks that are not along the heaviest chain. So, the throughput of the GHOST protocol is within a small factor of that resulting from the longest chain rule. This is sub-optimal since many blocks seen by the honest miners are eventually discarded, lowering the average confirmation rate per block.

Directed Acyclic Graphs (DAGs). Recent works have proposed mechanisms to include blocks that are *not* on the longest or the heaviest chain in Nakamoto consensus. One line of work proposes that instead of keeping a chain, the miners can keep a directed acyclic graph (DAG) of blocks seen in their local view [45, 46,60,64,65]. Each miner has its view of the blocks it has seen, partially ordered in the DAG. The DAG has edges called "reference edges" that point to those blocks that the miner saw before it mined the present block, in addition to usual hashchain edges. The protocol specifies how miners order the blocks at the same depth in their local views of the DAG, and agree on their diverging DAG views.

A number of rules have been proposed to agree and order DAGs, such as SPECTRE [65], PHANTOM [64], and Conflux [46]. For instance, the Conflux protocol shows one mechanism for achieving this by finding a "pivot chain" using the GHOST rule and then topologically sorting the blocks that are at the same depth as a block on the pivot chain. Miners union the DAG views they receive from other nodes. Blocks at the same depth are ordered on hash value of PoW puzzle difficulty solved. The security of Conflux reduces to that of the GHOST rule. The PHANTOM protocol selects a subtree rather than a single chain and sorts topologically. The Conflux paper presents a liveness attack on the PHANTOM protocol, which is shown to be effective with an adversary that controls 15% computational power. DAG based schemes are relatively recent, and their rigorous scrutiny deserves further attention.

5   Scalability Solutions Based on Byzantine Agreement

The difficulty of securing variants of Nakamoto consensus has led to an alternative line of protocols that leverage classical Byzantine agreement (or BA) protocols instead. Consensus in a Byzantine network has been extensively studied, see surveys [9,29,39]. However, directly applying BA algorithms in the assumption model of Bitcoin is not straightforward. One key difficulty is that commonly BA protocols assume a pre-established set of identities known to all participants running the protocol.

To achieve this starting point, several protocols propose different designs to establish identities from the assumptions (a)–(c). Wattenhofer et al. use the Nakamoto consensus protocol to arrive at a common prefix of blocks, which contain public keys (identities) of the participants [21]. The security of this step directly relies directly on the security of Nakamoto consensus variants utilized.

The use of Nakamoto consensus to establish identities as a pre-step is not necessary. A number of works including Elastico [47], Omniledger [41], and RapidChain [73] directly establish identities from PoW or related cryptographic constructs[5]. A number of these solutions further "shard" identities, i.e., assign different clusters/committees to identities implicitly which can operate in parallel [6,41,47,73]. More recent works show how to use more general cryptographic puzzles to bootstrap a "reconciled view" of the set of participants in a mining network without Nakamoto consensus and even without assumption (c) outlined in Sect. 1 [7,34,53].

The security of these designs depends directly on the size of the set of identities established to run the BA protocol. The larger the size of the identity set, the higher is the communication cost of establishing the identity sets between the participants and subsequently running the BA protocol instances. This sample size establishes limits on how often the identity establishment protocol can run, which is directly related to the constant c for which the fairness property holds. There is a trade-off in choosing the sample size that different designs make. The sample sizes picked in various designs vary, but typically are in hundreds, for acceptable levels of security and confirmation times in tens of seconds [32,41,47].

The set of identities is supposed to be chosen randomly by sampling the computational power or stake distribution. Therefore, the fraction of adversarial identities in the chosen set is f in expectation. For sets of size s, the probability of the adversarial identities deviating from the mean f is bounded by a function exponentially small in s, which follows from the standard Chernoff bounds (Chap. 4. [55]). We point out that these analyses of sample sizes for establishing identity sets are often the same for proof-of-work systems and proof-of-stake systems [32]. This is because the process of creating identities based on random

---

[5] Verifiable random functions (VRFs) have been used to probabilistically select identity sets without eagerly revealing the identities selected [32,41].

sampling, and counting how many identities (Byzantine and honest) end up in an identity set, is the same for many PoS- or PoW-based systems. In all these different protocols for establishing identities, the role of a formal framework to model the sampling process (often a Binomial random variable[6]) guides the robust choice of sample size parameters.

A second factor that dictates the set size is the fraction of adversaries the BA algorithm can tolerate in one instance. BA protocols designed original for fully asynchronous networks like PBFT [19] tolerate $\frac{1}{3}$ adversary or their more efficient versions (ByzCoin [40], Omniledger [41]). Recent works use synchronous BA protocols which can tolerate the optimal $\frac{1}{2}$ Byzantine fraction [29,61]. Protocols that can tolerate better adversarial fractions (e.g. $\frac{1}{2}$ vs. $\frac{1}{3}$) require further smaller sets of identities [73].

The use of BA agreement in blockchains has spurred further research in designing faster BA protocols. The trade-offs in designing BA protocols which are fast when the network delay δ is small while degrading gracefully on slower networks have been actively studied [41,54,59,61]. Several works have improved the communication costs of BA agreement protocols, trading off the performance between the honest case and when the overlay P2P graphs have Byzantine adversaries [40,67]. More efficient broadcast primitives have emerged, for instance, using collective signing [67] or erasure-coded information dispersal techniques [54,73].

As blockchains run continuously, multiple rounds of BA protocol are implicitly composed in sequence. In sharded blockchains, BA protocol instances are often composed in parallel as well. Some care must be taken when composing instances, especially for BA protocols that have probabilistic termination time like the BA* algorithm [32] or PBFT[7] [19]. When BFT protocol instances are running in parallel—as in sharding-based blockchain protocols—the expected running time for all of the instances generation may not be constant in expectation, as the slowest instance (out of many) dominates the stopping time [11]. Optionally, to mitigate this delay, a protocol may choose to run a BA protocol instance to synchronize the output of the parallel instances running on each shard [47]. Specifically, a final committee determines whether a shard has agreed upon a block or not within a predetermined time bound. This bounds the delay at each shard, however, it admits the possibility that in some rounds, empty blocks will be mined. However, the probability that the protocol does not make progress for a few rounds under the assumption (a) of Sect. 2.3 is negligibly small. Protocols may not choose to synchronize outputs of shards at each epoch,

---

[6] The probability of a picked identity being Byzantine in the sample set is f, and honest is $1 - f$. The analysis examines two Binomial random variables, the number of honest and Byzantine adversaries picked in an indentity set, such that their ratio does not exceed the tolerance of the BA algorithm. When Nakamoto-style PoW is used to create identities, the number of identities created per unit time (by setting an appropriate puzzle difficulty), is approximated well by a Poisson random variable.

[7] PBFT is a leader-based protocol and may have multiple rounds, which depends on the probability of a dishonest leader being chosen at a particular round triggering a "view change" sub-step.

but then additional mechanisms to ensure atomicity of cross-shard commits in an epoch are often utilized [41].

6   Conclusions

We survey known results about how well Nakamoto consensus guarantees desired security, when configured for faster confirmations. Guided by theoretical analyses, new designs and variants of the Nakamoto consensus protocol are under active investigation, searching for an optimal protocol. Careful analyses have dispelled folklore claims of safety against 51% attacks hold categorically when re-configuring the Nakamoto consensus protocol. We further summarize another recent paradigm of constructions that are based on using established Byzantine agreement protocols. We explain some of the commonalities and the factors that determine their confirmation latencies and security trade-offs.

Acknowledgements. We thank Hung Dang for his helpful comments on the work. We thank sponsors of the Crystal Center at NUS, which has supported this work. All opinions presented in this work are those of the authors only.

References

1. Feather-forks: enforcing a blacklist with sub-50. https://bitcointalk.org/index.php?topic=312668.0
2. Hash chain wiki. https://en.wikipedia.org/wiki/Hash_chain
3. Litecoin wiki. https://en.wikipedia.org/wiki/Litecoin
4. A next-generation smart contract and decentralized application platform. https://github.com/ethereum/wiki/wiki/White-Paper
5. Total market capital of cryptourrencies (2018). https://coinmarketcap.com
6. Al-Bassam, M., Sonnino, A., Bano, S., Hrycyszyn, D., Danezis, G.: Chainspace: a sharded smart contracts platform. arXiv preprint arXiv:1708.03778 (2017)
7. Andrychowicz, M., Dziembowski, S.: PoW-based distributed cryptography with no trusted setup. In: Gennaro, R., Robshaw, M. (eds.) CRYPTO 2015. LNCS, vol. 9216, pp. 379–399. Springer, Heidelberg (2015). https://doi.org/10.1007/978-3-662-48000-7_19
8. Apostolaki, M., Zohar, A., Vanbever, L.: Hijacking Bitcoin: routing attacks on cryptocurrencies. In: 2017 IEEE Symposium on Security and Privacy (SP), pp. 375–392. IEEE (2017)
9. Aspnes, J.: Randomized protocols for asynchronous consensus. Distrib. Comput. 16(2–3), 165–175 (2003)
10. Ben-Or, M.: Another advantage of free choice (extended abstract): completely asynchronous agreement protocols. In: Proceedings of the Second Annual ACM Symposium on Principles of Distributed Computing, pp. 27–30. ACM (1983)
11. Ben-Or, M., El-Yaniv, R.: Resilient-optimal interactive consistency in constant time. Distrib. Comput. 16(4), 249–262 (2003)
12. Ben-Or, M., Pavlov, E., Vaikuntanathan, V.: Byzantine agreement in the full-information model in O (log n) rounds. In: Proceedings of the Thirty-Eighth Annual ACM Symposium on Theory of Computing, pp. 179–186. ACM (2006)

13. Bentov, I., Gabizon, A., Zuckerman, D.: Bitcoin beacon. arXiv preprint arXiv:1605.04559 (2016)
14. Bitcoinst: 51 percent attack on Bitcoin cash (2018). https://bitcoinist.com/roger-ver-bitpico-hard-fork-bitcoin-cash/
15. Bolot, J.C.: End-to-end packet delay and loss behavior in the internet. In: ACM SIGCOMM Computer Communication Review, vol. 23, pp. 289–298. ACM (1993)
16. Bonneau, J., Clark, J., Goldfeder, S.: On bitcoin as a public randomness source. IACR Cryptology ePrint Archive 2015, 1015 (2015)
17. Bonneau, J., Miller, A., Clark, J., Narayanan, A., Kroll, J.A., Felten, E.W.: SoK: research perspectives and challenges for Bitcoin and cryptocurrencies. In: 2015 IEEE Symposium on Security and Privacy (SP), pp. 104–121. IEEE (2015)
18. Breidenbach, L., Daian, P., Tramer, F., Juels, A.: Enter the hydra: towards principled bug bounties and exploit-resistant smart contracts. In: Proceedings of the 27th USENIX Conference on Security Symposium. USENIX Association (2018)
19. Castro, M., Liskov, B., et al.: Practical Byzantine fault tolerance. In: Proceedings of the Third Symposium on Operating Systems Design and Implementation, pp. 173–186. USENIX Association (1999)
20. Daian, P., Pass, R., Shi, E.: Snow white: robustly reconfigurable consensus and applications to provably secure proofs of stake (2017)
21. Decker, C., Seidel, J., Wattenhofer, R.: Bitcoin meets strong consistency. In: Proceedings of the 17th International Conference on Distributed Computing and Networking, p. 13. ACM (2016)
22. Decker, C., Wattenhofer, R.: Information propagation in the Bitcoin network. In: 2013 IEEE Thirteenth International Conference on Peer-to-Peer Computing (P2P), pp. 1–10. IEEE (2013)
23. Douceur, J.R.: The sybil attack. In: Druschel, P., Kaashoek, F., Rowstron, A. (eds.) IPTPS 2002. LNCS, vol. 2429, pp. 251–260. Springer, Heidelberg (2002). https://doi.org/10.1007/3-540-45748-8_24
24. Dwork, C., Naor, M.: Pricing via processing or combatting junk mail. In: Brickell, E.F. (ed.) CRYPTO 1992. LNCS, vol. 740, pp. 139–147. Springer, Heidelberg (1993). https://doi.org/10.1007/3-540-48071-4_10
25. Eyal, I.: The miner's dilemma. In: 2015 IEEE Symposium on Security and Privacy (SP), pp. 89–103. IEEE (2015)
26. Eyal, I., Gencer, A.E., Sirer, E.G., Van Renesse, R.: Bitcoin-NG: a scalable blockchain protocol. In: NSDI, pp. 45–59 (2016)
27. Eyal, I., Sirer, E.G.: Majority is not enough: Bitcoin mining is vulnerable. Commun. ACM 61(7), 95–102 (2018)
28. Fischer, M.J., Lynch, N.A., Paterson, M.S.: Impossibility of distributed consensus with one faulty process. J. ACM (JACM) 32(2), 374–382 (1985)
29. Garay, J., Kiayias, A.: SoK: a consensus taxonomy in the blockchain era. Cryptology ePrint Archive, Report 2018/754 (2018). https://eprint.iacr.org/2018/754
30. Garay, J., Kiayias, A., Leonardos, N.: The Bitcoin backbone protocol: analysis and applications. In: Oswald, E., Fischlin, M. (eds.) EUROCRYPT 2015. LNCS, vol. 9057, pp. 281–310. Springer, Heidelberg (2015). https://doi.org/10.1007/978-3-662-46803-6_10
31. Gervais, A., Karame, G.O., Wüst, K., Glykantzis, V., Ritzdorf, H., Capkun, S.: On the security and performance of proof of work blockchains. In: Proceedings of the 2016 ACM SIGSAC Conference on Computer and Communications Security, pp. 3–16. ACM (2016)

32. Gilad, Y., Hemo, R., Micali, S., Vlachos, G., Zeldovich, N.: Algorand: scaling byzantine agreements for cryptocurrencies. In: Proceedings of the 26th Symposium on Operating Systems Principles, pp. 51–68. ACM (2017)
33. Heilman, E., Kendler, A., Zohar, A., Goldberg, S.: Eclipse attacks on Bitcoin's peer-to-peer network. In: USENIX Security Symposium, pp. 129–144 (2015)
34. Hou, R., Jahja, I., Luu, L., Saxena, P., Yu, H.: Randomized view reconciliation in permissionless distributed systems (2017)
35. Kalodner, H., Goldfeder, S., Chen, X., Weinberg, S.M., Felten, E.W.: Arbitrum: scalable, private smart contracts. In: Proceedings of the 27th USENIX Conference on Security Symposium, pp. 1353–1370. USENIX Association (2018)
36. Kiayias, A., Panagiotakos, G.: Speed-security tradeoffs in blockchain protocols (2015)
37. Kiayias, A., Panagiotakos, G.: On trees, chains and fast transactions in the blockchain. (2016)
38. Kiayias, A., Russell, A., David, B., Oliynykov, R.: Ouroboros: a provably secure proof-of-stake blockchain protocol. In: Katz, J., Shacham, H. (eds.) CRYPTO 2017. LNCS, vol. 10401, pp. 357–388. Springer, Cham (2017). https://doi.org/10.1007/978-3-319-63688-7_12
39. King, V., Saia, J.: Byzantine agreement in expected polynomial time. J. ACM (JACM) **63**(2), 13 (2016)
40. Kogias, E.K., Jovanovic, P., Gailly, N., Khoffi, I., Gasser, L., Ford, B.: Enhancing Bitcoin security and performance with strong consistency via collective signing. In: 25th USENIX Security Symposium (USENIX Security 2016), pp. 279–296 (2016)
41. Kokoris-Kogias, E., Jovanovic, P., Gasser, L., Gailly, N., Ford, B.: OmniLedger: a secure, scale-out, decentralized ledger. IACR Cryptology ePrint Archive 2017, 406 (2017)
42. Kroll, J.A., Davey, I.C., Felten, E.W.: The economics of Bitcoin mining, or Bitcoin in the presence of adversaries. In: Proceedings of WEIS, vol. 2013, p. 11 (2013)
43. Lamport, L.: How to make a multiprocessor computer that correctly executes multiprocess programs. IEEE Trans. Comput. **28**(9), 690–691 (1979). https://doi.org/10.1109/TC.1979.1675439
44. Lamport, L., Shostak, R., Pease, M.: The Byzantine generals problem. ACM Trans. Program. Lang. Syst. (TOPLAS) **4**(3), 382–401 (1982)
45. Lewenberg, Y., Sompolinsky, Y., Zohar, A.: Inclusive block chain protocols. In: Böhme, R., Okamoto, T. (eds.) FC 2015. LNCS, vol. 8975, pp. 528–547. Springer, Heidelberg (2015). https://doi.org/10.1007/978-3-662-47854-7_33
46. Li, C., Li, P., Xu, W., Long, F., Yao, A.C.: Scaling Nakamoto consensus to thousands of transactions per second. arXiv preprint arXiv:1805.03870 (2018)
47. Luu, L., Narayanan, V., Zheng, C., Baweja, K., Gilbert, S., Saxena, P.: Asecure sharding protocol for open blockchains. In: Proceedings of the 2016 ACM SIGSAC Conference on Computer and Communications Security, pp. 17–30. ACM (2016)
48. Luu, L., Saha, R., Parameshwaran, I., Saxena, P., Hobor, A.: On power splitting games in distributed computation: The case of Bitcoin pooled mining. In: 2015 IEEE 28th Computer Security Foundations Symposium (CSF), pp. 397–411. IEEE (2015)
49. Luu, L., Teutsch, J., Kulkarni, R., Saxena, P.: Demystifying incentives in the consensus computer. In: Proceedings of the 22nd ACM SIGSAC Conference on Computer and Communications Security, pp. 706–719. ACM (2015)
50. Luu, L., Velner, Y., Teutsch, J., Saxena, P.: Smart pool: practical decentralized pooled mining. IACR Cryptology ePrint Archive 2017, 19 (2017)

51. Lynch, N.A.: Distributed Algorithms. Elsevier, Amsterdam (1996)
52. Maurer, U.: Modelling a public-key infrastructure. In: Bertino, E., Kurth, H., Martella, G., Montolivo, E. (eds.) ESORICS 1996. LNCS, vol. 1146, pp. 325–350. Springer, Heidelberg (1996). https://doi.org/10.1007/3-540-61770-1_45
53. Miller, A., Kosba, A., Katz, J., Shi, E.: Nonoutsourceable scratch-off puzzlesto discourage Bitcoin mining coalitions. In: Proceedings of the 22nd ACMSIGSAC Conference on Computer and Communications Security, pp. 680–691. ACM(2015)
54. Miller, A., Xia, Y., Croman, K., Shi, E., Song, D.: The honey badger of BFT protocols. In: Proceedings of the 2016 ACM SIGSAC Conference on Computer and Communications Security, pp. 31–42. ACM (2016)
55. Mitzenmacher, M., Upfal, E.: Probability and Computing: Randomized Algorithms and Probabilistic Analysis. Cambridge University Press, Cambridge (2005)
56. Moon, S.B., Skelly, P., Towsley, D.: Estimation and removal of clock skew from network delay measurements. In: INFOCOM 1999 Proceedings of the Eighteenth Annual Joint Conference of the IEEE Computer and Communications Societies, vol. 1, pp. 227–234. IEEE (1999)
57. Nakamoto, S.: Bitcoin: a peer-to-peer electronic cash system (2008)
58. Pass, R., Seeman, L., Shelat, A.: Analysis of the blockchain protocol in asynchronous networks. In: Coron, J.-S., Nielsen, J.B. (eds.) EUROCRYPT 2017. LNCS, vol. 10211, pp. 643–673. Springer, Cham (2017). https://doi.org/10.1007/978-3-319-56614-6_22
59. Pass, R., Shi, E.: Thunderella: blockchains with optimistic instant confirmation. In: Nielsen, J.B., Rijmen, V. (eds.) EUROCRYPT 2018. LNCS, vol. 10821, pp. 3–33. Springer, Cham (2018). https://doi.org/10.1007/978-3-319-78375-8_1
60. Popov, S.: The tangle. cit. on, p. 131 (2016)
61. Ren, L., Nayak, K., Abraham, I., Devadas, S.: Practical synchronous byzantine consensus. arXiv preprint arXiv:1704.02397 (2017)
62. Rosenfeld, M.: Analysis of hashrate-based double spending. arXiv preprint arXiv:1402.2009 (2014)
63. Sapirshtein, A., Sompolinsky, Y., Zohar, A.: Optimal selfish mining strategies in Bitcoin. In: Grossklags, J., Preneel, B. (eds.) FC 2016. LNCS, vol. 9603, pp. 515–532. Springer, Heidelberg (2017). https://doi.org/10.1007/978-3-662-54970-4_30
64. Sompolinsky, Y., Zohar, A.: PHANTOM: a scalable BlockDAG protocol (2018)
65. Sompolinsky, Y., Lewenberg, Y., Zohar, A.: SPECTRE: a fast and scalable cryptocurrency protocol. IACR Cryptology ePrint Archive 2016, 1159 (2016)
66. Sompolinsky, Y., Zohar, A.: Secure high-rate transaction processing in Bitcoin. In: Böhme, R., Okamoto, T. (eds.) FC 2015. LNCS, vol. 8975, pp. 507–527. Springer, Heidelberg (2015). https://doi.org/10.1007/978-3-662-47854-7_32
67. Syta, E., et al.: Keeping authorities "honest or bust" with decentralized witness cosigning. In: 2016 IEEE Symposium on Security and Privacy (SP), pp. 526–545. IEEE (2016)
68. Szabo, N.: Smart contracts (1994). http://www.fon.hum.uva.nl/rob/Courses/InformationInSpeech/CDROM/Literature/LOTwinterschool2006/szabo.best.vwh.net/smart.contracts.html
69. Teutsch, J., Jain, S., Saxena, P.: When cryptocurrencies mine their own business. In: Grossklags, J., Preneel, B. (eds.) FC 2016. LNCS, vol. 9603, pp. 499–514. Springer, Heidelberg (2017). https://doi.org/10.1007/978-3-662-54970-4_29
70. Teutsch, J., Reitwießner, C.: A scalable verification solution for blockchains (2017). https://people.cs.uchicago.edu/teutsch/papers/truebitpdf

71. Vasek, M., Thornton, M., Moore, T.: Empirical analysis of denial-of-service attacks in the Bitcoin ecosystem. In: Böhme, R., Brenner, M., Moore, T., Smith, M. (eds.) FC 2014. LNCS, vol. 8438, pp. 57–71. Springer, Heidelberg (2014). https://doi.org/10.1007/978-3-662-44774-1_5

72. Wood, G.: Ethereum: a secure decentralised generalised transaction ledger. Ethereum Proj. Yellow Pap. **151**, 1–32 (2014)

73. Zamani, M., Movahedi, M., Raykova, M.: RapidChain: scaling blockchain via full sharding. In: Proceedings of the 2018 ACM SIGSAC Conference on Computer and Communications Security, pp. 931–948. ACM (2018)

74. Das, S., Ribeiro, V.J., Anand, A.: YODA: enabling computationally intensive contracts on blockchains with Byzantine and Selfish nodes. arXiv preprint arXiv:1811.03265 (2018)

Author Index